INTERNATIONAL CLIMAT

International Climate Change Law

DANIEL BODANSKY
JUTTA BRUNNÉE
LAVANYA RAJAMANI

OXFORD
UNIVERSITY PRESS

OXFORD

UNIVERSITY PRESS

Great Clarendon Street, Oxford, OX2 6DP,
United Kingdom

Oxford University Press is a department of the University of Oxford.
It furthers the University's objective of excellence in research, scholarship,
and education by publishing worldwide. Oxford is a registered trade mark of
Oxford University Press in the UK and in certain other countries

First Edition published in 2017

Published in the United States of America by Oxford University Press
198 Madison Avenue, New York, NY 10016, United States of America

British Library Cataloguing in Publication Data
Data available

ISBN 978-0-19-966430-6

Foreword

International climate change law presents a moving target. Since its birth in the early 1990s, it has been whiplashed by the vicissitudes of domestic politics. Even before its rules had been finalized, the Kyoto Protocol was pronounced dead by the newly elected administration of George W. Bush in spring 2001. And less than two decades later, years of arduous negotiations leading to the 2015 Paris Agreement are now at risk as a result of the election of President Donald Trump.

So writing a book about international climate change law poses a challenge. Given its chequered history, what can one say about the subject that is not in danger of becoming quickly obsolete? If we had completed this book in 2014, as originally intended, it would have missed the Paris Agreement, now the central element of international climate change law. And with the election of President Trump, climate change law may undergo yet another reversal in the coming years.

Nevertheless, we believe that a careful examination of the current elements of international climate change law is of enduring value. An enormous amount of effort and legal creativity has gone into the development of international climate change law. So whatever its ultimate fate, it is of significant interest from a scholarly perspective.

Even more importantly, we believe that international climate change law will continue to play a crucial role in practice. The Paris Agreement still commands very broad international support, changes in the United States notwithstanding, so it may well endure and flourish. Even if it does not, climate change is not going away as a problem. At some point states will be compelled to address it as a matter of urgent priority. And when they do, they will find a rich trove of ideas and approaches in the Framework Convention on Climate Change, the Kyoto Protocol, the Paris Agreement, and the other elements of international climate change law discussed in this book. For even when things change, they often stay the same. The UN climate regime, for one, has been remarkably resilient and its basic principles and procedural elements have remained salient throughout its meandering history.

Collectively, we have been involved in the UN climate regime for more than a half century. During this time, we have benefited from countless conversations with colleagues working in academia, government, non-governmental groups, and international institutions, and have accumulated far too many debts to acknowledge fully. But we would like to thank, in particular, Harro van Asselt, Susan Biniaz, Chad Carpenter, Michael Zammit Cutajar, Chandrashekar Dasgupta, Elliot Diringer, Navroz K. Dubash, Andrew Green, Andrew Higham, Jürgen Lefevere, Jane McAdam, Sebastian Oberthür, Franz Perez, Bryce Rudyk, Christina Voight, Jacob Werksman, and Harald Winkler for their insights and friendship over the years, and for their comments on some of the chapters of this book. If they had not given so generously of their knowledge and time, this book would not have been possible. We have also benefited from the dedicated support of Samuel Bayefksy,

Jordan Brunner, Elizabeth Christy, Robert Hersch, Vyoma Jha, Evan Singleton, and Raag Yadava, whose exceptional research assistance was indispensable. In particular, we want to thank Shibani Ghosh, whose extraordinary eye for detail and tremendous research skills have enriched this work beyond measure. Finally, we are grateful to our loving and supportive families for their patience and good cheer as we worked to complete this manuscript and long workdays grew longer still.

Daniel Bodansky
Jutta Brunnée
Lavanya Rajamani

February 2017

Table of Contents

Table of Cases

NATIONAL COURTS AND TRIBUNALS

Table of International Instruments and National Legislation

FCCC CONFERENCE OF
THE PARTIES DECISIONS

KYOTO MEETING OF
THE PARTIES DECISIONS

NATIONAL LEGISLATION

List of Acronyms

AAU	Assigned Amount Unit
ACESA	American Clean Energy and Security Act
ADP	Ad Hoc Working Group on the Durban Platform for Enhanced Action
AGBM	Ad Hoc Group on the Berlin Mandate
AIJ	Activities Implemented Jointly
AILAC	Independent Association of Latin America and the Caribbean
ALBA	Bolivarian Alliance for the Peoples of the Americas
AOSIS	Alliance of Small Island States
APA	Ad Hoc Working Group on the Paris Agreement
AWG-KP	Ad Hoc Working Group under the Kyoto Protocol
BASIC	Brazil, South Africa, India, and China
BAT	Best Available Technology
BR	Biennial Report
BTAs	Border Tax Adjustments
BUR	Biennial Update Report
CAEP	Committee on Aviation Environmental Protection
CAF	Cancun Adaptation Framework
CAIT	Climate Analysis Indicator Tool
CBDRRC	Common But Differentiated Responsibilities and Respective Capabilities
CCAC	Climate and Clean Air Coalition to Reduce Short-Lived Climate Pollutants
CCS	Carbon Capture and Storage
CDM	Clean Development Mechanism
CER	Certified Emission Reduction
CESCR	Committee on Economic, Social and Cultural Rights
CETA	EU-Canada Comprehensive Economic and Trade Agreement
CFCs	Chlorofluorocarbons
CITES	Convention on International Trade in Endangered Species of Wild Fauna and Flora
CMA	Conference of the Parties serving as the Meeting of the Parties to the Paris Agreement
CMP	Conference of the Parties serving as the Meeting of the Parties to the Kyoto Protocol
CO_2	Carbon dioxide
CO_2e	CO_2 equivalent
COP	Conference of the Parties
CSO	Civil Society Organization
DSB	Dispute Settlement Body
DSU	Dispute Settlement Understanding
ECJ	European Court of Justice
ECtHR	European Court of Human Rights

EEA	European Economic Area
EEDI	Energy Efficiency Design Index
EIA	Environmental Impact Assessment
EIG	Environmental Integrity Group
EITs	Economies in Transition
ERT	Expert Review Team
ERU	Emission Reduction Unit
ETS	Emissions Trading System
EU	European Union
EU ETS	European Union—Emissions Trading Scheme

FCCC	Framework Convention on Climate Change
FIELD	Foundation for International Environmental Law and Development
FIT	Feed-in-Tariff

G-77/China	Group of 77 and China
G-8	Group of Eight
GATS	General Agreement on Trade in Services
GATT	General Agreement on Tariffs and Trade
GCF	Green Climate Fund
GDP	Gross Domestic Product
GEF	Global Environment Facility
GHG	Greenhouse Gas
GPID	Guiding Principles on Internal Displacement
GWP	Global Warming Potential

HCFCs	Hydrochlorofluorocarbons
HFCs	Hydrofluorocarbons
HRC	Human Rights Council

IAComHR	Inter-American Commission on Human Rights
IACtHR	Inter-American Court of Human Rights
IAEA	International Atomic Energy Agency
IAR	International Assessment and Review
IASC	Inter-Agency Standing Committee
ICA	International Consultation and Analysis
ICAO	International Civil Aviation Organization
ICAP	International Carbon Action Partnership
ICCPR	International Covenant on Civil and Political Rights
ICESCR	International Covenant on Economic, Social and Cultural Rights
ICJ	International Court of Justice
ICLEI	International Council for Local Environmental Initiatives (now, Local Governments for Sustainability)
ICSID	International Centre for the Settlement of Investment Disputes
ICTSD	International Centre for Trade and Sustainable Development
IDMC	Internal Displacement Monitoring Centre
IISD	International Institute for Sustainable Development
ILA	International Law Association
ILC	International Law Commission

IMO	International Maritime Organization
INC	Intergovernmental Negotiating Committee for a Framework Convention on Climate Change
INDC	Intended Nationally Determined Contribution
IOM	International Organization for Migration
IPCC	Intergovernmental Panel on Climate Change
ISO	International Organization for Standardization
ITLOS	International Tribunal for the Law of the Sea
JI	Joint Implementation
JUSCANZ	Japan, United States, Canada, Australia, and New Zealand
JUSSCANNZ	Japan, United States, Switzerland, Canada, Australia, Norway, and New Zealand
JUSSCANZ	Japan, United States, Switzerland, Canada, Australia, and New Zealand
lCER	Long-term Certified Emission Reduction
LDCF	Least Developed Countries Fund
LDCs	Least Developed Countries
LMDCs	Like Minded Developing Countries
LPAA	Lima to Paris Action Agenda
LRTAP	Convention on Long-Range Transboundary Air Pollution
LULUCF	Land Use, Land Use Change, and Forestry
MBM	Market-Based Measure
MCP	Multilateral Consultative Process
MEA	Multilateral Environmental Agreement
MEF	Major Economies Forum on Energy and Climate
MEM	Major Economies Meeting on Energy Security and Climate Change
MEPC	Marine Environment Protection Committee
MFN	Most Favored Nation
MRV	Measurement, Reporting and Verification
NAFTA	North American Free Trade Agreement
NAMA	Nationally Appropriate Mitigation Action
NAP	National Adaptation Plan
NAPA	National Adaptation Programme of Action
NASA	National Aeronautics and Space Administration
NAZCA	Non-State Actor Zone for Climate Action
NCP	Non-Compliance Procedure
NDC	Nationally Determined Contribution
NGO	Non-Governmental Organization
NRC	Norwegian Refugee Council
NSMD	Non-State Market Driven
NWP	Nairobi Work Programme on Impacts, Vulnerability, and Adaptation to Climate Change
ODA	Official Development Assistance
ODS	Ozone Depleting Substances
OECD	Organisation for Economic Co-operation and Development

OHCHR	Office of the High Commissioner for Human Rights
OPEC	Organization of Petroleum Exporting Countries
PAM	Policy and Measure
PFCs	Perfluorocarbons
ppm	Parts Per Million
PPMs	Processes and Production Methods
QELRO	Quantified Emission Limitation and Reduction Objective
RCEP	Regional Comprehensive Economic Partnership
RED	Reductions in Emissions from Deforestation
REDD+	Reducing Emissions from Deforestation and Forest Degradation
REIO	Regional Economic Integration Organization
RGGI	Regional Greenhouse Gas Initiative
RMU	Removal Unit
SBI	Subsidiary Body for Implementation
SBSTA	Subsidiary Body for Scientific and Technological Advice
SCCF	Special Climate Change Fund
SCM Agreement	Agreement on Subsidies and Countervailing Measures
SDM	Sustainable Development Mechanism
SLCF	Short-Lived Climate Forcer
SPM	Summary for Policymakers
SPS Agreement	Agreement on the Application of Sanitary and Phytosanitary Measures
SWCC	Second World Climate Conference
TBT Agreement	Agreement on Technical Barriers To Trade
tCER	Temporary Certified Emission Reduction
TREM	Trade-Related Environmental Measure
TRIMs	Agreement on Trade-Related Investment Measures
TTIP	EU-US Transatlantic Trade and Investment Partnership
TPP	Trans-Pacific Partnership
UN	United Nations
UNCED	United Nations Conference on Environment and Development
UNDP	United Nations Development Programme
UNECE	United Nations Economic Commission for Europe
UNEP	United Nations Environment Programme
UNGA	United Nations General Assembly
UNHCR	United Nations High Commissioner for Refugees
UNTC	United Nations Treaty Collection
US	United States
USSR	Union of Soviet Socialist Republics
VCLT	Vienna Convention on the Law of Treaties
VCS	Verified Carbon Standard

WIM	Warsaw International Mechanism for Loss and Damage Associated with Climate Change Impacts
WMO	World Meteorological Organization
WRI	World Resources Institute
WTO Agreement	Agreement Establishing the World Trade Organization
WTO	World Trade Organization

1

Introduction

It is now beyond doubt that climate change is real, it is already happening, and human beings are largely responsible for it.[1] Humanity has acquired 'geological force' in the 'Anthropocene',[2] and is pushing up against planetary boundaries.[3] Since the beginning of the industrial revolution, when people began burning fossil fuels, atmospheric concentrations of carbon dioxide (CO_2)—the principal greenhouse gas (GHG)—have risen from about 280 parts per million (ppm) to more than 400 ppm, higher than at any time in the last 800,000 years.[4] Although many uncertainties remain, the Fifth Assessment Report of the Intergovernmental Panel on Climate Change (IPCC)[5] concluded that:

- The warming of the climate system is 'unequivocal'.[6] According to the latest data from the United Kingdom's Met Office, global average temperature is now almost 1° C higher than pre-industrial levels.[7]

---

[1] Intergovernmental Panel on Climate Change (IPCC), *Climate Change 2014: Synthesis Report* (2014) Summary for Policymakers (SPM), 4–5.

[2] The term 'Anthropocene' was coined by Eugene Stoermer in the 1980s and popularized by the Nobel Prize-winning chemist, Paul Crutzen, beginning around 2000. See Will Steffen *et al.*, 'The Anthropocene: Conceptual and Historical Perspectives', *Philosophical Transactions of the Royal Society*, 369/1938 (2011): 842.

[3] Johan Rockström *et al.*, 'Planetary Boundaries: Exploring the Safe Operating Space for Humanity', *Ecology and Society*, 14/2 (2009): 32.

[4] IPCC, *Climate Change 2014: Synthesis Report* (n 1) SPM, 4. According to the latest data from the Scripps Institution of Oceanography, which has been directly measuring atmospheric concentrations of CO_2 at its Mauna Loa Observatory in Hawaii since the late 1950s, CO_2 concentrations were 406 ppm as of 22 January 2017. Scripps Institution of Oceanography, 'The Keeling Curve' <https://scripps.ucsd.edu/programs/keelingcurve/> accessed 22 January 2017.

[5] 'The Intergovernmental Panel on Climate Change (IPCC) is the international body for assessing the science related to climate change. The IPCC was set up in 1988 by the World Meteorological Organization (WMO) and the United Nations Environment Programme (UNEP) to provide policymakers with regular assessments of the scientific basis of climate change, its impacts and future risks, and options for adaptation and mitigation.' IPCC, 'IPCC Factsheet: What is the IPCC?' <http://www.ipcc.ch/news_and_events/docs/factsheets/FS_what_ipcc.pdf> accessed 20 January 2017.

[6] IPCC, *Climate Change 2014: Synthesis Report* (n 1) SPM, 2.

[7] United Kingdom Met Office, 'Global Climate in Context as the World Approaches 1° C Above Pre-Industrial for the First Time' (9 November 2015) <http://www.metoffice.gov.uk/research/news/2015/global-average-temperature-2015> accessed 20 January 2017.

- It is 'extremely likely that human influence has been the dominant cause of the observed warming since the mid-20th century'.[8]

- '[M]any of the observed changes are unprecedented over decades to millennia. The atmosphere and ocean have warmed, the amounts of snow and ice have diminished, sea level has risen, and the concentrations of greenhouse gases have increased.'[9]

- These changes 'have caused impacts on natural and human systems on all continents and across all oceans'.[10]

- 'Continued emission of greenhouse gases will cause further warming…, increasing the likelihood of severe, pervasive and irreversible impacts….'[11]

This book provides an overview of the international legal response to this global threat.

I. CLIMATE CHANGE AS AN INTRACTABLE POLICY CHALLENGE

Climate change poses a complex, polycentric, and seemingly intractable policy challenge—a challenge some have characterized as 'super wicked'.[12] United Nations Secretary General Ban Ki-moon characterized it as the 'defining issue of our age'.[13] Certainly, it is one of the most difficult policy problems ever faced.

Several factors combine to make climate change an 'issue from hell'.[14] It is planetary in scope and—due to its long-term and potentially irreversible consequences—intergenerational in its impacts. It is caused by a wide range of production and consumption processes. Its causes and effects are global, and require complex collective action. It can be managed only if all states, or at least the major GHG emitters, cooperate in undertaking potentially costly, large-scale shifts in their economic and energy systems. Yet, because most of the benefits of climate change mitigation

---

[8] IPCC, *Climate Change 2013: The Physical Science Basis* (Cambridge University Press, 2013) SPM, 17.

[9] Ibid, SPM, 4.   [10] IPCC, *Climate Change 2014: Synthesis Report* (n 1) SPM, 6.

[11] Ibid, SPM, 8; IPCC, *Climate Change 2014: Mitigation of Climate Change* (Cambridge University Press, 2014) SPM, 8 (noting that without additional GHG mitigation efforts, global mean surface temperature is set to increase by 2100 from 3.7° C to 4.8° C above pre-industrial levels).

[12] Richard Lazarus, 'Super Wicked Problems and Climate Change: Restraining the Present to Liberate the Future', *Cornell Law Review*, 94/5 (2009): 1153; see generally Horst W.J. Rittel and Marvin M. Webber, 'Dilemmas in a General Theory of Planning', *Policy Science* 4/2 (1973): 155, 160 (introducing the concept of 'wicked' problems); Kelly Levin *et al.*, 'Playing it Forward: Path Dependency, Progressive Incrementalism, and the "Super Wicked" Problem of Global Climate Change' (7 July 2007) (paper prepared for delivery to the International Studies Association Convention Chicago, 28 February–3 March 2007) <http://citeseerx.ist.psu.edu/viewdoc/download?doi=10.1.1.464.5287&rep =rep1&type=pdf> accessed 20 January 2017.

[13] UN Secretary General Ban Ki-moon, 'Opening Remarks at 2014 Climate Summit' (23 September 2014) <http://www.un.org/apps/news/infocus/sgspeeches/statments_full.asp?statID=2355#. Vv21uBKANBc> accessed 20 January 2017.

[14] Al Gore, *The Future: Six Drivers of Global Change* (New York: Random House, 2013) 314.

do not accrue to the country taking action, but are instead shared by the international community as a whole, individual countries have little incentive to act on their own. Significant investments to reduce GHG emissions will be in a country's individual self-interest only if they are reciprocated by other states—only if a country's actions are part of a bargain involving significant action by other countries to address climate change.[15]

For a variety of reasons, however, it has proven extremely difficult to secure international agreement. Part of the explanation is familiar: international law generally has difficulty solving collective action problems because it lacks strong tools to secure participation and compliance and thus provides only a measure of assurance to states that, if they act, others will reciprocate.[16] But several particular features of the climate change problem exacerbate this general problem:

- First, climate change implicates virtually every aspect of a state's domestic policies—energy, agriculture, transportation, urban planning, and so forth—with potentially enormous economic stakes. As a result, in many countries it is enmeshed in the vicissitudes of domestic politics. In the United States (US), for example, climate change has become a highly partisan issue, with a majority of one of the two main political parties openly questioning the science of climate change, making legislative action all but impossible and limiting the kinds of international agreements the US can join.[17] And, in Australia, a government fell over the 'carbon tax'.[18]

- Second, because of the climate system's inertia, climate change requires people to act now to address a long-term and, in some cases, uncertain threat.[19] According to the IPCC, delaying concerted mitigation action beyond 2030 'will substantially increase the challenges' associated with meeting the target adopted in the Paris Agreement of limiting temperature increase to well below 2° C.[20] There is an even less chance of reaching a 1.5° C aspirational goal

---

[15] IPCC, *Climate Change 2014: Mitigation of Climate Change* (n 11) 5.

[16] See generally Scott Barrett, *Environment and Statecraft: The Strategy of Environmental Treaty-Making* (Oxford University Press, 2003).

[17] Kiley Kroh, Kristen Ellingboe, and Tiffany Germain, 'The Anti-Science Climate Denier Caucus: 114th Congress Edition' *ThinkProgress* (8 January 2015) <https://thinkprogress.org/the-anti-science-climate-denier-caucus-114th-congress-edition-c76c3f8bfedd#.71brt4r1r> accessed 27 October 2016.

[18] In September 2013, the Liberal Party defeated the Labour Party in general elections, after the Liberal Party leader, Tony Abbott, declared the election a 'referendum' on Australia's carbon tax. Christopher Rootes, 'A Referendum on the Carbon Tax? The 2013 Australian Election, the Greens, and the Environment', *Environmental Politics*, 23/1 (2014): 166. The following year, the Abbott government repealed the carbon tax.

[19] Levin *et al.*, Playing It Forward (n 12); See IPCC, *Climate Change 2014: Synthesis Report* (n 1); see for popular reportage of the IPCC Report, Sam Friell, 'UN: Time is Running Out for Climate Change Action', *Time* (13 April 2014) <http://time.com/60769/global-warming-ipcc-carbon-emissions/> accessed 27 October 2016.

[20] The IPCC notes that if concerted mitigation action is delayed, keeping to the temperature limit 'will require substantially higher rates of emissions reductions from 2030 to 2050; a much more rapid scale-up of low-carbon energy over this period; a larger reliance on [carbon dioxide removal] in the long term; and higher transitional and long-term economic impacts'. IPCC, *Climate Change*

without a considerable increase in mitigation ambition in the 2020 to 2030 period.[21] But there is comparatively little appetite in many countries to take costly action now to avert seemingly remote harms in the future. Short-term election cycles compel governments to prioritize immediate concerns such as poverty eradication, energy access, affordable transportation, and economic development over seemingly long-term problems such as climate change.

• Finally, states have very different interests, priorities, capacities, and perspectives, making agreement even harder. There are vast disparities between states in wealth, GHG emissions profiles, and vulnerabilities. The countries primarily responsible for causing the climate change problem are not the ones that will be most adversely affected. Addressing the problem could produce losers as well as winners. And states have very different views as to what would constitute a fair outcome. Small island states, for instance, at the frontlines of climate change impacts, have a compelling reason to act. Yet since their GHG emissions are inconsequential, their actions will have little impact on the trajectory of warming. By contrast, the Organization of Petroleum Exporting Countries (OPEC), the members of which are economically dependent on fossil fuels and have high per capita GHG emissions, have compelling reasons—at least in the short term—for inaction. And, many large developing countries still have the burden of providing energy access to vast swathes of their population.[22]

Given these challenges, it is not surprising that international law has had only modest success to date in addressing climate change.

II. THREE PERSPECTIVES ON THE CLIMATE CHANGE PROBLEM

The climate change problem can be understood in many ways—as a scientific, technological, or even religious problem.[23] But three perspectives have dominated the international policy response to climate change. First, European countries have tended to see it as an environmental problem, reflected in their representation for many years at the UN climate negotiations by their environment ministries. Small

---

2014: Synthesis Report (n 1) SPM, 24. See Decision 1/CP.21, 'Adoption of the Paris Agreement' (29 January 2016) FCCC/CP/2015/10/Add.1, 2, Annex: Paris Agreement (Paris Agreement).

[21] Carl-Friedrich Schleussner *et al.*, 'Science and Policy Characteristics of the Paris Agreement Temperature Goal', *Nature Climate Change*, 6/9 (2016): 827.

[22] In India, for example, climate change is dwarfed on the political agenda by the need to provide electricity to 300 million people. See eg India's Intended Nationally Determined Contribution, Working Towards Climate Justice (1 October 2015) <http://www4.unfccc.int/submissions/INDC/Published%20Documents/India/1/INDIA%20INDC%20TO%20UNFCCC.pdf> accessed 20 January 2017 (which notes that India is home to 'around 24% of the global population without access to electricity (304 million)').

[23] Pope Francis, 'Encyclical Letter *Laudato Si'* of the Holy Father Francis on Care for Our Common Home' (Vatican Press, 2015) <http://w2.vatican.va/content/dam/francesco/pdf/encyclicals/documents/papa-francesco_20150524_enciclica-laudato-si_en.pdf> accesssed 20 January 2017.

island states have, not surprisingly, been even more environmentally minded, given the existential threat posed by climate change. In contrast, many non-European developed countries (in particular, the US) have tended, almost from the start, to see climate change through an economic lens, with economists playing a major role in formulating policies.[24] Meanwhile, many developing countries understand climate politics as part of a larger pattern of historical and economic injustices—a continuation of the 1970s debate about the 'new international economic order', which grew out of the decolonization movement.[25] In their view, developed countries not only bear the primary historical responsibility for combating climate change, but should also support developing countries in their efforts to do so.[26] Indeed, some developing countries even claim 'compensation' and argue that developed countries must discharge their 'ecological debt'.[27]

A. Climate change as an environmental problem

Perhaps the most obvious perspective on climate change is to see it as an environmental problem.[28] Viewed in this way, the goal of international climate policy is to prevent dangerous anthropogenic climate change by reducing net GHG emissions. Given the persistence of CO_2 in the atmosphere, the goal of preventing dangerous climate change will eventually require completely eliminating net emissions, as the 2015 Paris Agreement recognizes.[29] But how much we need to reduce emissions at any particular point in time is a function of three factors: first, the level of temperature increase deemed safe; second, the concentration levels necessary to prevent warming from exceeding that temperature limit; and third, the choice

---

[24] See Daniel Bodansky, 'Transatlantic Environmental Relations', in John Peterson and Mark Pollack (eds), *Europe, America, and Bush* (London: Routledge, 2003) 58 (contrasting EU and US approaches to climate change).

[25] On the New International Economic Order, see generally Jagdish N. Bhagwati (ed), *The New International Economic Order: The North-South Debate* (Cambridge: MIT Press, 1977).

[26] Statement by Ambassador Nozipho Mxakato-Diseko from South Africa on Behalf of the Group of 77 and China, at the Opening Plenary of the 12th Part of the 2nd Session of the Ad Hoc Working Group on the Durban Platform for Enhanced Action (ADP 2-12), Paris, France (29 November 2015) <http://www4.unfccc.int/Submissions/Lists/OSPSubmissionUpload/219_137_130932914217320365-G77%20and%20China%20statement%20ADP2-12%2029%20Nov%202015.pdf> accessed 20 January 2017.

[27] Peter Neill, 'Ecological Debt and the Global Footprint Network' *The Huffington Post* (4 January 2015) <http://www.huffingtonpost.com/peter-neill/ecological-debt--the-glob_b_6101200.html> accessed 20 January 2017 (discussing the origins of the term 'ecological debt'); Plurinational State of Bolivia on Behalf of the Alianza Bolivariana Para Los Pueblos De Nuestra América—ALBA, UNFCCC -ADP 2.11 (19 October 2015) <http://www4.unfccc.int/Submissions/Lists/OSPSubmissionUpload/88_129_130897230954649738-Intervenci%C3%B3n%20Final%20ALBA%2019.10.15.pdf> accessed 20 January 2017; ALBA Countries, 'ALBA Declaration on Copenhagen Climate Summit' (28 December 2009) <https://venezuelanalysis.com/analysis/5038> accessed 20 January 2017.

[28] This sub-section and the next draw, in part, from Daniel Bodansky, *The Durban Platform Negotiations: Goals and Options* (Harvard Project on Climate Agreements, July 2012) <http://belfercenter.ksg.harvard.edu/files/bodansky_durban2_vp.pdf> accessed 20 January 2017; Daniel Bodansky, *The Art and Craft of International Environmental Law* (Cambridge, MA: Harvard University Press, 2010) 62–70.

[29] Paris Agreement, Art 4.1.

of an emissions pathway to achieve the necessary concentration level. In the Paris Agreement, states agreed to the goal of limiting temperature increase to 'well below' 2° C (compared to pre-industrial levels), and also to pursue efforts to limit global warming to 1.5° C.[30] Achievement of the 2° C limit would likely require stabilization of GHG concentrations at no more than 450 ppm, and global emissions to peak and then fall by 40–70% by 2050.[31]

Since we are not currently close to achieving these reductions, the environmental effectiveness of the international climate regime can be measured by the magnitude of global emissions reductions achieved over time—how close they come to putting the world on a pathway to reaching the 2° C or 1.5° C temperature limit. This might appear to depend on the stringency of the regime's emissions reduction commitments: the more stringent the commitments, the better. But environmental effectiveness is a function not only of the stringency of commitments, but also of the levels of participation and compliance by states.[32] Weakness along any of these three dimensions will undermine the climate regime's effectiveness, regardless of how well it does on the other two. And because stringency, participation, and compliance are interlinked, we must consider how varying one factor affects the others. More stringent requirements promote environmental effectiveness, all other things being equal. But they do not necessarily boost climate effectiveness if they result in lower participation and/or compliance. Conversely, high participation and compliance are desirable in and of themselves, but they do not necessarily make an agreement more environmentally effective if they are secured at the price of watering down the agreement's substantive requirements. Achieving the greatest emissions reductions requires solving an immensely complex equation involving all three factors. Moreover, since climate change depends on cumulative emissions rather than on emissions at any particular point in time,[33] we need to consider stringency and participation as dynamic variables. Less stringent commitments or participation now might produce greater environmental effectiveness in the long run, if they are part of an evolutionary framework that leads to greater action.

B. Climate change as an economic problem

Climate change can also be seen as an economic problem. From this perspective, the goal of climate policy is to achieve the 'efficient' outcome—that is, the outcome with the highest net benefits.[34] Accordingly, we should reduce emissions only so long as the benefits of further reductions outweigh the costs. And, to the extent

---

[30] Ibid, Art 2.1.

[31] IPCC, *Climate Change 2014: Mitigation of Climate Change* (n 11) 10–12.

[32] Barrett, *Environment and Statecraft* (n 16).

[33] IPCC, *Climate Change 2013: The Physical Science Basis* (n 8) SPM, 27.

[34] Examples of the economic perspective include William D. Nordhaus, *The Climate Casino: Risk, Uncertainty, and Economics for a Warming World* (New Haven, CT: Yale University Press, 2013); Nicholas Stern, *The Economics of Climate Change: The Stern Review* (Cambridge University Press, 2007); Gernot Wagner and Martin L. Weitzman, *Climate Shock: The Economic Consequences of a Hotter Planet* (Princeton University Press, 2015).

adaptation is cheaper than mitigation, then that should be the preferred policy. Calculating costs and benefits is extremely difficult, of course, particularly given that many of the benefits of reducing emissions involve non-market goods that are difficult to value and will be realized far in the future. Nevertheless, some rough weighing of costs and benefits, even if not explicit, is the basis of most decision-making.

In addition to defining a goal of efficiency, the economic perspective focuses on the means of achieving that goal, namely, by reducing emissions as cost-effectively as possible.[35] In general, a policy is cost-effective if it equalizes the marginal cost of compliance across time and place. If GHG emissions can be reduced more cheaply in the future than now, or by one country more cheaply than another, then it may be possible to achieve the same climate benefit at a lower cost by shifting some of the pollution reductions into the future or to countries with lower mitigation costs.[36] In the climate regime, cost-effectiveness has been the rationale for the use of market mechanisms such as emissions trading, which allow emissions to be reduced wherever this can be done most cheaply.[37]

C. Climate change as an ethical problem

A third perspective on the climate change problem is that of equity and climate justice.[38] Cost-benefit analysis simply seeks to maximize aggregate economic value and does not address the ethical issues raised by climate change. If one country receives the benefits from a polluting activity and another bears the costs, the policy is still efficient as long as, in the aggregate, the benefits exceed the costs. The ethical perspective, in contrast, focuses on issues of distributive and corrective justice, including: how do we equitably distribute the burdens of mitigating and adapting to climate change, and who, if anyone, is ethically responsible for the damages caused by climate change?

In contrast to environmental effectiveness and economic efficiency, for which there are relatively well-accepted metrics, there is little consensus about what equity and climate justice entail.[39] Some accounts focus on historical responsibility, others on duties to future generations, others on a fair division of burdens based on

---

[35] This paragraph and the next are based on Bodansky, *Art and Craft of International Environmental Law* (n 28) 68–9.

[36] The timing and location of emissions reductions generally do not affect the resulting climate benefits, because climate change is what economists refer to as a 'stocks' rather than a 'flows' problem. What matters to the climate system is not the level of emissions at any particular time and place, but cumulative global emissions over time.

[37] See Chapter 6, Section V.

[38] See generally Stephen M. Gardiner *et al.*, *Climate Ethics: Essential Readings* (Oxford University Press, 2010); Dale Jamieson, *Reason in a Dark Time: Why the Struggle Against Climate Change Failed – and What It Means for Our Future* (Oxford University Press, 2014); Henry Shue, *Climate Justice: Vulnerability and Protection* (Oxford University Press, 2014).

[39] John Ashton and Xueman Wang, 'Equity and Climate: In Principle and Practice', in Joseph E. Aldy *et al.*, *Beyond Kyoto: Advancing the International Effort against Climate Change* (Arlington, Virginia: Pew Center on Global Climate Change, December 2003) 61.

current capabilities, and yet others on the egalitarian principle that people have an equal right to the 'atmospheric space'.

Consider, for example, the question: how should we allocate emission reductions among countries? Developed countries account for the majority of cumulative CO_2 emissions, suggesting that they bear greater historical responsibility for the climate change problem.[40] In per capita terms, even today GHG emissions from indus-trialized countries are 2.5 times greater than those from developing countries.[41] However, total emissions from developing countries have overtaken those from industrialized countries,[42] and emissions from large developing countries are pro-jected to continue to rise sharply.[43] In 2005, China surpassed the United States as the world's largest emitter of CO_2;[44] in 2013, its share of global emissions was 29%, compared to 15% for the US and 11% for the European Union (EU). China's per capita emissions (7.4 tonnes) slightly exceeded those of the EU (7.3 tonnes), although both remained significantly below the per capita emissions of the US (16.6 tonnes).[45] Given these figures, it is unclear how emissions reductions are to be shared between countries, and on what basis. Several metrics have been suggested over the years. These range from emission-based indicators (such as cumulative emissions, total emissions, or per capita emissions) to those relating to a state's capabilities and developmental needs (such as gross domestic product per capita, the UN Development Programme's Human Development Index, or electrifica-tion rates).[46] Thus far, the parties to the UN climate regime have not agreed on any objective indicators or other means of allocating emissions reductions among states, except through political negotiations or national decision-making.

Climate justice issues are also raised by the fact that the countries most vul-nerable to climate change, such as small island states, have contributed the least

---

[40] CO_2 emissions from Annex I countries from 1850 to 2012 are 937,952 $MtCO_2$ and from non-Annex I are 388,623 $MtCO_2$. Data for Cumulative Total CO_2 Emissions Excluding Land-Use Change and Forestry from 1850 to selected years—2012 from World Resources Institute (WRI), 'CAIT Climate Data Explorer' <http://cait.wri.org/> accessed 20 January 2017. Note also that the preamble to the Framework Convention on Climate Change specifically acknowledges that 'the largest share of historical and current emissions has originated in developed countries', United Nations Framework Convention on Climate Change (adopted 9 May 1992, entered into force 21 March 1994) 1771 UNTS 107 (FCCC), preambular recital 3.

[41] IPCC, *Climate Change 2014: Mitigation of Climate Change* (n 11) 113.

[42] Ibid; see also Sheila M. Olmstead and Robert N. Stavins, 'Three Key Elements of a Post-2012 International Climate Policy Architecture', *Review of Environmental Economics and Policy*, 6/1 (2012): 65, 70.

[43] US Energy Information Administration, 'International Energy Outlook 2013' (July 2013) <http://www.eia.gov/forecasts/archive/ieo13/pdf/0484(2013).pdf> accessed 20 January 2017, 159–65. See also IPCC, *Climate Change 2014: Mitigation of Climate Change* (n 11) 125–30.

[44] Based on data from the WRI, CAIT Climate Data Explorer (n 40).

[45] Jos G.J. Olivier *et al.*, *Trends in Global CO_2 Emissions: 2014 Report* (The Hague: PBL Netherlands Environmental Assessment Agency, 2014) <http://edgar.jrc.ec.europa.eu/news_docs/jrc-2014-trends-in-global-co2-emissions-2014-report-93171.pdf> accessed 20 January 2017, 24.

[46] See eg Submission by Swaziland on behalf of the African Group under Workstream I of the ADP (8 October 2013) <https://unfccc.int/files/documentation/submissions_from_parties/adp/applica-tion/pdf/adp_african_group_workstream_1_20131008.pdf> accessed 20 January 2017.

to causing it.[47] Climate change is likely to disproportionately affect developing countries, many of which are acutely vulnerable.[48] It is projected 'to slow down economic growth, make poverty reduction more difficult, further erode food security, and prolong existing and create new poverty traps...'.[49] While developing countries need to adopt climate resilient sustainable development pathways, there are limits to adaptation. Some countries, communities, and ecosystems may be able to adapt to 1.5°–2° C warming, but few will be able to adapt to 3°–4° C warming. In the absence of robust international support mechanisms, the primary burden of adapting to climate change is likely to fall on such developing countries, diverting scarce resources from other critical human development priorities.

The World Bank estimates that the combined needs of developing countries for mitigation and adaptation will be approximately $275 billion per year by 2030,[50] and the FCCC estimates costs of tens and possibly hundreds of billions of dollars per year just for adaptation.[51] Industrialized countries have larger economic and technological capacity, but the extent of their responsibility for supporting developing countries is disputed. Needless to say, creating adequate funding in the system to address the demands of climate change is still a work in progress. It is clear, however, that current and projected demand for resources to mitigate and adapt to climate change vastly outstrips the funds that are available.

Finally, climate change raises issues of inter-generational equity, since most of the burdens of climate change will be borne by future generations, especially those from developing countries that are likely to have very limited resources to adapt. Does the present owe duties to the future? If so, what are those duties and what are their implications for climate policy?[52]

The environmental perspective can, at times, be in tension with the ethical perspective. Equity principles, for example, are often cited to argue that developed countries should bear the primary burden of reducing emissions, since they, as a group, have higher historical and per capita emissions than developing countries. But, from an environmental standpoint, reducing developing country emissions

---

[47] IPCC, *Climate Change 2014: Impacts, Adaptation and Vulnerability* (Cambridge University Press, 2014) SPM, 30–2.

[48] See generally, IPCC, *Climate Change 2014: Synthesis Report* (n 1) SPM, 13–16. See also FCCC, 'Climate Change: Impacts, Vulnerabilities and Adaptation in Developing Countries' (Bonn: UNFCCC, 2007) <http://unfccc.int/resource/docs/publications/impacts.pdf> accessed 20 January 2017; and The Climate Vulnerable Forum <http://www.thecvf.org/> accessed 20 January 2017.

[49] IPCC, *Climate Change 2014: Impacts, Adaptation and Vulnerability* (n 47) SPM, 20.

[50] World Bank, *World Development Report 2010: Development and Climate Change* (Washington, D.C.: World Bank, 2010). A 2007 FCCC secretariat report has similar figures, estimating that an additional $200–$210 billion per year would be needed in global investment and financial flows to reduce CO_2e emissions by 25% by the year 2030, roughly half of it in developing countries. FCCC, 'Investment and Financial Flows to Address Climate Change' (Bonn: UNFCCC, 2007) <http://unfccc.int/resource/docs/publications/financial_flows.pdf> accessed 20 January 2017.

[51] FCCC, ibid. See also UNEP, *Adaptation Finance Gap Report 2016* (Nairobi: UNEP, May 2016), notes that the cost of adapting to climate change in developing countries could rise to between $280 and $500 billion per year by 2050.

[52] See generally Edith Brown Weiss, *In Fairness to Future Generations: International Law, Common Patrimony, and Intergenerational Equity* (New York: Transnational Publishers, 1989).

is also crucial. For this reason, many industrialized countries insist on developing country participation as a matter of pragmatic problem solving, or even 'fairness'.[53]

Nevertheless, environmental effectiveness and ethics are also intertwined, since considerations of climate justice are important factors in determining what level of climate change (1.5° C or 2° C) is deemed environmentally acceptable. For example, one might prefer a 1.5° C rather than a 2° C limit because of concern about the injustice of inflicting catastrophic damage on small island and least developed countries. Yet a 1.5° C limit also raises equity issues, since it could dramatically shrink the carbon budget for those countries that have large populations without access to modern forms of energy, and need to increase their emissions to address energy poverty in their countries. In any case, unless climate policy is perceived as equitable, it is unlikely to be accepted and followed, making it less environmentally effective. The challenge is to find ways of reflecting ethical considerations that are acceptable to the major emitters, both developed and developing, so as not to discourage participation and compliance.

III. DEMARCATING INTERNATIONAL CLIMATE CHANGE LAW

Climate change has been a major international issue since the late 1980s, and states have developed a significant body of international law in response.[54] Much of that law has been treaty based, adopted under the auspices of the 1992 United Nations Framework Convention on Climate Change (FCCC), including the 1997 Kyoto Protocol,[55] the 2015 Paris Agreement, and the numerous decisions of the parties to these instruments. We will refer to this vast and complex web of principles, rules, regulations, and institutions as the UN climate regime. It serves a variety of functions, including to facilitate the ongoing negotiations; to track and enable the implementation of core commitments relating to mitigation, adaptation, and provision of support; and to supervise compliance. Chapter 3 provides a general introduction to treaty-based approaches, Chapter 4 traces the development of the UN climate regime, and Chapters 5–7 provide a detailed analysis of the principal agreements in the UN climate regime.

Although the UN climate regime forms the core of international climate change law, international climate change law, conceived more broadly, includes not only the UN regime, but also rules and principles of general international law relevant to climate change; norms developed by other treaty regimes and international bodies;

---

[53] See eg Umbrella Group Statement, High Level Segment, <http://unfccc.int/resource/docs/cop18_cmp8_hl_statements/Statement%20on%20behalf%20of%20the%20Umbrella%20Group.pdf> accessed 20 January 2017. See generally J. Timmons Roberts and Bradley C. Parks, *A Climate of Injustice: Global Inequality, North-South Politics, and Climate Policy* (MIT Press, 2007) ch. 5.

[54] See Chapter 4 for the history of the climate change issue.

[55] Kyoto Protocol to the United Nations Framework Convention on Climate Change (adopted 11 December 1997, entered into force 16 February 2005) 2303 UNTS 162 (Kyoto Protocol).

regulations, policies, and institutions at the regional, national, and sub-national levels; and judicial decisions of national, regional, and international courts.[56] Although the core of this book focuses on the UN climate regime, Chapter 2 considers general international law, notably customary law, and Chapter 8 surveys polycentric governance of the climate change problem. In addition, Chapter 9 examines the intersection of climate change law with other areas of international law, including human rights law, migration law, and trade law.

In referring to 'international climate change law', we do not mean to suggest that it is a discrete body of law with its own sources, methods of law-making, and principles, or that is it a self-contained regime. Quite the opposite, international climate change law sits squarely within the fields of international environmental law and public international law more broadly.[57] Indeed, Chapter 2 is devoted to locating international climate change law within the broader context of international law, including the rules and principles of general international law, the evolution of which helps account for the predominant role of treaty-based climate change law. Similarly, Chapter 3 explores treaty-based law-making in detail. And Chapter 9 examines the implications of climate change for other areas of international law, and vice versa. In short, this books attempts to avoid 'issue fragmentation' and to tease out the 'legal inter-relationships and commonalities' that exist across international law.[58] As the book reveals, international climate change law is, in some respects, an exemplar of international environmental law. In other respects, it is a potential portent of future risks for other areas of international law.[59] In either case, international climate change law, as it is emerging, functions as a laboratory for the development of international law more generally.

IV. THE SUBJECT MATTER OF INTERNATIONAL CLIMATE CHANGE LAW

International climate change law focuses on four basic issues: (1) mitigation of climate change—that is, limiting it or preventing it from happening; (2) adaptation to climate change, in order to limit its harmful effects; (3) financial and other means of support for mitigation and adaptation; and (4) international oversight to promote implementation, compliance, and effectiveness.

In the development of international climate change law, states have taken differing views on whether the climate regime should focus primarily on mitigation,

---

[56] For a brief discussion of climate change litigation, see Chapter 8, Section VI.

[57] Birnie, Boyle, and Redgwell make a similar argument in relation to 'international environmental law' and public international law. Patricia Birnie, Alan Boyle, and Catherine Redgwell, *International Law and the Environment* (Oxford University Press, 3rd edn, 2009) 2–4.

[58] Elizabeth Fisher *et al.*, 'Maturity and Methodology: Starting a Debate about Environmental Law Scholarship', *Journal of Environmental Law*, 21/2 (2009): 213, 241.

[59] See generally Duncan French and Lavanya Rajamani, 'Climate Change and International Environmental Law: Musings on a Journey to Somewhere', *Journal of Environmental Law*, 25/3 (2013): 437.

or should strike a balance between mitigation and adaptation. Although the objective of the FCCC refers to both mitigation and adaptation,[60] in the first decade of the UN climate regime's existence, the focus was squarely on mitigation. The negotiation and elaboration of the Kyoto Protocol, prescribing GHG mitigation targets and timetables for developed countries, preoccupied states from 1995 until 2001. It was only thereafter that the climate regime began seriously considering ways to enhance adaptation action, co-operation, and support. Meanwhile, throughout the history of the regime, developing countries, in particular, have been focused on financial assistance and other means of implementation, including technology transfer and capacity building. Finally, a major emphasis of the UN climate regime has been to develop a robust system of reporting and review, in order to promote transparency, and, perhaps less consistently over the years, to develop strong procedures to determine and impose consequences for non-compliance.

A. Mitigation

Much of international climate change law focuses on mitigation, which encompasses both measures to limit GHG emissions and measures to preserve or enhance sinks.[61] Policies to reduce emissions include energy efficiency standards, subsidies for renewable energy, a carbon tax, an emissions trading system, funding of urban mass transit systems, and technology research and development. Sinks policies generally relate to land use, land-use change, and forestry (LULUCF), and include measures to reduce emissions from deforestation and forest degradation (REDD+) and to encourage afforestation.

Issues relating to mitigation include:

- *Whether to address emissions on an economy-wide basis or at a sectoral level?* Generally, the UN climate regime has sought to address aggregate national emissions and has not separated out particular sectors such as electricity generation or buildings.[62] But a few sectors receive specific attention, including emissions from international maritime and air transport, which are addressed through the International Maritime Organization (IMO) and the International Civil Aviation Organization (ICAO), respectively,[63] and forestry, which is the subject of REDD+.[64]

- *Whether to regulate greenhouse gases comprehensively or gas-by-gas?* Although CO_2 accounts for more than two-thirds of total GHG emissions[65] and, except

---

[60] FCCC, Art 2.

[61] IPCC, *Climate Change 2014: Mitigation of Climate Change* (n 11) SPM, 4.

[62] Ibid. By contrast, the IPCC report on mitigation analyzes policy on a sectoral basis, with sections discussing energy supply, energy end-use sectors, land use, buildings, infrastructure, and so forth.

[63] See Chapter 8, Sections IV.A.1. and IV.A.2.

[64] See generally Christina Voight (ed), *Research Handbook on REDD+ and International Law* (Cheltenham: Edward Elgar Publishing, 2016).

[65] IPCC, *Climate Change 2014: Synthesis Report* (n 1) SPM, Figure SPM 1.2.

for emissions from land use, can be accurately accounted, the UN climate regime has not focused specifically on CO_2. Instead, it seeks to promote cost-effectiveness by addressing GHGs comprehensively, which allows states to focus on whichever gases can be reduced at the least cost.[66] In contrast, efforts to address climate change through the Montreal Protocol have focused on particular gases—hydrochlorofluorocarbons (HCFCs) initially and, currently, hydrofluorocarbons (HFCs).[67]

- *Whether to prescribe particular measures internationally or give states flexibility?* In general, international climate change law has not tried to prescribe particular mitigation measures. Instead, as discussed in Section V.2 below, it has adopted either a bottom-up approach that allows states to develop and report on their own policies, or, when it has prescribed rules internationally, the rules have been obligations of result—for example, to reduce emissions by some specified amount—which allow states to choose what policies they will use to achieve the required result. One exception to this general rule is IMO's work to limit emissions from maritime shipping under the International Convention for the Prevention of Pollution from Ships (MARPOL),[68] which has involved the adoption of mandatory energy efficiency standards for vessels.[69]

- *Whether to give states flexibility in deciding where to reduce emissions?* Market mechanisms such as emissions trading allow countries to implement their mitigation commitments through emissions reductions in another country. The FCCC contained an embryonic market mechanism by allowing parties to undertake activities jointly to reduce emissions.[70] The Kyoto Protocol employs market mechanisms much more extensively, by allowing states to (1) receive credits for undertaking emissions projects in another country through the Clean Development Mechanism and joint implementation; and (2) trade emissions allowances with other parties, selling to countries with higher mitigation costs and buying from countries with lower costs.[71]

- *The extent to which commitments of states should be tailored to their differing capabilities and responsibilities, and how?* The issue of differentiation has been one of the most controversial in the context of mitigation, and is discussed separately in Section V.C below.

---

[66] See Chapter 5, Section IV.B.2.

[67] Montreal Protocol on Substances that Deplete the Ozone Layer (adopted 16 September 1987, entered into force 1 January 1989) 1522 UNTS 3 (Montreal Protocol). For a discussion of the Montreal Protocol, see Chapter 8, Section IV.B.

[68] Protocol of 1978 Relating to the International Convention for the Prevention of Pollution from Ships (adopted 17 February 1978, entered into force 2 October 1983) 1340 UNTS 61 (MARPOL 73/78).

[69] See Chapter 8, Section IV.A.1.   [70] See Chapter 5, Section IV.B.3.

[71] These market mechanisms are discussed in detail in Chapter 6, Section V.

B. Adaptation

Scientists predict that climate change will have dramatic impacts on coastal areas, agriculture, forests, human health, and biodiversity, creating a need for adaptation. Adaptation involves 'anticipating the adverse effects of climate change and taking appropriate action to prevent or minimize the damage they can cause'.[72] Some adaptation activities focus specifically on climate change impacts, such as developing heat-resistant crops and building sea walls. But many adaptation activities are aimed at improving the resilience of societies against risks generally, by building capacity, reducing poverty, and strengthening disaster preparedness.

In contrast to mitigation, which requires collective action, adaptation can usually be undertaken by individual states. Moreover, states have an individual incentive to act, since the benefits of adaptation measures generally flow to the state undertaking them, rather than to the international community as a whole. For these reasons, the role of international cooperation is very different for adaptation than for mitigation. An international climate regime need not impose commitments to adapt, since states have an interest in doing so on their own. Instead, the primary function of international cooperation is to provide support for adaptation and to facilitate information sharing.

International action to address adaptation has three basic rationales. First, since the biggest impacts of climate change will fall on states that contribute little to the problem, such as small island states, the countries that are causing the problem should, as a matter of restorative justice, provide assistance to those that will bear a disproportionate share of the burden. Second, the countries most severely affected by climate change tend to be poor, with limited capacity to respond. So international assistance is needed to build their capacity. Finally, since the adaptation challenges faced by different countries are similar, states can learn from one another by exchanging information—for example, about tools for evaluating impacts or about successful policies and practices.

C. Finance

Finance emerged as a major issue in international environmental law in the late 1980s. The 1985 Vienna Convention for the Protection of the Ozone Layer did not provide for the transfer of financial resources.[73] Even the 1987 Montreal Protocol, which established specific control measures for developing countries, contained only a very weak commitment by developed countries to 'facilitate the provision of subsidies, aid, credits, guarantees or insurance programmes' to developing countries.[74] Following Montreal, however, developing countries began to assert that

---

[72] European Commission, Climate Action, 'Adaptation to Climate Change' <http://ec.europa.eu/clima/policies/adaptation/index_en.htm> accessed 20 January 2017.

[73] Vienna Convention for the Protection of the Ozone Layer (adopted 22 March 1985, entered into force 22 September 1988) 1513 UNTS 293.

[74] Montreal Protocol, Art 5.3.

they would accept obligations to limit their use of ozone-depleting substances only if developed states agreed to provide them with additional financial resources and technology. The 1990 London Amendments responded by establishing a World Bank-administered fund to help developing countries implement the Montreal Protocol.[75] For the most part, the UN climate regime picked up where the negotiations on the London Amendments left off.

Given the scale of resources required for mitigation and adaptation, and the arguable inequities inherent in visiting costly mitigation and adaptation measures on developing countries, especially those with negligible emissions and capacity, the extent of support offered to these countries is key to addressing climate change. But the world of finance brings its own set of complications, technocrats, and sensitivities. It involves many inter-related issues, which have plagued negotiators over the years:

- *What should be the overall magnitude of international funding?* As noted earlier, the World Bank and FCCC secretariat have estimated costs of hundreds of billions of dollars per year.[76] How much of these costs should be funded internationally? Although developed countries pledged at the 2009 Copenhagen conference (and again in the 2015 Paris Agreement) to mobilize $100 billion per year for climate finance,[77] this amount still falls well short of the World Bank and FCCC estimates. And, there are differing reports on the extent to which even this relatively modest commitment is on track to being fulfilled.[78]

- *Where should international funding come from—public sources, private sector investment flows, or automatic mechanisms such as a carbon tax?* The $100 billion mobilization pledge by developed countries includes funds mobilized from private sources (which, according to the FCCC secretariat, currently account for 86% of climate finance[79]).

---

[75] Amendment to the Montreal Protocol on Substances that Deplete the Ozone Layer (adopted 29 June 1990, entered into force 10 August 1992) (1991) 30 ILM 537.

[76] See nn 50–51 above and accompanying text.

[77] Decision 2/CP.15, 'Copenhagen Accord' (30 March 2010) FCCC/CP/2009/11/Add.1, 4 (Copenhagen Accord), para 8 (pledging to mobilize $100 billion per year by 2020); Decision 1/CP.21 (n 20) para 53 (extending $100 billion pledge through 2025).

[78] Compare Organisation for Economic Co-operation and Development (OECD), 'Climate Finance in 2013-2014 and USD 100 Billion Goal' (2015) <http://www.oecd.org/env/cc/Climate-Finance-in-2013-14-and-the-USD-billion-goal.pdf> accessed 20 January 2017 ($62 billion in climate finance mobilized in 2014) with Climate Change Finance Unit, Ministry of Finance, Government of India, 'Climate Change Finance, Analysis of a Recent OECD Report: Some Credible Facts Needed' (2015) <http://pibphoto.nic.in/documents/rlink/2015/nov/p2015112901.pdf > accessed 20 January 2017 (criticizing the methodology of the OECD report).

[79] FCCC, 'Fact sheet: Financing climate change action: Investment and financial flows for a strengthened response to climate change' <http://unfccc.int/press/fact_sheets/items/4982.php> accessed 20 January 2017. See generally Barbara Buchner et al., 'The Landscape of Climate Finance 2012' (Climate Policy Initiative, November 2012) <http://climatepolicyinitiative.org/wp-content/uploads/2012/12/The-Landscape-of-Climate-Finance-2012.pdf> accessed 20 January 2017; Smita Nakhooda, Neil Bird, and Liane Schalatek, 'Climate Finance Fundamentals Brief 3: Adaptation Finance' (Heinrich Böll Stiftung and Overseas Development Institute, November 2011).

- *If public funds are used, which countries should have funding obligations and how should the level of their contributions be determined?* Should provision of support, and the quantum, be mandatory or voluntary? The UN climate regime imposes obligations to provide finance only on countries included in Annex II to the FCCC (comprising members of the Organization of Economic and Cooperation and Development (OECD) as of 1992), but allows each Annex II party to decide on the amount of its contribution.

- *Which countries should be entitled to receive assistance?* Should all developing countries be included, a sub-set that have special circumstances such as Least Developed Countries (LDCs) and Small Island Developing States, or a broader group that includes economies in transition (EITs) and Turkey? The UN climate regime generally provides assistance only to developing countries,[80] but does not define exactly which countries count as developing.

- *What types of costs should be covered?* Should finance be provided only for the costs of preparing GHG inventories and reports or also for implementing measures to reduce emissions, for adapting to climate change, and for the 'loss and damage' caused by climate change? There is some appetite among developed countries to provide financial assistance for reporting, but little or none for the other categories of costs.

- *How should financial resources be administered?* Who should decide how the money is spent? Should spending be determined bilaterally through negotiations between the donor and recipient states? Or should financial assistance be administered multilaterally—for example, by an existing institution such as the Global Environment Facility (GEF) or by a new institution created under the FCCC? The FCCC established a multilateral financial mechanism (initially operated by the GEF, now also by the Green Climate Fund), but also recognized that states could provide assistance bilaterally.[81]

D. Oversight

International oversight encompasses mechanisms to promote implementation, compliance, and effectiveness. These can include: (1) national reporting on GHG emissions and on mitigation and adaptation measures, (2) expert review of information provided by states, (3) mechanisms to assess implementation and compliance, (4) reviews of effectiveness, and (5) formal dispute settlement. All but the latter figure prominently in international climate change law. The FCCC established reporting requirements, authorized the development of an expert review process, and provided for a review of effectiveness. The Kyoto Protocol created more stringent oversight for states with binding emissions targets, including a compliance mechanism that can take enforcement actions. And the Paris Agreement provides

---

[80] FCCC, Art 4.3.   [81] Ibid, Art 11.5.

for an enhanced transparency framework applicable to all parties, an implementation and compliance mechanism, and regular stocktakes of progress.

V. RECURRING THEMES IN
THE UN CLIMATE REGIME

In seeking to address the climate change problem, the UN climate regime has explored different solutions—tweaking, amending, and even changing course. Three recurring issues have characterized these explorations: the legal form of climate instruments and the legal character of provisions in them; the architecture of climate instruments; and differentiation among countries, in particular, between developed and developing countries.

The experimentation within the climate regime, in relation to all three recurring themes, reflects parties' sustained effort to develop a regime that is both effective and equitable.[82] For the regime to be effective, it must attract wide, if not universal, participation, it must provide for deep cuts in global emissions, and it must be complied with. However, securing universal participation as well as deep cuts has proven difficult because of concerns about reciprocity, economic harm, and fairness or equity in burden sharing. To be effective over time, the agreement also needs to be responsive to evolving science and technology as well as changing economic conditions and emissions profiles of countries and regions. This dimension too has proven difficult to secure in the UN climate regime. Many of the difficulties in securing participation, deep cuts, and evolution in the climate regime can be traced to a lack of trust among its participants. Ultimately, for an agreement to be effective it must generate a sense of ownership and commitment, which can only develop under conditions of mutual confidence and understanding. The climate regime's experiments with legal form and character, architecture, and differentiation speak to the issues of building trust, encouraging participation and promoting learning, dynamism, compliance, and effectiveness. These issues are further discussed in Chapter 3, and the three recurring themes introduced below provide the context and sub-text for much of the discussion in the subsequent chapters of this book.

A. Legal bindingness

The potentially high costs of climate change action, combined with the deeply discordant political context in which the climate regime has evolved, have led to considerable innovation in developing legal instruments and provisions of varying degrees of normative force,[83] thereby blurring the boundaries between

---

[82] See eg Kal Raustalia, 'Compliance and Effectiveness in International Regulatory Cooperation', *Case Western Reserve Journal International Law*, 32/3 (2000): 387.

[83] This section draws on material from French and Rajamani, Climate Change and International Environmental Law (n 59).

law and non-law. A legally binding instrument 'communicates expectations', 'produces reliance', and generates 'compliance pull'.[84] In these ways, it helps generate 'credible commitments',[85] and its violation entails higher reputational costs.[86] Legally binding instruments also typically are more durable and survive domestic political changes more than non-binding ones.[87] However, committing to a legally binding instrument also entails significant real and perceived 'sovereignty costs'.[88] States may lose autonomy over decision-making in some of the areas regulated by the agreement as well as expose national decision-making to international scrutiny.[89] There is a risk, therefore, that making an instrument legally binding will lead to less participation or less ambitious commitments, thereby negatively impacting its effectiveness.[90] For example, many states, including China, India, and the US, were unwilling to accept legally binding limits on their emissions in the Kyoto Protocol and, as a result, it covered only about a quarter of global emissions. In turn this outcome helped prompt innovation and experimentation with informal, soft, and hortatory norms, which could garner more widespread participation. These issues are discussed in further detail in Chapter 3.

1. Treaties

The 1992 FCCC, its 1997 Kyoto Protocol, and the 2015 Paris Agreement, as treaties, are legally binding instruments. However, provisions within these instruments vary in their legal force, ranging from those that merely provide context or narrative to those that establish legal obligations.[91] The legal 'bindingness' of a treaty provision depends on many factors, including:

- Where it occurs—in the preamble or operative part of an agreement.
- Who the provision addresses—states, collectively or individually, or others.
- Whether it uses mandatory or recommendatory language.
- How precise it is.

---

[84] Dinah Shelton, 'Introduction', in Dinah Shelton (ed), *Commitment and Compliance: The Role of Non-Binding Norms in the International Legal System* (Oxford University Press, 2000) 8; Thomas M. Franck, *The Power of Legitimacy Among Nations* (Oxford University Press, 1993).

[85] Kenneth Abbott and Duncan Snidal, 'Hard and Soft Law in International Governance', *International Organisation*, 54/3 (2000): 421, 426.

[86] Ibid, 427; see also Jacob Werksman, 'The Legal Character of International Environmental Obligations in the Wake of the Paris Climate Change Agreement' (Brodies Environmental Law Lecture Series, 2016).

[87] Werksman, ibid. There are exceptions of course. Consider the example of Canada, which signed and ratified the Kyoto Protocol under one government but changed its attitude toward, and eventually withdrew from, the protocol under another government.

[88] Abbott and Snidal (n 86) 436–41.   [89] Ibid.

[90] Daniel Bodansky, 'Legally-Binding versus Non-Legally Binding Instruments', in Scott Barrett, Carlo Carraro, and Jaime de Melo (eds), *Towards a Workable and Effective Climate Regime* (London: Centre for Economic Policy Research Press, 2015) 155.

[91] See Chapter 7, Section II.A.

- What institutional mechanisms exist for transparency, accountability, and compliance.[92]

Thus, for instance, the GHG mitigation obligation in the FCCC's Article 4.2 requiring developed countries to take policies and measures, 'with the aim of' returning to 1990 emissions levels, is a soft obligation or a 'quasi-target'.[93] The GHG mitigation obligation in Article 3 of the Kyoto Protocol requiring developed countries to meet their GHG targets listed in Annex B is a hard obligation (parties 'shall'),[94] as are the obligations in Article 4.2 of the Paris Agreement to prepare, communicate, and maintain nationally determined contributions (NDCs). The distinction between 'obligations of conduct' and 'obligations of result' is also significant, and the international climate regime is replete with instances of both. Kyoto Protocol Article 3 is an obligation of result in that parties are bound to achieve the targets listed in Annex B, in contrast to Paris Agreement Article 4.2, which establishes obligations of conduct (eg to 'prepare, communicate and maintain' NDCs).

2. Decisions of parties

In addition to treaties, the international climate regime contains hundreds of decisions taken by the conferences of parties to the FCCC and the Kyoto Protocol.[95] Conference of the parties (COP) decisions are not in a formal sense legally binding, unless the parent treaty provides explicit authority to the COP to take binding decisions.[96] COP decisions have come, however, to acquire tremendous operational and legal significance in the climate regime. They have enriched and expanded the normative core of the regime by fleshing out treaty provisions,[97] reviewing the adequacy of existing obligations,[98] and launching negotiations to adopt further agreements.[99] COP decisions have also created an elaborate institutional

---

[92] Lavanya Rajamani, 'The 2015 Paris Agreement: Interplay Between Hard, Soft and Non-Obligations', *Journal of Environmental Law*, 28/2 (2016): 337; see also Bodansky, Legally Binding versus Non-Legally Binding Instruments (n 90); Daniel Bodansky, 'The Legal Character of the Paris Agreement', *Review of European, Comparative and International Law*, 25/2 (2016): 142.

[93] Chapter 5, Section IV.B.1.   [94] Kyoto Protocol, Art 3.1.

[95] See FCCC, Art 7; Kyoto Protocol, Art 9; some argue that the legislative competencies provided in some multilateral environmental agreements to progressively develop the regime amount to 'powers of formal revision of the treaty'. See Volker Röben, 'Institutional Developments under Modern International Environmental Agreements', *Max Planck Yearbook of United Nations Law*, 4/1 (2000): 363, 391.

[96] From a formal legal perspective COP decisions are not, absent explicit authorization, legally binding. See Jutta Brunnée, 'COPing with Consent: Law-Making under Multilateral Environmental Agreements', *Leiden Journal of International Law*, 15/1 (2002): 1.

[97] See eg Kyoto Protocol, Arts 6.2, 12.7, and 17, and Decision 2/CMP.1, 'Principles, Nature and Scope of the Mechanisms pursuant to Article 6, 12 and 17 of the Kyoto Protocol' (30 March 2006) FCCC/KP/CMP/2005/8/Add.1.

[98] Pursuant to FCCC, Art 4.2(d).

[99] See eg Decision 1/CP.1, 'The Berlin Mandate: Review of the adequacy of Article 4, paragraph 2(a) and (b), of the Convention, including proposals related to a protocol and decisions on follow-up' (6 June 1995) FCCC/CP/1995/7/Add.1, 4 (Berlin Mandate); Decision 1/CP.17, 'Establishment of an Ad Hoc Working Group on the Durban Platform for Enhanced Action' (11 December 2011) FCCC/CP/2011/9/Add.1, 2 (Durban Platform).

architecture to supervise implementation and compliance.[100] The operational significance of COP decisions is further strengthened by the fact that treaty language in the climate regime is often marked by constructive ambiguity, reflecting and auguring protracted dissonance. Therefore, agreed language, even in COP decisions, is often highlighted, cited, and reproduced in subsequent legal texts. For instance, selective language from the Berlin Mandate, a COP decision, is reflected verbatim in operational provisions of the Kyoto Protocol.[101] In addition, COP decisions such as the Berlin Mandate, the Bali Action Plan,[102] and the Durban Platform, which launched new rounds of negotiations, created frameworks and attendant boundaries that parties seldom diverged from. The Berlin Mandate, for instance, specifically excluded new commitments for developing countries and the Kyoto Protocol consequently contained none.

COP decisions also often contain many of the characteristics that provide normative force, despite the fact they are not a formal source of law. They can be precise, as for instance decisions relating to the eligibility requirements to participate in emissions trading.[103] They, on occasion, use mandatory language ('shall').[104] As a result, COP decisions may influence and condition state behavior—indeed, even exert a compliance pull—to a greater extent than imprecise or hortatory treaty provisions.

3. *Political agreements*

In addition to treaties and decisions of parties, the international climate regime contains political agreements of tremendous salience, most notably the 2009 Copenhagen Accord.[105] The Copenhagen Accord was reached among heads of state and government of twenty-eight parties to the FCCC, including all major emitters and economies, as well as those representing the most vulnerable and least developed states, but was only noted by the COP, not formally adopted.[106] The Copenhagen Accord therefore was neither a COP decision that could be operationalized through the FCCC institutional architecture, nor an independent

---

[100] For example, bodies with considerable influence and consequences for state and non-state actors, such as the Clean Development Mechanism Executive Board, the Joint Implementation Supervisory Committee, and the Compliance Committee, were all constituted by COP decisions. See Decisions 2-24/CP.7, 'Marrakesh Accords' (21 January 2002) FCCC/CP/2001/13 (Marrakesh Accords).

[101] Compare paragraph 2(b), Berlin Mandate, and the chapeau of Article 10, Kyoto Protocol. Both contain language on not 'introducing any new commitments for Parties not included in Annex I, but reaffirming existing commitments'.

[102] Decision 1/CP.13, 'Bali Action Plan' (14 March 2008) FCCC/CP/2007/6/Add.1, 3 (Bali Action Plan).

[103] Decision 11/CMP.1, 'Modalities, rules and guidelines for emissions trading under Article 17 of the Kyoto Protocol' (30 March 2006) FCCC/KP/CMP/2005/8/Add.2.

[104] Brunnée, COPing with Consent (n 96) 26, 29.

[105] Other examples include Report of the Conference of the Parties on its Second Session, held at Geneva from 8 to 19 July 1996, Addendum (29 October 1996) FCCC/CP/1996/15/Add.1, Annex: The Geneva Ministerial Declaration; Decision 1/CP.8, 'Delhi Ministerial Declaration on Climate Change and Sustainable Development' (28 March 2003) FCCC/CP/2002/7/Add.1.

[106] Decision 2/CP.15 (n 77) preambular recital.

plurilateral agreement with its own operational architecture and legal commitments. The FCCC Secretariat, in fact, has made it clear that the Accord's provisions 'do not have any legal standing' in the UN climate regime.[107] Yet the Accord is arguably one of the most influential documents to have emerged from the climate negotiations. Its architecture, which privileges national sovereignty over international prescription,[108] captures self-selected targets and actions, and focuses on transparency provisions, represented a step change in the evolution of the climate regime, and provided a template for the design of the 2015 Paris Agreement.[109] The true significance of the Accord lies not in its legal character, but rather in the emerging political consensus that it reflects. First, unlike any multilateral agreement in living memory, the heads of state of the world's largest economies negotiated the Copenhagen Accord. It thus provides unparalleled political guidance in an area rife with discord.[110] Second, 141 states representing over 87%[111] of global emissions eventually associated themselves with the Accord.[112] By contrast, although the Kyoto Protocol has 192 parties, its emissions reductions commitments cover only a fraction of global emissions.[113] Third, the political compromises in the Accord were fleshed out and adopted into the formal UN process a year later through the Cancun Agreements adopted by COP16.[114] The influence of the Copenhagen Accord exemplifies the now increasingly credible thesis that, in international environmental law, 'informal, non-binding norms may come to shape practice quite effectively'.[115] In contrast, the Kyoto Protocol, despite its legally binding character

---

[107] See FCCC, 'Notification to Parties, Clarification relating to the Notification of 18 January 2010' (25 January 2010) <http://unfccc.int/files/parties_and_observers/notifications/application/pdf/100125_noti_clarification.pdf> accessed 20 January 2017.

[108] See Submission from the US 'Submission of the United States to the AWG-LCA Chair' (30 April 2010) FCCC/AWGLCA/2010/MISC.2, 79 (noting that '[t]he Accord text also usefully bows in the direction of national sovereignty').

[109] See Daniel Bodansky, 'The Paris Climate Agreement: A New Hope?', *American Journal of International Law*, 11/02 (2016): 288.

[110] See Submission from Japan (30 April 2010) FCCC/AWGLCA/2010/MISC.2, 66 (noting that the Accord is an 'extremely important document' and it provides 'high level political guidance'), Submission from New Zealand (30 April 2010) FCCC/AWGLCA/2010/MISC.2, 72 (noting that 'it is a clear letter of political intent and unprecedented in its conception'); the Submission from the United States (16 March 2010) FCCC/KP/AWG/2010/MISC.1 and FCCC/AWGLCA/2010/MISC.1, 48 (noting 'the historic nature' of the Copenhagen Conference).

[111] See US Climate Action Network, 'Who's On Board with the Copenhagen Accord?', <http://www.usclimatenetwork.org/policy/copenhagen-accord-commitments> accessed 20 January 2017.

[112] See FCCC, 'Copenhagen Accord' <http://unfccc.int/meetings/copenhagen_dec_2009/items/5262.php> accessed 20 January 2017.

[113] Japan cited this as the reason for its decision not to adopt second commitment period targets under Kyoto. See Ministry of Foreign Affairs, Government of Japan, 'Japan's Position Regarding the Kyoto Protocol' (December 2010) <http://www.mofa.go.jp/policy/environment/warm/cop/kp_pos_1012.html> accessed 20 January 2017.

[114] Decision 1/CP.16, 'The Cancun Agreements: Outcome of the work of the Ad Hoc Working Group on Long-term Cooperative Action under the Convention' (15 March 2011) FCCC/CP/2010/7/Add.1, 2 (Cancun Agreements LCA).

[115] Stephen J. Toope, 'Formality and Informality', in Daniel Bodansky, Jutta Brunnée, and Ellen Hey (eds), *Oxford Handbook of International Environmental Law* (Oxford University Press, 2007) 108, 119.

and its many innovations,[116] did not see much of its architecture survive in the 2015 agreement.

It is not unusual in international environmental law for a soft law instrument to act as a precursor for a hard law instrument,[117] as the Copenhagen Accord did for the Paris Agreement. What is unusual is that the soft law in this instance did not predate the entire formal regime, viz. the FCCC and Kyoto Protocol, but was resorted to at a particular stage in the evolution of the climate regime—an experimental stage that necessitated a roll back in the formality of the law. The progression of norms in the climate regime thus did not assume a linear trajectory from soft to hard. Rather, it meandered back and forth, from the comparatively vague and in some cases hortatory provisions of the FCCC, to the hard obligations of result in the Kyoto Protocol, to the political agreement reflected in the Copenhagen Accord, to the hard obligations of conduct in the Paris Agreement.

B. Architecture

International agreements vary widely in the latitude that they give participating states.[118] Some take a top-down approach, defining particular policies and measures that parties must undertake. Others adopt a more bottom-up approach, allowing each participating state to define its own commitments. In the environmental realm, the Convention on International Trade in Endangered Species (CITES)[119] illustrates the top-down approach. It prescribes which species to protect and how to do so (through a permitting system for imports and exports).[120] Similarly, MARPOL prescribes very specific rules regarding the construction, design, and performance of oil tankers.[121] Conversely, the US–Canada Air Quality Agreement illustrates a more bottom-up approach, largely codifying in an international agreement the domestic air pollution programs of the two participating states.[122]

---

[116] Differentiation in central obligations, and the enforcement branch of the compliance system, to name two.

[117] For example, in regulating trade in chemicals and pesticides, states initially negotiated the International Code of Conduct on the Distribution and Use of Pesticides (adopted on 28 November 1985 by Resolution 10/85 by the Food and Agriculture Organization of the United Nations Conference at its Twenty-third Session) and the London Guidelines for the Exchange of Information on Chemicals in International Trade (adopted by the UNEP Governing Council at its Fourteenth session). See UNEP Governing Council Decision 14/27 'Environmentally safe management of chemicals, in particular those that are banned and severely restricted in international trade' Official Records of the General Assembly, Forty-second Session (8–19 June 1987) (28 September 1987) Supplement No. 25 (A/42/25). These two documents became the basis for the Rotterdam Convention. See Rotterdam Convention on the Prior Informed Consent Procedure for Certain Hazardous Chemicals and Pesticides in International Trade (adopted 10 September 1998, entered into force 24 February 2004) 2244 UNTS 337.

[118] This paragraph is drawn from Daniel Bodansky, 'A Tale of Two Architectures: The Once and Future U.N. Climate Change Regime', *Arizona State Law Journal*, 43/6 (2011): 697.

[119] Convention on International Trade in Endangered Species of Wild Fauna and Flora (adopted 3 March 1973, entered into force 1 July 1975) 993 UNTS 243.

[120] Ibid.   [121] MARPOL 73/78 (n 69) Annex I.

[122] Agreement Between the Government of Canada and the Government of the United States of America on Air Quality (entered into force 31 March 1991) (1991) 30 ILM 676.

Similarly, the Ramsar Convention on Wetlands encourages countries to promote the conservation and 'wise use' of wetlands, but gives countries broad discretion to determine the policies and measures that they will use to do so.[123]

In the UN climate regime, states have continually grappled with the issue of how much latitude to give states in developing their own climate change policies. Some argue that the nature of climate change as a classic collective action problem demands a top-down approach, which prescribes collectively negotiated emissions targets for states. Others advocate a bottom-up, facilitative approach in which international pledges grow out of, and reflect, domestic policies.[124] They argue that such an approach is necessary, since climate change is not simply an international issue; it engages virtually every aspect of domestic policy.

In essence, the history of the UN climate regime ever since has consisted of variations on these two architectures:

- The FCCC had elements of both architectures. On the one hand, it established a system of 'pledge and review', in which states put forward nationally determined policies and measures subject to international review. On the other hand, it established an internationally negotiated emissions aim for the developed countries and other parties listed in Annex I to the FCCC.[125]

- The Kyoto Protocol reflected a more top-down prescriptive approach. Although it gave parties flexibility in deciding how to implement their emissions targets, the targets themselves were internationally negotiated rather than nationally determined.[126]

- The Copenhagen Accord/Cancun Agreements moved toward a bottom-up facilitative approach, centered around nationally determined pledges.[127]

- Finally, the Paris Agreement reflects a hybrid architecture, containing both bottom-up and top-down elements.[128]

As the Kyoto Protocol and the Copenhagen Accord illustrate, the top-down and bottom-up approach each have advantages and disadvantages. The Kyoto Protocol represents the archetypal 'top-down' architecture, with its pursuit of a common objective implemented through multilaterally negotiated targets and timetables, a strong measurement, reporting and verification (MRV) system, and a compliance mechanism with an enforcement branch.[129] However, while these elements all promoted ambition, they came at the expense of participation. The Kyoto Protocol

---

[123] Convention on Wetlands of International Importance especially as Waterfowl Habitat (adopted 2 February 1971, entered into force 21 December 1975) 996 UNTS 245 (Ramsar Convention) Art 3.1.

[124] Bodansky, Paris Climate Agreement (n 109).

[125] See generally Chapter 5, discussing the FCCC.

[126] See generally Chapter 6, discussing the Kyoto Protocol.

[127] See generally Bodansky, Tale of Two Architectures (n 118).

[128] See generally Chapter 7, discussing the Paris Agreement.

[129] For a defense of the top-down architecture, see William Hare *et al.*, 'The Architecture of the Global Climate Regime: A Top-Down Perspective', *Climate Policy*, 10/6 (2010): 600. See also Harald Winkler and Judy Beaumont, 'Fair and Effective Multilateralism in the Post-Copenhagen Climate Negotiations', *Climate Policy*, 10/6 (2010): 638.

excluded developing countries' emissions from the ambit of its emissions targets, and failed to attract the participation of the US. Moreover, participation further shrunk in the Kyoto Protocol's second commitment period running from 2013 to 2020, with several developed countries opting out, including Japan and Russia.[130] Although the parties with emissions targets were all assessed in compliance at the end of first commitment period in 2012, they accounted for only 24% of 2010 global emissions,[131] and the Kyoto Protocol will cover an even smaller fraction of global emissions in its second commitment period, assuming the relevant amendment enters into force.[132]

In contrast, the FCCC, the Copenhagen Accord, and the Cancun Agreements all, to varying degrees, endorse a 'bottom-up' approach, and garnered much greater participation. Although a top-down approach is not necessarily incompatible with flexibility, a bottom-up approach grants more discretion and autonomy to states and therefore, arguably, is better suited to their diversity of national circumstances, political constraints, and developmental choices.[133] The FCCC has attracted universal participation, and 141 countries put forward emissions pledges under the Copenhagen Accord, representing more than 85% of global emissions.[134] This broader participation not only increases the regime's environmental effectiveness; it can also reduce costs by including more low cost mitigation options across a larger market.[135] Nevertheless, greater participation does not necessarily produce greater effectiveness, since greater heterogeneity of participants often comes at the expense of ambition and rigor.[136] The Copenhagen/Cancun pledges were modest in their

---

[130] See Letter to Ms Christiana Figueres, Executive Secretary of the UNFCCC, from the Head of Roshydromet, National Climate Change Coordinator, The Russian Federation (8 December 2010) <http://unfccc.int/files/meetings/cop_15/copenhagen_accord/application/pdf/russianfederation_cph10.pdf> accessed 20 January 2017; Letter to Ms Christiana Figueres, Executive Secretary of the UNFCCC, from the Japanese Ambassador for COP16 of the UNFCCC (10 December 2010) <http://unfccc.int/files/meetings/ad_hoc_working_groups/kp/application/pdf/japan_awgkp15.pdf> accessed 20 January 2017. New Zealand has decided not to accept an emissions target in Kyoto's second commitment period, see Tim Groser, 'New Zealand Commits to UN Framework Convention', *Government of New Zealand Press Release* (9 November 2012) <https://www.beehive.govt.nz/release/new-zealand-commits-un-framework-convention> accessed 20 January 2017. Canada has formally withdrawn from the Kyoto Protocol. See United Nations, Kyoto Protocol to the United Nations Framework Convention on Climate Change, 11 December 1997, 'Canada: Withdrawal' (16 December 2011) C.N.796.2011.TREATIES-1 <http://unfccc.int/files/kyoto_protocol/background/application/pdf/canada.pdf.pdf> accessed 20 January 2017.
[131] Igor Shishlov, Romain Morel, and Valentin Bellassen, 'Compliance of the Parties to the Kyoto Protocol in the First Commitment Period', *Climate Policy*, 16/6 (2016): 768.
[132] Australia, Belarus, the EU, Iceland, Kazakhstan, Norway, Switzerland, and Ukraine between them account for 13.96% of global GHG emissions in 2010, excluding emissions from the land sector. Even if contributions to the global carbon stock or historical responsibility is factored in, these countries will account only for 24% of global CO_2 emissions. Cumulative CO_2 emissions excluding LULUCF during 1850–2012 (in % of world total)—the EU (24%), Australia (0.01%), Norway (0.001%), Switzerland (0.002%). See WRI, CAIT Climate Data Explorer (n 40).
[133] For a defense of the bottom-up architecture see Steve Rayner, 'How to Eat an Elephant: A Bottom-up Approach to Climate Policy', *Climate Policy*, 10/6 (2010): 615.
[134] US Climate Action Network, Copenhagen Accord (n 111).
[135] See discussion in IPCC, *Climate Change 2014: Mitigation of Climate Change* (n 11) 1014.
[136] As the LDCs warned in the Durban Platform negotiations, '[a] voluntary, non-binding, pledge and review regime is unable to deliver what is required by science to address the climate challenge

ambition and also, in some cases, heavily qualified and conditioned on actions by others.[137] As a result, their aggregate effect[138] fell well short of the emissions pathways consistent with the goal of limiting global average temperature increase to below 2° C above pre-industrial levels.[139]

The Paris Agreement seeks to find a middle ground, through a hybrid architecture that combines a bottom-up approach to promote flexibility and participation with a top-down system of international rules to promote ambition and accountability.[140] The bottom-up element comprises the NDCs of parties.[141] Although these are subject to expectations of 'progression' and 'highest possible ambition'[142] for all and leadership for developed countries, they are ultimately self-determined, making it possible for countries across the entire spectrum of differing national circumstances to participate. The top-down elements comprise these expectations referred to, the five-year cycles of global stocktake to assess collective progress toward long-term goals and successive NDCs,[143] a transparency framework applicable to all,[144] and a facilitative compliance system.[145] The Paris Agreement, with its hybrid architecture, has proven its ability to attract virtually universal participation: 191 states,[146] accounting for 99% of global emissions,[147] have submitted NDCs in the context of the Paris Agreement. A record 175 FCCC parties signed the Agreement on 22 April 2016,[148] when it opened for signature, and the Paris Agreement entered into force on 4 November 2016, less than a year after it was adopted.[149] However, the contributions submitted by parties so far, like the pledges submitted under the Copenhagen Accord and Cancun Agreements, are not consistent with limiting temperature rise to 2° C.[150] Moreover, many of the top-down

and could lead towards 4° C warming world'. Submission by Nepal on behalf of the Least Developed Countries Group on the ADP Work Stream 1: The 2015 Agreement, Building on the Conclusions of the ADP 1-2 (3 September 2013) <http://unfccc.int/files/documentation/submissions_from_parties/adp/application/pdf/adp_ldcs_20130903.pdf> accessed 20 January 2017.

[137] See generally Lavanya Rajamani, 'The Making and Unmaking of the Copenhagen Accord', *International and Comparative Law Quarterly*, 59/3 (2010): 824.

[138] Compilation of economy-wide emission reduction targets to be implemented by Parties included in Annex I to the Convention, Revised note by the secretariat (7 June 2011) FCCC/SB/2011/INF.1/Rev.1; Compilation of information on nationally appropriate mitigation actions to be implemented by Parties not included in Annex I to the Convention, Note by the secretariat (18 March 2011) FCCC/AWGLCA/2011/INF.1.

[139] UNEP, 'Bridging the Emissions Gap – A UNEP Synthesis Report' (UNEP, 2011).

[140] Bodansky, Paris Climate Agreement (n 109).   [141] Paris Agreement, Art 4.2.

[142] Ibid, Art 4.3.   [143] Ibid, Art 14.   [144] Ibid, Art 13.   [145] Ibid, Art 15.

[146] FCCC, 'INDCs as communicated by the Parties' <http://www4.unfccc.int/submissions/indc/Submission%20Pages/submissions.aspx>, accessed 20 January 2017.

[147] FCCC, Aggregate Effect of the Intended Nationally Determined Contributions: An Update, Synthesis report by the secretariat (2 May 2016) FCCC/CP/2016/2, 4.

[148] See for a list of signatories, FCCC, 'List of 175 signatories to Paris Agreement' <http://newsroom.unfccc.int/paris-agreement/175-states-sign-paris-agreement/> accessed 20 January 2017.

[149] See for the status of ratification, FCCC, 'Paris Agreement - Status of Ratification' <http://unfccc.int/paris_agreement/items/9485.php> accessed 20 January 2017.

[150] UNEP, 'The Emissions Gap Report 2015' (Nairobi: UNEP, November 2015) 26 (INDCs are most consistent with long-term scenarios that limit global average temperature increase to below 3–3.5° C by the end of the century with >66% chance); FCCC, Aggregate Effect of the Intended Nationally Determined Contributions (n 147) 13. (According to the AR5, the total global cumulative emissions since 2011 that are consistent with a global average temperature rise of less than 2° C above

elements of the Agreement have yet to be fleshed out, and it remains to be seen how rigorous they will be.

As this history of the UN climate regime illustrates, trade-offs between breadth of participation and depth of commitments are central to the design of international instruments. In essence, the top-down and bottom-up architectures reflect two contrasting strategies for developing a treaty regime over time: a start-deep-and-broaden strategy, and a start-broad-and-deepen strategy. The top-down approach of the Kyoto Protocol sought to achieve depth of commitments first, in the expectation that breadth of participation would develop over time. But when participation in the Kyoto system instead shrunk, parties changed course and adopted the Copenhagen/Cancun approach, which sought to achieve breadth of participation first.[151] The Paris Agreement continues this focus on breadth, but also establishes an expectation of 'progression' and thus of greater depth over time. It remains to be seen whether this hybrid approach will be adequate to respond to the urgency of the climate challenge.

In general, the approach to oversight in international climate change law has reflected the 'managerial' rather than the 'enforcement' model—that is, it has tried to encourage and facilitate national action through transparency, peer pressure, and capacity building, rather than to force states to act through legal prescriptions and sanctions.[152] As explored in Chapters 6 and 7, the Kyoto Protocol experimented with an enforcement-oriented approach, to ensure compliance with its legally-binding emissions targets, but the Paris Agreement returns international climate change law to the managerial model.

C. Differentiation

Like the questions of legal bindingness and architecture, differentiation[153] has been a central issue in the development of international climate change law. The

---

pre-industrial levels at a likely (>66%) probability are 1,000 Gt CO_2. Considering the aggregate effect of the INDCs, global cumulative CO_2 emissions are expected to equal 53% (51–6%) by 2025 and 74% (70–7%) by 2030 of that 1,000 Gt CO_2.)

[151] See discussion in IPCC, *Climate Change 2014: Mitigation of Climate Change* (n 11) 1014–15.

[152] Abram Chayes and Antonia Handler Chayes, *The New Sovereignty: Compliance with International Regulatory Agreements* (Cambridge US: Harvard University Press, 1996) ch. 1.

[153] On CBDRRC, see generally Tuula Honkonen, *The Common But Differentiated Responsibility Principle in Multilateral Environmental Agreements: Regulatory and Policy Aspects* (Alphen aan den Rijn: Kluwer Law International, 2009); Lavanya Rajamani, *Differential Treatment in International Environmental Law* (Oxford University Press, 2006); Christopher D. Stone, 'Common But Differentiated Responsibilities in International Law', *American Journal of International Law*, 98/2 (2004): 276; Jutta Brunnée and Charlotte Streck, 'The UNFCCC as a Negotiation Forum: Towards Common but More Differentiated Responsibilities', *Climate Policy*, 13/5 (2013): 589; Philippe Cullet, 'Principle 7: Common but Differentiated Responsibilities', in Jorge E. Viñuales (ed), *The Rio Declaration on Environment and Development: A Commentary* (Oxford University Press, 2015); D.B. Magraw, 'Legal Treatment of Developing Countries: Differential, Contextual and Absolute Norms', *Colorado Journal of Environmental Law and Policy*, 1/1 (1990): 69; Lavanya Rajamani, 'The Reach and Limits of the Principle of Common but Differentiated Responsibilities and Respective Capabilities in the Climate Change Regime', in Navroz K. Dubash (ed), *Handbook of Climate Change and India:*

principle of common but differentiated responsibilities and respective capabilities (CBDRRC), first articulated in the FCCC, represents a departure from the traditional approach of international agreements, namely, to define a common set of obligations for all parties. It gives expression to the profound equity concerns raised by the climate change challenge, by providing that the climate change commitments of parties should be differentiated, based on their different responsibilities and capabilities.

The principle of CBDRRC is deeply embedded in the UN climate regime. It is anchored in FCCC Article 3. It also features in the Kyoto Protocol,[154] and in several provisions of the Paris Agreement, although in the Paris Agreement it contains the qualifier 'in light of different national circumstances'.[155] Furthermore, the CBDRRC principle is highlighted in numerous COP decisions,[156] and finds reflection in the Copenhagen Accord of 2009.[157]

Although there is universal support for the principle of CBDRRC, there is very little agreement on its rationale, core content, and application in particular situations.[158] With respect to the rationale for differentiation, developing countries have tended to focus on the term 'responsibilities', which they understand to be a function of 'historical emissions', whereas some developed countries—the US, in particular—have focused on the term 'capabilities'. If the different historical contributions of countries to the climate change problem provide the basis for differentiation, as developing countries contend, then differentiation will change relatively slowly. In contrast, if capabilities provide the basis for differentiation, then a country's obligations could evolve more rapidly, as it develops and gains greater financial, technological, and administrative capabilities. The principle of CBDRRC preserves the positions of both sides in this debate, by including both 'responsibilities' and 'respective capabilities' as bases for differentiation.

CBDRRC also does not specify *how* commitments should be differentiated. The Montreal Protocol differentiates the commitments of developed and developing countries in terms of timing. The same control measures apply to all countries, but developing countries get an additional ten years in which to comply.[159] In contrast, the climate regime has differentiated the substantive content of countries' commitments. Some apply to all states, and others only to particular groups of states. The Kyoto Protocol takes differentiation the furthest, establishing quantified emissions limitation targets for Annex I countries but not for non-Annex I countries.

Development, Politics and Governance (New Delhi: Oxford University Press, 2011); Harold Winkler and Lavanya Rajamani, 'CBDR&RC in a Regime Applicable to All', *Climate Policy*, 14/1 (2014): 50.

[154] Kyoto Protocol, Art 10.   [155] Paris Agreement, Art 2.2; see Chapter 7.

[156] See eg Berlin Mandate; Bali Action Plan; Cancun Agreements LCA; Decision 1/CMP.6, 'The Cancun Agreements: Outcome of the work of the Ad Hoc Working Group on Further Commitments for Annex I Parties under the Kyoto Protocol at its fifteenth session' (15 March 2011) FCCC/KP/CMP/2010/12/Add.1.

[157] Copenhagen Accord, para 1.

[158] For a detailed analysis see Rajamani, CBDRRC Reach and Limits (n 153) 118.

[159] Montreal Protocol, Art 5.

Finally, CBDRRC is usually associated with the division between 'developed' and 'developing' countries (and the associated division in the FCCC and the Kyoto Protocol between Annex I and non-Annex I parties), but this is not the only basis on which countries might be differentiated. Certainly, in the climate regime, CBDRRC has focused on the respective commitments of developed and developing countries, and the invocation of CBDRRC is followed in FCCC Article 3.1 by the statement, '[a]ccordingly, the developed country Parties should take the lead in combating climate change and the adverse effects thereof', and then, in FCCC Article 3.2, by a recognition of the specific needs and special circumstances of developing countries. But the UN climate regime also recognizes other bases for differentiation, including countries' economic structures and resource bases and their vulnerability to climate change.[160]

The continuing controversies over the issue of differentiation have led to considerable innovation and experimentation in international climate change law.[161] The FCCC and the Kyoto Protocol take a categorical approach to differentiation: that is, they categorize parties into different groups and match particular commitments to particular categories of parties. The FCCC establishes four such categories: (1) parties listed in Annex I (often equated with 'developed countries'), (2) parties listed in Annex II, (3) parties listed in Annex I but not Annex II (the EITs), and (4) parties not listed in Annex I (often equated with 'developing countries'). The norms of differential treatment in evidence in the FCCC and its Kyoto Protocol are of several general types:[162] first, provisions that differentiate between Annex I and non-Annex I parties with respect to the central obligations contained in the treaty, such as emissions reduction targets and timetables, and reporting requirements;[163] second, provisions that differentiate between different categories of parties with respect to implementation, such as delayed compliance schedules,[164] permission to adopt subsequent base years,[165] delayed reporting schedules,[166] and softer approaches to non-compliance;[167] and third, provisions that grant assistance to developing countries, inter alia, financial[168] and technological.[169] Of these, the provisions that differentiate between Annex I and non-Annex I parties with respect to central obligations—such that Annex I parties have targets and timetables for GHG mitigation, while non-Annex I parties do not[170]—have proven the most

---

[160] The FCCC recognizes differences between countries in their economic structures and resources bases, available technologies, and other individual circumstances (Art 4.2(a)). Moreover, it differentiates the commitments not only of Annex I and non-Annex I countries, but also of countries with EITs (Art 4.6), and highlights several other categories of countries, including especially vulnerable states (Arts 3.2, 4.8), least-developed states (Art 4.9), and countries that are highly dependent on fossil fuels (Art 4.10).

[161] See generally Rajamani, *Differential Treatment* (n 153).   [162] Ibid, 93–114.

[163] See eg Kyoto Protocol, Art 3.   [164] Ibid, Art 3.5.   [165] Ibid.

[166] See eg FCCC, Art 12.5.

[167] See eg Decision 24/CP.7, 'Procedures and Mechanisms Relating to Compliance under the Kyoto Protocol' (21 January 2002) FCCC/CP/2001/13/Add.3, 64.

[168] See eg FCCC, Art 4.3.   [169] Ibid, Art 4.5.   [170] Kyoto Protocol, Art 3.

controversial, and the US rejection of the Kyoto Protocol in 2001 can be sourced, in part, to such differentiation.[171]

In the negotiations since the Kyoto Protocol, and in particular since its rejection by the US, there has been a gradual erosion of categorical, annex-based differentiation and a move toward self-differentiation.[172] This shift occurred in response to consistent demands from developed countries that specific mitigation commitments be extended to developing countries. Many developing countries, for their part, vigorously resisted such efforts; some even came together in a negotiating coalition—the Like Minded Developing Countries (LMDCs)—expressly to preserve annex-based differentiation. In Paris, a compromise was struck on differentiation that bypassed the FCCC annexes, built on self-differentiation, and took different approaches to differentiation in different issues areas. In contrast to the explicit categorization of countries seen in the FCCC and Kyoto Protocol annexes, the self-differentiation approach allows parties to define their own commitments, tailor these to their national circumstances, capacities, and constraints, and thus differentiate themselves from each other. The 2009 Copenhagen Accord was built around this type of self-differentiation, and the 2013 Warsaw decision inviting parties to 'initiate or intensify domestic preparations for their intended nationally determined contributions'[173] presaged such a self-differentiated approach in the 2015 Paris Agreement. The development of this approach represented a step change in the climate regime, and set the stage for a more nuanced approach to differentiation in the Paris Agreement. The Paris Agreement neither creates explicit categories of parties nor tailors commitments to categories of parties as the FCCC and the Kyoto Protocol do. Rather, it tailors differentiation to the specificities of each issue area it addresses—mitigation, adaptation, finance, technology, capacity building, and transparency.[174] In effect, this approach has resulted in different forms of differentiation in different issue areas. In the area of mitigation, for instance, the Paris Agreement combines self-differentiation with normative expectations for all countries of 'progression' and 'highest possible ambition', and for developed countries of leadership.[175] In contrast, in the area of transparency, differentiation is tailored to capacities, by providing flexibility to those developing countries 'that need it in the light of their capacities'.[176]

While this fine-grained operationalization of differentiation in the Paris Agreement proved sufficient to secure agreement, it nevertheless leaves several

---

[171] Text of a Letter from the President to Senators Hagel, Helms, Craig, and Roberts (The White House, Office of the Press Secretary, 13 March 2001) <https://georgewbush-whitehouse.archives.gov/news/releases/2001/03/20010314.html> accessed 20 January 2017.

[172] See generally, Lavanya Rajamani, 'The Changing Fortunes of Differential Treatment in International Environmental Law', *International Affairs*, 88/3 (2012): 605.

[173] Decision 1/CP.19, 'Further advancing the Durban Platform' (31 January 2014) FCCC/CP/2013/10/Add.1 (Warsaw decision).

[174] Lavanya Rajamani, 'Ambition and Differentiation in the 2015 Paris Agreement: Interpretative Possibilities and Underlying Politics', *International and Comparative Law Quarterly*, 65/2 (2016): 493.

[175] See Chapter 7, Section II.D.2.a.   [176] Ibid, Section II.D.2.b.

lingering equity concerns unaddressed.[177] For instance, the Paris Agreement uses the terms 'developed' and 'developing' countries without either defining them or using lists as the FCCC and Kyoto Protocol do. Some developing countries may suggest using the FCCC annexes to provide concrete content to these terms. Further in relation to transparency, parties will need to consider which developing countries need flexibility, what kind of flexibility will be provided,[178] and for how long. In these and other areas, the devil of differentiation will lie in the details of the post-Paris negotiations.

Over its more than two-decade evolution, the UN climate regime has explored a variety of approaches to differentiation. In this time, the nature and extent of differentiation has shifted gradually but significantly—from differentiation in central obligations in the Kyoto Protocol, to bounded self-differentiation and tailored flexibility in the Paris Agreement. Yet equity and differentiation remain salient in the regime, and will continue to evolve as the regime evolves.

VI. THE BROADER CONTEXT FOR INTERNATIONAL CLIMATE CHANGE LAW

Responses to the climate change challenge have emerged at multiple levels, in multiple forums across levels, and involve a multitude of actors.[179] The landscape of climate cooperation at the international level includes: action taken under other multilateral environmental agreements; action taken by other treaty regimes and international bodies; and, policy guidance and political signals provided by multilateral, plurilateral, and bilateral 'clubs'.[180] In addition, there is informal cooperation among state and non-state actors across levels and across countries. Cooperation across the full landscape of climate agreements, institutions, and actors plays a critical role in filling gaps in and bolstering, complementing, and implementing international climate change law.

Nearly all human activities contribute to climate change. And climate change will, in turn, have enormous impacts on both humans and the natural environment. Not surprisingly, then, climate change engages many different areas of international law:

- Both climate change and climate change policies could affect the enjoyment of human rights. Climate change, for example, could threaten the rights to life, food, housing, and health,[181] while mitigation and adaptation measures could

---

[177] See eg T. Jayaraman and Tejal Kanitkar, 'The Paris Agreement', *Economic and Political Weekly*, 51/3 (2016): 10.

[178] Decision 1/CP.21 (n 20) para 89 specifies flexibility in 'scope, frequency, and level of detail of reporting, and in the scope of review'.

[179] See IPCC, *Climate Change 2014: Mitigation of Climate Change* (n 11) Fig 13.1.

[180] Robert O. Keohane and David G. Victor, 'The Regime Complex for Climate Change', *Perspectives on Politics*, 9/1 (2011): 7.

[181] Office of the High Commissioner for Human Rights (OHCHR), 'Understanding Human Rights and Climate Change: Submission of the Office of the High Commissioner for Human Rights

impinge on indigenous rights. In 2008, the Office of the High Commissioner of Human Rights initiated a stream of work on Human Rights and Climate Change,[182] and the Human Rights Council has adopted a series of resolutions alerting states to the inter-connections between human rights and climate change, and reminding them of their obligations under human rights instruments.[183] Due in large part to these interventions, and those of various non-state actors, the 2015 Paris Agreement recognizes the intersections between human rights and climate change, albeit in a preambular recital.[184]

- Rising temperatures and ocean acidification will affect the marine environment and, in particular, coral reefs, thereby raising law of the sea issues. In addition, sea level rise will change the baselines from which states' maritime zones are measured and is likely to submerge some low-lying island states—issues also addressed by the law of the sea.

- Rising sea levels and extreme weather events may force people to move within and across national borders. The United Nations High Commissioner for Refugees and the International Organization on Migration, among others, have a range of policy, research, and operational activities to prevent forced migration, to the extent possible, assist affected populations where migration occurs, and facilitate migration as an adaptation strategy.[185] However, existing international legal frameworks are poorly designed to respond to such large-scale movements of persons due to climate and other factors.[186]

- Climate change is likely to severely impact biodiversity and sensitive eco-systems and thus has enormous implications for other multilateral environmental regimes, including the Biological Diversity Convention,[187] the Ramsar Wetlands Convention, and the World Heritage Convention.[188] In

to the 21st Conference of the Parties to the United Nations Framework Convention on Climate Change' (26 November 2015) <http://www.ohchr.org/Documents/Issues/ClimateChange/COP21.pdf> accessed 20 January 2017.

[182] See generally OHCHR, 'Human Rights and Climate Change' <http://www.ohchr.org/EN/Issues/HRAndClimateChange/Pages/HRClimateChangeIndex.aspx> accessed 20 January 2017.

[183] See Human Rights Council Res 32/33, 'Human Rights and Climate Change' (28 June 2016) A/HRC/32/L.34; Human Rights Council Res 29/15, 'Human Rights and Climate Change' (30 June 2015) A/HRC/29/L.21; Human Rights Council Res 26/27, 'Human Rights and Climate Change' (25 June 2014) A/HRC/26/L.33/Rev.1; Human Rights Council Res 18/22, 'Human Rights and Climate Change' (28 September 2011) A/HRC/18/L.26/Rev.1.

[184] Paris Agreement, preambular recital 11.

[185] International Organization for Migration (IOM), 'Migration and Climate Change' <https://www.iom.int/migration-and-climate-change> accessed 20 January 2017; United Nations High Commissioner for Refugees (UNHCR), 'Climate Change and Disasters' <http://www.unhcr.org/pages/49e4a5096.html> accessed 20 January 2017.

[186] See Chapter 9, Section III.

[187] Convention on Biological Diversity (adopted 5 June 1992, entered into force 29 December 1993) 1760 UNTS 79.

[188] Convention for the Protection of the World Cultural and Natural Heritage (adopted 16 November 1972, entered into force 17 December 1975) 1037 UNTS 151 (World Heritage Convention); see generally Catherine Redgwell, 'Climate Change and International Environmental Law', in Rosemary Gail Rayfuse and Shirley V. Scott (eds), *International Law in the Era of Climate Change* (Cheltenham: Edward Elgar Publishing, 2012) 119.

response, these regimes have all begun to consider climate change in various ways. Parties to the Biodiversity Convention have taken a series of decisions to encourage coherence and mutual supportiveness between the biodiversity and climate regimes,[189] including with respect to measures to respond to climate change that could have impacts on species and habitat protection.[190] Ramsar Wetlands Convention conferences have adopted resolutions encouraging parties, inter alia, to increase the resilience of wetlands, promote and restore wetlands that are significant GHG sinks, and ensure that forest-based mitigation measures do not damage the ecological character of wetlands.[191] And the World Heritage Committee has launched initiatives to assess the impacts of climate change on world heritage and define appropriate management responses.[192]

• Climate change could also have security implications. It could act as a 'threat multiplier' for national and international security, exacerbating other sources of violence and conflict.[193] In the last decade the UN Security Council has held several debates on climate change. The first of these led to a UN General Assembly Resolution[194] and a Report by the Secretary-General.[195]

• Measures to address climate change could affect competitiveness and trade flows between countries. Conversely, measures to promote international trade could affect climate change both positively and negatively. As a result, there is the potential for both synergy and conflict between the climate change and trade regimes.

In general, these relationships between climate change and other areas of international law fall into one of two general baskets. In a few cases, other international regimes directly seek to address climate change. The work of the International

---

[189] See eg Decision XI/19, 'Biodiversity and Climate Change related issues: advice on the application of relevant safeguards for biodiversity with regard to policy approaches and positive incentives on issues relating to emissions from deforestation and forest degradation in developing countries; and the role of conservation, sustainable management of forests and enhancement of forest carbon stocks in developing countries' (5 December 2012) UNEP/CBD/COP/DEC/XI/19.

[190] Ibid. For example, reforestation could have positive impacts on biodiversity protection, while ocean iron fertilization could have negative impacts on marine biodiversity.

[191] See eg Resolution XI.14, 'Climate change and wetlands: implications for the Ramsar Covention on Wetlands' (6–13 July 2012).

[192] United Nations Educational, Scientific and Cultural Organization (UNESCO), 'Climate Change and World Heritage' (World Heritage Reports 22, UNESCO, May 2007) <http://whc.unesco.org/en/series/22/> accessed 20 January 2017; UNESCO, 'Development of Policy Document on Impacts of Climate Change and World Heritage' (UNESCO, 2008) <http://whc.unesco.org/en/CC-policy-document/> accessed 20 January 2017; and see generally UNESCO, 'Climate Change: Climate Change and World Heritage' <http://whc.unesco.org/en/climatechange/> accessed 20 January 2017. See also Redgwell, Climate Change and International Environmental Law (n 188).

[193] Permanent Mission of Spain to the United Nations, 'Security Council open Arria-formula meeting on the role of Climate Change as a threat multiplier for Global Security' *Press Office* <http://www.spainun.org/climatechange/> accessed 20 January 2017.

[194] United Nations General Assembly Res 63/281, 'Climate Change and its Possible Security Implications' (11 June 2009) UN Doc A/RES/63/281.

[195] UN Secretary-General, 'Climate Change and its Possible Security Implications' (11 September 2009) UN Doc A/64/350.

Maritime Organization to limit maritime emissions and that of the Montreal Protocol regime to limit HFCs fall into this basket. These will be considered in Chapter 8 as part of the fabric of polycentric climate governance. A much broader array of international legal regimes will be engaged by climate change, but do not (yet) exercise governance functions. Since this book cannot be a book about everything, we will necessarily be selective in 'mapping the edges' of international climate change law, focusing in Chapter 9 on the intersection of climate change law with human rights law, migration law, and trade law.

Climate change is also addressed in various multilateral or plurilateral 'clubs'.[196] Clubs can act as forums for dialogue or focus on implementation.[197] The most prominent among those focused on dialogue is the Major Economies Forum on Climate Change and Energy (MEF). The MEF consists of seventeen developed and developing countries[198] between them accounting for about 80% of the world's emissions.[199] Several 'G' clubs also provide political direction to the climate regime. These 'G' clubs are distinguishable from negotiating coalitions and groups[200] in that they have formal membership, their members have objectively similar characteristics, they have rotating Presidencies, and their mandates cover a broader universe than climate change. 'G' clubs forge common positions, but typically for the purpose of setting a standard rather than negotiating as a block. The G-8, G-8+5, and the G-20 have all played a prominent role, albeit to varying degrees. In addition to these multilateral and plurilateral clubs, bilateral climate cooperation between countries has also played a critical role in reaching a climate deal and shaping its contours, and will likely play a role in implementing it. These 'clubs' will be discussed in greater detail in Chapter 8.

The proliferation of multilateral, plurilateral, and bilateral initiatives to address climate change, and the many inter-connections between climate change law and other areas of international law, have led to a vibrant debate about the fragmentation of global climate governance architecture,[201] the utility and continuing relevance of the FCCC process,[202] and the potential for such clubs to be 'transformational'.[203] Although these debates are of continuing relevance, the 2015 Paris Agreement marks a new phase in international climate cooperation, reflecting a

---

[196] Keohane and Victor, Regime Complex (n 180).

[197] See Lutz Weischer, Jennifer Morgan, and Milap Patel, 'Climate Clubs: Can Small Groups of Countries Make a Big Difference in Addressing Climate Change?', *Review of European, Comparative and International Environmental Law*, 21/3 (2012): 177.

[198] The participants of the MEF include Australia, Brazil, Canada, China, the EU, France, Germany, India, Indonesia, Italy, Japan, Korea, Mexico, Russia, South Africa, the United Kingdom, and the US. 'Major Economies Forum on Energy and Climate' <http://www.majoreconomiesforum.org/> accessed 20 January 2017.

[199] WRI, CAIT Climate Data Explorer (n 40).

[200] The negotiating coalitions active in the climate change negotiations are discussed in Chapter 3, Section II.

[201] Frank Biermann *et al.*, 'The Fragmentation of Global Governance Architectures: A Framework for Analysis', *Global Environmental Politics*, 9/4 (2009): 14.

[202] See eg Keohane and Victor, Regime Complex (n 180) and, compare with Harald Winkler and Judy Beaumont, 'Fair and Effective Multilateralism in the Post-Copenhagen Climate Negotiations', *Climate Policy*, 10/6 (2010): 638.

[203] See Weischer *et al.*, Climate Clubs (n 197).

greater degree of political will and sense of ownership among states. But activities at many other levels, by many other actors, will continue to play a significant role in international climate change law. What will be essential is that these activities by other international institutions, sub-and non-state actors, and clubs of public and private actors complement rather than compete with the FCCC process.

SELECT BIBLIOGRAPHY

Bodansky D., *The Art and Craft of International Environmental Law* (Cambridge, MA: Harvard University Press, 2010).

Carlarne C.P., Gray K.R., and Tarasofsky R. (eds), *The Oxford Handbook of International Climate Change Law* (Oxford University Press, 2016).

Dessler A. and Parson E.A., *The Science and Politics of Global Climate Change: A Guide to the Debate* (Cambridge University Press, 2nd edn, 2010).

Farber D.A. and Peeters M. (eds), *Climate Change Law* (Cheltenham, UK: Edward Elgar, 2016).

French D. and Rajamani L., 'Climate Change and International Environmental Law: Musings on a Journey to Somewhere', *Journal of Environmental Law*, 25/3 (2013): 437.

Gardiner S.M. *et al.* (eds), *Climate Ethics: Essential Readings* (Oxford University Press, 2010).

Lazarus R., 'Super Wicked Problems and Climate Change: Restraining the Present to Liberate the Future', *Cornell Law Review*, 94/5 (2009): 1153.

Nordhaus W.D., *The Climate Casino: Risk, Uncertainty, and Economics for a Warming World* (New Haven, CT: Yale University Press, 2013).

2

Climate Change and International Law

I. INTRODUCTION

International climate change law does not operate in isolation. It is anchored in international environmental law, and in rules of general international law on foundational issues such as state sovereignty, law-making, and state responsibility. This broader legal landscape, the key features of which are explored in this chapter, provides important context for understanding the emergence and evolution of international climate change law.[1]

The chapter begins with a brief overview of the processes through which international legal norms are developed—the 'sources' of international law. It then surveys the evolution of the main rules and principles of international environmental law relevant to climate change. Historically, international law was focused on proven interferences with an individual state's sovereign interests. It was not conceptually equipped to address merely potential or future impacts, the protection of the global commons, or the preservation of a shared natural system, such as the global climate. Due to its focus on states' rights and obligations, classic international law also provided limited recourse to individuals or groups suffering from transboundary harms. Even today, the conceptual framework of international law fails to fully address the many dimensions of the climate challenge.[2] The applicability of international human rights law to climate change issues is considered in Chapter 9. This chapter focuses on the scope, and limitations, of the rules and principles that apply between states. It examines in some detail the general rule whereby states must strive to avert significant transboundary harm (the no-harm rule), a norm that, along with related procedural duties (considered in Section

---

[1] This chapter draws on Jutta Brunnée, 'Common Areas, Common Heritage and Common Concern', in Daniel Bodansky, Jutta Brunnée, and Ellen Hey (eds), *Oxford Handbook of International Environmental Law* (Oxford University Press, 2007) 550; Jutta Brunnée, 'Climate Change and Compliance and Enforcement Processes', in Rosemary Rayfuse and Shirley Scott (eds), *International Law in the Era of Climate Change* (Cheltenham: Edward Elgar Publishing, 2012) 290; Jutta Brunnée, 'The Global Climate Regime: Wither Common Concern?', in Holger P. Hestermeyer *et al.* (eds), *Coexistence, Cooperation and Solidarity: Liber Amicorum Rüdiger Wolfrum* (Leiden, NL; Boston: Martinus Nijhoff Publishers, 2012) 721; and Jutta Brunnée, 'The Sources of International Environmental Law: Interactional Law', in Samantha Besson and Jean d'Aspremont (eds), *The Oxford Handbook on the Sources of International Law* (Oxford University Press, 2017 forthcoming).

[2] See Chapter 1, Section I.

III.A.2 below), remains the conceptual foundation of international environmental law. In considering these core rules of international environmental law, the chapter also canvasses the salient features and constraints of the law of state responsibility and touches upon the main dispute settlement forums available to states. It then traces the emergence of newer norms, such as the duty to conduct environmental impact assessments (EIA), the notion of common concern of humankind, the principle of common but differentiated responsibilities, the precautionary principle, and the concept of sustainable development. While these norms may better capture the inter-temporal and global nature of the climate challenge, they arguably have not become binding international law but remain so-called 'soft law'.

As will become apparent, general international law, while it does serve important functions, is not well suited to tackling complex, global environmental problems, including climate change. That fact helps explain the emergence of treaty-based environmental regimes, specifically designed to address such problems. The key challenges in pursuing climate policy through such regimes flow from the need to induce sufficient numbers of key actors to consent to be bound by the underlying treaty, to develop the regime as the understanding or parameters of the problem evolve, to make meaningful commitments, and to meet those commitments. This chapter highlights these challenges, and the main strategies through which multilateral environmental agreements (MEAs) attempt to address them—treaty development over time, treaty design to induce participation, and treaty-based processes to promote implementation and compliance, all of which have played significant roles in the evolution of international climate change law.

II. THE SOURCES OF INTERNATIONAL LAW

The classic 'sources' of international law include treaties, customary law, and general principles of law.[3] Over time, other norm-setting processes have emerged through which 'soft law' norms are developed, which seek to guide behavior but are not legally binding. All of these traditional and newer sources of international norms play a role in shaping the legal responses to global climate change. By contrast, international or national courts, designed to resolve disputes about the existence and interpretation of binding international law,[4] have played a limited role in the climate context to date.[5]

---

[3] Article 38 of the Statute of the International Court of Justice (ICJ Statute) enumerates the 'sources' of the international legal rules that the Court is to apply. See ICJ Statute (26 June 1945) (1945) 39 AJIL Supp 215. For a more expansive analysis of the 'sources' question, see Brunnée, Sources of International Environmental Law (n 1).

[4] See ibid., ICJ Statute, Art 38.1(d), which provides that judicial decisions are not a 'source' of law, but a 'subsidiary means for the determination of international law'.

[5] But see Christina Voigt, 'The Potential Roles of the ICJ in Climate Change-related Claims', in Daniel A. Farber and Marjan Peeters (eds), *Elgar Encyclopedia of Environmental Law vol 1: Climate Change Law* (Cheltenham, UK: Edward Elgar, 2016) 152; Jacqueline Peel and Hari Osofsky, *Climate Change Litigation: Regulatory Pathways to Cleaner Energy* (Cambridge University Press, 2015) (exploring

Customary international law emerges from the consistent and widespread practice of states, pursued out of a sense of legal obligation (*opinio juris*).[6] Although customary law, therefore, is in principle dynamic, it usually develops slowly and incrementally. States' practices and legal opinions tend to maintain existing rules, and initiating a shift in the practices and views of a sufficient number of states to generate a new customary norm is relatively difficult. As a result, customary rules typically provide general background principles for interaction, rather than specific rules of behavior. Methodologically, as the International Court of Justice (ICJ) has consistently stressed,[7] establishing that a given norm is binding as custom requires evidence of both elements—state practice and *opinio juris*. However, providing such evidence is more difficult than one might assume at first glance. Determining whether state practice is sufficiently consistent and widespread to create a customary rule is a challenging task—in particular, when there is a significant gap between states' physical and verbal practice, that is, between what states say and what they do.[8] Proving that state practice is accompanied by the requisite *opinio juris* can be an even more complicated exercise, since it requires evidence for the views of states, which often are not directly expressed.[9]

Background principles for state interaction can also arise in the guise of the 'general principles' contemplated in Article 38.1 (c) of the ICJ Statute. However, as a 'source' of law, general principles are beset by even greater methodological challenges, notably due to the lingering disagreements about what counts as a general principle in the first place. Some commentators ground general principles in natural law.[10] Others consider the term to refer to principles of domestic law that are found in all major legal systems, such that they can be considered to be 'general

---

the potential of domestic climate litigation in Australia and the United States). See also Sections III.B.2 and III.C below, as well as Chapter 8, Section VI.

[6] For a more detailed treatment, see Brunnée, Sources of International Environmental Law (n 1).

[7] See *North Sea Continental Shelf Cases (Federal Republic of Germany/ Denmark, Federal Republic of Germany/ Netherlands)* (Judgment) [1969] ICJ Rep 3, 44–5 (paras 77–8); *Nicaragua Case (Nicaragua v United States)* (Judgment) [1986] ICJ Rep 14, 108–9 (para 107); and *Jurisdictional Immunities of the State (Germany v Italy: Greece Intervening)* (Judgment) [2012] ICJ Rep 99, 123 (para 55).

[8] See Daniel Bodansky, 'Customary (and Not So Customary) International Environmental Law', *Indiana Journal of Global Legal Studies*, 3/1 (1995): 105, 113 (noting that gathering evidence of actual state practice is much more complex than the orthodox account allows, with systematic surveys generally lacking).

[9] Many observers consider that the best approach is to infer *opinio juris*, with all due caution, from the practice of states. But this approach remains controversial. For a vivid illustration of the debate, see Jean-Marie Henckaerts, 'Study on Customary International Humanitarian Law: A Contribution to the Understanding and Respect for the Rule of Law in Armed Conflict', *International Review of the Red Cross*, 87/857 (2005): 175, 181–2 (providing a well-reasoned account of the inference approach); and John B. Bellinger III and William J. Haynes II, 'A US Government Response to the International Committee of the Red Cross Study Customary International Humanitarian Law', *International Review of the Red Cross*, 89/866 (2007): 443, 446 (insisting that 'although the same action may serve as evidence both of State practice and *opinio juris*, the United States does not agree that *opinio juris* simply can be inferred from practice').

[10] See eg Judge Cançado Trinidade, *Case concerning Pulp Mills on the River Uruguay (Argentina v Uruguay)* (Separate Opinion) [2010] ICJ Rep 135, 142 (para 17), 151 (para 39), 207 (paras 191–3).

principles' of international law. Yet others maintain that evidence is needed that a principle has found support directly in international law, such that it has become a part of customary international law.[11]

Does customary law or do general principles provide a more plausible 'source' for the basic norms of international environmental law?[12] For present purposes, suffice it to say that both give rise to general international law. The term 'general international law' denotes international legal rules and principles that apply to all states, in contrast to treaties, which bind only states that have explicitly consented to be bound and are therefore parties to the agreement.

International climate change law consists in part of rules and principles of general international law, such as the no-harm rule considered in the next section, and in (much larger) part of treaty-based regimes, the key features of which are considered in Section IV of this chapter. Treaties differ from customary law and general principles not only by virtue of the fact that they apply exclusively to those states that explicitly consent to be bound by them, but also through the widely agreed, and much more detailed, rules that govern law-making. The most important rules and practices of treaty-based law-making are considered in Chapter 3, setting the stage for the detailed review, in Chapters 4–7, of the legal instruments through which international climate change law has been developed.

'Soft law' can provide both standards intended to be of general application and standards that operate in a treaty setting. Notwithstanding its prevalence and growing significance in many areas of international law,[13] the very notion of 'soft law' remains contentious.[14] Indeed, 'soft law' is made in a range of ways and

---

[11] See overview in Hugh Thirlway, *The Sources of International Law* (Oxford University Press, 2014) 94–6.

[12] See Daniel Bodansky, *The Art and Craft of International Environmental Law* (Cambridge, MA: Harvard University Press, 2010) 199–203. For a manifestation of the 'custom or general principle' question in the caselaw of the ICJ, see nn 31–32 below and accompanying text.

[13] See eg Joost Pauwelyn, Ramses A. Wessel, and Jan Wouters, 'When Structures Become Shackles: Stagnation and Dynamics in International Law-making', *European Journal of International Law*, 25/3 (2015): 733; Dinah Shelton (ed), *Commitment and Compliance: The Role of Non-Binding Norms in the International Legal System* (Oxford University Press, 2000); Pierre-Marie Dupuy, 'Soft Law and the International Law of the Environment', *Michigan Journal of International Law*, 12/2 (1991): 420.

[14] See eg Malcolm N. Shaw, *International Law* (Cambridge University Press, 7th edn, 2014) 83 (stating categorically that soft law is not law); Jan Klabbers, 'The Redundancy of Soft Law', *Nordic Journal of International Law*, 65/2 (1996): 167, 167–8 (considering that the traditional binary conception of law can serve soft law's purported functions); and Prosper Weil, 'Towards Relative Normativity in International Law?', *American Journal of International Law*, 77 (1983): 413 (considering soft law to be a danger to international law). But see also Alan Boyle, 'Soft Law in International Law-Making', in Malcolm D. Evans (ed), *International Law* (Oxford University Press, 3rd edn, 2010) 118, 122–4 (accepting that soft law is a relevant, albeit fluid, category that encompasses norms with a range of legal effects). See also Kenneth W. Abbott and Duncan Snidal, 'Hard and Soft Law in International Governance', *International Organization*, 54/3 (2000): 421 (proceeding from a rational choice perspective and relying on obligation, precision, and delegation as indicators of a norm's hard- or softness).

comes in a great variety of forms, many of which interact or overlap with one or more of the traditional 'sources' of law.[15] For example, some 'soft' norms are precursors to customary law;[16] others are generated by states 'in non-binding form according to traditional modes of law-making'; yet others may be produced by or directed at non-state actors.[17] However, distinctions between 'hard' and 'soft' law in terms of content and effects can be difficult to draw.[18] For example, 'hard' law is sometimes combined with 'soft' dispute settlement processes or 'soft' sanctions.[19] Conversely, although 'soft' norms do not figure in the 'causes of action' allowed in international adjudication, they can figure in practical legal reasoning of courts, states, and other international actors.[20] And, just as binding treaties may contain non-obligatory or vague terms,[21] 'soft' standards may contain mandatory and extremely detailed terms.[22] All of these manifestations of 'soft law' can be found in international climate change law, where an array of 'soft' norm-setting processes have come to play a significant role, especially in the UN climate regime, along with recourse to 'soft' content in otherwise 'hard' instruments, as the Paris Agreement illustrates.[23]

Finally, while an understanding of the customary, treaty-based, and 'soft' law-making processes dominated by states is important, it is also important to appreciate the growing role of standard-setting by non- and sub-state actors and by international organizations. The most important of such standard-setting processes outside of the UN climate regime are surveyed in Chapter 8 on 'polycentric' or 'multi-level' climate governance.

---

[15] See Boyle, ibid.　　[16] Ibid, 134–7.

[17] See Christine Chinkin, 'Normative Development in the International Legal System', in Dinah Shelton (ed), *Commitment and Compliance: The Role of Non-Binding Norms in the International Legal System* (Oxford University Press, 2000) 21, 30–1.

[18] See Bodansky, *Art and Craft of International Environmental Law* (n 12) 96–107 (arguing that 'legal' / 'non-legal' are not always the most salient norm qualities). Daniel Bodansky, 'Legally Binding Versus Non-Legally Binding Instruments', in Scott Barrett, Carlo Carraro, and Jaime de Melo (eds), *Towards a Workable and Effective Climate Regime* (London: Centre for Economic Policy Research Press, 2015) 155 (distinguishing between legal bindingness, precision, judicial application, and enforcement).

[19] Chinkin, Normative Development (n 17) 40.

[20] Christine Chinkin, 'The Challenge of Soft Law: Development and Change in International Law', *International & Comparative Law Quarterly*, 38/14 (1989): 850, 850–1. See also Committee on the Legal Principles relating to Climate Change, 'Legal Principles Relating to Climate Change' (International Law Association (ILA), Washington, D.C., 2014) (ILA Legal Principles) Art 2 and Commentary (explaining why both emerging and binding principles are included).

[21] Boyle, Soft Law (n 14) 130–2; Bodansky, *Art and Craft of International Environmental Law* (n 12) 13–14.

[22] See Jutta Brunnée, 'COPing with Consent: Lawmaking under Multilateral Environmental Agreements', *Leiden Journal of International Law*, 15/1 (2002): 1.

[23] For a detailed discussion of the issue of legal form, see Chapter 1, Section V.A. For a discussion of the legal instruments used in the UN climate regime, see Chapter 4. For the regime's treaties, see Chapters 4–7.

III. KEY PRINCIPLES OF INTERNATIONAL ENVIRONMENTAL LAW

A. The no-harm rule and related principles

Contemporary international environmental law has its roots in concepts that aim to balance competing sovereign interests.[24] Under the foundational no-harm rule, states' sovereign right to use their territories and resources finds its limits when significant transboundary harm is inflicted; neighboring states must tolerate harm that remains below that threshold. This rule found early expression in the 1941 *Trail Smelter Arbitration*, which concerned air pollution originating from a smelter located in the Canadian province of British Columbia that caused damage to livestock and farmland in the US state of Washington.[25] The arbitral tribunal held that no state had 'the right to use or permit the use of its territory in such a manner as to cause injury by fumes in or to the territory of another', and specified that the injury in question had to be 'of serious consequence' and 'established by clear and convincing evidence'.[26] The tribunal confirmed that Canada was not only required to compensate for the transboundary harm that had been caused, but was also required to introduce control measures that would prevent future damage.[27]

The notion that states are responsible for transboundary harm caused by activities undertaken in their territory has since been affirmed and fleshed out through a series of MEAs and other international instruments, as well as several decisions of the ICJ. According to Principle 21 of the 1972 Stockholm Declaration of the United Nations Conference on the Human Environment, states have the 'sovereign right to exploit their own resources pursuant to their own environmental policies, and the responsibility to ensure that activities within their jurisdiction or control do not cause damage to the environment of other States or of areas beyond the limits of national jurisdiction'.[28] The wording of Principle 21 suggested that the no-harm rule applies also to global commons, such as the high seas or Antarctica and, by extension, the Earth's atmosphere. Principle 2 of the 1992 Rio Declaration on Environment and Development restated the Stockholm formulation, adding that states are entitled to exploit their resources pursuant to their environmental and 'developmental' policies.[29] This wording, also found in the preamble to the FCCC, reflects the Rio Conference's broader effort to balance environmental and

---

[24] See *Island of Palmas Case (The Netherlands v United States)* (1928) 2 RIAA 829, 839 (holding that '[t]erritorial sovereignty...has as corollary a duty: the obligation to protect within the territory the rights of other States, in particular their right to integrity and inviolability').

[25] *Trail Smelter Arbitration (United States v Canada)* (1938 and 1941) 3 RIAA 1905.

[26] Ibid, 1965.   [27] Ibid, 1974–8 and 1980–1.

[28] UN Conference on the Human Environment, 'Declaration of the United Nations Conference on the Human Environment' (16 June 1972) UN Doc A/CONF.48/14/Rev 1, 3, reprinted in 11 ILM 1416 (1972) (Stockholm Declaration).

[29] UN Conference on Environment and Development, 'Rio Declaration on Environment and Development' (14 June 1992) UN Doc A/CONF.151/26/Rev 1 vol I, 3, reprinted in 31 ILM 874 (1992) (Rio Declaration).

developmental concerns;[30] but in substance it arguably does little more than high-light rights that flow naturally from sovereignty.

The ICJ first confirmed in 1996, in its Advisory Opinion on the *Legality of the Threat or Use of Nuclear Weapons*, that 'the general obligation of States to ensure that activities within their jurisdiction and control respect the environment of other States or of areas beyond national control is now part of the corpus of international law relating to the environment', but did not specify whether this obligation was customary in nature or was a general principle of law.[31] The Court reiterated this conclusion in its 1997 decision in the *Gabčíkovo-Nagymaros Case* and clarified in its 2010 decision in the *Pulp Mills Case* that the obligation is in fact customary law.[32]

1. Harm prevention and due diligence

In the *Pulp Mills Case*, the ICJ emphasized two important features of the no-harm rule. First, as suggested already by the *Trail Smelter* decision, the no-harm rule encompasses an obligation to take appropriate measures to *prevent* harm to the environment of other states or to the global commons.[33] Second, 'the principle of prevention, as a customary rule, has its origins in the due diligence that is required of a State in its territory'.[34] In turn, the obligation to act with due diligence entails 'not only the adoption of appropriate rules and measures, but also a certain level of vigilance in their enforcement and the exercise of administrative control applicable to public and private operators'.[35]

The Seabed Disputes Chamber of the International Tribunal for the Law of the Sea (ITLOS), in its 2012 Advisory Opinion on *Responsibilities in the Area*, built on this approach and highlighted the contextual nature of the due diligence standard.[36] According to the Chamber, the due diligence standard 'may change over time as measures considered sufficiently diligent at a certain moment may become not diligent enough in light, for instance, of new scientific or technological knowledge. It may also change in relation to the risks involved in the activity… [and] be more

---

[30] See nn 127–137 below and accompanying text.

[31] *Legality of the Threat or Use of Nuclear Weapons* (Advisory Opinion) [1996] ICJ Rep 226, 242 (para 29).

[32] *Gabčíkovo-Nagymaros Project (Hungary/Slovakia)* (Judgment) [1997] ICJ Rep 7, 41 (para 53); *Case concerning Pulp Mills on the River Uruguay (Argentina v Uruguay)* (Judgment) [2010] ICJ Rep 14, 55 (para 101).

[33] See also ILA Legal Principles (n 20) Art 7A(1) and Commentary.

[34] *Pulp Mills* (n 32) 55 (para 101). See also *Certain Activities Carried Out by Nicaragua in the Border Area (Costa Rica/Nicaragua)* and *Construction of a Road in Costa Rica along the San Juan River (Nicaragua/Costa Rica)*, (Judgment) [2015] ICJ <http://www.icj-cij.org/docket/index.php?p1=3&p2=1&case=150> accessed 27 October 2016.

[35] *Pulp Mills*, ibid, 79 (para 197). See also ILA Legal Principles (n 20) Art 7A(2) and Commentary. See also ILA Study Group on Due Diligence in International Law, 'First Report' (7 March 2014) and 'Second Report' (July 2016) (both providing overarching assessments of the due diligence concept, spanning different areas of international law).

[36] *Responsibilities and Obligations of States Sponsoring Person and Entities with Respect to Activities in the Area* (Advisory Opinion, Order of 1 February 2011) ITLOS Reports 2011, 10 (*Responsibilities in the Area*) paras 115, 117.

severe for the riskier activities'.[37] Furthermore, the due diligence standard may vary in light of the capacity of the state concerned,[38] although this point appears to be more controversial. Some leading commentators, citing numerous international instruments—including the FCCC—that accommodate the lesser technological and regulatory capacities of developing countries, compare the flexibility of the due diligence standard to the principle of common but differentiated responsibilities.[39] However, the Seabed Disputes Chamber of ITLOS made a point of emphasizing that differential treatment for developed and developing states is warranted only when the underlying international legal obligations provide for it.[40] Indeed, in relation to the principle of common but differentiated responsibilities, which was considered in Chapter 1 and to which the discussion returns later in this chapter and in Chapter 4, the United States (US) sought to guard against the potential implications of its wording by repeatedly stating its opposition to any interpretation that 'would imply a recognition or acceptance . . . of . . . any diminution of the responsibilities of developing countries under international law'.[41]

2. Procedural obligations

The no-harm rule is buttressed by a series of procedural obligations,[42] including the obligation to notify or warn potentially affected states;[43] the obligation to exchange information, consult, and negotiate;[44] and the general obligation to cooperate to prevent transboundary environmental harm.[45] The *Pulp Mills Case*, the ITLOS Advisory Opinion on *Responsibilities in the Area*, and the ICJ's 2015 decisions in the inter-connected *Costa Rica/Nicaragua* and *Nicaragua/Costa Rica Cases* all confirmed that states' procedural obligations under customary international law now include the obligation to conduct an EIA when activities under their jurisdiction or control may have a significant adverse effect outside their borders.[46] While these procedural

---

[37] Ibid, para 117.

[38] See International Law Commission (ILC), 'Text of the Draft Articles on Prevention of Transboundary Harm from Hazardous Activities, with commentaries', in *Report of the International Law Commission on the work of its fifty-third session* (21 April–1 June and 2 July–10 August 2001) UN Doc A/56/10, 370, Art 3 and Commentary, paras 12–13; see also ILA Legal Principles (n 20) Art 7A(3) and Commentary.

[39] Patricia Birnie, Alan Boyle, and Catherine Redgwell, *International Law and the Environment* (Oxford University Press, 3rd edn, 2009) 149.

[40] *Responsibilities in the Area* (n 36) paras 151–63.

[41] US Department of State, 'U.S. interpretive statement on World Summit on Sustainable Development declaration' (2002) <http://www.state.gov/s/l/38717.htm> accessed 20 January 2017 (reiterating a statement made at the 1992 UN Conference on Environment and Development).

[42] See also ILA Legal Principles (n 20) Art 7A(1) and Commentary.

[43] *Corfu Channel (United Kingdom of Great Britain and Northern Ireland v Albania)* (Merits) [1949] ICJ Rep 4, 22 (affirming states' general 'obligation not to allow knowingly its territory to be used for acts contrary to the rights of others States').

[44] *Lake Lanoux Arbitration (Spain v France)* (1957) 12 RIAA 281.

[45] See *Pulp Mills* (n 32) 67 (para 145) (tracing the obligation to cooperate to the good faith principle in international law).

[46] Ibid, 83 (paras 204–5); *Responsibilities in the Area* (n 36) para 145; *Costa Rica/Nicaragua* and *Nicaragua/Costa Rica* (n 34) para 104.

obligations have a separate existence as customary norms, through the due diligence standard they arguably are also implied in the substantive obligation to prevent environmental harm.[47] For example, conducting an assessment of potential transboundary environmental impacts will typically be among the measures that a state must take to discharge its obligation of due diligence.[48]

3. Prevention and precaution

The requirement of due diligence furthermore appears to have emerged as a bridge between the duty to prevent environmental harm and the proposition that 'the precautionary approach shall be widely applied by states according to their capabilities'.[49] Traditionally, the no-harm rule was engaged in the event of a known or objectively determined risk of significant environmental harm.[50] By contrast, the precautionary principle, as articulated in Principle 15 of the Rio Declaration, does not require 'full scientific certainty' where there are 'threats of serious or irreversible damage',[51] and its lower evidentiary threshold could strengthen the protective potential of international environmental law. However, although Principle 15 constitutes the most commonly invoked version of the precautionary principle,[52] debate persists among states and academic commentators about the precise contents of the principle, and whether or not it has acquired customary law status.[53]

International courts and tribunals, while alluding to the wisdom of precautionary approaches to environmental protection,[54] have avoided making pronouncements on the legal status of the precautionary principle.[55] In its Advisory Opinion on *Responsibilities in the Area*, the ITLOS Seabed Disputes Chamber followed this

---

[47] See Birnie *et al.*, *International Law and the Environment* (n 39) 147–50. But see also Jutta Brunnée, 'Procedure and Substance in International Environmental Law: Confused at a Higher Level?', *ESIL Reflections*, 5/6 (2016) <http://www.esil-sedi.eu/sites/default/files/ESIL%20Reflection%20Brunnée.pdf> accessed 20 January 2017 (discussing the ambiguities introduced by the ICJ's *Costa Rica/Nicaragua* and *Nicaragua/Costa Rica* decisions regarding the relationship between procedural and substantive obligations, and the requirement of due diligence).

[48] *Pulp Mills* (n 32) 83 (para 204) (noting that 'due diligence, and the duty of vigilance and prevention which it implies, would not be considered to have been exercised, if a party... did not undertake an environmental impact assessment[.]'); *Costa Rica/Nicaragua* and *Nicaragua/Costa Rica* (n 34) para 104.

[49] See Rio Declaration, Principle 15.

[50] See Birnie *et al.*, International Law and the Environment (n 39) 153.

[51] But see ILA Legal Principles (n 20) Art 7B and Commentary (criticizing the notion of 'lack of scientific certainty' as too imprecise and opting instead for the notion of 'reasonable foreseeability').

[52] See also FCCC, Art 3.3 (employing a modified version of Rio Principle 15).

[53] See Birnie *et al.*, International Law and the Environment (n 39) 154–64. See also Daniel Bodansky, 'Deconstructing the Precautionary Principle', in David D. Caron and Harry N. Scheiber (eds), *Bringing New Law to Ocean Waters* (Leiden/Boston: Brill, 2004) 382.

[54] See *Gabčíkovo-Nagymaros* (n 32) 78 (para 140); *Pulp Mills* (n 32) 71 (para 164) and 76–7 (para 185). See also *Southern Bluefin Tuna Cases (Australia and New Zealand v Japan)* (Order of 27 August 1999) ITLOS Cases Nos 3 and 4, para 77 <https://www.itlos.org/fileadmin/itlos/documents/cases/case_no_3_4/Order.27.08.99.E.pdf> accessed 20 January 2017.

[55] See *European Communities - Measures Concerning Meat and Meat Products (EC–Hormones) - Report of the Appellate Body* (16 January 1998) WT/DS48/AB/R, para 123; *European Communities - Measures Affecting the Approval and Marketing of Biotech Products - Reports of the Panel* (29 September 2006) WT/DS291/R, para 7.89.

cautious approach by noting that the 'growing number of international treaties and other instruments' that incorporate the precautionary approach as articulated in Principle 15 of the Rio Declaration have 'initiated a trend towards making [it] part of customary international law'.[56] However, elsewhere in its opinion, the Chamber engaged in the above-mentioned 'bridge-building' between prevention and precaution by observing that 'the precautionary approach is also an integral part of the general obligation of due diligence'.[57] According to the Chamber, this obligation requires states 'to take all appropriate measures to prevent damage... [and] applies in situations where scientific evidence concerning the scope and potential negative impact of the activity in question is insufficient but where there are plausible indications of potential risks'.[58] The Chamber concluded that a state 'would not meet its obligation of due diligence if it disregarded those risks'.[59] These observations are certainly in line with the Chamber's view that the standard of diligence will vary, *inter alia*, 'in relation to the risks involved'.[60] But while this perspective seems sensible in many respects, it remains to be seen whether its sliding scale approach to prevention and precaution will be embraced in international practice.[61]

B. Establishing state responsibility for violation of the no-harm rule

1. General considerations

What happens if one state violates its duty to use due diligence to prevent significant transboundary harm to another, or fails to meet the attendant procedural obligations? General international law, through the 'secondary' rules of the law of state responsibility,[62] provides an answer. Under these rules, an injured state can invoke the responsibility of another state for violations of international law.[63] Hence, a state that is owed obligations under the no-harm rule or its related procedural obligations is entitled to demand cessation of the violation and claim reparation from the responsible state.[64] Should that state not comply with these secondary obligations,

---

[56] *Responsibilities in the Area* (n 36) para 135.   [57] Ibid, para 131.   [58] Ibid.
[59] Ibid.   [60] See n 36 above and accompanying text.
[61] The Chamber may have spelled out what the ICJ merely alluded to in its *Gabčíkovo-Nagymaros* and *Pulp Mills* decisions by noting that 'in the field of environmental protection, vigilance and prevention are required on account of the often irreversible character of damage to the environment and of the limitations inherent in the very mechanism of reparation of this type of damage'. See *Gabčíkovo-Nagymaros* (n 32) 78 (para 140); *Pulp Mills* (n 32) 76–7 (para 185). See also ILA Legal Principles (n 20) Art 7A and 7B and Commentary. However, the ICJ in *Costa Rica/Nicaragua* and *Nicaragua/Costa Rica* did not take up the opportunity to pronounce itself on the question. See Brunnée, Procedure and Substance (n 47) 6.
[62] The 'secondary obligations' of the law of state responsibility are triggered by breaches of the 'primary obligations' of international law, such as the no-harm rule. See Jutta Brunnée, 'International Legal Accountability Through the Lens of the Law of State Responsibility', *Netherlands Yearbook of International Law*, 36/1 (2005): 21, 23.
[63] See ILC, 'Text of the Draft Articles on Responsibility of States for internationally wrongful acts', in Report of the ILC (n 38) 43 (Draft Articles on State Responsibility) Art 42.
[64] Ibid, Arts 30 and 31.

the injured state would be entitled to take countermeasures against the responsible state.[65] In other words, in order to induce the responsible state to cease the violation or provide reparation, an injured state may resort to what would otherwise be violations of international law. The question whether this adversarial posture of the law of state responsibility is suited to dealing with global environmental challenges like climate change is considered later in this chapter.[66] For now, suffice it to say that, in principle, the law of state responsibility authorizes individual states to take certain 'self-help' measures in response to violations of the no-harm duty, if the responsible state does not cease its wrongful activities.

How, then, does the customary law framework perform in dealing with the impacts of climate change on states? For an individual state to have a legal basis to challenge the conduct of another state for climate-related injuries or threats, it would have to show that the other state had breached the no-harm rule or its related procedural duties. This would require demonstrating that activities under the jurisdiction or control of the other state have caused, or entail a quantifiable risk of causing, significant harm in the claimant state's territory. Showing significant harm should not be difficult when impacts such as displacements, deaths, or destruction as a result of sea level rise, floods, droughts, or heatwaves actually occur. However, although modeling and attribution capacities are steadily improving, it may still be difficult to establish with sufficient probability that a particular weather event or impact was in fact caused by human action, as opposed to other factors,[67] let alone be attributed to the conduct of a specific state. It may be easier to demonstrate that human-induced climate change is likely to cause the types of harm mentioned above.[68] But a claimant state would still have to establish the other state's causal contribution to that risk.

A perhaps even greater obstacle to a successful action is the fact that states are required only to exercise due diligence in the prevention of climate change.[69] A claimant state would need to establish that the defendant state had failed to take reasonable and appropriate regulatory and enforcement measures to curb greenhouse gas emissions from activities under its jurisdiction. Even leaving aside the question whether lesser technological and regulatory capacity lowers the due diligence standard applicable to a developing country, customary international law provides no general, bright line standard for due diligence, let alone climate change-related diligence. Ironically, the recent evolution of the UN climate regime may have made it easier for states to demonstrate their due diligence. After all, the Paris Agreement accommodates a wide range of national contributions, raising

---

[65] Ibid, Art 49.   [66] See Section IV.C below.

[67] See Myles Allen, 'The Scientific Basis for Climate Change Liability', in Richard Lord *et al.* (eds), *Climate Change Liability: Transnational Law and Practice* (Cambridge University Press, 2012) 8. For an accessible survey of recent developments, see Robert McSweeney, 'Q &A: How scientists link extreme weather events to climate change' (CarbonBrief, 14 January 2016) <https://www.carbonbrief.org/qa-how-scientists-link-extreme-weather-to-climate-change> accessed 20 January 2017 (interviewing Myles Allen and Friederike Otto).

[68] On the evidence concerning human-induced climate change and its likely impacts, see Chapter 1.

[69] See Section III.A.1 above.

the question whether it would be possible to argue that a state that meets its commitments under the agreement is not exercising due diligence.[70] Furthermore, although the world now appears to agree on the need to keep global warming to 'well below 2° C' and to pursue efforts to limit it to '1.5° C above pre-industrial levels',[71] a chorus of voices suggests that these temperature goals are unattainable.[72]

2. Legal action for climate harm—some examples

Does this grim assessment mean that the law of state responsibility has no role to play at all? Not quite. So far, states have not formally invoked the law of state responsibility for climate change-related injuries. But, there has been an uptick in states bringing environmental issues before international courts, resulting in important clarifications of the core principles.[73] In the climate context, small island states, perhaps not surprisingly, have been most enterprising in considering legal options beyond active involvement in the UN climate regime. It is no coincidence that in ratifying the FCCC, the Kyoto Protocol, and the Paris Agreement, respectively, some island states declared their 'understanding that signature and subsequent ratification ... shall in no way constitute a renunciation of any rights under international law concerning State responsibility for the adverse effects of climate change and that no provision in the Protocol can be interpreted as derogating from principles of general international law'.[74]

---

[70] See Christina Voigt, 'The Paris Agreement: What is the Standard of Conduct for Parties' (24 March 2016) <http://www.qil-qdi.org/paris-agreement-standard-conduct-parties/> accessed 20 January 2017 (exploring the relationship between the Paris Agreement and the due diligence standard). However, since the Paris Agreement stipulates that each party's nationally determined contribution 'will ... reflect its highest possible ambition' (Art 4.3), it has been argued that the agreement establishes a due diligence standard whereby each party is to 'do as well as it can'. See Christina Voigt, 'On the Paris Agreement's Imminent Entry into Force (Part II of II)' (12 October 2016) <http://www.ejiltalk. org/on-the-paris-agreements-imminent-entering-into-force-what-are-the-consequences-of-the-paris-agreements-entering-into-force-part-ii/> accessed 20 January 2017.

[71] See Paris Agreement, Art 2.1(a).

[72] Oliver Geden, 'Warming World: It's Time to Give Up the 2 Degree Target', *Spiegel Online* (7 June 2013) <http://www.spiegel.de/international/world/climate-change-target-of-two-degrees-celsius-needs-revision-a-904219.html> accessed 20 January 2017. But see also Intergovernmental Panel on Climate Change (IPCC), *Climate Change 2014: Synthesis Report* (IPCC, 2015) 81–9 (maintaining that the temperature targets are still achievable with timely and assertive emission reductions); and United Nations Environment Programme (UNEP), *The Emissions Gap Report 2015* (Nairobi: UNEP, 2015) xvi (noting that '[s]taying below 2° C temperature rise implies that CO_2 emissions are reduced to net zero by 2060–2075').

[73] See *Pulp Mills* (n 32); *Responsibilities in the Area* (n 36); *Costa Rica/Nicaragua* and *Nicaragua/Costa Rica* (n 34). See generally, Tim Stephens, *International Courts and Environmental Protection* (Cambridge University Press, 2009).

[74] See eg, FCCC, 'Declarations by Parties - United Nations Framework Convention on Climate Change', Declarations by Fiji, Kiribati, Nauru, Papa New Guinea, Solomon Islands and Tuvalu <http:// unfccc.int/essential_background/convention/items/5410.php> accessed 20 January 2017; FCCC, 'Declarations by Parties - Kyoto Protocol', Declarations by Cook Islands, Kiribati, Nauru and Niue <http://unfccc.int/kyoto_protocol/status_of_ratification/items/5424.php> accessed 20 January 2017; and FCCC, 'Paris Agreement - Status of Ratification', Declarations by Cook Islands, Marshall Islands, Micronesia, Nauru, Solomon Islands, Tuvalu and Vanuatu <http://unfccc.int/paris_agreement/items/ 9444.php> accessed 20 January 2017.

In 2002, Tuvalu publicly mused about bringing Australia and the US before the ICJ for their contributions to climate change.[75] Given the various considerations outlined above, it is unclear how strong a case Tuvalu could have mounted. An additional obstacle with respect to the US would have been the need for its consent to the ICJ's jurisdiction.[76] In any event, Tuvalu ultimately did not pursue a contentious case before the ICJ.

In 2011, another small island nation, Palau, announced its plan to seek an advisory opinion from the ICJ on states' 'legal responsibility to ensure that any activities on their territory that emit greenhouse gases do not harm other States'.[77] While some states appeared supportive, others were concerned about interference with the FCCC process,[78] and Palau has not pursued its initiative. The ICJ's jurisdiction to give an Advisory Opinion would not need the consent of individual states; but it would have to be requested in accordance with the UN Charter.[79] Pursuant to Article 96 of the Charter, the most likely avenue would be a request by the General Assembly, which would require a two-thirds majority vote.

The perhaps most intriguing illustration to date of how the harm prevention principles might be harnessed was the intervention of the Federated States of Micronesia in the environmental assessment of the plan to modernize a large coal-fired power plant in the Czech Republic, the Prunéřov II plant. Under Czech law, any state whose territory could suffer significant environmental impacts due to a project may participate in the EIA process.[80] In a letter to the Czech Ministry of the Environment, Micronesia asserted that the project's climate change impacts could affect its territory and requested that a transboundary EIA be undertaken in accordance with Czech law.[81] It further asserted that the planned modernizations failed to meet the best available technology (BAT) standard imposed by relevant EU and Czech law,[82] an argument also advanced by several environmental

---

[75] See Rebecca Elizabeth Jacobs, 'Treading Deep Waters: Substantive Law Issues in Tuvalu's Threat to Sue the United States In the International Court of Justice', *Pacific Rim Law & Policy Journal*, 14/1 (2005): 103.

[76] Australia has declared its general acceptance of the ICJ's compulsory jurisdiction under Article 36.2 of the ICJ Statute. See ICJ, 'Declarations Recognizing the Jurisdiction of the Court as Compulsory', Australia (22 March 2002) <http://www.icj-cij.org/jurisdiction/?p1=5&p2=1&p3=3&code=AU> accessed 20 January 2017.

[77] See UN News Centre, 'Palau seeks UN World Court opinion on damage caused by greenhouse gases' (22 September 2011) <http://www.un.org/apps/news/story.asp?NewsID=39710&Cr=pacific+island&Cr1#.UbtgAr5zYeg> accessed 20 January 2017.

[78] UN Department of Public Information, 'Press Conference on Request for International Court of Justice Advisory Opinion on Climate Change' (3 February 2012) <http://www.un.org/News/briefings/docs/2012/120203_ICJ.doc.htm> accessed 20 January 2017.

[79] Charter of the United Nations (entered into force 24 October 1945) 1 UNTS xvi.

[80] Greenpeace, 'Legal Steps taken by the Federated States of Micronesia against the Prunéřov II coal-fired power plant, Czech Republic' (2010) <http://www.greenpeace.org/international/Global/international/planet-2/report/2010/3/teia_fsm.pdf> accessed 20 January 2017.

[81] See Paulo A. Lopes, 'FSM v. Czech: A New "Standing" for Climate Change', *Sustainable Development Law & Policy*, 10/2 (2010): 24, 25.

[82] See René Lefeber, 'Climate Change and State Responsibility', in Rosemary Rayfuse and Shirley Scott (eds), *International Law in the Era of Climate Change* (Cheltenham: Edward Elgar Publishing, 2012) 321, 336.

organizations.[83]

The Czech Ministry of the Environment retained a Norwegian consulting firm for a third party assessment of the modernization project. This assessment concluded that the project did not meet the BAT standard and calculated that an additional 205,082 tons of CO_2 would be emitted by Prunéřov II as a result.[84] The Ministry of the Environment nonetheless approved the modernization without requiring that it conform to the BAT standard. However, it asked the proponent power company to propose 'compensation measures' at its other power plants to offset the excess emissions.[85]

The Prunéřov II episode is interesting for at least two reasons. First, Micronesia's argument, while relying upon Czech law, effectively rested on the due diligence requirements that attach to the no-harm rule, as well as on the obligation to conduct assessments of transboundary impacts. Although the Czech authorities neither acknowledged a legal obligation to offset the project's climate impact, nor indeed Micronesia's request, it is conceivable that the Czech government was aware of the ICJ's judgment in the *Pulp Mills Case*, which was delivered around the same time.[86]

Second, although the emissions of one power plant could hardly be said to cause sea level rise or other climate impacts, the episode suggests that challenges against individual, large emissions sources like Prunéřov II have potential bite.[87] Would a failure to abide by national or other applicable BAT standards amount to a lack of due diligence?[88] If so, even without clear evidence of present or future harm, a state could well be found to have violated its obligation of due diligence or its obligation to conduct an EIA. In its *Pulp Mills* decision, at least, the ICJ opined that states' procedural obligations, while related to the substantive harm prevention duty, also have an independent existence.[89] And, according to the ITLOS Seabed Chamber, 'plausible indications of potential risks' are sufficient to trigger such procedural obligations.[90] Either way, procedural obligations can be useful when states, or judges, are reluctant to entertain substantive arguments, or find it difficult to establish that environmental harm has been, or is being, caused by another state. Generally speaking, violations of procedural obligations are more easily established.

---

[83] See Bonnie Malkin, 'Micronesia mounts unprecedented legal challenge over Czech power station', *The Telegraph* (24 May 2011) <http://www.telegraph.co.uk/news/earth/environment/climatechange/8532796/Micronesia-mounts-unprecedented-legal-challenge-over-Czech-power-station.html> accessed 20 January 2017.

[84] Justice and Environment, 'Climate change aspects within EIA proceedings - Czech Republic: Prunéřov II Power Plant' (2012) <http://www.justiceandenvironment.org/_files/file/2012/CC%20EIA%20case%20study%20Czech%20Republic.pdf> accessed 20 January 2017, 6 (fn 11).

[85] Ibid.   [86] See n 32 above and accompanying text.

[87] If modernized as planned, *Prunéřov II* would be the largest source of CO_2 emissions in the Czech Republic and one of the largest in Europe. See Malkin, Micronesia (n 83). See also Jan Srytr, 'Pacific Island Nation makes legal history', *Frank Bold* (29 March 2012) <http://en.frankbold.org/news/pacific-island-nation-makes-legal-history> accessed 20 January 2017 (suggesting that procedural approaches, such as reliance on EIA obligations, could be strong tools).

[88] See Birnie *et al.*, *International Law and the Environment* (n 39) 148–9.

[89] See *Pulp Mills* (n 32) paras 78–9. But see again Brunnée, Procedure and Substance (n 47) 4 (commenting on the ICJ's far more ambiguous stance in *Costa Rica/Nicaragua* and *Nicaragua/Costa Rica*).

[90] See *Responsibilities in the Area* (n 36) para 131 and accompanying text.

By holding states to their procedural duties, they can sometimes be prompted to correct harmful conduct, or at least to take more effective preventive measures going forward. In this way, procedural obligations can strengthen the preventive aspects of the no-harm rule, as well as flesh out its due diligence standard.

C. Invoking state responsibility for harm to the global commons

The preceding section explored the no-harm rule as it might apply to instances of transboundary harm caused by one state to another. Such situations fit within the traditional 'bilateral' structure of international law, which entails that only a directly injured state can invoke the responsibility of another for violations.[91] However, since the *obiter dictum* of the ICJ in the 1970 *Barcelona Traction Case*, it is has come to be accepted that there also exist certain 'obligations of a State towards the international community as a whole'[92]—that is, they may be owed *erga omnes*. These obligations, 'by their very nature...are the concern of all States', and 'all States can be held to have a legal interest in their protection'.[93] Environmental obligations have not been explicitly identified by the ICJ as having *erga omnes* quality. Yet as we have seen, the Court has confirmed repeatedly that the no-harm rule and related procedural rules apply to adverse environmental impacts in areas beyond national control and to the global commons.[94]

Assuming that the no-harm rule includes an *erga omnes* component, do individual states have standing to hold violators to account? For many commentators, the right of each state to invoke responsibility for violations is inherent in the very concept of obligations *erga omnes*.[95] But the ICJ has not pronounced itself on this point, nor is there clear state practice.[96] New Zealand, in its 1973 application to the ICJ for interim measures to stop nuclear testing in the South Pacific, complained *inter alia* about France's violation of the rights of all members of the international community to be free from nuclear fall-out and contamination of the high seas and atmosphere.[97] Given France's unilateral declaration that it would end testing, the Court never decided the merits of the case brought by New Zealand, and of Australia's parallel case. But various separate or dissenting opinions revealed that the judges were divided on the standing question. Some judges noted that while 'the existence of a so-called *actio popularis* in international law is a matter of controversy', it 'may be considered as capable of rational legal argument and a proper

---

[91] See Draft Articles on State Responsibility (n 63) Art 42.

[92] *Barcelona Traction, Light and Power Company, Ltd. (Belgium v Spain)* (Judgment) [1970] ICJ Rep 3, 32 (para 33).

[93] Ibid; but see also at 47 (para 91) (requiring a concrete treaty mechanism to provide standing).

[94] See nn 28–32 above and accompanying text.

[95] For an overview, see Brunnée, 'International Legal Accountability' (n 62).

[96] Ibid, 32.

[97] *Nuclear Tests (New Zealand v France)* (Interim Measures) [1973] ICJ Rep 135, 139 (para 23). Australia, in a parallel case, did not frame its claim explicitly in terms of the rights of all members of the international community. It did, however, argue that the French tests would infringe the freedom of the high seas. See also *Nuclear Tests (Australia v France)* (Interim Measures) [1973] ICJ Rep 99, 103 (para 22).

subject of litigation'.[98] For others, the applicant states had 'no legal title...to act as spokesman for the international community'.[99] At any rate, options for judicial settlement of disputes pertaining to the commons are generally limited, in practice, by the previously mentioned requirement that all parties must accept the ICJ's jurisdiction on a reciprocal basis.[100]

Meanwhile, the International Law Commission's (ILC)[101] Draft Articles on State Responsibility endorsed the idea of collective interest standing but also imposed limitations on remedies and countermeasures. According to the ILC Draft Articles, any state may invoke the responsibility of another for breaches of obligations owed to the international community.[102] Similarly, obligations owed to a group of states on the basis of a treaty (obligations *erga omnes partes*) enable any party to demand compliance.[103] However, unless a state is 'specially affected' by the violation, it may seek only the cessation of the violation, not claim reparations except in the interest of those injured.[104] Subtle differences between 'specially affected' states and all other beneficiaries of *erga omnes* obligations also characterize the ILC's approach to countermeasures. Specially affected states may resort to countermeasures.[105] By contrast, all other states may take only 'lawful measures' against the violating state, leaving open the precise scope of permissible responses.[106]

Whereas a small number of states have at least contemplated legal action for climate change-related damage to their territories, none have done so in relation to harm to the global commons.[107] In addition to the obstacles an injured state would have to surmount in raising a successful challenge,[108] even the basis for legal action by individual states to protect the global climate remains uncertain. Furthermore, while this is arguably true more generally speaking, the adversarial mode of the law of state responsibility is especially ill-suited to promoting the collective action and close cooperation that is needed to tackle climate change.[109] In short, individual

---

[98] *Nuclear Tests (Australia v France)* (Judgment) [1974] ICJ Rep 253, 370 (para 117) (Judges Onyeama, Dillard, Jiminez de Arechega, and Waldock).

[99] See ibid, 390 (Judge de Castro).

[100] See n 76 above and accompanying text. See also *Gabčíkovo-Nagymaros* (n 32), Separate Opinion of Vice-President Weeramantry, 88, 117 (pointing to the additional problems that flow from the fact that the Court's procedures, focused as they are upon disputes between specific state parties, are ill-suited to doing 'justice to rights and obligations of an *erga omnes* character').

[101] The ILC is a UN body composed of legal experts nominated by states parties, and tasked with the codification and progressive development of international law.

[102] Draft Articles on State Responsibility (n 63) Art 48.1 (b).	[103] Ibid, Art 48.1 (a).

[104] Ibid. States that are 'specially affected' are considered to be 'injured states' and so may seek both cessation of the violation and reparation of the injury (Arts 42, 30, and 31).

[105] See n 65 above and accompanying text.

[106] Draft Articles on State Responsibility (n 63) Art 54.

[107] For a helpful discussion of the basic options, see Jacqueline Peel, 'New State Responsibility Rules and Compliance with Multilateral Environmental Obligations: Some Case Studies of How the New Rules Might Apply in the International Environmental Context', *Review of European Community and International Environmental Law*, 10/1 (2001): 82.

[108] See nn 67–72 above and accompanying text.

[109] But see Patrick Hamilton, 'Counter(measure)ing Climate Change: The ILC, Third State Countermeasures and Climate Change', *International Journal of Sustainable Development Law and Policy*, 4/2 (2008): 83 (exploring the strengths and weaknesses of countermeasures in addressing collective interests).

states are unlikely to be able to pursue a public interest action to promote climate protection. Yet if the ICJ were indeed asked to deliver an Advisory Opinion on climate change,[110] it may well find reason to offer comments on the legal implications of the no-harm rule for the protection of the environment both within states' territory and beyond.

D. Common concern and common but differentiated responsibilities and respective capabilities

The preamble of the FCCC begins by acknowledging that 'change in the Earth's climate and its adverse effects are a common concern of humankind'. In order to appreciate the role and approach of the UN climate regime, it is worth exploring what status, if any, the concept of common concern has in international law, and what its legal implications may be in the context of climate change. Recall that, according to the ICJ, *erga omnes* obligations 'are the concern of all States' and all states 'have a legal interest in their protection'.[111] But if *erga omnes* obligations imply 'common concern', does 'common concern' imply *erga omnes* obligations?

International practice suggests that the concept of common concern is applicable both to environmental concerns that arise within individual states as well as those beyond the jurisdiction of states.[112] The thrust of the concept is not that areas or resources are 'commons', but rather that certain environmental processes or protective actions raise common concerns.[113] Hence, under the FCCC, it is changes in the climate and attendant adverse effects that are said to be of concern to all states.

In practice, the notion of 'common concern' has gained prominence mainly as a conceptual underpinning for the urgently needed cooperation among states. Moreover, it suggests that states' freedom of action might be subject to legitimate criticism by others, even when other states' sovereign rights are not affected in a manner that would engage the no-harm principle.

But the concept of common concern does not entail specific rules governing the conduct of states. And the practice of states does not establish that the concept of common concern entails legal obligations that are owed *erga omnes*.[114] Indeed, it is less than certain that, in the absence of a treaty that identifies a concern as 'common', the concept has legal effects at all.[115] In any case, although the Rio

---

[110] See nn 77–78 above and accompanying text. See also Philippe Sands, 'Climate Change and International Law: Adjudicating the Future in International Law', *Journal of Environmental Law* 28/1 (2016): 19 (reviewing the challenges and opportunities of bringing climate change before an international court or tribunal, including by way of a request for an Advisory Opinion).

[111] *Barcelona Traction* (n 93).

[112] See Birnie *et al.*, *International Law and the Environment* (n 39) 128–9.

[113] See Brunnée, Common Concern (n 1).

[114] See Birnie *et al.*, *International Law and the Environment* (n 39) 130.

[115] See here the pointed debate within the ILC on the concept of 'common concern', eg ILC, 'Provisional summary record of the 3244th meeting', Sixty-seventh session (first part), 6 May 2015 (18

Declaration calls upon states 'to cooperate in a spirit of global partnership to conserve, protect and restore the health and integrity of the Earth's ecosystem',[116] it has been more typical for states to identify specific common concerns, such as climate change, through a treaty.

According to some observers, the concept of common but differentiated responsibilities and respective capabilities (CBDRRC) is the conceptual flipside of common concern.[117] The FCCC does not make this connection. But the preamble to the convention does acknowledge that 'the global nature of climate change calls for the widest possible cooperation by all countries and their participation in an effective and appropriate international response, in accordance with their common but differentiated responsibilities and respective capabilities and their social and economic conditions'.[118] The Paris Agreement, for its part, in acknowledging climate change as a common concern, connects it to a series of other considerations, including human rights, rights of various groups, the right to development, and intergenerational equity.[119]

The CBDRRC principle purports to moderate international law's premise of equal rights and obligations for notionally equal sovereign actors. As such, it aims to enable a more nuanced approach to international environmental cooperation, acknowledging the deep inequalities between and differing priorities of developed and developing countries.[120] The evolution of the CBDRRC principle is considered in Chapter 1. Suffice it to note for present purposes that, despite its prominence in international environmental law, the principle has not achieved acceptance as customary international law.[121] In the climate regime, as Chapters 4–7 amply illustrate, the evolving CBDRRC principle has underpinned the difficult burden sharing issues that arise in the quest for agreement on a global regime of climate change mitigation and adaptation actions.

December 2015) UN Doc A/CN.4/SR.3246 (Statements by Mr Murphy and Mr Nolte). See also ILC, *Report of the International Law Commission on the Work of Its Sixty-Seventh Session* (4 May–5 June and 6 July–7 August 2015) UN Doc A/70/10, 22, para 53 (adopting a compromise formulation, 'pressing concern of the international community as a whole').

[116] See Rio Declaration, Principle 7.

[117] See Birnie *et al.*, *International Law and the Environment* (n 39) 132–6. See also ILA Legal Principles (n 20) Art 2 and Commentary (noting that 'the idea that climate change is a common concern is universally accepted, as is the proposition that all states have a common responsibility to take appropriate measures to address the concern'—footnote omitted).

[118] See ILA Legal Principles (n 20) Art 5(2) and Commentary (noting that 'common responsibility could be said to flow from the common concern occasioned by climate change and its adverse effects').

[119] Paris Agreement, preamble.

[120] For a comprehensive analysis, see Lavanya Rajamani, *Differential Treatment in International Environmental Law* (Oxford University Press, 2006). See also Ulrich Beyerlin and Thilo Marauhn, *International Environmental Law* (Oxford: Hart Publishing, 2011) 61–6.

[121] See eg Thomas Deleuil, 'The Common but Differentiated Responsibilities Principle: Changes in Continuity after the Durban Conference of the Parties', *Review of European, Comparative and International Environmental Law*, 21/3 (2012): 271.

E. Precaution, sustainable development, and the intertemporal reach of international environmental law

The discussion so far of the conceptual framework of international environmental law has illustrated that, initially, its rules and principles focused on the prevention of harm within state territory. International environmental law, however, has evolved to address the spatial gap that resulted from the original, narrow focus of the no-harm rule. The harm prevention rule extends to areas beyond the jurisdiction of states, and newer principles of international environmental law call upon states to co-operate to address common environmental concerns that are not directly connected to states' territorial interests. What, then, of the temporal gap in the traditional rule framework that was identified in the introduction to this chapter? Has international environmental law evolved to reflect the fact that states' actions have impacts not only in the present, but also in the future? In particular, what about the long-term, uncertain but potentially irreversible, impacts of today's actions on the global climate?

Of course, the basic duty to prevent environmental harm does have an eye to the future. Its reach into the future is extended by the precautionary principle. The earlier discussion of states' obligation to prevent harm suggests that the precautionary principle, as a matter of general international law, may be most likely to be relevant in heightening the requisite standard of due diligence in the face of threats of serious or irreversible damage.[122] This effect can be further strengthened through contextualized articulations of the precautionary principle in individual treaty regimes. In that context, precaution can also help frame the overall approach of the regime.

Arguably, the precautionary principle serves the latter function in the climate regime, where it is among the principles that guide parties' actions under the FCCC,[123] and will be considered more closely in Chapter 5. But whether the adapted version of Rio Principle 15 that appears in the FCCC makes the due diligence standard for climate action more concrete or instead dilutes it is open to debate. The notion that FCCC parties 'take precautionary measures to anticipate, prevent or minimize the cause of climate change and mitigate its adverse effects' seems more assertive than Principle 15's proviso that precautionary measures be taken 'to protect the environment'.[124] However, the FCCC merely stipulates that parties 'should' take such measures, and further suggests that lack of full scientific certainty 'should' not be used as a reason for postponing them.[125] That wording is considerably weaker than Principle 15's stipulation that 'the precautionary approach shall be widely applied' and that lack of full scientific certainty 'shall' not be a reason for postponing relevant measures.[126]

Another concept that aims to extend international environmental law's focus into the future is the notion of sustainable development. Like the notion of common but differentiated responsibilities and respective capabilities, the concept of sustainable development is concerned with the relationship between environmental and

---

[122] See nn 49–61 above and accompanying text.   [123] See FCCC, Art 3.3.
[124] Ibid; Rio Declaration, Principle 15.   [125] Ibid.   [126] Ibid.

developmental considerations. Yet, whereas CBDRRC highlights considerations of intragenerational equity, sustainable development focuses on the intergenerational aspects of this relationship as well.[127] This linkage is reflected in the Brundtland Commission's influential definition of sustainable development as 'development that meets the needs of the present without compromising the ability of future generations to meet their own needs'.[128] However, many developing countries have been concerned about articulations of the concept that might be read to imply limitations on their development priorities. These concerns found expression in the elliptical Principle 3 of the Rio Declaration, which states that '[t]he right to development must be fulfilled so as to equitably meet developmental and environmental needs of present and future generations'.[129]

The Rio Declaration uses the term 'sustainable development' in twelve of its twenty-seven principles. But the precise content and contours of this basic concept remain elusive. Rather than offer a definition, the declaration outlines various elements of sustainable development.[130] One important element is that development, while essential, must remain within the carrying capacity of the environment and, therefore, that environmental protection must be part of the development process.[131] As such, the notion of sustainable development reinforces the already noted expansion and shifts in the conceptual structure of international environmental law. Like the concept of common concern, sustainable development aims to elevate certain aspects of domestic resource management to matters of international concern. Further, appropriate resource use and development are not measured solely against the extent of transboundary or global impact, but are defined according to what the environment can sustain in the longer term.

The concept of sustainable development has been described as an 'interstitial norm', a norm that, without being legally binding or clearly defined, shapes the interpretation and application of customary or treaty norms.[132] Indeed, the concept has served this shaping function in a range of contexts. For example, in the *Gabčíkovo-Nagymaros Case*, the ICJ observed that, due to 'new scientific insights and to a growing awareness of the risks for mankind—for present and future

---

[127] See eg Stockholm Declaration, Principle 1 (proclaiming that 'man . . . bears a solemn responsibility to protect and improve the environment for present and future generations').

[128] World Commission on Environment and Development, *Our Common Future* (Oxford University Press, 1987) 43.

[129] Rio Declaration, Principle 3. For another illustration, see Chapter 3, Section II.D.5 (discussing the drafting history of FCCC, Art 3.4).

[130] See Birnie *et al.*, *International Law and the Environment* (n 39) 116–23—suggesting that the declaration sets out the concept's substantive elements (such as the integration of environment and development, the right to development, sustainable utilization of natural resources, and intra- and intergenerational equity) as well as procedural elements (such as cooperation, public participation in environmental decision-making, and EIA).

[131] See ILA Legal Principles (n 20) Art 3(4–5) and Commentary (on the concept of sustainable development and the importance of integration of environmental, economic and social matters).

[132] Vaughn Lowe, 'Sustainable Development and Unsustainable Arguments', in Alan Boyle and David Freestone (eds), *International Law and Sustainable Development: Past Achievements and Future Challenges* (Oxford University Press, 1999) 19, 31.

generations... new norms and standards have been developed... [and] have to be taken into consideration'.[133] According to the ICJ, the 'need to reconcile economic development with protection of the environment is aptly expressed in the concept of sustainable development'.[134]

In the climate regime, sustainable development is also one of the guiding principles. The FCCC echoes the Rio Declaration when it stipulates that parties 'have a right to, and should, promote sustainable development'.[135] The role of the concept in the FCCC and the other instruments of the climate regime will be examined in detail in Chapters 5–7. Suffice it to note here that the uneasy compromise in the Rio Declaration and FCCC reflects the continuing debate on how to balance environment and development. Whereas developing countries have asserted a 'right' to develop, industrialized countries have sought to emphasize the need to develop sustainably. The US specifically stated that its support of the Rio Declaration did not 'change its long-standing opposition to the so-called "right to development"',[136] a position that is unlikely to have changed, notwithstanding the reference to 'the right to development', along with a series of other rights, in the preamble of the Paris Agreement.[137]

IV. TREATY-BASED APPROACHES TO ENVIRONMENTAL PROTECTION

The discussion of the legal rules on harm prevention has illustrated that customary international environmental law holds some potential for addressing the climate change problem, however limited states' actual recourse to it may have been to date. Also, the conceptual framework of international law has developed beyond the confines of the no-harm rule to address collective environmental concerns as well as concerns about potential future impacts. The latter developments, however, have manifested themselves not so much in the evolution and application of customary law as in the emergence of soft law and in the development of treaty-based regimes. Treaty-based regimes can enshrine concrete commitments that build on concepts such as common concern, common but differentiated responsibilities,

---

[133] See *Gabčíkovo-Nagymaros* (n 32) 78 (para 140).

[134] Ibid. See also *Pulp Mills* (n 32) 48–9 (paras 75–6), 75 (paras 177–84); and *United States – Import Prohibition of Certain Shrimp and Shrimp Products: Report of the Appellate Body* (12 October 1998) WT/DS58/AB/R, 48–50 (paras 129–31) and 57–8 (paras 152–3).

[135] FCCC, Art 3.4.

[136] Report of the United Nations Conference on Environment and Development (Rio de Janeiro, 3–14 June 1992) UN Doc. A/CONF.151/26 (Vol IV) (28 September 1992) Chapter IV.B, para 16. See also Daniel Bodansky, 'The United Nations Framework Convention on Climate Change: A Commentary', *Yale Journal of International Law*, 18/2 (1993): 451, 504–5 (on the negotiating history of the principle in the FCCC).

[137] See Paris Agreement, preamble. See n 119 above and accompanying text. For a detailed discussion, see Chapter 7.

or sustainable development. Treaties can also provide more specific guidance than the harm prevention or precautionary principles. For example, a treaty can provide for concrete remedial or preventive obligations, such as specific emission reduction obligations, can stipulate detailed procedural requirements, and can provide for oversight mechanisms tailored to the circumstances at hand.

Effective environmental regime-building, however, is anything but straightforward. Since treaties apply only to states that have expressed their consent to be bound, the overarching challenge is to encourage the participation of all relevant actors while also ensuring that the regime is ambitious enough to provide for an effective response to the problem.[138] This challenge is all the more difficult when global collective action is needed and when states must be induced to take potentially costly action now in order to address long-term and uncertain harms.[139] Since their emergence in the 1970s, modern environmental treaty regimes have developed a range of strategies and features to better meet the collective action challenge. The following overview focuses on three broad themes: treaty development over time, treaty design to induce participation, and promotion of implementation and compliance.[140]

A. Treaty development over time

The reference above to 'regimes' highlights the first important point: MEAs are not one-off contracts between states, but establish open-ended 'sets of implicit or explicit principles, norms, rules, and decision-making procedures around which actors' expectations converge'.[141] In other words, the adoption of an MEA is usually not the endpoint of the international legal process but rather the beginning. Such dynamic, long-term regimes typically have several intertwined features—the framework-protocol model, institutionalization, and ongoing standard-setting processes.[142]

---

[138] See Scott Barrett, *Environment and Statecraft: The Strategy of Environmental Treaty-making* (Oxford University Press, 2003) (emphasizing the importance of participation, and suggesting that it be theorized jointly with compliance).

[139] See eg Jo Cofino, 'It is profitable to let the world go to hell', *The Guardian* (19 January 2015) <https://www.theguardian.com/sustainable-business/2015/jan/19/davos-climate-action-democracy-failure-jorgen-randers> accessed 20 January 2017.

[140] For a detailed discussion of these issues, see Bodansky, *Art and Craft of International Environmental Law* (n 12) chs 8, 10, and 11.

[141] Steven Krasner, 'Structural Causes and Consequences: Regimes as Intervening Variables', *International Organization*, 36/2 (1982): 185, 186.

[142] For a pioneering and still trenchant analysis, see Thomas Gehring, *Dynamic International Regimes: Institutions for International Environmental Governance* (Frankfurt: Peter Lang, 1994). See also Thomas Gehring, 'Treaty-Making and Treaty Evolution', in Bodansky *et al.* (eds), *Oxford Handbook of International Environmental Law* (n 1) 491; Catherine Redgwell, 'Multilateral Environmental Treaty-Making', in Vera Gowland-Debbas (ed), *Multilateral Treaty-Making: The Current Status of Challenges to and Reforms Needed in the International Legislative Process* (Dordrecht: Springer, 2000) 89, 90 (describing the approach as 'permanent environmental diplomacy').

1. The framework-protocol model

Modern MEAs tend to employ a 'framework-protocol' model to regime building. In this approach, states first negotiate a framework convention, establishing general obligations concerning basic matters such as scientific research and exchange of information, as well as a skeletal legal and institutional framework for future action. The framework convention then becomes the basis for developing protocols that contain specific regulatory measures (for example, emissions limitation commitments) and more detailed implementation mechanisms.[143]

The framework-protocol model serves two basic functions. First, it allows work to proceed in an incremental manner. States can begin to address a problem without waiting for a consensus to emerge on appropriate response measures, or even before there is agreement that a problem exists. Second, framework conventions can create positive feedback loops, making the adoption of specific substantive commitments more likely. States that are initially reluctant to undertake substantive commitments, but that acquiesce in the seemingly innocuous process set in motion by the framework convention, may feel increasing pressure not to fall out of step as that process gains momentum, allowing the international law-making process to take on a momentum of its own.[144]

2. Institutionalization

The framework-protocol model goes hand-in-hand with institutionalization, which typically occurs at a number of levels. Many environmental regimes establish, or collaborate with, bodies that facilitate exchange among scientific or technical experts. For example, the FCCC established a permanent Subsidiary Body for Scientific and Technological Advice, and another Subsidiary Body for Implementation.[145] The climate regime also draws upon the expertise of the Intergovernmental Panel on Climate Change (IPCC), which operates under the auspices of the World Meteorological Organization and the United Nations Environment Programme.[146] Expert forums such as these are important in building consensus around the nature of collective concerns and the collective action that is required to address them.[147]

---

[143] For a more detailed exploration of the attendant treaty development issues, see Chapter 3, Section II.D. On the framework-protocol approach see generally Daniel Bodansky, *The Framework Convention/Protocol Approach*, WHO/NCD/TFI/99.1 (World Health Organization, 1999), on which this section draws. For a skeptical view of the effectiveness of the framework-protocol approach, see George W. Downs, Kyle W. Danish, and Peter N. Barsoom, 'The Transformational Model of International Regime Design: Triumph of Hope or Experience?', *Columbia Journal of Transnational Law*, 38/3 (2000): 465–514.

[144] See Chapter 3, Section II.D.1. See also Bodansky, *Art and Craft of International Environmental Law* (n 12) 186–7.

[145] FCCC, Arts 9 and 10.

[146] See IPCC, 'Organization' <http://www.ipcc.ch/organization/organization.shtml#.UcCt5b5zYeg> accessed 20 January 2017. See also FCCC, 'Science'<http://unfccc.int/science/items/6990.php> accessed 20 January 2017.

[147] See generally Peter Haas, 'Epistemic Communities', in Bodansky *et al.* (ed), *Oxford Handbook of International Environmental Law* (n 1) 791.

Scientific or technical expert bodies also make important contributions in the further elaboration, refinement, or adjustment of regulatory strategies. In the climate context, for example, the work of the IPCC has helped clarify what constitutes 'dangerous anthropogenic interference with the climate system',[148] and what sorts of global emission reductions would have to be accomplished on what schedule to avert the danger.[149] Although this type of contribution is indispensable for effective regime development, the climate regime has illustrated that it is not necessarily sufficient to prompt political agreement, let alone action.[150]

The development of the regime is usually in the hands of the plenary bodies established by the framework convention and any subsequent protocols or other agreements. Some observers argue that, due to the emergence of these conferences of the parties (COPs), MEAs increasingly resemble international organizations.[151] For others, COPs are essentially diplomatic conferences,[152] with the important difference being that they facilitate regular, long-term engagements between technical experts, policy-makers, and lawyers. Either way, COPs and their subsidiary bodies have become central venues for international regulatory activities around collective concerns. In the climate regime, two plenary bodies, the FCCC COP and the Conference of Parties serving as the Meeting of the Parties to the Kyoto Protocol (CMP) to the Kyoto Protocol, have played these roles to date.[153] Upon entry into force of the Paris Agreement, they were joined by a third such body, the Conference of Parties serving as the Meeting of the Parties to the Paris Agreement (CMA).[154] Distinct bodies are needed because, notwithstanding their close connection, the FCCC, the Kyoto Protocol, and the Paris Agreement are separate treaties, with slightly different rosters of parties.[155] For reasons of efficiency, the two existing bodies meet in conjunction with one another and the Paris Agreement similarly provides that the CMA meet together with the FCCC COP.[156]

---

[148] FCCC, Art 2.

[149] For a detailed discussion, see Jutta Brunnée and Stephen J. Toope, *Legitimacy and Legality in International Law: An Interactional Account* (Cambridge University Press, 2010) 146–51.

[150] See nn 71–72 above and accompanying text.

[151] Robin Churchill and Geir Ulfstein, 'Autonomous Institutional Arrangements in Multilateral Environmental Agreements: A Little-Noticed Phenomenon in International Law', *American Journal of International Law*, 94/4 (2000): 623.

[152] Alan E. Boyle, 'Saving the World? Implementation and Enforcement of International Environmental Law Through International Institutions', *Journal of Environmental Law*, 3/2 (1991): 229.

[153] See FCCC, Art 7; Kyoto Protocol, Art 13.

[154] See Paris Agreement, Art 16. See also Chapters 3 and 7.

[155] The FCCC has 197 parties, whereas the Kyoto Protocol has 192. Andorra, Canada, Palestine, South Sudan, and the US are not parties to the Protocol. See FCCC, 'Status of Ratification of the Convention' <http://unfccc.int/essential_background/convention/status_of_ratification/items/2631. php> accessed 20 January 2017; FCCC, 'Status of Ratification of the Kyoto Protocol' <http://unfccc. int/kyoto_protocol/status_of_ratification/items/2613.php> accessed 20 January 2017. For the current status of signatures and ratifications, see FCCC, 'Paris Agreement - Status of Ratification' <http:// unfccc.int/paris_agreement/items/9444.php> accessed 20 January 2017. On the 'related-but-separate' nature of framework agreements and their protocols, see Chapter 3, Section II.D.1.

[156] Kyoto Protocol, Art 13.1. Paris Agreement, Art 16 similarly envisages that, upon entry into force, the FCCC COP will convene to serve as its meeting of the parties.

3. Ongoing standard-setting processes

The phenomenon of treaty-based regulatory processes, which is explored in greater detail in Chapter 3, is the third characteristic of dynamic treaty development over time. Arguably, this phenomenon is of particular significance in the collective action context because it enhances the potential for legitimate outcomes.[157] MEAs enshrine the background assumption that standard-setting is a collective enterprise, and settle the parameters for engaging in it. Specifically, while states' sovereignty is respected through consent requirements, the consent processes in many MEAs are structured so as to maximize opportunities for collective outcomes. To be sure, much regime development under MEAs still occurs through ordinary consent-based methods. For example, when an agreement is amended, or when an additional treaty, such as a protocol, is adopted, individual states are bound only when they consent to these instruments. But a range of strategies are deployed to address the need for timely collective action.[158] For example, under many MEAs, especially when technical issues are involved, relevant standards can be changed or expanded with effect for all parties except those that explicitly opt out.[159]

Perhaps most importantly, an ever-growing range of treaty-based standard-setting occurs not through protocols or formal amendments, but through decisions of the above-mentioned plenary bodies, without subsequent formal consent by individual states. For example, under the FCCC and its Kyoto Protocol, much of the regulatory detail to make the treaties operational was adopted through COP decisions.[160] Except in the rare cases where the relevant treaty invests the COP with authority to adopt a binding rule, the resulting standards are not legally binding, notwithstanding the mandatory language they may contain.[161] Thus, provisions on central matters ranging from inventory and monitoring requirements to the protocol's mechanisms for trading of emission units or reduction credits were adopted in soft law form.[162] The Paris Agreement envisages a similar approach for the adoption of standards on key issues.[163] As the experience with the climate regime illustrates, even such soft standards are often subject to protracted negotiations. Nonetheless, this approach does facilitate agreement on collective action

---

[157] On legitimacy, see generally Daniel Bodansky, 'The Legitimacy of International Governance: A Coming Challenge for International Environmental Law?', *American Journal of International Law*, 93/3 (1999): 596.

[158] See Brunnée, COPing with Consent (n 22). In the climate regime, however, it has turned out to be difficult to employ these strategies, in part due to the consensus requirement and in part due to the sensitive nature of most regime-development issues. For a detailed discussion of the law-making processes in the climate regime, see Chapter 3.

[159] Brunnée, ibid.

[160] For further discussion of the role of decisions, see Chapter 3, Section II.D.3.

[161] Ibid.

[162] But see Churchill and Ulfstein, Autonomous Institutional Arrangements (n 151) 639–40 (arguing that the Kyoto Protocol empowered the COP to adopt legally binding decisions on certain matters, such as international emissions trading). On the notion of 'soft law', see nn 14–23 above and accompanying text.

[163] See Paris Agreement, eg Arts 4.8, 4.9, 4.13, and 13.13. See also Chapter 3.

and adoption of standards that are applicable to all parties—important features for efforts to address collective concerns.

Equally important is that soft regulatory processes enable speedier regime development and adjustment than processes that require subsequent ratification by individual states. This dynamism of MEA-based standard-setting is beneficial because environmental problems, the scientific understanding of them, and political circumstances all typically evolve over time, often rapidly. The climate regime is a case in point. However, one notorious feature of its decision-making process has undercut these beneficial effects on numerous occasions: in elaborating the rules of procedure for the COP, the parties were unable to agree on the voting rules.[164] Pending agreement on this crucial point, the FCCC parties have adopted the general UN practice of consensus decision-making.[165] This practice has enabled small numbers of parties to prevent the adoption of decisions in the regime. One high-profile example is the 2009 Copenhagen Accord, which the COP was unable to adopt due to the objections of a handful of states.[166]

One further dimension of regime-based regulatory processes is of interest. Environmental treaty regimes provide an arena in which non-state actors, such as international organizations, non-governmental organizations, or business entities can be directly engaged.[167] In the climate regime, non-state actors participate in myriad ways. For example, the meetings of the treaty bodies in principle are accessible to accredited observers,[168] although many of the key meetings are closed to observers in practice. The FCCC process also envisages that observers may make interventions,[169] albeit subject to the approval of the chairperson and, in practice, only in a very limited way. Roughly 100 inter-governmental organizations and almost 1,600 non-governmental entities are accredited with the FCCC.[170]

---

[164] At COP1, it was decided that the draft Rules of Procedure would be applied provisionally, with the exception of Rule 42 on voting. The draft Rules of Procedure are reproduced in FCCC, Organizational Matters: Adoption of the Rules of Procedure - Note by the Secretariat (22 May 1996) FCCC/CP/1996/2.

[165] See Patrick Széll, 'Decision Making under Multilateral Environmental Agreements', *Environmental Policy and Law*, 26/5 (1996): 210.

[166] For more on the consensus issues in the climate regime see Chapter 3, Section II.B.2 and Chapter 4.

[167] See Jutta Brunnée and Ellen Hey, 'Transparency and International Environmental Institutions', in Andrea Bianchi and Anne Peters (eds), *Transparency in International Law* (Cambridge University Press, 2013) 23, 30–2.

[168] FCCC, Art 7.6; Kyoto Protocol, Art 13.8 (both stipulating that observer entities must be 'qualified in matters covered by the Convention').

[169] FCCC, *A Guide to the Climate Change Convention Process* (Bonn: Climate Change Secretariat, 2002) <http://unfccc.int/resource/process/guideprocess-p.pdf> accessed 20 January 2017.

[170] FCCC, 'Parties and Observers' <http://unfccc.int/parties_and_observers/items/2704.php> accessed 20 January 2017. The Paris Agreement contains the most comprehensive articulation yet of whose interests are engaged, without, however, granting non-state actors specific rights or status under the regime. See Paris Agreement, preamble (acknowledging that 'climate change is a common concern of humankind, Parties should, when taking action to address climate change, respect, promote and consider their respective obligations on human rights, the right to health, the rights of indigenous peoples, local communities, migrants, children, persons with disabilities and people in vulnerable situations and the right to development, as well as gender equality, empowerment of women and intergenerational equity').

Non-governmental entities may distribute information or policy papers, meet with or even be part of official delegations, and report on negotiations.[171] Although, in a formal sense, standard-setting remains in the hands of states, non-state actors thus have considerable opportunities to provide input into law-making processes or even to help shape their outcomes.

B. Treaty design to induce participation

The framework-protocol model surveyed above, which takes an incremental approach to treaty development, also ranks among the design features that MEAs deploy to promote participation. The framework treaty encourages participation through the very general nature of the commitments initially imposed upon parties, coupled with the fact that the opportunity to actively shape subsequent commitments is reserved to treaty parties. Participation in a framework treaty, in other words, provides access and influence, at a relatively low level of commitment. Although the framework convention makes it increasingly difficult for parties to resist further development of the regime,[172] individual states are under no legal obligation to consent to new or more ambitious commitments.

The basic thrust of the framework-protocol model, in other words, is to engender broad participation and then to deepen parties' commitments over time.[173] The institutionalization and reliance on a spectrum of law-making processes highlighted in the preceding section are meant to facilitate this 'deepening' process. Most modern MEAs, including the FCCC, reflect this 'broad-then-deep' approach. An alternative approach is to start with a deeper level of commitment by a smaller group of parties and then to work toward a broadening of participation.[174] In the climate regime, the Kyoto Protocol is an example of this 'deep-then-broad' approach, with industrialized countries and countries with economies in transition taking the lead in assuming binding greenhouse gas emission reduction commitments.[175] Needless to say, it has proven to be exceedingly difficult to extend concrete emissions commitments beyond the states covered by the Kyoto Protocol. Years of negotiation and experimentation with various aspects of regime design were needed to achieve, through the Paris Agreement, an instrument that is genuinely global in scope. With the Paris Agreement, the climate regime could be said to have returned to a 'broad-then-deep' approach, reflected, in particular, in the notion that parties' nationally determined climate actions 'will represent a progression over time'.[176]

---

[171] For example, the *Earth Negotiations Bulletin*, produced by a Canadian non-profit organization, publishes daily summaries of the main developments in climate negotiations through the Internet. IISD Reporting Services, 'ENB Archives' <http://www.iisd.ca/voltoc.html> accessed 20 January 2017.

[172] See n 144 above and accompanying text.

[173] See Bodansky, *Art and Craft of International Environmental Law* (n 12) 185–7 (on treaty design that begins with broad participation and subsequently deepens commitments).

[174] See ibid, 184–6.

[175] Notwithstanding the fact that many observers at the time considered the protocol's emission reduction targets to be insufficient, they required the parties to take costly measures, considerably beyond 'business-as-usual'. For a discussion, see Chapter 6, Section IV.B.2.

[176] See Paris Agreement, Arts 3 and 4.3. For a detailed discussion, see Chapter 7, Section V.C.

Other regime design features can be employed in conjunction with the basic models surveyed above to promote broader participation.[177] In this vein, MEAs have made extensive use of differential standards of various kinds. The Montreal Protocol, for example, imposed the same control measures on all countries, but granted developing countries additional time in which to comply.[178] This approach was designed to bring developing countries, whose participation was crucial to achieving a global phase-out of the production and consumption of ozone depleting substances, into the Montreal Protocol. In contrast, the climate regime attempted to gain global support by differentiating the substantive content of countries' commitments. For example, the Kyoto Protocol established quantified emission limitation targets for industrialized countries and countries with economies in transition, but not for developing countries.[179] With the Paris Agreement, the climate regime now has moved to a much more nuanced approach to differentiation. The principle of CBDRRC is qualified by the phrase 'in the light of different national circumstances', and differentiation is tailored to the demands of each issue area.[180] For instance, in relation to mitigation, each party is permitted to decide upon its level of commitment, subject to certain normative expectations in relation to differentiation, progression, and highest possible ambition.[181]

The Paris Agreement's 'nationally determined contributions' (NDCs) also serve to promote participation, since they provide parties with considerable flexibility in the standards to which they must adhere. Flexible standards help induce participation because they lower the risks inherent in taking on longer-term commitments in an often rapidly evolving social, economic, or technological context.[182] In the case of the Paris Agreement's NDCs, flexibility flows from the fact that the content of individual parties' NDCs is not binding under international law, and that parties are free to adjust their domestic policy choices so long as they meet the above-mentioned broad parameters set by the Paris Agreement, including progression and highest possible ambition over time.[183] Of course, a range of other approaches to flexibility are conceivable as well, some of which have been tested in the climate regime. The Kyoto Protocol, for example, permits parties to rely upon emissions trading and other market mechanisms to help meet their commitments, and allows

[177] See Bodansky, *Art and Craft of International Environmental Law* (n 12) 182.

[178] Montreal Protocol, Art 5.

[179] For a detailed review of the Kyoto Protocol, see Chapter 6. For in-depth discussion of the various types of differentiation in the climate regime, see also Chapter 1, Section V.C.

[180] See eg Paris Agreement, preamble and Art 4. For a detailed discussion of the evolution of CBDRRC, see Chapter 1, Section V.C. and Chapter 7, Section II.D.

[181] See Paris Agreement, Art 4.2. For a detailed discussion of Article 4, see Chapter 7, Section V.

[182] See Daniel Bodansky and Elliot Diringer, 'Building Flexibility and Ambition into a 2015 Climate Agreement' (June 2014) <http://www.c2es.org/publications/building-flexibility-ambition-2015-climate-agreement> accessed 27 October 2016 (discussing the importance of, and options for, flexibility in the climate regime).

[183] For a detailed discussion of the normative expectations set out in the Paris Agreement, see Chapter 7, Section V.

parties to pool their emission targets and be assessed as a group in meeting their combined target.[184]

Differentiated and flexible standards, however, are not always sufficient to prompt broad participation in an MEA. Some countries, notably developing countries, face economic, technological, and regulatory capacity limitations that make it difficult, or even impossible, for them to implement emissions-related or other environmental commitments. MEAs, therefore, tend to take a proactive approach and provide for various kinds of implementation assistance.[185] In the case of the Montreal Protocol, for example, the differentiated commitment regime for developed countries was insufficient, even in combination with certain leverage mechanism through which the regime sought to induce participation,[186] to prompt major developing countries like China and India to join the regime.[187] The Montreal Protocol, therefore, was amended to establish a funding mechanism that provided financial support to cover the costs of industrial conversion in developing countries, as well as technical assistance, training and capacity-building.[188] Indeed, the Montreal Protocol links developing countries' compliance with the effective implementation of financial and technology transfer commitments by developed countries.[189] The Montreal Protocol also established a compliance mechanism that was primarily designed to assist parties in achieving compliance.[190] Both mechanisms were instrumental in bringing about universal participation in the Montreal Protocol, as well as broad compliance with its progressively tightened control measures.[191] The Montreal Protocol's approach to financial and technical assistance has loomed large over the climate negotiations, but is unlikely to be replicated, given the much larger scale and complexity of the climate challenge.[192]

As already alluded to above, some MEAs have employed mechanisms to leverage participation.[193] However, reliance on such leverage generally has been contingent on the particular features of the environmental problem at hand.

---

[184] See Kyoto Protocol, Arts 4, 6, 12, and 17.

[185] See, generally, Bodansky, *Art and Craft of International Environmental Law* (n 12) 243–5.

[186] See nn 188–192 below and accompanying text.

[187] See Matthew J. Hoffmann, *Ozone Depletion and Climate Change: Constructing a Global Response* (Albany, NY: SUNY Press, 2012) 107.

[188] See Amendment to the Montreal Protocol on Substances that deplete the Ozone Layer (adopted on 29 June 1990, entered into force 10 August 1992) (1991) 30 ILM 537 (London Amendment) Art 10. Since its inception, the funding mechanism had disbursed US $3.32 billion; the total budget for 2015–17 is US $ 507.5 million. See 'Multilateral Fund for the Implementation of the Montreal Protocol' <http://www.multilateralfund.org/default.aspx> accessed 20 January 2017.

[189] See Montreal Protocol, Art 5.5.

[190] See Report of the Tenth Meeting of the Parties to Montreal Protocol on Substances that Deplete the Ozone Layer (3 December 1998) UN Doc UNEP/OzL.Pro.10/9, Annex II: Non-compliance procedure (1998) (Montreal Protocol NCP).

[191] On the success of the Montreal Protocol, see UNEP—Ozone Secretariat, *The Montreal Protocol on Substances that Deplete the Ozone Layer: Achievements in Stratospheric Ozone Depletion—Progress Report 1987 - 2012* (Nairobi: UNEP - Ozone Secretariat, 2012).

[192] On the protracted debates about financial and technical assistance in the climate context see Chapter 5, Section IV.D.

[193] See generally, Bodansky, *Art and Craft of International Environmental Law* (n 12) 183.

The Montreal Protocol again serves to illustrate the point.[194] Since the protocol was concerned with the elimination of the production and consumption of specific categories of harmful substances, it was possible to design the regime in such a way as to take advantage of trade leverage. Specifically, the protocol required parties to ban both the import of ozone depleting substances from states not parties to the agreement and the export of such substances to non-parties.[195] The goal was to deprive non-parties of the market for their production of ozone depleting substances, as well as of access to such substances for purposes of consumption. However, it turned out that even these leverage mechanisms were insufficient to induce China and India to join the Montreal Protocol, both of which had major and growing domestic markets for ozone depleting substances.[196] Ultimately, as noted, the provision of financial and technical assistance was necessary to convince these two states to join. In the climate context, recourse to trade measures has been mooted in the literature,[197] but the climate regime does not provide the same opportunities to deploy trade measures as did the ozone regime.[198] In any case, as discussed in more detail in Chapter 9, to date the climate regime has limited itself to emphasizing the importance of a 'supportive and open international economic system', and to stating that 'measures taken to combat climate change, including unilateral ones, should not constitute a means of arbitrary or unjustifiable discrimination or a disguised restriction on international trade'.[199]

C. Promotion of implementation and compliance

The third key feature shared by most modern environmental regimes is their emphasis on promoting implementation and compliance. MEAs generally rely on two inter-related approaches: first, measurement, reporting and technical review processes to enhance transparency regarding parties' implementation efforts, and second, the creation of regime-specific mechanisms to facilitate compliance and respond to non-compliance.

---

[194] See ibid. Some other MEAs deal with environmental issues that are exacerbated or even caused by the international trade of certain items, such as endangered species or hazardous wastes. Both the endangered species and the hazardous waste regimes restrict trade with non-parties unless a non-party state has comparable requirements in place.

[195] See Montreal Protocol, Arts 2, 2A-I, 4, 4A.

[196] See Hoffmann, *Ozone Depletion* (n 187) 108.

[197] See eg Meinhard Doelle, 'Climate Change and the WTO: Opportunities to Motivate State Action on Climate Change through the World Trade Organization', *Review of European Community and International Environmental Law*, 85/13 (2004); ZhongXiang Zhang, 'Multilateral Trade Measures in a Post–2012 Climate Change Regime? What Can Be Taken from the Montreal Protocol and the WTO?', *Energy Policy*, 37/12 (2009): 5105.

[198] See Scott Barrett and Richard Stavins, 'Increasing Participation and Compliance in International Climate Change Agreements', *International Environmental Agreements: Politics, Law and Economics*, 3/4 (2003): 349, 364–6. On the trade law issues that might be raised by climate policy measures, see Chapter 9, Section IV.

[199] FCCC, Art 3.5.

1. Emergence of the implementation and compliance focus

MEAs initially had only limited compliance-related features. These involved requirements for reporting by parties on their performance,[200] and assembly and publication of information on parties' performance through treaty bodies such as secretariats or COPs.[201] In addition, MEAs generally made provision for the resolution of disputes related to the interpretation or application of the agreement.[202] Such dispute resolution clauses tended to be rudimentary, and required agreement of all concerned parties.[203] Some clauses enabled a single party to trigger dispute settlement. However, in these cases, outcomes were limited to purely recommendatory awards.[204]

As the number and complexity of MEAs increased, attention began to focus more and more on mechanisms to actively promote compliance. It became apparent that MEAs had performance problems related to both procedural obligations, such as reporting requirements, and substantive commitments, such as emission reduction targets.[205] MEAs, it seemed, were not equipped to address these compliance problems. Parties did not make use of available dispute settlement processes.[206] And, as highlighted earlier in this chapter, conventional dispute settlement procedures, which tend to be adversarial, backward-looking, and legalistic, are ill-suited to dealing with ongoing global concerns,[207] let alone with the compliance problems that arise in the context of MEAs.[208] Because the harms resulting from global commons problems such as climate change are widely distributed, states are unlikely to have sufficient incentive to engage in bilateral dispute settlement, and in any event, the object is not to sanction wrongdoers, but rather to promote compliance going forward, which requires action by the widest possible range of states.[209]

2. Modern multilateral environmental agreements and compliance

MEAs today employ a broad spectrum of compliance techniques.[210] First, measurement, reporting and verification (MRV) requirements have assumed even greater importance. In the climate regime, for example, MRV requirements have always

---

[200] See eg Vienna Convention for the Protection of the Ozone Layer (adopted on 22 March 1985, entered into force 22 September 1988) 1513 UNTS 293 (Vienna Convention) Art 5; Convention on Long-Range Transboundary Air Pollution (adopted 13 November 1979, entered into force 16 March 1983) 1302 UNTS 217 (LRTAP Convention) Art 4. For an overview, see Kamen Sachariev, 'Promoting Compliance with International Environmental Legal Standards: Reflections on Monitoring and Reporting Mechanisms', *Yearbook of International Environmental Law*, 2/1 (1991): 31.
[201] See eg Vienna Convention, Arts 6(2)(b) and 7(1)(b).
[202] See UNEP, '*Study on Dispute Avoidance and Dispute Settlement in International Environmental Law*' (1999) UN Doc UNEP/GC.20/INF/16, 54–6.
[203] See eg LRTAP Convention, Art 8.   [204] See eg Vienna Convention, Art 11.
[205] Edith Brown Weiss, 'Understanding Compliance with International Environmental Agreements: The Baker's Dozen Myths', *University of Richmond Law Review*, 32 (1999): 1555, 1560–1.
[206] Ibid, 1582.   [207] See nn 107–109 above and accompanying text.
[208] See Malgosia A. Fitzmaurice and Catherine Redgwell, 'Environmental Non-Compliance Procedures and International Law', *Netherlands Yearbook of International Law*, 31 (2000): 35, 37.
[209] See also Bodansky, *Art and Craft of International Environmental Law* (n 12) 245–7.
[210] See generally, ibid, Chapter 11. See also Sandrine Maljean-Dubois and Lavanya Rajamani (eds), *Implementation of International Environmental Law* (Center for Studies and Research in International

been central,[211] and they again took center-stage in the Paris Agreement.[212] MRV requirements provide the necessary foundation for any subsequent compliance assessment, but they also compile, and make publically accessible, reliable information about individual parties' performance. MRV processes thereby can assure other parties of a 'level playing field' as they take the potentially costly actions to implement a treaty. Furthermore, exposure to the scrutiny of other treaty parties, as well as civil society actors and the general public, exerts pressure upon parties to meet commitments and to improve implementation measures where performance has been revealed as falling short.

Second, MEAs have seen the emergence of dedicated procedures and mechanisms to assess parties' compliance with their treaty commitments and provide for a range of measures to facilitate or compel compliance.[213] MEA non-compliance procedures (NCPs) can typically be triggered by any state party, including by a state about its own performance. The bodies established to assess whether or not a party has been in compliance, generally, are not composed of independent experts but of government negotiators, reflecting their diplomatic rather than judicial nature.[214] The procedures also reflect the underlying collective interest of parties in compliance matters. For example, under the Montreal Protocol's NCP, the treaty's secretariat can and does sometimes trigger the procedure.[215] The Kyoto Protocol's NCP is automatically triggered when an expert review process reveals questions about a party's implementation of its commitments.[216] However, while both procedures thus allow for a form of collective interest trigger, they remain firmly focused on inter-state concerns. For example, under the Kyoto procedure, non-governmental organizations may submit 'factual and technical information' relevant to the compliance review,[217] have access to meetings of the compliance bodies unless parties object,[218] and have access to the findings of the compliance body.[219] But they cannot trigger the procedure or make formal submissions.

Third, in keeping with the insights of what has been termed a 'managerial' approach,[220] MEA-based responses to non-compliance typically take account of the causes of non-compliance and of the differing circumstances of non-complying

---

Law and International Relations, Hague Academy of International Law, Leiden/Boston: Martinus Nijhoff Publishers, 2011).

[211] On the MRV provisions of the FCCC and Kyoto Protocol, see Chapter 5, Section VI, and Chapter 6, Section VI.A.

[212] On the MRV provisions of the Paris Agreement, see Chapter 7, Section X.A.

[213] See Günther Handl, 'Compliance Control Mechanisms and International Environmental Obligations', *Tulane Journal of International & Comparative Law*, 5/1 (1997): 29.

[214] See Bodansky, *Art and Craft of International Environmental Law* (n 12) 248.

[215] See Montreal Protocol NCP (n 190) para 3.

[216] See Decision 24/CP.7, 'Procedures and Mechanisms Relating to Compliance under the Kyoto Protocol' (21 January 2002) FCCC/CP/2001/13/Add.3, 64, Annex: Procedures and Mechanisms Relating to Compliance under the Kyoto Protocol, Section VI, para 1. For a more detailed discussion of the protocol's compliance regime, see Chapter 6, Section VI.B.

[217] Decision 24/CP.7, ibid. Section VIII, para 4.   [218] Ibid, Section IX, para 2.

[219] Ibid, Section VIII, para 7.

[220] Abram Chayes and Antonia Handler Chayes, *The New Sovereignty: Compliance with International Regulatory Agreements* (Cambridge, MA: Harvard University Press, 1995).

states. The compliance procedure under the Montreal Protocol pioneered this approach in the MEA context, stipulating that the compliance committee 'identify the facts and possible causes relating to individual cases of non-compliance'.[221] Transparency, justificatory discourse, and capacity-building—highlighted by managerialism as best suited to addressing the majority of compliance problems—also play central roles in promoting compliance with MEAs.[222] All NCPs place heavy emphasis on justificatory discourse: once the procedure has been triggered, the party in question must explain its performance through written and oral exchanges with the compliance body.[223]

Fourth, cooperative facilitation of compliance is the primary objective of the majority of NCPs.[224] The NCP under the Montreal Protocol encapsulates this approach when it states that it is aimed at 'securing an amicable solution... on the basis of respect for the provisions of the Protocol'.[225] In view of this focus on facilitation of compliance, many NCPs also place strong emphasis on financial and technical assistance and other capacity-building measures,[226] above and beyond the financial and technical assistance that may otherwise be provided for in the treaty.[227] This pragmatic approach recognizes that non-complying parties in many global agreements, such as the Montreal Protocol, are most likely to be states with genuine capacity limitations, and that parties' collective interest in achieving regime goals tends to be better served by promoting full compliance than by punishing non-compliance.

However, is a facilitative, cooperative approach to promoting compliance sufficient to deal with all compliance failures? Managerialists suggest that enforcement-oriented measures may be needed in those (relatively rare) instances in which a party deliberately violates a treaty commitment.[228] Other commentators argue, more broadly, that a facilitative approach is likely to fall short whenever an agreement requires parties to take measures that go beyond the business-as-usual steps that they would have taken even in the absence of the agreement.[229]

The existing MEA compliance regimes reflect these considerations to varying degrees. Even NCPs that are cast as primarily facilitative are not completely devoid

---

[221] See Montreal Protocol NCP (n 190) para 7(d).

[222] Chayes and Chayes, *The New Sovereignty* (n 220) 22–6.

[223] See eg Montreal Protocol NCP (n 190) paras 3–4, 7(c), 8, 11.

[224] See Bodansky, *Art and Craft of International Environmental Law* (n 12) 227.

[225] See Montreal Protocol NCP (n 190) para 8. See also LRTAP Convention, '*Report of the Fifteenth Session of the Executive Body*', (January 1998) ECE/EB.AIR/53, Annex III para 3(b) (describing itself as designed to secure 'a constructive solution').

[226] See eg Annex V: Indicative List of Measures that Might be Taken by a Meeting of the Parties in Respect of Non-Compliance with the Protocol in Report of the Fourth Meeting of the Parties (n 190).

[227] See nn 182–189 above and accompanying text.

[228] Chayes and Chayes, *The New Sovereignty* (n 220) 3–10 (on the most common causes of non-compliance).

[229] See George W. Downs, David M. Rocke, and Peter N. Barsoom, 'Is the Good News about Compliance Good News about Cooperation?', *International Organization*, 50/3 (1996): 379; and George W. Downs, 'Enforcement and the Evolution of Cooperation', *Michigan Journal of International Law*, 19/2 (1998): 319.

of harder-edged features.[230] For example, parties' compliance records are typically publicized, and compliance bodies can issue 'cautions' to non-complying parties.[231] Some procedures, such as the Montreal Protocol NCP, also envisage the suspension of certain 'privileges' under the MEA when a party fails to meet its commitments.[232] Nonetheless, it is fair to say that the conventional wisdom underpinning MEA-based NCPs remains that cooperative and facilitative approaches generally are better suited to promoting compliance than adversarial and enforcement-oriented responses to non-compliance. One might add that this 'softer touch' on compliance has also been easier to sell to states than a harder-edged approach would have been.[233]

Under the Kyoto Protocol, however, only industrialized countries and countries with economies in transition had emission reduction commitments. Therefore, capacity-building and financial assistance were less appropriate in promoting compliance than, for example, in the case of the Montreal Protocol. Furthermore, the Kyoto Protocol regime had certain unique features, such as its emissions trading mechanisms, which necessitated a tougher approach to compliance. Hence, the Kyoto Protocol's compliance procedure, which is reviewed in more detail in Chapter 6, sets itself apart from other NCPs by explicitly declaring its goals to be to 'facilitate, promote and *enforce* compliance'.[234] By contrast, the Paris Agreement, given its reliance on nationally determined, rather than internationally negotiated, emission reduction contributions, reverts to a 'mechanism to facilitate implementation ... and promote compliance'.[235] It will consist of a committee that is 'expert-based and facilitative in nature and function in a manner that is transparent, non-adversarial and non-punitive', and that is meant to be attentive to 'the respective national capabilities and circumstances of Parties'.[236]

V. CONCLUSION

The no-harm rule remains the conceptual cornerstone of international environmental law. From its origins in the balancing of competing state rights to the use of territory, the rule has undergone a considerable evolution, allowing it to retain its relevance. Now understood as an obligation to exercise due diligence to prevent harm to the environment of other states and the global environment, the no-harm rule is obviously relevant to the problem of climate change, although its precise

---

[230] See O. Yoshida, ' "Soft Enforcement" of Treaty: The Montreal Non-Compliance Procedure and the Functions of Internal International Institutions', *Colorado Journal of International Environmental Law and Policy*, 10/1 (1999): 95.

[231] See eg Indicative List of Measures (n 227).   [232] See ibid.

[233] See Jana von Stein, 'The International Law and Politics of Climate Change: Ratification of the United Nations Framework Convention and the Kyoto Protocol', *Journal of Conflict Resolution*, 52/2 (2008): 243–4.

[234] See Decision 24/CP.7 (n 217) Annex, Section I (emphasis added). See also Chapter 6, Section VI.B.

[235] See Paris Agreement, Art 15.1.   [236] Ibid, Art 15.2.

implications remain unclear. In other contexts, the no-harm rule has been used by individual states to take legal action against other states. Its potential force is strengthened by the gradual elaboration of the rule's due diligence, precautionary, and procedural elements, including through recent international caselaw.

Given the growth in the environmental caseload of the ICJ and other international tribunals, it is not inconceivable that a contentious or advisory case involving climate change will come before an international court. Furthermore, the Prunéřov II episode suggests that the customary international law framework could potentially shape state conduct even without recourse to formal dispute settlement or enforcement action. Unilateral action by key states can sometimes dramatize an issue and exert the pressure necessary to achieve progress, or circumvent the blockages of collective decision-making.[237]

That said, legal action or argument on the basis of customary law can take climate action only so far. The rules and principles of international environmental law are too open-textured to allow for the finely calibrated and wide-ranging response actions required to tackle climate change. Furthermore, the rules on state responsibility offer relatively limited avenues for holding states to account for failures to comply with their obligations, and even more limited options for enforcing compliance. A cooperative problem-solving approach will generally be better suited than adjudication to solving collective action problems like climate change.

In this connection, perhaps the most important role of international environmental norms is to support policy demands and negotiating positions, and more generally, to shape international environmental regimes, including the climate regime. This role is not contingent on the status of a norm as customary international law. A number of principles of uncertain legal status have proven to be influential, albeit to vaying degrees, in shaping the debates under the auspices of the FCCC, including precaution, common concern, common but differentiated responsibilities, and sustainable development.

Overall, a treaty-based approach is better able than customary law to address the multiple facets of climate change that were highlighted in Chapter 1, as well as the complex linkages between them. Indeed, the FCCC is remarkable in the extent to which it acknowledges the multidimensional nature of the climate challenge and embraces the rules and principles of international environmental law discussed in this chapter. The climate regime can also draw upon a rich repository of experience gained through other environmental regimes. As this chapter has illustrated, MEAs have spawned an array of features and approaches to promote meaningful collective action among states, ranging from the institutionalization and ongoing standard-setting processes that characterize the gradual regime-building approach

---

[237] See Daniel Bodansky, 'What's So Bad about Unilateral Action to Protect the Environment', *European Journal of International Law*, 11/2 (2000): 339. See also the example of *Whaling in the Antarctic (Australia v Japan: New Zealand Intervening)* (Judgment) [2014] ICJ Rep 223 (in this case, Australia challenged Japan's whaling practice, in the interest of all parties to the 1946 International Convention for the Regulating of Whaling (adopted on 2 December 1946, entered into force 10 November 1948) 161 UNTS 72.

of the framework-protocol model, to the many techniques employed to encourage participation, to the spectrum of elements designed to promote implementation and compliance. However, each international environmental problem has its own features and policy context. What may work in dealing with one issue is not necessarily suited to dealing with another. The sheer complexity of climate change and the high stakes of climate politics have vexed regime-building efforts, notwithstanding the recourse to the framework-protocol model and many other tried and tested regime-design elements. Climate negotiators have had to abandon some of the familiar approaches and experiment with new ones. More than twenty years after its adoption, the climate regime remains a work in progress.

As this chapter has sought to show, the structure and processes of general international law and international environmental law have significantly shaped, and continue to underpin, international climate change law. It may be too soon to say whether, in turn, the ongoing development of the climate regime will have broader implications for international law. As far back as twenty-five years ago, a prominent observer of international law worried that the flexibility of commitments, the informality of NCPs, the absence of findings of breaches of international law, the absence of sanctions, and the provision of assistance to non-compliant parties in MEAs risked diluting the obligatory nature of international law.[238] As another commentator put it, the cost of more effective management of environmental problems may well be 'giving up the rule of law in favour of a specific set of goals' and making 'the binding force of international law...negotiable'.[239] The Paris Agreement, with its reliance on non-legally binding, nationally determined 'contributions' and commensurably soft compliance features, is unlikely to allay these concerns. However, they may at once misjudge the role that international law, as traditionally conceived, realistically can play in dealing with complex policy challenges such as global climate change, and underestimate the role that international environmental law, as it has evolved, has played and continues to play in the global climate regime. The following chapters will enable readers to make their own assessments.

SELECT BIBLIOGRAPHY

Barrett S., *Environment and Statecraft: The Strategy of Environmental Treaty-making* (Oxford University Press, 2003).

Birnie P., Boyle A., and Redgwell C., *International Law and the Environment* (Oxford University Press, 3rd edn, 2009).

Bodansky D., *The Art and Craft of International Environmental Law* (Cambridge, MA: Harvard University Press, 2010).

---

[238] See Martti Koskenniemi, 'Breach of Treaty or Non-Compliance? Reflections on the Enforcement of the Montreal Protocol', *Yearbook of International Environmental Law*, 3/1 (1992): 123.

[239] Jan Klabbers, 'Compliance Procedures', in Bodansky *et al.* (eds), *Oxford Handbook of International Environmental Law* (n 1) 995, 1007–8.

Brunnée J., 'The Sources of International Environmental Law: Interactional Law', in Besson S. and d'Aspremont J. (eds), *The Oxford Handbook on the Sources of International Law* (Oxford University Press, 2017 forthcoming).

Chayes A. and Chayes A.H., *The New Sovereignty: Compliance with International Regulatory Agreements* (Cambridge, MA: Harvard University Press, 1995).

Committee on the Legal Principles relating to Climate Change, 'Legal Principles Relating to Climate Change' (International Law Association (ILA), Washington, D.C., 2014).

Gehring T., 'Treaty-Making and Treaty Evolution', in Bodansky D., Brunnée J., and Hey E. (eds), *Oxford Handbook of International Environmental Law* (Oxford University Press, 2007) 491.

Peel J., 'New State Responsibility Rules and Compliance with Multilateral Environmental Obligations: Some Case Studies of How the New Rules Might Apply in the International Environmental Context', *Review of European Community and International Environmental Law*, 10/1 (2001): 82.

Sands P., 'Climate Change and International Law: Adjudicating the Future in International Law', *Journal of Environmental Law*, 28/1 (2016): 19.

Shelton D. (ed), *Commitment and Compliance: The Role of Non-Binding Norms in the International Legal System* (Oxford University Press, 2000).

3

Treaty-Based Law-Making

Rules, Tools, and Techniques

I. INTRODUCTION

As discussed in Chapter 2, modern multilateral environmental agreements (MEAs) typically establish long-term regimes, characterized by institutionalization of expert networks, the instantiation of a range of iterative law-making and standard-setting modes, and the development of treaty-based transparency and accountability mechanisms. International climate change law has followed this model, with the FCCC as the hub of global regime-building and standard-setting efforts. The elements and evolution of the climate regime are considered in detail in Chapters 4–7. However, navigating the UN climate regime and working with the various types of instruments it comprises require an understanding of the basic concepts, processes, and devices of treaty law.[1] This chapter provides an overview.

II. TREATIES AND TREATY-BASED LAW-MAKING

A. What is a treaty?

Under customary law, treaties can be oral and can be concluded between all international legal persons that have treaty-making capacity (ie states and, within the bounds of their competences, international organizations). In contrast, the Vienna Convention on the Law of Treaties (VCLT) defines 'treaty' more narrowly as 'an international agreement concluded between States in written form and governed by international law'.[2] The discussion in this chapter focuses on treaties as defined in the VCLT. Such treaties can be embodied in a single instrument or in two or more

---

[1] See United Nations Environment Program (UNEP), *Multilateral Agreement Negotiator's Handbook* (Joensuu, Finland: University of Joensuu, 2nd edn, 2007). See also Joyeeta Gupta, *'On Behalf of my Delegation ...' – A Survival Guide for Developing Country Climate Negotiators* (Washington D.C., Center for Sustainable Development in the Americas, 2000).

[2] Vienna Convention on the Law of Treaties (adopted 23 May 1969, entered into force 27 January 1980) 1155 UNTS 331 (VCLT), Art 2.1(a). The phrase 'governed by international law' is meant to distinguish treaties from other arrangements between states, such as political agreements or contracts governed by private international law.

related instruments, an 'instrument' being a written act of a state or states. The basic rules of treaty law are codified in the VCLT, but are considered today to be universally binding as customary international law.[3]

Whether or not an agreement between states constitutes a treaty within the meaning of the VCLT depends solely on whether it meets the above requirements, rather than on what the instrument is called. The climate regime illustrates this point. The UN Framework 'Convention' on Climate Change is a treaty, as is the Kyoto 'Protocol' and the Paris 'Agreement'.[4] By contrast, the Copenhagen 'Accord' is a political agreement between certain states, and the Cancun 'Agreements' comprise a set of decisions of the FCCC Conference of the Parties (COP).[5]

B. Treaty negotiations

International law does not provide general rules to govern treaty negotiations, but certain common practices prevail in the pre-negotiation and negotiation phases.

1. *The pre-negotiation phase: issue, forum, and mandate*

Even before formal negotiations begin, considerable time may be taken up by identifying and framing the principal issues and, if the decision is made to initiate negotiations, by agreeing upon a forum and a negotiating mandate.[6] Climate change is a case in point. Although climate change emerged as a major international concern in the 1980s, it took states until December 1990 to formally launch the negotiations through General Assembly Resolution 45/212, which established the Intergovernmental Negotiating Committee for a Framework Convention on Climate Change (INC).[7] Adopting the mandates for the subsequent negotiations of the Kyoto Protocol and the Paris Agreement proved even more contentious, with parties trying to lock in key positions before even agreeing to initiate a formal negotiating process.

The negotiating mandate for what became the FCCC specified that the INC was to prepare 'an effective framework convention on climate change, containing appropriate commitments, and any related instruments as might be agreed upon'.[8] Through this mandate, states pre-determined what type of legal outcome

---

[3] For an excellent overview, see Duncan Hollis, 'Defining Treaties', in Duncan B. Hollis (ed), *The Oxford Guide to Treaties* (Oxford University Press, 2012) 11.

[4] See United Nations, 'Definition of key terms used in the UN Treaty Collection' <http://training.itcilo.it/actrav_cdrom1/english/global/law/keyterm.htm > accessed 20 January 2017.

[5] The different types of instruments that are produced under the auspices of the climate regime are considered below, in Section II.D on 'Treaty Development'. See also Chapter 7, Section II.A.1 (on the nomenclature of the Paris Agreement).

[6] On the importance of choice of forum and framing of mandates, see Daniel Bodansky, *The Art and Craft of International Environmental Law* (Harvard University Press, 2010) 167–9.

[7] United Nations General Assembly Res 45/212, 'Protection of global climate for present and future generations of mankind' (21 December 1990) UN Doc A/RES/45/212. For a detailed review see Chapter 4, Section II on 'agenda setting'.

[8] Ibid, para 1.

the negotiations were to yield, while leaving the nature of the commitments in the agreement relatively open-ended. The phrase 'any related instruments as might be agreed upon' also left open the possibility of adopting additional instruments at the same time.

In 1995, when the parties to the FCCC turned their attention to additional climate commitments, the negotiating mandate for what became the Kyoto Protocol was an intensely controversial matter, and developing countries agreed to it only on the condition that it explicitly exclude them from any new commitments—a feature of the Kyoto Protocol that would remain a flashpoint.[9] The so-called Berlin Mandate adopted by COP1 settled a number of other key issues, including the legal form of the new instrument (a treaty),[10] and the type of commitments it would contain (emission targets). But the negotiating mandate left open whether the emission targets to be negotiated would be legally binding, an issue not settled until the following year in the Geneva Ministerial Declaration.[11]

Fast-forward sixteen years to 2011, when FCCC parties were finally ready to agree on a negotiating mandate to further advance the climate regime—the Durban Platform. It established a process to 'develop a protocol, another legal instrument or an agreed outcome with legal force under the Convention applicable to all Parties'.[12] The Durban Platform also specified the time frame that parties were to pursue, calling for adoption of the new agreement by 2015, and for it to 'come into effect and be implemented from 2020'.[13] Unlike the earlier mandates, the Durban Platform left more scope for parties to decide on the legal form and architecture of the future agreement.[14] This flexibility helped parties reach agreement that the new instrument would apply to both developed and developing countries. By specifying that the agreement would be 'under the Convention', the Durban Platform implicitly imported the convention's objective and principles, while avoiding the challenge of addressing various fraught issues in the mandate itself.[15]

Settling on a forum and parameters for negotiations, as the preceding overview illustrates, is a politically delicate task and the choices made at this preliminary stage have significant implications for the process, form, and substance of legal development. But agreement on the mandate marks only the beginning of many years of

---

[9] Berlin Mandate, para 2(b).

[10] Ibid, preambular recital 3 (specifying that the outcome would be a 'protocol or another legal instrument').

[11] Ibid, para 2(a) (on emission targets). See also Report of the Conference of the Parties on its Second Session, held at Geneva from 8 to 19 July 1996, Addendum (29 October 1996) FCCC/CP/1996/15/Add.1, Annex: The Geneva Ministerial Declaration (Geneva Ministerial Declaration) para 8.

[12] Durban Platform, para 2. For a detailed analysis of the decision, see Lavanya Rajamani, 'The Durban Platform for Enhanced Action and the Future of the Climate Regime', *International and Comparative Law Quarterly*, 61/2 (2012): 501.

[13] Durban Platform, para 4.

[14] Although the requirement that the outcome have 'legal force' pointed toward a treaty. See Daniel Bodansky and Lavanya Rajamani, 'Key Legal Issues in the 2015 Climate Negotiations' (Center for Climate and Energy Solutions, June 2015) <http://www.c2es.org/docUploads/legal-issues-brief-06-2015.pdf> accessed 20 January 2017.

[15] See below, Section II.D.5, for a discussion of the role of compromise language and interpretation in the practice of the climate regime. For an in-depth analysis, see Rajamani, Durban Platform (n 12).

hard work that typically go into negotiating a major environmental agreement. The FCCC, perhaps surprisingly, was negotiated in less than two years. It was adopted at the Rio Earth Summit in June 1992. The Kyoto Protocol too was negotiated in two years, and was adopted in 1997, at the third meeting of the FCCC parties (COP3). Then, however, the pace of climate negotiations slowed dramatically, at least as far as the negotiation of legally binding instruments was concerned. In the meantime, of course, the convention's COP and the protocol's Conference of the Parties serving as the Meeting of the Parties (CMP) negotiated and adopted an array of decisions that flesh out or aim to develop the climate regime.[16]

2. The negotiating process

It is difficult to overstate the challenges posed by climate negotiations: the issues are complex and multifaceted, the stakes are high, and agreement must be forged between all states in the world, including states with widely diverging circumstances, perspectives, and priorities.[17] While the number of participating states was slightly lower when the FCCC was first negotiated, the convention is a truly universal agreement today, counting 196 states and the European Union (EU) among its parties.[18] Not surprisingly, then, negotiations tend to be difficult and time-consuming.

When negotiations start from scratch, rules of procedure, including voting rules, must be agreed upon. Since global climate negotiations now unfold under the auspices of the FCCC, the rules of procedure for the COP—or, more accurately, the draft rules of procedure—apply to all decision-making. The adoption of the rules was, and continues to be, blocked, due to disagreement on the voting rule.[19] Hence, throughout its history, the FCCC has operated on the basis of a general agreement that decisions be taken by consensus.[20] However, even the question of what exactly constitutes 'consensus' in the climate regime is contentious.

Generally speaking, following UN practice, 'consensus' is distinct from unanimity; only an explicit objection will break consensus.[21] Consensus breaking is relatively rare. More frequently, the threat of a negative vote suffices to prevent a question from being put in the first place. Alternatively, as the early practice of the climate regime illustrates, presiding officers can sometimes head off challenges

---

[16] See below, Section II.D.3.

[17] For a helpful exploration of the organizational and procedural dimensions of climate negotiations, see Joanna Depledge, *The Organization of Global Negotiations: Constructing the Climate Change Regime* (London: Earthscan, 2015).

[18] See FCCC, 'Status of Ratification of the Convention' <http://unfccc.int/essential_background/convention/status_of_ratification/items/2631.php> accessed 20 January 2017.

[19] Rule 42 of the Draft Rules of procedure sets forth two options, one requiring substantive decisions to be made by consensus and the other allowing decisions to be made by two-thirds majority vote, with some exceptions, if consensus is impossible. FCCC, Draft Rules of Procedure of the Conference of the Parties and its Subsidiary Bodies (22 May 1996) FCCC/CP/1996/2, 2, Rule 42.

[20] See Antto Vihma, 'Climate of Consensus: Managing Decision Making in the UN Climate Change Negotiations', *Review of European Community & International Environmental Law*, 24/1 (2015): 58, 62.

[21] See UNEP, *Negotiator's Handbook* (n 1) 3–12.

by presuming consensus and gaveling through a decision without giving the floor
to a party looking to voice opposition.[22] Still, since the inception of the climate
regime, there have been four instances of explicit objections, at COP2 in Geneva in
1996, at COP15 in Copenhagen in 2009, at COP16 in Cancun, and at COP18 in
Doha.[23] The failure of COP15 to adopt the Copenhagen Accord, which had been
hammered out by leaders of most of the major economies and negotiating groups
in the waning hours of the meeting, provides a vivid illustration. An acrimonious
session of the COP was suspended when a small group of countries objected to a
COP decision to 'adopt' the Accord.[24] The compromise decision to 'take [...] note'
of the Accord followed the practice of COP2,[25] which had taken note of—rather
than adopted—the Geneva Ministerial Declaration.[26] The consensus challenge
arose again the following year, at COP16, when parties sought to bring key elements of the Copenhagen Accord into the UN climate regime by adopting a set of
decisions dubbed the Cancun Agreements. This time, a single party, Bolivia, voiced
express opposition, on procedural and substantive grounds. However, the presiding officers of the COP nevertheless gaveled through the decision and declared the
Cancun Agreements adopted by consensus.[27] Similarly, at COP18, Russia's express
objections were overruled, enabling the adoption of the Doha Amendment to the
Kyoto Protocol.[28]

This experience illustrates the pitfalls of the consensus process. Ideally, consensus decision-making ensures that all participants, including less powerful groups,
have an opportunity to shape the outcome, and that the resultant decision contains
a feasible and legitimate approach.[29] However, the obvious drawbacks of the consensus process are that it may push decision-making toward the lowest common
denominator and enable a very small group of states to prevent an overwhelming

---

[22] See Lavanya Rajamani, 'The Cancun Climate Agreements: Reading the Text, Subtext and Tea
Leaves', *International and Comparative Law Quarterly*, 60/2 (2011): 499, 515–16 (providing the
examples of Organization of Petroleum Exporting Countries (OPEC) opposition to the adoption
of the FCCC by the INC, and to the adoption of the Berlin Mandate at COP1); Vihma, Climate of
Consensus (n 20) 62–3. See also Depledge, *Organization of Global Negotiations* (n 17) ch 4 (on the role
of presiding officers).

[23] For detailed consideration of the evolving consensus practice in the climate regime, see
Rajamani, ibid, 514–18; Duncan French and Lavanya Rajamani, 'Climate Change and International
Environmental Law: Musings on a Journey to Somewhere', *Journal of Environmental Law*, 25/3
(2013): 437, 448–51.

[24] For detailed discussions, see Daniel Bodansky, 'The Copenhagen Climate Change Conference:
A Post-Mortem', *American Journal of International Law*, 104/2 (2010): 230; Lavanya Rajamani, 'The
Making and Unmaking of the Copenhagen Accord', *International and Comparative Law Quarterly*,
59/3 (2010): 824.

[25] Decision 2/CP.15, 'Copenhagen Accord' (30 March 2010) FCCC/CP/2009/11/Add.1, 4,
introductory text.

[26] See FCCC, Report of the COP on its Second Session (n 11) 70. See also below, Section II.D.4
(on the role political agreements in the climate regime).

[27] For a detailed discussion of the varying theories of consensus articulated in Cancun, see Rajamani,
Cancun Climate Agreements (n 22) 514–15.

[28] See French and Rajamani, Climate Change and International Environmental Law (n 23) 449.
On amendments, including the Doha Amendment, see below, Section II.D.2.

[29] See Rajamani, Cancun Climate Agreements (n 22) 517–18 (providing a finely grained discussion
of the attendant considerations).

majority from moving ahead. The approach taken at Cancun and Doha, however, may not present a viable solution to the dilemma in the longer run.[30] In rejecting express objections by parties, the Cancun and Doha decisions went beyond the general understanding of consensus in the UN system and raised difficult conceptual and threshold questions. Is the new rule within the UN climate regime one of 'quasi-consensus', 'general agreement', or 'consensus-minus-one'?[31] And, what happens if two or three states voice objections, or a very small group, as was the case in Copenhagen? All of these difficulties notwithstanding, there still does not appear to be sufficient support among key countries for abandoning consensus decision-making in favor of other options, such as qualified majority voting (eg two-thirds or three-quarters majority voting).[32]

The consensus issue may be an especially stark example of the procedural struggles in the climate regime. But it is hardly the only one. Procedural questions of various kinds tend to run throughout the negotiations. Often, procedural matters are proxy battlegrounds for substantive disagreements, and process questions are deployed to block, delay, or limit substantive progress. Needless to say, preparing the ground for, and achieving, substantive progress is where the real challenges of climate negotiations lie. A wide range of strategies are deployed to foster common ground and manage multiple, interrelated issues.

Especially in the early stages of a negotiating process, efforts may be made to provide depoliticized opportunities for exchange of views on sensitive issues, such as workshops involving expert presentations on a given topic.[33] Such events, hosted under the auspices of the climate regime, or sponsored by parties or even non-governmental entities, can also serve capacity-building functions, assisting smaller delegations in getting a better sense of the issues and the range of options for solving them. During the negotiating sessions, too, much important work happens away from the public sessions in which positions are stated and texts adopted. Delegates have informal 'corridor' discussions, or meet off the record to work out key issues.[34]

---

[30] As noted in the text, the Doha Amendment was adopted over Russia's objections. The following year, in June 2013, as an expression of its displeasure, Russia proposed the inclusion of a new agenda item on 'procedural and legal issues related to decision-making' by the COP. When some countries objected to this new agenda item, Russia prevented the Subsidiary Body for Implementation (SBI) from adopting its agenda, thereby preventing the SBI from conducting any business. See Report of the Subsidiary Body for Implementation on its thirty-eighth session, held in Bonn from 3 to 14 June 2013 (27 August 2013) FCCC/SBI/2013/10, 4. The issue was not defused until the Warsaw COP later that year, when the COP President agreed to hold consultations on Russia's proposed new agenda item, which are ongoing as of 2016.

[31] See Rajamani, Cancun Climate Agreements (n 22) 516–17; French and Rajamani, Climate Change and International Environmental Law (n 23) 450.

[32] See Vihma, Climate of Consensus (n 20) 63–4 (noting that the reluctant parties include the US and the EU, if only to avoid the political and legal transaction costs of reform).

[33] For an overview, see Depledge, Organization of Global Negotiations (n 17) ch 10. See the series of ADP workshops held in 2013, for instance, FCCC, 'Workshop on scope, structure and design of the 2015 agreement' <http://unfccc.int/meetings/bonn_apr_2013/workshop/7488.php> accessed 20 January 2017.

[34] See Bodansky, *Art and Craft of International Environmental Law* (n 6) 170.

The negotiations themselves are usually broken into various sub-issues, with different working groups being charged with advancing them.[35] Deliberations usually begin with the solicitation of written position statements or proposals from parties. At a certain point, the working group chair(s) invite proposals for draft text. Ultimately, the goal is to identify the elements of the future agreement and to develop a single composite text. The advantage of this approach, which has been predominant in the climate regime, is that all parties have the opportunity for input. The downside is that parties feel compelled to insert all of their preferred options into the text. The resulting text can become unwieldy, complicating the task of narrowing down the issues and options into a workable agreement.

For example, the initial compilation text for the Copenhagen climate conference was fifty-three pages long. Once parties had refined and clarified their positions, the draft text had ballooned to almost 200 pages,[36] presenting the Copenhagen meeting with a nearly impossible task, even leaving aside political differences. The evolution of the negotiating text for the 2015 Paris meeting followed a similar although less extreme pattern, moving back and forth between shorter and longer texts. In December 2014, the co-chairs of the working group produced a thirty-nine page paper containing 'elements for a draft negotiating text'.[37] By the time the parties adopted a draft negotiating text at their Geneva meetings in February 2015, the co-chairs' elements paper had expanded into ninety pages of options and square brackets,[38] which reflected the parties' proposed insertions. At the beginning of October, however, the co-chairs presented a document of twenty pages, with carefully selected brackets, that reflected their view of where compromises might be struck, and what the key outstanding issues were. However, it was rejected by many developing countries, so the Paris COP opened with a much longer draft text that included all of the parties' proposals and was riddled with some 1600 square brackets.[39]

In order for a desired formulation or option to remain on the negotiating table, parties must ensure the relevant text is included in the official draft. Square brackets are the device used in negotiations to identify options proposed by at least one party, but objected to by one or more other parties.[40] This approach accounts for

<hr />

[35] See Depledge, Organization of Global Negotiations (n 17) ch 9 and ch 11.

[36] Pamela Chasek, Lynn Wagner, and I. William Zartman, 'Six Ways to Make Climate Negotiations More Effective' (Policy Brief—Fixing Climate Governance Series, No 3, June 2015) <https://www.cigionline.org/sites/default/files/fixing_climate_governance_pb_no3_3.pdf> accessed 20 January 2017, 2.

[37] Decision 1/CP.20, 'Lima Call for Climate Action' (2 February 2015) FCCC/CP/2014/10/Add.1, 2 (Lima Call for Climate Action) Annex: Elements of a Draft Negotiating Text.

[38] Ad Hoc Working Group on the Durban Platform for Enhanced Action (ADP), 'Negotiating Text' (25 February 2015) FCCC/ADP/2015/1.

[39] Frank McDonald, 'It's all in the detail: time for hardball talks on climate change', *The Irish Times* (2 December 2015); see also ADP, Draft agreement and draft decision on workstreams 1 and 2 of the Ad Hoc Working Group on the Durban Platform for Enhanced Action (10 November 2015) ADP.2015.11.InformalNote.

[40] McDonald, ibid; R.P. Barston, *Modern Diplomacy* (London and New York: Routledge, 4th edn, 2014) 87.

the phenomenon of ballooning negotiating texts described above. One of the central tasks for the final stages of a negotiation is to whittle down the negotiating text, reducing the number of options for each provision and square brackets within provisions, thereby revealing the contours of a possible outcome. In the process, the 'crunch issues'—the big disagreements between the parties—are highlighted. These issues typically remain unresolved until the last few days, even hours, of the negotiating round.

The means of resolving crunch issues to reach agreement has varied over the twenty-five-year history of the UN climate regime. In the FCCC negotiations, the chair of the INC quietly convened a small group referred to as the 'extended bureau', which consisted of about twenty-five key countries, including the officers of the INC and its two working groups (the 'bureau') and other countries selected by the INC chair. The extended bureau met inter-sessionally before the final meeting of the INC, and requested the INC chair to prepare a compromise text, which proved vital in reaching agreement. Then, in the final meeting of the INC at the UN headquarters in New York, after giving all delegations an opportunity to express their views, the INC chair reconvened the extended bureau, which met practically around the clock during the last few days of the meeting in a small conference room in the upper reaches of the headquarters building, far removed from the negotiating rooms below, to hammer out compromises on the outstanding issues.[41]

The strategy of convening a small group of key countries, often referred to as the 'friends of the chair', in the final days and hours of COPs to resolve 'crunch' issues was the norm throughout much of the FCCC's history, and was used extensively during the negotiation of the Kyoto Protocol.[42] This approach requires deference by the many delegations excluded from the final negotiations to the compromises reached by a small group behind closed doors. This deference, however, began to fray in the negotiations leading up to the 2009 Copenhagen conference, as a wider array of countries became active in the climate negotiations. It broke down entirely at the Copenhagen conference, when, as mentioned above,[43] a small group of countries prevented adoption of the Copenhagen Accord, which had been negotiated by the leaders of twenty-eight key countries (including all of the major economies and negotiating groups) in a 'friends of the president' process.

The demise of the closed-door, 'friends of the chair' approach in Copenhagen led to experimentation with other modes of resolving crunch issues. At the Durban meeting in 2011, the South African COP President convened so-called 'indabas'—a traditional meeting technique from southern Africa, which anyone can attend but at which only leaders may speak in order to state positions and propose possible compromise solutions.[44] When the Durban indabas failed to resolve the key issue

---

[41] This discussion is drawn from Daniel Bodansky, 'The United Nations Framework Convention on Climate Change: A Commentary', *Yale Journal of International Law*, 18/2 (1991): 451, 491–2.

[42] See Depledge, *Organization of Global Negotiations* (n 17) 122–31.

[43] See nn 24–26 above and accompanying text.

[44] J.G.S. de Wet, 'Highlights from the Office of the Chief State Law Adviser (International Law)', *South African Yearbook of International Law*, 36 (2011): 146, 156, 159; and see Sandrine

of the legal form of the new agreement to be negotiated, the COP President asked the main disputants to 'huddle' on the plenary floor to work out their differences.[45] This huddle produced the phrase, 'agreed outcome with legal force', which broke the impasse preventing adoption of the Durban Platform.[46] 'Huddles' were again used in Warsaw to resolve difficult issues, but soon came to be seen as problematic too, for example because some felt they favored physical strength and stature (in jostling to the center).

In part due to such concerns, COP21 in Paris did not use the 'huddle' approach. Instead, a variety of other means were used to produce the ultimate text. During the first week, the parties, with the assistance of the Ad Hoc Working Group on the Durban Platform for Enhanced Action (ADP) co-chairs and facilitators for each issue area, trimmed the large number of square brackets.[47] They did this, inter alia, by projecting negotiating text on screen and painstakingly working through the text, bracket by bracket, and making use of 'bridging proposals' that facilitators offered based on their judgment of where the compromises lay. At this stage, parties played a direct role in drafting. In the second week, in contrast, the French Presidency chose to adopt a different process, one in which it retained the 'drafting pen' as it were. It convened a set of ministerial meetings on key issues, followed by 'indaba' style meetings with all parties and several rounds of bilateral consultations with key groups of parties. Intense negotiations between small groups of parties continued in parallel, some convened at the request of the Presidency, others convened by interested parties. The President relied on inputs, textual and conceptual, from all of these meetings to assess where the compromises lay, and together with a core secretariat drafting team produced three sets of 'President's proposals' in the second week. These proposals iteratively eliminated all the brackets in the text. The last of the square brackets to be lifted related to 'crunch issues' such as the legal nature of the agreement, the level of ambition, matters of transparency and accountability, climate finance issues, and questions around 'loss and damage' due to climate change.[48] In seeking to eliminate brackets, the Presidency had to find solutions on text, broker agreements, and strike an equilibrium acceptable to all, while striving toward the highest possible ambition. The Presidency and

---

Maljean-Dubois and Matthieu Wemaere, 'After Durban, What Legal Form for the Future International Climate Regime?', *Carbon & Climate Law Review*, 2012/3 (2012): 160, 187, 189.

[45] See Lavanya Rajamani, 'The Warsaw Climate Negotiations: Emerging Understandings and Battle Lines on the Road to the 2015 Climate Agreement', *International and Comparative Law Quarterly*, 63/3 (2014): 721, 724–5.

[46] Navroz K. Dubash and Lavanya Rajamani, 'Multilateral Diplomacy on Climate Change', in David M. Malone, C. Raja Mohan, and Srinath Raghavan (eds), *Oxford Handbook of Indian Foreign Policy* (Oxford University Press, 2015) 663, 666. On the Durban Platform, and see nn 12–15 above and accompanying text.

[47] See ADP, Draft Paris Outcome, Revised draft conclusions proposed by the Co-Chairs (5 December 2015) FCCC/ADP/2015/L.6/Rev.1, Annex I: Draft Agreement and Draft Decision.

[48] Daniel Bodansky, 'Crunch Issues in Paris', *Opinio Juris* (6 December 2015) <http://opiniojuris.org/2015/12/06/crunch-issues-in-paris/> accessed 20 January 2017.

the Paris negotiations succeeded in this respect, enabling the adoption of the Paris Agreement on 12 December 2015.[49]

In this process of gradually streamlining the text and delivering agreement, negotiating groups play a key role. These groups allow individual states to reinforce and leverage their negotiating positions through alliances. At the same time, they help 'bundle' parties' priorities and gradually reduce the range of positions that the negotiating process must manage. Some countries negotiate primarily through one or more of these groups, others such as the US, China, and India negotiate both through these groups as well as independently.

At the outset of the climate negotiations, the number of negotiating groups was comparatively small. The Group of 77 and China (G-77/ China), comprising 134 developing countries, was the biggest, leveraging the combined power of larger and smaller developing states. Within the G-77/China, two other groups, with vastly different priorities, had a distinct identity—the Organization of Petroleum Exporting Countries (OPEC), comprising fourteen countries, and the Alliance of Small Island States (AOSIS), comprising forty-four countries—although they tended to join ranks in the interests of G-77/China solidarity.

But, over the last two decades, the number of negotiating groups has proliferated. Within the G-77/China, these groups include the Least Developed Countries (LDCs), comprising forty-eight countries; the African Group, comprising fifty-four countries; the Bolivarian Alliance for the Peoples of our America (ALBA), consisting of eleven Marxist-oriented Latin American countries; the Coalition for Rainforest Nations, a loose coalition of over forty countries; the BASIC Group, comprising four emerging economies (Brazil, South Africa, India, and China), which gained prominence in the lead up to the Copenhagen conference and played a decisive role in Copenhagen and thereafter; the like-minded developing countries (LMDCs) group, which emerged in the aftermath of the Durban conference and includes Bolivia, China, India, Malaysia, the Philippines, Saudi Arabia, and Venezuela, among others; and the Independent Association of Latin America and the Caribbean (AILAC), consisting of seven progressive Latin American countries.

Among developed states, the main groupings are the EU and the Umbrella Group, which includes Australia, Canada, Iceland, Japan, Kazakhstan, New Zealand, Norway, Russia, Ukraine, and the US. The precursor to the Umbrella Group in the negotiations was JUSCANZ (Japan, US, Canada, Australia, and New Zealand). It would at times include Switzerland and take on an extra 'S' to become JUSSCANZ, or Norway and take on an extra 'N' to become JUSSCANNZ.

Finally, in the last decade, a number of groups have formed that include both developed and developing countries. These include the Environmental Integrity Group (EIG), consisting of Mexico, Liechtenstein, Monaco, the Republic of Korea, and Switzerland, and the Cartagena Dialogue for Progressive Action, consisting of

---

[49] See generally FCCC, Adoption of The Paris Agreement, Proposal by the President (12 December 2015) FCCC/CP/2015/L.9/Rev.1. See Decision 1/CP.21, 'Adoption of the Paris Agreement' (29 January 2016) FCCC/CP/2015/10/Add.1, 2.

thirty-two countries cutting across the full spectrum of negotiating groups. The Cartagena Dialogue occasionally delivers common statements, but its members do not typically negotiate together.

There is overlapping membership between these various groups, as for instance between the LDCs and the African Group, and between BASIC and the LMDCs. Some of these groups have an existence independent of the climate negotiations, and in some instances, predate the climate negotiations, as for instance the G-77/China and the LDCs. Other groups have emerged from the climate negotiating process, as for instance BASIC and the LMDCs. Some of these groups are relatively homogeneous and share objective characteristics (eg AILAC), and others such as the Cartagena Dialogue have few objective characteristics in common but share goals and seek to forge common positions. The relationships fostered in these groups, both at the negotiator and ministerial level, can prove critical at key moments in the negotiations. For example, the 'high ambition coalition', a ministerial coalition that emerged organically from the Cartagena Dialogue in the lead-up to the Paris conference, strengthened the hand of the French Presidency in delivering the Paris Agreement, in particular the reference to the '1.5° C' aspirational long-term temperature goal.[50]

Inter-sessional discussions between particular countries and groups of countries can also play a crucial role in advancing the climate negotiations, especially given the cumbersome nature of the consensus process. For example, the bilateral, off-line discussions between the United Kingdom (acting on behalf of the EU) and the US resolved one of the critical issues in the FCCC negotiations, namely, emission targets for developed countries. Similarly, in the Kyoto context, in the negotiations on what became the Marrakesh Accords, informal dialogues among negotiators led to increasing acceptance of Kyoto's market mechanisms. Most recently, the bilateral, off-line discussions between China and the US, leading to their November 2014 Joint Announcement on Climate Change,[51] illustrate the momentum that can be provided when key parties find common ground.

C. Adoption, signature, ratification, and entry into force of treaties

The 'adoption' of a treaty marks the end of (successful) negotiations, signifying the finalization of the treaty text. In the UN climate regime, new agreements are adopted by the COP. The FCCC provides specific voting rules for the adoption of

---

[50] According to Minister Tony de Brum, Republic of the Marshall Islands, this coalition was not a negotiating group but 'joining the voices of all those who are committed to an ambitious agreement and a safe climate future' 'big and small, rich and poor'. See Lisa Friedman, 'Glimmers of a Climate Deal Emerge in Paris', *Scientific American* (10 December 2015) <https://www.scientificamerican.com/article/glimmers-of-a-climate-deal-emerge-in-paris/> accessed 20 January 2017.

[51] The White House, 'U.S.-China Joint Announcement on Climate Change' (11 November 2014) <https://obamawhitehouse.archives.gov/the-press-office/2014/11/11/us-china-joint-announcement-climate-change> accessed 20 January 2017. See Chapter 7, Section II.D.

amendments and annexes;[52] otherwise, the adoption of an agreement requires consensus, like any other COP decision.

Adoption of a treaty does not mean that states are legally bound by its terms. In the case of multilateral treaties like the FCCC, Kyoto Protocol, and Paris Agreement, becoming legally bound requires two additional steps. First, individual states must express their consent to be bound; and second, a sufficient number of states must do so in order for the agreement to 'enter into force'. The two questions—when and how individual states consent to be bound and when a treaty enters into force—are distinct but intertwined. Whereas each party controls whether and when it formally consents to be bound, entry into force is contingent upon the consent threshold and any other entry-into-force requirements stipulated in the treaty being met.

The first step in this process begins with opening the treaty for signature, which generally occurs shortly after the treaty is adopted.[53] For example, the Paris Agreement provides for signature anytime between 22 April 2016 and 21 April 2017.[54] Perhaps to underscore their sense of urgency, an unprecedented 175 parties signed the Paris Agreement on the first possible day.[55] Signature does not bind a state to the treaty,[56] but it usually is a preliminary step toward formal consent. It serves a number of important functions in the treaty-making process, especially in the context of multilateral treaties. First, the signature stage gives states an opportunity to indicate their support for the treaty while taking time to prepare for formal consent, which, in many constitutional systems, requires legislative approval, and may also require adoption of regulatory and policy measures to enable compliance. Second, although signature does not make the terms of the treaty binding on a state, it does entail an obligation to refrain from acts that would 'defeat the object and purpose of the treaty'.[57] In other words, signature is not an empty gesture; it expresses a state's intention, in the normal course of events, to become a treaty party. That states take the signature step seriously was illustrated, for example, by the US decision to go back on its initial signature of the Kyoto Protocol and express the intention *not* to become a party.[58] Therefore, third, signatures send important signals to other states regarding the degree of support for the treaty and its chances

---

[52] See FCCC, Arts 15 and 16.

[53] For example, the FCCC was opened for signature at the Rio Summit in June 1992, a month after it was adopted, and remained open for a year, through 19 June 1993 (FCCC, Art 20.1). Similarly, the Kyoto Protocol was opened for signature on 16 March 1998, three months after its adoption, and remained open through 15 March 1999 (Kyoto Protocol, Art 24.1).

[54] Paris Agreement, Art 20.1.

[55] For the current list of signatories, see FCCC, 'Status of Ratification—Paris Agreement' <http://unfccc.int/paris_agreement/items/9444.php> accessed 20 January 2017.

[56] Unless otherwise provided—see VCLT (n 2) Art 12. Note that bilateral treaties sometimes stipulate that signature signifies consent.

[57] See ibid, Art 18.

[58] See ibid, Art 18 (a). See also 'Text of a Letter from the President to Senators Hagel, Helms, Craig, and Roberts' (13 March 2001) <http://georgewbush-whitehouse.archives.gov/news/releases/2001/03/20010314.html> accessed 20 January 2017.

of eventual entry into force. In turn, fixed periods during which a treaty is open for signature (usually, a year) help accelerate and compress this signaling process.

The fact that a treaty is open for signature for only a limited period of time does not mean that non-signatory states cannot become parties to it. It means only that such states must move directly to what would normally be the second step in the process: formal consent to be bound. Hence, the FCCC has 197 parties, but only 165 signatories,[59] and the Kyoto Protocol has 192 parties, but only eighty-three signatories.[60] Conversely, although signature generally signals a state's intention to join a treaty, it does not entail any obligation to do so. Formal consent by signatories is generally termed 'ratification',[61] but is sometimes also referred to as 'acceptance' or 'approval'—terms that recognize the diversity of domestic practices. The consent of a non-signatory state is generally referred to as 'accession'.[62]

Consent to a treaty is a necessary condition for a state to be bound, but it is not a sufficient condition. A treaty becomes binding on consenting states only once it enters into force.[63] As result, if a state ratifies a treaty that is already in force, it becomes legally bound, usually with a short delay stipulated in the treaty.[64] But if a state submits its ratification before the treaty enters into force, it will not be bound by its terms until the treaty takes effect. Since treaties often take a considerable time to enter into force, there can be a significant lag period between a state's consent and its becoming legally bound. For example, while the FCCC entered into force less than two years after its adoption, the Kyoto Protocol took more than eight years to do so.[65]

One of the reasons the Kyoto Protocol took so long to enter into force was that many of its provisions required fleshing out. While states agreed in the Kyoto Protocol to reporting and review requirements, emissions trading mechanisms, and procedures and mechanisms for compliance assessment, they left the development of detailed rules and guidelines on each of these subjects to a later stage. However, without knowing the conditions under which emissions allowances or credits could be traded, the costs of compliance, and the consequences of non-compliance, few states were willing to ratify the Kyoto Protocol. Hence, negotiation of these and other details resumed almost immediately upon adoption of the protocol. Only after the necessary package of decisions had been adopted, in the Marrakesh Accords of 2001,[66] did a sufficient number of states ratify the Kyoto Protocol to bring it into force in 2005. This further delay was due in part to the decision of the

---

[59] See FCCC, Status of Ratification—Convention (n 18).
[60] See FCCC, 'Status of Ratification of the Kyoto Protocol' <http://unfccc.int/kyoto_protocol/status_of_ratification/items/2613.php> accessed 20 January 2017.
[61] VCLT (n 2) Art 14.
[62] Ibid, Art 15; see also FCCC, Art 22.1; Kyoto Protocol, Art 24.1; Paris Agreement, Art 21.1.
[63] VCLT, Art 26.   [64] See eg, FCCC, Art 23.2 (stipulating 90 days).
[65] See FCCC, Status of Ratification—Convention (n 18); FCCC, Status of Ratification—Kyoto Protocol (n 60).
[66] The legal status of the Marrakesh Accords and other COP decisions is considered further in Section II.D 3 below.

US not to ratify the protocol, which made it harder to meet the entry-into-force threshold discussed below.

The speed of a treaty's entry into force also depends on the treaty's requirements in this respect. Indeed, a treaty's entry-into-force formula is of great political and practical importance. It must strike a balance between the desire to bring the treaty into effect as soon as possible, and the need to ensure that the treaty has a sufficient number of parties to be credible. Moreover, if an agreement requires states to take on demanding and costly emission reduction commitments, few states will be inclined to join unless they are assured that a sufficient number of other major emitters are similarly committed to yield net benefits. The climate regime illustrates these considerations. The FCCC did not include legally binding emission targets, so its entry-into-force provision simply required that fifty states join,[67] a number that ensures broad participation but still allows treaties to enter into force relatively quickly, and that is commonly used in global treaties. In contrast, both the Kyoto Protocol and the Paris Agreement provide for specified emission reductions by parties, so they included 'double trigger' requirements, which made entry into force contingent not simply on ratification by a particular number of states, but also by states whose emissions represent a significant proportion of the problem—55% of Annex I emissions in the case of the Kyoto Protocol,[68] and 55% of global emissions in the case of the Paris Agreement.[69]

D. Treaty development

A central feature of MEAs is that they are designed to operate as long-term regimes, allowing for treaty development through repeated cycles of interlocking expert, diplomatic and standard-setting processes. The main legal tools for treaty development are new treaties adopted under the umbrella of the framework convention (usually, but not necessarily, called 'protocols'), amendments to an existing treaty (the framework treaty or a protocol), or decisions of the relevant treaty bodies.[70] On occasion, political agreements can also serve as stepping stones toward subsequent legal agreements. Finally, treaty development can be effected by interpretative processes

---

[67] FCCC, Art 23.1.   [68] Kyoto Protocol, Art 25.1.

[69] Paris Agreement, Art 21.1. The Paris Agreement crossed its entry into force threshold on 5 October 2016, triggering its entry into force on 4 November 2016. See FCCC, Status of Ratification—Paris Agreement (n 55). For the relevant emission shares, see Report of the Conference of the Parties on its twenty-first session, held in Paris from 30 November to 13 December 2015 (29 January 2016) FCCC/CP/2015/10, Annex I. See also FCCC Legal Affairs Programme, 'Entry into force of the Paris Agreement: legal requirements and implications' (7 April 2016) <http://unfccc.int/files/paris_agreement/application/pdf/entry_into_force_of_pa.pdf> accessed 20 January 2017 (providing a detailed discussion of the Paris Agreement's entry into force requirements and the legal and procedural issues that arise given the agreement enters into force before 2020, when it was meant to take effect). On the entry into force of the Paris Agreement, see also Chapter 7, Section XII.

[70] For an overview, see Jutta Brunnée, 'Environment, Multilateral Agreements', in Rüdiger Wolfrum (ed), *Max Planck Encyclopedia of Public International Law* (Oxford University Press, 2011). See also Jutta Brunnée, 'COPing with Consent: Lawmaking under Multilateral Environmental Agreements', *Leiden Journal of International Law*, 15/1 (2002): 1, 15–31.

and subsequent practice under the treaty, often enabled by deliberate vagueness or ambiguity in the treaty text. In this section, each of these devices is explored in turn.

1. New treaties to supplement the framework

As noted at the beginning of this chapter, modern MEAs tend to be anchored by a framework treaty. The purpose of the framework treaty is to enshrine the treaty objective, basic principles to guide action under the treaty, and general obligations to work toward the treaty objective. Framework treaties also often provide for scientific and technical exchange and establish treaty bodies and decision-making procedures, including the procedures for treaty development.[71] But they postpone difficult issues, such as the negotiation of specific, potentially costly, commitments, for which the time may not yet be ripe, due to divergent views or lack of scientific or technical knowledge or consensus. Parties can then focus the negotiations of supplemental treaties, usually referred to as 'protocols', on these difficult substantive issues, having already settled many basic questions concerning treaty objectives, institutions, and procedures. Furthermore, they can take advantage of the 'related but separate' legal nature of supplemental treaties to tailor certain aspects of the new treaty to the specificities of the issues at hand.

The FCCC was designed along these lines and envisaged that parties might adopt one or more protocols.[72] In the context of MEAs, 'protocol' is the most commonly used term for supplemental treaties, but a 'related but separate' treaty need not be called a 'protocol'. The 2015 Paris Agreement is a case in point. For political reasons, explored in Chapter 7, it was styled an 'agreement' rather than a 'protocol'. But, its title notwithstanding, it was adopted under and supplements the FCCC, like the Kyoto Protocol.

The 'related but separate' character of protocols and other supplemental agreements has several dimensions. First, in many environmental treaty regimes, including the climate regime, only states that are parties to the framework treaty can become parties to the supplemental treaty,[73] in part because the purpose of the latter is to further the objective of the umbrella treaty.[74] But since the supplement is nonetheless a separate treaty, each framework treaty party can decide whether and when to join the supplemental treaty.[75] Second, supplemental treaties typically draw on the framework treaty for basic institutional and procedural arrangements, which is another reason why parties to the former must also be parties to the latter.

On the institutional front, the bodies serving the FCCC, such as its secretariat and the subsidiary bodies for scientific and technological advice and for implementation, serve the Kyoto Protocol and Paris Agreement as well.[76] Indeed, the FCCC

---

[71] Brunnée, ibid, para 32.   [72] FCCC, Art 17.

[73] Ibid, Art 17.4; Kyoto Protocol, preamble and Art 24; Paris Agreement, Art 20.1.

[74] Kyoto Protocol, preamble; Paris Agreement, preamble and Art 2.1.

[75] The list of ratifications of the Kyoto Protocol provides a good illustration. See FCCC, Status of Ratification—Kyoto Protocol (n 60).

[76] Kyoto Protocol, Arts 14 and 15; Paris Agreement, Arts 17 and 18.

COP functions as the CMP for the Kyoto Protocol as well as the Conference of the Parties serving as the Meeting of the Parties to the Paris Agreement (CMA). Hence, the 2016 Marrakesh conference constituted the twenty-second conference of the parties to the FCCC, the twelfth meeting of the parties to the Kyoto Protocol, and the first meeting of the parties to the Paris Agreement.[77] However, when the COP meets as the CMP or the CMA, it includes only those FCCC parties that are also parties to the Kyoto Protocol or Paris Agreement, respectively.[78] This difference reflects the fact that the FCCC, Kyoto Protocol, and Paris Agreement, although closely related, are separate treaties, with overlapping but distinct memberships. Therefore, when it comes to decisions under the Kyoto Protocol or Paris Agreement, only parties to the relevant treaty can vote.[79] The same applies to all treaty bodies that are composed of party representatives.[80] Still, in view of the close connections between the treaties, the practice in the climate regime has been inclusive. For example, FCCC parties that are not parties to the Kyoto Protocol have been permitted to make interventions and submit textual proposals in the deliberations under the auspices of the protocol.[81]

On the procedural front, supplemental treaties typically draw upon the framework treaty in several key respects. For example, the Paris Agreement declares the FCCC's amendment rules to be applicable *mutatis mutandis*.[82] Both the Kyoto Protocol and the Paris Agreement emulate the FCCC's dispute settlement, voting, signature, ratification, reservations, and withdrawal provisions, and its rules regarding 'regional economic integration organizations' (ie the EU).[83] At the same time, since they are separate treaties, supplemental agreements can also make different arrangements when warranted. The different entry-into-force formulas of the FCCC, Kyoto Protocol, and Paris Agreement, respectively, provide a good illustration.[84] Another example is the Kyoto Protocol's amendment process, which is considered in more detail in the next section. For present purposes, suffice it to say that the Kyoto Protocol follows the FCCC approach for amendments to the protocol itself, but deviates from it for the amendment of Annexes A and B.[85] Generally speaking, annexes to MEAs contain material that is 'of a scientific, technical, procedural or administrative character',[86] and employ a simplified amendment procedure, whereby annexes or amendments to annexes enter into force for

---

[77] FCCC, 'Marrakech Climate Change Conference—November 2016' <http://unfccc.int/meetings/marrakech_nov_2016/meeting/9567.php> accessed 20 January 2017.
[78] Kyoto Protocol, Art 13; Paris Agreement, Art 16.
[79] Kyoto Protocol, Art 13.2; Paris Agreement, Art 16.2.   [80] Kyoto Protocol, Art 15.2.
[81] FCCC Legal Affairs Programme, Entry into force of the Paris Agreement (n 69) para 19. Note that, in an effort to create a 'bridge' that would help parties meet across the Kyoto and FCCC tracks, the Cancun Agreements placed mitigation proposals from all developed countries in an information document that was deliberately ambiguous as to whether it related to the FCCC or to the Kyoto Protocol.
[82] Paris Agreement, Arts 22 and 23; FCCC, Arts 15 and 16.
[83] FCCC, Arts 14, 18, 20, 22, 23.2, 23.3, 24, and 25; Kyoto Protocol, Arts 19, 22, 24, 25.3, 25.4, 26, and 27; Paris Agreement, Arts 20, 21.3, 21.4, 24, 25, 27, and 28.
[84] See nn 67–69 above and accompanying text.
[85] FCCC, Arts 15–16; Kyoto Protocol, Arts 20 and 21.   [86] FCCC, Art 16.1.

all parties within six months, except for those parties that explicitly notify their non-acceptance prior to expiry of that period.[87] However, because Annexes A and B to the Kyoto Protocol specify important aspects of parties' emission reduction commitments, the protocol excludes them from this 'opt out' process, and subjects them instead to the standard 'opt in' amendment process, requiring written consent in the case of Annex B.[88]

2. Amendments

Whereas a protocol or other supplemental agreement constitutes a separate treaty and leaves the original treaty untouched, amendments effect changes to the underlying treaty itself, be it the framework treaty or a supplemental agreement. For example, the 2012 Doha Amendment to the Kyoto Protocol is intended to establish a second commitment period, running from 2013 to 2020.[89] To that end, it provides for additions to the text of the protocol, and changes to its abovementioned two annexes. The changes to Annex A add one gas to the list of greenhouse gases covered by the protocol.[90] The changes to Annex B specify new emission reduction commitments by those protocol parties that indicated willingness to participate in a second commitment period.[91]

As indicated in the previous section, amendments to the Kyoto Protocol as well as to its Annexes A and B require parties to join the amendment through formal acceptance.[92] This approach has two important implications. First, only protocol parties that do join the Doha Amendment in this way will be subject to new, binding emission reduction requirements in the protocol's second commitment period. In this respect an amendment resembles a protocol or other treaty—it binds only those states that formally consent. The second key feature of the standard amendment process is that the amendment, and with it the new commitments that it would entail, enter into force only when a specified number of acceptances has been reached. In the case of the Kyoto Protocol, the relevant threshold is high, requiring acceptance of the Doha Amendment by three-fourths of the parties to the protocol.[93] Given this extremely high threshold, it is uncertain whether the Doha Amendment will ever garner the 144 acceptances that would be required for its entry into force.[94]

As the example of the Doha Amendment serves to illustrate, the standard amendment process entails that a treaty may evolve at 'different speeds'—some

---

[87] FCCC, Art 16.3; Kyoto Protocol, Art 16.5; Paris Agreement, Art 23.

[88] Kyoto Protocol, Art 21.7, Annexes A and B. See also section II.D.2.

[89] Decision 1/CMP.8, 'Amendment to the Kyoto Protocol pursuant to its Article 3, para 9 (the Doha Amendment)' (28 February 2013) FCCC/KP/CMP/2012/13/Add.1, 2, Annex I: Doha Amendment to the Kyoto Protocol (Doha Amendment), Art 1, Section F.

[90] Ibid, Art 1, Section B.   [91] Ibid, Art 1, Section A.

[92] Kyoto Protocol, Arts 20.4 and 21.7.   [93] Ibid. See also Doha Amendment, Art 2.

[94] As on 29 December 2016, only seventy-five parties had ratified the Doha Amendment. See FCCC, 'Status of the Doha Amendment' <http://unfccc.int/kyoto_protocol/doha_amendment/items/7362.php> accessed 20 January 2017.

treaty parties may have new and more ambitious commitments while others do not.[95] What is more, due to the high entry-into-force threshold stipulated by the FCCC and the Kyoto Protocol, this formal process can slow or even stall treaty development. In most MEAs, therefore, it is generally reserved for changes to an agreement's core obligations, or its procedural or institutional structure, which do not require frequent changes.[96]

In contrast, the more technical regulatory details of MEAs, such as lists of regulated substances, which are expected to require more frequent updating in light of new information or changing circumstances, are usually amendable through the simplified opt-out process referred to in the previous section.[97] This simplified process removes the need for formal acceptance of an amendment by individual parties and dispenses with the time-consuming requirement of meeting an entry-into-force threshold. Instead, the relevant amendment enters into force for all parties except those that opt out within a specified period of time. However, although the FCCC, Kyoto Protocol, and Paris Agreement each provide for an opt-out process for annex amendments,[98] to date these simplified amendment procedures have either been inapplicable, as has been the case with the Kyoto Protocol's Annexes A and B,[99] or have faltered because parties had trouble agreeing on the relevant amendment. The latter difficulties can arise because, before the opt-out process comes into play, the text of the amendment must first be adopted by decision of the parties. Although such a decision could be taken, as a last resort, by a three-fourths majority,[100] the practice of the climate regime has been to seek consensus.[101] A notorious example of the resulting challenges relates to the difficulties in adding or removing parties, even at their request, from the lists of parties in Annexes I and II to the FCCC.[102]

The climate regime's most flexible treaty development process is set out in the Doha Amendment to the Kyoto Protocol, which allows parties listed in Annex B to tighten their own commitments by proposing an 'adjustment' to the emissions reduction specified for them in the annex.[103] The adjustment is then 'considered adopted' by the CMP 'unless more than three-fourths of the Parties present and voting object' and becomes 'binding upon Parties' on 1 January of the following

---

[95] Jutta Brunnée, Environment, Multilateral Agreements (n 70) para 33. See also Peter Sand, 'Lessons Learned in Global Environmental Governance', *Boston College Environmental Affairs Law Review*, 18/2 (1991): 213, 236–48.

[96] See Jutta Brunnée, 'Treaty Amendments', in Hollis (ed), *Oxford Guide* (n 3) 347, 351–2.

[97] See generally Brunnée, Environment, Multilateral Agreements (n 70) para 34.

[98] See n 87 above and accompanying text.   [99] See n 88 above and accompanying text.

[100] FCCC, Arts 15.3 and 16.2.

[101] See nn 21–32 above and accompanying text (on the challenges of the consensus process). See also Farhana Yamin and Joanna Depledge, *The International Climate Change Regime: A Guide to Rules, Institutions and Procedures* (Cambridge University Press, 2004) 437, 442–5.

[102] See Yamin, ibid 105–6. See also FCCC, 'Proposals to Amend the Lists in Annexes I and II of the Convention' <http://unfccc.int/cop7/issues/propamlist.html> accessed 20 January 2017 (reporting on the efforts of Turkey to be removed from Annex II and Kazakhstan to become an Annex I party). See also Chapter 5, Section II.D.

[103] Doha Amendment, Art 1, Section D. On the use of adjustments in MEAs more generally, see Jutta Brunnée, 'International Legislation', in Rüdiger Wolfrum, *Max Planck Encyclopedia of Public International Law* (Oxford University Press, 2010) paras 31–3.

year.[104] This approach effectively reverses the normal process, whereby an amendment requires *acceptance* by three-fourths of the parties to enter into force. The purpose of the *objection* requirement is to remove the barriers to stronger emissions reduction commitments that are inherent not only in the standard amendment process but, potentially, also in the simplified amendment process, as the example of amendments to FCCC Annexes I and II illustrates. However, given that the fate of the Doha Amendment is uncertain and that, even if it were to enter into force, its commitment period extends only to 2020,[105] it is unlikely that this adjustment process will ever come into play.

3. Decisions of the parties

Supplemental treaties and amendments are adopted under the auspices of a regime's plenary body, which plays the principal role in treaty development. Yet, with respect to these law-making devices, each treaty party remains sovereign to decide through a subsequent step, be it explicit consent (protocol and standard amendment) or refraining from opting-out (simplified amendment), whether or not to be bound by a new instrument. Moreover, the instrument does not enter into force until its entry-into-force requirements are satisfied. The plenary body thus does not directly establish standards; its adoption of a supplemental agreement or amendment is merely an intermediate stage in the standard-setting process.[106]

Plenary bodies exercise more direct standard-setting authority when they adopt decisions pursuant to their general decision-making authority,[107] or pursuant to more specific authorities provided by their governing treaty. In the UN climate regime, the COP and CMP have adopted decisions containing a vast array of regulatory detail, which flesh out the FCCC and Kyoto Protocol, respectively, and make them operational. Through this decision-making practice, the climate regime's plenary bodies have come closer to exercising something akin to a 'legislative' function. Typically adopted by consensus, decisions take immediate effect for all parties precisely because, unlike new treaties or amendments, they do not require subsequent ratification or approval by parties. In principle, therefore, they enable speedier, more responsive standard-setting, and avoid the differentiation of treaty commitments among parties that can result from supplemental agreements. Ordinarily, plenary body decisions are not legally binding, unless the governing treaty gives the plenary body authority to adopt a binding decision on a particular subject. Nevertheless, even non-binding decisions are sometimes phrased in

---

[104] Doha Amendment, Art 1, Section E.

[105] See nn 89–94 above and accompanying text, and Chapter 6, Section X.

[106] See Brunnée, COPing with Consent (n 70) 16; Alan E. Boyle, 'Saving the World? Implementation and Enforcement of International Environmental Law through International Institutions', *Journal of Environmental Law*, 3/2 (1991): 235. See also International Law Commission, *Report of the International Law Commission on the Work of Its Sixty-sixth Session* (5 May–6 June and 7 July–8 August 2014) UN Doc A/69/10, 205–17 (offering a recent assessment of state practice and scholarship).

[107] FCCC, Art 7.2; Kyoto Protocol, Art 13.4. See also Paris Agreement, Art 16.4.

mandatory terms, using language normally reserved for binding law ('shall').[108] In many respects, these treaty-based standards resemble regulations or guidelines adopted pursuant to national legislation. And, indeed, they are often treated by states in ways not dissimilar to binding international law—they are negotiated with considerable care and tend to be implemented domestically as carefully as binding international law.[109]

The Marrakesh Accords, mentioned above,[110] are a good example. They consist of a set of CMP decisions establishing rules on crucial matters ranging from inventory and reporting requirements (pursuant to Articles 5 and 7 of the Kyoto Protocol), to the mechanisms for trading of emission units or reduction credits (pursuant to Articles 6, 12, and 17 of the Kyoto Protocol), to the protocol's non-compliance procedure (pursuant to Article 18 of the Kyoto Protocol). The decisions impose extensive requirements on parties to the Kyoto Protocol. Indeed, non-compliance with some of these decisions, such as inventory and reporting requirements, have specific consequences for states, notably the loss of eligibility to participate in the market mechanisms.[111] What is more, protocol parties accept both the need to comply with these requirements and the authority of the non-compliance regime, notwithstanding their ostensibly non-binding nature.[112]

The outcome of the 2015 Paris conference represents a continuation of the varied standard-setting practice under the FCCC. The Paris Agreement was accompanied by a COP decision that adopted the treaty text and supplemented it in many key respects.[113] Furthermore, the Paris Agreement itself envisages extensive recourse to CMA decisions, for example to specify the content of and manner in which parties are to communicate their nationally determined contributions (NDCs), to provide guidance on the accounting of NDCs, and to adopt the 'modalities and procedures' for the agreement's implementation and compliance mechanism.[114] Indeed, by providing that parties 'shall' communicate their NDCs in accordance with the relevant CMA decisions, the Paris Agreement requires parties to comply with these decisions, effectively rendering them legally binding.[115]

4. Political agreements

The evolution of the climate regime demonstrates that even formally non-binding instruments are subject to difficult negotiations, with agreement by no means guaranteed. The fate of the Copenhagen Accord, which could not be adopted as a COP decision, is a case in point.[116] It also illustrates the fact that, sometimes, a political rather

---

[108] See Brunnée, COPing with Consent (n 70) 26.   [109] See ibid, 23–31.

[110] See n 66 above and accompanying text.

[111] Decision 27/CMP.1, 'Procedures and mechanisms relating to compliance under the Kyoto Protocol' (30 March 2006) FCCC/KP/CMP/2005/8/Add.3, Annex, Section XV, para 4.

[112] See Jutta Brunnée and Stephen J. Toope, *Legitimacy and Legality in International Law: An Interactional Account* (Cambridge University Press, 2010) 201–4.

[113] See Decision 1/CP.21 (n 49).   [114] Paris Agreement, Arts 3, 4.8, 4.9, and 15.3.

[115] Ibid, Art 4.8. For a more detailed discussion, see Chapter 7, Section V.A.

[116] See nn 24–26 above and accompanying text.

than legal agreement can serve a crucial track-setting function and facilitate subsequent regime development. The Copenhagen Accord, after all, sketched out the shift from the Kyoto Protocol's ('top down') reliance on internationally-negotiated emissions reduction commitments to the Paris Agreement's ('bottom-up') NDC approach, and helped advance the erosion of the sharp, Kyoto-style, differentiation between developed and developing country parties.[117] The accord was unusual in that it was negotiated by the heads of state of twenty-eight key parties to the FCCC, on the margins of the official meetings but outside of the COP process.[118] Due to the high-level genesis of the political compromises that it embodied, the Copenhagen Accord was a turning point for the climate regime, notwithstanding the fact that its provisions 'do not have any legal standing' in the FCCC process.[119] The Copenhagen Accord was not the first time states resorted to a political agreement to advance climate negotiations. An earlier, not quite as dramatic but nonetheless highly significant, example was the 1996 Geneva Ministerial Declaration,[120] in which ministers and other heads of delegation 'recognized and endorsed' the second assessment report of the Intergovernmental Panel of Climate Change as a scientific basis for accelerating the negotiations on what became the Kyoto Protocol, and clarified that the emission targets being developed in the Kyoto Protocol negotiations would be legally binding.[121]

5. Ambiguity, interpretation, and subsequent practice

The discussion so far has shown that parties can develop a treaty regime through a variety of instruments, ranging from formal amendments to plenary body decisions to political agreements. Before concluding the chapter, it is worth highlighting briefly that there exist a range of drafting techniques and interpretative and practice-based devices that parties can use to deal with lack of agreement or to accommodate the evolution of understandings on specific issues.

Carefully crafted ambiguity, such that a given passage is capable of more than one interpretation, is a frequently used device in the treaty negotiators' toolkit, across many areas of international law.[122] The history of the climate regime is replete with

---

[117] See Daniel Bodansky, 'The Paris Climate Change Agreement: A New Hope?', *American Journal of International Law*, 110/2 (2016): 292. See also Jutta Brunnée and Charlotte Streck, 'The UNFCCC as a negotiation forum: towards common but more differentiated responsibilities', *Climate Policy*, 13/5 (2013): 589 (tracing the differentiation principle's evolution).

[118] See French and Rajamani, Climate Change and International Environmental Law (n 23) 446–8.

[119] See FCCC, 'Notification to Parties, Clarification relating to the Notification of 18 January 2010' (25 January 2010), <https://unfccc.int/files/parties_and_observers/notifications/application/pdf/100125_noti_clarification.pdf> accessed 20 January 2017.

[120] Geneva Ministerial Declaration (n 11).

[121] See Sebastian Oberthür and Hermann Ott, *The Kyoto Protocol: International Climate Policy for the 21st Century* (Berlin-Heidelberg: Springer Verlag, 1999) 52–4.

[122] See eg, 'The Ambiguity of GATT Article XXI: Subtle Success or Rampant Failure?', *Duke Law Journal* 52/6 (2003): 1277; Itay Fishhendler, 'Ambiguity in Transboundary Environmental Dispute Resolution: The Israeli - Jordanian Water Agreement', *Journal of Peace Research*, 45/1 (2008): 91; John Tobin, 'Seeking to Persuade: A Constructive Approach to Human Rights Treaty Interpretation', *Harvard Human Rights Journal*, 23 (2010):1, Maya Jegen and Frédéric Mérand, 'Constructive Ambiguity: Comparing the EU's Energy and Defence Policies', *Western European Politics*, 37 (2014):182.

examples of such 'constructive' ambiguity,[123] many of which are discussed in other parts of the book. Suffice it for present purposes to provide a flavor of how ambiguity can be deployed.

First, it can help parties to agree on an instrument notwithstanding lingering differences on a particular issue. For example, the idea of a legal 'right to development', strongly advocated by many developing countries, and its relationship to the notion of sustainable development, a concept generally preferred by the US and other developed countries, have been the subject of long-standing disagreements, including in the climate negotiations.[124] The FCCC negotiators ended up finding a compromise formulation that drew together references to the notion of a 'right' and to the notion of 'sustainable development' in such a way as to leave the implications of each ambiguous. An initial proposal for inclusion in the convention's Article 3 on 'principles' was to stipulate that parties 'have a right to, and should promote, sustainable development'.[125] However, this formulation could have been read as implying acceptance of a 'right to sustainable development', which some parties did not support. The negotiators solved the problem by moving the second comma in the passage above. The ultimately agreed wording of what became FCCC Article 3.4 provides that the parties 'have a right to, and should, promote sustainable development', enabling parties so inclined to maintain that the right, and duty, in question pertain to the promotion of sustainable development, not sustainable development as such.[126]

A second important function of intentional ambiguity is inherent in the first one: to the extent that recourse to ambiguity enables parties to adopt an instrument notwithstanding remaining disagreements, it also allows them to postpone politically sensitive or otherwise difficult issues to a later stage. This latter dimension of ambiguity can be extremely important to individual parties as they work to balance international pressures to reach agreement with strong domestic or regional views on particular questions. In complex, multi-issue negotiations such as those on climate change, this function of ambiguity assumes particular importance, although it does not, of course, guarantee a successful outcome in the long run. Nonetheless, the climate regime does provide many examples of recourse to ambiguity that enabled parties to maintain their preferred positions and leave the issue to be resolved at a later stage. A good illustration is provided by the Durban Platform's language on the legal form of what would become the Paris Agreement.[127] Another illustration

---

[123] For a wide range of examples of ambiguity and other drafting techniques see Susan Biniaz, 'Comma But Differentiated Responsibilities: Punctuation and 30 Other Ways Negotiators Have Resolved Issues in the International Climate Change Regime' (Columbia Law School – Sabin Center for Climate Change Law Working Paper, June 2016) <https://web.law.columbia.edu/sites/default/files/microsites/climate-change/files/Publications/biniaz_2016_june_comma_diff_responsibilities.pdf> accessed 20 January 2017.

[124] See Chapter 2, Section III.E and, especially, Chapter 5, Section III.C.4.

[125] See Biniaz, Comma But Differentiated (n 123) 9. For more on Article 3, see Chapter 5, Section III.C.

[126] See Biniaz, ibid.

[127] See n 12 above and accompanying text. See also detailed discussion in Chapter 7, Section I.A.1.

is found in the many efforts to build textual bridges across the deep disagreements about the role and meaning of the common but differentiated responsibilities and respective capabilities principle in the climate regime.[128] In both cases, ambiguity in the earlier text helped keep parties at the negotiating table and engaged in the subsequent development of the regime. The Paris Agreement speaks to the potential value of this approach, illustrating the evolution of parties' original positions on both issues—through its hybrid legal form in the first case and through its nuanced, issue-specific approach to differentiation in the second.[129]

Textual ambiguity in a legal instrument, of course, is closely connected to the subsequent processes of interpretation and application of the instrument. Pursuant to the VCLT, treaties are to be interpreted 'in good faith in accordance with the ordinary meaning to be given to the terms of the treaty in their context and in the light of its object and purpose'.[130] In some areas of international law, courts and tribunals have stepped into the interpretative role.[131] In the climate regime, judicial interpretation has not played a significant role, if any.[132] Nonetheless, interpretative processes are inherent in the practice of any treaty regime. According to the VCLT, subsequent agreements between the parties concerning the interpretation of a treaty, and subsequent practice in the application of the treaty, are to be taken into account in illuminating its meaning.[133] In this way, protocols or COP decisions adopted under a framework treaty can serve to maintain or reduce ambiguities in earlier instruments, or shift the meaning of certain terms.[134] At the same time, unless there is evidence to the contrary, the provisions and understandings of the framework treaty remain relevant in the interpretation and application of subsequent instruments adopted in the regime. That is why in the climate regime, in the negotiation of the Paris Agreement, some believed that the question of its relationship to the FCCC was of considerable consequence.[135]

III. CONCLUSION

The preceding overview of treaty law and treaty-based law-making is intended to give readers a sense of the reservoir of rules that guide parties in their efforts to

---

[128] For detailed treatments of the evolution of these debates, along with the recourse to drafting solutions, see Chapters 1 and Chapters 4–7.

[129] See detailed discussion in Chapters 4 and 7.   [130] VCLT (n 2) Art 31.1.

[131] See eg Joost Pauwelyn and Manfred Elsig, 'The Politics of Treaty Interpretation', in Jeffrey L. Dunoff and Mark A. Pollack (eds), *Interdisciplinary Perspectives on International Law and International Relations: The State of the Art* (Cambridge University Press, 2013) 445.

[132] See Chapters 2 and 8.   [133] VCLT (n 2) Art 31.3.

[134] See for example the long-running efforts of some parties in the climate regime to defend particular understandings of the common but differentiated responsibilities and respective capabilities principle articulated in the FCCC, and of other parties to instantiate an alternative understanding. See Chapters 1 and Chapters 4–7.

[135] See Chapters 7, Section I.D.1.See above, Section II.D.1. See also nn 12–15 above on the role of the Durban Platform.

further develop the UN climate regime, and the rich array of legal devices and techniques that they have at their disposal. Chapters 4–7 build on this background, and provide detailed illustrations of how the rules, tools, and techniques of treaty-based law-making have been deployed in the development of the climate regime.

SELECT BIBLIOGRAPHY

Bodansky D., *The Art and Craft of International Environmental Law* (Cambridge, MA: Harvard University Press, 2010).

Brunnée J., 'Environment, Multilateral Agreements', in Wolfrum R. (ed), *Max Planck Encyclopedia of Public International Law* (Oxford University Press, 2011).

Depledge J., *The Organization of Global Negotiations: Constructing the Climate Change Regime* (London: Earthscan, 2015).

French D. and Rajamani L., 'Climate Change and International Environmental Law: Musings on a Journey to Somewhere', *Journal of Environmental Law*, 25/3 (2013): 437.

Gupta J., '*On Behalf of my Delegation ...*' – *A Survival Guide for Developing Country Climate Negotiators* (Washington, D.C., Center for Sustainable Development in the Americas, 2000).

Hollis D.B. (ed), *The Oxford Guide to Treaties* (Oxford University Press, 2012).

Vihma A., 'Climate of Consensus: Managing Decision Making in the UN Climate Change Negotiations', *Review of European, Comparative and International Environmental Law*, 24/1 (2015): 58.

4

Evolution of the United Nations Climate Regime

I. INTRODUCTION

The development of the UN climate regime can be broken into four phases.[1] The first was an agenda-setting phase, extending through 1990. The second was a constitutional phase, when the basic framework of the UN climate regime was put in place, beginning in 1991, when the UN General Assembly initiated negotiation of a framework convention on climate change, and continuing through 1994, when the FCCC entered into force. The third phase was regulatory, focusing on the negotiation, elaboration, and operationalization of the Kyoto Protocol, which required industrialized countries to reduce their emissions of carbon dioxide (CO_2) and five other gases that contribute to the greenhouse effect. It extended from 1995, when the Berlin Mandate launched the negotiations, through the Kyoto Protocol's entry into force in 2004, and included the adoption of the 2001 Marrakesh Accords, which set forth detailed rules regarding how the Kyoto Protocol would work. Finally, the period since 2005 has focused on what to do after 2012, when the Kyoto Protocol's first commitment period ended. Milestones of this phase include the 2007 Bali Action Plan; the 2009 Copenhagen Accord; the 2011 Durban Platform, which initiated a new round of negotiations to address the period from 2020; the 2012 Doha Amendment, which extended the Kyoto Protocol through 2020; and the 2015 Paris Agreement, which addresses the period from 2020 onward.

---

[1] This chapter draws on materials from Daniel Bodansky, 'The United Nations Framework Convention on Climate Change: A Commentary', *Yale Journal of International Law*, 18/2 (1993): 451; Daniel Bodansky, 'Prologue to the Climate Change Convention', in Irving Mintzer and J.A. Leonard (eds), *Negotiating Climate Change: The Inside Story of the Rio Convention* (Cambridge University Press, 1994) 45; Daniel Bodansky, 'The Copenhagen Climate Change Conference: A Postmortem', *American Journal of International Law*, 104/2 (2010): 230; Daniel Bodansky, 'A Tale of Two Architectures: The Once and Future UN Climate Change Regime', *Arizona State Law Journal*, 43/1 (2011): 697; Daniel Bodansky, 'The Durban Platform Negotiations: Goals and Options' (Harvard Project on Climate Agreements, July 2012) <http://belfercenter.ksg.harvard.edu/files/bodansky_durban2_vp.pdf> accessed 20 January 2017; Daniel Bodansky and Lavanya Rajamani, 'The Evolution and Governance Architecture of the Climate Change Regime', in Urs Luterbacher and Detlef Sprinz (eds), *Global Climate Change in an International Context* (Cambridge, MA: MIT Press, 2017 forthcoming).

II. AGENDA-SETTING (1985–1990)

Although the general theory of greenhouse warming has been understood by scientists since the end of the nineteenth century, an international regime to address the problem of climate change began to develop only in the 1980s.[2] As late as 1979, efforts by the organizers of the First World Climate Conference to attract participation by policymakers proved unsuccessful, and even in 1985, when a major workshop on climate change was held in Villach, Austria, the United States (US) government officials who participated did so without specific instructions. By the late 1980s, in contrast, the US Congress was holding frequent hearings on global warming; the issue was raised and discussed in the UN General Assembly; and international meetings such as the 1988 Toronto Conference, the 1989 Hague and Noordwijk Conferences, and the 1990 Second World Climate Conference (SWCC) attracted numerous ministers and even some heads of state.

The development of the climate change issue initially took place in the scientific arena, as a result of better understanding of the problem.[3] Through careful measurements at remote observatories such as Mauna Loa, Hawaii, scientists established in the early 1960s that atmospheric concentrations of CO_2 (the primary greenhouse gas (GHG)) were, in fact, increasing. The 'Keeling Curve',[4] which shows this rise, is one of the few undisputed facts in the climate change controversy and led to the initial growth of scientific concern in the late 1960s and early 1970s. During the 1970s and 1980s, improvements in computing power allowed scientists to develop more sophisticated computer models of the atmosphere, which, while still subject to considerable uncertainty, led to increased confidence in global warming predictions. Based on a review of these models, a 1979 report by the US National Academy of Sciences concluded that, if CO_2 in the atmosphere continued to increase, there would be 'no reason to doubt that climate change will result and no reason to believe that these changes will be negligible'.[5] Moreover, in the mid-1980s, scientists recognized that human emissions of other trace gases such as methane and nitrous oxide also contribute to the greenhouse effect, making the problem even more serious than previously believed. Finally, careful reassessments of the historical temperature record in the 1980s indicated that the global average temperature had indeed been increasing since the middle of the twentieth century.

Despite these advances, whether improved scientific knowledge would have been enough to spur political action is doubtful, particularly given scientific uncertainties

---

[2] Bodansky, UNFCCC Commentary, ibid; Rafe Pomerance, 'The Dangers from Climate Warming: A Public Awakening', in Dean E. Abrahamson (ed), *The Challenge of Global Warming* (Washington, D.C.: Island Press, 1989) 259.

[3] On the development of the science of climate change, see generally Spencer R. Weart, *The Discovery of Global Warming* (Cambridge, MA: Harvard University Press, 2008).

[4] Scripps Institution of Oceanography, 'The Keeling Curve' <https://scripps.ucsd.edu/programs/keelingcurve/> accessed 20 January 2017.

[5] National Research Council, *Carbon Dioxide and Climate: A Scientific Assessment* (Washington, D.C.: National Academies Press, 1979) viii.

about climate change, which persist even now. Although the development of scientific knowledge was significant in laying a foundation for the development of public and political interest, three additional factors acted as the direct catalysts for governmental action.

First, a small group of environmentally-oriented developed-country scientists—including Bert Bolin of Sweden, who would later become the first chair of the Intergovernmental Panel on Climate Change (IPCC)—worked to promote the climate change issue on the international agenda. As major figures in the international science establishment, with close ties to the World Meteorological Organization (WMO) and the United Nations Environment Programme (UNEP), these scientists acted as 'knowledge-brokers' and entrepreneurs, helping to translate and publicize the emerging scientific knowledge about the greenhouse effect through workshops and conferences, articles in non-specialist journals, and personal contacts with policymakers. The 1985 and 1987 Villach meetings, the establishment of the Advisory Group on Greenhouse Gases under the joint auspices of WMO and UNEP, the report of the Enquete Commission in Germany,[6] the testimony of climate modelers such as James Hansen of the National Aeronautics and Space Administration (NASA) before US Congressional committees in 1987 and 1988—all of these developments helped to familiarize policymakers with climate change and to convert it from a speculative theory into a real-world possibility.

Second, the development of the climate regime in the late 1980s and early 1990s rode a wave of environmental activity that began in 1987 with the adoption of the Montreal Protocol on Substances that Deplete the Ozone Layer and the publication of the Brundtland Commission report, *Our Common Future*,[7] and crested at the 1992 UN Conference on Environment and Development (UNCED) in Rio de Janeiro. The latter half of the 1980s was a period of increased concern about global environmental issues generally, including depletion of the stratospheric ozone layer, deforestation, loss of biological diversity, pollution of the oceans, and international trade in hazardous wastes. The discovery of the Antarctic 'ozone hole' in 1985, followed by the confirmation that it resulted from emissions of chlorofluorocarbons (CFCs), dramatically demonstrated that human activities can indeed affect the global atmosphere and raised the prominence of atmospheric issues generally. Initially, public concern about global warming rode on the coattails of the ozone issue.

Finally, the North American heatwave and drought of the summer of 1988 gave an enormous popular boost to global warming concerns, particularly in the US and Canada. By the end of 1988, global environmental issues were so prominent that *Time* magazine named endangered Earth 'Newsmaker of the Year'. A conference organized by the Canadian government in June 1988 called for global emissions of CO_2 to be reduced by 20% by the year 2005; the development of a global

---

[6] Enquete Commission of the 11th German Bundestag, *Protecting the Earth's Atmosphere: An International Challenge* (Bonn: Deutscher Bundestag Referat Öffentlichkeitsarbeit, 1989).

[7] World Commission on Environment and Development, *Our Common Future* (Oxford University Press, 1987).

framework convention to protect the atmosphere; and the establishment of a world atmosphere fund financed in part by a tax on fossil fuels.[8]

The year 1988 marked a watershed moment in the emergence of climate change as an intergovernmental issue. During the agenda-setting stage, the distinction between governmental and non-governmental actors had been blurred. The climate change issue was dominated essentially by non-governmental actors—primarily environmentally-oriented scientists. Although some were government employees, their actions did not reflect official national positions. Moreover, the series of quasi-official meetings that they helped organize—which were influential in communicating the scientific consensus about climate change and articulating a set of initial policy responses—were *non*-governmental rather than *inter*-governmental in character.

The period from 1988 to 1990 was transitional: non-governmental actors still had considerable influence, but governments began to play a greater role. The IPCC reflected this ambivalence. Established by WMO and UNEP in 1988 at the instigation of governments, in part as a means of reasserting governmental control over the climate change issue, the IPCC's most influential outputs have been its scientific assessments of global warming—products of the international scientific community more than of governments.

Among the landmarks of the pre-negotiation phase of the climate change issue were:

- The 1988 UN General Assembly resolution on climate change, characterizing the climate as the 'common concern of mankind'.[9]

- The 1989 Hague Summit, attended by seventeen heads of state, which called for the development of a 'new institutional authority' to preserve the earth's atmosphere and combat global warming.[10]

- The 1989 Noordwijk ministerial meeting, the first high-level intergovernmental meeting focusing specifically on the climate change issue.[11]

- The November 1990 SWCC, which in contrast to its forerunner a decade earlier, was a major political event, held at the ministerial level.[12]

By the time the SWCC convened in 1990, the three basic dynamics in the climate change negotiations had already begun to manifest themselves:

- First, a split among developed countries between supporters and opponents of legally binding, quantitative limits on GHG emissions.

[8] Proceedings of the World Conference on the Changing Atmosphere: Implications for Global Security, held in Toronto from 27 to 30 June 1988 (1988) WMO No 710.

[9] UN General Assembly (UNGA) Res 43/53, 'Protection of global climate for present and future generations of mankind' (6 December 1988) UN Doc A/RES/43/53.

[10] Hague Declaration on the Environment (11 March 1989) reprinted in (1989) 28 ILM 1308.

[11] Pier Vellinga, Peter Kendall, and Joyeeta Gupta (eds), *Noordwijk Conference Report* (Netherlands Ministry of Housing, Physical Planning and Environment, 1989).

[12] Jill Jäger and Howard Ferguson (eds), *Climate Change: Science, Impacts and Policy: Proceedings of the Second World Climate Conference* (Cambridge University Press, 1991).

Table 4.1 Milestones in the development of the UN climate regime

1988	UN General Assembly adopts first resolution on climate change, declaring that climate change is of common concern
1990	UN General Assembly establishes the INC, to negotiate a framework convention on climate change containing appropriate commitments
1992	FCCC adopted, opened for signature at UNCED
1994	FCCC enters into force
1995	Berlin Mandate adopted, authorizing the negotiation of a protocol containing quantified emission limitation objectives for developed countries, but excluding any new commitments for developing countries
1997	Kyoto Protocol adopted
2001	Marrakesh Accords adopted, operationalizing the Kyoto Protocol
2004	Kyoto Protocol enters into force
2007	Bali Action Plan adopted, initiating a comprehensive process to address long-term cooperative action on climate change
2009	Heads of state adopt the Copenhagen Accord. But COP fails to agree to a new climate agreement or to adopt the Accord
2011	Durban Platform adopted, launching a new round of negotiations to address the period from 2020
2012	Doha Amendment adopted, extending the Kyoto Protocol through 2020
2013	Warsaw COP decision invites parties to submit INDCs in the context of the 2015 agreement
2014	Lima Call to Climate Action adopted, agreeing on the 'elements of a draft negotiating text' and providing guidance on INDCs
2015	Paris Agreement adopted

Source: Adapted from Daniel Bodansky, *The Art and Craft of International Environmental Law* (Cambridge, MA: Harvard University Press, 2010) 20.

- Second, a split between developed and developing countries over their respective responsibilities for addressing climate change.
- Finally, a split among developing countries between those worried more about climate change and those worried more about economic development.

The split among developed countries was the first dynamic to emerge. Developed countries conducted the bulk of the scientific research on climate change, had the most active environmental constituencies and ministries and, as a result, were the first countries to become seriously concerned about the climate change problem. At the 1989 Noordwijk meeting, the divergence among them became apparent. On the one hand, most European countries supported the approach that had been used to address the acid rain and ozone depletion problems, namely, establishing quantitative limitations on national emission levels of GHGs ('targets and timetables'). On the other hand, the US—supported at Noordwijk by Japan and the Soviet Union—challenged this approach on the grounds that targets and timetables were too rigid, did not take into account differing national circumstances, and would be largely symbolic. Instead, the US argued that emphasis should be placed on further scientific research and on developing national, rather than international, strategies and programs—the position to which the second Bush Administration later reverted more than a decade later.

The SWCC also saw the emergence of a second fault-line in the climate change negotiations: the divide between developed countries and developing countries, which negotiate collectively as the Group of 77 and China (G-77/China, now comprised of 134 countries). Earlier in 1990, at the London ozone conference, developing countries had successfully pressed for the establishment of a special fund to help them implement the Montreal Protocol on Substances that Deplete the Ozone Layer,[13] and, in the UN General Assembly, they had insisted that the environmental conference scheduled to be held in Rio de Janeiro in 1992 give equal weight to environment and development.[14] In the climate change context, developing countries sought greater representation and argued that climate change should be viewed not simply as an environmental issue but as a development issue as well. For both reasons, they pushed to move the negotiations from the comparatively technical, narrow confines of the IPCC, in which they found it difficult to participate on an equal basis with industrialized countries, to the UN General Assembly. Their efforts proved successful, and the December 1990 resolution authorizing the initiation of negotiations placed the negotiations under the auspices of the General Assembly rather than the IPCC, UNEP, or WMO, as developed countries would have preferred.[15]

As early as 1990, however, the split among developing countries had also become apparent. Developing countries agreed on the need for financial assistance and technology transfer, but on little else. At one end of the spectrum, the small island developing countries, fearing inundation from sea level rise, supported strong commitments to limit emissions. At the SWCC, they organized themselves into the Alliance of Small Island States (AOSIS), a group that continues to play a major role in pushing for stronger action. At the other end of the spectrum, the oil-producing countries questioned the science of climate change and argued for a 'go slow' approach. In the middle, the large developing countries such as Brazil, India, and China insisted that measures to combat climate change should not infringe on their sovereignty—in particular, their right to develop economically. They argued that they were not responsible for creating the climate change problem and had other more pressing priorities, in particular, economic development and poverty alleviation. In their view, since developed countries were historically responsible for

---

[13] Amendment to the Montreal Protocol on Substances that Deplete the Ozone Layer (adopted 29 June 1990, entered into force 10 August 1992) 1598 UNTS 469.

[14] UNGA Res 44/228, 'United Nations Conference on Environment and Development' (22 December 1989) UN Doc A/RES/44/228.

[15] UNGA Res 45/212, 'Protection of global climate for present and future generations of mankind' (21 December 1990) UN Doc A/RES/45/212. For a discussion of the role of negotiating mandates, see Chapter 3, Section II.B.1.

creating the climate change problem, developed countries should also be responsible for solving it. This position has generally persisted among developing countries to this day, leading them to reject efforts by developed countries to have them accept legally binding emissions limitation targets.

III. CONSTITUTIONAL PHASE: NEGOTIATION AND ENTRY INTO FORCE OF THE FCCC (1990–1995)

Although international environmental law underwent impressive growth in the 1970s and 1980s,[16] it had little to say about climate change when the issue first appeared on the international agenda in the late 1980s.[17] The only existing air pollution conventions addressed transboundary air pollution in Europe and North America[18] and the depletion of the stratospheric ozone layer. While customary international law articulates general principles relevant to atmospheric pollution,[19] these principles do not have the specificity and certainty needed to address the climate change problem effectively.[20] Therefore, when calls began to be made to take international action to address climate change, the unquestioned assumption was that this would require the negotiation of a new treaty.

The formal treaty-making process, from the commencement of negotiations to the entry into force of the FCCC, took little more than three years, a comparatively short period for international environmental negotiations. The process began in December 1990, when the UN General Assembly established the Intergovernmental Negotiating Committee for a Framework Convention on Climate Change (INC), with the mandate to negotiate a convention containing 'appropriate commitments' in time for signature in June 1992 at UNCED.[21] Between February 1991 and May 1992, the INC held five sessions. It adopted the FCCC on 9 May 1992, and the convention entered into force less than two years later on 21 March 1994, as a result of its ratification by fifty countries.

---

[16] See generally Bodansky, UNFCCC Commentary (n 1); Donald M. Goldberg, 'As the World Burns: Negotiating the Framework Convention on Climate Change', *Georgetown International Environmental Law Review*, 5/2 (1993): 239; Irving Mintzer and J. Amber Leonard (eds), *Negotiating Climate Change: The Inside Story of the Rio Convention* (Cambridge University Press, 1994).

[17] Daniel B. Magraw, 'Global Change and International Law', *Colorado Journal of International Environmental Law and Policy*, 1/1 (1990): 1; Durwood Zaelke and James Cameron, 'Global Warming and Climate Change - An Overview of the International Legal Process', *American University Journal of International Law and Policy*, 5/2 (1990): 249.

[18] Convention on Long-Range Transboundary Air Pollution (adopted 13 November 1979, entered into force 16 March 1983) 1302 UNTS 217.

[19] For example, the principle of prevention provides that states should 'ensure that activities within their jurisdiction or control do not cause damage to the environment of other States or of areas beyond the limits of national jurisdiction'. See Stockholm Declaration, principle 21.

[20] For more on the application of principles of customary international law to climate change, see Chapter 2, Section II.

[21] UNGA Res 45/212 (n 15). For more on the role of negotiating mandates, see Chapter 3, Section II.B.1.

In understanding the INC process, four factors are critical. First, the June 1992 UNCED deadline exerted substantial pressure on governments. Given the public visibility of the UNCED process, most countries wished to have a convention ready for signature in Rio. Second, in contrast to the agenda-setting and pre-negotiation phases, governments were very much in control and non-governmental actors played a limited role. Even the IPCC did not have a substantial effect on the actual negotiations.[22] Third, although many of the principal issues in the FCCC negotiations were real issues with potentially substantial implications for national interests, the negotiations often focused more on semantics than on substance. Words were debated and selected as much for their political as for their legal significance. Proposed formulations took on a symbolic and even talismanic quality, only distantly connected to the actual meaning of the words.[23] Linguistic debates became a proxy for political confrontation, with success or failure measured not just by the substantive outcomes but also by the inclusion or exclusion of particular terms. Fourth, the desire for consensus decision-making gave individual countries (in particular, the US) substantial leverage—if not a complete veto—over the final outcome.

The negotiation of the FCCC (and later the Kyoto Protocol, the Marrakesh Accords, and the Paris Agreement) followed a pattern common to international environmental negotiations. At first, little progress was apparent, as countries debated process issues and repeated their positions rather than seek compromise formulations. But, while frustrating to those hoping for rapid progress, this sparring process allowed countries to voice their views and concerns, to learn about and gauge the strength of other states' views, and to send up trial balloons. Real negotiations, however, began only in the final months (or even hours) before the negotiations were scheduled to conclude, when governments realized that they would need to compromise if they wished to avoid failure, and typically involved only a small group of key delegations (generally referred to as the 'friends of the chair').[24]

Two of the three basic dynamics established during the agenda-setting phase were particularly strong during the FCCC negotiations: first, the split between developed and developing countries; and second, the split among developed countries. Reflecting the split between developed and developing countries, the FCCC provided that developed countries should take the lead in addressing climate change (Article 3.1), articulated the principle of 'common but differentiated responsibilities and respective capabilities' (CBDRRC) (Article 3.1), and distinguished between the commitments of 'Annex I' and 'non-Annex I' countries (usually equated with developed and developing countries, respectively). Non-Annex

---

[22] The one exception was the role played by a British environmental law group, the Foundation for International Environmental Law and Development (FIELD), which helped organize and support the then newly-formed Alliance of Small Island States (AOSIS).

[23] For example, developing and developed countries argued for hours over whether economic development should be characterized as 'essential' or a 'prerequisite' for developing countries' response measures.

[24] For further discussion of the use of 'friends of the chair', see Chapter 3, Section II.B.2.

I countries were subjected only to very general common commitments to address the climate change issue (Article 4.1), while Annex I countries were subjected to more stringent reporting requirements and review (Article 12.2) and, in the case of countries listed in Annex II (a subset of Annex I that excludes the former Soviet bloc), to general financial and technological commitments (Articles 4.3–4.5).

Reflecting the split among developed countries, the US and the European Union (EU) differed strongly over whether to include binding emission reduction targets. In a compromise provision brokered by the United Kingdom in the closing months of the negotiations, the FCCC established only a heavily-qualified, non-binding quasi-target for developed countries to aim to return emissions to 1990 levels by the year 2000 (Article 4.2).

By contrast, the split among developing countries was largely set aside during the negotiation of the FCCC. Although observers continually predicted the demise of the G-77/China, the coalition of developing countries maintained its unity throughout the negotiations, pushing to limit the commitments of developing countries and to impose stronger commitments on developed countries.

The initial baseline for the FCCC negotiations was the 'framework agreement' model used in the preceding decade to address the issues of acid rain and ozone depletion.[25] Virtually all countries agreed that the FCCC should include, at a minimum, the basic elements of a framework convention. The main question was whether to include additional provisions of a more regulatory nature. As a whole, the FCCC reflected the US preference for what might be called a 'framework convention plus'. As a framework convention, the FCCC focuses on establishing the regime's basic system of governance, including its objective (Article 2), principles (Article 3), institutions (Articles 7–10), and law-making procedures (Articles 15–17). To the extent it establishes substantive obligations, they are very general in nature, rather than legally binding emissions targets, as the EU and AOSIS had wished (Articles 4–6). But the FCCC goes beyond previous framework conventions by establishing a financial mechanism (Article 11) and comparatively strong implementation machinery, including detailed reporting requirements (Article 12) and international review (Article 7.2(e)).[26]

On most issues, however, the various sides in the negotiation fought each other to a standstill. They did not resolve issues so much as paper over them, either through formulations that preserved the positions of all sides,[27] that were deliberately ambiguous,[28] or that deferred issues until later.[29] From this perspective,

---

[25] For more on framework conventions, see Chapter 2, Section IV.A.1.

[26] For a detailed discussion of the FCCC, see Chapter 5.

[27] See eg FCCC, Art 11 (financial mechanism).

[28] See eg ibid, Art 4.2 (commitments by industrialized countries to limit emissions).

[29] See eg ibid, Art 13 (directing COP to consider establishing a multilateral consultative procedure to resolve implementation questions). For a fascinating catalogue of these drafting techniques, see Susan Biniaz, 'Comma But Differentiated Responsibilities: Punctuation and 30 Other Ways Negotiators Have Resolved Issues in the International Climate Change Regime' (Columbia Law School – Sabin Center for Climate Change Law, 2016) <https://web.law.columbia.edu/sites/default/files/microsites/climate-change/files/Publications/biniaz_2016_june_comma_diff_responsibilities.pdf> accessed 20 January 2017.

the adoption of the convention in 1992 represented not an end point, but rather a punctuation mark in an ongoing process of negotiation—a process that continues to this day.

IV. REGULATORY PHASE: NEGOTIATION AND ELABORATION OF THE KYOTO PROTOCOL (1995–2005)

The ink had barely dried on the FCCC[30] before most countries began to argue that the convention's 'commitments' were inadequate and needed to be supplemented by more specific emission limitation targets. In response, the first Conference of the Parties (COP1), meeting in Berlin in 1995, adopted the 'Berlin Mandate', which established the Ad Hoc Group on the Berlin Mandate (AGBM) to negotiate a new legal instrument.[31] The negotiations continued for two years, ending in the adoption of the Kyoto Protocol in December 1997.[32]

The architecture established by the Kyoto Protocol has four main features: (1) a top-down regulatory approach, involving internationally-negotiated emissions targets and accounting rules; (2) sharp differentiation between developed and developing countries; (3) legal bindingness, including a strong compliance system; and (4) market mechanisms to allow cost-effective implementation.

The Berlin Mandate largely settled the first feature—the Kyoto Protocol's top-down regulatory approach—by calling for the negotiation of quantified emission limitation and reduction objectives (QELROs), rather than allowing each country to nationally determine its climate policies, as the FCCC had done. Much of the Kyoto Protocol negotiation focused on defining the nature and stringency of these internationally-defined emissions targets. The EU proposed a comparatively strong target, requiring a 10% cut in GHG emissions below 1990 levels by the year 2010, while other industrialized countries such as the US and Australia proposed much weaker targets, with Japan somewhere in the middle. In the end, the protocol established individualized QELROs for each developed country party (listed in Annex B of the protocol), ranging from a minus 8% target for the EU states to a plus 8% target for Australia, rather than a common target for developed countries as a whole.

The Berlin Mandate also largely resolved the second issue—namely differentiation—by calling for the negotiation of QELROs only for developed countries, while explicitly excluding the negotiation of any new commitments for developing countries.[33] Under strong pressure from then-German environment minister Angela Merkel, who presided over the Berlin meeting, the US reluctantly accepted this approach, despite its failure to leave open the possibility of new mitigation commitments for developing countries such as China and India. But

---

[30] See generally Sebastian Oberthür and Hermann E. Ott, *The Kyoto Protocol: International Climate Policy for the 21st Century* (Berlin-Heidelberg: Springer-Verlag, 1999) ch 4.

[31] For more on the role of negotiating mandates, see Chapter 3, Section II.B.1.

[32] For a detailed discussion of the Kyoto Protocol, see Chapter 6.

[33] Berlin Mandate, paras 2(a) and 2(b).

in the AGBM negotiations, the US pressed for the inclusion of a mechanism to allow developing countries to 'voluntarily' assume emission limitation objectives.[34] Not surprisingly, most developing countries strongly opposed such an approach, arguing that any new commitments for developing countries, even if voluntarily assumed, were expressly excluded by the Berlin Mandate.[35]

The Berlin Mandate left open the third issue, namely, whether the internationally-negotiated emissions targets would be legally binding—that is why the Berlin Mandate described them as quantified emission limitation and reduction 'objectives' rather than 'commitments'. The decision to make QELROs legally binding was not made until the following year at COP2, in the Geneva Ministerial Declaration, when US negotiators acceded to EU demands that the targets under negotiation be legally binding.[36]

Finally, the debate on the fourth issue about whether to establish market mechanisms such as emissions trading proved divisive throughout the Kyoto Protocol negotiations and even after. The US and other members of the 'Umbrella Group' (which includes Australia, Canada, Iceland, Japan, New Zealand, Norway, and Russia) sought mechanisms to allow developed countries to achieve their emissions targets in the most flexible, cost-effective manner possible, for example by allowing a country to receive credit for emissions reduction projects it undertakes in other countries as well as for forest and agricultural activities that remove CO_2 from the atmosphere ('sink activities'). The EU, generally supported by developing countries, wanted to limit the use of market mechanisms on the grounds that developed countries should meet their emissions targets primarily through domestic measures to reduce their GHG emissions.

In essence, the Kyoto Protocol represents a trade-off between EU victory on the stringency and legal character of the emissions targets, US (and Umbrella Group) victory on the market mechanisms, and developing country victory on differentiation. In Kyoto, the US accepted a much stronger emissions limitation target (minus 7% from 1990 levels) than it had wanted, but succeeded in incorporating significant flexibility into the protocol. Most importantly, the protocol:

- Provided for the development of an international emissions trading system (Article 17).

---

[34] The Byrd-Hagel Resolution (25 July 1997) S.Res.98, 105th Cong., adopted by the US Senate by a vote of 95–0 shortly before the Kyoto Conference, expressed the sense of the Senate that it would not consent to any treaty that imposed emissions limitation commitments on the US unless it also imposed new emissions limitation commitments on developing countries within the same compliance period.

[35] Berlin Mandate, para 2(b) (expressly excluding 'any new commitments' for non-Annex I parties). For a discussion of the negotiating history, see Chapter 6, Section II.D.3; see also Joanna Depledge, 'Tracing the Origins of the Kyoto Protocol: An Article-by-Article Textual History' (25 November 2000) FCCC/TP/2000/2, 102–5.

[36] Report of the Conference of the Parties on its Second Session, held at Geneva from 8 to 19 July 1996, Addendum (29 October 1996) FCCC/CP/1996/15/Add.1, Annex: The Geneva Ministerial Declaration, para 8.

- Established the Clean Development Mechanism (CDM), which allows industrialized countries to receive credit for emission reduction projects in developing countries (Article 12).

- Allowed states to receive credits for certain sink activities (Articles 3.3 and 3.4).

Developing countries, however, successfully resisted strong US pressure to establish a process by which they could voluntarily assume quantitative emissions targets.

While a tremendous achievement, the Kyoto Protocol deferred to future negotiations most of the detailed issues about how it would work, thereby creating an opening for states to renegotiate the protocol under the guise of elaborating its rules. The EU, for example, attempted to place quantitative limits ('concrete ceilings') on the use of emissions trading by developed countries to meet their emissions limitation targets.[37] Similarly, the US sought to weaken its own emissions target through the inclusion of expansive credits for sink activities, as well as to persuade at least some developing countries to accept emissions targets of their own.

The scope of the negotiations that followed Kyoto was decided at COP4 in Buenos Aires, where the parties adopted a comprehensive plan to complete work on the Kyoto Protocol rules (known as 'the Buenos Aires Plan of Action').[38] Initially, negotiations were scheduled to conclude in November 2000 at COP6 in The Hague. But when The Hague conference broke down at the eleventh hour, principally over the issue of credits for sink activities, the parties agreed to reconvene the following summer to make one final effort to reach agreement.[39]

In the initial aftermath of The Hague conference, the prospects for an agreement on the Kyoto rules looked remote. The rejection of the Kyoto Protocol by the newly elected Bush Administration in March 2001 led many to predict the protocol's demise.[40] Ironically, however, the peremptory nature of the Bush Administration's action—rejecting the protocol without proposing any alternative—had the opposite effect. It galvanized other countries into action, particularly the EU, and led them to make the necessary compromises for the November 2001 adoption of the Marrakesh Accords, which set forth detailed rules fleshing out the Kyoto Protocol's often skeletal provisions.[41] Also ironically, given the withdrawal by the US from the Kyoto Protocol, the Marrakesh Accords largely reflected US positions during the post-Kyoto negotiations. In particular, they did not impose any quantitative limits on the use of the market mechanisms (as the EU had initially sought), and allowed

---

[37] In arguing for concrete ceilings, the EU relied on the language in Article 17 of the Kyoto Protocol providing that emissions trading shall be 'supplemental' to domestic action.

[38] Decision 1/CP.4, 'The Buenos Aires Plan of Action' (25 January 1999) FCCC/CP/1998/16/Add.1, 4.

[39] On the Hague Conference, see Lavanya Rajamani, 'Renegotiating Kyoto: A Review of the Sixth Conference of Parties to the Framework Convention on Climate Change', *Colorado Journal of International Environmental Law and Policy*, 12/1 (2001): 201.

[40] See eg David G. Victor, *The Collapse of the Kyoto Protocol and the Struggle to Slow Global Warming* (Princeton University Press, 2004).

[41] On the Marrakesh Accords, see generally Suraje Dessai and Emma Lisa Schipper, 'The Marrakesh Accords to the Kyoto Protocol: Analysis and Future Prospects', *Global Environmental Change*, 13/2 (2003): 149.

significant credits for sink activities. As a result of Russia's ratification, the Kyoto Protocol entered into force on 16 February 2005.

V. SECOND CONSTITUTIONAL PHASE: NEGOTIATING THE FUTURE CLIMATE REGIME (2005–2016)

Although the Kyoto Protocol was a considerable achievement, it had two significant limitations. First, it set targets for only a five-year commitment period running from 2008 through 2012, and did not limit emissions in 2013 and thereafter. Second, its emissions targets encompassed less than 24% of global GHG emissions,[42] both because of US non-participation and because of the protocol's failure to establish any emissions limitation commitments for China (which in 2005 surpassed the US as the world's biggest current emitter[43]) and other developing countries.

Following the Kyoto Protocol's entry into force, attention shifted to the problem of what to do after 2012, when the protocol's first commitment period was set to end.[44] One option was to extend the Kyoto Protocol through the adoption of a second commitment period, with a new round of emission reduction targets for developed country parties. A second option was to extend the protocol, in conjunction with negotiating a new agreement under the FCCC that would address the emissions of countries that either are not parties to the protocol (eg, the US) or do not have Kyoto emissions targets (eg, developing countries). A third option was to adopt a single new agreement that would replace the Kyoto Protocol and be more comprehensive in coverage, addressing both developed and developing country emissions. In general, developing countries preferred the first option (preferably, with the US joining the protocol in its second iteration), which would have left their emissions unaddressed, while most developed countries (the US during most of the Bush Administration excepted) preferred the second or third option, which attempted to encompass the emissions of the US and of large developing countries such as China, India, and Brazil.

The task of addressing the post-2012 period proceeded along two tracks, one under the Kyoto Protocol and the other under the FCCC. At the first meeting of the parties to the Kyoto Protocol (CMP1) in 2005, states initiated a process to negotiate a new round of commitments under the protocol.[45] In parallel, the

---

[42] Igor Shishlov, Romain Morel, and Valentin Bellassen, 'Compliance of the Parties to the Kyoto Protocol in the First Commitment Period', *Climate Policy*, 16/6 (2016): 768.

[43] These figures are based on the World Resource Institute's Climate Analysis Indicator Tool (CAIT), which compiles figures on global and national emissions. World Resource Institute (WRI), 'CAIT Climate Data Explorer' <http://cait.wri.org/> accessed 20 January 2017.

[44] See Chapter 6, Section X.

[45] Decision 1/CMP.1, 'Consideration of commitments for subsequent periods for Parties included in Annex I to the Convention under Article 3, paragraph 9 of the Kyoto Protocol' (30 March 2006) FCCC/KP/CMP/2005/8/Add.1, 3.

parties to the FCCC established a dialogue on long-term cooperative action, which was succeeded in 2007 by the Bali Plan of Action and then, in turn, by the 2012 Durban Platform for Enhanced Action.[46]

Perhaps the most consequential feature of this most recent phase in the climate change negotiations has been the push by developed countries to address developing country emissions, which already represent more than half of global emissions and are predicted to account for most of the emissions increases between now and 2050.[47] For the first decade of the climate regime, from the initiation of the negotiations in 1991 to the adoption of the Marrakesh Accords in 2001, climate change negotiations focused almost exclusively on developed country emissions. Although the US fitfully pushed to address the issue of 'developing country participation', the Berlin Mandate effectively took this issue off the table by specifically excluding any new commitments for non-Annex I countries. As a result, the primary axis in the negotiations was the split among developed countries: between the US (generally joined by its Umbrella Group allies) and the EU.[48] On one side, the EU pushed for strong emissions reduction targets implemented domestically; on the other side, the US initially resisted a targets-based approach during the FCCC negotiations, then embraced it under President Bill Clinton, but insisted on allowing targets to be met through the use of international market mechanisms such as emissions trading and through sink activities. Although developing countries engaged in these debates, the negotiations largely focused on what developed countries would do.

After 2001, when the Marrakesh conference adopted the detailed rules for operationalizing the Kyoto Protocol, the basic dynamic in the climate negotiations changed. The issue of reducing developed country emissions continued to be central, but developed countries became increasingly insistent on addressing developing country emissions as well. This brought to the fore the second main axis in the climate change negotiations: the split between developed and developing countries.

The new negotiating dynamic began to emerge at the 2002 New Delhi conference, when European countries—fresh from their success in finalizing the Kyoto Protocol—began pressing for action from developing countries. For most of the next few years, however, the shift in the negotiating dynamic was overshadowed by the Bush Administration's decision to reject the Kyoto Protocol. But when the negotiations began to regain momentum during the final years of the Bush Administration, the shift in dynamics became apparent. The developed-developing country divide moved to center stage at the Bali conference in 2007 and has stayed there ever since.

---

[46] See below Section V.D.
[47] OECD, *OECD Environmental Outlook to 2050: The Consequences of Inaction* (OECD, 2012) 80, Figure 3.5.
[48] For further discussion of negotiating groups, see Chapter 3, Section II.B.2.

Action Plan

The 2007 Bali conference was the first key climate meeting since the adoption of the Kyoto Protocol's rulebook at the Marrakesh conference in 2001. In the Bali Action Plan, states agreed to launch a 'comprehensive process' to reach an 'agreed outcome' under the FCCC, encompassing all aspects of the climate change issue, including mitigation, adaptation, finance, and technology.[49] The use of the term 'agreed outcome' was neutral as to the question of legal form, and left open whether the Bali Action Plan would result in a new treaty, a decision of the parties, or some other type of instrument.

Although the Bali Action Plan addressed mitigation by both developed and developing countries and thus began to shift away from the Berlin Mandate approach, it continued to distinguish between the two. For developed countries, it spoke of 'measurable, reportable and verifiable' commitments, including QELROs, while for developing countries, it referred to 'nationally appropriate mitigation actions' (NAMAs). Many developing countries argued that this distinction between developed country 'commitments' and developing country 'actions' maintained the 'firewall' between developed and developing countries that, in their view, had been established by the Berlin Mandate and Kyoto Protocol, and they resisted efforts to consider developed and developing country mitigation together. This was one of the main reasons why, five years later at the Durban conference, the US pressed to terminate the work of the Bali Action Plan and replace it with the Durban Platform.

B. Copenhagen Accord

The Copenhagen conference,[50] held in December 2009, was originally intended as the end point of the parallel negotiating tracks organized under the FCCC and the Kyoto Protocol, and many expected it to produce a new legal agreement (or agreements) addressing the post-2012 period—a view reflected in the unofficial slogan of the conference, 'seal the deal'. The already sky-high expectations were only heightened by the decision by more than 100 heads of state to attend, including President Obama and the leaders of China, India, Brazil, South Africa, Japan, the United Kingdom, France, and Germany. Thus, when states failed to reach agreement on a new legal instrument, many were bitterly disappointed.

But although the Copenhagen conference failed to adopt a legally binding agreement, it did produce the Copenhagen Accord, a political agreement negotiated in the closing hours of the meeting by the leaders of twenty-eight countries, including all of the major economies and emitters, representatives of all of the UN regional groups, and representatives of the most vulnerable and least developed states. Inelegant and extremely brief, the Copenhagen Accord nevertheless addressed

---

[49] Bali Action Plan, para 1. See for a detailed discussion of the Bali Action Plan, Lavanya Rajamani, 'From Berlin to Bali and Beyond: Killing Kyoto Softly', *International and Comparative Law Quarterly*, 57/4 (2008): 909.

[50] This section draws on material from Bodansky, Copenhagen Climate Change Conference (n 1).

many of the principal elements under negotiation, including mitigation, adaptation, finance, technology, forestry, and verification. Among its key elements, it:

- Set a long-term aspirational goal of limiting temperature rise to no more than 2° C (para 1).

- Established a process for recording the mitigation targets and actions to be implemented by developed and developing countries, respectively (which the principal countries had put forward prior to the meeting) (paras 4–5).

- Put significant new money on the table for climate change mitigation and adaptation by developing countries, including 'fast-start' funding for the 2010–2012 period 'approaching' $30 billion and a goal of mobilizing $100 billion per year by 2020 (para 8).

- Provided for 'international consultation and analysis' of developing country mitigation actions, plus fuller measurement, reporting, and verification of developed country targets and financing, as well of developing country mitigation actions that receive international support (para 5).

At the same time, the Copenhagen Accord fell short in important respects, for example, by failing to reach agreement on a long-term emissions reduction target, such as the 50% reduction by 2050 ('50-by-50') goal agreed to by the Group of Eight (G-8) the previous year in Japan.[51]

As a political necessity, the Copenhagen Accord continued to reflect the principle of CBDRRC. But it began to break down the firewall between developed and developing countries that had been erected in the Berlin Mandate and Kyoto Protocol. For the first time, the major developing countries agreed to reflect their national emissions reduction pledges in an international instrument, to report on their GHG inventories and their mitigation actions in biennial national communications, and to subject their actions to 'international consultation and analysis'. In doing so, developing countries effectively 'internationalized' their national climate change policies, at least partially.

The Copenhagen conference is also notable, from a process standpoint, for several shifts in the negotiating dynamic. China (negotiating as part of the BASIC group, which also includes Brazil, India, and South Africa) was much more assertive than previously, reflecting its emergence as a global power; indeed, at one point, it thumbed its nose at the US by sending a mid-level official to negotiate with President Obama. Conversely, the EU played a less central role. The fractures within the developing country negotiating bloc (the G-77/China) were more evident than ever; indeed, during the final session, the negotiator for Papua New Guinea publicly blamed the big developing countries for the failure to make more progress. And the willingness and ability of a small group of countries (including Bolivia, Sudan, Tuvalu, and Venezuela) to block the adoption of the Copenhagen

---

[51] 'G-8 Hokkaido Toyako Summit Leaders Declaration' (8 July 2008) <http://www.mofa.go.jp/policy/economy/summit/2008/doc/doc080714__en.html> accessed 20 January 2017, para 23.

Accord, which had been negotiated among the leaders of all of the world's principal economies, highlighted the problematic nature of the COP's consensus decision-making rule.[52]

Finally, the Copenhagen Accord is notable for embracing a fundamentally different architecture than the Kyoto Protocol. Rather than defining emissions targets from the top-down through international negotiations, the Copenhagen Accord established a bottom-up process that allowed each party to self-define its own commitments and actions.[53] The Accord specified that developed countries would put forward national emissions targets in the 2020 time frame, but allowed each party to determine its own target level, base year, and accounting rules. Meanwhile, developing countries were given even greater latitude in formulating NAMAs.

Although the Copenhagen Accord reflected a significant reorientation of the climate regime, its status coming out of Copenhagen was unclear. On the one hand, it had been adopted by the leaders of all of the world's major economies, giving it considerable political weight. On the other hand, when it was brought back to the official conference in the waning hours of the meeting, the COP could agree only to 'take [...] note' of the Accord,[54] rather than to adopt it. As a result, the Copenhagen Accord was given no official status within the FCCC process.[55]

C. Cancun Agreements

The uncertain status of the Copenhagen Accord was addressed the following year at COP16 in Cancun. The Cancun Agreements not only brought the core elements of the Copenhagen Accord into the FCCC process, through decisions of the parties, but also elaborated the Accord's three-page text into thirty pages of decision language.[56] Key elements of the Cancun Agreements included:

- A reiteration of the long-term goal of limiting temperature increase to below 2° C (para 4).
- Anchoring of the emissions targets and actions pledged pursuant to the Copenhagen Accord in the FCCC process, through inclusion in two 'INF' (information) documents: one for emissions targets to be implemented by developed countries (para 36), the other for NAMAs to be implemented by developing countries (para 49).
- Establishment of a registry for listing NAMAs for which developing countries sought international support (para 53).

---

[52] For more on the consensus decision-making rule, see Chapter 3, Section II.B.2.

[53] Bodansky, Tale of Two Architectures (n 1) 705. For a general discussion of top-down versus bottom-up architectures, see Chapter 1, Section V.B.

[54] Decision 2/CP.15, 'Copenhagen Accord' (30 March 2010) FCCC/CP/2009/11/Add.1, 4, introductory text.

[55] See generally Lavanya Rajamani, 'The Making and Unmaking of the Copenhagen Accord', *International and Comparative Law Quarterly*, 59/3 (2010): 824.

[56] See generally Lavanya Rajamani, 'The Cancun Climate Agreements: Reading the Text, Subtext and Tea Leaves', *International and Comparative Law Quarterly*, 60/2 (2011): 499.

- Establishment of the Green Climate Fund, under the manage
  four-member board of directors and administered initially |
  (paras 102–3, 107).
- Reiteration of the collective commitment in Copenhagen by developeu ~
  tries to provide an amount approaching $30 billion in fast-start financing for
  the 2010 to 2012 period, balanced between mitigation and adaptation, as well
  as of the longer-term goal of mobilizing $100 billion per year by 2020, a 'sig-
  nificant portion' of which should flow through the newly-established Green
  Climate Fund (paras 95, 98, 100).
- Elaboration of the process of international consultation and analysis of developing country mitigation actions, to be performed by the Subsidiary Body on
  Implementation of the FCCC (para 63).
- Establishment of a new technology mechanism to facilitate technology devel-
  opment and transfer (para 117).
- Establishment of a framework for reducing emissions from deforestation and
  forest degradation in developing countries (REDD+) (paras 68–79).
- Adoption of the Cancun Adaptation Framework (para 13).

D. Durban Platform and Doha Amendment

Although the 2010 Cancun meeting made significant progress in regularizing and
elaborating the Copenhagen Accord, it failed to resolve the question of whether to
extend the Kyoto Protocol's emissions targets beyond 2012. Moreover, it left open
whether to negotiate a new legal agreement, either in addition to or as a replace-
ment for the Kyoto Protocol, to address the emissions of states that do not have
Kyoto targets. These issues were the focus of COP17 in Durban.

The Durban conference set a new record for length, lasting more than a day
and a half beyond its scheduled conclusion.[57] In the end, states agreed to a finely-
balanced compromise consisting of three pillars:

First, the Durban Platform for Enhanced Action provided the mandate for the
Paris Agreement negotiations, by establishing a new negotiating group (the Ad
Hoc Working Group on the Durban Platform for Enhanced Action, or ADP) to
develop 'a protocol, another legal instrument or an agreed outcome with legal force
under the convention applicable to all parties'.[58] The Durban Platform called for
completion of the new instrument by 2015 and decided that it would 'come into
effect and be implemented from 2020'.[59] At the insistence of small-island and
least-developed countries (which, together with the EU, formed what some have
called an 'ambitious majority' in Durban), the Durban Platform also sought to

---

[57] On the Durban conference, see generally Bodansky, Durban Platform Negotiations (n 1) and
Lavanya Rajamani, 'The Durban Platform for Enhanced Action and the Future of the Climate Regime',
International and Comparative Law Quarterly, 61/2 (2012): 501.
[58] Durban Platform, para 2.   [59] Ibid, para 4.

enhance the level of ambition of countries' mitigation efforts prior to 2020, in order to address the 'ambition gap' between the pledges made under the Copenhagen/Cancun framework and the aggregate emissions pathways necessary to hold global warming below 2° C.[60]

Second, in exchange for agreement by developing countries to launch a new negotiating process, the EU agreed to extend the Kyoto Protocol through 2020, meeting the chief demand of the BASIC group and other developing countries. The formal amendment establishing a second commitment period was adopted in 2012 at COP18 in Doha, and covers an eight-year period running from 2013 to 2020. Because Canada had withdrawn from the protocol, and Japan and Russia declined to accept new emissions targets, the Doha Amendment established emissions targets for only a small number of parties, representing less than 12% of global GHG emissions.[61]

Third, the Durban COP adopted a series of decisions that elaborate and operationalize various elements of the Cancun Agreements, perhaps most importantly by formally adopting the governing instrument of the Green Climate Fund.[62]

The Durban Platform continued the move away from the firewall between developed and developing countries embodied in the Berlin Mandate and the Kyoto Protocol. In contrast to these earlier instruments, the Durban Platform called for 'the widest possible cooperation by all countries and their participation in an effective and appropriate international response' (preambular para 1), and provided that the agreed outcome would be 'applicable to all parties' (para 2). These provisions reflected the US insistence that any new negotiating mandate be 'symmetrical' in its application to developing as well as developed countries.

Along similar lines, the Durban Platform made no reference to the principle of equity or to the principle of CBDRRC, nor did it repeat the FCCC's language that developed countries should 'take the lead' in combating climate change. Indeed, the Durban Platform contained no reference to 'developing', 'developed', 'Annex I', or 'non-Annex I' parties—the categories that had previously dominated the FCCC regime. Although the principles of equity and CBDRRC were implicitly incorporated by the statement that the Durban Platform outcome would be 'under the Convention',[63] the lack of any explicit reference to these principles represented a significant shift in how the Durban Platform framed the Paris Agreement negotiations.[64]

---

[60] Ibid, paras 6–7.

[61] This includes the emissions share of Australia, Belarus, EU-28, Iceland, Kazakhstan, Norway, Switzerland, and Ukraine in 2010, excluding land use, land use change, and forestry. WRI, CAIT Climate Data Explorer (n 43). For a list of parties with emissions targets, see Doha Amendment, Art 1, Section A, which replaces the table in Annex B to the protocol with a new Annex B listing the second commitment period targets.

[62] Report of the Conference of the Parties on its Seventeenth Session, held in Durban from 28 November to 11 December 2011, Addendum (15 March 2012) FCCC/CP/2011/9/Add.1, 58, Annex: Governing Instrument for the Green Climate Fund.

[63] Durban Platform, para 2.

[64] See generally Lavanya Rajamani, 'Differentiation in the Emerging Climate Regime', *Theoretical Inquiries in Law*, 14/1 (2013): 151.

Finally, in contrast to the Kyoto Protocol negotiating mandate, which specifically called for a new legal agreement, the Durban Platform left the issue of legal form open, providing three alternatives: a protocol, another legal instrument, or an agreed outcome with legal force. The inclusion of the third option, 'an agreed outcome with legal force', reflected the unwillingness of some countries (most notably, India) to concede that the new round of negotiations should result in a new legal agreement. The phrase emerged from what became known as the 'huddle'—a discussion among the key negotiators on the floor of the closing plenary. It does not have any established meaning in international law and was deliberately ambiguous, in order to allow delegations skeptical of a new legal agreement to argue that a non-legal option had not been foreclosed.[65]

The ADP met fifteen times in the four years between the Durban and Paris conferences. Milestones of the ADP process included the 2013 Warsaw decision on 'Further Advancing the Durban Platform', which first articulated the hybrid structure of the new agreement and called on states to submit their intended nationally determined contributions (INDCs) well in advance of the Paris conference, and the 2014 Lima Call for Climate Action, which elaborated informational norms for parties' INDCs. The ADP produced a draft negotiating text in February 2015.[66] Later that year, countries began submitting their INDCs and, by the time the Paris conference began, 182 states had done so. The ADP concluded its work at the end of the first week in Paris, forwarding its draft negotiating text to ministers.[67]

In the UN climate regime, the end game of COPs is typically a process of trench warfare, in which virtually every word is fought over, and gains and losses are measured in brackets and commas. One has to be a COP-ologist, familiar with the subtle history and nuance of every provision, to follow the to and fro. The Paris conference was no exception. What was exceptional was the skillful performance of the COP Presidency (headed by the French foreign minister, Laurent Fabius) and FCCC secretariat in managing the negotiations. The result was a generally positive spirit in the final week, with little of the sniping typical of COPs. After one last kerfuffle at the end, discussed in Chapter 7, the Paris Agreement was adopted by acclamation on 12 December 2015, a momentous event in the development of the UN climate regime.

VI. CONCLUSION

In many respects, the dynamics of the climate change negotiations have remained remarkably constant in the more than twenty years since the negotiations began.

---

[65] See Chapter 7, Section I.A.

[66] Ad Hoc Working Group on the Durban Platform for Enhanced Action (ADP), Negotiating Text (25 February 2015) FCCC/ADP/2015/1.

[67] ADP, Draft Paris Outcome, Revised draft conclusions proposed by the Co-Chairs (5 December 2015) FCCC/ADP/2015/L.6/Rev.1.

Despite numerous changes in governments within many of the key states, dramatic economic shifts—most importantly, the emergence of China as an economic power—and much stronger scientific evidence of the likelihood and dangers of climate change, the international climate change negotiations have stayed much the same. The EU has consistently pushed for strong, legally binding emissions targets. The US has consistently argued for domestic flexibility. And China and India have consistently resisted the imposition of binding emissions targets on themselves. These elements of continuity reflect enduring national interests and domestic political dynamics.

Nevertheless, the climate regime today is quite different from when it first emerged in the early 1990s:

- An increasing number of states and groups play significant roles in the negotiations. In addition to the groups that were influential from the start—the EU and its member states; the US and its Umbrella Group partners; big developing states such as Brazil, China, India, and South Africa, which now negotiate as the BASIC group; AOSIS; and the oil-producing states (led by Saudi Arabia)—new players have emerged. These include least-developed states in Africa, which joined with AOSIS and the EU to form an 'ambitious majority' in Durban; Mexico and Korea, which now are members of the Organisation for Economic Cooperation and Development (OECD), the club of advanced market-oriented economies; and left-leaning Latin American countries such as Bolivia, Cuba, Ecuador, and Venezuela, which form the Bolivarian Alliance for the Peoples of the Americas (ALBA).[68]

- The influence of the G-77/China—the developing country negotiating group—has declined, as developing countries increasingly negotiate in smaller groups such as BASIC, LMDCs, AOSIS, and ALBA, which better reflect their interests and ideology.

- The FCCC secretariat has grown tremendously in size and responsibilities.

- An elaborate system of measurement, reporting, and review has developed.

- The benefits of using market mechanisms, such as emissions trading, to reduce costs have become widely accepted, including by the EU, which in the Kyoto Protocol negotiations had sought to limit their use.

- The climate regime has moved beyond a narrow focus on developed country emissions to an approach that addresses global emissions.

- Finally—and perhaps most importantly—an increasing number of states have implemented national climate change policies, in some cases quite strong policies, despite their reluctance to accept international emissions reduction targets.

---

[68] For further discussion of negotiating groups, see Chapter 3, Section II.B.2.

SELECT BIBLIOGRAPHY

Bodansky D., 'The Copenhagen Climate Change Conference: A Postmortem', *American Journal of International Law*, 104/2 (2010): 230.

Bodansky D., 'A Tale of Two Architectures: The Once and Future UN Climate Change Regime', *Arizona State Law Journal*, 43/1 (2011): 697.

Bodansky D. and Rajamani L., 'The Evolution and Governance Architecture of the Climate Change Regime', in Luterbacher U. and Sprinz D. (eds), *Global Climate Change in an International Context* (Cambridge, MA: MIT Press, 2017 forthcoming).

Chasek P. and Wagner L.M. (eds), *The Roads from Rio: Twenty Years of Multilateral Environmental Negotiations* (New York: RFF Press, 2012).

Depledge J., 'Tracing the Origins of the Kyoto Protocol: An Article-by-Article Textual History', FCCC/TP/2000/2 (25 November 2000).

Leggett J., *The Carbon War: Global Warming and the End of the Oil Era* (New York: Routledge, 2001).

Mintzer I. and Leonard J.A. (eds), *Negotiating Climate Change: The Inside Story of the Rio Convention* (Cambridge University Press, 1994).

Pomerance R., 'The Dangers from Climate Warming: A Public Awakening', in Abrahamson D.E. (ed), *The Challenge of Global Warming* (Washington, D.C.: Island Press, 1989) 259.

Rajamani L., 'From Berlin to Bali and Beyond: Killing Kyoto Softly', *International and Comparative Law Quarterly*, 57/4 (2008): 909.

Rajamani L., 'The Making and Unmaking of the Copenhagen Accord', *International and Comparative Law Quarterly*, 59/3 (2010): 824.

Rajamani L., 'The Durban Platform for Enhanced Action and the Future of the Climate Regime', *International and Comparative Law Quarterly*, 61/2 (2012): 501.

Rajamani L., 'The Warsaw Climate Negotiations: Emerging Understandings and Battle Lines on the Road to the 2015 Climate Agreement', *International and Comparative Law Quarterly*, 63/3 (2014): 721–40.

Weart S.R., *The Discovery of Global Warming* (Cambridge, MA: Harvard University Press, 2008).

5

The Framework Convention
on Climate Change

I. INTRODUCTION

The FCCC[1] established the governance structure for the international climate regime, reflecting its role as a framework convention. It also provided the regime's initial architecture and approach to differentiation. Broadly speaking, the FCCC can be divided into four parts: (1) the introductory provisions, setting forth the basic definitions, principles, and objectives of the regime (Articles 1–3); (2) the commitments relating to mitigation of, and adaptation to, climate change, including commitments relating to finance and technology transfer (Articles 4–6); (3) institutional and procedural mechanisms to implement the convention (Articles 7–14); and (4) final clauses dealing with such matters as protocols, annexes, amendment, ratification, and entry into force (Articles 15–26).

After more than two decades, the FCCC remains the foundation of the UN climate regime. The 1997 Kyoto Protocol and the 2015 Paris Agreement were both adopted under its auspices, as well as the 2007 Bali Action Plan, the 2010 Cancun Agreements, and the 2011 Durban Platform. The FCCC's comparatively spare provisions have also been elaborated by numerous decisions of the parties, together with an extensive body of practice.

In the almost twenty-five years since the FCCC's adoption on 9 May 1992, some of the controversies that raged during its negotiation have been settled—perhaps most importantly, the debate about whether to allow states to use market mechanisms to implement their commitments to reduce emissions. This issue was resolved in favor of market mechanisms during the Kyoto Protocol negotiations, and the Paris Agreement continues to recognize their use. Other issues have narrowed significantly but still persist—for example, how to differentiate among the commitments of different parties or groups of parties. The Paris Agreement reflects a new, more nuanced, approach to differentiation, which does not employ the FCCC's annex structure. But debates about differentiation will likely continue in

---

[1] This chapter is based on Daniel Bodansky, 'The United Nations Framework Convention on Climate Change: A Commentary', *Yale Journal of International Law*, 18/2 (1993): 451, with substantial revisions and updates. It also draws on materials from Daniel Bodansky, *The Art and Craft of International Environmental Law* (Cambridge, MA: Harvard University Press, 2010).

the process of elaborating the Paris Agreement's rules. Finally, some issues remain as controversial as ever—for example, the extent to which developed countries should be required to support mitigation and adaptation efforts by developing countries.

II. OVERARCHING ISSUES

A. Legal bindingness

The FCCC takes a similar approach to the issue of legal bindingness as the Paris Agreement more than two decades later—by distinguishing between the legal form of the overall instrument and the legal character of its constituent provisions.[2] In the year leading up to the initiation of negotiations in 1990, a broad consensus had emerged to negotiate a legal agreement addressing climate change—that is, a treaty.[3] The UN General Assembly resolution establishing the Intergovernmental Negotiating Committee for a Framework Convention on Climate Change (INC) embodied this view by charging the INC with drafting 'an effective framework convention on climate change',[4] thus effectively deciding the issue of legal form. But the General Assembly mandate provided only that the FCCC would contain 'appropriate commitments', without any indication of what these commitments should be. The question of which provisions to formulate as legal commitments and which to formulate in softer terms thus remained a persistent issue throughout the INC process, as it was in the Paris Agreement negotiations.

Early proposals for a climate change agreement were influenced by the framework-protocol model that had emerged in the 1970s and 1980s to address the problems of regional seas, acid rain, and depletion of the stratospheric ozone layer. Framework conventions are largely procedural, establishing a basis for future action, with few if any substantive obligations. But despite the advantages and historical successes of this model, many countries wanted the INC to do more than produce a framework convention. Given the perceived urgency of the climate change problem as well as the extensive preparatory work of the Intergovernmental Panel on Climate Change (IPCC), they viewed the two-step, framework convention/protocol process as unnecessarily slow, and pushed for an agreement containing strong substantive obligations to limit emissions.

The debate between the framework and substantive approaches persisted right up to the end of the negotiations, when the INC considered whether the title of the agreement should be the 'UN Convention on Climate Change', or—as was ultimately agreed—the 'UN *Framework* Convention on Climate Change'. Despite its title, however, the FCCC lies somewhere between a framework and a substantive

---

[2] See Chapter 7, Section II.A for a discussion of the Paris Agreement's legal bindingness.
[3] Bodansky, UNFCCC Commentary (n 1) 473–4.
[4] United Nations General Assembly (UNGA) Res 45/212, 'Protection of global climate for present and future generations of mankind' (21 December 1990) UN Doc A/RES/45/212. For a general discussion of negotiating mandates, see Chapter 3, Section II.B.1.

agreement. It establishes more extensive commitments than those contained in Long-Range Transboundary Air Pollution Convention[5] or the Vienna Convention for the Protection of the Ozone Layer,[6] but not nearly as specific as those in a regulatory agreement like the Montreal Protocol on Substances that Deplete the Ozone Layer. Instead, its only specific provision to limit greenhouse gas (GHG) emissions is formulated as a non-binding aim, rather than as a legal commitment.[7]

B. Architecture

In the development of the FCCC, the top-down approach of the Montreal Protocol initially served as a major inspiration for many countries. Given the Montreal Protocol's perceived success, many viewed it as a model for the climate change issue and proposed using the same top-down regulatory approach, involving internationally negotiated commitments. In contrast, the United States (US) and Japan argued for a more bottom-up system of 'pledge and review', in which states' pledges would be nationally determined.

Ultimately, the FCCC is a hybrid that includes aspects of both approaches. Article 4.1 reflects a bottom-up approach, requiring all parties to develop (and report on) national policies and measures to combat climate change—albeit with the hybrid element of international review.[8] Meanwhile, Article 4.2 reflects a top-down model, establishing an internationally determined emissions target for parties listed in Annex I[9] to return emissions to 1990 levels in the year 2000, albeit formulated in convoluted and non-binding terms.[10] Interestingly, the bottom-up requirements of Article 4.1 are legally binding, while the top-down target in Article 4.2 was not, illustrating that the issue of top-down vs bottom-up is distinct from that of legally binding vs non-legally binding. In the subsequent development of the UN climate regime, the Kyoto Protocol sought to strengthen and legalize the top-down approach of Article 4.2, while the Copenhagen/Cancun framework and the Paris Agreement moved back toward the more bottom-up approach of Article 4.1.

C. Scope

As a framework convention, intended to establish the general system of governance of the UN climate regime, the FCCC has a broad scope, addressing all aspects of the climate change issue, including mitigation, adaptation, finance, technology transfer, transparency, and compliance. The main issue in the negotiations relating to scope was whether the FCCC should focus on CO_2 emissions or take a more

---

[5] Convention on Long-Range Transboundary Air Pollution (adopted 13 November 1979, entered into force 16 March 1983) 1302 UNTS 217.

[6] Vienna Convention for the Protection of the Ozone Layer (adopted 22 March 1985, entered into force 22 September 1988) 1513 UNTS 293.

[7] FCCC, Art 4.2. For further discussion, see Section IV.B.1 below.

[8] Bodansky, UNFCCC Commentary (n 1) 486–7, 508.

[9] For a discussion of Annex I parties, see n 12 below and accompanying text.

[10] See generally Bodansky, UNFCCC Commentary (n 1) 508–17.

comprehensive approach that addresses emissions of other GHGs as well as removals by sinks. As discussed in Section IV.B.2, states ultimately agreed to adopt the comprehensive approach in the FCCC.

D. Differentiation

Although it was clear from the outset of the INC negotiations that the FCCC would contain differentiated commitments for developed and developing countries, delegations did not decide until the final negotiating session on what categories of parties to recognize, which countries to include in each category, and the categories' respective commitments. Most developing states argued that the agreement should recognize only two categories of countries, 'developed' and 'developing', but the Alliance of Small Island States (AOSIS) supported a more complex and multivariate differentiation, focusing on special vulnerability to climate change. Several developed states proposed the additional categories of 'newly industrialized states' and 'countries with economies in transition' (ie the states of Eastern Europe and the former Soviet Union, which at the time were transitioning from communism to market economies). In the end, although the FCCC uses 'developed' and 'developing' countries as the primary categories, it also recognizes several additional categories of countries, including:

- 'Countries with economies in transition' (EITs), which are given 'a certain degree of flexibility' in implementing their emissions reduction targets (Article 4.6).
- 'Least developed states' (LDCs), whose special needs are to be taken into 'full account' in actions regarding funding and technology transfer (Article 4.9).

The FCCC also includes provisions requiring parties to give consideration to the special needs of states that are especially vulnerable to climate change (Article 4.8) or to the effects of mitigation measures (Article 4.10).[11]

Proposals on how to determine which countries fit within the two basic categories—developed and developing—broke down into three approaches: (1) defining 'developed' and 'developing' countries by objective criteria such as per capita income; (2) listing particular states to which specific commitments would apply; or (3) using a combination of both methods. The first approach has the benefit of flexibility since, as countries meet the criteria of 'developed country', they graduate into that status. On the other hand, the list method avoids ambiguities about whether a state meets the definition of 'developed' versus 'developing'.

---

[11] Articles 4.8 and 4.10 contain subtle differences. Under Article 4.8, parties are to give 'full consideration to what actions are necessary... to meet the specific needs and concerns of developing country Parties arising from the adverse effects of climate change and/or the impact of the implementation of response measures'. By comparison, Article 4.10 contains weaker language, requiring parties to 'take into consideration... the situation of Parties [both developed and developing] with economies that are vulnerable to the adverse effects of the implementation of [response] measures'.

The INC ultimately decided to use lists rather than criteria to categorize countries. The FCCC establishes two such lists:

- Annex I, which includes the members, as of 1992, of the Organization of Economic Co-operation and Development (OECD)—the advanced market-oriented economies—and EITs, which are indicated in Annex I by an asterisk.
- Annex II, a subset of Annex I that is limited to OECD members.

Parties not listed in Annex I are usually referred to as 'non-Annex I parties', and are subject only to the general commitments applicable to all parties (Articles 4.1, 5, 6, 12.1). Annex I parties have additional, more specific commitments relating to mitigation and reporting (Articles 4.2 and 12.2), while Annex II parties have additional commitments with respect to financial assistance and technology transfer (Articles 4.3–4.5).

Although the division between Annex I and non-Annex I parties is often equated with the division between developed and developing countries, the FCCC does not make this association explicit, nor does it contain any definition of the terms 'developed country' or 'developing country'. Indeed, the convention's first reference to Annex I, which occurs in Article 4.2, refers to 'developed countries and other Parties included in Annex I', suggesting that Annex I includes parties other than developed countries.[12]

The lists of countries in Annexes I and II were compiled in haste, in the closing hours of the FCCC negotiations, and little consideration was given to which countries to include on which list. As a result, Annex I contains several anomalies. On the one hand, Israel and South Africa were not included in Annex I, even though they arguably qualified as developed countries at the time.[13] On the other hand, Turkey was included in Annexes I and II because of its membership in the OECD, even though, as of 1992, it might equally well have been characterized as a developing country.[14]

When the FCCC was adopted, these anomalies did not occasion significant concern, both because the obligations placed on Annex I and Annex II parties were relatively modest, and because the FCCC made provision for the annexes to evolve, by allowing the annexes to be revised by a three-quarters majority vote (Article 16.2) and expressly calling on the Conference of the Parties (COP) to review the annexes by the end of 1998, 'with a view to taking decisions regarding such amendments to the lists in Annexes I and II as may be appropriate' (Article 4.2 (f)). However, in the ensuing years, the annexes proved remarkably resistant to change, notwithstanding

---

[12] The phrase 'other parties' has two possible meanings in this context. One interpretation is that the phrase refers to the EU, which is a regional economic integration organization (REIO), not a developed *country*. Alternatively, 'other parties' might refer to EITs, some of which objected to being characterized as 'developed', fearing that such a label might subject them to financial or other additional obligations in the future.

[13] Israel is not included in the analogous list of 'Article 5' parties under the Montreal Protocol.

[14] Turkey was subsequently removed from Annex II by an amendment adopted by COP7 and was not given an emissions limitation target under the Kyoto Protocol. See Decision 26/CP.7, 'Amendment to the list in Annex II to the Convention' (21 January 2002) FCCC/CP/2001/13/Add.4, 5.

massive shifts in the world economy, which made many non-Annex I countries richer on a per capita basis than some of the poorest Annex I countries,[15] brought Chile, Korea, and Mexico into the OECD, and resulted in China becoming the world's biggest GHG emitter on an absolute basis (although not on an historical or per capita basis). A few non-controversial amendments were made to Annex I to reflect the breakup of Czechoslovakia and Yugoslavia in the 1990s and the accession of Cyprus and Malta to the European Union (EU) in 2004. But efforts by Annex I countries to add countries whose economies had grown and that, arguably, were no longer 'developing' countries (by 2015, for example, Singapore had become the richest country in the world on a per capita basis), never got off the ground, due to strong opposition by non-Annex I parties, which viewed the division between Annex I and non-Annex I countries as sacrosanct. Even the attempt by Kazakhstan in 1999 to voluntarily join Annex I was opposed by important developing countries.[16] As a result, the FCCC annexes remain essentially the same, even today, as when they were adopted in 1992.

III. PREAMBLE, OBJECTIVE, AND PRINCIPLES (ARTICLES 2 AND 3)

The FCCC includes not only a preamble but also articles setting forth the 'ultimate objective' of the agreement (Article 2) and outlining general principles to guide the parties in implementing its provisions (Article 3).

A. Preamble

Preambles to international agreements generally state the background, purposes, and context of the agreement.[17] The preamble to the FCCC refers to several existing or emerging concepts of international environmental law, including the characterization of climate as the 'common concern of mankind',[18] Principle 21 of the

---

[15] According to the International Monetary Fund's World Economic Outlook database, approximately fifty non-Annex I countries now have a higher per capita income than Ukraine, the poorest Annex I country, seventeen are richer than Russia, and four non-Annex I countries (Qatar, Singapore, Brunei, and the United Arab Emirates) are among the ten richest countries in the world. International Monetary Fund, 'World Economic Outlook Database' (April 2013) <http://www.imf.org/external/pubs/ft/weo/2013/01/weodata/index.aspx> accessed 20 January 2017.

[16] Joanna Depledge, 'The Road Less Travelled: Difficulties in Moving Between Annexes in the Climate Change Regime', *Climate Policy*, 9/3 (2009): 273, 279. Because there was no consensus to amend Annex I to add Kazakhstan, and countries were unwilling to take a vote, Kazakhstan used the alternative procedure of making a unilateral declaration pursuant to Article 4.2(g) of the FCCC, indicating its intent to be bound by the obligations of Annex I parties under Articles 4.2(a) and 4.2(b).

[17] György Haraszti, *Some Fundamental Problems of the Law of Treaties* (Budapest: Akademiai Kiaddo, 1973) 106–7.

[18] The characterization of climate change as a 'common concern of humankind' was first stated in UNGA Res 43/53, 'Protection of global climate for present and future generations of mankind' (6 December 1988) UN Doc A/RES/43/53.

Stockholm Declaration (in the slightly modified form of the Rio Declaration on Environment and Development), and the principle of inter-generational equity.[19]

Several preambular recitals address particular concerns of developing countries. Perhaps the most significant of these is recital 3, which notes 'that the largest share of historical and current global emissions of greenhouse gases has originated in developed countries, that per capita emissions in developing countries are still relatively low and that the share of global emissions originating in developing countries will grow to meet their social and development needs'.[20] While this recital contains much that is helpful to developing countries, it represents a substantial compromise on their part. Developing countries had sought to include the so-called 'main responsibility' principle, which posits that the climate change problem results primarily from the over-consumptive and profligate lifestyles of developed countries, and that developed countries therefore bear the main responsibility for combating it.[21] A version of the main responsibility principle had been included in the General Assembly resolution establishing the INC,[22] but the opening clause of recital 3 reflects only the first half of the principle and is formulated as a neutral factual statement, severed from the corollary that 'developed country parties should take the lead in combating climate change', which appears only later in the convention (in Article 3.1). Similarly, the reference in the second clause to 'per capita emissions' is all that remains of an Indian proposal that the convention should promote the convergence of GHG emissions at a common per capita level.[23] Finally, the concluding clause, referring to the growth in emissions of developing countries, was originally proposed for the principles article rather than the preamble and phrased in mandatory rather than descriptive terms.

The preamble also addresses developing country concerns by:

- Linking the level of response measures to the 'differentiated responsibilities and respective capabilities' of the parties (recital 6).
- Reaffirming the principle of sovereignty (recital 9).
- Recognizing that 'standards applied by some countries may be inappropriate and of unwarranted economic and social cost to other countries, in particular developing countries' (recital 10).

---

[19] For a more general discussion of these principles, see Chapter 2, Section III.

[20] Identical language was proposed for inclusion in the Paris Agreement, but did not make its way into the final text. See Draft Paris Outcome: Revised draft conclusions proposed by the Co-Chairs (5 December 2015) FCCC/ADP/2015/L.6/Rev.1.

[21] The 'main responsibility' principle was first articulated in the Beijing Ministerial Declaration on Environment and Development (adopted 19 June 1991) UN Doc A/CONF.151/PC/85, Annex, para. 7.

[22] UNGA Res 45/212 (n 4) preambular recital 8 ('noting the fact that the largest part of the current emission of pollutants into the environment originates in developed countries, and recognizing therefore that those countries have the main responsibility for combating such pollution').

[23] Report of the Intergovernmental Negotiating Committee for a Framework Convention on Its Fourth Session, 9–20 December 1991 (29 January 1992) A/AC.237/15, Annex II: Consolidated Working Document, Art III.2.

- Taking into 'full account the legitimate priority needs of developing countries for the achievement of sustained economic growth and the eradication of poverty' (recital 21).

- Recognizing that developing countries in particular 'need access to resources in order to achieve sustainable social and economic development' and that, 'in order... to progress towards that goal, their energy consumption will need to grow' (recital 22).

However, the preamble does not include several provisions that developing countries supported but that raised concerns for developed countries, such as references to the need for 'adequate, new and additional financial resources' and transfer of technology on 'preferential, concessional and non-commercial terms'; a paragraph characterizing improvement in the international economic environment as a 'prerequisite' for developing country action to address climate change; and language opposing any new 'conditionality' in aid or development financing.[24]

Other noteworthy provisions of the preamble stress the importance of basing response measures on 'scientific, technical and economic considerations' (recital 16); recognize the 'no regrets' principle (ie that some actions to address climate change can be justified in their own right, independent of the climate change issue) (recital 17); and contain the only surviving reference in the convention to energy efficiency (recital 22).

B. Objective (Article 2)

Article 2 establishes the 'ultimate' objective of the FCCC as the stabilization of GHG concentrations at a safe level—that is, a level that would 'prevent dangerous anthropogenic interference with the climate system'. This level is to be achieved within a time frame that: (1) allows ecosystems to adapt naturally to climate change; (2) ensures that food production is not threatened; and (3) enables economic development to proceed in a sustainable manner.[25]

Four features of this objective are noteworthy. First, it focuses on atmospheric *concentrations* of GHGs, rather than on *emissions*. This focus is justified from a scientific standpoint, since climate change is what economists call a 'stock' rather than a 'flow' problem: it depends on the overall level of GHGs in the atmosphere, rather than on the emissions at any particular point in time.[26] Second, the objective addresses not only concentration levels, but also rates of change. Third, the references to sustainable economic development and food production legitimize the consideration of economic and social as well as environmental factors in addressing climate change. Finally, specifying what concentration level is safe involves value

---

[24] Ibid, preambular recitals 10, 16, and 20.
[25] Michael Oppenheimer and Annie Petsonk, 'Article 2 of the FCCC: Historical Origins, Recent Interpretations', *Climatic Change*, 73/3 (2005): 195.
[26] Glenn W. Harrison, 'Stocks and Flows', in Steven N. Durlauf and Lawrence E. Blume (eds), *The New Palgrave Dictionary of Economics* (Basingstoke, UK: Palgrave Macmillan, 2nd edn, 2008).

judgments, and cannot be answered by science alone. Ultimately, it requires political choices about how to balance economic, social, and environmental factors.

The exact legal status of the convention's stabilization objective is uncertain. Article 2 in its final form uses declarative language and does not characterize the objective as a commitment. Also unclear is whether the Article 2 objective specifies the 'object and purpose' of the FCCC, within the meaning of the Vienna Convention on the Law of Treaties, which precludes reservations that are incompatible with the 'object and purpose' of an agreement, and requires signatories to refrain from actions that would 'defeat the object and purpose' of the agreement.[27] In what may have been an attempt to prevent 'objective' from being equated with 'object and purpose', Article 2 adds the qualification 'ultimate'.

In the twenty years since the FCCC's adoption, parties have still not been able to specify the GHG concentration level that the regime should seek to achieve, pursuant to Article 2. Instead, they have been able to agree only on objectives defined in terms of temperature change and long-term emissions. The 2010 Cancun Agreements set a goal of limiting global warming to no more than 2° C above pre-industrial levels, and provided for a review no later than 2015 to consider strengthening this temperature limit to 1.5° C,[28] the level that small island states argue is necessary to avoid unacceptable risks from sea-level rise. In the 2015 Paris Agreement, states agreed to strengthen this goal to 'well below' 2° C and 'to pursue efforts to limit the temperature increase to 1.5° C above pre-industrial levels'.[29] In addition, they defined medium and long-term emissions objectives, calling for a peaking of global emissions 'as soon as possible' and for net zero emissions in the second half of this century.[30]

C. Principles (Article 3)

1. Background

US was against this

During the negotiation of the FCCC, most developing countries supported the inclusion of an article on general principles, arguing that it would serve as the lodestar or compass to guide the parties in implementing and developing the agreement.[31] Some even argued that the FCCC should include only principles, and leave commitments to future protocols. In contrast, developed countries generally questioned the need for a principles article. The US, in particular, opposed its inclusion, arguing that its legal status would be unclear. If the principles merely stated the intentions of the parties or provided a context for interpreting the FCCC's

[27] Vienna Convention on the Law of Treaties (adopted 23 May 1969, entered into force 27 January 1980) 1155 UNTS 331, Arts 18 and 19.

[28] Cancun Agreements LCA, para 4.

[29] Paris Agreement, Art 2.1(a). For more on the Paris Agreement, see Chapter 7, Section IV.

[30] Ibid, Art 4.1.

[31] An article on general principles was first proposed by China. See INC, Set of informal papers provided by delegations related to the preparation of a Framework Convention on Climate Change (23 July 1991) A/AC.237/Misc.1/Add.4/Rev.1, 3, 4–5.

commitments, the US argued, then they should be included in the preamble rather than in the operative part of the agreement. On the other hand, if the principles were themselves commitments, then they should be designated as such in the convention.

The US reasoning, however, failed to take into account that principles may serve a third function, different from those of either preambles or commitments: unlike preambular paragraphs, principles may embody legal standards, but standards that are more general than commitments and do not specify particular actions.[32] In essence, the principles in the FCCC establish the general framework for the development of the UN climate regime. They provide benchmarks against which to evaluate specific proposals—for example, relating to emissions targets or financial assistance. Some are climate specific, but most reflect more general principles of international law, such as the principle of common but differentiated responsibilities and respective capabilities (CBDRRC), intra- and inter-general equity, and sustainable development.[33]

Although developing countries ultimately prevailed in obtaining the inclusion of a principles article, the US successfully pressed for several changes to reduce its potential legal implications. First, a *chapeau* was added, specifying that the principles are to 'guide' the parties in their actions to achieve the objectives of the convention and to implement its provisions. Second, the term 'states' was replaced by 'parties', in order to forestall arguments that the principles in Article 3 reflect customary international law and bind states generally. Instead, the principles clearly apply only to the parties and only in relation to the FCCC, not as general international law. Finally, the term 'inter alia' was added to the *chapeau* to indicate that Article 3 is not an exhaustive list and that the parties may take into account other relevant principles in developing and implementing the convention.

Developing countries also accepted compromises on the substance of the principles. In some cases, developed country opposition led to the transfer of a proposed principle to the preamble; in other cases, principles proposed by developing countries were not included in the final text at all. In general, developed countries were able to define the principles more narrowly than in the parallel negotiations on the Rio Declaration, possibly because the INC was a less politicized, less public forum than the preparatory committee for the Rio Conference.

2. Principle of common but differentiated responsibilities and respective capabilities

The most widely-cited and -discussed principle of the climate regime is the principle of CBDRRC, which is stated in the preamble and again in Article 3.1.[34] In

---

[32] Ronald Dworkin, *Taking Rights Seriously* (Cambridge, MA: Harvard University Press, 1977) 24–6.

[33] Nicolas De Sadeleer, *Environmental Principles: From Political Slogans to Legal Rules* (Oxford University Press, 2002). For a discussion of these principles, see Chapter 2, Section III.

[34] For a general discussion of CBDRRC, see Chapter 1, Section V.C.

contrast to the Rio Declaration, which bases differentiation only on the different contributions of states to environmental degradation,[35] the FCCC focuses on the respective capabilities of states as well as on their different responsibilities. This was important for some developed countries—the US, in particular. If the different historical contributions of countries to the climate change problem provide the basis for differentiation, as developing countries contended in the FCCC negotiations, then differentiation would change relatively slowly. In contrast, if capabilities provide the basis for differentiation, then a country's obligations could evolve more rapidly, as it develops and gains greater financial, technological, and administrative capabilities.

Although CBDRRC is usually associated with the division between 'developed' and 'developing' countries (and the associated division in the FCCC between Annex I and non-Annex I parties), the FCCC also recognizes other bases of differentiation, including differences between countries in their economic structures and resources bases, available technologies, and other individual circumstances (Article 4.2(a)). Moreover, as noted in Section II.D above, the FCCC differentiates the commitments not only of Annex I and non-Annex I countries, but also of EITs (Article 4.6), and highlights several other categories of countries, including especially vulnerable states (Articles 3.2, 4.8), least-developed states (Article 4.9), and countries that are highly dependent on fossil fuels (Article 4.10).

3. Precaution and cost-effectiveness

The precautionary principle states that where there is a threat of serious or irreversible damage, scientific uncertainty should not be used as a reason to postpone precautionary measures to anticipate, prevent, or minimize the harm. Various formulations of the precautionary principle now appear regularly in international environmental agreements and declarations.[36] In the FCCC negotiations, the main issue was whether to include a reference to 'cost-effectiveness', thereby introducing economic considerations into what would otherwise be a purely environmental standard. The 1990 Second World Climate Conference Ministerial Declaration had spoken of 'cost-effective' precautionary measures,[37] and the G-77/China proposal on principles used a similar formulation. Ultimately, the precautionary principle paragraph was combined with a separate paragraph in the Chair's text on cost-effectiveness.[38] The principle, as adopted, also endorses the comprehensive approach and joint implementation (JI), discussed in Sections IV.B.2 and IV.B.3 of this chapter.

---

[35] Rio Declaration, principle 7.

[36] Daniel Bodansky, 'Deconstructing the Precautionary Principle', in D.D. Caron and H.N. Scheiber (eds), *Bringing New Law to Ocean Waters* (Leiden: Brill, 2004) 381.

[37] Second World Climate Conference Ministerial Declaration, para 7, in Jill Jäger and H.L. Ferguson (eds), *Climate Change: Science, Impacts and Policy – Proceedings of the Second World Climate Conference* (Cambridge University Press, 1991).

[38] Working Papers by the Chairman, A/AC.237/CRP.1 and Adds 1–8 (1992) Art 2.3 (precautionary principle) and Art 2.4 (cost-effectiveness).

4. Sustainable development

The FCCC recognizes in Article 3.4 that states have a right to promote sustainable development. Initially, developing countries proposed language recognizing that 'the right to development is an inalienable human right' and that '[a]ll peoples have an equal right in matters relating to reasonable living standards'.[39] Meanwhile, some developed countries sought to include a principle that states have a duty to aim at sustainable development. Both proposals raised serious problems for some delegations. On the one hand, the US questioned inclusion of the 'right to development', on the grounds that it is vague and could be used by developing countries to demand financial assistance from developed countries.[40] In contrast, developing countries expressed doubts about the concept of 'sustainable development', fearing that 'sustainability' might become a new conditionality on financial assistance and ultimately inhibit their development plans.

Article 3.4 finesses both issues by stating that 'the Parties have a right to, and should, promote sustainable development'. By using the language of 'rights' rather than 'duties', this formulation satisfied developing countries.[41] And by framing the right, not as a 'right to development', but rather as a right to 'promote sustainable development', it satisfied the US as well.

5. Supportive and open economic system

The final principle (Article 3.5) concerns the need for 'a supportive and open international economic system', and addresses in particular the relationship between environmental measures and trade, an increasingly contentious issue (see Chapter 9, Section IV). Article 3.5 reiterates the rule contained in Article XX of the General Agreement on Tariffs and Trade (GATT), which prohibits measures that 'constitute a means of arbitrary or unjustifiable discrimination between countries... or a disguised restriction on international trade'.[42] Like GATT Article XX, Article 3.5 is neutral in effect, since it does not define what types of trade measures constitute 'arbitrary or unjustifiable' discrimination or are a 'disguised restriction' on trade. Thus, it neither condones nor forbids using trade measures, like those contained

[39] INC, Joint Statement of the Group of 77, made by its Chairman (Ghana) at the fourth session of the Intergovernmental Negotiating Committee for a Framework Convention on Climate Change (19 December 1991) A/AC.237/WG.1/L.8. For a discussion of human rights and climate change, see Chapter 9, Section II.

[40] Reflecting this view, the US voted several years earlier against adoption of the UN Declaration on the Right to Development, UNGA Res 41/128, 'Declaration on the Right to Development' (4 December 1986) UN Doc A/RES/41/128.

[41] In addition, Article 3.4 contains a number of caveats that address developing country concerns, including the recognition that environmental policies and measures should be 'appropriate for the specific conditions of each party' and should be integrated with national development plans, and that 'economic development is essential for adopting measures to address climate change'.

[42] General Agreement on Tariffs and Trade (adopted 30 October 1947, entered into force 1 January 1948) 55 UNTS 194, Art XX. For a discussion of Article XX, see Chapter 9, Section IV.

in the Montreal Protocol,[43] to encourage participation in the FCCC or to punish non-compliance.

IV. COMMITMENTS (ARTICLES 4–6 AND 12)

The FCCC sets forth different commitments for different categories of countries, including (1) general commitments that apply to all parties, both developed and developing (Articles 4.1, 5, 6, and 12.1); (2) specific commitments relating to mitigation and reporting that apply only to Annex I parties (Articles 4.2 and 12.2); and (3) specific commitments on financial resources and technology transfer that apply only to Annex II parties (Articles 4.3–4.5). This structure reflects the FCCC's initial premise that developing countries should not have the same commitments as developed countries.

A. General commitments (Articles 4.1, 5, 6, and 12.1)

The general commitments in Articles 4.1, 5, 6, and 12.1 apply to all parties, both developed and developing. An extensive list of general commitments was proposed during the negotiations, including use of best available technology to limit GHG emissions; promotion of energy efficiency and conservation; development of renewable energy sources; promotion of sustainable forest management; removal of subsidies that contribute to global warming; harmonization of national policies, taxes, and efficiency standards; internalization of costs; and development and coordination of market instruments. As the negotiations proceeded, however, these proposals were slowly pared away or watered down, and the general commitments became general not only in their application to all parties, but also in their content. For the most part, the FCCC's general commitments do not compel particular actions. Rather, like the 2015 Paris Agreement, they encourage countries to formulate and implement their own national programs to mitigate climate change (Article 4.1(b)), to cooperate in preparing for adaptation to the impacts of climate change (Article 4.1(d)), to take climate change into account in their existing policies (Article 4.1(f)), to exchange information (Article 4.1(h)), and to promote scientific research, education, training, and public awareness (Articles 4.1(g), 4.1(i), 5, and 6).

Without question, the most significant general commitments in the FCCC relate to national inventories and reporting. Every party, both developed and developing, is required to prepare, periodically update, and publish a national inventory of its emissions by sources and removals by sinks of GHGs, using 'comparable methodologies' to be agreed on by the COP (Article 4.1(a)), and to communicate information to the COP on its inventory and the steps it has taken to implement the convention (Article 12.1).

---

[43] Montreal Protocol, Art 4 (prohibiting trade with non-parties of controlled substances and products containing controlled substances).

The general commitments in Article 4 contain several qualifications to make them acceptable to developing countries. Article 4.1 allows parties, in carrying out their commitments, to 'tak[e] into account their common but differentiated responsibilities and their specific national and regional development priorities, objectives and circumstances'. Moreover, Article 4.7 specifically recognizes that 'the first and overriding priorities' of developing countries are 'economic and social development and poverty eradication'. Developing countries, however, did not succeed in including a provision explicitly making their commitments legally contingent on the provision of adequate financial resources and technology. Instead, Article 4.7 uses more neutral language, stating that developing country performance 'will depend' on the fulfillment of developed country commitments—a formulation that could be interpreted as either asserting a factual rather than a legal dependency (as developed countries do), or as creating a pre-condition to effective performance by developing countries of their commitments (as developing countries do).[44] Similarly, developing countries sought to include language suggesting that they would implement climate change measures only to the extent that the measures were 'without detriment' to their national development goals and policies. As adopted, however, Article 4.7 provides simply that developing country implementation 'will take fully into account' their socio-economic priorities.

B. Mitigation (Articles 4.1(b)–(d) and 4.2)

As noted above, Article 4.1 creates only a general obligation on parties to 'formulate, implement, publish and regularly update national and, where appropriate, regional programmes containing measures to mitigate climate change'. Proposals for more extensive general commitments were rejected by one side or another in the course of the negotiations. Oil-producing states such as Saudi Arabia and Kuwait objected to the stricter regulation of sources, while countries with large forests such as Malaysia and Brazil fought the inclusion of strong commitments relating to sinks. As a result, Article 4.1(c), which addresses emission reduction technologies, makes no mention of energy efficiency measures or renewable energy sources, and places all relevant economic sectors (energy, transport, industry, agriculture, forestry, and waste management) on an equal footing. Similarly, Article 4.1(d), which requires states to promote the sustainable management and enhancement of sinks and reservoirs, fails to single out forests for special consideration. The general commitments in Article 4.1 were also weakened by the omission of proposals to require parties to conduct environmental impact assessments[45] and to 'coordinate' or 'harmonize' economic and administrative instruments, such as taxes, subsidies, and

---

[44] For further discussion of Article 4.7 and similar provisions in other multilateral environmental agreements, see Lavanya Rajamani, 'The Nature, Promise and Limits of Differential Treatment in the Climate Change Regime', *Yearbook of International Environmental Law*, 16 (2007): 81, 103–7.

[45] Instead, Article 4.1(f) lists environmental impact assessment only as one of several possible methods to integrate climate considerations into policymaking.

charges (which was made a specific commitment applicable only to Annex I parties under Article 4.2(e)).

In addition to the general commitments in Article 4.1, Annex I parties also have specific commitments relating to mitigation. First, each Annex I party must adopt national policies and measures to limit GHG emissions and to protect and enhance its sinks and reservoirs, with the goal of returning emissions to 1990 levels by the year 2000 (Article 4.2(a)–(b)). In addition, Annex I parties must coordinate relevant economic and administrative instruments and identify and periodically review their policies and practices that contribute to increased GHG emissions (eg subsidies and energy pricing policies) (Article 4.2(e)).

Three issues dominated the mitigation negotiations: (1) whether to include legally binding, internationally negotiated, quantitative limits on the emissions of developed countries; (2) whether to adopt a 'comprehensive' approach that allows states to address all sources and sinks of GHGs collectively; and (3) whether to allow Annex I countries to get credit for emission reduction projects in developing countries that they undertake or support.

1. Targets and timetables

Perhaps the most controversial issue in the entire FCCC negotiation was whether to include a target and timetable to limit the emissions of developed countries. Although, in common parlance, the term 'target' means an object or goal, in the context of international environmental law it can also refer to a legally binding commitment. A target and timetable creates an obligation to achieve a particular result (the target) by a particular date (the timetable). As an 'obligation of result' rather than an 'obligation of conduct', a target and timetable gives states flexibility in how to implement their international commitment domestically. In 1991, when the FCCC negotiations began, internationally defined targets and timetables had been used in a number of recent environmental agreements, including the 1987 Montreal Protocol, and were viewed by most countries other than the US as the preferred mode of international regulation of GHG emissions. By contrast, obligations of conduct, such as energy efficiency standards or a carbon tax, were discussed only marginally in the FCCC negotiations.

Prior to the initiation of the negotiations in 1991, a number of international conferences had stressed the need to stabilize emissions as soon as possible, and in the INC, most Western states pressed vigorously for the adoption of an internationally-defined stabilization target, particularly for CO_2 emissions. For example, the EU supported a commitment by developed countries to stabilize CO_2 emissions at 1990 levels by the year 2000, while Canada, Australia, and New Zealand proposed a stabilization target for all GHGs not controlled by the Montreal Protocol.[46] The main holdout against the adoption of an emissions stabilization target was the US, which criticized the EU proposal as rigid and inequitable, given the differences

---

[46] Consolidated Working Document (n 23) Art IV.2.1(b), Alternative A1.

between countries in national circumstances and implementation costs. The US was supported by Japan, which preferred a 'best efforts' approach rather than a binding emissions target, and proposed the 'pledge and review' formula at the June 1991 session of the INC.

Through the mediation of the United Kingdom, the US and the EU ultimately reached a compromise, reflected in two highly convoluted subparagraphs of Article 4.2. Article 4.2(a) obliquely articulates a timetable for reducing emissions, by 'recognizing' that 'the return by the end of the present decade [ie the year 2000] to earlier levels of...emissions...would contribute to the modification' of developed country emissions trends. Meanwhile, Article 4.2(b) suggests an emissions target, by requiring Annex I parties to communicate information on their policies and measures, 'with the aim of returning individually or jointly' to 1990 emissions levels. Together, the two paragraphs are usually interpreted as establishing a non-binding quasi-target and -timetable to return emissions to 1990 levels by the year 2000. Whether these nebulous provisions actually did establish a target and timetable is an interesting theoretical question, but the question is now moot, since the putative target and timetable addressed emissions only through the year 2000 and has now expired. Moreover, even while it was in effect, the target and timetable was non-binding, since it was expressed as an 'aim' rather than a legal requirement. Binding or not, the target was nonetheless met, according to data compiled by the FCCC secretariat, which show that total GHG emissions of Annex I countries declined by 3% from 1990 to 2000.[47] This decline, however, resulted primarily from the lower emissions of Russia and the other EITs, whose economies collapsed in the 1990s following the fall of communism, rather than from the FCCC.

2. *Comprehensive approach*

The so-called 'comprehensive approach' provides that climate change mitigation should address all sources and sinks of GHGs collectively. Under the comprehensive approach, global warming potentials (GWPs) are calculated for each GHG to permit emissions of different gases to be compared according to a single CO_2-equivalent (CO_2e) metric. States may then take measures to limit their net contribution to the greenhouse effect, either by controlling their aggregate CO_2e emissions or by enhancing their removal of GHGs by sinks.

In the negotiations, supporters of the comprehensive approach—which included the US, Canada, Australia, New Zealand, and most Nordic countries—justified it on both economic and environmental grounds. Economically, the comprehensive approach allows states to choose which gases and sinks to focus on, so that they can determine for themselves which mitigation measures are most cost-effective. Environmentally, it eliminates incentives to switch from one type of polluting

---

[47] Subsidiary Body for Implementation (SBI), National Communications from Parties included in Annex I to the Convention: Compilation and Synthesis of Third National Communications (16 May 2003) FCCC/SBI/2003/7, 4, para 11.

activity to another, by focusing on aggregate levels of GHG emissions, rather than on any specific gas, sink, or sector.[48]

Most delegations accepted the theoretical merits of the comprehensive approach, and it is mentioned favorably in both the preamble and Article 3 of the FCCC. In the context of targets and timetables, however, some delegations argued that the comprehensive approach was not feasible because of insufficient knowledge both about sources of GHGs other than carbon dioxide (CO_2) and about removals of GHGs by sinks.

Article 4.2 refers to 'levels of anthropogenic emissions of CO_2 and other greenhouse gases not controlled by the Montreal Protocol', without specifying whether emissions levels of GHGs should be considered collectively or whether each gas should be accounted for separately. In any event, Article 4.2 is notable both for singling out CO_2 and for clearly excluding GHGs controlled by the Montreal Protocol. Article 4.2 also does not fully resolve the question of whether the FCCC should focus on gross emissions or net emissions (subtracting removals by sinks). On the one hand, it refers several times to 'emissions by sources and removals by sinks' as a package; on the other hand, its quasi-target and timetable relates only to emissions.

3. Joint implementation

GHGs remain in the atmosphere for a long time and migrate globally, so the location of emissions reductions makes little difference to climate change. This suggests a further extension of the comprehensive approach: namely, allowing countries to implement their mitigation commitments through emissions reductions in another country, through market mechanisms such as JI or emissions trading.

In the FCCC negotiations, the primary question concerning market mechanisms was their geographic scope—whether to allow JI only among Annex I parties, which have emissions reduction targets, or whether to allow it on a general basis, encompassing both non-Annex I and Annex I parties.[49] This last option drew the greatest criticism, both because of the difficulties of determining the baseline against which to measure emissions reductions in developing countries, and because many believed it would be unethical to allow a developed state to achieve its emissions reduction commitments in a developing country instead of taking responsibility at home.[50]

The FCCC provides for flexibility to a limited degree, under the rubric of JI. Article 3.3 states that '[e]fforts to address climate change may be carried out

---

[48] Richard B. Stewart and Jonathan B. Wiener, 'The Comprehensive Approach to Global Climate Policy: Issues of Design and Practicability', *Arizona Journal of International and Comparative Law*, 9/1 (1992): 83.

[49] In the Kyoto Protocol, the first option became Articles 6 and 17, which allow joint implementation and emissions trading among Annex I parties, and the second option became Article 12, which creates the Clean Development Mechanism.

[50] These same issues were prominent in the Kyoto Protocol negotiations, discussed in Chapter 6.

cooperatively by interested Parties', and Article 4.2(a) permits states to 'implement...policies and measures jointly with other Parties'. Since these provisions do not restrict which states may participate in JI, they leave open the possibility of JI between developed and developing countries.

In practice, JI has played only a limited role under the FCCC. In Decision 5/CP.1, which launched a 'pilot phase' of 'activities implemented jointly' (AIJ), the COP significantly circumscribed JI, by agreeing (1) that activities implemented jointly between Annex I and non-Annex parties would 'not be seen as fulfillment of current commitments of Annex I Parties under Article 4.2(b)', and (2) that JI activities are 'supplemental, and should be treated as a subsidiary means of achieving the objective of the convention'.[51] Under the pilot phase of AIJ, only 157 projects were initiated, none since 2002.[52] Instead, most 'joint implementation' has been undertaken under the Kyoto Protocol, either through Article 6, which allows JI among Annex I countries, or Article 12, which allows joint implementation between Annex I and non-Annex I countries through the Clean Development Mechanism.[53] As discussed in Chapter 7, the Paris Agreement also authorizes the use of market mechanisms, by recognizing that states may use 'internationally transferred mitigation outcomes' in achieving their nationally determined contributions, and by creating a new market mechanism.[54]

C. Adaptation (Articles 4.1(b) and (e), 4.8, and 4.9)

Mitigation and adaptation are, in theory, on an equal footing in the UN climate regime. Nevertheless, the FCCC contains relatively few provisions on adaptation. Article 3.3 articulates the principle that policies and measures relating to climate change should be comprehensive and address adaptation. Article 4.1(b) creates a general commitment to 'formulate, implement, publish and regularly update national and, where appropriate, regional programmes containing...measures to facilitate adequate adaptation to climate change'. Article 4.1(e) creates a general commitment to cooperate in preparing for adaptation to the impacts of climate change. Article 4.4 imposes an obligation on Annex II countries to 'assist the developing country Parties that are particularly vulnerable to the adverse effects of climate change in meeting the costs of adaptation to those adverse effects'. And Articles 4.8 and 4.9 focus attention on developing states that are particularly vulnerable to the adverse effects of climate change, including low-lying and small island states, least developed states, developing states with fragile mountain ecosystems, and states prone to drought and desertification.

---

[51] Decision 5/CP.1, 'Activities implemented jointly under the pilot phase' (6 June 1995) FCCC/CP/1995/7/Add.1, 18, preambular recitals 4(b) and 4(c).

[52] Subsidiary Body for Scientific and Technological Advice (SBSTA), Activities Implemented Jointly under the Pilot Phase: Seventh Synthesis Report (13 September 2006) FCCC/SBSTA/2006/8.

[53] For a discussion of the Kyoto Protocol's market mechanisms, see Chapter 6, Section V.

[54] Paris Agreement, Art 6. For a discussion of the Paris Agreement's market mechanisms, see Chapter 7, Section VI.

Most of the work under the UN climate regime to address the issue of adaptation has occurred since the FCCC's adoption, through decisions of the parties, focusing primarily on adaptation planning and assistance. In 2001, the Marrakesh COP adopted the least developed countries (LDC) work programme,[55] which:

- Provided for the preparation by LDCs of national adaptation programmes of action (NAPAs).[56]

- Established a least developed country group of experts to provide technical guidance to LDCs in the preparation of NAPAs.[57]

- Created two new funds focusing on adaptation, the Least Developed Countries Fund (LDCF) and the Special Climate Change Fund (SCCF).[58]

- Authorized the Global Environment Facility (GEF) and the LDCF to provide support for the preparation and implementation of NAPAs.[59]

The first NAPA was submitted by Mauritania in November 2004 and, as of January 2017, fifty-one LDCs had completed NAPAs. Submitting a NAPA is a prerequisite for receiving assistance from the LDCF for implementation activities.

In 2006, COP12 (dubbed by some the 'Adaptation COP') adopted the Nairobi work programme on impacts, vulnerability, and adaptation to climate change (NWP), to help developing countries make better informed decisions about possible policy responses.[60] The NWP was originally intended to involve a five-year study by the Subsidiary Body for Scientific and Technological Advice (SBSTA), but was extended in 2010 and, as of October 2016, was still ongoing, with the SBSTA now focused on how the NWP can assist in the implementation of the Paris Agreement.[61]

In 2011, COP16 adopted the Cancun Adaptation Framework (CAF),[62] which establishes an Adaptation Committee and provides for the formulation and implementation by LDCs of national adaptation plans (NAPs), building on their experience with NAPAs. The Adaptation Committee is comprised of sixteen members serving in their personal capacity, nominated by the parties and elected by the COP.

---

[55] Decision 5/CP.7, 'Implementation of Article 4, paragraphs 8 and 9 of the Convention' (21 January 2002) FCCC/CP/2001/13/Add.1, 32, para 11.

[56] Decision 28/CP.7, 'Guidelines for the preparation of national adaptation programmes of action' (21 January 2002) FCCC/CP/2001/13/Add.4, 7.

[57] Decision 29/CP.7, 'Establishment of a least developed countries expert group' (21 January 2002) FCCC/CP/2001/13/Add.4, 14.

[58] Decision 7/CP.7, 'Funding under the Convention' (21 January 2002) FCCC/CP/2001/13/Add.1, 43.

[59] Decision 6/CP.7, 'Additional guidance to an operating entity of the financial mechanism' (21 January 2002) FCCC/CP/2001/13/Add.1, 40, para 1(a).

[60] Report of Subsidiary Body for Scientific and Technological Advice on its Twenty-Fifth Session, held at Nairobi from 6 to 14 November 2006 (1 February 2007) FCCC/SBSTA/2006/11, paras 11–71. The five-year work programme was initiated at COP11 by Decision 2/CP.11, and was renamed the NWP at COP12.

[61] SBSTA, Nairobi work programme on impacts, vulnerability and adaptation to climate change, Draft conclusions proposed by the Chair (24 May 2016) FCCC/SBSTA/2016/L.9, para 6.

[62] Cancun Agreements LCA, paras 11–35.

At the urging of small island and least developed states, the CAF also established a work program on 'loss and damage' resulting from climate change in particularly vulnerable developing countries.[63] Loss and damage refers generally to the negative impacts of climate change on vulnerable states. There is a distinction between loss and damage in that 'loss' refers to 'negative impacts in relation to which reparation or restoration is impossible', while 'damage' refers to 'negative impacts in relation to which reparation or restoration is possible'.[64] Loss and damage has been a highly controversial issue in the UN climate regime, because it raises the prospect of financial compensation for adverse climate change impacts—for example, through insurance or legal liability—which the US and other developed countries strongly oppose. One particular problem in addressing loss and damage is attributing particular losses and damages to anthropogenic climate change, as opposed to, say, natural variability, lack of resilience, or poor institutional planning.[65] At the 2013 Warsaw COP, parties established the Warsaw International Mechanism for Loss and Damage Associated with Climate Change Impacts (WIM).[66] A key issue at the time was whether loss and damage should be addressed as part of adaptation or as a distinct issue.[67] Some believe that loss and damage goes well beyond adaptation, and touches on issues of liability and compensation, while others sought to keep the issue of loss and damage contained within the less-contentious framework of adaptation. The decision establishing the WIM placed it under the CAF, but recognized that loss and damage 'in some cases involves more than that which can be reduced by adaptation',[68] and called for a review of the mechanism in 2016. The Paris Agreement also includes an article addressing the issue of loss and damage.[69]

D. Financial support (Articles 4.3 and 4.4)

The FCCC establishes the basic financial commitments of states under the UN climate regime, as well as a financial mechanism for the provision of resources (discussed in Section V.E below). Since the FCCC's adoption, these core financial provisions have been supplemented by decisions of the parties, which have established new climate-related funds, specified the types of projects eligible to receive assistance, and adopted overall political goals concerning the magnitude of funding.

---

[63] Ibid, para 26.

[64] SBI, A literature review on the topics in the context of thematic area 2 of the work programme on loss and damage: a range of approaches to address loss and damage associated with the adverse effects of climate change (15 November 2012) FCCC/SBI/2012/INF.14, para 2.

[65] Mike Hulme, 'Can (and Should) "Loss and Damage" Be Attributed to Climate Change?' (Fletcher Forum of World Affairs, 27 February 2013) <http://www.fletcherforum.org/home/2016/8/22/can-and-should-loss-and-damage-be-attributed-to-climate-change?rq=mike%20hulme> accessed 20 January 2017.

[66] Decision 2/CP.19, 'Warsaw International Mechanism for Loss and Damage Associated with Climate Change Impacts' (31 January 2014) FCCC/CP/2013/10/Add.1, 6.

[67] Karen Elizabeth McNamara, 'Exploring Loss and Damage at the International Climate Change Talks', *International Journal of Disaster Risk Science*, 5/3 (2014): 242.

[68] Decision 2/CP.19 (n 66) preambular recital 4.

[69] Paris Agreement, Art 8. See Chapter 7, Section VIII.

The basic financial commitments of the UN climate regime are established in Articles 4.3 and 4.4 of the FCCC, which require Annex II parties to provide financial resources to developing countries for three general purposes: (1) to prepare emissions inventories and national reports; (2) to implement measures to reduce emissions; and (3) to meet the costs of adapting to the adverse effects of climate change (for example, by building sea walls or developing drought-resistant crops). The FCCC negotiations focused primarily on the first two purposes—funding for reporting and mitigation—and decided to include a provision on adaptation financing only in the final stage of the negotiations. This emphasis on reporting and mitigation rather than on adaptation is not surprising. Financing emissions reduction measures by developing countries serves the interests, at least to some degree, of developed countries, since mitigation provides global benefits. In contrast, adaptation measures generate primarily local benefits, so developed countries have less incentive to fund adaptation measures in developing states.

In contrast to the specific commitments of Annex I parties on mitigation and reporting, which are expressed as individual commitments of 'each Annex I party', the financial and technology commitments set forth in Articles 4.3–4.5 are expressed as collective commitments of 'the developed country Parties and other developed Parties included in Annex II'.[70] As a result, it is unclear whether individual Annex II parties have specific obligations relating to finance and technology. Moreover, Article 4.3 does not mandate any particular level of funding or provide for assessed contributions. Instead, it simply stresses the 'need for adequacy and predictability in the flow of funds and the importance of appropriate burden sharing among the developed country Parties'—a formulation that allows each Annex II party to determine for itself the size of its own financial contribution.

Instead of seeking specific minimum sums, some developing countries sought a more general commitment by developed countries to provide 'adequate, new and additional' financial resources, in order to preclude developed countries from diverting money from existing development aid (usually referred to as Official Development Assistance, or ODA). In the INC, developed countries were ultimately willing to accept language in Article 4.3 requiring the provision of 'new and additional' financial resources, although the US opposed this formulation until near the end of the negotiations.

Article 4.3 distinguishes between the financial commitments of Annex II parties relating to reporting and mitigation. Developing countries were most immediately concerned with the costs of reporting, because those were their only definite costs of joining the FCCC. Annex II countries were amenable to underwriting these costs fully, both because they wanted developing countries to develop and publish emissions inventories and reports, and because the costs of doing so are relatively low. Accordingly, Article 4.3 provides that Annex II parties will provide 'new and

---

[70] For example, Article 4.3 uses the formulation, 'they [Annex II parties] shall...provide...financial resources', rather than, 'each Annex II party shall provide financial resources'.

additional' financial resources to pay for the 'agreed full costs' of reporting pursuant to Article 12.1.

In contrast, Article 4.3 provides more limited funding for the costs of mitigation measures by developing states, since these costs are open-ended and potentially huge. Annex II countries, particularly the US and the United Kingdom, wanted to ensure that, in joining the convention, they were not writing a blank check. They did so by insisting, first, that the obligation in Article 4.3 to provide assistance for mitigation was only for projects to which the FCCC's financial mechanism agreed and, second, that the convention's financial mechanism be entrusted to the GEF, where donor countries have a significant voice.

In addition, Article 4.3 provides that financial assistance should cover only the 'incremental' costs of mitigation measures under Article 4.1, rather than the 'full' costs, as is the case for developing country inventories and reports. The convention does not define 'incremental costs', but the GEF did so in a 1996 policy paper, which defined incremental costs as the 'additional...costs on countries beyond the costs that are strictly necessary for achieving their own development goals, but nevertheless generate additional benefits that the world as a whole can share'.[71] Although this concept is clear, identifying the incremental costs of a project can be very difficult in practice, since, for many types of actions, there is no clear baseline of ordinary costs from which to measure the additional costs of generating global environmental benefits.

Adaptation assistance is addressed in Article 4.4 of the convention, which is quite brief and establishes only a weak obligation on Annex II parties. During the negotiations, AOSIS had proposed that the convention establish an insurance fund that would provide compensation for damages suffered as a result of sea-level rise, but this proposal was successively whittled down, and the only remaining trace in the FCCC is a reference in Article 4.8 to insurance as one of the possible measures to meet the specific needs and concerns of developing countries. In its place, AOSIS succeeded during the closing days of the negotiations in adding Article 4.4, which provides that developed countries 'shall also assist the developing country Parties that are particularly vulnerable to the adverse effects of climate change in meeting costs of adaptation to those adverse effects'.

Articles 4.3 and 4.4 provide for funding by Annex II countries of 'developing country' costs, rather than non-Annex I country costs. During the negotiations, the US suggested that EITs be eligible to receive financial assistance, but this proposal received little support, even from EITs themselves. Instead, eastern European states were satisfied with an exemption from any obligation to provide financial resources, through their exclusion from Annex II.

The only source of financial resources contemplated under Articles 4.3 and 4.4 is public funds. Prior to the negotiations, the 1988 Toronto Conference Statement had proposed raising money for climate change measures by imposing a levy on

---

[71] Global Environment Facility, 'Incremental Costs' (29 February 1996) GEF/C.7/Inf.5, 3.

fossil fuel consumption.[72] In the INC, however, there was little discussion of creating an automatic mechanism to generate financial resources, such as a carbon tax, emissions fees, or fines. Instead, the FCCC provides only for contributions by states, either through the convention's financial mechanism or 'through bilateral, regional, or other multilateral channels' (Article 11.5). In contrast, the voluntary pledge by developed countries in the Copenhagen Accord to mobilize $100 billion per year by 2020—extended to 2025 by the 2015 Paris COP decision—explicitly applies to a 'wide variety of sources', including both public and private sources, as well as 'alternative sources of finance'.[73]

E. Technology transfer (Article 4.5)

Technology cooperation and transfer is closely related to the issue of financial resources. In the FCCC negotiations, delegations generally agreed on the importance of technology transfer and on the need to view technology broadly, including 'know-how' as well as hardware. The debates centered instead on the terms of technology transfer. Developing countries sought a commitment by developed countries to transfer technology on 'concessional and preferential terms', arguing that they need access to environmentally sound technologies at an affordable cost. Some developing countries even suggested that the convention provide for assured access to technology or compulsory licensing.[74] In contrast, developed countries emphasized technology 'cooperation' rather than 'transfer' and the need to protect intellectual property rights in order to preserve incentives for innovation. Most developed countries were willing to agree only to the transfer of technology on 'fair and most favorable terms'.

In the end, developing states accepted a quite modest provision on technology transfer, which does not define the terms on which transfers will occur. Instead, Article 4.5 requires developed countries 'to take all practicable steps to promote, facilitate and finance, as appropriate, the transfer of, or access to, environmentally sound technologies and know-how to other Parties', and to support the 'development and enhancement of endogenous capacities and technologies of developing country Parties'.

The FCCC did not create any institution focusing specifically on technology transfer. Most delegations felt, at the time, that it would be more efficient to have a single institution addressing both financial resources and technology transfer, and focused their attention on the role of the financial mechanism in technology

---

[72] Proceedings of the World Conference on the Changing Atmosphere: Implications for Global Security, held in Toronto from 27 to 30 June 1988 (1988) WMO Doc. 710.

[73] Copenhagen Accord, para 8; Decision 1/CP.21, 'Adoption of the Paris Agreement' (29 January 2016) FCCC/CP/2015/10/Add.1, para 53.

[74] INC, Set of informal papers provided by delegations, related to the preparation of a Framework Convention on Climate Change (22 October 1991) A/AC.237/Misc.1/Add.15, 3 (submission of Ghana on behalf of the G-77).

transfer, rather than on proposals to establish a separate technology mechanism or clearinghouse.

Most of the current system relating to technology transfer was thus established through decisions of the parties, rather than by the FCCC directly. In 2001, COP7 adopted a framework for technology transfer, consisting of three components: technology needs assessments, a technology information clearing house, and capacity-building.[75] In 2008, COP14 adopted the Poznan Strategic Program on Technology Transfer, which was developed by the GEF and focuses on technology needs assessments, pilot technology projects, and dissemination of successfully demonstrated technologies.[76] Two years later, COP16 established the Technology Mechanism, consisting of a policy-oriented Technology Executive Committee (comprised of twenty high-level experts) and a Climate Technology Centre and Network hosted by a UNEP-led consortium of institutions.[77] The Paris Agreement incorporates the Technology Mechanism and establishes a technology framework to give it 'overarching guidance'.[78]

F. Transparency (Articles 4.1(a) and 12)

As noted above, each party must prepare and communicate an emissions inventory and report in general terms on its steps to implement the convention (Article 12.1). In addition, Annex I parties must report in detail on their implementation measures and Annex II parties must report on their transfers of financial resources and technology (Article 12.2). The FCCC's provisions relating to reporting and review are further discussed in Section VI.B below.

V. INSTITUTIONS (ARTICLES 7–11)

When climate change first emerged as a policy issue in the late 1980s, some leaders felt that it required the development of supranational bodies, with authority to adopt and enforce international regulatory standards to limit GHG emissions. At the 1989 Hague Conference, seventeen heads of state called for the establishment of 'new institutional authority' to address climate change, with power to make decisions even when 'unanimous agreement has not been achieved'.[79] This radical proposal was never pursued in the FCCC negotiations, however. Instead, the FCCC relies on more traditional types of international institutions, which are essentially inter-governmental rather than supra-national in nature and play a primarily coordinating and facilitative role.

---

[75] Decision 4/CP.7, 'Development and transfer of technologies' (21 January 2002) FCCC/CP/2001/13/Add.1, 22.

[76] Decision 2/CP.14, 'Development and transfer of technologies' (18 March 2009) FCCC/CP/2008/7/Add.1.

[77] Cancun Agreements LCA, para 117.   [78] Paris Agreement, Arts 10.3 and 10.4.

[79] Hague Declaration on the Environment (11 March 1989) (1989) 28 ILM 1308.

The FCCC establishes or defines five institutions: (a) a COP, (b) a secretariat, (c) a SBSTA, (d) a Subsidiary Body for Implementation (SBI), and (e) a financial mechanism. During the negotiations, delegations generally agreed on the need for both a COP to provide general policy review and guidance, and a secretariat to provide technical support. However, they differed about what additional bodies to create. Developed states generally supported establishing subsidiary bodies with technical functions relating to science and implementation, but not a new climate fund, which they feared might be controlled by developing countries. In contrast, developing states, led by India and China, sought to establish a climate fund, but questioned the need for subsidiary bodies on science and implementation. They feared that developed country experts would dominate the convention's machinery and use it to intrude on their sovereignty, by reviewing their national policies and actions.

The FCCC reflects a compromise between these two contrasting perspectives. It creates two subsidiary bodies, as developed countries proposed—one to provide scientific and technological advice and the other to facilitate implementation—but makes their membership consist of government representatives rather than independent experts. In addition, it defines a financial mechanism, as developing countries proposed, but provisionally entrusts its operation to an existing institution, the GEF. The more ambitious ideas raised in the FCCC negotiations did not come to fruition until almost two decades later, in the 2010 Cancun Agreements, which established a Green Climate Fund (GCF) and a Technology Mechanism, and adopted procedures for international consultation, assessment, and review.[80]

A. Conference of the Parties (Article 7)

COPs have become the most distinctive type of international environmental institution.[81] Virtually every multilateral agreement establishes a COP, which meets on a periodic basis (in the case of the FCCC COP, annually) and serves as the 'supreme' decision-making body of the treaty regime (Article 7.2). Notable climate COPs include COP3 in 1997, which adopted the Kyoto Protocol; COP7 in 2001, which adopted the Marrakesh Accords; COP15 in 2009, which served as the venue for negotiating the Copenhagen Accord; COP16 in 2010, which adopted the Cancun Agreements; and COP21 in 2015, which adopted the Paris Agreement.

The COP's primary functions are to make the decisions necessary to promote the implementation of the convention, and to review the convention's effectiveness. Formally, COP decisions are not legally binding, except in cases where the COP is acting under express authority given to it by the FCCC—for example, to define

---

[80] Cancun Agreements LCA, paras 44, 63, 100, 102, and 117.
[81] See generally Robin C. Churchill and Geir Ulfstein, 'Autonomous Institutional Arrangements in Multilateral Environmental Agreements: A Little-Noticed Phenomenon in International Law', *American Journal of International Law*, 94/4 (2000): 623. This section and the next draw on Bodansky, *Art and Craft of International Environmental Law* (n 1) 119–22.

methodologies for calculating national emissions of GHGs (Article 4.1(a)).[82] Instead, to create new legal obligations, the COP must adopt a protocol or amendment to the convention, which then requires acceptance by states before it enters into force (Articles 15–17). Nevertheless, the COP has significant authority. It can review the adequacy of existing commitments and decide to initiate new negotiations, as it did in the Berlin Mandate in 1995, the Bali Action Plan in 2007, and the Durban Platform in 2011. It can establish new bodies such as the GCF and the Technology Mechanism. And it can define new procedures such as those for 'international consultation and analysis' (ICA), which were adopted by COP17 in Durban.[83] Moreover, the COP serves as the central forum for consideration of the climate change issue, focuses public attention on the problem, and helps bring peer and public pressure on states to comply with and strengthen their commitments under the convention.

The FCCC provides that the COP shall adopt its rules of procedure by consensus (Article 7.3), but after almost twenty-five years, this has still proved impossible, due to disagreements about whether the COP's voting rule should provide for two-thirds majority voting or consensus.[84] As a result, the COP continues to operate under draft rules of procedure and, in the absence of any agreed voting rule, requires consensus in order to make decisions.[85]

B. Secretariat (Article 8)

In addition to a regular meeting of the parties, most international environmental regimes have recognized the utility of a permanent secretariat. Treaty secretariats serve a variety of functions, ranging from the provision of administrative support for intergovernmental meetings to more substantive roles such as commissioning studies, setting agendas, compiling and analyzing data, providing technical expertise, mediating between states, making compromise proposals, monitoring compliance, and providing financial and technical assistance.[86]

---

[82] Jutta Brunnée, 'COPing with Consent: Law-Making under Multilateral Environmental Agreements', *Leiden Journal of International Law*, 15/1 (2002): 1; Lavanya Rajamani, 'The Devilish Details: Key Legal Issues in the 2015 Climate Negotiations', *Modern Law Review*, 78/5 (2015): 826, 839–40. For more on the law-making role of COPs, see Chapter 3, Section II.D.3.

[83] Decision 2/CP.17, 'Outcome of the work of the Ad Hoc Working Group on Long-term Cooperative Action under the Convention' (15 March 2012) FCCC/CP/2011/9/Add.1, Annex IV.

[84] FCCC, Draft Rules of Procedure of the Conference of the Parties and Its Subsidiary Bodies (22 May 1996) FCCC/CP/1996/2, 2, Rule 42.

[85] For a discussion of the consensus rule, see Chapter 3, Section II.B.2.

[86] On environmental secretariats, see Bharat H. Desai, *Multilateral Environmental Agreements: Legal Status of the Secretariats* (Cambridge University Press, 2013); Steffen Bauer, 'Does Bureaucracy Really Matter? The Authority of Intergovernmental Treaty Secretariats in Global Environmental Politics', *Global Environmental Politics,* 6/1 (2006): 23; Rosemary Sandford, 'International Environmental Treaty Secretariats: Stage-Hands or Actors?', in Helge Ole Bergesen and Georg Parmann (eds), *Green Globe Yearbook of International Cooperation on Environment and Development 1994* (Oxford University Press, 1994) 17–19. For a survey of multilateral environmental agreement secretariats, see Secretary-General's High-Level Panel on UN System-Wide Coherence in the Areas of Development, Humanitarian Assistance, and the Environment, 'Basic Information on Secretariats of Multilateral

In the FCCC negotiations, the principal issue regarding the secretariat was the scope of its authority. Some commentators and delegations suggested a broad role for the secretariat in monitoring compliance, modeled on the verification functions of the International Atomic Energy Agency. However, most delegations preferred to establish a secretariat with strictly administrative functions. Some even raised questions about the scope of the secretariat's power to prepare reports, fearing that the secretariat's reports might reflect adversely on particular parties. Thus, Article 8 authorizes the secretariat to perform administrative tasks, such as arranging for sessions of the COP, facilitating assistance to parties in preparing their reports, compiling reports submitted to it by others, and coordinating with secretariats established under other international agreements. But it does not authorize the secretariat to play a compliance function, for example, by collecting data or by reviewing or reporting on the implementation by parties of the FCCC.

C. Subsidiary Body for Scientific and Technological Advice (Article 9)

Although the FCCC provides that decisions by the COP are to be based on the best available scientific information, not all states were convinced of the merits of establishing a new scientific body. Some developing countries contended that the IPCC could adequately provide scientific assessments and advice to the COP. In response, developed states argued that a new committee would help keep politics out of the IPCC, and serve as a useful interface between outside scientific groups and the FCCC's institutions. During the negotiations, it seemed at times that these differences would preclude the establishment of a science body. In the end, however, Article 9 established SBSTA and specified its composition and functions.

SBSTA is open to all parties and is composed of government representatives 'competent in the relevant field of expertise' (Article 9.1). AOSIS and some European states had preferred a more independent group of experts with limited membership. However, most developing countries insisted on making SBSTA a meeting of government representatives, and the US argued that an open-ended, inter-governmental group would best be able to serve as a liaison between primarily scientific bodies (such as the IPCC) and the politically-oriented COP. As a concession to developing countries, who were particularly concerned about technology development and transfer, the mandate of SBSTA includes technological as well as scientific matters. Among other issues, the SBSTA has played a significant role in providing scientific and technological advice on adaptation, reductions in emissions from deforestation and forest degradation, technology transfer, and emissions inventory guidelines.

D. Subsidiary Body for Implementation (Article 10)

Article 10 establishes the SBI. Initially, it appeared possible that states would agree to establish an implementation committee with authority to review implementation by individual parties. Indeed, Austria suggested giving the new institution quasi-adjudicative authority to resolve questions regarding a country's compliance with the convention. However, a number of developing countries, in particular India and China, objected strongly to international review of their national policies, and threatened to block the adoption of the convention if it provided for an implementation committee.

An eleventh-hour compromise that narrowly defined the powers of the implementation body broke the impasse. Article 10 gives SBI authority only to assess 'the overall aggregated effect of the steps taken by the Parties', not the steps taken by individual developing states to implement the convention. Like SBSTA, SBI's membership is open-ended and consists of government representatives who are expert on matters related to climate change. In addition to addressing budgetary and administrative matters, SBI has played a particularly important role in developing the system of monitoring, reporting, and verification established by the Cancun Agreements, discussed in Sections VI.B and VI.C below.

E. Financial mechanism (Articles 11 and 21.3)

Beside the targets and timetable issue (see Section IV.B.1 above), the FCCC's financial mechanism was perhaps the most controversial issue in the negotiations. The basic question was whether the FCCC should establish a new financial institution—a so-called 'climate' or 'green' fund—or channel financial assistance through the GEF, which was established in 1991 by the World Bank, United Nations Development Programme, and United Nations Environment Programme (UNEP) to fund projects in developing countries that provide global environmental benefits. On one side, developed countries did not wish to entrust their money to a new and untested institution, potentially under the sway of developing countries. Instead, they argued that the GEF should serve as the financial mechanism for the convention. On the other side, developing countries argued that channeling financial assistance through existing development institutions such as the World Bank would be inappropriate, because donor countries dominate these institutions. Developing countries opposed the GEF in particular, arguing that its decision-making was not transparent (since at the time the FCCC was negotiated, non-governmental organizations had no right of access to documents and meetings) or democratic (since the World Bank, which at the time chaired and administered the GEF, uses a system of weighted voting). Instead, developing countries proposed establishing a completely new institution that would operate under the collective authority of the FCCC parties.

In the end, developed and developing countries agreed on a compromise solution that neither established a new institution nor conclusively designated the GEF as the convention's financial mechanism. Instead, the convention simply 'defines' a financial mechanism by setting forth the mechanism's general characteristics and governance (Article 11), and then entrusts the operation of the financial mechanism on an interim basis to the GEF (Article 21). This compromise left open the possibility of creating a new institution, which the parties finally did almost twenty years later at COP16 in Cancun, when they established the GCF as a separate operating entity of the FCCC's financial mechanism.[87]

An important issue in the FCCC negotiations involved the relationship between the COP and the financial mechanism. Developed states wished to maintain the autonomy of the GEF, particularly in deciding which projects to fund, while developing countries wanted the financial mechanism to be under the 'authority' or 'supervision' of the COP. Article 11 resolves this difference by distinguishing between general policy guidance and specific funding decisions. It provides that the COP is to decide on policies, programme priorities, and eligibility criteria, but does not give the COP decision-making authority in project selection. Instead, Article 11 provides only that the COP and the financial mechanism agree on modalities 'to ensure that the funded projects...are in conformity with the policies, programme priorities', and eligibility criteria established by the Conference of the Parties', as well as on modalities by which funding decisions may be 'reconsidered'. Article 11 does provide that the financial mechanism is to be 'accountable to the COP'—a term that suggests something between 'authority' and 'guidance'.

As noted above, Article 21 designates the GEF as the convention's interim financial mechanism. In order to meet the requirements of Article 11, which requires the financial mechanism to have 'an equitable and balanced representation of all parties within a transparent system of governance', Article 21 called for the GEF to be 'appropriately restructured' and expanded so that it had 'universal' membership. Consistent with this mandate, the GEF adopted a new governing instrument in 1994, which established it as an independent entity rather than an arm of the World Bank and reformed its governance arrangements.[88]

In 1998, COP4 ended the GEF's provisional status and designated it as an operating entity of the financial mechanism on an ongoing basis, subject to reviews every four years.[89] Under a Memorandum of Understanding between the FCCC and the GEF Council,[90] the GEF is to report regularly to the COP on its activities

---

[87] Cancun Agreements LCA, para 102.

[88] Global Environment Facility (GEF), 'Instrument for the Establishment of the Restructured Global Environment Facility 1994' (Washington, D.C.: GEF, 1994). The restructured GEF is governed by an Assembly that meets every 3–4 years and consists of all member states; a Council comprised of thirty-two members, sixteen from developing (recipient) states, fourteen from developed (donor) states, and two from EITs; and a secretariat. The Council serves as the primary decision-making body, and makes decisions by weighted, double-majority voting, consisting of 60% of the total participants and 60% of total contributions. See generally Laurence Boisson de Chazournes, 'The Global Environment Facility: A Unique and Crucial Institution', *Review of European, Comparative and International Environmental Law*, 14/3 (2005): 193.

[89] Decision 3/CP.4, 'Review of the financial mechanism' (25 January 1999) FCCC/CP/1998/16/Add.1, 8.

[90] Decision 12/CP.2, 'Memorandum of Understanding between the Conference of the Parties and the Council of the Global Environment Facility' (29 October 1996) FCCC/CP/1996/15/Add.1, 55.

related to the convention. The COP may ask the GEF Council to clarify and recon-
sider a funding decision if it believes that the decision does not comply with the
COP's policy guidance, but it cannot directly change funding decisions.[91]

Although Article 11 states that the financial mechanism is to provide financial
resources on a grant or concessional basis, it does not specify the purposes for which
financial resources may be provided. In particular, it does not state whether the
financial mechanism may be used to fund adaptation measures. At the time the
FCCC was adopted, the GEF was not authorized to make grants for projects that
have local rather than global benefits. As a result, it could not provide funding
for adaptation costs, and the US successfully opposed AOSIS proposals to insert
a phrase in Article 11 that would have explicitly encompassed compensation for
adaptation costs. Subsequently, however, the GEF's mandate was expanded to
include adaptation funding.[92]

Since the FCCC's entry into force, the parties have also established a number of
specialized funds, including the SCCF and the LDCF, which were created in 2001
by the Marrakesh Accords[93] and are operated by the GEF. The SCCF's mandate
encompasses a broad range of activities in developing countries relating to mitigation and adaptation. The LDCF's mandate focuses more specifically on the preparation and implementation of NAPAs by LDCs.

Article 11 explicitly authorizes developed country parties to provide financial
resources through bilateral, regional, and other multilateral channels, rather than
through the FCCC's financial mechanism (Article 11.5). Although the financial
mechanism has received much of the attention in the UN climate regime, most
of the public funding for mitigation and adaptation activities has been provided
not through the financial mechanism, but through bilateral channels such as the
Agence Française de Développement, the Japan International Cooperation Agency,
the German International Climate Initiative, and the US Agency for International
Development; through regional institutions such as the European Investment
Bank; and through multilateral funds administered by the World Bank, such as the
Clean Technology Fund (which, by itself, is considerably larger than the GEF). In
2010, bilateral development agencies provided more than $10 billion in climate
finance, compared to less than $1 billion from the GEF.[94]

In the 2009 Copenhagen Accord, participating states agreed to create the GCF
to support developing country activities, and developed countries agreed that a
'significant portion' of the new funding provided under the Accord should 'flow
through' the new fund.[95] The GCF was formally established the following year
by COP16 as an operating entity of the FCCC's financial mechanism,[96] and

---

[91] Ibid, Annex, para 5. [92] Decision 6/CP.7 (n 59) 40.

[93] Decision 7/CP.7 (n 58) 43.

[94] On bilateral assistance, see United Nations Environment Programme (UNEP), 'Bilateral Finance
Institutions and Climate Change: A Mapping of Public Financial Flows for Mitigation and Adaptation
to Developing Countries in 2010' (UNEP, 2011). On climate-related assistance from the GEF, see
Report of the Global Environment Facility to the Conference of the Parties, Note by the secretariat (27
August 2013) FCCC/CP/2013/3.

[95] Copenhagen Accord, paras 8 and 10. [96] Cancun Agreements LCA, paras 102–11.

its governing instrument was adopted in 2011 by the Durban COP. Under the Cancun Agreements, the GCF's mandate is to provide support to developing countries to combat climate change, for example, by supporting low-emission development strategies, nationally appropriate mitigation actions, and NAPs. The GCF has separate windows for mitigation and adaptation activities, with resources balanced equally between the two.[97] Although the World Bank is serving as interim trustee of the GCF for three years, the GCF possesses international legal personality, and has its own governing instrument, governing board (comprised of twenty-four members, twelve each from developed and developing countries), and 'fully independent' secretariat, based in Korea. The GCF's governing board has 'full responsibility' for funding decisions, subject to policy guidance from the COP.[98]

In 2015, COP21, when adopting the Paris Agreement, decided that the FCCC's financial institutions, including the GCF, the SCCF, and the LDCF, would serve the new agreement.[99]

VI. IMPLEMENTATION AND COMPLIANCE MECHANISMS (ARTICLES 7.2 AND 12–14)

A. Overview

The FCCC establishes a relatively weak implementation system, consisting of so-called 'pledge and review'. First, countries are required under Article 12 to communicate information on their GHG emissions and implementation measures. While this reporting requirement falls well short of a binding 'pledge', it nonetheless forces parties to state publicly what they are doing and thereby serves as a prod to national action. Then, Article 7.2(e) provides for international review of parties' reports by the COP.

For many years, the FCCC's implementation system applied primarily to Annex I parties, both because many non-Annex I parties took a long time to file their initial national communications and because there was no agreement to subject non-Annex I reports to any international review. The Copenhagen Accord and Cancun Agreements strengthened the FCCC's pledge and review system, particularly for developing countries, by requiring more frequent reports (every two years) and by creating a process of ICA to assess non-Annex I reports. The Paris Agreement, in essence, institutionalizes this same general approach in a legally binding instrument.

In addition to the pledge and review process, the FCCC contemplates two mechanisms to review individual parties' compliance. First, the FCCC provides for the possible establishment of a multilateral consultative mechanism, modeled on

---

[97] Decision 3/CP.17, 'Launching the Green Climate Fund' (15 March 2012) FCCC/CP/2011/9/Add.1, 55, para 8.

[98] Ibid, Annex: Governing Instrument for the Green Climate Fund, paras 5 (board will have 'full responsibility'), 19 ('fully independent' secretariat).

[99] Decision 1/CP.21 (n 73) para 58. For more on the Paris Agreement, see Chapter 7.

the non-compliance procedure of the Montreal Protocol (Article 13). Second, the FCCC contains a boilerplate dispute settlement article, which provides for negotiation, conciliation, and non-compulsory arbitration or adjudication (Article 14). To date, neither of these compliance mechanisms has had any effect, dispute settlement because it has never been invoked, and the multilateral consultative process because it was never established.

B. Reporting (Article 12)

Reporting requirements promote transparency and thereby facilitate international review of a country's performance. Initially, some developed countries sought to include ambitious reporting requirements in the FCCC, either by specifying in an annex the information that national reports should include or by directing the COP to adopt agreed common formats for reports. One proposal would have required parties to establish a 'national assessment body' to prepare reports and to allow review and comments by non-governmental organizations.[100] These proposals were eventually abandoned, however, as the difficulty of adopting even a simple reporting requirement became apparent.

Although many international agreements include reporting requirements, some developing countries were reluctant to accept such a requirement in the FCCC. They argued that reports would be burdensome and should be voluntary rather than mandatory. Some developing countries even objected to the term 'reporting', contending that it suggested an intrusive, interventionist process. As a result, the convention uses the more neutral phrase, 'communication of information'. Against this backdrop, the reporting requirements in Article 12, although modest, still represent a significant step forward.

Article 12 differentiates the reporting requirements in three ways, for different categories of countries. First, the required content of non-Annex I, Annex I, and Annex II reports differ. All parties must communicate information on their national inventory of GHG emissions and removals (to the extent their capabilities permit), as well as on the steps taken or planned to implement the convention (Article 12.1). Annex I parties must, in addition, submit a detailed description of their policies and measures to implement their specific commitments, as well as an estimate of the effect of these policies and measures on their emissions by sources and removals by sinks (Article 12.2). Finally, Annex II parties must report on their transfers of financial resources and technology under Articles 4.3–4.5 (Article 12.3). These differences in the requirements for Annex I and non-Annex I reports have been elaborated in guidance adopted by the COP, which establish

---

[100] INC, Set of informal papers provided by delegations related to the preparation of a Framework Convention on Climate Change, Addendum (22 May 1991) A/AC.237/Misc.1/Add.1, 3 (submission of Australia).

more detailed and demanding guidelines for the communications and inventories of Annex I parties than for those of non-Annex I parties.[101]

Second, non-Annex I countries are entitled to financial and technical support in preparing their inventories and national communications (Article 12.7). Until they receive such assistance, they have no obligation to communicate any information.

Finally, Article 12 differentiates the timing of Annex I and non-Annex I communications. For Annex I parties, Article 12.3 gives them six months from the FCCC's entry into force to submit their initial national communication. Thereafter, the COP has determined that Annex I parties must submit inventories annually and national communications every four to five years. As of 2016, Annex I parties had submitted six national communications, with their seventh due in 2018. By contrast, Article 12.3 gives non-Annex I parties three years from the time they receive assistance to submit their initial national communication and, prior to the 2010 Cancun Agreements, the COP never adopted a timetable for the submission of subsequent inventories and communications.[102] For many years, some developing countries declined to accept funds for their national communications and therefore did not trigger the three-year clock. Five years after the FCCC's entry into force, only ten developing countries had submitted their initial communication. The slow pace of non-Annex I submissions led COP5 to create a consultative group of experts on non-Annex I communications in 1999,[103] which led to an improved pace of submissions. Nevertheless, Brazil, China, and India did not submit their initial communications until late 2004, more than ten years after the FCCC entered into force. As of October 2016, 147 non-Annex I parties had submitted their first national communication and 127 their second, but only twenty-seven had submitted their third communication, and only Mexico had submitted its fourth and fifth communications.[104]

The 2009 Copenhagen Accord and 2010 Cancun Agreements establish supplemental reporting requirements for both developed and developing countries, although these are phrased in hortatory rather than mandatory language ('should' rather than 'shall'). Developed country parties are required to submit biennial

---

[101] Compare FCCC, Review of the Implementation of Commitments and of Other Provisions of the Convention: UNFCCC guidelines on reporting and review (16 February 2000) FCCC/CP/1999/7 (Annex I guidelines); and Review of the Implementation of Commitments and of Other Provisions of the Convention, National Communications: Greenhouse gas inventories from Parties included in Annex I to the Convention: Guidelines on reporting and review (28 March 2003) FCCC/CP/2002/8 with Decision 17/CP.8, 'Guidelines for the preparation of national communications from Parties not included in Annex I to the Convention' (28 March 2003) FCCC/CP/2002/7/Add.2, 2, Annex. For example, Annex I countries are required to use the IPCC inventory guidelines in preparing their inventories and must include detailed documentation of their methods and data sources. By contrast, use of the IPCC inventory guidelines by non-Annex I parties is encouraged but not required.

[102] In addition, Article 12.3 allows least developed countries to submit their initial national communication at their discretion.

[103] Decision 8/CP.5, 'Other matters related to communications from Parties not included in Annex I to the Convention' (2 February 2000) FCCC/CP/1999/6/Add.1, 17, para 3.

[104] FCCC, 'Submitted National Communications from Non-Annex I Parties' <http://unfccc.int/national_reports/non-annex_i_natcom/submitted_natcom/items/653.php> accessed 20 January 2017.

reports (BRs) addressing their progress in achieving emission reductions and in providing financial and technology support to non-Annex I parties,[105] in additional to their quadrennial national communications and annual inventories. For the first time, non-Annex I parties also have a timetable for submitting their national communications (every four years). In addition, they are to submit biennial update reports (BURs), containing a national inventory report and information on mitigation actions, needs, and support received.[106] Guidelines for the preparation of BRs[107] and BURs[108] were adopted in 2011 at COP17. All of the Annex I parties have submitted an initial BR, with the second due in 2020. Although the first BUR by non-Annex I parties was due in December 2014, only thirty-four non-Annex I parties had submitted BURs as of October 2016.[109]

C. International review (Article 7.2)

Monitoring and verification procedures serve several functions. They provide information to other parties about whether potential competitors are complying with their obligations and help deter free riders through public embarrassment. They also facilitate international review of a country's performance and serve as a trigger for the application of sanctions.

The FCCC negotiating group considered a number of ambitious verification procedures, in some cases modeled on procedures used in other international agreements. Options included giving an existing organization such as the World Meteorological Organization or UNEP monitoring responsibilities, establishing a permanent review committee composed of independent technical experts, or using ad hoc teams of experts.[110]

Only remnants of these proposals remain in the FCCC, partly because the failure to agree on a binding target and timetable made monitoring and verification procedures less urgent. In addition, most delegations worked from the assumption that parties would act in good faith, and that failure to comply with the FCCC would result from circumstances beyond a party's control, such as lack of financial or technical resources. They felt the negotiations should focus on elaborating mechanisms to help countries fulfill their obligations, rather than on verification procedures. Finally, the entire question of monitoring and verification was extremely sensitive politically for many developing country delegations. Indeed, some developing countries objected to the use of such terms as 'monitoring', 'compliance', and

---

[105] Cancun Agreements LCA, para 40(a).   [106] Ibid, para 60.

[107] Decision 2/CP.17 (n 83) Annex I: UNFCCC biennial reporting guidelines for developed country Parties.

[108] Ibid, Annex III: UNFCCC biennial update reporting guidelines for Parties not included in Annex I to the Convention.

[109] FCCC, 'Submitted biennial update reports (BURs) from non-Annex I Parties' <http://unfccc.int/national_reports/non-annex_i_natcom/reporting_on_climate_change/items/8722.php> accessed 20 January 2017.

[110] INC, Single Text on Elements Relating to Mechanisms, Note by the Co-Chairmen of Working Group II (21 August 1991) A/AC.237/Misc.8, 24, 25, 32.

'verification'; the first because it had too activist and intrusive a tone, the last two because they suggested that countries might act in bad faith and willfully violate their obligations. As a result, the convention uses more neutral, descriptive language: 'monitor' was replaced by 'assess', 'compliance' by 'implementation', and 'verification' by 'resolution of questions'.

As it became increasingly clear that the FCCC would not establish international monitoring or fact-finding mechanisms, attention shifted to international review of national reports. Delegations identified several different types of potential review: (1) a procedural review to determine whether reports had been submitted and whether they conformed to any reporting guidelines; (2) a technical review of, for example, the methodologies used and whether particular national measures are likely to reduce emissions by the stated amount; and (3) a more substantive review, evaluating a party's compliance with its obligations under the convention.

The FCCC assigns the primary review function to the COP, which has the mandate to '[a]ssess, on the basis of all information made available to it in accordance with the provisions of the Convention, the implementation of the Convention by the parties, the overall effects of the measures taken pursuant to the Convention, ... and the extent to which progress towards the objective of the Convention is being achieved' (Article 7.2(e)). Although the use of the plural in the phrase, 'implementation of the Convention by the Parties', can be read to suggest that the provision is aimed at review of the parties' collective implementation, such an interpretation would make the provision redundant, since the following clause ('the overall effects of the measures taken') addresses collective implementation. If each clause is to be understood as a distinct mandate to the COP, the former clause must be read to address individual review. Thus, although Article 7.2(e) does not unambiguously authorize review of individual countries' performance, the provision as a whole suggests that the parties intended to permit individual review.

Whatever the correct legal interpretation of Article 7.2(e), developing countries were unwilling to have their national communications reviewed, so COP1 authorized in-depth expert reviews only of Annex I party communications and inventories.[111] Initially, expert reviews consisted primarily of paper reviews; country visits were the exception and required the prior approval of the country concerned. But, today, reviews of national communications ordinarily include country visits by the expert review team, and in-depth reviews of inventories are to include an in-country review at least once every five years. The outcome of the review process is a report prepared by the expert review team, which is published on the FCCC website.

The Copenhagen Accord and Cancun Agreements establish an additional review process for Annex I parties, as well as the first procedure for international scrutiny of non-Annex I communications. For Annex I parties, the Cancun Agreements establish a process of international assessment and review (IAR), conducted by SBI, consisting of two steps: first, a technical review of the BRs, inventories, and

---

[111] Decision 2/CP.1, 'Review of first communications from the Parties included in Annex I to the Convention' (6 June 1995) FCCC/CP/1995/7/Add.1, 7.

national communications of Annex I parties; and, second, a multilateral assessment of Annex I parties' progress in reducing emissions.[112] Seventeen Annex I parties were assessed by the SBI in 2014 in the first round of multilateral assessment, and twenty-four in 2015 in the second round.

For non-Annex I parties, the Cancun Agreements provide for a process of ICA under the SBI, in order to increase the transparency of developing country mitigation actions.[113] The information considered by the ICA process includes the non-Annex I party's inventory reports, as well as information on its mitigation actions and domestic measurement, reporting, and verification. According to the Cancun Agreements, ICA is to be 'non-intrusive, non-punitive and respectful of national sovereignty'.[114] The guidelines adopted for ICA by COP17 provide that ICA, like IAR, consists of two steps: first, a technical analysis by a team of experts of each non-Annex I party's BUR, examining the party's national inventory, mitigation actions, domestic measurement, reporting, and verification, and support received; and, second, a facilitative sharing of views among the parties, in which each party makes a brief presentation on its BUR, followed by an oral question and answer session.[115] For least developed and small island states, participation in ICA is voluntary.[116] As of October 2016, thirty-two non-Annex I BURs had undergone technical analysis, the first step in the ICA process.[117]

D. Multilateral consultative process to resolve questions regarding implementation (Article 13)

To resolve questions regarding a party's compliance with the convention, many felt that a multilateral, non-adversarial procedure would be preferable to traditional dispute settlement. Adversarial procedures seemed inappropriate because climate change is a global concern; non-compliance would therefore affect all the parties collectively, not simply the party bringing a challenge. Moreover, a non-adjudicative mechanism would promote cooperative relations by allowing questions to be resolved in a non-contentious manner.[118]

Although reservations by some developing states ultimately prevented the FCCC from directly establishing a multilateral compliance mechanism, a significant degree of consensus did emerge. For example, delegations generally agreed that

---

[112] Decision 2/CP.17 (n 83) Annex II: Modalities and procedures for international assessment and review.

[113] Cancun Agreements LCA, para 63.   [114] Ibid.

[115] Decision 2/CP.17 (n 83) Annex IV: Modalities and guidelines for international consultation and analysis, para 3.

[116] Ibid, para 58(d).

[117] FCCC, 'Measurement, reporting and verification (MRV) for Developing Country Parties' <http://unfccc.int/national_reports/non-annex_i_parties/ica/items/8621.php> accessed 20 January 2017.

[118] See generally Jutta Brunnée, 'Promoting Compliance with Multilateral Environmental Agreements', in Jutta Brunnée, Meinhard Doelle, and Lavanya Rajamani (eds), *Promoting Compliance in an Evolving Climate Regime* (Cambridge University Press, 2012) 38.

a compliance mechanism should be forward- rather than backward-looking: its main goal should be to help parties come into compliance with the convention rather than to adjudicate blame or impose sanctions. In this respect, the mechanism would be similar to the non-compliance procedure established under the Montreal Protocol.[119] Two primary alternatives were suggested regarding who should conduct the procedure: ad hoc panels established by the COP (modeled on GATT dispute resolution panels) or a standing implementation committee. Given the political nature of the compliance procedure, some delegations questioned whether the COP would agree to establish ad hoc panels; therefore, they preferred to entrust this function to a standing committee. Others felt that if the implementation committee had a technical character, it should not perform a quasi-political function such as compliance review; alternatively, if it had an open-ended membership (as was ultimately decided), it would be too unwieldy (and possibly too political) to undertake this type of detailed review. Two other options—namely to establish a standing, semi-adjudicative body or to make the establishment of panels automatic rather than dependent on a decision of the COP—were not extensively discussed during the negotiations.

Rather than establish a multilateral consultative process (MCP) immediately, Article 13 called on the COP to consider the establishment of such a mechanism at its first session. Accordingly, COP1 established an ad hoc group on Article 13 to draft terms of reference for the MCP.[120] The ad hoc group completed its work on the terms of reference in 1998, but was unable to agree on the composition of the multilateral consultative committee, preventing the adoption of the term of reference at COP4.[121] Although COP4 called for further consideration of the issue the following year, attention shifted to the establishment of a compliance system under the Kyoto Protocol, and the MCP was never pursued further. As a result, a multilateral consultative committee has never been established and the MCP is still inchoate.

E. Dispute settlement (Article 14)

In addition to the MCP, most delegations believed the convention should provide for traditional bilateral dispute settlement. The main question was whether the procedure should be mandatory or voluntary, and binding or non-binding. At one extreme, some developing countries wanted a purely voluntary, non-binding procedure, under which states with disputes would engage first in negotiations and then, if negotiations failed, in non-binding conciliation. Alternatively, some suggested

---

[119] 'Non-Compliance Procedure' (25 November 1992) UN Doc UNEP/OzL.Pro.4/15, 44, Annex IV.

[120] Decision 20/CP.1, 'Establishment of a multilateral consultative process for the resolution of questions regarding the implementation of the Convention' (6 June 1995) FCCC/CP/1995/7/1/ Add.1, 59.

[121] Decision 10/CP.4, 'Multilateral consultative process' (25 January 1999) FCCC/CP/1998/16/ Add.1, 43, Annex.

the possibility of compulsory arbitration if parties were unable to resolve a dispute through negotiation or conciliation.[122]

Article 14 represents a compromise, modeled on the dispute settlement provisions of other international environmental agreements. In the event of a dispute, the states concerned must first seek to settle it through negotiations or some other peaceful means. If that effort is unsuccessful, either state may request the creation of a conciliation commission, composed of an equal number of members appointed by each party and a chair chosen by the other members of the commission. The conciliation commission has the authority only to make 'recommendatory' awards, which the parties are to 'consider in good faith'. However, if both parties have accepted in advance the jurisdiction of the International Court of Justice (ICJ) or compulsory arbitration under Article 14.2, then these compulsory procedures may be used.[123]

Thus far, the dispute settlement procedure provided for in Article 14 has not been used. This is consistent with the experience in other environmental regimes. Even though dispute settlement procedures are common in multilateral environmental agreements, states rarely use them, both because no one state is particularly affected by another state's lack of compliance and because states generally seek to avoid adversarial proceedings with one another.[124] Indeed, interest in the FCCC's dispute settlement procedures has been so limited that the COP has still not adopted annexes establishing procedures on conciliation and arbitration, despite Article 14's admonition that the COP do so 'as soon as practicable'.

VII. FINAL CLAUSES (ARTICLES 15–25)

A. Amendments, annexes, and protocols to the convention (Articles 15, 16, and 17)

Of the final clauses,[125] Article 15 enables the FCCC to respond to new information and issues by allowing amendments to be made by a qualified majority. An amendment may be adopted in this manner, however, only if all efforts at consensus have been exhausted and if three-quarters of the parties vote for and ratify it. Even then, the amendment applies only to those parties that affirmatively accept it.

---

[122] INC, Revised Single Text on Elements Relating to Mechanisms (30 October 1991) A/AC.237/Misc.13, 37-9.

[123] As of October 2016, the Netherlands, Solomon Islands, and Tuvalu were the only parties that had accepted the arbitration procedure as compulsory, and of these only the Netherlands had accepted the compulsory jurisdiction of the International Court of Justice. FCCC, 'Declarations by Parties—United Nations Framework Convention on Climate Change' <http://unfccc.int/essential_background/convention/items/5410.php> accessed 20 January 2017.

[124] Cesare Romano, 'International Dispute Settlement', in Daniel Bodansky, Jutta Brunnée, and Ellen Hey (eds), *Oxford Handbook of International Environmental Law* (Oxford University Press, 2007) 1036, 1041.

[125] For a general discussion of the issues addressed in this section, see Chapter 3, Sections II.C, II.D.1, and II.D.2.

Article 16 establishes a more flexible procedure for the adoption and amendment of annexes. In contrast to amendments to the convention, a new annex or an amendment to an annex does not require ratification or acceptance by states in order to enter into force; it binds parties automatically unless a party notifies the depositary in writing of its non-acceptance. In effect, even though an amendment to an annex, like an amendment to the convention, cannot bind a state against its will, the presumption is reversed in the two situations. A convention amendment binds only those parties that accept it, whereas a new annex or an amendment to an annex binds a party unless the party opts out. Because of the comparative ease with which annexes may be adopted and amended, some delegations sought to limit the permissible content of annexes, in order to ensure that new legal requirements could not be imposed through an annex. Accordingly, Article 16.1 restricts annexes to 'lists, forms and any other material of a descriptive nature that is of a scientific, technical, procedural, or administrative character'.

Article 17 provides for the adoption by the COP of protocols to the convention. States disagreed about the need for protocols, and the FCCC does not call for the negotiation of any protocols, let alone establish a timetable for doing so. Instead, this question was left to future discussion. To maximize flexibility, Article 17 does not specify the requirements for entry into force or amendment of protocols. While framework conventions rarely require particular procedures, they often provide default rules that apply unless a protocol otherwise provides. Such default procedures save time by eliminating the need to renegotiate the same issues over and over for each individual protocol. The INC considered specifying default procedures, but ultimately decided not to do so. As a result, the Kyoto Protocol had to provide for its own entry into force conditions (Kyoto Protocol, Article 25.1).[126]

B. Voting rights, signature, and ratification (Articles 18, 20, and 22)

Because of the global nature of the climate change problem, the FCCC allows any state to sign and become a party. Members of the UN or of any of its specialized agencies may sign, as may parties to the Statute of the ICJ. Regional economic integration organizations (REIOs) (ie the EU) are also eligible to become parties to the convention. The FCCC includes what has become the standard provision regarding ratification by REIOs, namely that REIOs, in their instruments of ratification, must declare the extent of their competence on matters governed by the convention. REIOs have the number of votes equal to the number of their member states that are party to the convention, but may not vote on a matter if any member state exercises its right to vote.

---

[126] See Chapter 6, Section IX.

C. Entry into force (Article 23)

The FCCC's entry into force provision, requiring ratification by fifty states, strikes a balance. If the number of ratifications necessary for entry into force had been low, then the FCCC might have entered into force very early, with only a small number of parties entitled to participate in the first COP, when many important decisions were to be made. On the other hand, if the requirements for entry into force had been too strict, then entry into force might have been substantially delayed. In the end, the INC decided to require ratification by fifty states for entry into force, choosing the midpoint of the various numbers proposed.

Some states suggested an additional condition for entry into force, requiring ratification by states representing a minimum percentage of global GHG emissions, the approach used in the Montreal Protocol[127] and a variety of International Maritime Organization (IMO) marine pollution conventions.[128] A minimum emissions approach has two related purposes. First, it gives a convention credibility by requiring ratification by the states that contribute most to the problem, ie, the big GHG emitters. Second, it minimizes the risk of any one state being put at a competitive disadvantage by accepting an agreement, since it ensures that the agreement will enter into force only if a critical mass of other states also join. In contrast to the Kyoto Protocol and the Paris Agreement, both of which include an emissions threshold for entry into force,[129] an emissions threshold was deemed unnecessary for the FCCC, because it establishes only general obligations that do not impose high costs on parties initially.

D. Reservations and withdrawal (Articles 24 and 25)

Like many international environmental agreements, the FCCC does not allow reservations. This 'no reservations' rule is intended to ensure uniformity of obligations among the parties and to minimize free riders. However, if a party is sufficiently dissatisfied with the convention, it may withdraw after three years, by giving written notice, effective one year from the date of receipt by the depositary.

While the FCCC prohibits reservations, parties may make interpretive statements (often referred to as 'understandings' or 'declarations') at the time of signature or ratification. Fiji, Kiribati, Nauru, and Papua New Guinea all submitted declarations either when they signed or ratified the FCCC, stating their understanding that their action in accepting the FCCC 'shall in no way constitute a renunciation of any rights under international law concerning state responsibility

---

[127] Montreal Protocol, Art 16.1.

[128] See eg International Convention for the Prevention of Pollution from Ships (adopted 2 November 1973, entered into force 2 October 1983) 1340 UNTS 184, amended by Protocol of 1978 Relating to the International Convention for the Prevention of Pollution from Ships (adopted 17 February 1978, entered into force 2 October 1983) 1340 UNTS 61, Art 15(1).

[129] Kyoto Protocol, Art 25.1 (55 FCCC parties plus 55% of Annex I CO_2 emissions in 1990); Paris Agreement, Art 21.1 (55 FCCC parties plus 55% of global GHG emissions).

for the adverse effects of climate change and that no provisions in the convention can be interpreted as derogating from the principles of general international law'.[130]

VIII. CONCLUSION

The FCCC reflects a delicate compromise designed to encourage maximum participation by states. It avoids legally binding targets and timetables, which were opposed by the US. It limits the obligations of developing countries and requires that they be provided financial and technical assistance. At the same time, it focuses attention on the climate change problem, as European and small island states wanted. Ultimately, the proof was in the pudding: at the Rio Conference, the FCCC was signed by 154 states, and now has 197 parties.

As a framework convention, the FCCC aims to create a flexible system of governance for the climate change problem. It authorizes the COP to establish new institutions or change the mandate of existing ones. It allows amendments, annexes, and amendments to annexes to be approved by a three-quarters majority vote. In addition, it provides for regular reviews of its specific commitments on sources and sinks, as well as of the annexes, with a view to their possible amendment.

For much of its existence, however, the UN climate regime has in practice been quite rigid. The principles articulated in Article 3 became sacrosanct, as did the categorization of countries in Annexes I and II. Moreover, the requirement that decisions be made by consensus, in the absence of agreed rules of procedure, has promoted policy gridlock.

Nevertheless, the FCCC laid a basis for further action, which was realized in the 2015 Paris Agreement. By requiring parties to develop GHG inventories, formulate national strategies and measures, and cooperate in scientific research, it has promoted national planning and helped generate a better information base for future negotiations and decisions.

SELECT BIBLIOGRAPHY

Bodansky D., 'The United Nations Framework Convention on Climate Change: A Commentary', *Yale Journal of International Law*, 18/2 (1993): 451.

Depledge J., 'The Road Less Travelled: Difficulties in Moving Between Annexes in the Climate Change Regime', *Climate Policy*, 9/3 (2009): 273.

Freestone D., 'The United Nations Framework Convention on Climate Change – The Basis for the Climate Change Regime', in Carlarne C.P., Gray K.R., and Tarasofsky R.G. (eds), *The Oxford Handbook of International Climate Change Law* (Oxford University Press, 2016) 97.

Goldberg D.M., 'As the World Burns: Negotiating the Framework Convention on Climate Change', *Georgetown International Environmental Law Review*, 5/2 (1993): 239.

---

[130] See FCCC, Declarations by Parties (n 123).

Mintzer I.R. and Leonard J.A. (eds), *Negotiating Climate Change: The Inside Story of the Rio Convention* (Cambridge University Press, 1994).

Oppenheimer M. and Petsonk A., 'Article 2 of the FCCC: Historical Origins, Recent Interpretations', *Climatic Change*, 73/3 (2005): 195.

Rajamani L., 'The United Nations Framework Convention on Climate Change: A Framework Approach to Climate Change', in Farber D.A. and Peeters M. (eds), *Elgar Encyclopedia of Environmental Law vol 1: Climate Change Law* (Cheltenham, UK: Edward Elgar, 2016) 205.

Yamin F. and Depledge J., *The International Climate Change Regime: A Guide to Rules, Institutions and Procedures* (Cambridge University Press, 2004).

6

Kyoto Protocol

I. INTRODUCTION

The 1997 Kyoto Protocol supplements the framework laid out in the FCCC, by establishing internationally-negotiated, legally binding, quantitative emissions targets for Annex I parties. Although the Kyoto negotiations were hard fought, the range of issues was much narrower than in the FCCC or Paris processes, since the Kyoto negotiations focused only on Annex I emissions, and Annex I parties generally agreed on the need for legally binding targets. That left two central issues in contention: (1) the stringency of the targets, and (2) the flexibility states would have in implementing them. On one side, the European Union (EU) favored strong targets and limited flexibility; on the other, the United States (US) and other non-EU developed states generally favored weaker targets and greater flexibility. The Kyoto Protocol represents a trade-off between the EU preference for stringency and the US preference for flexibility. It established comparatively strong, economy-wide emissions targets for Annex I parties, backed by stringent requirements for reporting and review as well as enforcement measures. But it gave states considerable flexibility in meeting their targets: flexibility in choosing which sectors and greenhouse gases (GHGs) to focus on, and what specific measures to use (for example, energy efficiency standards, a carbon tax, and so forth); flexibility as to when to reduce emissions (as a result of the protocol's five-year commitment period and the option to bank emissions units for later use); and flexibility in where to reduce emissions (as a result of the protocol's market mechanisms, including emissions trading and the Clean Development Mechanism (CDM)).

The Kyoto Protocol was finalized and adopted in December 1997, but many of its key provisions were skeletal in character and required further elaboration. Matters requiring further work included:

- The rules for accounting of removals of carbon dioxide (CO_2) by carbon sinks.
- The system for reporting and review of Annex I emissions.
- The rules for the protocol's market mechanisms.
- The rules and procedures for the protocol's compliance mechanism.

Because these issues had huge implications for states' obligations under the protocol, many states were unwilling to ratify the protocol until they had been resolved. As discussed in Chapter 4, it took an additional four years of negotiations to elaborate the detailed rules needed to make the Kyoto Protocol operational. This work was completed in 2001 with the adoption of the Marrakesh Accords, which serve as the Kyoto Protocol's rule-book.[1]

The Kyoto Protocol is one of the most complex and ambitious environmental agreements ever negotiated. Not surprisingly, it has proven deeply controversial and, as a result, has had a chequered history. The US rejected the protocol shortly after President George W. Bush came into office in 2001, and, without US support, it took eight years to enter into force. Negotiations for Kyoto's second commitment period took an additional seven years, were deeply contentious and resulted in amendments that may never enter into force (although they are being provisionally applied). Even if these amendments do enter into force, they run only through 2020 and the future of the Kyoto Protocol beyond 2020 is doubtful. Nevertheless, the Kyoto Protocol has played a decisive role in the evolution of the climate regime. The experience under the protocol has also provided valuable lessons for the design and implementation of future climate agreements. Its many innovative provisions, including those pertaining to emissions targets, market mechanisms and compliance, thus merit close examination.

This chapter discusses the Kyoto Protocol in depth, first by exploring four overarching issues, cutting across the three instruments in the UN climate regime—the FCCC, the Kyoto Protocol, and the Paris Agreement—and then through a detailed analysis of the protocol's key provisions.

II. OVERARCHING ISSUES

In contrast to the Paris Agreement negotiations, the mandate for which left virtually every issue open, many of the key features of the Kyoto Protocol were decided, at the outset, by the 1995 Berlin Mandate, which initiated the negotiations and established the Ad Hoc Group on the Berlin Mandate (AGBM): (1) the Kyoto Protocol would be a treaty; (2) its architecture would have a significant top-down element, in the form of internationally-negotiated emissions targets; (3) its scope would be limited almost entirely to mitigation; and (4) it would be highly differentiated, establishing emissions targets for Annex I parties, but no new commitments for non-Annex I parties.

A. Legal bindingness

The Berlin Mandate stipulated that the outcome of the process was to be a 'protocol or another legal instrument'.[2] At the time, it was clear that 'another legal

---

[1] Decisions 2-24/CP.7, 'The Marrakesh Accords' (21 January 2002) FCCC/CP/2001/13/Add.1-3. The Marrakesh Accords were ratified by the first meeting of the Kyoto Protocol parties in 2005. See Decisions 2-30/CMP.1 (30 March 2006) FCCC/KP/CMP/2005/8/Add.1-4.
[2] Berlin Mandate, preambular recital 3.

instrument' referred to an amendment.[3] So, in essence, the Berlin Mandate was to negotiate either a protocol or an amendment to the FCCC. An amendment would have required only a three-fourths majority vote for its adoption,[4] whereas a protocol in practice required consensus, since the FCCC does not specify a voting procedure for the adoption of protocols and the Conference of the Parties (COP) has never been able to agree on rules of procedure.[5] Some parties favored keeping both options on the table over concerns about gathering the consensus necessary for the adoption of a protocol. By the Kyoto conference, however, agreement had emerged on adopting a protocol to the FCCC, and the option for an amendment was deleted from the negotiating text.[6]

The legal character of the GHG targets in the Kyoto Protocol was also at issue in the negotiations, but in a far more muted form than in the negotiation of the Paris Agreement. The Berlin Mandate required the AGBM process to aim, 'in the process of strengthening the commitments in Article 4.2(a) and (b) of the Convention … to set quantified limitation and reduction objectives within specified time-frames'.[7] The commitments in Article 4.2(a) and (b), discussed in Chapter 5, are non-binding targets.[8] The reference in the Berlin Mandate to strengthening these non-binding targets could be interpreted as tipping the balance toward legally binding targets in the Kyoto Protocol. But the Berlin Mandate did not provide explicit guidance on the legal character of the GHG targets to be negotiated. The EU and Alliance of Small Island States (AOSIS) favored legally binding GHG targets from the beginning of the negotiations, and at the 1996 Geneva Conference that marked the mid-point of the two-year negotiating process, the US also expressed a preference for legally binding targets.[9] The Geneva Ministerial Declaration, taken note of by the Geneva COP, endorsed 'quantified legally-binding objectives'.[10] In Geneva, Australia alone remained opposed to legally binding targets, and disassociated itself from this part of the Declaration, but by the time the Kyoto conference convened, its opposition too had fallen away, and the negotiating text used mandatory terms ('shall') in relation to individual emissions commitments.[11]

There was thus clarity by the Kyoto conference, both about the legal form of the instrument to be adopted, as well as the legal character of its mitigation commitments—the Kyoto Protocol would be a legally binding instrument with

---

[3] Joanna Depledge, 'Tracing the Origins of the Kyoto Protocol: An Article-by-Article Textual History' (25 November 2000) FCCC/TP/2000/2, 11–12.

[4] FCCC, Art 15.

[5] Ibid, Art 17. On the requirements for amendments in the climate regime, and the consensus issue, see Chapter 3, Sections II.D.1 and 2, and II.B.2.

[6] Depledge, Tracing the Origins of Kyoto Protocol (n 3) 11–12.

[7] Berlin Mandate, para 2(a).   [8] See Chapter 5, Section IV.B.

[9] Depledge, Tracing the Origins of Kyoto Protocol (n 3) 32.

[10] Report of the Conference of the Parties on its second session, held in Geneva from 8 to 19 July 1996, Addendum (29 October 1996) FCCC/CP/1996/15/Add.1, Annex: The Geneva Ministerial Declaration.

[11] Ad Hoc Group on the Berlin Mandate, Completion of a protocol or another legal instrument, Consolidated negotiating text by the Chairman (13 October 1997) FCCC/AGBM/1997/7. See also Depledge, Tracing the Origins of Kyoto Protocol (n 3) 31.

legally binding mitigation targets. In this regard, the Kyoto and Paris negotiations were very different, since in the Paris process, the questions of legal form and legal character were deeply contentious and remained at issue until the end. This contrast can, at least in part, be attributed to the instruments' respective approaches to differentiation. The Berlin Mandate stipulated that the Kyoto Protocol's commitments were to apply to Annex I parties alone, whereas the Paris Agreement's negotiating mandate provided that it would be 'applicable to all'.[12] Since developed countries were much more willing than developing countries to accept legally binding commitments, the limitation of commitments to developed countries meant that legal bindingness was less of an issue in the Kyoto than the Paris negotiations. The early agreement on the issue of legal bindingness, in turn, allowed states to begin considering, in advance of the Kyoto conference, the processes and mechanisms to facilitate implementation of these commitments and to promote compliance.[13]

B. Architecture

The architecture of the Kyoto Protocol was also pre-determined by its negotiating mandate. Inspired by the 1987 Montreal Protocol, the Berlin Mandate launched a process to set quantified emission limitation and reduction objectives (QELROs) within specified time frames for developed countries. Although parties initially proposed their own targets, these targets were multilaterally negotiated thereafter. In addition, many aspects of these targets were multilaterally determined, including the fact that the targets were absolute and virtually economy-wide, covered the six gases listed in Kyoto Annex A, and, with some exceptions, had a common base year (Article 3). The targets were also subject to multilaterally agreed accounting procedures, and elaborate reporting, review, and compliance procedures (Articles 5, 7, 8, and 18). In addition, parties negotiated a common set of rules relating to the market mechanisms (Articles 6, 12, and 17). The Kyoto Protocol is thus considered a 'top-down' international agreement.[14]

C. Scope

The Kyoto Protocol has a much narrower scope than the FCCC. As specified in the Berlin Mandate, its primary purpose is to strengthen the mitigation commitments of Annex I parties in Article 4.2 of the FCCC.[15] The Kyoto Protocol does so through targets and timetables. The Kyoto Protocol addresses adaptation only in passing, by reiterating the obligation of all parties under Article 4.1(b) of the FCCC to formulate, implement, publish, and regularly update programs containing

---

[12] See Chapter 7, Section II.D.
[13] Depledge, Tracing the Origins of Kyoto Protocol (n 3) 86.
[14] Navroz K. Dubash and Lavanya Rajamani, 'Beyond Copenhagen: Next Steps', *Climate Policy* 10/6 (2010): 593; See also Daniel Bodansky, 'A Tale of Two Architectures: The Once and Future U.N. Climate Change Regime', *Arizona State Law Journal*, 43/6 (2011): 697.
[15] Berlin Mandate, preambular recital 4.

measures to facilitate adaptation.[16] And it establishes a dedicated stream of funding for adaptation, by channelling 2% of the proceeds from the CDM, one of the market mechanisms, to an Adaptation Fund.[17] The focus of the Kyoto Protocol, however, is squarely on mitigation. And, since this focus was established in the Berlin Mandate, it was not in dispute during the AGBM negotiations.

The main issues in the Kyoto Protocol negotiations relating to scope concerned the gases and sectors to be covered. Parties had differing views on whether the Kyoto Protocol should focus on CO_2 emissions alone, address three gases –CO_2, methane (CH_4), and nitrous oxide (N_2O)—or take a more comprehensive approach that addresses emissions of other GHGs including hydrofluorocarbons (HFCs), perfluorocarbons (PFCs), and sulphur hexafluoride (SF_6). Serious disagreements persisted throughout the negotiations on whether the three synthetic gases—HFCs, PFCs, and SF_6—should be included. These gases have high global warming potentials (GWPs), and their use has grown rapidly. The US and other Umbrella Group countries, such as Australia, Canada, and Norway, supported their inclusion, in order to enhance states' flexibility in achieving their Kyoto targets. The EU, however, was concerned about the uncertainties regarding sources and sinks of different GHGs, and proposed that these gases be added later. Japan was concerned about the 1990 base year, which would have disadvantaged them given the rapid increase in their use of HFCs since that year.[18] The protocol struck a balance between these concerns by covering all six gases, but offering parties the option of using a later baseline of 1995 for HFCs, PFCs, and SF_6.[19] Given the rapid increases in the emissions of these gases between 1990 and 1995, the later baseline translated into a more modest reduction required of parties. The 2012 Doha Amendment, yet to enter into force, added a seventh gas, nitrogen trifluoride, to Annex A for the second commitment period.[20]

The Kyoto Protocol identifies in Annex A the six gases covered. It regulates these gases in a 'basket of gases' rather than a 'gas by gas' approach. The 'basket of gases' approach, favored by the US, permits all gases to be considered together for the purposes of achieving the Kyoto targets.[21] This approach requires defining the GWP of each gas listed in Annex A[22] in order to have a common metric to compare and measure their relative contributions to global warming.[23] Using their GWPs,

---

[16] Kyoto Protocol, Art 10(b).

[17] Decision 10/CP.7, 'Funding under the Kyoto Protocol' (21 January 2002) FCCC/CP/2001/13/Add.1, 52.

[18] Depledge, Tracing the Origins of Kyoto Protocol (n 3) 33–35. See generally Clare Breidenich *et al.*, 'The Kyoto Protocol to the United Nations Framework Convention on Climate Change', *American Journal of International Law*, 92/2 (1998): 315, 321–2.

[19] Kyoto Protocol, Art 3.8.   [20] Doha Amendment, Art 1, Section B.

[21] Depledge, Tracing the Origins of Kyoto Protocol (n 3) 35.

[22] The GWPs listed in Annex A are those accepted by the Intergovernmental Panel on Climate Change (IPCC), as provided for in Kyoto Protocol, Article 5.3.

[23] See Farhana Yamin and Joanna Depledge, *The International Climate Change Regime: A Guide to Rules, Institutions and Procedures* (Cambridge University Press, 2004) 78 (noting that GWPs are calculated as the ratio of the radiative forcing that would result from the emission of 1 kg of a GHG to that from the emission of 1 kg of CO_2 over a specified period of time).

emissions of non-CO_2 gases can be translated into CO_2 equivalent (CO_2e) terms.[24] The emissions limitation targets specified in the protocol apply to a party's CO_2e emissions. The protocol also identifies in Annex A the sectors covered, which are energy, industrial processes, solvents and other product use, agriculture, and waste. The 'basket of gases' approach, coupled with the wide range of sectors identified in Annex A, allows parties considerable flexibility in choosing which gases and sectors to focus on in implementing their targets.[25]

Although the Kyoto Protocol is broad in its coverage, it does not regulate all GHGs and GHG-intensive sectors. GHGs controlled by the Montreal Protocol are explicitly excluded from the Kyoto commitments.[26] Furthermore, the protocol provides that emissions from international civil aviation and maritime transport should be regulated through the International Civil Aviation Organization (ICAO) and the International Maritime Organization (IMO), respectively,[27] although the protocol does require parties to report on both domestic and international emissions from aviation and maritime fuels ('bunker fuels').[28]

Finally, the question of whether, and to what extent, emissions and removals by sinks should be covered under the Kyoto Protocol was highly controversial.[29] The protocol requires parties to report on emissions and removals by sinks.[30] There was a range of views, however, regarding how such emissions and removals should count toward achievement of parties' Kyoto targets. In a carefully balanced compromise, the protocol provides that parties may receive credit, up to specified limits, for the removal of CO_2 from the atmosphere through certain sink activities such as afforestation, reforestation, forest management and agricultural lands management, and may also receive credit through the CDM for certain sink projects in developing countries.[31]

D. Differentiation

The Berlin Mandate provided for radical differentiation in the Kyoto Protocol by limiting GHG targets and timetables to Annex I countries, and by explicitly excluding 'any new commitments' for non-Annex I parties.[32] Even proposals by

---

[24] Ibid.   [25] Ibid.

[26] Kyoto Protocol, Arts 2.1(a)(ii), 2.2, 5.1, 5.2, 7.1, and 10(a).

[27] Ibid, Art 2.2. See Chapter 8, Section IV.A.1 and 2.

[28] See Decision 24/CP.19, 'Revision of the UNFCCC reporting guidelines on annual inventories for Parties included in Annex I to the Convention' (31 January 2014) FCCC/CP/2013/10/Add.3, 2; Decision 3/CP.5, 'Guidelines for the preparation of national communications by Parties included in Annex I to the Convention, Part I: UNFCCC reporting guidelines on annual inventories' (2 February 2000) FCCC/CP/1999/6/Add.1, 6. For a discussion of the new data collection requirements under the International Maritime Organization, which dovetail with the reporting obligations in the UN climate regime, see Chapter 8, Section IV.A.1.

[29] 'A sink is a process, activity or mechanism that removes GHGs from the atmosphere; a reservoir is part of the climate system that allows a GHG to be stored.' FCCC, *United Nations Framework Convention on Climate Change* (Bonn: FCCC Secretariat, 2006) 24.

[30] Decision 2/CP.3, 'Methodological issues related to the Kyoto Protocol' (25 March 1998) FCCC/CP/1997/7/Add.1, 31, para 1.

[31] See below Section IV.B.2.f.   [32] Berlin Mandate, para 2(a) and (b).

the US and other developed countries to allow developing countries to 'voluntarily' accept emissions targets were rejected by developing countries on the grounds that such proposals were inconsistent with the Berlin Mandate. The sharp differentiation between countries with respect to central mitigation obligations—such that Annex I countries have GHG targets and timetables while non-Annex I countries do not—proved increasingly controversial over time. The US rejection of the Kyoto Protocol in 2001,[33] and the eventual withdrawal of many major developed countries from the Kyoto Protocol's second commitment period, can be traced, in part, to concerns about such differentiation in the Kyoto Protocol.

The Kyoto Protocol contains only one explicit reference, and a few implied references, to the principle of common but differentiated responsibilities and respective capabilities (CBDRRC). The preamble refers to FCCC Article 3 and the Berlin Mandate, both of which include the CBDRRC principle. Kyoto Article 10, discussed below, containing commitments for all parties, refers to 'common but differentiated responsibilities' and 'specific national and regional development priorities, objectives and circumstances'. Nevertheless, the differentiation in the Kyoto Protocol is traced by most commentators to this principle, and the associated notion of developed country leadership. Indeed, the climate regime, in particular the Kyoto Protocol, has been characterized as the 'clearest attempt to transform, activate and operationalize CBDR from a legal concept into a policy instrument'.[34]

The following sections explore the protocol's stark differentiation between Annex I and non-Annex I countries,[35] as well as the differentiation within the category of Annex I countries. They also consider more closely the (failed) attempt to introduce 'voluntary commitments' for developing countries during the Kyoto negotiations, which would have partially bridged the Annex I—non-Annex I divide.

1. Differentiation between Annex I and non-Annex I parties

The sharp differentiation between Annex I and non-Annex I countries in the Kyoto Protocol is illustrated most clearly by the fact that GHG mitigation targets and timetables are limited to Annex I countries. Indeed, this focus on Annex I is envisioned even for subsequent commitment periods, although the protocol does allow

---

[33] See Text of a Letter from the President to Senators Hagel, Helms, Craig, and Roberts (The White House, Office of the Press Secretary, 13 March 2001) <https://georgewbush-whitehouse.archives.gov/news/releases/2001/03/20010314.html> accessed 20 January 2017.

[34] Remarks by Christopher C. Joyner, 'Common but Differentiated Responsibilities', *American Society of International Law Proceedings*, 96 (2002): 358. See also Christopher D. Stone, 'Common but Differentiated Responsibilities in International Law', *American Journal of International Law*, 98/ 2 (2004): 276, 281; and Michael Weisslitz, 'Rethinking the Equitable Principle of Common but Differentiated Responsibility: Differential versus Absolute Norms of Compliance and Contribution in the Global Climate Change Context', *Colorado Journal of International Environmental Law and Policy*, 13/2 (2002): 473, 483 (referring to the Kyoto Protocol as 'CBDR in its most rigid application').

[35] The Kyoto Protocol employs the FCCC lists and categories of parties. See Kyoto Protocol, Art 1.7. Annex I to the FCCC and Annex B to the Kyoto Protocol were not, however, identical, as some Annex I Parties (Turkey and Belarus) had not ratified the FCCC when the Kyoto Protocol was being negotiated.

for the possibility of non-Annex I parties assuming emissions targets at some point in the future by establishing an amendment procedure for Annex B.[36]

Since emissions targets apply only to Annex I parties, the provisions of the protocol designed to monitor compliance with the targets are limited to Annex I parties, including the obligation to establish a national system for the estimation of GHG emissions by sources and removals by sinks,[37] the informational requirements in relation to annual inventories and national communications,[38] and the expert review processes.[39] The Kyoto Protocol's compliance procedure, considered below, is also tailored to the differentiated obligations of parties, and thus establishes an enforcement-oriented approach to compliance by Annex I parties with their emissions targets and related procedural commitments, and a facilitative approach to compliance by non-Annex I parties with the protocol's general and much more flexible and contextualized commitments.[40] In keeping with this bifurcation, the Compliance Committee consists of two branches, an enforcement and a facilitative branch.[41] The facilitative branch, which is empowered to provide financial and technical assistance and/or advice, is required to do so 'taking into account the principle of common but differentiated responsibilities and respective capabilities'.[42] In addition, the facilitative branch may 'formulat[e] … recommendations … taking into account Article 4, paragraph 7, of the Convention'[43]—a provision stressing the centrality of financial assistance and technology transfer to the performance of obligations by developing countries.[44]

In addition, the Kyoto Protocol draws on the FCCC and specifies a range of obligations for Annex II parties to assist non-Annex I parties, outlined below.[45] The protocol also creates an Adaptation Fund drawing on a share of the proceeds from the CDM.[46]

2. *Differentiation within the category of Annex I parties*

In addition to the differentiation between Annex I and non-Annex I parties, the Kyoto Protocol contains several provisions that differentiate among Annex I parties in relation to defining and implementing commitments. For instance, economies

---

[36] Kyoto Protocol, Art 3.9 which provides that 'commitments for subsequent periods for Parties included in Annex I shall be established in amendments to Annex B to this Protocol'.

[37] Ibid, Art 5.   [38] Ibid, Art 7.   [39] Ibid, Art 8.

[40] See Decision 27/CMP.1, 'Procedures and mechanisms relating to compliance under the Kyoto Protocol' (30 March 2006) FCCC/KP/CMP/2005/8/Add.3, 92.

[41] This is evident from the provisions relating to the mandate of the enforcement branch, which cover Annex I commitments alone (ie compliance with Kyoto Protocol Arts 3.1, 5.1, 5.2, 7.1, and 7.4, and eligibility requirements under Kyoto Protocol, Arts 6, 12, and 17). See ibid, Annex, Section V, para 4. The mandate of the facilitative branch extends generally to 'promoting compliance by Parties with their commitments under the Protocol'. Ibid, Annex, Section IV, para 4.

[42] Ibid, Annex, Section IV, para 4.   [43] Ibid, Annex, Section XIV, para (d).

[44] See for further details on the negotiating history of the Compliance Committee, Lavanya Rajamani, *Differential Treatment in International Environmental Law* (Oxford University Press, 2006) 203–5.

[45] Kyoto Protocol, Art 11.

[46] Decision 10/CP.7 (n 17). The share of proceeds was extended to emissions trading and joint implementation by the Doha Amendment. See below Section X.

in transition (EITs) are allowed to adopt a base year or period other than 1990 in defining their emissions targets.[47] Annex I parties also have different 'targets and timetables'. This differentiation is considered below, in the context of 'targets and timetables'.

3. Voluntary commitments for developing countries

A number of parties, including the members of AOSIS, the US, Australia, New Zealand, the EU, Japan, Poland, and Switzerland, aired concerns during the AGBM negotiations about the lack of emissions targets for non-Annex I parties.[48] In response, the AGBM Chair inserted a provision in the draft negotiating text on 'voluntary commitments for non-Annex I parties',[49] aiming to allow developing countries to assume voluntary country-specific emissions limitation or reduction commitments and thereby become eligible to participate in joint implementation and emissions trading.[50] However, in Kyoto, discussions on the proposed voluntary commitments article were acrimonious. The strongest opposition came from China and India. These countries questioned both the legality of creating a new category of parties under the convention and the 'voluntary' nature of the commitments under discussion.[51] Meanwhile the question of the 'evolution' of the commitment regime was raised as well. The US had originally introduced the concept of evolution in 1996, proposing that 'the Parties shall adopt, by [2005], binding provisions so that all Parties have quantitative greenhouse gas emissions obligations and so that there is a mechanism for automatic application of progressive greenhouse gas emissions obligations to Parties based upon agreed criteria'.[52] At the Kyoto COP, New Zealand called for 'progressive engagement' of developing countries according to their relative levels of development. It recommended launching a review process in 1998, to be concluded in 2002, to set legally binding commitments for all parties (except least developed countries (LDCs)) for future commitment periods.[53] This suggestion was rejected by the EU as 'not helpful to the negotiations and contrary to the Berlin Mandate',[54] and by the G-77/China because it was 'not the time to address developing country commitments, but to strengthen developed country commitments'.[55] The G-77/China threatened to boycott the negotiations if the proposal on evolution of commitments was not dropped.[56] Their reaction to this

---

[47] Kyoto Protocol, Art 3.5.
[48] Depledge, Tracing the Origins of Kyoto Protocol (n 3) 102.
[49] The Chair's text differed considerably from the text put forward by the parties. See ibid, 102–5, 103.
[50] Completion of a protocol or another legal instrument (n 11) Art 10.
[51] International Institute for Sustainable Development (IISD), 'Summary of the Third Conference of Parties to the UNFCCC, 1–11 December, 1997', *Earth Negotiations Bulletin*, 12/76 (1997): 1, 13.
[52] Depledge, Tracing the Origins of Kyoto Protocol (n 3) 83.
[53] See IISD, Summary of the Third Conference of the Parties to the FCCC (n 51). The proposal was supported by Australia, Canada, Japan, Poland, Slovenia, Switzerland and the US.
[54] Ibid, 5.
[55] Ibid,13. See Depledge, Tracing the Origins of Kyoto Protocol (n 3) 83. The proposal provoked forty-six interventions, mostly from non-Annex I countries recording their strong opposition to it.
[56] Ibid, 14.

proposal dovetailed with their reaction to the notion of voluntary commitments. As a result, both the voluntary commitments article and the proposal on 'evolution' were discarded.[57] Commentators note that, although the US was successful in shaping many aspects of the protocol, including in particular the protocol's market and other flexibility mechanisms, it suffered a 'decisive defeat' on the issue of new commitments for developing countries.[58] Developing countries may still voluntarily assume targets, but only through an amendment to Annex B—a lengthy and cumbersome process.[59]

III. PREAMBLE AND DEFINITIONS (ARTICLE 1)

The Kyoto Protocol, unlike both the FCCC and the Paris Agreement, contains a short preamble, confined to referencing the objective, provisions, and principles of the convention, as well as the Berlin Mandate that launched negotiations toward the Kyoto Protocol.

The Kyoto Protocol's definition section is similarly short, incorporating by reference the definitions contained in the FCCC. In addition, it defines: 'Conference of the Parties', 'Convention', 'Intergovernmental Panel on Climate Change', 'Montreal Protocol', 'Party', and 'Party included in Annex I'.[60]

IV. COMMITMENTS (ARTICLES 2, 3, 5, 7, 8, 10, AND 11)

Like the FCCC, the Kyoto Protocol sets out different commitments for different categories of parties including: (1) general commitments that apply to all parties, both developed and developing, which track existing commitments under Article 4.1 of the FCCC (Article 10); (2) new commitments relating to policies and measures, GHG mitigation targets and timetables, reporting, and review that apply only to Annex I parties (Articles 2, 3, 5, 7, and 8); and (3) specific commitments on financial resources that apply only to Annex II parties (Article 11). In keeping with

---

[57] See Depledge, Tracing the Origins of Kyoto Protocol (n 3) 80–3.

[58] See Andreas Missbach, 'Regulation Theory and Climate Change Policy', in Paul G. Harris (ed), *Climate Change and American Foreign Policy* (New York: Palgrave Macmillan US, 2000) 140–2.

[59] A non-Annex I party can choose voluntarily to become an Annex I party for the purposes of the Kyoto Protocol by the simple act of depositing a notification under FCCC, Article 4.2(g); however, if it wishes to take on an emissions limitation target, it needs to propose a formal amendment to Annex B, which requires acceptance by three-fourths of all Kyoto parties to enter into force, pursuant to Kyoto Protocol, Article 20.4. Belarus announced its intention to join Annex B in 2003, and after lengthy negotiations with other parties agreed to an emissions reduction target of 8% from 1990 levels, considerably stronger than its originally proposed stabilization target. Joanna Depledge, 'The Road Less Travelled: Difficulties in Moving between Annexes in the Climate Change Regime', *Climate Policy*, 9/3 (2009): 273, 282. The decision to amend Annex B to include Belarus was adopted in 2006, but has yet to enter into force. See Decision 10/CMP.2, 'Proposal from Belarus to amend Annex B to the Kyoto Protocol' (2 March 2007) FCCC/KP/CMP/2006/10/Add.1, 36.

[60] Kyoto Protocol, Art 1.

the Berlin Mandate, this structure reflects the Kyoto Protocol's focus on advancing the mitigation commitments of Annex I parties.

A. General commitments

Article 10 sets forth general commitments for all parties, which serve 'to advance the implementation' of Article 4.1 of the FCCC and 'to achieve sustainable development'. Since Article 10 applies to both developed and developing countries, it contains several contextualizing and qualifying phrases. In particular, it provides that parties are to take into account their 'common but differentiated responsibilities and their specific national and regional development priorities, objectives and circumstances'. It also specifically states that it does not introduce 'any new commitments' for non-Annex I parties, but rather 'reaffirm[s] existing commitments' under Article 4.1 of the FCCC. Moreover, it specifically 'tak[es] into account Article 4, paragraphs 3, 5, and 7, of the Convention',[61] thereby linking the implementation of commitments in Article 4.1 to the FCCC's commitments on financial assistance and technology transfer.

The negotiating history of Article 10 is instructive. Developing countries argued that advancing the implementation of existing commitments would need to be coupled with similar advances in the implementation of financial commitments by Annex II parties.[62] Indeed, there was considerable resistance from the G-77/China to Article 10(b) on mitigation and adaptation programs, even though it merely reiterated existing commitments under the FCCC, and it had to be gavelled through by the Chair over their objections.[63] In the context of Article 10, a proposal for the creation of a specific fund was discussed at length, but eventually discarded. Article 10 was, however, placed immediately before the article on the financial mechanism, to reflect the view that the issues addressed by the two articles were related: advancing commitments for developing countries would require increased financial support.[64]

B. Specific commitments for Annex I and Annex II parties

1. Policies and measures (Article 2)

Kyoto Article 2 requires Annex I parties to implement and/or further elaborate policies and measures (PAMs) in accordance with their national circumstances. It proceeds to list areas, in an illustrative manner ('such as'), in which PAMs could be taken, including enhancement of energy efficiency; protection and enhancement of GHG sinks; promotion of sustainable agriculture; research on renewable energies, carbon sequestration, and other environmentally-sound technologies; progressive reduction or phasing out of subsidies and other market imperfections in GHG

---

[61] Kyoto Protocol, Art 10, chapeau.
[62] Depledge, Tracing the Origins of Kyoto Protocol (n 3) 71.   [63] Ibid, 73.
[64] Ibid.

emitting sectors; reforms in relevant sectors (including, in particular, the transport sector) to limit and/or reduce GHG emissions; and limitation or reduction of methane emissions (Article 2.1(a)). In negotiating this article, parties disagreed on whether it should identify specific mandatory policies and measures. The EU favored including an annex identifying PAMs that all parties would be required to adopt and implement.[65] In contrast, the US, Australia, Canada, and New Zealand believed parties should retain flexibility in selecting PAMs.[66] Eventually the latter view prevailed, but the listing of specific PAMs in Article 2 generates expectations that parties will consider these in implementing the protocol.[67] This debate, among others, illustrates the long-standing and deep-seated differences between states on whether international climate regulation should be prescriptive or facilitative. These differences have existed from the inception of the UN climate regime and played a key role in shaping the 2015 Paris Agreement.

Article 2 requires parties to cooperate to enhance the effectiveness of their PAMs, including by exchanging information (Article 2.1(b)). Further, it provides that the Conference of Parties serving as the Meeting of the Parties to the Protocol (CMP) shall consider ways and means to elaborate such coordination, if it decides that cooperation would be beneficial (Article 2.4). These provisions are remnants of proposals by the EU and AOSIS requiring parties to coordinate the implementation of PAMs. The US, Australia, and other Umbrella Group countries did not favor such mandatory coordination, and the text reflects their view. Parties have since tasked the Subsidiary Body for Scientific and Technological Advice (SBSTA) with facilitating information exchange and sharing of experiences on PAMs of Annex I parties.

2. Mitigation targets and timetables (Article 3)

Article 3 contains the core commitments of Annex I parties under the protocol. Article 3.1 reads: 'The Parties included in Annex I shall, individually or jointly, ensure that their aggregate anthropogenic carbon dioxide equivalent emissions of the greenhouse gases listed in Annex A do not exceed their assigned amounts, calculated pursuant to their quantified emissions limitation and reduction commitments inscribed in Annex B with a view to reducing their overall emissions of such gases by at least 5% below 1990 levels in the commitment period 2008 to 2012'.

The Kyoto Protocol's approach to emissions targets is innovative, and strikes a balance between strictness and flexibility. On the one hand, the targets are legally binding, quantitative (and hence precise), absolute, and economy-wide. On the other hand, the protocol allows parties to achieve their targets in a flexible manner. Noteworthy features of Article 3 including the following.

---

[65] Ibid, 19.   [66] Ibid, 20.
[67] Yamin and Depledge, *International Climate Change Regime* (n 23) 111.

a) Legal character

Article 3.1 uses mandatory terms ('shall') in relation to the individual targets of Annex I parties and is clear and precise, thus rendering these targets, as discussed above, legally binding obligations of result.

b) Differentiated targets

Each Annex I party has an individual, differentiated target listed in Annex B, covering a basket of six gases listed in Annex A to the protocol. The individual country targets were the outcome of intense negotiations, and reflected politics rather than science. The G-77/China, the EU, AOSIS, and others initially proposed uniform targets for all Annex I parties, whereas the US, Australia, Japan, and other Umbrella Group countries supported differentiated commitments tailored to national circumstances.[68] Proposed criteria for differentiation included CO_2e emissions per capita, CO_2e emissions per unit of GDP, GDP per capita, and GDP per capita growth.[69] The disagreements between those that supported uniform targets and those that supported differentiated targets—and within the latter group, between those supporting different objective criteria for differentiation—persisted until the Kyoto conference. In Kyoto, however, the EU softened its stance and began seeking 'equivalence of effort' rather than a uniform target.[70] No agreement on objective criteria was forthcoming but targets had begun to filter through the process in the lead up to and in Kyoto. The Chair exerted pressure on parties to negotiate these targets at Kyoto. However, when no agreement emerged, the Chair drew up a list of targets based on announcements by parties and his consultations. After a series of bilateral meetings with parties to gather their reactions to his list of targets, the Chair left Annex B blank, and, in the final plenary, he invited parties to submit their revised, final targets to the podium. As parties did so, their targets were inserted into Annex B by the secretariat.[71]

This historical context is instructive, and offers a useful comparison with the process of establishing nationally determined contributions (NDCs) under the Paris Agreement. Both the initial Kyoto targets announced by parties and the NDCs offered by parties in the context of the Paris Agreement were nationally determined. But, in Kyoto, the targets were the subject of intensive negotiations among Annex I parties, whereas in Paris, multilateral negotiation of NDCs was never even proposed. Hence, in Kyoto, unlike in Paris, the targets of key countries and groups changed over the course of the conference, as a result of negotiations with other parties and persuasion by the AGBM Chair, Raul Estrada. The outcome (in some cases) was stronger targets than initially proposed.[72] For example, the US initially

---

[68] Breidenich *et al.*, Kyoto Protocol to the UNFCCC (n 18) 320.

[69] Completion of a protocol or another legal instrument (n 11) Annex C.

[70] Depledge, Tracing the Origins of Kyoto Protocol (n 3) 42.

[71] Ibid, 46. See also Breidenich *et al.*, Kyoto Protocol to the UNFCCC (n 18); and Hermann E. Ott, 'The Kyoto Protocol: Unfinished Business', *Environment*, 40/6 (1998): 16.

[72] Depledge, Tracing the Origins of Kyoto Protocol (n 3) 46. Sebastian Oberthür and Hermann E. Ott, *The Kyoto Protocol: International Climate Policy for the 21st Century* (Springer-Verlag Berlin Heidelberg, 1999) 120 (noting that the final numbers were negotiated between the US, the EU, and Japan).

proposed a GHG stabilization target at 1990 levels, the AGBM chair assigned them a reduction of 5% from 1990 levels, and on the last day the US accepted a reduction of 7% from 1990 levels.[73] Similarly, Canada initially proposed a reduction of 3% from 1990 levels, the chair assigned them a reduction of 5% from 1990 levels, and on the last day Canada accepted a reduction of 6% from 1990 levels.[74] Annex B contains a list of differentiated targets for thirty-eight countries, ranging from an 8% reduction from 1990 levels for the EU and a 7% reduction for the USA, to an 8% increase from 1990 levels for Australia and a 10% increase for Iceland.[75] Emissions in most Annex I countries were projected to increase due to economic growth, so the targets for most Kyoto countries represented a bigger departure from business-as-usual than the target numbers themselves suggested.[76] The targets for Russia and Ukraine were notable exceptions. Since these countries' targets were considerably higher than their expected emissions, their targets gave them a large supply of surplus credits (popularly known as 'hot air') that they could potentially sell to other countries through the emissions trading mechanism.[77]

The thirty-eight Annex B countries accounted for 39% of 2010 global GHG emissions.[78] Excluding the US (which rejected the protocol) and Canada (which withdrew from it), the remaining thirty-six countries accounted for 24% of 2010 global GHG emissions. These thirty-six Kyoto parties were in full compliance with their first commitment period targets.[79]

The 2012 Doha Amendment, yet to enter into force, contains individual differentiated targets for Annex B parties for the second commitment period, 2013–20. These are consistent with the targets Annex B parties put forward under the Cancun Agreements for 2020.[80] For instance, the EU's Kyoto target is a reduction of 20% from 1990 levels, the same as its Cancun pledge. Moreover, in a footnote to its Kyoto target, the EU reiterated the conditional offer made in its Cancun pledge to move up to a 30% reduction from 1990 levels, if other developed countries committed themselves to comparable emissions reductions and developing countries contributed adequately according to their responsibilities and

---

[73] See FCCC, Conference of the Parties on its third session, held in Kyoto from 1 to 10 December 1997 (9 December 1997) FCCC/CP/1997/CRP.4, Agenda Item 5; and Depledge, Tracing the Origins of Kyoto Protocol (n 3) 45.

[74] Oberthür and Ott, Kyoto Protocol (n 72) 118. See also Depledge, ibid.

[75] The targets in Annex B of the Protocol are defined in terms of an assigned amount of emissions for each country listed in Annex B. Some argue that the targets that allow an increase in emissions (those of Australia, Iceland, and Norway) are the result of 'intransigence, chutzpah and tough negotiating': Ott, Kyoto Protocol—Unfinished Business (n 71) 20. Others question the 'leadership' demonstrated in such targets. See Duncan French, '1997 Kyoto Protocol to the 1992 UN Framework Convention on Climate Change', *Journal of Environmental Law*, 10/2 (1998): 227, 233.

[76] For example, if the US had joined the Protocol it would have needed to reduce its emissions by about a third from business-as-usual scenarios for the 2008–12 period.

[77] David G. Victor, Nebojša Nakićenović, and Nadejda Victor, 'The Kyoto Protocol Emission Allocations: Windfall Surpluses for Russia and Ukraine', *Climatic Change*, 49/3 (2001): 263. See below Section IV.B.2.h. and V.A.

[78] Igor Shishlov, Romain Morel, and Valentin Bellassen, 'Compliance of the Parties to the Kyoto Protocol in the First Commitment Period', *Climate Policy*, 16/6 (2016): 768.

[79] Ibid.   [80] See Chapter 4, Section V.C.

respective capabilities.[81] Similarly, some countries, such as Australia, had pledged in Cancun reductions from reference years other than 1990. In these cases, the Doha Amendment lists the party's Kyoto target with reference both to the 1990 base year as well as the reference year chosen by the party, but clarifies that only the former is internationally legally binding.[82]

c) Collective target

In addition to the individual targets listed in Annex B, Article 3 contains a collective target for Annex I parties of 'at least 5% below 1990 levels'. This collective target was introduced to address G-77/China fears that including targets only in an annex to the protocol rather than in the protocol itself would marginalize the targets.[83] The Article 3 collective target was not negotiated separately or chosen based on environmental grounds (for example, based on an assessment of the reduction in Annex I emissions necessary to put the world onto a safe emissions pathway). Rather, it merely reflects the sum of the individual country targets listed in Annex B. Moreover, the legal character of this collective target differs from that of the individual targets listed in Annex B.[84] Unlike the mandatory terms that frame the individual targets, the collective target is prefaced by the phrase 'with a view to'. This wording signals an objective or goal rather than a legal obligation. In any case, the collective target was based on the assumption that all Annex B parties would become parties to the protocol. As this outcome was not within the control of individual parties, a collective target could not have been rendered as a legal obligation. Without the US and Canada, the effective collective target dropped to a 4% decrease in emissions for the thirty-six remaining Annex B parties.[85] The 2012 Doha Amendment, yet to enter into force, contains a collective target of 18% below 1990 levels for the second commitment period, 2013–20.[86]

d) Base year

The targets are generally set to a 1990 base year.[87] Early agreement emerged on the choice of 1990 as the base year, in part because it was the FCCC base year, and in part because reliable data was not available for the period before 1990. In line with the flexibility offered to EITs in the FCCC, the Kyoto Protocol also allows EITs to use a base year other than 1990,[88] and five countries—Bulgaria, Romania, Hungary, Poland,[89] and Slovenia[90]—did so. In order not to disadvantage Annex

---

[81] Doha Amendment, Art 1, Section A, fn 7.   [82] Ibid, fn 1.
[83] Depledge, Tracing the Origins of Kyoto Protocol (n 3) 46.
[84] See French, 1997 Kyoto Protocol (n 75) 232.
[85] Shishlov *et al.*, Compliance of the Parties (n 78).
[86] Doha Amendment, Art 1, Section C.   [87] Kyoto Protocol, Art 3.1.
[88] Ibid, Art 3.5.
[89] Decision 9/CP.2, 'Communications from Parties included in Annex I to the Convention: guidelines, schedule and process for consideration' (29 October 1996) FCCC/CP/1996/15/Add.1, 15.
[90] Decision 11/CP.4, 'National communications from Parties included in Annex I to the Convention' (25 January 1999) FCCC/CP/1998/16/Add.1, 47.

I parties that had taken early action on HFCs, PFCs, and SF_6, Annex I countries are allowed to choose between 1990 and 1995 base years for these gases.[91]

e) Assigned amount units

The Kyoto targets are expressed in terms of 'assigned amount units' (AAUs), each representing one ton of CO_2e emissions. At the beginning of a commitment period, a party's initial assigned amount is calculated by taking its base year CO_2e emissions, multiplied by the number of years in the commitment period, and then multiplied again by the party's emissions target. By way of example, if a country emitted one million tons of CO_2e in 1990, and was assigned a minus 6% emissions target for the first commitment period (ie a target allowing it to emit 94% of its base year emissions), its initial assigned amount would have been 4.7 million tons (1 million times 5 times .94). After a party's initial assigned amount is issued according to this formula, it is deposited in a registry maintained by the secretariat and can be added to or subtracted from, over the course of the commitment period, using the market mechanisms described in Section V below, as well as through sink activities that generate removal units (RMUs).[92] In order to comply with its emissions target, a party must have enough units in its account to cover its actual emissions over the commitment period.[93] Parties have adopted detailed modalities for the accounting of assigned amounts.[94]

f) Sinks

The Kyoto Protocol allows Annex I parties to take into account afforestation,[95] reforestation,[96] and deforestation[97] and other agreed land use, land-use change, and forestry (LULUCF) activities in meeting their commitments under Article 3.[98] Critical links exist between LULUCF activities and climate change. Forests, croplands, and grazing lands can be sources, sinks, or reservoirs of GHGs.[99] When they are damaged or destroyed, they release CO_2 and other GHGs into the atmosphere. When they are restored, they remove GHGs from the atmosphere.

The negotiations on sinks proved to be among the most contentious, both in Kyoto and in the post-Kyoto negotiations leading to the Marrakesh Accords.[100]

---

[91] Kyoto Protocol, Art 3.8.   [92] Ibid, Arts 3.10, 3.11, and 312.

[93] At the end of each commitment period, parties are given a brief period of time to 'true-up' their accounts through emissions trading, before compliance is determined.

[94] Decision 13/CMP.1, 'Modalities for the accounting of assigned amounts under Article 7, paragraph 4, of the Kyoto Protocol' (30 March 2006) FCCC/KP/CMP/2005/8/Add.2, 23.

[95] Afforestation refers to the 'planting of new forests on lands which, historically, have not contained forests'. See Intergovernmental Panel on Climate Change (IPCC), *Special Report on Land Use, Land-Use Change and Forestry (LULUCF)* (Cambridge University Press, 2000) ch 2.2.3.1.

[96] Reforestation refers to 'the establishment of trees on land that has been cleared of forest within the relatively recent past'. See ibid, ch 2.2.3.2.

[97] Deforestation refers to the 'permanent removal of forest cover and withdrawal of land from forest use, whether deliberately or circumstantially'. See ibid, ch 2.2.3.3.

[98] Kyoto Protocol, Arts 3.3 and 3.4.

[99] The definition of 'forest' has generated considerable debate in the climate change negotiations. See IPCC, Special Report on LULUCF (n 95) chs 2.2.2.1, 2.2.4.

[100] Oberthür and Ott, Kyoto Protocol (n 72) 124–6; Michael Grubb *et al.*, *The Kyoto Protocol: A Guide and Assessment* (London: Earthscan, 1999) 76–80.

One issue concerned accounting of sinks, since there are considerable uncertainties surrounding the storage rate of biospheric sinks, and inherent difficulties in defining, monitoring, and accounting for them. Many Annex I parties did not report on LULUCF in their national communications at the time and among those that did, the methodologies used were not consistent or comparable; in some cases, uncertainty estimates were very high. Nevertheless, many Umbrella Group countries, including Australia, Canada, New Zealand, and the US, favored the inclusion of sinks in the first commitment period to assist parties in meeting their GHG targets. Among them, Australia preferred a 'net-net' approach, which would have taken sinks into account both in calculating a Party's base year emissions as well as its emissions during the commitment period. New Zealand advocated a 'gross-net' approach, in which sinks are taken into account only in calculating a party's net emissions during the commitment period, for the purposes of assessing compliance with targets.[101] The majority of developing countries, including in particular the small island states, opposed the inclusion of sinks on the grounds that it would weaken the environmental integrity of the targets. The EU initially opposed the inclusion of sinks, but changed its position in the course of the negotiations.

The compromise in Article 3.3 specifically allows a limited set of LULUCF activities—afforestation, reforestation, and deforestation—undertaken since 1990 to be counted toward compliance with Kyoto targets (a 'gross-net' approach). The changes in emissions, however, must be the result of 'direct human induced land use change and forestry activities'. In addition, Article 3.4 authorizes the CMP to allow parties to count emissions and removals of GHGs by other sink activities. The Marrakesh Accords decision on sinks provides for the crediting of human-induced removals of GHGs by cropland, forest, and grazing land management—a major win for Umbrella Group states—but imposes country-specific caps on credits for forest management and provides for net-net accounting of agricultural and grazing lands management,[102] thus limiting the overall number of sinks credits (RMUs) allowed into the Kyoto system.[103]

g) Multi-year commitment period

The Kyoto targets apply to a multi-year commitment period—for the first commitment period, a five-year period running from 2008–12, and for the second commitment period, if it enters into force, an eight-year period running from 2013–20. This multi-year approach emerged from a US proposal supported by Japan, New Zealand, Norway, and the Russian Federation. A multi-year target,

[101] See Oberthür and Ott, Kyoto Protocol (n 72) 132–4; Grubb *et al.*, Kyoto Protocol (n 100) 76–80; and Yamin and Depledge, International Climate Change Regime (n 23) 80–2.

[102] Decision 16/CMP.1, 'Land use, land-use change and forestry' (30 March 2006) FCCC/KP/CMP/2005/8/Add.3, 3, Annex: Definitions, modalities, rules and guidelines relating to land-use, land-use change and forestry, paras 6–11.

[103] For a detailed analysis of decisions relating to LULUCF in the climate regime see Ian Fry, 'More Twists, Turns and Stumbles in the Jungle: A Further Exploration of Land Use, Land-Use Change and Forestry Decisions within the Kyoto Protocol', *Review of European Community and International Environmental Law*, 16/3 (2007): 341.

they argued, would offer greater flexibility to countries to take into account annual fluctuations, and better complement the market mechanisms the US had also proposed.[104] The G-77/China, AOSIS, and the EU preferred a single-year target, but the Chair worked to persuade them of the transparency, verifiability, and quantifiability of multi-year targets, and ultimately they accepted this approach. The start date of the first commitment period, 2008, was also subject to debate. While AOSIS, the EU and many countries and groups favored earlier single-year or multi-year time frames, the US and Canada were insistent on 2008–12. Although the 2008–12 commitment period was eventually accepted, as a compromise it was coupled with a requirement for 'demonstrable progress' by 2005.[105] The requirement for 'demonstrable progress' was framed in mandatory terms ('Parties shall ... have made ... demonstrable progress'). Nevertheless, since 'demonstrable progress' is an undefined concept, the actual legal impact of this provision was limited.[106] Parties agreed through a series of decisions to request reports by 1 January 2006 from Annex I parties demonstrating progress with their Kyoto targets,[107] and they tasked the secretariat with preparing a synthesis report.[108] The second CMP considered this synthesis report, acknowledged the progress made by those Annex I parties that had submitted reports, noted that much of the decrease in total aggregate emissions was from Annex I EITs, and urged parties to intensify their efforts to meet their Kyoto targets.[109]

h) Banking

The Kyoto Protocol allows parties to bank their excess AAUs from one commitment period for use in subsequent commitment periods.[110] This provision was proposed by the US, New Zealand, and Russia,[111] among others, and was also designed, like multi-year targets, to offer parties flexibility to determine when they reduce their emissions. The US also proposed 'borrowing' from future commitment periods, but this idea was not accepted.[112] The final negotiations

---

[104] Breidenich *et al.*, Kyoto Protocol to the UNFCCC (n 18) 321; and Depledge, Tracing the Origins of Kyoto Protocol (n 3) 36–7.

[105] Depledge, ibid, 38. See Kyoto Protocol, Art 3.2.

[106] See nn 286–287 below and accompanying text.

[107] Decision 22/CP.7, 'Guidelines for the preparation of the information required under Article 7 of the Kyoto Protocol' (21 January 2002) FCCC/CP/2001/13/Add.3, 14; and Decision 25/CP.8, 'Demonstrable progress under Article 3, paragraph 2, of the Kyoto Protocol' (28 March 2003) FCCC/CP/2002/7/Add.3, 54.

[108] Decision 25/CP.8, ibid; and Subsidiary Body for Implementation, Synthesis of reports demonstrating progress in accordance with Article 3, paragraph 2, of the Kyoto Protocol, Note by the secretariat (9 May 2006) FCCC/SBI/2006/INF.2 (only half of the Annex B parties had submitted these reports by the deadline).

[109] Decision 7/CMP.3, 'Demonstration of progress in achieving commitments under the Kyoto Protocol by Parties included in Annex I to the Convention' (14 March 2008) FCCC/KP/CMP/2007/9/Add.1, 23.

[110] Kyoto Protocol, Art 3.13.

[111] Depledge, Tracing the Origins of Kyoto Protocol (n 3) 54.

[112] Oberthür and Ott, Kyoto Protocol (n 72) 117 (describing the US proposal that parties should have the flexibility to transfer emissions allowances from the next budget period to the current, if required).

for the second commitment period proved difficult in part because Russia, Ukraine, and some EU member states (most vocally Poland) sought to bank, without restriction, their excess AAUs from the first commitment period, characterized by Ukraine as 'legitimately acquired sovereign property'.[113] As noted earlier, these countries' targets gave them a large number of surplus allowances, because the targets were based on their 1990 emissions, before their emissions plunged as a result of the collapse and restructuring of their economies following the break-up of the USSR. Allowing these countries to bank and then trade their 'hot air' from the first commitment period would have limited the effort needed from other countries, as well as diluted the environmental integrity of the second commitment period of the Kyoto Protocol. Ultimately, the Doha Amendment resolved this issue by allowing banking, but restricting the extent to which banked units can be traded.[114] Moreover, several Annex I parties, including the EU, Australia, Norway, Japan and Switzerland, recorded political declarations that they would not use surplus AAUs carried over from the first commitment period to meet their targets under the second commitment period.[115]

i) Joint fulfilment

The phrase 'individually or jointly' allows any group of Annex I parties to meet their emissions targets jointly. Article 4 contains further authorization for and operational details on 'joint fulfilment' of emissions targets. The EU-15 (at the time) established a collective target under Article 4 with a burden sharing agreement that reallocated the Kyoto targets amongst the EU member states. Thus, for instance, although the common EU target for the first commitment period was an 8% reduction from 1990 levels, Germany agreed to a 21% reduction and Portugal was allowed to increase its emissions by 28% over 1990 levels under the internal EU burden-sharing agreement.[116] The understanding at the time was that only the EU would avail itself of Article 4, but this understanding is not reflected in the text, as others were unwilling to create a special deal for the EU. The Doha Amendment targets are also premised on joint fulfilment by the EU.[117]

---

[113] 'Information on the quantified emission reduction and limitation objectives (QELROs) of Ukraine for the second commitment period of the Kyoto Protocol' <https://unfccc.int/files/meetings/ad_hoc_working_groups/kp/application/pdf/awgkp_ukraine_qerlo_06122012.pdf> accessed 20 January 2016.

[114] Decision 1/CMP.8 'Amendment to the Kyoto Protocol pursuant to its Art 3, paragraph 9 (the Doha Amendment)' (28 February 2013). FCCC/KP/CMP/2012/13/Add.1, 2, paras 23–6.

[115] Ibid, Annex II.

[116] Council Decision 2002/358/EC of 25 April 2002 concerning the approval, on behalf of the European Community, of the Kyoto Protocol to the United Nations Framework Convention on Climate Change and the joint fulfilment of commitments thereunder [2002] OJ L130/1, Annex II.

[117] Doha Amendment, Art 1, Section A, footnote 4.

3. *Financial Support (Article 11)*

In addition to mitigation commitments, the protocol reiterates the financial commitments of Annex II parties under Articles 4.3 and 4.5 of the FCCC, including to provide 'new and additional financial resources to meet the agreed full costs' incurred by developing countries in improving the quality of data/models for the preparation of national inventories, and the 'agreed full incremental costs' for the implementation of existing commitments that are 'agreed' between the developing country and the operational entity of the financial mechanism.[118]

Like the FCCC, the protocol provides that the implementation of Annex II parties' existing commitments shall 'take into account the need for adequacy and predictability in the flow of funds and the importance of appropriate burden sharing among developed country Parties'.[119] The lack of precision in these terms provides Annex II parties with considerable flexibility, particularly since no guidance exists on what constitutes an adequate and predictable flow of funds, and, no formula exists to determine what might be an appropriate sharing of the burden.

V. MECHANISMS (ARTICLES 6, 12, AND 17)

From almost the beginning of the Kyoto Protocol negotiations, the US made it clear that its acceptance of binding emissions targets would be conditional on the inclusion of market-based approaches, which would allow Annex I parties to achieve their targets cost-effectively.[120] The Kyoto Protocol largely reflects the US position by establishing three market mechanisms—although, in an ironic twist, this did not stop the US from later rejecting the protocol. Two of these mechanisms are project-based: joint implementation (JI) and the CDM. The third mechanism is emissions trading.

The three market mechanisms are intended to assist parties in achieving compliance with their GHG emissions targets. They are based on the rationale that emissions reductions have the same effect in slowing global warming wherever they occur, and that therefore reductions should be made where it is most cost-effective to do so. The protocol prescribes, however, that the market mechanisms are to be 'supplemental to domestic action'.[121] This 'supplementarity' qualification was a result of bitter and protracted negotiations on the limits to which use of these market mechanisms should be subject.[122] Many developing countries opposed the

---

[118] Compare FCCC, Art 11 and Kyoto Protocol, Art 10(a).
[119] Kyoto Protocol, Art 11.2.
[120] Depledge, Tracing the Origins of Kyoto Protocol (n 3) 83.
[121] Kyoto Protocol, Arts 6.1(d) and 17.
[122] Article 6 of the Kyoto Protocol states that the parties' acquisition of ERUs shall be 'supplemental' to domestic actions for the purposes of meeting emissions reduction commitments. Article 12 of the protocol specifies that Annex I parties may use certified emission reductions (CERs) accruing from CDM activities to contribute to compliance only with 'part of' their emission reduction commitments. Article 17 permits Annex B parties to participate in emissions trading to meet their commitments under the protocol, provided such trading is 'supplemental' to domestic actions.

unrestricted use of the mechanisms, as they believed that domestic action in Annex I parties would better serve equity. The EU and others also wanted to limit use of the mechanisms because of concerns about their impact on the integrity of the protocol, including due to 'hot air' in the system.[123] For the US and other Umbrella Group countries, however, acceptance of the Kyoto targets was premised on being able to use the market mechanisms without any quantitative limits (known in the negotiations as 'concrete ceilings'). Thus, in the end, only a qualitative restriction on the use of the mechanisms proved possible, namely, that 'domestic action shall … constitute a significant element of the effort' made by Annex I parties in meeting their targets,[124] and this requirement was put within the purview of the compliance committee's facilitative rather than enforcement branch.[125]

The Kyoto Protocol's mechanisms involve transfers of four types of emissions units: (1) AAUs, generated directly from a party's emissions target, (2) RMUs, generated by afforestation, reforestation, forest management, and other sink activities undertaken pursuant to Articles 3.3 and 3.4; (3) emission reduction units (ERUs), generated by JI, and (4) certified emission reductions (CERs), generated by the CDM.[126] To ensure that all the Kyoto units can be traded in a single market,[127] each is denominated as a unit equal to one metric ton of CO_2e and there is full fungibility (or interchangeability) between them.[128]

A. Joint implementation (Article 6)

The JI mechanism[129] builds on provisions of the FCCC, in particular on Activities Implemented Jointly, discussed in Chapter 5.[130] Many of the proposals for JI in the AGBM negotiations envisaged projects between Annex I and non-Annex I countries. The G-77/China, however, opposed such projects both because they believed action should primarily be taken by and in Annex I countries and because they believed the terms of such arrangements would favor Annex I countries.[131] When the CDM emerged in the final days of the Kyoto conference as a mechanism

---

[123] Lavanya Rajamani, 'Re-negotiating Kyoto: A Review of the Sixth Conference of Parties to the Framework Convention on Climate Change', *Colorado Journal of International Environmental Law and Policy,* 12/1 (2001): 201, 216–17.

[124] Decision 15/CP.7, 'Principles, nature and scope of the mechanisms pursuant to Articles 6, 12 and 17 of the Kyoto Protocol' (21 January 2002) FCCC/CP/2001/13/Add.2, 2, preambular recital 7.

[125] See Decision 27/CMP.1 (n 40) Annex, Section IV, para 5(b).

[126] Kyoto Protocol, Arts 3, 6, 12, and 17.

[127] It is worth noting, however, that there are distinctions between these units in relation to banking. CERs and ERUs can be banked up to 2.5% of a party's AAU, whereas RMUs cannot be banked. Decision 13/CMP.1 (n 94) Annex, paras 15–16.

[128] Ibid, Annex, paras 1–4. See generally on fungibility, Farhana Yamin (ed), *Climate Change and Carbon Markets: A Handbook of Emission Reduction Mechanisms* (London: Earthscan, 2005) 17–19.

[129] The term 'joint implementation' does not occur in the text of Article 6, but this mechanism has from the start been called 'joint implementation', including in official FCCC documents.

[130] FCCC, Arts 3.3 and 4.2 (a) and (b), and Decision 5/CP.1, 'Activities implemented jointly under the pilot phase' (6 June 1995) FCCC/1995/7/Add.1, 18. See Chapter 5, Section IV.B.3.

[131] Oberthür and Ott, Kyoto Protocol (n 72) 152.

allowing Annex I parties to undertake projects in non-Annex I parties, the JI mechanism came to be limited to Annex I countries.

The JI mechanism allows one Annex I party to receive credits (ERUs) for projects in another Annex I party that reduce emissions or enhance the removal of GHGs by sinks, provided such emissions reductions or enhanced removals are 'additional' to any that would have otherwise occurred.[132] The protocol provides that the parties 'may' elaborate guidelines for JI, including guidelines for verification and accounting,[133] which were adopted as part of the Marrakech Accords.[134]

The Marrakesh Accords established an Article 6 Supervisory Committee, under the authority of the CMP, inter alia, to supervise the verification of ERUs generated through Article 6 projects.[135] The Article 6 guidelines identify eligibility requirements for parties to participate in JI: they must be a Kyoto party, their assigned amount must have been duly calculated and recorded,[136] and they must have fulfilled their commitments under Articles 5 and 7, discussed above.[137] If a host party meets these eligibility requirements, it can approve projects, verify for itself that emissions reductions from a JI project are 'additional', and issue the appropriate quantity of ERUs.[138] In contrast, if a party does not meet all of the eligibility requirements, the verification of 'additionality' must occur through the Article 6 Supervisory Committee.[139] The former procedure is termed 'Track 1' and the latter 'Track 2'. When ERUs are transferred between parties, they are subtracted from one party's registry and added to the other's to ensure that there is no double counting of emissions reductions.[140]

In JI, unlike in the CDM, AAUs are converted into an equivalent number of ERUs before they are issued, so JI merely involves the transfer of existing units between Annex I parties, rather than the creation of additional emissions units that would expand the overall emissions budget of Annex I parties. Nevertheless, the limited international oversight as well as transparency of JI Track 1 activities has led many to question their environmental integrity,[141] in particular in relation to the quality of auditing services, the use of inappropriate and inconsistent methodological approaches, project approval, and monitoring of emissions reductions.[142] Indeed, some studies find that JI may have enabled global GHG emissions to be about 600 million tonnes of carbon dioxide equivalent (tCO_2e) higher than they would have been if each Annex I party had met its emissions target domestically.[143]

---

[132] Kyoto Protocol, Art 6.   [133] Ibid, Art 6.2.

[134] Decision 9/CMP.1, 'Guidelines for the implementation of Article 6 of the Kyoto Protocol' (30 March 2006) FCCC/KP/CMP/2005/8/Add.2, 2.

[135] Ibid, para 3.   [136] In accordance with Decision 13/CMP.1 (n 94).

[137] Decision 9/CMP.1 (n 134) Annex, para 21.   [138] Ibid, para 22.

[139] Ibid, para 23.   [140] Kyoto Protocol, Arts 3.10 and 3.11.

[141] Anja Kollmuss, Lambert Schneider, and Vladyslav Zhezherin, 'Has Joint Implementation reduced GHG emissions? Lessons learned for the design of carbon market mechanisms' (Stockholm Environment Institute Working Paper No. 2015-07, 2015) <https://www.sei-international.org/mediamanager/documents/Publications/Climate/SEI-WP-2015-07-JI-lessons-for-carbon-mechs.pdf> accessed 20 January 2017.

[142] FCCC, Joint Implementation, Concept note: Input from the Joint Implementation Supervisory Committee to CMP 12, Version 01.0 (3 March 2016) JI-JISC38-AA-A05.

[143] Kollmuss *et al.*, Has Joint Implementation reduced GHG emissions? (n 141) 1.

As of 1 January 2016, 871 million ERUs had been issued, the overwhelming majority for Track 1 activities.[144] Nearly 60% of these ERUs have been issued by Ukraine and 30% by Russia.[145] As these countries have large surpluses of AAUs, some NGOs have argued that they are engaging in 'hot-air laundering', ie exporting surplus AAUs in the form of ERUs, rather than actually undertaking additional emissions reduction projects.[146] Independent studies flag 'significant environmental integrity concerns' with 80% of ERUs issued by Ukraine and Russia.[147] This would, if true, compromise both the environmental integrity of the Kyoto Protocol as well as the stability of the carbon market. The Doha CMP requested the Subsidiary Body for Implementation (SBI) to draft revised joint implementation guidelines for consideration by parties.[148] It identified the key attributes that should characterize the future operation of the JI, including a single unified track for JI projects, closely aligned or unified accreditation procedures for JI and CDM, clear and transparent information, and clear, transparent, and objective requirements to ensure reductions are additional to those that would have occurred anyway.[149] The future of JI as well as of the other Kyoto mechanisms, however, is unclear at this moment, as discussed below.[150]

At the heart of the environmental integrity concerns that have beset the operation of JI thus far is the issue of 'additionality', ie whether the emissions reduction would have happened anyway, in the absence of the project activity. As this is a key issue for both project-based mechanisms—JI and the CDM—it will be discussed below.

B. Clean Development Mechanism (Article 12)

The CDM owes its origins to a Brazilian Proposal for a clean development fund, which sought to impose financial penalties on Annex I parties for non-compliance and to channel the funds to non-Annex I parties for addressing climate change.[151] In the course of the negotiations, Brazil's clean development fund and a similar proposal by the G-77/China transformed into the CDM,[152] which gives Annex I parties additional flexibility in meeting their targets, and involves developing countries in emissions mitigation efforts. The CDM drew inspiration from ideas raised in the

---

[144] FCCC, 'Emissions Reductions Units (ERUs) Issued' <http://ji.unfccc.int/statistics/2015/ERU_Issuance_2015_10_15_1200.pdf> accessed 20 January 2017.

[145] Calculation based on FCCC data, ibid.

[146] Climate Action Network, 'Submission on Joint Implementation' (15 February 2013) <http://unfccc.int/resource/docs/2013/smsn/ngo/298.pdf> accessed 20 January 2017.

[147] Kollmuss *et al.*, Has Joint Implementation reduced GHG emissions? (n 141) 9.

[148] Decision 6/CMP.8, 'Guidance on the implementation of Article 6 of the Kyoto Protocol' (28 February 2013) FCCC/KP/CMP/2012/13/Add.2, 14, paras 14–16.

[149] Ibid, para 15. The proposed modalities and procedures for Joint Implementation are currently under consideration by the SBI. SBI, Review of the Joint Implementation Guidelines, Draft Conclusions Proposed by the Chair (3 December 2015) FCCC/SBI/2015/L.30.

[150] See Section V.D. below.

[151] Depledge, Tracing the Origins of Kyoto Protocol (n 3) 60.

[152] See Ken Johnson, 'Brazil and the Politics of the Climate Change Negotiations', *The Journal of Environment and Development,* 10/2 (2001): 178.

context of the negotiations on JI and from activities implemented jointly under the convention,[153] and, in essence, became a mechanism for joint implementation between Annex I and non-Annex I parties.

The CDM allows Annex I parties to undertake or invest in project activities in non-Annex I countries and to use the CERs that accrue from the project toward compliance with their Kyoto emissions targets.[154] The purpose of the CDM is 'to assist Parties not included in Annex I in achieving sustainable development and in contributing to the ultimate objective of the convention, and to assist Parties included in Annex I in achieving compliance with their quantified emission limitation and reduction commitments under Article 3'. To generate CERs, the emissions reductions from CDM projects must be 'additional' to any that would have otherwise occurred.[155] The protocol provides that the CDM shall be subject to the authority and guidance of the CMP, and be supervised by the CDM Executive Board.[156] It also provides that parties 'shall' elaborate modalities and procedures with the objective of ensuring transparency, efficiency, and accountability through independent auditing and verification of project activities.[157]

The Marrakesh Accords specify modalities and procedures for the operation of the CDM.[158] These list the eligibility requirements for participation in the CDM,[159] and outline a rigorous process of monitoring, verification, and certification for emissions reductions from CDM projects.[160] Parties also launched the CDM ('prompt start') in advance of entry into force of the Kyoto Protocol.[161] As of 31 December 2016, the CDM Executive Board had registered 754 projects, expected to produce CERs amounting to over 8.48 billion tonnes of CO_2e.[162] Several issues have arisen in the course of the CDM's operations that offer lessons for the design of any future market mechanisms under the climate regime. These include the following.

1. Additionality

Additionality, a key requirement in the context of both JI and the CDM, has proven difficult to define, implement, and secure. The Kyoto Protocol requires CERs to

---

[153] See Jacob Werksman, 'The Clean Development Mechanism: Unwrapping the Kyoto Surprise', *Review of European, Comparative and International Environmental Law*, 7/2 (1998): 147.

[154] Kyoto Protocol, Art 12.   [155] Ibid, Art 12.5(c).   [156] Ibid, Art 12.4.

[157] Ibid, Art 12.7.

[158] Decision 3/CMP.1, 'Modalities and procedures for a clean development mechanism as defined in Article 12 of the Kyoto Protocol' (30 March 2006) FCCC/KP/CMP/2005/8/Add.1, 6.

[159] For a non-Annex I country, it must be a Party to the Kyoto Protocol, and for an Annex I country its assigned amount must have been duly calculated and recorded, and it must have fulfilled its commitments under Articles 5 and 7. Decision 3/CMP.1, ibid, Annex, paras 30 and 31.

[160] Ibid, Annex, paras 53–63.

[161] Decision 17/CP.7, 'Modalities and procedures for a clean development mechanism, as defined in Article 12 of the Kyoto Protocol' (21 January 2002) FCCC/CP/2001/13/Add.2, 20. Kyoto Article 12.10 permits CERs obtained from 2000 up to 2008 to be used to achieve compliance in the first commitment period.

[162] FCCC, 'Project Activities' <http://cdm.unfccc.int/Statistics/Public/CDMinsights/index.html> accessed 20 January 2017.

be certified as 'additional to any that would occur in the absence of the certified project activity'.[163] The Marrakesh Accords define additionality in similarly general terms.[164] Additionality is assessed in relation to a business-as-usual 'baseline'—that is, what would have occurred in the absence of the CDM project activity.[165] The climate change process has struggled to clearly define additionality and set baselines. The CDM methodologies panel, which supports the CDM Executive Board, has over time developed and refined detailed guidance, including 'tools' to demonstrate and assess additionality and identify baselines.[166] Nevertheless, assessing additionality and setting baselines involves considerable subjectivity.[167]

Additionality is critical to the environmental integrity of the protocol, even more so in the case of the CDM than JI. As noted earlier, JI involves the transfer of emissions allowances between two Annex I parties, both of which have targets, and thus does not increase the overall number of allowances in the system. In contrast, CDM projects generate additional emissions allowances, since they are undertaken in non-Annex I parties, which do not have any emissions targets. CERs thus loosen the cap on Annex I emissions. As a result, if CERs are generated from emissions reductions that are not additional, in that they would have occurred anyway, the environmental integrity of the Annex I targets is undermined.[168] For this reason, Article 12.5 requires that CERs from CDM projects be certified internationally before they are created, by an operational entity designated by the CDM Executive Board. Nevertheless, many studies over the years have questioned the extent to which CDM projects have resulted in emissions reductions that are truly additional.[169] Further, the very notion of additionality can create perverse incentives for developing countries to refrain from adopting progressive climate regulations and

---

[163] Kyoto Protocol, Art 12.5(c).

[164] Decision 3/CMP.1 (n 158) Annex, para 43; see generally Axel Michaelowa, 'Interpreting the Additionality of CDM Projects: Changes in Additionality Definitions and Regulatory Practices over Time', in David Freestone and Charlotte Streck (eds), *Legal Aspects of Carbon Trading: Kyoto, Copenhagen and Beyond* (Oxford University Press, 2009) 248.

[165] Michael Gillenwater, 'What is Additionality?' (Greenhouse Gas Management Institute, January 2012) <http://ghginstitute.org/wp-content/uploads/2015/04/AdditionalityPaper_Part-1ver3FINAL.pdf> accessed 20 January 2017; Michael W. Wara and David G. Victor, 'A Realistic Policy on International Carbon Offsets' (April 2008) Stanford University, Program on Energy and Sustainable Development, Working Paper #74 <http://pesd.fsi.stanford.edu/sites/default/files/WP74_final_final.pdf> accessed 20 January 2017; and World Bank, *10 Years of Experience in Carbon Finance: Insights from working with the Kyoto mechanisms* (Washington, D.C.: World Bank, 2009).

[166] See FCCC, Clean Development Mechanism, 'Methodological tool: Combined tool to identify the baseline scenario and demonstrate additionality, Version 06.0' (24 July 2015) <https://cdm.unfccc.int/methodologies/PAmethodologies/tools/am-tool-02-v6.0.pdf> accessed 20 January 2017; and 'Clean Development Mechanism, Methodological tool: tool for the demonstration and assessment of additionality, Version 07.0.0' (23 November 2012) <https://cdm.unfccc.int/methodologies/PAmethodologies/tools/am-tool-01-v7.0.0.pdf> accessed 20 January 2017.

[167] See eg Lambert Schneider, 'Assessing the Additionality of CDM Projects: Practical Experiences and Lessons Learned', *Climate Policy*, 9/3 (2009): 242; and Axel Michaelowa, 'Strengths and Weaknesses of the CDM in Comparison with New and Emerging Market Mechanisms' (Paper No. 2 for the CDM Policy Dialogue, June 2012) <http://www.cdmpolicydialogue.org/research/1030_strengths.pdf> accessed 20 January 2017.

[168] Werksman, Clean Development Mechanism (n 153) 154–5.   [169] See n 167 above.

measures, as these will then be built into their baseline, making additionality more difficult to demonstrate in the future.[170]

2. Sustainable development

Sustainable development, the stated purpose of the CDM in relation to developing countries,[171] has also proven difficult to define, implement and secure. The notion of sustainable development is defined neither in the FCCC nor in the Kyoto Protocol. Efforts to introduce sustainable development indicators in the climate negotiations proved fruitless, and the Marrakesh Accords chose merely to characterize sustainable development as a host country 'prerogative'.[172] A designated national authority in each country has to confirm that project participation is voluntary, and that the project helps it achieve sustainable development.[173]

The extent to which the CDM has contributed to sustainable development in developing countries is difficult to assess, yet available evidence suggests that the benefits have been limited.[174] There is a variance in definitions and approaches across host countries. Developing countries have relied on different approaches to determine if CDM projects contribute to their sustainable development. These can be broadly categorized into: the guidelines approach, where broad (generally ambiguous and indeterminate) guidelines are prescribed; the checklist approach, where either a positive and/or negative checklist is developed (for instance, renewable energy development and energy efficiency may be part of the positive checklist, and large hydro development part of the negative checklist); and, the scoring approach, where projects are rated based on set criteria.[175] Brazil uses a combination of the guidelines, checklist, and scoring approaches,[176] China combines the guidelines and checklist approach,[177] and India employs a pure guidelines approach,

---

[170] See eg Christiana Figueres, 'Sectoral CDM: Opening the CDM to the Yet Unrealized Goal of Sustainable Development', *McGill International Journal of Sustainable Development Law and Policy*, 2/1 (2006): 5.

[171] Kyoto Protocol, Art 12.2.   [172] Decision 17/CP.7 (n 161) preambular recital 4.

[173] Ibid, Annex, para 40(a).

[174] Johannes Alexeew et al., 'An Analysis of the Relationship between the Additionality of CDM projects and their Contribution to Sustainable Development', *International Environmental Agreements*, 10/3 (2010): 233. For a review of earlier literature, see Karen Holm Olsen, 'The Clean Development Mechanism's Contribution to Sustainable Development - A Review of the Literature', *Climate Change*, 84/1 (2007): 59.

[175] Anne Olhoff et al., *CDM Sustainable Development Impacts* (Roskilde: UNEP Risoe Centre, 2004) 49–51.

[176] Brazil identifies nuclear energy, large hydro, unsustainable biomass energy, among others, as ineligible under the CDM. Brazil, Ministry of Environment, Eligibility Criteria and Sustainability Indicators to Assess Projects that Contribute to the Mitigation of Climate Change and to Promoting Sustainable Development (2002), 42.

[177] China identifies renewable energy, methane recovery, and energy efficiency as priority areas, and encourages transfer of environmentally sound technology to China. See Department of Climate Change, National Development and Reform Commission, Clean Development Mechanism, 'Measures for Operation and Management of Clean Development Mechanism Projects in China' (21 November 2005) <http://cdm-en.ccchina.gov.cn/Detail.aspx?newsId=5628&TId=37> accessed 20 January 2017, Arts 4, 6, and 10.

which invests its designated national authority with considerable discretion.[178] It is fair to say that host countries have an incentive to compete for CDM projects by lowering 'sustainable development' requirements. Some scholars note that the 'reality' of CDM projects is that they focus on maximizing CERs rather than promoting sustainable development.[179] In response to the perceived failures of a decentralized system for assessing sustainable development in relation to the CDM, in 2003 the World Wildlife Fund and other international NGOs established the 'gold standard'. The Gold Standard is a standard and certification body that has created a best practice benchmark for energy projects incorporating sustainability criteria such as access to basic services and improving health, income and gender equality.[180] Thus far, it has certified over 1100 projects in seventy countries.[181] These projects trade for a premium in the carbon market.

3. Project eligibility

In light of the CDM's sustainable development requirement, the negotiations leading to the Marrakesh Accords focused on the types of projects permitted under the CDM. The EU proposed a 'positive list' of safe and environmentally sound projects from which CDM projects could be drawn,[182] including renewable energy, energy efficiency, and demand-side management projects.[183] The EU argued that a positive list would ensure environmental integrity, increase certainty for investors, and help garner political and public support. While the Umbrella Group believed such a list to be unnecessary, others disagreed over which types of projects should be included on the list.[184] For instance, India and China wished to allow nuclear energy projects under the CDM, while AOSIS and the Organization of the Petroleum Exporting Countries (OPEC) opposed allowing them. Similarly, the Umbrella Group and several South and Central American countries wished to

---

[178] National CDM Authority, Ministry of Environment and Forests (Climate Change Division), Order (16 April 2004) <http://ncdmaindia.gov.in/ViewPDF.aspx?pub=notification.pdf> accessed 20 January 2017.

[179] Christina Voigt, 'Climate Law Reporter: Is the Clean Development Mechanism Sustainable? Some Critical Aspects', *Sustainable Development Law and Policy*, 8/2 (2008): 15, 18; and Bharathi Pillai, 'Moving Forward to 2012: An Evaluation of the Clean Development Mechanism', *New York University Environmental Law Journal*, 18/2 (2010): 357.

[180] See 'Gold Standard' <http://www.goldstandard.org/> accessed 20 January 2017.

[181] Ibid. See for a contrasting view, Sam Headon, 'Whose Sustainable Development? Sustainable Development under the Kyoto Protocol, the "Coldplay Effect" and the CDM Gold Standard', *Colorado Journal of International Environmental Law and Policy*, 20/2 (2009): 127, 128 (arguing that proposals for furthering sustainable development should not focus on mandatory universal standards but on building capacity in developing countries to have and maintain rigorous standards).

[182] The issue was raised and discussed at the Thirteenth Session of the Subsidiary Bodies, held in Lyon, from 11 to 15 September 2000.

[183] See Preparations for the First Session of the Conference of the Parties Serving as the Meeting of the Parties to the Kyoto Protocol (Decision 8/CP.4), Work Programme on Mechanisms (Decision 7/CP.4 and 14/CP.5), Article 12 of the Kyoto Protocol, Note by the President (24 November 2000) FCCC/CP/2000/CRP.2, para 8.

[184] Rajamani, Re-negotiating Kyoto (n 123) 218.

include sinks projects in the CDM, while the EU, AOSIS, Brazil, China, and India opposed such projects.[185]

The negotiations on whether to allow sinks projects proved particularly contentious. In addition to the concerns over measurement and uncertainty, referred to earlier, sinks projects raise concerns relating to non-permanence and leakage. Non-permanence is a risk because the enhancement of carbon stocks from sinks projects is potentially reversible through human activities, natural disturbances, and environmental change, including climate change.[186] Also, the reduction of deforestation in one area does not necessarily imply a reduction in deforestation worldwide. In fact, the resulting decrease in timber supply in one area might accelerate deforestation elsewhere. When this phenomenon—termed leakage—occurs, allowing credits under the CDM causes overall global GHG levels to increase, because global deforestation continues while Annex I parties use the credits they have acquired through the CDM projects to offset additional domestic GHG emissions.

Nevertheless, many developing countries were keen to use their natural capital and engage in sinks projects, and the Umbrella Group strongly supported the inclusion of sinks projects in the CDM. The compromise reached in the Marrakesh Accords allows sinks projects, but limits them to reforestation and afforestation projects, not projects to avoid deforestation.[187]

To address broader concerns with sinks projects, specific methodologies have since been developed for afforestation and reforestation projects,[188] and GHG removals from such projects can only be used to help meet emissions targets up to 1% of a party's base year emissions for each year of the commitment period.[189] To address non-permanence, the rules distinguish between temporary CERs (tCERs) and long-term CERs (lCERs).[190] In relation to nuclear projects, the Marrakesh Accords urge parties 'to refrain from using certified emissions reductions generated from nuclear facilities to meet their targets.[191] Beyond these two restrictions, however, parties are free to choose any type of CDM project. In practice, however,

---

[185] Emily Boyd, Esteve Corbera, and Manuel Estrada, 'UNFCCC Negotiations (Pre-Kyoto to COP-9): What the Process Says about the Politics of CDM-Sinks', *International Environmental Agreements: Politics, Law and Economics,* 8/2 (2008): 95, 101.

[186] See generally IPCC, *IPCC Special Report on Land Use, Land-Use Change and Forestry, Summary for Policymakers* (Cambridge University Press, 2000) 10, para 40.

[187] Decision 17/CP.7 (n 161) para 7(a). To address the issue of avoided deforestation, Papua New Guinea and Costa Rica, on behalf of a Coalition for Rainforest Nations, launched the RED initiative (standing for Reductions in Emissions from Deforestation) at COP11 in 2006. The following year, RED become REDD+, with the addition of forest degradation within its ambit, and it featured in the Bali Action Plan as one of five 'building blocks'. See generally Christina Voight (ed), *Research Handbook on REDD+ and International Law* (Cheltenham, UK: Edward Elgar, 2016).

[188] FCCC, 'CDM Methodologies' <http://cdm.unfccc.int/methodologies/index.html> accessed 20 January 2017.

[189] Decision 16/CMP.1 (n 102) Annex, para 14.

[190] Decision 5/CMP.1, 'Modalities and procedures for afforestation and reforestation project activities under the clean development mechanism in the first commitment period of the Kyoto Protocol' (30 March 2006) FCCC/KP/CMP/2005/8/Add.1, 61, Annex, para 1.

[191] Decision 17/CP.7 (n 161) preambular recital 5. A similar restriction also applies to JI, Decision 16/CP.7, 'Guidelines for the implementation of Article 6 of the Kyoto Protocol' (21 January 2002) FCCC/CP/2001/13/Add.2, 5, preambular recital 4.

the market for credits from certain types of projects has been shaped by buyer preferences. The EU, the principal buyer of CDM credits, has qualitative and quantitative restrictions on the credits that can be brought into the EU market.[192] In addition, individual EU member states have incorporated qualitative and quantitative restrictions into their state-funded programs for purchasing CDM (and JI) credits.[193]

4. Project types

a) Unilateral CDM
The permissive nature of the Marrakesh Accords has also given rise to innovative institutional arrangements for CDM projects such as 'unilateral CDM'.[194] Unilateral CDM projects are developed, financed, and implemented directly by developing countries, with no Annex I country investor and no identified buyers before certification of the emissions reductions.[195] As of 31 July 2016, 30% of all CDM projects are unilateral,[196] many in India.

b) Programmatic CDM
Given the limited impact that single projects can have on emissions trends and the high transaction costs, the CDM Executive Board has permitted project developers to register a 'programme of activities' consisting of several component project activities under the CDM.[197] Such programs encourage coordinated implementation of policies, reduce transaction costs, and decrease project risk and uncertainties.

c) Other project types
In a similar vein, the CDM Executive Board has developed simplified modalities and procedures[198] as well as tailored methodologies for small-scale

---

[192] The EU bans the use of credits from nuclear energy projects, sinks projects, and projects involving the destruction of industrial gases (HFC-23 and N_2O). It accepts credits from large hydro projects only if certain conditions are fulfilled. European Commission, Climate Action, 'Use of International Credits' <http://ec.europa.eu/clima/policies/ets/credits_en> accessed 20 January 2017.

[193] See eg 'Directive for the Austrian JI/CDM Programme' <https://ji.unfccc.int/UserManagement/FileStorage/UM5XOG3J6Y69SN5F24RT8W4SC7WJJ3> accessed 20 January 2017.

[194] The CDM Executive Board's Project Design Document Template envisages such unilateral CDM projects. See FCCC, 'Forms' <https://cdm.unfccc.int/Reference/PDDs_Forms/index.html> accessed 20 January 2017.

[195] Axel Michaelowa *et al.*, 'Unilateral CDM: Chances and Pitfalls' (Eschborn: Deutsche Gesellschaft für Technische Zusammenarbeit, November 2003); UNEP, *Legal Issues Guidebook to the Clean Development Mechanism (The UNEP Project CD4CDM)* (Roskilde: UNEP Risoe Centre, June 2004) 48–9.

[196] FCCC, 'Distribution of Registered Projects by Other Party' <http://cdm.unfccc.int/Statistics/Public/files/201607/proj_reg_byOther.pdf> accessed 20 January 2017 (unilateral projects are captured under the category 'none' in relation to any other (than the host) party listed).

[197] FCCC, 'CDM Programmes of Activities' <https://cdm.unfccc.int/ProgrammeOfActivities/index.html> accessed 20 January 2017.

[198] Decision 17/CP.7 (n 161). The term 'modalities and procedures' refers to the rules associated with operationalizing mechanisms such as the CDM or project activities such as afforestation and reforestation.

projects.[199] Modalities and procedures, as well as methodologies, were adopted also for carbon capture and storage projects.[200] These were adopted after protracted negotiations due to concerns over the additionality, permanence, and sustainability of such projects.[201]

5. Equitable geographical distribution of CDM projects

Even as the CDM and its rules were being negotiated, many LDCs and African nations expressed concerns that, given the limited scale of emissions reductions possible in their countries, they would receive very few CDM projects. These concerns have proven to be well founded. The vast majority of the 8.4 billion CERs anticipated from the CDM thus far will be generated from projects located in China (nearly 50%), followed by India (20%).[202] Only a miniscule number of projects are located in Africa.[203] The African Group had sought, early in the negotiations of the Marrakesh Accords, to introduce the concept of 'emissions avoidance', arguing that the CDM should be designed to reward not just projects that reduce emissions, but also projects that avoid emissions by promoting sustainable development using clean technologies. This proposal was not accepted. But persistent calls from LDCs, the African Group, and small island developing states to ensure 'equitable geographical distribution of CDM projects' has led to efforts to address the lack of CDM projects in LDCs and small island states,[204] including through financial and other support to enhance skills and to strengthen human and institutional capacity

[199] FCCC, CDM Methodologies (n 188). The term 'methodologies' refers to approaches to individual project activities reflecting aspects such as sector and region. There are two types of methodologies—baseline and monitoring. Baseline methodologies are a means to estimate the emissions that would have occurred in the most plausible alternative scenario to the project activity, and monitoring methodologies are the means to estimate the actual emissions reductions from the project. See 'What is a methodology?', in *CDM Rulebook: Clean Development Mechanism Rules, Practice & Procedures* <http://www.cdmrulebook.org/404.html> accessed 20 January 2017.

[200] Carbon capture and storage (CCS) is defined as 'the capture and transport of carbon dioxide from anthropogenic sources of emissions, and the injection of the captured carbon dioxide into an underground geological storage site for long-term isolation from the atmosphere'. Decision 10/CMP.7, 'Modalities and procedures for carbon dioxide capture and storage in geological formations as clean development mechanism project activities' (15 March 2012) FCCC/KP/CMP/2011/10/Add.2, 13, Annex, A.1. See also FCCC, CDM Methodologies (n 188).

[201] See generally Katherine A. Abend, 'Deploying Carbon Capture and Storage in Developing Countries: Risks and Opportunities', *Georgetown International Environmental Law Review,* 23/3 (2011): 397; and Anatole Boute, 'Carbon Capture and Storage under the Clean Development Mechanism – An Overview of Regulatory Challenges', *Carbon and Climate Law Review,* 2/4 (2008): 339.

[202] FCCC, 'Distribution of Registered Projects by Host Party' <http://cdm.unfccc.int/Statistics/ Public/files/201607/proj_reg_byHost.pdf> accessed 20 January 2017.

[203] FCCC, 'Distribution of Registered Projects by UN Region and Sub-region' <http://cdm.unfccc.int/Statistics/Public/files/201607/proj_reg_bySubregion.pdf> accessed 20 January 2017.

[204] See eg Decision 7/CMP.1, 'Further guidance relating to the clean development mechanism' (30 March 2006) FCCC/KP/CMP/2005/8/Add.1, 93, para 32; and Equitable distribution of clean development mechanism project activities: Submissions from Parties (14 August 2006) FCCC/KP/CMP/ 2006/MISC.1. The CDM Executive Board's analysis of submissions is in FCCC, 'Equitable distribution of clean development mechanism project activities - analysis of submissions' <https://cdm.unfccc. int/EB/026/eb26annagan4.pdf> accessed 20 January 2017.

to develop CDM projects.[205] Simplified modalities and procedures as well as tailored methodologies for small-scale projects have also proven helpful. Ultimately, however, market forces drive the private sector to low-risk, high-opportunity locations and projects, and the skewed distribution of CDM projects has continued. Note, however, that EU rules have permitted new CERs only from projects based in LDCs to enter the EU emissions trading system (EU-ETS) from 2013.[206]

6. Share of proceeds

The Kyoto Protocol requires a 'share of the proceeds' from CDM projects to be used to cover the CDM's administrative costs, as well as to assist developing country parties that are particularly vulnerable to climate change.[207] The Marrakesh Accords set the share of proceeds at 2% of the CERs issued for a CDM project activity, and channel these CERs to the Adaptation Fund.[208] The accords exempt CDM projects in LDCs from this requirement. For the second commitment period, in response to a long-standing call by LDCs, the share of proceeds levy has been extended to JI and emissions trading.[209]

C. Emissions trading (Article 17)

The US, New Zealand, Canada, Australia, Norway, and France submitted proposals in favor of emissions trading.[210] The EU, however, took a more cautious approach, due to concerns that unrestricted emissions trading would allow the available 'hot air' in the system to dilute the effort required to meet the Kyoto targets.[211] The US and other developed countries argued that the EU's joint-fulfilment was in effect emissions trading, and that other developed countries should be offered the same opportunity.[212] After considerable negotiation, Annex I parties reached a compromise that struck a balance between the strength of the Kyoto targets and flexibility in achieving them. However, developing countries, in particular China and India, continued to oppose emissions trading on principle, arguing that it could be interpreted as a right to pollute.[213] Their opposition until the final hours of the Kyoto conference resulted in a bare bones Article 17, far shorter than the provisions

---

[205] See Decision 8/CMP.7, 'Further guidance relating to the clean development mechanism' (15 March 2012) FCCC/KP/CMP/2011/10/Add.2, 6, paras 30–3.

[206] See for further information, European Commission, Climate Action, Use of International Credits (n 192). See generally European Commission, Climate Action, 'The EU Emissions Trading System (EU ETS)' <http://ec.europa.eu/clima/policies/ets_en > accessed 20 January 2017.

[207] Kyoto Protocol, Art 12.8.

[208] Decision 17/CP.7 (n 161) para 15; and Decision 10/CP.7 (n 17).

[209] Decision 1/CMP.8 (n 114) para 21.

[210] Depledge, Tracing the Origins of Kyoto Protocol (n 3) 82.   [211] Ibid.

[212] Breidenich *et al.*, Kyoto Protocol to the UNFCCC (n 18) 324.

[213] Oberthür and Ott, Kyoto Protocol (n 72) 188–9; Ott, Kyoto Protocol—Unfinished Business (n 71) 41. In response to these concerns, the Marrakesh Accords specifically include a principle stating that Kyoto has 'not created or bestowed any right, title, or entitlement to emissions' on Annex I parties. Decision 15/CP.7 (n 124) preambular recital 5.

on CDM and JI, and much whittled down from the earlier provision on emissions trading in the negotiating text.[214]

Kyoto Article 17 permits an Annex I party[215] to engage in 'emissions trading'—transferring or acquiring AAUs, ERUs, CERs, or RMUs to or from another Annex I party—to meet its commitments under the protocol, provided that such trading is 'supplemental' to domestic actions. The protocol ensures environmental integrity by requiring the transferring party to deduct the transferred units from its assigned amount before the acquiring party can add the transfer to (and thus increase) its assigned amount.[216]

The protocol provides that parties 'shall define the relevant principles, modalities, rules and guidelines, in particular for verification, reporting and accountability for emissions trading'.[217] These rules were finalized, along with the rules for the CDM and JI, in the Marrakesh Accords.[218] The modalities, rules, and guidelines list the eligibility requirements for participation in emissions trading.[219] They also establish a 'commitment period reserve', set at 90% of a party's assigned amount.[220] A commitment period reserve is the minimum number of emissions units (AAUs, ERUs, CERs, and RMUs) a country must have in its national registry at any given time. The reserve is designed to limit a party's ability to over-sell allowances and end up in breach of its Kyoto targets.[221] The accords set out detailed modalities for the accounting of assigned amounts, including institutional requirements relating to the establishment of national registries, and an independent international transaction log, maintained by the FCCC secretariat, to verify the validity of transactions[222] and to prevent double counting.[223]

---

[214] Depledge, Tracing the Origins of Kyoto Protocol (n 3) 85.

[215] Article 17 uses the phrase 'Annex B party' rather than 'Annex I party'—the only instance in the protocol where reference is made to an Annex B Party. The two annexes are almost identical. For the protocol's first commitment period, the protocol's Annex B includes all of the FCCC Annex I parties as of 1997, when the protocol was adopted, with the exception of Turkey. Belarus joined the FCCC on 9 August 2000 as an Annex I party, and has proposed an amendment that would add it to Annex B, but the amendment has not yet received sufficient acceptances to enter into force. For the protocol's second commitment period, all of the Annex I parties that have indicated their intention to become parties to the Doha Amendment have Annex B targets, with the exception of New Zealand.

[216] Kyoto Protocol, Arts 3.10 and 3.11.

[217] Article 17 directs the COP (not CMP) to develop the modalities, rules, and guidelines. It thus left open the possibility for interim trading, in advance of the entry into force of the protocol. See Yamin and Depledge, International Climate Change Regime (n 23) 157.

[218] Decision 11/CMP.1, 'Modalities, rules and guidelines for emissions trading under Article 17 of the Kyoto Protocol' (30 March 2006) FCCC/KP/CMP/2005/8/Add.2, 17.

[219] In order to engage in emissions trading, a party must be an Annex I party, its assigned amount must have been duly calculated and recorded, and it must have fulfilled its commitments under Articles 5 and 7. Decision 11/CMP.1, ibid, Annex, paras 2 and 3. See generally Yamin and Depledge, International Climate Change Regime (n 23) 148–56.

[220] Decision 11/CMP.1, ibid, Annex, para 6.

[221] Yamin and Depledge, International Climate Change Regime (n 23) 158.

[222] Decision 13/CMP.1 (n 94) Annex, para 38. Registries are set up under Decision 3/CMP.1 (n 158) and Decision 13/CMP.1 (n 94). See for more information FCCC, 'International Transaction Log' <http://unfccc.int/kyoto_protocol/registry_systems/itl/items/4065.php> accessed 20 January 2016.

[223] Decision 13/CMP.1 (n 94).

The Kyoto emissions trading system provided the impetus for the creation of emissions trading schemes at the regional level by the EU, at the national level by countries like Kazakhstan, New Zealand, South Korea, and Switzerland, and at the subnational level by individual states, provinces, and cities, including British Columbia, California, Ontario, Quebec, Saitama, and Tokyo.[224] China is also set to launch its emissions trading scheme, expected to be the world's largest, in 2017.[225] The options for linking these carbon markets are also being actively explored. Linking carbon markets can increase cost-effectiveness, improve market liquidity, and reduce price volatility, although it can also undermine environmental effectiveness.[226] The EU ETS, launched in 2005, now in its third phase, covers over 11,000 installations in thirty-one countries and airlines operating between these countries.[227] In total, it covers around 45% of the EU's GHG emissions.[228] Although the EU initially resisted the inclusion of an emissions trading option in the Kyoto Protocol, today the international carbon market, valued at 48 billion Euro,[229] is primarily driven by the EU ETS.[230]

D. Outlook

There is considerable uncertainty about the future of the Kyoto mechanisms. The demand for ERUs and CERs has dried up in recent years.[231] The price of credits has dropped dramatically,[232] attributed by scholars to the oversupply of credits, quantitative limits on their use in the EU ETS, and reduced demand due in part to the post-2007 economic crisis.[233] In addition, the 2020 targets have not been strengthened by parties, which would have increased demand for Kyoto credits. And, it is unclear whether and how the CDM and the JI will be used beyond 2020.

---

[224] Torbjorg Jevnaker and Jorgen Wettestad, 'Linked Carbon Markets: Silver Bullet, or Castle in the Air?', *Climate Law*, 6/1–2 (2016): 142, 144.

[225] Jeff Schwartz, 'China's National Emissions Trading System: Implications for Carbon Markets and Trade' (Geneva: International Centre for Trade and Sustainable Development, March 2016) <http://www.ieta.org/resources/China/Chinas_National_ETS_Implications_for_Carbon_Markets_and_Trade_ICTSD_March2016_Jeff_Swartz.pdf> accessed 20 January 2017.

[226] Jevnaker and Wettestad, Linked Carbon Markets (n 224) 144.

[227] See EU Emissions Trading System (n 206).   [228] Ibid.

[229] 'Carbon Market Monitor: America to the Rescue – Review of Global Markets in 2015 and Outlook for 2016-18' (Thomson Reuters, 11 January 2016) <http://climateobserver.org/wp-content/uploads/2016/01/Carbon-Market-Review-2016.pdf> accessed 20 January 2017.

[230] See Javier de Cendra de Larragan, 'The Kyoto Protocol, with a Special Focus on the Flexible Mechanisms', in Daniel A. Farber and Marjan Peeters (eds), *Elgar Encyclopedia of Environmental Law Series vol 1: Climate Change Law* (Cheltenham: Edward Elgar Publishing, 2016) 227, 232.

[231] Annual report of the Executive Board of the Clean Development Mechanism to the Conference of the Parties serving as the meeting of the Parties to the Kyoto Protocol (12 November 2015) FCCC/KP/CMP/2015/5. See also World Bank Group: Climate Change, *State and Trends of Carbon Pricing* (Washington, D.C.: World Bank, October 2016) 36.

[232] The average CER price on the secondary market was €0.17/tCO$_2$e (US$0.19) in 2014, more than 50% lower than in 2013, and the ERU price in December 2014 was €0.03 (US$0.03). See World Bank, *State and Trends of Carbon Pricing* (Washington, D.C.: World Bank, 2015) 36.

[233] Nicolas Koch *et al.*, 'Causes of the EU ETS Price Drop: Recession, CDM, Renewable Policies or a Bit of Everything? New Evidence', *Energy Policy*, 73 (2014): 676. See generally European Commission, Climate Action, Use of International Credits (n 192).

All of these factors have had a chilling effect on the registration of new projects.[234] Indeed, half of the projects that had issued CERs by 2012 ceased issuance beyond this point.[235] The Paris Agreement and its accompanying decision are silent on the future of the JI and CDM, but the decision accompanying the Paris Agreement encourages parties to promote voluntary cancellation of Kyoto credits.[236] The Paris Agreement establishes a new mechanism (christened by some as the sustainable development mechanism (SDM)), which merges the functionality of the CDM and JI by encompassing emissions reductions in both developed and developing countries.[237] The Conference of the Parties serving as the Meeting of the Parties to the Paris Agreement (CMA) is tasked with developing rules, modalities, and procedures for this mechanism,[238] inter alia based on '[e]xperience gained with and lessons learned from existing mechanisms and approaches adopted under the Convention and its related legal instruments'.[239] Although the Kyoto Protocol is not explicitly mentioned, due to sensitivities among non-Kyoto parties, the Kyoto Protocol is a 'related legal instrument', so lessons learned from the Kyoto mechanisms are clearly relevant. It is possible that the SDM will build on elements of JI and CDM but it is unclear, at this stage, how and in what ways this will occur.

VI. REPORTING, REVIEW, AND COMPLIANCE (ARTICLES 5, 7, 8, AND 18)

A. Reporting and review (Articles 5, 7, and 8)

A strong measurement, reporting and verification (MRV) regime is an essential component of any compliance system.[240] In the case of the Kyoto Protocol, a rigorous approach was seen as especially important in promoting and assessing compliance with emissions-related commitments, and in securing the operation and integrity of the Kyoto mechanisms.[241] The Kyoto Protocol, therefore, provides for a robust MRV system, building on the national GHG inventories and national communications already required under the FCCC,[242] but also supplementing these with additional requirements to fit the specific needs of the protocol.[243] The US

---

[234] Ibid.   [235] Annual report of CDM Executive Board (n 231).

[236] Decision 1/CP.21, 'Adoption of the Paris Agreement' (29 January 2016) FCCC/CP/2015/10/Add.1, 2, para 106.

[237] See Chapter 7, Section VI.   [238] Paris Agreement, Art 6.7.

[239] Decision 1/CP.21 (n 236) para 37(f).

[240] This discussion draws on Jutta Brunnée, 'A Fine Balance: Facilitation and Enforcement in the Design of a Compliance System for the Kyoto Protocol', *Tulane Environmental Law Journal*, 13/2 (2000): 223, 239–41. See also Chapter 2, Section IV. C.

[241] On the connections between the protocol's compliance system and the Kyoto mechanisms, see below Section VI.B.

[242] See Chapter 5, Section VI.B.

[243] For a detailed discussion of the protocol's MRV system, see Anke Herold, 'Experiences with Articles 5, 7 and 8 Defining the Monitoring, Reporting and Verification System under the Kyoto Protocol', in Jutta Brunnée, Meinhard Doelle, and Lavanya Rajamani (eds), *Promoting Compliance in an Evolving Climate Change Regime* (Cambridge University Press, 2012) 122.

and the EU played a key role in crafting the reporting regime, and with Japan, the review process.[244]

Article 5 of the protocol requires Annex I parties to have in place a national system for the estimation of anthropogenic emissions by sources and removals by sinks of GHGs.[245] Guidelines for such national systems, incorporating methodologies adopted by the IPCC,[246] were included in the Marrakesh Accords.[247] The national monitoring systems required by Article 5 are intended to facilitate the preparation by each Annex I party of an annual inventory of greenhouse gas emissions and removals, required under Article 7.[248] These requirements enable the assessment of parties' compliance with their emissions reduction commitments. Inventory and reporting commitments, then, provide a crucial interface between parties' implementation efforts and the compliance assessment process. Article 7 of the protocol builds on the FCCC's extensive reporting obligations.[249] It regulates the collection and submission of supplementary information necessary to demonstrate compliance with the provisions of the protocol.[250] Guidelines for the preparation of this information were also part of the Marrakesh Accords.[251]

Again emulating the approach of the FCCC,[252] expert review teams (ERTs) are to undertake an initial assessment of the information submitted by each Annex I party pursuant to Article 7 of the protocol. According to Article 8, these reviews of individual countries are to provide 'a thorough and comprehensive technical assessment of all aspects of the implementation by a Party of [the] Protocol'.[253] On the basis of these reviews, the ERTs are to identify 'any potential problems', raising 'questions of implementation' for further consideration.[254] The idea was to carve out a technical, depoliticized role for ERTs and to clearly separate them from potentially sensitive assessments of compliance with protocol commitments. Therefore, ERTs are comprised of technical experts rather than state representatives, chosen from a roster of experts maintained by the FCCC.[255] However, ERTs have

---

[244] See Depledge, Tracing the Origins of Kyoto Protocol (n 3) 59–61, 64–8.

[245] Kyoto Protocol, Art 5.1.

[246] Ibid, Arts 5.1 and 5.2. See also IPCC, *Revised 1996 IPCC Guidelines for National Greenhouse Gas Inventories* (Geneva: IPCC, UNEP, and WMO, 1996); and IPCC, *Good Practice Guidance and Uncertainty Management in National Greenhouse Gas Inventories* (Geneva: IPCC, UNEP, and WMO, 2000).

[247] Decision 19/CMP.1, 'Guidelines for national systems under Article 5, paragraph 1, of the Kyoto Protocol' (30 March 2006) FCCC/KP/CMP/2005/8/Add.3, 14.

[248] Kyoto Protocol, Art 7.1.

[249] FCCC, Art 12.1 (outlining the requirements for 'national communications' to allow for the evaluation of the emissions performance of individual Annex I parties, but also imposing certain reporting obligations on all parties, Annex I and non-Annex I alike). See also Chapter 5, Section VI.B.

[250] Kyoto Protocol, Arts 7.1 and 7.2.

[251] Decision 15/CMP.1, 'Guidelines for the preparation of the information required under Article 7 of the Kyoto Protocol' (30 March 2006) FCCC/KP/CMP/2005/8/Add.2, 54; and Decision 13/CMP.1 (n 94).

[252] See FCCC, 'Review Process' <http://unfccc.int/national_reports/annex_i_ghg_inventories/review_process/items/2762.php> accessed 20 January 2017.

[253] Kyoto Protocol, Art 8.3.   [254] Ibid.

[255] See FCCC, 'Roster of Experts' <http://www4.unfccc.int/sites/roe/Pages/Home.aspx> accessed 20 January 2017. But see also Anna Huggins, 'The Desirability of Depoliticization: Compliance in the International Climate Regime', *Transnational Environmental Law*, 4/1 (2015): 101, 110 (noting

come to play a larger, and according to some observers more politicized,[256] role in the Kyoto Protocol's compliance system than originally envisaged. Not only do ERTs, through the abovementioned 'questions of implementation', provide a 'trigger' for the involvement of the protocol's Compliance Committee, but they have also come to take on the work that was meant to be undertaken by the Compliance Committee's 'facilitative branch', as discussed in Section VI.B.3 below.[257]

B. Compliance procedures and mechanisms

1. Context and goals

Article 18 of the Kyoto Protocol called for the development of 'appropriate and effective procedures and mechanisms to determine and address cases of non-compliance'.[258] Negotiators recognized early on that the compliance regime could not simply adopt existing models, such as the Montreal Protocol's non-compliance procedure,[259] but had to be tailored to the unique features of the protocol.[260] AOSIS, the EU, Canada, Japan, Norway, and the US played a key role in advocating compliance procedures and mechanisms during the Kyoto negotiations.[261]

In order to understand the protocol's compliance system, it is important to recall that central components are contained in several articles, not only in Article 18. An essential foundation for the Article 18 'procedures and mechanisms' is provided by the protocol's elaborate MRV system, consisting of the aforementioned inventory and reporting requirements under Articles 5 and 7, and the expert review process operating under Article 8.[262] Indeed, until the final months of the AGBM negotiations, compliance was discussed in the context of Article 8, and there was no separate article in the negotiating text on compliance.[263]

In addition, the rules governing the Kyoto mechanisms, set out in the Marrakesh Accords,[264] contain important elements of the protocol's compliance strategy. Most notably, the mechanism eligibility rules make participation contingent upon

---

a range of challenges to the intended impartiality of ERT members, including that almost all of them work in national government departments and 'many are involved in the preparation of their own country's emissions inventory').

[256] See Huggins, ibid, 110–14.

[257] On the greater role of the ERTs, see Sebastian Oberthür, 'Compliance under the Evolving Climate Change Regime', in Cinnamon P. Carlane, Kevin R. Gray, and Richard Tarasofsky (eds), *The Oxford Handbook of International Climate Change Law* (Oxford University Press, 2016) 120, 123–4; and Huggins, ibid.

[258] The following discussion draws on Jutta Brunnée, 'Climate Change and Compliance and Enforcement Processes', in Rosemary Rayfuse and Shirley Scott (eds), *International Law in the Era of Climate Change* (Cheltenham: Edward Elgar Publishing, 2012) 290.

[259] On key features of that procedure, see Chapter 2, Section IV.C.2.

[260] See Brunnée, Fine Balance (n 240) 229.

[261] Depledge, Tracing the Origins of Kyoto Protocol (n 3) 86–8.

[262] On the elements of the MRV system, see Section VI.A above.

[263] Depledge, Tracing the Origins of Kyoto Protocol (n 3) 86–8.

[264] On the Kyoto Mechanisms, see Section V above.

compliance with the inventory and reporting commitments in Articles 5 and 7.[265] These eligibility requirements seek to ensure the availability of reliable information on parties' emissions reduction performance, and to help prevent uses of the mechanisms that would detract from rather than support the protocol's emissions reduction goals.

The Kyoto Protocol's compliance system[266] remains the most ambitious and elaborate of the multilateral environmental agreements' (MEA) compliance regimes in operation today. Notably, to account for the unique features of the Kyoto Protocol, including the strong differentiation between Annex I and non-Annex I party commitments and the reliance on the Kyoto mechanisms, the purposes of the 'procedures and mechanisms' are to 'facilitate, promote and *enforce* compliance' with the protocol.[267] The explicit reference to enforcement of compliance distinguishes these procedures and mechanisms from the largely facilitative range of approaches of existing non-compliance procedures.[268]

2. Triggers

The compliance process can be triggered by questions of implementation raised by the expert reviews or by a protocol party, either with respect to itself or with respect to another party.[269] The expert review trigger is intended to ensure that *all* questions of implementation pertaining to emissions-related commitments come before the Compliance Committee, a feature that is designed to enhance transparency with respect to parties' performance, as well as the predictability and credibility of the compliance procedure.[270] Indeed, in the practice of the compliance regime, all but one submission, by South Africa on behalf of the G-77/China,[271] has come to the Compliance Committee through questions of implementation raised by ERTs. However, according to some observers, the quasi-automatic nature of the ERT trigger has been diluted by a growing practice of ERTs to exercise a degree of discretion in determining whether and when to identify an issue as a question of implementation for mandatory review by the Compliance Committee.[272]

---

[265] See Decision 9/CMP.1 (n 134) paras 21–9; Decision 3/CMP.1 (n 158) paras 31–4; and Decision 11/CMP.1 (n 218) paras 2–4.

[266] See Decision 27/CMP.1 (n 40) Annex.

[267] See ibid, Annex, Section I (emphasis added).

[268] See Chapter 2, Section IV.C.2. See also Jutta Brunnée, 'The Kyoto Protocol: A Testing Ground for Compliance Theories?', *Zeitschrift für ausländisches öffentliches Recht und Völkerrecht (Heidelberg Journal of International Law)*, 63 (2003): 255; Geir Ulfstein and Jacob Werksman, 'The Kyoto Compliance System: Towards Hard Enforcement', in Olav Schram Stokke, Jon Hovi, and Geir Ulfstein (eds), *Implementing the Climate Regime* (London: Earthscan, 2005) 59; René Lefeber and Sebastian Oberthür, 'Key Features of the Kyoto Protocol's Compliance System', in Brunnée *et al.*, Promoting Compliance in an Evolving Climate Change Regime (n 243) 77.

[269] Decision 27/CMP.1 (n 40) Annex, Section VI, para 1.

[270] See Lefeber and Oberthür, Key Features of the Kyoto Protocol's Compliance System (n 268).

[271] See n 287 below and accompanying text.

[272] See Huggins, Desirability of Depoliticization (n 255) 112.

3. *The Compliance Committee and its process*

In view of its facilitative as well as enforcement purposes, the Kyoto regime includes distinctive institutional and procedural arrangements. The Compliance Committee established under the protocol has a 'facilitative branch' and an 'enforcement branch'.[273] The full committee has twenty members, with each branch comprising ten members.[274] Elected by the meeting of the parties to the protocol, committee members are experts who serve in their personal capacities.[275] Each branch must include one member from each of the five UN regional groups and one member from a small island developing state. Of the remaining four members, each branch must include two Annex I and two non-Annex I party members.[276] When a question of implementation is received by the Compliance Committee, its bureau (ic the chairs and co-chairs of each branch) decides to which branch to allocate the issue.[277]

a) The facilitative branch

As set out in the Marrakesh Accords, the task of the facilitative branch is to promote compliance with protocol commitments through advice and assistance, taking into account the FCCC's CBDRRC principle.[278] The facilitative branch is responsible for questions concerning the implementation of protocol commitments other than those related to Annex I parties' emissions reduction commitments.[279] Emissions reduction commitments and the related inventory and reporting commitments are within the purview of the facilitative branch only when referred to it by the enforcement branch, or prior to and during a given commitment period, when the facilitative branch can play an 'early warning' role.[280] In keeping with the role of the facilitative branch, the compliance tools at its disposal include advice and facilitation of assistance to individual parties, facilitation of financial and technical assistance, and recommendations to the party concerned.[281]

In practice, the facilitative branch has been almost entirely dormant.[282] Its inactivity is due in large part to the larger than anticipated facilitative role played by expert reviews.[283] In effect, ERTs removed the need for additional facilitation by resolving issues in cooperation with the party during the review process.[284] As a result, during the protocol's first commitment period, not a single question of implementation was referred to the facilitative branch.[285] Only one submission, by South Africa on behalf of the G-77/China, was made to the facilitative branch in 2006, pertaining to the alleged failure by several developed countries to submit

---

[273] Decision 27/CMP.1 (n 40) Annex, Section II, para 2.   [274] Ibid, Section II, para 3.
[275] Ibid, Section II, paras 3 and 6.   [276] Ibid, Sections IV, para 1 and V, para 1.
[277] Ibid, Section VII, para 1.   [278] Ibid, Sections IV, para 4 and XIV.
[279] Ibid, Section IV.5, para 5.   [280] Ibid, Sections IV, para 6 and IX, para 12.
[281] Ibid, Section XIV, paras (a)–(d).
[282] See Oberthür, Compliance under the Evolving Climate Change Regime (n 257) 125.
[283] Decision 27/CMP.1 (n 40) Annex, Section III, para 2(b).
[284] See Oberthür, Compliance under the Evolving Climate Change Regime (n 257) 124–5.
[285] Ibid.

reports on their progress in achieving their targets, as required by Article 3.2 of the protocol.[286] This submission, however, did not proceed to the merits because the members of the facilitative branch could not reach a decision on whether a submission by the G-77/China met the requirement of a submission by a party.[287]

b) The enforcement branch

The mandate of the enforcement branch is to resolve all questions relating to Annex I parties' compliance with their emissions reduction commitments, the attendant inventory and reporting commitments, and the eligibility requirements for the Kyoto mechanisms.[288] The enforcement branch both determines whether a party is in compliance with its commitments and applies 'consequences' in the event of non-compliance.[289]

The consequences that can be applied by the enforcement branch for non-compliance differ depending on the commitment that is at issue.[290] In cases of non-compliance with inventory or reporting commitments, consequences consist in a declaration of non-compliance and in the requirement that the party prepare a 'compliance action plan'.[291] That plan must include an analysis of the causes of non-compliance, the measures that the party intends to take to remedy the non-compliance, and a timetable for their implementation. Progress in the implementation of the plan must be reported to the enforcement branch.[292] Where the enforcement branch has determined that a party has not met one or more of the eligibility requirements for the Kyoto mechanisms, the consequence is suspension of the party from participation in the mechanisms.[293]

The process concerning parties' emissions reduction targets includes a 'true-up' period after the completion of the expert review, during which parties can acquire emissions allowances or credits to bring themselves into compliance.[294] When a party nonetheless exceeds its emissions target, it will be suspended from eligibility to transfer emissions units under Article 17, and will be required to develop a compliance action plan.[295] In addition, the excess emissions will be subtracted, at a rate of 1.3 times the amount of excess emissions, from that party's assigned amount for the next commitment period.[296] This 1.3 rate for 'subtraction of tons' (as this consequence was generally called) was intended to discourage parties from simply postponing their emissions reductions to the subsequent commitment period, effectively 'borrowing' from a future allowance.[297] It is worth noting that since all

---

[286] See Meinhard Doelle, 'Experience with the Facilitative and Enforcement Branches of the Kyoto Compliance System', in Brunnée *et al.*, Promoting Compliance in an Evolving Climate Change Regime (n 243) 102, 103–4.

[287] Ibid.   [288] Decision 27/CMP.1 (n 40) Annex, Section V, para 4.

[289] Ibid, Sections I, V, para 6 and XV.

[290] Regarding the compliance tools available to the facilitative branch, see n 281 above and accompanying text.

[291] Decision 27/CMP.1 (n 40) Annex, Section XV, para 1.

[292] Ibid, Section XV, paras 2 and 3.   [293] Ibid, Section XV, para 4.

[294] Ibid, Sections XIII and XV, para 5.

[295] Ibid, Section XV, paras 5(a) and (b), 6, and 7.   [296] Ibid, Section XV, para 5(c).

[297] On 'borrowing', see n 112 above and accompanying text.

protocol parties complied with their first commitment period targets, there was no need to apply this consequence.[298]

An additional aspect of these consequences is worth highlighting: the Compliance Committee itself does not determine whether or not to impose consequences, or which consequences to impose. Its role is only to determine whether a party is in non-compliance and, if so, to apply consequences that were predetermined by the protocol parties in the procedures and mechanisms adopted pursuant to Article 18. This 'pre-determined' nature of the consequences was meant both to depoliticize the role of the Compliance Committee and to make the compliance regime more predictable for parties.[299]

Formally, the consequences applied by the enforcement branch are not legally binding, since the protocol provides that any procedure entailing binding consequences must be adopted by an amendment to the protocol,[300] rather than by a CMP decision, as was the case. Nevertheless, the enforcement branch process has been described as the 'most judicial' compliance mechanism among MEAs.[301] This assessment is no doubt accurate. In view of its mandate and the role of its decisions in the operation of the Kyoto Protocol (notably in relation to the Kyoto mechanisms), the timelines and steps for the enforcement branch process are tightly specified.[302] Furthermore, the procedures and mechanisms set out a series of due process elements, such as rights to written submissions and hearings.[303] Perhaps most unusually for an MEA-based compliance regime, the procedures and mechanisms allow for an appeal to the CMP of enforcement branch decisions relating to a party's compliance with its emissions target. Since these decisions expose parties to the most significant consequences, the procedures and mechanisms permit an appeal if the affected party 'believes it has been denied due process'.[304] However, save for this limited right of appeal,[305] the decisions of the enforcement branch are final.

During the protocol's first commitment period, the enforcement branch successfully handled questions of implementation regarding the compliance of eight

---

[298] See nn 78–9 above and accompanying text. For a discussion, see Michael Grubb, 'Full Legal Compliance with the Kyoto Protocol's First Commitment Period – Some Lessons', *Climate Policy*, 16/6 (2016): 673.

[299] See Huggins, Desirability of Depoliticization (n 255) 119.

[300] Kyoto Protocol, Art 18.

[301] See Oberthür, Compliance under the Evolving Climate Change Regime (n 257) 123. See also FCCC, 'Procedural requirements and the scope and content of applicable law for the consideration of appeals under decision 27/CMP.1 and other relevant decisions of the Conference of the Parties serving as the meeting of the Parties to the Kyoto Protocol, as well as the approach taken by other relevant international bodies relating to denial of due process', Technical Paper (15 September 2011) FCCC/TP/2011/6, para 43 (referring to the function of the enforcement branch as 'quasi-judicial').

[302] See Decision 27/CMP.1 (n 40) Annex, Section IX.   [303] Ibid, Section XI.

[304] Ibid, Section XI, para 1.

[305] The CMP cannot revisit the substance of the enforcement branch decision but can focus only on procedural considerations. See ibid, Sections XI, para 3 and XI, para 4. Furthermore, the CMP must agree by a three-fourths majority vote to override the decision of the enforcement branch and send the matter back for review. See ibid, Section XI, para 3.

parties with inventory and reporting commitments, and eligibility for participation in the Kyoto mechanisms.[306] Except for one case, involving Ukraine,[307] the branch did not have occasion to apply the consequences that attach to non-compliance with parties' emissions targets.

4. Outlook

The most distinctive features of the Kyoto Protocol's compliance mechanism are tightly connected to the protocol's binding emissions targets, MRV regime, market mechanisms, and sharp differentiation between Annex I and non-Annex I parties. So the protocol's compliance system is not likely to exert significant influence on the development of the Paris Agreement's implementation and compliance mechanism, since the Paris Agreement relies upon 'nationally determined' contributions, which do not establish legally binding targets and are applicable to all, rather than only developed states. In particular, the enforcement-oriented, 'quasi-judicial', aspects of the Kyoto Protocol's approach to compliance are unlikely to be replicated under the Paris Agreement.[308] Nevertheless, the experience with the enforcement branch provides useful lessons, which could influence the design of other MEA compliance regimes. As far as the Paris Agreement is concerned, the facilitative aspects of Kyoto's procedures and mechanisms constitute a more likely repository of ideas for the design of the agreement's mechanism to 'facilitate implementation' and 'promote compliance'.

VII. INSTITUTIONS (ARTICLES 13, 14, AND 15)

The Kyoto Protocol uses the existing institutional structure of the FCCC—the Conference of Parties to the FCCC serves as the Meeting of Parties to the Kyoto Protocol. Those states that are not party to the Kyoto Protocol can participate as observers.[309] The subsidiary bodies to the FCCC serve the Kyoto Protocol,[310] and both the FCCC and the Kyoto Protocol share a secretariat.[311] The Kyoto Protocol also established the CDM Executive Board.[312] In addition to operationalizing the CDM Executive Board, the Marrakesh Accords created a range of new institutions

---

[306] See FCCC, 'Compliance under the Kyoto Protocol' <http://unfccc.int/kyoto_protocol/compliance/items/2875.php> accessed 20 January 2017. See also Doelle, Experience with the Facilitative and Enforcement Branches (n 286) 105–20 (providing a detailed review of four enforcement branch proceedings).

[307] Final Decision of the Enforcement Branch of the Compliance Committee for Party Concerned: Ukraine (7 September 2016) CC-2016-1-6 /Ukraine/EB <http://unfccc.int/files/kyoto_protocol/compliance/questions_of_implementation/application/pdf/cc-2016-1-6_ukraine_eb_final_decision.pdf> accessed 20 January 2017.

[308] See generally Stine Aakre, 'The Political Feasibility of Potent Enforcement in a Post-Kyoto Climate Agreement', *International Environmental Agreements*, 16/1 (2016): 145. For a discussion of the Paris Agreement's implementation and compliance mechanism, see Chapter 7, Section X.C.

[309] Kyoto Protocol, Art 13.   [310] Ibid, Art 15.   [311] Ibid, Art 14.

[312] Ibid, Art 12.4.

including the joint implementation Supervisory Committee and the Compliance Committee.

VIII. MULTILATERAL CONSULTATIVE PROCESS (ARTICLE 16)

The Kyoto Protocol requires parties to consider applying the convention's multilateral consultative process (MCP) to the protocol.[313] As discussed in Chapter 5, since parties were unable to agree upon the composition of the multilateral consultative committee, the MCP is not in operation. In the Kyoto Protocol, the creation of a facilitative branch within the Compliance Committee under Article 18 removed the need for the application of the MCP.

IX. FINAL CLAUSES (ARTICLES 19–28)

The Kyoto Protocol includes a standard set of final clauses. Parties must express their consent to be bound by means of ratification, acceptance, or approval.[314] Entry into force involves a 'double trigger', requiring acceptance by at least fifty-five states that account for at least 55% of Annex I greenhouse gas emissions.[315] The protocol entered into force on 16 February 2005.

The Kyoto Protocol incorporates by reference the FCCC's provision on dispute settlement.[316] Reservations are expressly disallowed,[317] but parties may withdraw beginning three years after the agreement's entry into force by giving one year's notice.[318] Canada withdrew in 2011.[319] Amendments can be proposed by any party, are subject to a six-month notice rule, and in the absence of consensus can be adopted by a three-fourths majority.[320] Annexes are an integral part of the protocol. Similarly, annexes and amendments to annexes can be proposed by any party, are subject to the six-month notice rule, and in the absence of consensus can be adopted by a three-fourths majority.[321] As discussed in Chapter 3, the protocol specifies that Annex B amendments require the written consent of the party concerned (Article 21.7).

---

[313] See FCCC, Art 13. See also Decision 10/CP.4, 'Multilateral Consultative Process' (25 January 1999) FCCC/CP/1998/16/Add.1, 42.

[314] Kyoto Protocol, Art 24. On ratification, acceptance, and approval, see also Chapter 3, Section II.C.

[315] Ibid, Art 25. On entry into force, see also Chapter 3, Section II.C.

[316] Ibid, Art 19.   [317] Ibid, Art 26.   [318] Ibid, Art 27.

[319] United Nations, Kyoto Protocol to the United Nations Framework Convention on Climate Change Kyoto, 11 December 1997, 'Canada: Withdrawal' (16 December 2011) C.N.796.2011. TREATIES-1 (Depositary Notification) <https://unfccc.int/files/kyoto_protocol/background/application/pdf/canada.pdf.pdf> accessed 20 January 2017.

[320] Kyoto Protocol, Art 20. On amendments, see also Chapter 3, Section II.D.2.

[321] Ibid, Art 21.

X. THE SECOND AND FUTURE COMMITMENT
PERIODS OF THE KYOTO PROTOCOL

Climate pundits had begun proclaiming the death of the Kyoto Protocol even before the US rejection of it in 2001.[322] Scholarly commentary too frequently referred to a 'post-Kyoto' climate regime, conflating the end of the first commitment period with the end of the Kyoto regime. Kyoto, however, was intended to establish a long-term architecture, with multiple commitment periods. Its Article 3.9 specified the process for establishing commitments for the second commitment period, calling for the initiation of negotiations no later than 2005, seven years before the end of the first commitment period. Developing countries, for which the Kyoto model has obvious attractions because they are exempt from emissions targets, were keen to extend the protocol for a second and future commitment periods. Kyoto Annex B parties, in contrast, were reluctant to do so, for some countries because of Kyoto's prescriptive architecture, and for others because they did not want to be subject to emissions targets if the US, China, and other large emitters were not.[323]

At the protocol's first CMP, parties launched an Ad Hoc Open-Ended Working Group to consider further commitments for developed countries beyond 2012 under the Kyoto Protocol (AWG-KP), in accordance with Article 3.9.[324] The AWG-KP process took seven years to reach agreement. The process was hampered from the start by considerable political uncertainty. It was unclear, given the ongoing parallel negotiations under the FCCC, whether the outcome of the FCCC process would complement or supplant the Kyoto Protocol.[325] If it were to complement the Kyoto Protocol, it was unclear how any commitments of the US under the FCCC process could be matched in legal character, ambition and accountability with the commitments of other developed countries under Kyoto's second commitment period. At the same time, it was clear that an FCCC outcome that was applicable to all countries could not be structured in a prescriptive, Kyoto-like manner. While the AWG-KP negotiations continued, parties put forward actions and commitments in a parallel process under the 2009 Copenhagen Accord. These were later incorporated into the 2010 Cancun Agreements. Japan and Russia indicated that they would not take on second commitment period targets under the Kyoto Protocol, but undertook climate commitments under the Cancun Agreements.[326]

---

[322] See eg David G. Victor, *The Collapse of the Kyoto Protocol and the Struggle to Slow Global Warming* (Princeton University Press, 2001).

[323] Lavanya Rajamani, 'Addressing the Post-Kyoto Stress Disorder: Reflections on the Emerging Legal Architecture of the Climate Regime', *International and Comparative Law Quarterly*, 58/4 (2009): 803.

[324] Decision 1/CMP.1, 'Consideration of Commitments for Subsequent Periods for Parties Included in Annex I to the Convention under Article 3, Paragraph 9 of the Kyoto Protocol' (30 March 2006) FCCC/KP/CMP/2005/8/Add.1, 3.

[325] Rajamani, Addressing the Post-Kyoto Stress Disorder (n 323) 809.

[326] See John Vidal, 'Cancun Climate Change Summit: Japan refuses to extend Kyoto Protocol', *The Guardian* (1 December 2010) <https://www.theguardian.com/environment/2010/dec/01/cancun-climate-change-summit-japan-kyoto> accessed 20 January 2017; Suzanne Goldenberg,

In an effort to create a 'bridge' between the Kyoto and FCCC tracks, the Cancun Agreements placed mitigation proposals from all developed countries in an information document[327] that was deliberately ambiguous as to whether it related to the FCCC or to the Kyoto Protocol.[328]

Ending years of speculation and uncertainty, parties agreed in Durban in 2011 to extend the Kyoto Protocol for a second commitment period. The EU struck a deal with developing countries at Durban that they would accept Kyoto second commitment period targets if developing countries joined the consensus on launching negotiations toward a 2015 agreement 'applicable to all'. The details of the Kyoto amendment, however, were not worked out until the following year in Doha. Parties disagreed on several issues including: the length of the commitment period—whether it should be five years (like the first commitment period) or eight years (to coincide with the scheduled launch of the 2015 agreement); the scale and ambition of the collective and individual targets; the extent to which parties not participating in Kyoto's second commitment period could continue to use the Kyoto mechanisms; and the extent to which surplus assigned amount units could be banked for use in subsequent commitment periods. In the Doha Amendment, parties agreed to:

- Expand the list of GHGs in Annex A to include nitrogen trifluoride.

- Extend the second commitment period to 2020.

- Accept a collective target of 18% below 1990 levels.

- Accept individual targets consistent with the ones Annex B parties had agreed to under the Cancun Agreements, but translated into quantified emissions limitation and reduction objectives for the entire commitment period, 2013–20.

- Revisit targets by 2014 in line with a reduction of 25 to 40% below 1990 levels by 2020.

'Cancun Climate Change Conference: Russia will not renew Kyoto Protocol', *The Guardian* (10 December 2010) <https://www.theguardian.com/environment/2010/dec/10/cancun-climate-change-conference-kyoto> accessed 20 January 2017; and Brian Fallow, 'NZ backs off Kyoto climate change route', *New Zealand Herald* (10 November 2012) <http://www.nzherald.co.nz/business/news/article.cfm?c_id=3&objectid=10846305> accessed 20 January 2017.

[327] Information documents provide information on a specific negotiating issue. They are not translated into all the UN languages. See FCCC, 'Introductory Guide to Documents' <http://unfccc.int/documentation/introductory_guide_to_documents/items/2644.php> accessed 20 January 2017. See Compilation of economy-wide emission reduction targets to be implemented by Parties included in Annex I to the Convention, Revised note by the Secretariat (7 June 2011) FCCC/SB/2011/INF.1. The document number listed in the Kyoto Outcome Decision in relation to mitigation targets for developed countries is identical to that in the LCA Outcome Decision. See Doha Amendment, Art 1, Section A, footnote 2; Cancun Agreements LCA, para 36; Decision 1/CMP.6, 'The Cancun Agreements: Outcome of the work of the Ad Hoc Working Group on Further Commitments for Annex I Parties under the Kyoto Protocol at its fifteenth session' (15 March 2011) FCCC/KP/CMP/2010/12/Add.1, para 3.

[328] Subsidiary bodies under the FCCC serve as the subsidiary bodies under the protocol, and sessions of these bodies under the FCCC and Kyoto Protocol are held in conjunction with each other. Kyoto Protocol, Art 15, and FCCC, Arts 9 and 10.

- Restrict the eligibility of non-Doha Amendment parties to participate in the Kyoto mechanisms.

- Allow banking of excess AAUs, but restrict the extent to which and conditions under which these can be traded.[329]

- Automatically adjust the Doha Amendment targets so as to disallow any growth in emissions as against the average of a party's annual emissions from 2008 to 2010.[330]

- Continue the 2% share of proceeds of the CDM and extend its application to the first international transfers of AAUs and the issuance of ERUs for JI projects.[331]

The Doha Amendment will enter into force when 144 parties have deposited their instruments of acceptance.[332] To date, only seventy five have done so, including only a handful of Annex B parties.[333] Among the developed countries, New Zealand has crafted a special position for itself. It has accepted the Doha Amendment but without a target under Annex B. In practice, this means that New Zealand will be held accountable only for the protocol's reporting and review requirements, and not for the achievement of a target. Parties provided for provisional application of the Doha Amendment, pending entry into force. Parties that choose not to apply it provisionally are nonetheless required to 'implement their commitments and other responsibilities in relation to the second commitment period, in a manner consistent with their national legislation or domestic processes'.[334] This provision is significant, in that it allows for de facto application of the Doha Amendment, even if it never enters into force.

In 2014, a high-level ministerial round table took place, as required by the Doha Amendment, on revisiting the ambition of Annex B targets.[335] The FCCC secretariat received four submissions—the EU and Iceland, Norway, Liechtenstein, and Australia—in time for the round table, and no commitments for enhanced ambition were made at the meeting or thereafter. The G-77/China proposed a contact group on the issue, but Australia, Switzerland, the EU, and Norway opposed this proposal, and the issue has been deferred to future sessions.

What is the future of the Kyoto Protocol? In the two decades it has been in existence, major developed countries—including the US, Canada, Russia, and Japan—have disassociated themselves from the Kyoto Protocol, and only a subset

---

[329] Decision 1/CMP.8 (n 114) paras 4, 7, 15, and 24, Doha Amendment, Art 1, Section A, footnotes 3, 10, 11, Section B and Section C.

[330] Doha Amendment, Art 1, Section G.   [331] Ibid, Section J.

[332] Kyoto Protocol, Arts 21 and 20.

[333] Australia, Switzerland, New Zealand, Norway, Iceland, Italy, Hungary. See United Nations Treaty Collection, 'Chapter XXVII: Environment, 7. c Doha Amendment to the Kyoto Protocol' <https://treaties.un.org/Pages/ViewDetails.aspx?src=TREATY&mtdsg_no=XXVII-7-c&chapter=27&clang=_en#EndDec> accessed 20 January 2017.

[334] Decision 1/CMP.8 (n 114) paras 5 and 6.

[335] Report on the high-level ministerial round table on increased ambition of Kyoto Protocol commitments, Note by the Secretariat (4 September 2014) FCCC/KP/CMP/2014/3.

of Annex B parties—the EU, Australia, Iceland, Liechtenstein, Monaco, Norway, and Switzerland—have adopted targets for the second commitment period, covering only a fraction of global GHG emissions.[336] Indeed, the second commitment period amendment was adopted only because many developing countries made it a pre-condition for securing their agreement to launch negotiations toward a 2015 Paris Agreement 'applicable to all'. At that critical juncture in the negotiations, such an extension was an indispensable confidence-building gesture.

Neither the Doha Amendment nor the 2015 Paris Agreement offers any clarity on the survival (or termination) of the Kyoto Protocol beyond 2020. However, the near universal support for the Paris Agreement—its scope, coverage, and breadth, its hybrid architecture, and its distinctive approach to differentiation—is a strong signal that the political commitment underpinning the Kyoto Protocol has long since dissipated. The political appetite among developed countries for extending the Kyoto Protocol beyond 2020 does not exist. Indeed, the eight-year duration of the second commitment period was chosen so as to end when the Paris Agreement's NDCs were expected to take effect, and thus to avoid a commitment gap.

The Kyoto Protocol does not contain a provision on its termination. In the absence of such a provision, its termination may take place in one of three ways: (1) 'by consent of all the Parties after consultation with other contracting States',[337] (2) by 'conclusion of a later treaty relating to the same subject-matter',[338] or (3) by desuetude or abrogation by virtue of non-application over a prolonged period of time.[339]

In relation to the first option, it is unlikely that developing and industrialized countries will agree on terminating Kyoto. Instead, some (or many) Annex I parties may choose to withdraw from it.[340] Even if these withdrawals lead to a situation in which the number of parties representing the necessary proportion of Annex I GHG emissions falls below the requirements for entry into force,[341] Kyoto will not terminate as a result.[342] But it will have little effect, since it will not be binding on those countries that have withdrawn, and there may be little of Kyoto left to operationalize.

In relation to the second option for treaty termination, parties must have 'intended that the matter should be governed' by the later treaty, or the provisions of the later treaty must be so incompatible with the earlier one that they are not

---

[336] The Kyoto Protocol's second commitment period covers only 11.8% of 2012 global GHG emissions. This includes the emissions share of Australia, Belarus, EU-28, Iceland, Kazakhstan, Norway, Switzerland, Ukraine in 2010, excluding LULUCF. World Resources Institute (WRI), 'CAIT Climate Data Explorer' <http://cait.wri.org/> accessed 20 January 2017.

[337] Vienna Convention on the Law of Treaties (adopted 23 May 1969, entered into force 27 January 1980) 1155 UNTS 331 (VCLT), Art 54.

[338] Ibid, Art 59.

[339] See Olivier Corten and Pierre Klein (eds), *The Vienna Convention on the Law of Treaties: A Commentary*, vol 1 (Oxford University Press, 2011) 1022–5.

[340] Kyoto Protocol, Art 27 permits states to withdraw after three years after the protocol's entry into force. Any such withdrawal will take effect one year after the notice of withdrawal.

[341] Ibid, Art 25.

[342] VCLT, Art 55 (n 337), provides that 'a multilateral treaty does not terminate by reason only of the fact that the number of the parties falls below the number necessary for its entry into force'.

capable of being applied at the same time.[343] If neither of these conditions is satisfied, either because of lack of appropriate 'intention' (which is notoriously difficult to determine) or because some aspects of the later treaty can be applied in conjunction with the protocol, then Kyoto will not be terminated or suspended, and Article 30 of the VCLT will govern the relations between the two treaties. If the parties to Kyoto are also parties to the later one, the earlier treaty applies only to the extent that it is compatible with the later treaty. If the parties are not entirely the same, as is likely to be the case here, the situation is rather more complex.[344]

In relation to the third option, desuetude or obsolescence, a treaty is terminated through disuse over a long period of time. This route to termination, however, is premised on the implied consent of parties as evidenced by their conduct.[345] Kyoto is unlikely to merely fall into disuse through neglect, since there are institutional and budgetary implications to Kyoto's continued existence. As long as states remain parties to Kyoto, they will have budgetary responsibilities.[346] Parties also have reporting obligations under Kyoto that will not end merely because the second commitment period does. In the circumstances, if no agreement on its termination is reached, states are likely to withdraw from Kyoto after 2020.

XI. CONCLUSION

The Kyoto Protocol has generated considerable controversy in the two decades it has been in existence. It took only two years to be negotiated, but another eight years to enter into force. It took a further seven years for its second commitment period targets to be negotiated, and the Doha Amendment is yet to (and may never) enter into force.

The Paris Agreement, set to take over from the Kyoto Protocol, represents a significant departure from the protocol: it has a hybrid architecture; it does not impose an obligation to achieve parties' NDCs; and its principal mitigation commitments are applicable to all, albeit with some differences in the normative expectations placed on different parties or groups of parties. Reflecting this departure, the Paris Agreement does not specifically import elements from the Kyoto Protocol. It recognizes that the Kyoto Protocol Adaptation Fund 'may serve' the Agreement,[347] but this is the only Kyoto Protocol body with an identified role in the network of institutional arrangements the Paris Agreement utilizes.

---

[343] Ibid, Art 59(a) and (b).

[344] Ibid, Art 30.4. The treaty, earlier or later, that both states are party to, will govern their mutual rights and obligations.

[345] Anthony Aust, *Modern Treaty Law and Practice* (Cambridge University Press, 3rd edn, 2013) 306–7.

[346] See eg Decision 12/CMP.11, 'Programme budget for the biennium 2016–2017' (29 January 2016) FCCC/KP/CMP/2015/8/Add.2, 18, for the most recent budget, and indicative scale of contributions from parties.

[347] Decision 1/CP.21 (n 236) paras 60 and 61.

Nevertheless, the Kyoto Protocol is likely to leave an enduring imprint on the climate regime. The Kyoto Protocol has catalyzed a vibrant carbon market. Although in the negotiations of the Kyoto Protocol, the Umbrella Group alone was wholeheartedly in favor of market instruments to address climate change, there has been a rapid scale-up of interest and engagement in market-based approaches in the decades that followed. More than half the NDCs submitted in the context of the Paris Agreement contain references to carbon markets.[348] Paris Agreement Article 6 recognizes that parties may engage in cooperative approaches, which may facilitate linking of national carbon markets.[349] Many of these markets developed in response to the price that the Kyoto mechanisms placed on carbon. The new market mechanism established by the Paris Agreement may draw on the experience of the Kyoto mechanisms, as discussed above, in particular in relation to additionality, sustainable development, project eligibility, and methodologies.

The Kyoto Protocol also generated valuable experience with the building blocks for well-functioning carbon markets, including national inventories, a common accounting system, common time frames and uniform reporting formats. The transparency framework under the Paris Agreement is to build on and enhance the transparency arrangements under the convention,[350] rather than the Kyoto Protocol. However, it is likely that Kyoto Protocol parties will draw on their experience with Kyoto Articles 5, 7, and 8 in developing modalities, procedures and guidelines for the transparency of action and support under the Paris Agreement. This is so particularly for the EU, since the procedures in Articles 5, 7, and 8 of the Kyoto Protocol are entrenched in EU legislation,[351] and have proven to be a reliable and workable system. Those currently using the system will likely continue to use it in some form, and will seek to insert elements of it into the Paris Agreement's transparency framework.

Thus, even if the Kyoto Protocol is eventually terminated or withers away, it has contributed significantly to the international policy response to the climate change problem. It created a complex global system essentially from scratch, triggered valuable experiments, generated useful experience, and built capacity to account, report, and manage GHG emissions. Arguably the Kyoto Protocol sought to do too much too quickly, and in advance of the requisite political will to maintain the regime it established. Yet its novelty, complexity, and ambition is a testament to the perseverance and creativity of those who negotiated it, and it will leave an enduring legacy in the climate regime.

---

[348] Environmental Defense Fund and International Emissions Trading Association, 'Carbon Pricing: the Paris Agreement's Key Ingredient' (April 2016) <http://www.ieta.org/resources/Resources/Reports/Carbon_Pricing_The_Paris_Agreements_Key_Ingredient.pdf> accessed 20 January 2017; International Carbon Action Partnership (ICAP), 'Emissions Trading Worldwide: International Carbon Action Partnership: Status Report 2016' (Berlin: ICAP, 2016) (Sixty-four INDCs said they planned to use markets, and twenty-five said they were considering using markets).

[349] 'Carbon Pricing', ibid.   [350] Paris Agreement, Art 13.3 and Art 13.4.

[351] See European Commission, Climate Action, 'Emissions Monitoring and Reporting' <http://ec.europa.eu/clima/policies/strategies/progress/monitoring/index_en.htm> accessed 20 January 2017.

SELECT BIBLIOGRAPHY

Breidenich C., *et al.*, 'The Kyoto Protocol to the United Nations Framework Convention on Climate Change', *American Journal of International Law*, 92/2 (1998): 315.

Brunnée J., 'A Fine Balance: Facilitation and Enforcement in the Design of a Compliance System for the Kyoto Protocol', *Tulane Environmental Law Journal*, 13/2 (2000): 223.

Brunnée J., 'The Kyoto Protocol: A Testing Ground for Compliance Theories?', *Zeitschrift für ausländisches öffentliches Recht und Völkerrecht (Heidelberg Journal of International Law)*, 63 (2003): 255.

Brunnée J., Doelle M., and Rajamani L. (eds), *Promoting Compliance in an Evolving Climate Change Regime* (Cambridge University Press, 2012).

de Cendra de Larragan J., 'The Kyoto Protocol, with a Special Focus on the Flexible Mechanisms', in Farber D.A. and Peeters M. (eds), *Elgar Encyclopedia of Environmental Law, vol 1: Climate Change Law* (Cheltenham, UK: Edward Elgar, 2016) 227.

Depledge J., 'Tracing the Origins of the Kyoto Protocol: An Article-by-Article Textual History' (25 November 2000) FCCC/TP/2000/2.

French D., '1997 Kyoto Protocol to the 1992 UN Framework Convention on Climate Change', *Journal of Environmental Law*, 10/2 (1998): 227.

Grubb M., *et al.*, *The Kyoto Protocol: A Guide and Assessment* (London: Earthscan, 1999) 76.

Jacur F.R., 'The Kyoto Protocol's Compliance Mechanism', in Farber D.A. and Peeters M. (eds), *Elgar Encyclopedia of Environmental Law vol 1: Climate Change Law* (Cheltenham: Edward Elgar Publishing, 2016) 239.

Oberthür S., 'Compliance under the Evolving Climate Change Regime', in Carlane C.P., Gray K.R., and Tarasofsky R. (eds), *The Oxford Handbook of International Climate Change Law* (Oxford University Press, 2016) 120.

Oberthür S. and Ott H.E., *The Kyoto Protocol: International Climate Policy for the 21st Century* (Berlin/Heidelberg: Springer-Verlag, 1999).

Rajamani L., 'Addressing the Post-Kyoto Stress Disorder: Reflections on the Emerging Legal Architecture of the Climate Regime', *International and Comparative Law Quarterly*, 58/4 (2009): 803.

Shishlov I., Morel R., and Bellassen V., 'Compliance of the Parties to the Kyoto Protocol in the First Commitment Period', *Climate Policy*, 16/6 (2016): 768.

Ulfstein G. and Werksman J., 'The Kyoto Compliance System: Towards Hard Enforcement', in Stokke OS., Hovi J., and Ulfstein G. (eds), *Implementing the Climate Regime* (London: Earthscan, 2005) 59.

Yamin F. and Depledge J., *The International Climate Change Regime: A Guide to Rules, Institutions and Procedures* (Cambridge University Press, 2004).

7

Paris Agreement

I. INTRODUCTION

UN Secretary General Ban Ki-moon characterized the 2015 Paris Agreement,[1] adopted after years of deeply contentious multilateral negotiations, as a 'monumental triumph'.[2] Others have, in a similar vein, hailed the Agreement as 'historic',[3] a 'landmark',[4] the 'world's greatest diplomatic success',[5] and a 'big, big deal'.[6] To the extent these claims are true, it is not because the Paris Agreement either decisively resolves the climate crisis or is novel in its approach, but because the agreement represents a considerable achievement in multilateral diplomacy. Negotiations rife with fundamental and seemingly intractable disagreements wound their way to a successful conclusion in Paris on 12 December 2015. These negotiations, driven by unprecedented political will,[7] were expected to reach an agreement. However, the fact that they reached a long-term, balanced and virtually universally accepted agreement,[8] despite the many crisscrossing red lines of parties, was not a foregone conclusion.

---

[1] This chapter draws on Lavanya Rajamani, 'Ambition and Differentiation in the 2015 Paris Agreement: Interpretative Possibilities and Underlying Politics', *International and Comparative Law Quarterly*, 65/2 (2016): 493; Lavanya Rajamani, 'The 2015 Paris Agreement: Interplay Between Hard, Soft and Non-Obligations', *Journal of Environmental Law*, 28/2 (2016): 337; Daniel Bodansky, 'The Paris Climate Agreement: A New Hope?', *American Journal of International Law*, 110/2 (2016): 288.

[2] 'COP21: UN chief hails new climate change agreement as "monumental triumph"', *UN News Centre* (12 December 2015) <http://www.un.org/apps/news/story.asp?NewsID=52802#.Vrh45fl96Uk> accessed 20 January 2017.

[3] Joby Warrick and Chris Mooney, '196 Countries Approve Historic Climate Agreement', *The Washington Post* (12 December 2015) <https://www.washingtonpost.com/news/energy-environment/wp/2015/12/12/proposed-historic-climate-pact-nears-final-vote/> accessed 20 January 2017.

[4] Coral Davenport, 'Nations Approve Landmark Climate Accord in Paris', *The New York Times* (13 December 2015) A1.

[5] Fiona Harvey, 'Paris Climate Change Agreement: The World's Greatest Diplomatic Success', *The Guardian* (14 December 2015) <https://www.theguardian.com/environment/2015/dec/13/paris-climate-deal-cop-diplomacy-developing-united-nations> accessed 20 January 2017.

[6] Thomas L. Friedman, 'Paris Climate Accord Is a Big, Big Deal', *The New York Times* (16 December 2015) A35.

[7] 150 Heads of State and Government attended the leaders event, see 'Leaders Event and High Level Segment' *Paris COP Information Hub* <http://newsroom.unfccc.int/cop21parisinformationhub/cop-21cmp-11-information-hub-leaders-and-high-level-segment/> accessed 20 January 2017.

[8] At the signing ceremony on 22 April 2016, only Bolivia voiced objections to the agreement.

The Paris Agreement sets an ambitious direction for the climate regime, and complements this direction with a set of common core obligations for all countries, including legally binding obligations of conduct in relation to parties' nationally determined mitigation contributions, and an expectation of progression over time. It also establishes a common transparency and accountability framework and an iterative process, in which parties take stock, every five years, of their collective progress and put forward emission reduction contributions for the next five-year period. The Paris Agreement, moreover, commands universal or near universal acceptance, and is applicable to all. As of 20 January 2017, over 190 countries representing roughly 99% of global emissions had put forward intended nationally determined contributions (INDCs).[9]

This chapter considers the 2015 Paris Agreement in depth, first by exploring four overarching issues, and then through a detailed analysis of its key provisions.

II. OVERARCHING ISSUES

The negotiations leading up to what became the Paris Agreement were beset by disagreements in at least four key overarching areas: (1) the legal form of the 2015 agreement, and the legal character of provisions within it; (2) the architecture of the 2015 agreement; (3) the scope of the 2015 agreement; and (4) the nature and extent of differentiation it contains. The design of the 2015 agreement reflects the compromises struck in these four key areas.

A. Legal bindingness

1. Legal form of the 2015 agreement

The legal form of the 2015 agreement was at issue from the start. The options for legal form ranged from legal agreements such as protocols and amendments that are treaties within the meaning of the Vienna Convention on the Law of Treaties (VCLT),[10] to soft law options such as decisions taken by the Conference of the Parties (COP), which are not, save in the exception, legally binding.[11] The Alliance of Small Island States (AOSIS) and other vulnerable countries have long argued that anything short of a legally binding instrument would be an affront to their existential crisis. The European Union (EU), the United States (US), and other

---

[9] World Resources Institute (WRI), 'CAIT Climate Data Explorer' <http://cait.wri.org/indc/> accessed 20 January 2017. For a listing of the INDCs submitted, see INDCs as communicated by the Parties, <http://www4.unfccc.int/submissions/INDC/Submission%20Pages/submissions.aspx> accessed 20 January 2017. For the process of conversion from 'intended' nationally determined contributions to NDCs, see n 301 below and accompanying text.

[10] Vienna Convention on the Law of Treaties (adopted 23 May 1969, entered into force 27 January 1980) 1155 UNTS 331 (VCLT), Art 2.1(a) (definition of 'treaties').

[11] See Chapter 1, Section V.A for a discussion of the different dimensions of legal bindingness and Chapter 3, Section II.D.3 for the legal status of COP decisions.

developed countries also consistently favored a global and comprehensive legally binding agreement under the FCCC. Brazil, China, and India, concerned about the constraints of a new legal agreement on their development prospects, were initially reluctant to endorse the call for a legally binding instrument, but, in the final hours of the 2011 Durban conference, which launched the negotiations for the 2015 agreement, only India remained firm in its opposition to such an instrument. India feared that a legally binding instrument would contain binding mitigation commitments that would pose challenges for its development aspirations. Eventually, the EU prevailed upon India to accept a compromise that called for the development of a 'protocol, another legal instrument or an agreed outcome with legal force under the Convention applicable to all Parties'.[12] In India's view, this wording was sufficiently open-ended that it preserved the option of an instrument other than a treaty.[13]

Parties chose not to decide the legal form of the 2015 agreement and the legal character of its constituent provisions until the end of the four-year negotiating process.[14] Nevertheless, by the time parties arrived in Paris, there was emerging consensus that the 2015 agreement would take the form of a legally binding instrument. The US was willing to accept a legally binding instrument, despite significant domestic political constraints, so long as developed and developing countries were equally bound by the agreement.[15] India, despite its historical reluctance to accept a legally binding instrument, had softened its stance. Other

---

[12] Durban Platform, para 2. See generally Lavanya Rajamani, 'The Durban Platform for Enhanced Action and the Future of the Climate Regime', *International and Comparative Law Quarterly*, 61/2 (2012): 501. See also Daniel Bodansky, 'The Durban Platform Negotiations: Goals and Options' (Harvard Project on Climate Agreements, 2012) <http://belfercenter.ksg.harvard.edu/files/bodansky_durban2_vp.pdf> accessed 20 January 2017.

[13] Submission from India (30 April 2012) FCCC/ADP/2012/MISC.3, 33.

[14] In 2013, the Warsaw conference invited parties to submit 'intended nationally determined contributions' (INDCs) in the context of the 2015 agreement, but left unresolved the legal form of the 2015 agreement and, explicitly, the legal nature or character of nationally determined contributions. Warsaw decision, para 2(b) and (c). The 'Elements text' for the 2015 agreement, produced by the 2014 Lima conference, and the 'Geneva Negotiating Text' also contained footnoted disclaimers in relation to the legal form and character of the agreement and its provisions. See Lima Call for Climate Action, Annex: Elements for a draft negotiating text; Ad Hoc Working Group on the Durban Platform for Enhanced Action (ADP), 'Negotiating text' (25 February 2015) FCCC/ADP/2015/1 (Geneva Negotiating Text).

[15] Throughout the ADP negotiations, the US envisioned the 2015 agreement as having 'final clauses', thus signalling that the 2015 agreement would be a treaty within the meaning of the VCLT. U.S. Submission on Elements of the 2015 Agreement (12 February 2014) <http://unfccc.int/files/documentation/submissions_from_parties/adp/application/pdf/u.s._submission_on_elements_of_the_2105_agreement.pdf> accessed 20 January 2017, 10–11. However, the US preferred that the 2015 agreement not be characterized as a 'treaty', since the term 'treaty' has specific connotations in US constitutional law. See Daniel Bodansky and Lavanya Rajamani, 'Key Legal Issues in the 2015 Climate Negotiations' (Arlington, VA: Center for Climate and Energy Solutions, June 2015) <http://www.c2es.org/docUploads/legal-issues-brief-06-2015.pdf> accessed 20 January 2016, note 7; Lavanya Rajamani, 'The Devilish Details: Key Legal Issues in the 2015 Climate Negotiations', *Modern Law Review*, 78/5 (2015): 826; see also Jacob Werksman, 'The Legal Character of International Environmental Obligations in the Wake of the Paris Climate Change Agreement' (University of Edinburgh: Brodies Environmental Law Lecture Series, 9 February 2016) <http://www.law.ed.ac.uk/other_areas_of_interest/events/brodies_lectures_on_environmental_law> accessed 20 January 2017.

developing countries were more concerned with particular provisions of the agreement than its legal form. The softening of positions in relation to legal form can be traced to at least three developments. First, a powerful political momentum had built up over time, due to the efforts of the EU and many vulnerable countries, toward adoption of a legally binding instrument. Second, the reluctance of many countries across the developed–developing country divide to take on internationally-negotiated commitments had led to the emergence and gathering traction of the notion of 'nationally determined contributions' (NDCs)—an approach that, by privileging sovereign autonomy, respecting national circumstances, and permitting self-differentiation, significantly reduced the sovereignty costs of a legally binding instrument. Third, due to the efforts of the US and others, there was increasing recognition and acceptance by states of the distinction between the legal form of the instrument (ie could be binding) and the legal character of national determined contributions (ie could be non-binding).

Two key points are worth noting about the Paris Agreement. First, it is a treaty, as defined in the VCLT.[16] It is titled the 'Paris Agreement' rather than the Paris Protocol, in deference to US political sensitivities,[17] and was not explicitly adopted under FCCC Article 17, which governs the adoption of 'Protocols'. However, the nomenclature of an instrument is legally irrelevant.[18]

Second, the Paris Agreement is an agreement 'under the United Nations Framework Convention on Climate Change'.[19] As such, the provisions of the FCCC that apply to 'related legal instruments' apply to the Paris Agreement, including the FCCC's ultimate objective.[20] Furthermore, Article 2 of the Paris Agreement links the 'purpose'[21] of the agreement with 'enhancing the implementation of the Convention',[22] which some parties argue ensures the centrality of the convention in the evolution of the climate regime.[23] The Paris Agreement also makes use of many of the FCCC's institutions, including the COP and financial mechanism.[24]

---

[16] VCLT, Art 2.1(a).

[17] For appearances sake, the US wanted to distinguish the Paris Agreement as much as possible from the Kyoto Protocol, which the US had rejected, including with respect to its title. For a full discussion, see Rajamani, Devilish Details (n 15) 835.

[18] See Chapter 3, Section II.A.

[19] Decision 1/CP.21, 'Adoption of the Paris Agreement' (29 January 2016) FCCC/CP/2015/10/Add.1, 2, para 1. This is in keeping with the Durban Platform, pursuant to which the Paris Agreement was adopted. See Paris Agreement, preambular recital 1.

[20] Other provisions of the FCCC that apply to related legal instruments include the power of the COP under Article 7.2 to review implementation and Article 14 on dispute settlement.

[21] See Paris Agreement, Art 3 (characterizing Article 2 as the purpose of the agreement).

[22] For a discussion of interpretive possibilities relating to this provision, see Rajamani, Ambition and Differentiation (n 1). See also Annalisa Savaresi, 'The Paris Agreement: A Rejoinder', *Blog of the European Journal of International Law* (16 February 2016) <http://www.ejiltalk.org/the-paris-agreement-a-rejoinder/> accessed 20 January 2016.

[23] For further discussion of this issue, see nn 91–93 below and accompanying text.

[24] Paris Agreement, Art 9.8.

2. *Legal character of the provisions in the 2015 agreement*

Parties agreed to a legally binding 2015 agreement on the understanding that it would contain a range of provisions, some with greater legal force and authority than others.[25] The legal character of a provision, as discussed in Chapter 1, depends on a variety of factors including—location (where the provision occurs), subjects (who the provision addresses), normative content (what requirements, obligations or standards the provision contains), language (whether the provision uses mandatory, hortatory, or advisory language), precision (whether the provision uses contextual, qualifying, or discretionary clauses), and what institutional mechanisms exist for transparency, accountability, and compliance.[26] Taking these factors into account, the Paris Agreement contains provisions that span the spectrum of legal character. Table 7.1 provides a rough sketch of this spread of provisions, and the cascading levels of treaty norms designed collectively to further the purpose of the agreement.[27] It tabulates provisions based on their nature and subjects. At one end of the spectrum are provisions that create rights and obligations for parties and lend themselves to assessments of compliance and non-compliance. This is, for instance, the case with individual ('each Party') obligations, framed in mandatory terms ('shall'), with clear and precise normative content, and no qualifying or discretionary elements. Such provisions can be characterized as 'hard law'.[28] In the middle of the spectrum are provisions that identify actors ('each Party' or 'all Parties') and set standards, but include qualifying or discretionary elements or are formulated in hortatory or advisory terms ('should' or 'encourage'). These provisions can be characterized, in varying ways, as 'soft law'.[29] At the other end of the spectrum are provisions lacking normative content that capture understandings between parties, provide context, or offer a narrative regarding the need for the provision or its location in the broader picture. Even when these provisions are found in the operational part of a legally binding instrument, they are contextual or descriptive and thus might be characterized as 'non-law'—a purely descriptive term that should not be interpreted as denigrating their critical importance in the Paris Agreement.[30] These three categories of provisions—hard law, soft law, and non-law—are fluid, and there are no bright lines between them. Each provision of the Paris Agreement contains a unique blend of elements, and thus occupies its own place in the spectrum of

[25] The US, for instance, envisioned that only some elements would be 'internationally legally binding': US Submission (n 15) 7.

[26] See Chapter 1, Section V.A.

[27] Table 7.1 is intended to be illustrative rather than comprehensive, and focuses on provisions that are addressed to states, not those that create obligations for the Conference of the Parties serving as the Meeting of the Parties to the Paris Agreement (CMA) (such as Art 14).

[28] See Dinah Shelton, 'Introduction', in Dinah Shelton (ed) *Commitment and Compliance: The Role of Non-Binding Norms in the International Legal System* (Oxford University Press, 2000) 1, 10–13.

[29] There are several definitions of 'soft law'. For an overview see Jutta Brunnée, 'The Sources of International Environmental Law: Interactional Law', in Samantha Besson and Jean d'Aspremont (eds), *Oxford Handbook on the Sources of International Law* (Oxford University Press, 2017 forthcoming). See also Chapter 1, Section V.A and Chapter 2, Section II.

[30] See discussion on Article 7 in Section VII below.

legal character. For instance, on adaptation, an individual obligation ('each party') phrased in mandatory terms ('shall') is combined with discretionary language ('as appropriate').[31] The combination of elements in each provision is a reflection of the demands of the relevant issue area as well as the particular politics that drove its negotiation. The legal character of particular provisions, including non-law provisions, will be discussed in the detailed analysis of key provisions below.

B. Architecture

A second issue that vexed negotiators was the issue of architecture—whether the Paris Agreement should reflect a top-down or a bottom-up approach. In contrast to the mandate for the Kyoto Protocol negotiations, which called for the negotiation of quantitative emission limitation and reduction objectives,[32] the Durban Platform did not offer any concrete guidance on the issue of architecture, although it recognized in a preambular recital that fulfilling the convention's objective 'will require strengthening of the multilateral, rules-based regime'.[33] It became clear from the submissions of parties after Durban, however, that although some parties favored a top-down architecture and others were keen to retain as much autonomy as possible, there was growing convergence on a hybrid approach that merged the two, by adding top-down elements to the bottom-up approach of the Copenhagen Accord and Cancun Agreements.[34] The decision that parties took in 2013 at the Warsaw COP to prepare INDCs in the context of the 2015 agreement reflected this emerging convergence. It laid the ground for a bottom-up process, in which each state would be able to define the stringency, scope, and form of its contribution. But the decision also introduced some international discipline, by calling on parties to communicate their INDCs 'in a manner that facilitates ... clarity, transparency, and understanding',[35] and by suggesting they do so, if possible, in the first quarter of 2015, to leave time before Paris for a process of informal, *ex ante* review.[36]

The Paris Agreement crystallizes this emerging hybrid architecture, in which bottom-up substance to promote participation (contained in parties' NDCs) is combined with a top-down process to promote ambition and accountability (contained in the agreement's internationally-determined provisions on progression and highest possible ambition, accounting, transparency, stocktake, and compliance). The bottom-up component of the Paris Agreement's hybrid architecture was

---

[31] Paris Agreement, Art 7.9.   [32] Berlin Mandate, para 2.
[33] Durban Platform, preambular recital 3.
[34] See eg 'Submission by Japan: Information, views and proposals on matters related to the work of Ad Hoc Working Group on the Durban Platform for Enhanced Action (ADP)' (10 September 2013) <http://unfccc.int/files/documentation/submissions_from_parties/adp/application/pdf/adp_japan_workstream_1_and_2_20130910.pdf> accessed 20 January 2017, arguing for a 'flexible hybrid system'.
[35] Warsaw decision, para 2(b).
[36] Ibid. The Lima Call for Climate Action, adopted the following year at COP-20, contributed additional details, identifying (but not prescribing) information that states might provide in connection with their NDCs, including assumptions and methodological approaches, time frames, scope, and coverage. Lima Call for Climate Action, para 14.

nearly complete by the time the Paris conference began. Over the course of 2015, virtually every state submitted an INDC.[37] The Paris Conference focused on the other half of the hybrid equation: the development of strong international rules to promote ambition and accountability. The Paris agreement does not include a number of important proposals, such as that NDCs be quantified or quantifiable and include an unconditional element, and that proposed NDCs be subject to a formal process of *ex ante* review to consider their ambition, comparability, and fairness. Nevertheless, the so-called 'friends of rules' group of countries in Paris ultimately proved successful in including comparatively strong rules on transparency, accounting, and updating.[38] The rules that were successfully incorporated into the agreement are at the outer edge of what was politically achievable given the experience of the previous four years of negotiations.[39]

C. Scope

A third overarching issue that negotiators grappled with through the course of the four-year negotiating process was the scope or coverage of the 2015 agreement. The Durban Platform decision required consideration of 'mitigation, adaptation, finance, technology development and transfer, transparency of action, and support, and capacity-building'.[40] In the discussions on the content of the 2015 agreement, developed countries sought to focus on mitigation, transparency, and market instruments, while some developing countries sought to spread the focus across the other 'pillars' of the Bali Action Plan, namely adaptation, finance, and technology development.

The submissions and interventions of parties in the Ad Hoc Working Group on the Durban Platform (ADP) negotiations continued these debates. The US argued that 'mitigation is the main issue that needs updating',[41] Australia believed that 'mitigation must be central to the 2015 agreement',[42] and the Independent Association of Latin America and the Caribbean (AILAC) that 'mitigation will necessarily be at the core of the 2015 agreement'.[43] China and India, among

---

[37] 154 INDCs of 182 states had been by submitted by 1 December 2015 when the Paris conference began. 163 INDCs of 191 states have been submitted as of 20 January 2017. See INDCs as communicated by the Parties (n 9). 119 INDCs of 147 states had been submitted by 1 October 2015, and were taken into account in the FCCC secretariat's first Synthesis Report on the aggregate effect of the INDCs. FCCC, 'Synthesis Report on the Aggregate Effect of the Intended Nationally Determined Contributions' (30 October 2015) FCCC/CP/2015/7.

[38] See below Section V.A.   [39] Rajamani, Ambition and Differentiation (n 1).

[40] Durban Platform, para 5.

[41] ADP Workstream 1: 2015 Agreement, Submission of the United States (11 March 2013) <https://unfccc.int/files/documentation/submissions_from_parties/adp/application/pdf/adp_usa_workstream_1_20130312.pdf> accessed 20 January 2017.

[42] Australia, Submission under the Durban Platform for Enhanced Action, The 2015 climate change agreement, ADP (26 March 2013) <http://unfccc.int/files/documentation/submissions_from_parties/adp/application/pdf/adp_australia_workstream_1_20130326.pdf> accessed 20 January 2017.

[43] Submission by the Independent Alliance of Latin America and the Caribbean—AILAC, ADP—Planning of Work in 2013 (1 March 2013) <http://unfccc.int/files/documentation/submissions_from_parties/adp/application/pdf/adp_ailac_workstream1_20130301.pdf> accessed 20 January 2017.

others, disagreed. India argued that 'enhanced action under the Durban Platform is related not just to the mitigation but to other pillars of climate action decided upon in the Bali Action Plan and subsequent COP decisions'.[44] China argued that all the elements should be addressed 'on an equal footing and in a holistic, balanced and coordinated manner' and, with India, that unresolved issues from the Bali process—such as equitable access to sustainable development, trade and unilateral measures, and technology-related intellectual property rights—should also be addressed.[45] The African Group, the Least Developed Countries (LDCs), and AILAC were insistent that there should be political parity between the treatment of adaptation and mitigation. In addition, some parties suggested that the 2015 agreement address loss and damage,[46] and compliance.[47] Given the lack of specificity in the Durban Platform and the divergence in positions of states, it was thus unclear at the start of the four-year negotiating process what attention, if any, different elements in the Durban Platform would ultimately receive in the 2015 agreement. It was also unclear if elements not explicitly identified in the Durban Platform would feature in the 2015 agreement.

As noted above, the Warsaw conference in 2013 invited parties to prepare and submit INDCs in 2015. In the course of the following year, however, it became clear that the carefully negotiated language of the Warsaw decision raised further issues, including:

- Whether INDCs would cover only mitigation or also adaptation, finance, technology and capacity-building.

- Whether mitigation would be a compulsory or optional component of a party's INDC.

---

[44] Submission by India on the work of the Ad-hoc Working Group on the Durban Platform for Enhanced Action Work-stream I (9 March 2013) <http://unfccc.int/files/documentation/submissions_from_parties/adp/application/pdf/adp_india_workstream_2_20130309.pdf> accessed 20 January 2017, para 5.13.

[45] China's Submission on the Work of the Ad Hoc Working Group on Durban Platform for Enhanced Action (5 March 2013) <http://unfccc.int/files/documentation/submissions_from_parties/adp/application/pdf/adp_china_workstream_1_20130305.pdf> accessed 20 January 2017, para 5; see also Joint Statement issued at the Conclusion of the 13th BASIC Ministerial Meeting on Climate Change Beijing, China 19–20 November 2012 (Beijing: Embassy of India, 21 November 2012) <http://www.indianembassy.org.cn/newsDetails.aspx?NewsId=381> accessed 20 January 2017.

[46] AOSIS submission on the Plan of Work of the Ad Hoc Working Group on Durban Platform for Enhanced Action (1 May 2012) <http://aosis.org/wp-content/uploads/2013/05/AOSIS-Submission-ADP-Final-May-2012.pdf> accessed 20 January 2017, para 19.

[47] Submission by Swaziland on behalf of the African Group on adaptation in the 2015 Agreement (8 October 2013) <http://unfccc.int/files/documentation/submissions_from_parties/adp/application/pdf/adp_african_group_workstream_1_adaptation_20131008.pdf> accessed 20 January 2017; South African Submission on Mitigation under the Ad Hoc Working Group on the Durban Platform for Enhanced Action (30 September 2013) <http://unfccc.int/files/documentation/submissions_from_parties/adp/application/pdf/adp_south_africa_workstream_1__mitigation_20130930.pdf> accessed 20 January 2017; Submission by India (n 44) para 5.21; Submission by Lithuania and the European Commission on behalf of the European Union and its Member States (16 September 2013) <http://unfccc.int/files/documentation/submissions_from_parties/adp/application/pdf/adp_eu_workstream_1_design_of_2015_agreement_20130916.pdf> accessed 30 January 2017.

- Whether parties could submit conditional INDCs—conditioned on the provision of support or on action by other parties—or only unconditional ones.

There were a range of views on these issues cutting across developed-developing country lines, with some states insisting that contributions should cover only mitigation and others arguing that mitigation and adaptation should be accorded legal and material parity. In addition, many developing countries, including the Like Minded Developing Countries (LMDCs),[48] argued that if they were required to submit mitigation contributions, there had to be a corresponding increase in the provision of technical and financial support. This, in their view, could best be ensured by requiring developed countries to submit contributions on finance.[49] Needless to say, this proved difficult to achieve. The Lima outcome therefore merely repeated Warsaw language inviting parties to communicate their INDCs. It encouraged parties to consider including an adaptation component in their contributions,[50] but was silent on a financial component. Parties were therefore free to offer a full and diverse range of contributions, and they did so: some focused on mitigation alone,[51] while others covered all areas;[52] some were unconditional,[53] while others contained both conditional[54] and unconditional elements.[55]

The Paris Agreement addresses all of the elements listed in the Durban decision in a comprehensive manner: 'mitigation, adaptation, finance, technology development and transfer, transparency of action, and support and capacity-building'. In addition, it addresses loss and damage,[56] an issue of importance to small island states and LDCs, as well as compliance,[57] of interest to a broader coalition of developed and developing countries. Although the agreement is broad in its coverage, its

---

[48] The LMDCs are a coalition of developing countries that include Bolivia, China, Cuba, Dominica, Ecuador, Egypt, El Salvador, India, Iran, Iraq, Malaysia, Mali, Nicaragua, Philippines, Saudi Arabia, Sri Lanka, Sudan, and Venezuela. See Chapter 3, Section II.B.2.
[49] Proposal from the Like Minded Developing Countries in Climate Change, Decision X/CP.20 Elements for a Draft Negotiating Text of the 2015 ADP Agreed Outcome of the UNFCCC (3 June 2014) <http://unfccc.int/files/documentation/submissions_from_parties/adp/application/pdf/adp2-5_submission_by_malaysia_on_behalf_of_the_lmdc_crp.pdf> accessed 20 January 2017.
[50] Lima Call for Climate Action, para 12.
[51] See eg Switzerland's intended nationally determined contribution and clarifying information (27 February 2015); Submission by Latvia and the European Commission on behalf of the European Union and its Member States (6 March 2015); Submission by Norway to the ADP, Norway's Intended Nationally Determined Contribution (27 March 2015); US Cover Note, INDC and Accompanying Information (31 March 2015); and the Russian Submission (1 April 2015) <http://www4.unfccc.int/submissions/indc/Submission%20Pages/submissions.aspx> accessed 20 January 2017.
[52] See eg Contribution of Gabon (1 April 2015), and India's Intended Nationally Determined Contribution: Working Towards Climate Justice (1 October 2015) <http://www4.unfccc.int/submissions/indc/Submission%20Pages/submissions.aspx> accessed 20 January 2017.
[53] See eg Submission by Latvia and the EC (n 51).
[54] See eg Russian Submission (n 51) (conditioning their INDC on the 'maximum possible account of absorbing capacity of forests').
[55] See eg INDC of Malaysia (27 November 2015) <http://www4.unfccc.int/submissions/INDC/Submission%20Pages/submissions.aspx> accessed 20 January 2017 (pledging to reduce the emissions intensity of its GDP by 45% from 2005 levels by 2030, 10% of which will be conditional on provision of international support, the rest unconditional).
[56] Paris Agreement, Art 8.   [57] Ibid, Art 15.

treatment of these issues and the legal character of provisions in different areas vary, as illustrated in the sections below where the specific provisions of the agreement are considered in detail.[58]

Article 3, which contains overarching obligations that cut across issue areas, reflects the comprehensive scope of the Paris Agreement. It reads, in pertinent part,

[a]s nationally determined contributions to the global response to climate change, all Parties are to undertake and communicate ambitious efforts as defined in Articles 4, 7, 9, 10, 11 and 13 with a view to achieving the purpose of this Agreement as set out in Article 2. The efforts of all Parties will represent a progression over time ...

The term 'contributions' in this context could be read either as the term of art it had become after Warsaw, or in its commonsensical meaning as an offering toward the global response to climate change. Further, the term 'efforts' was used so as to preclude the need to characterize the full range of actions across the Paris Agreement as 'contributions'. This range of actions includes mitigation contributions,[59] adaptation planning and implementation,[60] and provision of financial resources to developing countries.[61]

In contrast to Article 3's comprehensive coverage, the Paris Agreement requires parties to submit NDCs only in relation to mitigation.[62] This issue proved contentious, with the LMDCs insisting until the final hours of the Paris negotiations that parties should be able to offer NDCs in areas other than mitigation, such as adaptation and means of implementation (finance, technology, and capacity-building). Their concern is addressed in Article 7.11, which recognizes that an adaptation communication can be submitted as part of a state's NDC.[63] It is also addressed through Article 3 in so far as the ambiguous reference to 'contributions' in that article can be interpreted as cutting across issue areas.

It is worth noting that the references in Article 3 to the specific articles that address mitigation, adaptation, finance, capacity-building, technology, and transparency were introduced to ensure that the obligations in each issue area would be determined by these articles, and that Article 3 would not create any new (potentially conflicting or confusing) obligations in relation to these areas. The one substantive new element in Article 3 is that the progression requirement applies beyond mitigation to areas such as adaptation and support. However, this provision applies to 'all Parties' not 'each Party', indicating that it could be interpreted as a collective rather than an individual requirement. Further, it uses the auxiliary verb 'will' rather than the imperative 'shall' and thus sets strong expectations (rather than obligations) of more ambitious actions over time.

The legal character of the provisions in each issue area is also different. Table 7.1 demonstrates that the provisions on mitigation and transparency create several new

---

[58] See Rajamani, 2015 Paris Agreement (n 1).   [59] Paris Agreement, Art 4.2.
[60] Ibid, Art 7.9.   [61] Ibid, Art 9.1.   [62] Ibid, Art 4.2.
[63] It is worth noting that 137 parties included an adaptation component in their INDCs. FCCC, 'Aggregate Effect of the Intended Nationally Determined Contributions: An Update' (2 May 2016) FCCC/CP/2016/2, para 7.

legal obligations for individual parties ('Each Party shall'). In contrast, the provision on finance generally continues existing obligations rather than creates new substantive obligations. Finally, in the areas of adaptation, technology, capacity-building, and loss and damage, the provisions primarily recommend, encourage or set aspirations, rather than bind parties.

D. Differentiation

Perhaps the most divisive overarching issue in the Paris Agreement negotiations was the issue of differentiation. Differentiation in the climate regime is founded on the principle of common but differentiated responsibilities and respective capabilities (CBDRRC), as discussed in Chapter 1. This principle has been operationalized in several ways, most sharply in the Kyoto Protocol, which established quantitative emission reduction targets for developed countries but not developing countries. Although the Kyoto model of differentiation was, from the outset, contentious, it began to seriously erode only with the negotiation of the Bali Action Plan in 2007. The trajectory of the climate negotiations since Bali indicates a move away from a bifurcated approach to differentiation, toward a more nuanced approach, with greater symmetry or parallelism.[64] Of particular significance is the text of the Durban Platform decision that launched the negotiation of the Paris Agreement.

In marked contrast to previous COP negotiating mandates,[65] the Durban Platform decision did not contain a reference to 'equity' or 'common but differentiated responsibilities and respective capabilities', because of differences over how such a reference should be formulated.[66] Developed countries insisted that any reference to 'common but differentiated responsibilities' be qualified with a statement that this principle must be interpreted in the light of contemporary economic realities.[67] The 2015 agreement, the EU argued, must contain a broader spectrum of differentiation in the obligations among parties than is the case under the convention. These proposals, however, were unacceptable to developing countries. India, in particular, argued that qualifying CBDRRC in this manner would be tantamount to amending the FCCC.[68] The compromise reached was to omit any

---

[64] See Lavanya Rajamani, 'Differentiation in the Emerging Climate Regime', *Theoretical Inquiries in Law*, 14/1 (2013): 151. See also Harald Winkler and Lavanya Rajamani, 'CBDR&RC in a Regime Applicable to All', *Climate Policy*, 14/1 (2014): 102.

[65] See eg Berlin Mandate, para 1(a); Bali Action Plan, para 1(a).

[66] The analysis of the Durban Platform decision that follows is drawn from Rajamani, Durban Platform (n 12).

[67] See eg Submission of Australia (10 December 2008) FCCC/AWGLCA/2008/Misc.5/Add.2 (Part I), 73; Submission of Japan (27 October 2008) FCCC/AWGLCA/2008/MISC.5, 40, 41; Submission of the United States (27 October 2008) FCCC/AWGLCA/2008/MISC.5, 106. It is worth noting that several international tribunals have approached treaties as 'living instruments' and applied the 'evolutionary' method of treaty interpretation. See generally for a discussion of these, Isabelle Van Damme, *Treaty Interpretation by the WTO Appellate Body* (Oxford University Press, 2009); George Letsas, 'Strasbourg's Interpretive Ethic: Lessons for the International Lawyer', *European Journal of International Law*, 21/3 (2010): 509.

[68] The FCCC permits non-Annex I parties to graduate to Annex I, through amendment to the annexes, should they wish to do so. See FCCC, Art 16. Thus far, the only cases of such graduation

reference to CBDRRC in the Durban Platform and instead simply provide that the 2015 agreement would be 'under the Convention'[69]– thereby implicitly engaging the FCCC's principles, including the principle of CBDRRC. Many developing countries believed that this reference to the FCCC would hold at bay efforts to reinterpret and qualify CBDRRC. But the debate over CBDRRC in Durban, and its eventual resolution, reflected a recasting of differentiation in the 2015 climate regime.

Another indicator of the shifting approach to differentiation can be found in the Durban Platform's provision that the 2015 agreement would be 'applicable to all Parties'.[70] Developed countries, in particular the US, Japan, and Australia, were insistent on including this language. However, the mere fact that an instrument is applicable to all does not imply that it is applicable in a symmetrical manner. Universality of application does not automatically signal uniformity of application. The phrase 'applicable to all', therefore, had political rather than legal significance. It was a signal that the 2015 agreement would move toward symmetrical obligations, at least in so far as the nature and form of the obligations (even if not their stringency) were concerned.[71] In a similar vein, preambular recitals in the Durban Platform decision called for 'all Parties' to urgently address climate change, and for the widest possible cooperation 'by all countries'.[72]

The 2012 Doha ADP decision explicitly reintroduced into the negotiations, through a preambular recital, a reference to the principles of the convention.[73] The Warsaw decision of 2013 similarly contained a general reference to 'principles' of the convention,[74] but no specific reference to CBDRRC. The Lima Call for Climate Action of 2014, in contrast, contained an explicit reference to the CBDRRC principle, but qualified by the clause 'in the light of different national circumstances'.[75] This qualification—which represents a compromise arrived at between the US and China[76]—arguably shifts the interpretation of CBDRRC. Although it could be

have been Malta and Cyprus (yet to enter into force), and both have sought such graduation as a consequence of their joining the EU.

[69] Durban Platform, para 2.   [70] Ibid.

[71] See eg the comment by Todd Stern, the US Climate Change Envoy, after Durban, '[f]undamentally, we got the kind of symmetry we have been focused on since the beginning of the Obama administration', quoted in Lisa Friedman and Jean Chemnick, 'Durban talks create "platform" for new climate treaty that could include all nations', *ClimateWire* (12 December 2011) <http://www.eenews.net/stories/1059957503> accessed 20 January 2017. See also reaction of Connie Hedegaard, EU climate commissioner, after Durban: 'The big thing is that now all big economies, all parties have to commit in the future in a legal way and that's what we came here for', in 'Reaction to UN climate deal', *BBC News Science and Environment* (11 December 2011) <http://www.bbc.co.uk/news/science-environment-16129762> accessed 20 January 2017.

[72] Durban Platform, preambular recital 1.

[73] Decision 2/CP.18, 'Advancing the Durban Platform' (28 February 2013) FCCC/CP/2012/8/Add.1, 19, preambular recital 7.

[74] See Decision 1/CP.18, 'Agreed outcome pursuant to the Bali Action Plan' (28 February 2013) FCCC/CP/2012/8/Add.1, 3, recital to Part I; and Warsaw decision, preambular recital 9.

[75] Lima Call for Climate Action, para 3.

[76] See US-China Joint Announcement on Climate Change (Beijing, China, 12 November 2014) <https://www.whitehouse.gov/the-press-office/2014/11/11/us-china-joint-announcement-climate-change> accessed 20 January 2017, para 2.

argued that the principle, even in its original formulation, is dynamic, because historical responsibilities and respective capabilities both evolve, the qualification of the principle by a reference to 'different national circumstances' represented a political signal of flexibility and dynamism. As national circumstances evolve, so too will the common but differentiated responsibilities of parties. Moreover, given the differences in national circumstances among states, a simple categorization of states as developed or developing might not be appropriate. It is this version of the principle of common but differentiated responsibilities, with the qualifier 'in the light of different national circumstances', that features in the Paris Agreement.

1. The CBDRRC principle in the Paris Agreement[77]

The Paris Agreement contains references to the CBDRRC principle in a preambular recital,[78] and in the provisions relating to the purpose of the agreement,[79] progression,[80] and long-term low greenhouse gas (GHG) development strategies,[81] but always with the qualification, 'in light of different national circumstances'. The most significant of these references appears in Article 2, which sets the regime's long-term temperature goal and frames the implementation of the entire agreement. It reads: '[t]his Agreement will be implemented to reflect equity and the principle of common but differentiated responsibilities and respective capabilities, in the light of different national circumstances'.[82] This language generates an expectation that the agreement will reflect CBDRRC ('will be implemented to reflect') and preserves a range of interpretative possibilities for developing countries, yet stops short of prescribing CBDRRC in the implementation of the agreement.

In addition to the CBDRRC principle, the Paris Agreement contains references to the related notions of equity,[83] sustainable development,[84] equitable access to sustainable development,[85] poverty eradication,[86] and climate justice.[87] While some of these notions feature in the FCCC and others in COP decisions, they are formulated differently in the Paris Agreement. For instance, the references in the FCCC to poverty eradication recognize it either as a 'legitimate priority need'[88] or as an 'overriding priorit[y]',[89] whereas in the Paris Agreement it is recognized as part of the 'context' for action.[90]

---

[77] See for an in depth discussion Lavanya Rajamani and Emmanuel Guérin, 'Central Concepts in the Paris Agreement and How They Evolved', in Daniel Klein *et al.* (eds), *The Paris Climate Agreement: Analysis and Commentary* (Oxford University Press, forthcoming 2017); Lavanya Rajamani, 'Guiding Principles and General Obligations (Article 2.2 and Article 3)', in Klein *et al.*, ibid. See also Christina Voigt and Felipe Ferriera, 'Differentiation in the Paris Agreement', *Climate Law Special Issue*, 6/1–2 (2016): 58–74; Sandrine Maljean-Dubois, 'The Paris Agreement: A New Step in the Gradual Evolution of Differential Treatment in the Climate Regime', *Review of European, Comparative and International Environmental Law*, 25/2 (2016): 151–60.

[78] Paris Agreement, preambular recital 3.　　[79] Ibid, Art 2.2.　　[80] Ibid, Art 4.3.
[81] Ibid, Art 4.19.　　[82] Ibid, Art 2.2.
[83] Ibid, preambular recital 3, Arts 2.2, 4.1, and 14.1.
[84] Ibid, preambular recital 8, Arts 2.1, 4.1, 6, 7.1, 8.1, and 10.5.
[85] Ibid, preambular recital 8.　　[86] Ibid, preambular recital 8, Arts 2.1, 4.1, and 6.8.
[87] Ibid, preambular recital 13.　　[88] FCCC, preambular recital 21.
[89] Ibid, Art 4.7.　　[90] See eg Paris Agreement, Arts 2.1, 4.1, and 6.8.

The issue of CBDRRC also underlays debates about the relationship of the 2015 Paris Agreement to the FCCC, discussed above.[91] Developed countries were insistent that the Paris Agreement abandon the FCCC and Kyoto Protocol's annex-based approach to differentiation, which they regard as outdated and rigid, and they successfully excluded any reference to the annexes in the Paris Agreement. But many developing countries were equally insistent that the agreement contain a hook for arguments to reintroduce what they regard as the continuing balance of responsibilities between developed and developing countries reflected in the annex-based approach to differentiation. They sought to do this indirectly, through the inclusion of general language tying the Paris Agreement to the FCCC, which they believed would implicitly engage the entirety of the FCCC, including its annexes. The shadow boxing over this issue rippled through the negotiations of the entire text. It can be seen in the debate about whether to call the agreement simply the 'Paris Agreement' or the 'Paris Implementing Agreement'. And it was in particular evidence in the negotiations over whether to include language in Article 2's chapeau stating that the Paris Agreement should enhance the implementation of the convention, as most developing countries argued it should, or just the objective of the convention,[92] as most developed countries favored. For many developing countries, implemention of the convention implies the continued relevance of all the convention's principles and provisions, in particular the balance of responsibilities reflected in FCCC Article 4, and the corresponding annexes. Developed countries, in contrast, believe the Paris Agreement represents a paradigm shift in which the annex-based structure of the FCCC no longer has any continuing relevance, and sought to reinforce this position by referring only to the Paris Agreement's role in implementing the convention's objective. Ultimately, the parties reached a carefully balanced compromise in Article 2, which reads: '[t]his Agreement, in enhancing the implementation of the Convention, including its objective, aims to strengthen the global response to the threat of climate change, in the context of sustainable development and efforts to eradicate poverty, … '.[93] The intense negotiations over this somewhat convoluted provision illustrate the importance placed on language in the UN climate process and the difficulties of resolving disagreements definitively.

2. *Operationalizing the CBDRRC principle in the Paris Agreement*

The Paris Agreement operationalizes the CBDRRC principle not through the FCCC and Kyoto Protocol's annex structure, but in a tailored way, which takes into account the specificities of each of the Durban pillars—mitigation, adaptation, finance, technology, capacity-building, and transparency.[94] This more nuanced approach has resulted in different approaches to differentiation in different areas.

---

[91] See nn 19–23 above and acccompanying text.   [92] FCCC, Art 2.
[93] Paris Agreement, Art 2.1, chapeau.
[94] Lavanya Rajamani, 'Differentiation in a 2015 Climate Agreement' (Arlington, VA: Center for Climate and Energy Solutions, June 2015) <http://www.c2es.org/docUploads/differentiation-brief-06-2015.pdf> accessed 20 January 2017.

a) Differentiation in mitigation

The mitigation provisions of the Paris Agreement embrace a 'bounded self-differentiation' model, discussed below. The Warsaw decision invited parties to submit INDCs in the context of the 2015 agreement.[95] In submitting these contributions, parties were able to determine the scope, form, and rigor of their contributions, as well as the information that accompanied them. In so far as parties chose their own contributions and tailored these to their national circumstances, capacities and constraints, they differentiated themselves from every other nation. This form of differentiation has come to be characterized as self-differentiation. The mitigation section of the Paris Agreement contains self-differentiation, albeit modulated by several normative expectations placed on parties, as discussed below.

In contrast to the Kyoto Protocol, all of the legal obligations of parties relating to mitigation, with one exception,[96] are undifferentiated, including the obligations to prepare, communicate, and maintain successive NDCs; to provide the information necessary for clarity, transparency, and understanding; to communicate a successive NDC every five years; and to account for their NDCs.[97] The provisions that incorporate differentiation are all couched as recommendations or expectations,[98] rather than as binding obligations,[99] and even many of these reflect a self-differentiation (albeit bounded) model. For instance, in relation to the expectation that successive mitigation contributions will represent a progression beyond current contributions and will reflect a party's highest possible level of ambition, as discussed later,[100] it is for each party to determine, at least initially, what contribution constitutes progression and reflects its highest possible ambition, given the CBRDRC principle. Similarly, in relation to the provision that all parties should strive to formulate and communicate long-term low GHG emission development strategies,[101] it is for each party to take CBDRRC into account in determining its strategies.

The undifferentiated legal obligations, however, are 'bounded' or 'modulated' by several normative expectations placed on parties. Perhaps the most important of these, reflecting a categorical approach to differentiation, is in Article 4, which reads: '[d]eveloped country Parties should continue taking the lead by undertaking economy-wide absolute emission reduction targets. Developing country Parties should continue enhancing their mitigation efforts, and are encouraged to move over time towards economy-wide emission reduction or limitation targets in the light of different national circumstances'.[102] The use of the terms 'developed country Parties' and 'developing country Parties' and the notion of leadership are reminiscent of the FCCC. The paragraph sets strong normative expectations, but does not create any new obligations for parties, given the use of the term 'should'.

---

[95] See Warsaw decision, para 2(b).
[96] Article 4.5 states that 'support shall be provided' to developing countries. Read in conjunction with Article 9.1, it follows that developed countries are to provide this support.
[97] See nn 168–170 below and accompanying text.
[98] Paris Agreement, Art 4.4 and 4.19.   [99] Ibid, Art 4.3.
[100] See nn 187–193 below and accompanying text.   [101] Paris Agreement, Art 4.19.
[102] Ibid, Art 4.4.

Indeed, it is precisely because this provision creates no new obligations that the US was able to accept the Paris Agreement. This provision was at the center of the 'shall/should' controversy that nearly unraveled the Paris deal in the final hours.[103] The 'take it or leave it' text presented by the French contained mandatory language ('shall') in relation to developed country targets, and recommendatory language ('should') in relation to developing country mitigation efforts. In addition to the lack of parallelism in the legal character of requirements placed on developed and developing countries, the use of mandatory language for developed countries' targets posed a problem for the US. In the light of long-standing and intractable resistance to climate treaties in the Senate, the US had worked throughout the negotiations to ensure that the Paris Agreement could be accepted by it as a Presidential-executive agreement. This approach would have been put in jeopardy, arguably, if the agreement required the US to have a quantitative emissions target, since such a target is not currently part of US law.[104] However, the LMDCs objected to changes in what had been presented as a 'take it or leave it' text. Eventually, after furious huddling in the plenary room, and high-level negotiations outside it, the 'shall' was declared a typographical error and changed to a 'should' by the FCCC secretariat.

In addition to Article 4.4's differentiation between developed and developing countries, the Paris Agreement also recognizes that peaking of emissions will take longer in developing countries,[105] and that support shall be provided to developing countries for the implementation of this article.[106]

Thus, the mitigation section of the Paris Agreement operationalizes the CBDRRC principle through self-differentiation, but sets normative expectations in relation to the types of actions developed and developing country parties should take, and recognizes the need for flexibility and support for developing countries. It also sets normative expectations in relation to progression and 'highest possible ambition' through successive cycles of contributions. Self-differentiation was broadly acceptable to states because it provides flexibility and privileges sovereign autonomy. Given the lack of collective agreement about states' differentiated responsibilities and respective capabilities, self-differentiation was a pragmatic choice intended to encourage broad participation. But the Paris Agreement includes 'modulators' or boundaries to this self-differentiation that encourage ambition and recognize differences.

b) Differentiation in transparency

The transparency provisions of the Paris Agreement provide for flexibility to parties based on their capacities rather than on their categorization as developing countries. Parties rejected a bifurcated transparency system, on the table until the end, in favor of a framework applicable to all countries, albeit with 'built-in flexibility' tailored to parties' differing capacities as well as the provision of support to developing

---

[103] John Vidal, 'How a 'Typo' Nearly Derailed the Paris Climate Deal', *The Guardian* (16 December 2015) <http://www.theguardian.com/environment/blog/2015/dec/16/how-a-typo-nearly-derailed-the-paris-climate-deal> accessed 20 January 2017.
[104] Ibid.   [105] Paris Agreement, Art 4.1   [106] Ibid, Art 4.5 read with Art 9.1.

countries.[107] These provisions place uniform informational requirements on parties in relation to mitigation and adaptation.[108] But since parties have differentiated obligations in relation to support, the associated informational requirements are accordingly differentiated.[109] Reporting and review are also similarly differentiated.

Differentiation in the transparency provisions is thus a pragmatic tailoring of informational demands to capacities. While distinct from the bounded self-differentiation in the mitigation provisions, the transparency provisions too represent a significant departure from the FCCC, which places different informational burdens set to different time frames on Annex I and non-Annex I parties.[110]

This less categorical approach to differentiation proved possible in part because the Paris Agreement provides a number of hooks that developing countries could try to use to reintroduce bifurcation between developed and developing countries in the future. For example, the agreement provides that the enhanced framework shall 'build on' the transparency arrangements under the convention,[111] and that these arrangements, including the bifurcated system of international assessment and review (IAR) and international consultation and analysis (ICA),[112] 'shall form part of the experience drawn upon' in developing the framework's rules.[113] Moreover, the decision accompanying the Paris Agreement 'decides' that those developing countries that need flexibility in light of their national capacities 'shall' be provided flexibility in implementing the transparency framework, 'including in the scope, frequency, and level of detail of reporting, and in the scope of review'.[114] However, any attempt to reintroduce bifurcation in the transparency framework would need to overcome the Paris Agreement's characterization of the framework's modalities, procedures, and guidelines as 'common'—a characterization that is seemingly at odds with a bifurcated approach.

c) Differentiation in finance

The finance article of the Paris Agreement is perhaps most similar to the FCCC in the form of differentiation it embodies. It requires developed country parties to provide financial resources to developing country parties[115] 'in continuation of their existing obligations under the Convention', and to provide biennial reports.[116] It also recommends that developed countries continue to take the lead in mobilizing climate finance.[117] This recommendation is given concrete content in the decision accompanying the Paris Agreement, which captures an agreement to continue the developed countries' existing collective mobilization goal through 2025.[118]

Although the responsibility for provision and mobilization of financial resources is placed primarily on developed countries, the Paris Agreement, in a departure

---

[107] Ibid, Arts 13.1 and 13.2.   [108] Ibid, Arts 13.7 and 13.8.
[109] Ibid, Arts 13.9 and 13.10.
[110] FCCC, Art 12; Cancun Agreements LCA, para 40 (Annex I parties), and para 60 (non-Annex I parties).
[111] Paris Agreement, Art 13.3.   [112] See Chapter 5, Section VI.C.
[113] Paris Agreement, Art 13.4.   [114] Decision 1/CP.21 (n 19) para 89.
[115] Paris Agreement, Art 9.1.   [116] Ibid, Art 9.5.   [117] Ibid, Art 9.3.
[118] Decision 1/CP.21 (n 19) para 53.

from the FCCC,[119] expands the donor base to '[o]ther parties'.[120] Other parties—presumably, developing country parties—are 'encouraged' to provide such support 'voluntarily'.[121] And, they have correspondingly less demanding reporting requirements placed on them in relation to such support.[122] It is because of this potentially expanded donor base in the Paris Agreement that provisions on support across the agreement are phrased in the passive voice ('support shall be provided'),[123] which precludes the need to identify who is to provide such support. The agreement thus reflects a compromise, in which the provision of support to developing countries remains a central crosscutting feature of the climate regime, but the base of potential donors is expanded. The Paris Agreement also recognizes that enhanced support for developing countries will allow for higher ambition in their actions,[124] and that developing countries will need to be supported to ensure effective implementation of the agreement.[125]

In contrast to the annex-based approach of the FCCC and the Kyoto Protocol, the Paris Agreement does not list which countries qualify as 'developed' and 'developing', nor does the agreement contain a more general definition of these terms. In Paris, countries with 'economies in transition' as well as those whose 'special circumstances are recognized' by the COP, viz, Turkey, sought to ensure that they would be included in the category of 'developing countries' and thus be entitled to any benefits that might flow thereon.[126] This proved contentious until the end, but the term 'developing countries' was eventually left open and undefined.

Differentiation in the finance provisions is thus relatively close to the type of differentiation seen in the FCCC. Although the expansion of the donor base introduces a new element, the finance provisions represent a less radical departure from the FCCC's bifurcated, categorical approach than, for instance, the nature of differentiation seen in the mitigation provisions.

III. PREAMBLE

The preamble to the Paris Agreement identifies a series of contextual factors that could prove helpful in interpreting the agreement. These include: the CBDRRC principle;[127] best available scientific knowledge;[128] special circumstances of particularly vulnerable nations;[129] special needs and situations of the LDCs;[130] equitable access to sustainable development and eradication of poverty;[131] food

---

[119] See FCCC, Art 4.3.   [120] Paris Agreement, Art 9.2.   [121] Ibid.
[122] Ibid, Arts 9.5 and 9.7.   [123] See eg ibid, Arts 4.5, 7.13, 10.6, and 13.14.
[124] Ibid, Art 4.5.   [125] Ibid, Art 3.
[126] Draft Text on COP 21 agenda item 4 (b) Durban Platform for Enhanced Action (decision 1/CP.17): Adoption of a protocol, another legal instrument, or an agreed outcome with legal force under the Convention applicable to all Parties, Version 1 of 9 December 2015 at 15:00, Draft Paris Outcome, Proposal by the President <http://unfccc.int/resource/docs/2015/cop21/eng/da01.pdf> accessed 20 January 2017, footnote 7.
[127] Paris Agreement, preambular recital 3.   [128] Ibid, preambular recital 4.
[129] Ibid, preambular recital 5.   [130] Ibid, preambular recital 6.
[131] Ibid, preambular recital 8.

security;[132] just transition of the work force;[133] human rights;[134] conservation and enhancement of sinks;[135] ecosystem integrity;[136] climate justice;[137] environmental education, awareness, training and participation;[138] multi-level governance;[139] and sustainable patterns of consumption and production.[140] Of this long list, perhaps the most significant and hotly debated reference is that to human rights.[141]

Climate change threatens a variety of human rights, including the rights to life, health, food, and housing, and the measures taken to mitigate and adapt to climate change can raise human rights concerns as well.[142] The intersection of international climate change law and human rights law is discussed in Chapter 9. In the lead-up to Paris, many parties,[143] non-governmental organizations,[144] and international bodies[145] urged the inclusion of human rights concerns in the Paris Agreement.[146] Although some parties sought a reference to human rights in an operative provision of the agreement, for various reasons, discussed in Chapter 9, the only explicit reference to human rights in the Paris Agreement occurs in the preamble.

Preambular recital 11 reads:

Parties should, when taking action to address climate change, respect, promote, and consider their respective obligations on human rights, the right to health, the rights of indigenous peoples, local communities, migrants, children, persons with disabilities and people in vulnerable situations, and the right to development, as well as gender equality, empowerment of women, and intergenerational equity.

This formulation carefully circumscribes the impact of the reference to human rights. First, it addresses the human rights aspects only of response measures ('when taking action'), not of climate change itself. This is a narrower approach than that

---

[132] Ibid, preambular recital 9.   [133] Ibid, preambular recital 10.
[134] Ibid, preambular recital 11.   [135] Ibid, preambular recital 12.
[136] Ibid, preambular recital 13.
[137] Ibid (albeit qualified with the phrase 'importance for some').
[138] Ibid, preambular recital 14.   [139] Ibid, preambular recital 15.
[140] Ibid, preambular recital 16.
[141] The discussion on the human rights recital of the Paris Agreement draws on Lavanya Rajamani, 'Human Rights in the Climate Change Regime: From Rio to Paris', in John H. Knox and Ramin Pejan (eds), *The Human Right to a Healthy Environment* (Cambridge University Press, 2017, forthcoming). See Chapter 9, Section II.G.
[142] Office of the High Commissioner for Human Rights (OHCHR), 'Understanding Human Rights and Climate Change: Submission to COP21' (26 November 2015) <http://www.ohchr.org/Documents/Issues/ClimateChange/COP21.pdf> accessed 20 January 2017.
[143] See eg Submission of Chile on behalf of AILAC to the ADP on Human Rights and Climate Change (31 May 2015) <http://www4.unfccc.int/Submissions/Lists/OSPSubmissionUpload/195_99_130775585079215037-Chile%20on%20behalf%20of%20AILAC%20HR%20and%20CC.docx> accessed 20 January 2017.
[144] See eg Submission to the Ad Hoc Working Group on the Durban Platform for Enhanced Action Calling for Human Rights Protections in the 2015 Climate Agreement (7 February 2015) <http://unfccc.int/files/documentation/submissions_from_non-party_stakeholders/application/pdf/489.pdf> accessed 20 January 2017.
[145] See eg OHCHR, 'A New Climate Change Agreement Must Include Human Rights Protections for All' (17 October 2014) <http://www.ohchr.org/Documents/HRBodies/SP/SP_To_UNFCCC.pdf> accessed 20 January 2017.
[146] See generally for a recap of the advocacy movement on human rights in the lead up to Paris, Benoit Mayer, 'Human Rights in the Paris Agreement', *Climate Law*, 6/1–2 (2016): 109.

advocated by the Office of the High Commissioner of Human Rights (OHCHR), which considers that states are obliged to 'take affirmative measures to prevent human rights harms caused by climate change, including foreseeable long-term harms'.[147] The Paris Agreement, in contrast, recommends that states respect, promote, and consider human rights when taking response measures, but is silent with respect to whether they should take human rights considerations into account in determining the ambition, scope and scale of their mitigation or adaptation actions.

Second, the preambular provision recommends that parties 'respect, promote and consider' their human rights obligations, not 'respect, protect, promote *and fulfill*'[148] their obligations, as the OHCHR had urged states to do.[149] Thus, while the Paris Agreement urges states to refrain from taking actions that might interfere with the listed human rights, it does not, by itself, urge them either to prevent others from interfering with these rights or to adopt measures toward full realization.

Third, the preambular recital refers to parties' 'respective obligations'. It is thus limited to parties' existing human rights obligations, and is not intended to imply any new ones. States had differing views on the existence, characterization, relative importance, and boundaries of human rights relating to climate change. In these circumstances, restricting the application of specific rights to those individual parties that already have obligations in relation to those rights was considered desirable.

Notwithstanding the fact that the only explicit reference to human rights in the Paris Agreement is carefully circumscribed, its very inclusion is novel, and may signal enhanced receptivity to rights concerns and discourses.

IV. PURPOSE (ARTICLES 2 AND 4.1)

The 'purpose' of the 2015 agreement is to strengthen the global response to the threat of climate change.[150] In relation to mitigation, parties have explored different options for expressing long-term goals. Long-term mitigation goals can be formulated in terms of limiting temperature increase (2° C or 1.5° C above pre-industrial levels); as a GHG emissions reduction goal (for instance, 50% by 2050); or as a time frame for peaking of emissions.

Of these options for defining a long-term goal, the temperature goal has thus far acquired greater currency in the UN climate regime. The 2° C goal was

---

[147] See OHCHR, Understanding Human Rights and Climate Change (n 142).

[148] See ibid (emphasis added). See also OHCHR, 'Letter from the Special Rapporteur on human rights and the environment' (4 May 2016) <http://srenvironment.org/wp-content/uploads/2016/06/Letter-to-SBSTA-UNFCCC-final.pdf> accessed 20 January 2017.

[149] See OHCHR, New Climate Change Agreement (n 145); OHCHR, 'The Effects of Climate Change on the Full Enjoyment of Human Rights' (30 April 2015) <http://www.thecvf.org/wp-content/uploads/2015/05/humanrightsSRHRE.pdf> accessed 20 January 2017.

[150] Paris Agreement, Art 2.1. Although the Paris Agreement articles do not have titles, Article 3 identifies Article 2 as the 'purpose' of the agreement.

first recognized by the G-8 in L'Aquila in 2009.[151] It was incorporated into the Copenhagen Accord later that year,[152] and into the Cancun Agreements in 2010.[153] It also features in the Durban Platform decision that launched the negotiations toward a 2015 agreement, in a preambular recital that notes the significant gap between parties' mitigation pledges and the required emissions pathways to reach the 2° C temperature goal.[154] The Durban Platform, however, also references the 1.5° C goal as an alternative to the 2° C goal, thereby leaving open the option of strengthening the global temperature goal in the future. AOSIS, LDCs and the African Group, among others, have long argued for a 1.5° C global temperature goal.[155] For many of these countries, even a 2° C temperature increase poses an existential threat.

The Paris Agreement resolves to hold the increase in global average temperature to 'well below 2° C' above pre-industrial levels, and to pursue efforts toward a 1.5° C temperature limit.[156] The world is not currently on a pathway to 1.5° C, far from it.[157] Such a pathway would dramatically shrink the remaining carbon space, with troubling implications for countries like India that have yet to lift the vast majority of their citizens from the scourge of poverty.[158] Nevertheless, the aspirational 1.5° C goal sets a direction of travel for the climate regime and signals solidarity with the small island states on the frontlines of climate impacts.

The long-term temperature goal is to be achieved, as set out in Article 4.1, inter alia, through global peaking of GHG emissions as soon as possible (with a recognition that peaking will take longer in developing countries), and rapid reductions thereafter, 'so as to achieve a balance between anthropogenic emissions by sources and removals by sinks of GHGs in the second half of the century'.[159] Although parties had proposed quantitative global emission goals with specific peaking dates or percentage reductions from 2010 levels,[160] in the end it proved possible to reach agreement only on goals that lacked specific time lines.

---

[151] See Declaration of the Leaders of the Major Economies Forum on Energy and Climate (L'Aquila, Italy, 9 July 2009) <http://www.majoreconomiesforum.org/past-meetings/the-first-leaders-meeting.html> accessed 20 January 2017. See Chapter 8, Section IV.E.2 for a discussion of 'G clubs'.

[152] Copenhagen Accord, para 2.   [153] Cancun Agreements LCA, para 4.

[154] Durban Platform, preambular recital 2.

[155] Submission by Nepal on behalf of the Least Developed Countries Group on the ADP Work Stream 1: The 2015 Agreement, Building on the Conclusions of the ADP 1-2 (3 September 2013) <http://unfccc.int/files/documentation/submissions_from_parties/adp/application/pdf/adp_ldcs_20130903.pdf> accessed 20 January 2017; Submission by Swaziland on behalf of the Africa Group in respect of Workstream I: 2015 Agreement under the ADP (30 April 2013) <http://unfccc.int/files/bodies/awg/application/pdf/adp_2_african_group_29042013.pdf> accessed 20 January 2017.

[156] Paris Agreement, Art 2.1.

[157] Carbon Brief, 'Six years worth of current emissions would blow the carbon budget for 1.5 degrees' (13 November 2014) <https://www.carbonbrief.org/six-years-worth-of-current-emissions-would-blow-the-carbon-budget-for-1-5-degrees> accessed 20 January 2017.

[158] See T. Jayaraman and Tejal Kanitkar, 'The Paris Agreement: Deepening the Climate Crisis', *Economic and Political Weekly*, 51/3 (2016): 10.

[159] Paris Agreement, Art 4.1.

[160] See ADP, Draft agreement and draft decision on workstreams 1 and 2 of the Ad Hoc Working Group on the Durban Platform for Enhanced Action, Work of the ADP contact group (6 November 2015, reissued on 10 November 2015) ADP.2015.11.InformalNote, Art 3.

The net zero concept requires anthropogenic GHG emissions to be reduced rapidly, with the remainder made up through enhanced removals of GHGs by sinks.[161] In the lead-up to Paris, significant support had emerged for a longer-term decarbonization goal, in line with the conclusion of the Intergovernmental Panel on Climate Change (IPCC) that temperature stabilization will require zero net carbon emissions.[162] G-7 leaders had included such a goal in their 2015 summit declaration.[163] But fossil fuel-producing states did not want to single out carbon dioxide or focus only on emissions from sources to the exclusion of removal by sinks; hence the compromise formulation in Article 4.1, which is neutral as between carbon dioxide and other GHGs and as between reduced emissions and enhanced removals.

These global mitigation goals are to be achieved 'on the basis of equity, and in the context of sustainable development and efforts to eradicate poverty'.[164] As noted before, these terms are framed differently in the Paris Agreement than in the FCCC.[165] The Paris Agreement also recommends that parties 'strive to formulate and implement' long-term low GHG emission development strategies.[166] These are likely to play a critical role in shifting development trajectories and investment patterns toward meeting the long-term temperature goal. In a regime that permits countries to choose the nature, form and stringency of their contributions, this provision provides a mechanism for catalyzing national strategic thinking to ensure short-term actions are in line with long-term goals, and for aggregating the efforts of the parties.[167]

In order to address all of the elements of the Durban Platform in a balanced manner, the Paris Agreement also defines aims for adaptation and finance, albeit in general, qualitative terms (rather than in quantitative terms, as proposed by the African Group). For adaptation, Article 2 expresses the aim of increasing adaptive capacity, fostering climate resilience, and reducing vulnerability—aims reiterated in Article 7, which deals specifically with adaptation. The finance aim—namely, to make 'finance flows consistent with a pathway towards low greenhouse gas emissions and climate-resilient development'—addresses private as well as public flows, and provides support for efforts to phase out climate-unfriendly investments.

---

[161] See Kelly Levin, Jennifer Morgan, and Jiawei Song, 'Insider: Understanding the Paris Agreement's Long-term Goal to Limit Global Warming' (World Resources Institute, 15 December 2015) <http://www.wri.org/blog/2015/12/insider-understanding-paris-agreement%E2%80%99s-long-term-goal-limit-global-warming> accessed 20 January 2017.

[162] IPCC, *Climate Change 2014: Synthesis Report* (Cambridge University Press, 2014) Summary for Policy Makers, 20.

[163] G-7 Leaders' Declaration (Schloss Elmau, Germany, 8 June 2015) <https://www.whitehouse.gov/the-press-office/2015/06/08/g-7-leaders-declaration> accessed 20 January 2017. See Chapter 8, Section IV.E.2 for a discussion of 'G clubs'.

[164] Paris Agreement, Art 4.1.   [165] See nn 83–90 above and accompanying text.

[166] Paris Agreement, Art 4.19.

[167] For examples of such strategies, see the Deep Decarbonization Pathways Project, *Synthesis Reports* <http://deepdecarbonization.org/ddpp-reports/> accessed 20 January 2017.

V. MITIGATION (ARTICLE 4)

A. Obligations in relation to nationally determined contributions (NDCs)

The most significant legal obligations in the Paris Agreement are to be found in its mitigation article. In order to meet the long-term temperature goal, parties are subject to binding obligations of conduct in relation to their nationally determined mitigation contributions.[168] The most significant of these are contained in Article 4.2, which reads:

Each Party shall prepare, communicate and maintain successive nationally determined contributions that it intends to achieve. Parties shall pursue domestic mitigation measures, with the aim of achieving the objectives of such contributions.

There are many drafting treasures to be mined in this carefully negotiated text. First, unlike the majority of provisions in the Paris Agreement that apply to 'Parties',[169] the first sentence of this provision applies to 'each Party', thus creating individual obligations. Second, this provision, like selective provisions in the Paris Agreement, uses the imperative 'shall' both in relation to preparing, communicating and maintaining national contributions, as well as pursuing domestic mitigation measures. Third, while these are binding obligations, they are obligations of conduct rather than result. The term 'intends to achieve' in the first sentence establishes a good faith expectation that each party intends to achieve its NDC, but stops short of requiring it to do so. The second clause in the second sentence performs a similar function. It requires parties to pursue measures 'with the aim of achieving the objectives of [their] contributions'.[170]

Parties thus have binding obligations of conduct to prepare, communicate and maintain contributions, as well as to pursue domestic measures. There is also a good faith expectation that parties intend to and will aim to achieve the objectives of their contributions. In the lead up to Paris, many parties, including the EU, South Africa, and the small island states, had argued that parties should be required to achieve their NDCs, thus imposing an obligation of result. This was strenuously opposed by the US, China, and India, among others, who did not wish to subject themselves to legally binding obligations of result. The Paris Agreement deferred to the latter in this respect. However, to help ensure that parties act in good faith, the agreement requires each party to provide the information necessary to track

---

[168] See contra, Richard Falk, ' "Voluntary" International Law and the Paris Agreement' (16 January 2016) <https://richardfalk.wordpress.com/2016/01/16/voluntary-international-law-and-the-paris-agreement/> accessed 20 January 2017.

[169] Paris Agreement, Arts 3, 4.1, 4.2, 4.8, 4.13, 4.15, 4.16, 4.19, 5.1, 5.2, 6.1, 6.3, 6.8, 7.2, 7.4, 7.5, 7.6, 7.7, 8.1, 8.3, 9.2, 10.1, 10.2, 11.4, 12, and 14.3.

[170] The comma ensures that the final clause modifies parties who 'pursue' those measures rather than the measures themselves. Thus the 'with' functions not as a preposition qualifying 'measures' but as a conjunction qualifying 'pursue'.

progress in implementing and achieving its nationally determined contribution,[171] and subjects parties to a 'facilitative, multilateral consideration of progress' with respect to such implementation and achievement.[172]

The NDCs parties have submitted are formulated in a variety of ways. Some are quantitative (such as absolute emission reduction targets)[173] and others are qualitative (such as goals to adopt climate friendly paths);[174] some are conditional (as for instance on the provision of international support)[175] while others are unconditional.[176] In the circumstances, an obligation of result, if one had been created, may not have lent itself to enforcement.

In addition to the binding obligation to prepare, communicate and maintain contributions as well as to take domestic measures, parties are subject to further procedural obligations. Each party is required to communicate a contribution every five years.[177] When communicating their NDCs, parties are required to provide the information necessary for clarity, transparency, and understanding.[178] These provisions are phrased in mandatory terms ('shall'), and thus constitute binding obligations for parties. Some also oblige parties to act in accordance with 'relevant decisions' to be taken by the Conference of the Parties serving as the Meeting of the Parties to the Paris Agreement (CMA), thus effectively giving the CMA authority to adopt legally binding decisions.[179] It is worth noting, however, that the 'relevant decisions' may provide parties with discretion. For instance, decision 1/CP.21 provides that parties '*may* include, as appropriate, inter alia' several listed pieces of information, but does not require them to do so.[180]

The Paris Agreement also requires parties to account for their NDCs in accordance with 'guidance' adopted by the CMA.[181] Although this provision is phrased in mandatory terms ('shall'), the use of the word 'guidance' could be interpreted

---

[171] Paris Agreement, Art 13.7(b).   [172] Ibid, Art 13.11.

[173] See eg United States' Intended Nationally Determined Contribution (31 March 2015) <http://www4.unfccc.int/submissions/indc/Submission%20Pages/submissions.aspx> accessed 20 January 2017.

[174] India's Intended Nationally Determined Contribution (1 October 2015) <http://www4.unfccc.int/submissions/indc/Submission%20Pages/submissions.aspx> accessed 20 January 2017. In addition to quantitative emissions intensity targets, India's INDC identifies qualitative objectives such as to 'propagate a healthy and sustainable way of living based on traditions and values of conservation and moderation'.

[175] Arguably India's. See India's INDC, ibid.

[176] See eg Brazil, Intended Nationally Determined Contribution Towards Achieving the Objective of the United Nations Framework Convention on Climate Change (28 September 2015) <http://www4.unfccc.int/submissions/indc/Submission%20Pages/submissions.aspx> accessed 20 January 2017. It is worth noting that parties considered the possibility of requiring all contributions to be unconditional. No agreement proved possible on this in Paris, but the Ad hoc Working Group on the Paris Agreement (APA) has been tasked with developing further guidance on 'features' of nationally determined contributions for consideration and adoption by the CMA. See Decision 1/CP.21 (n 19) para 26.

[177] Paris Agreement, Art 4.9.   [178] Ibid, Art 4.8.

[179] These decisions are to be negotiated in the next few years and adopted by the CMA in 2018.

[180] Decision 1/CP.21 (n 19) para 27 (emphasis added).

[181] Paris Agreement, Art 4.13. See also Decision 1/CP.21 (n 19) paras 31 and 32. It is worth noting that the guidance on accounting applies only to second and subsequent contributions, although parties could choose to apply it before.

as implying that a CMA decision containing accounting guidance would not bind parties. Alternatively, it could be interpreted as meaning that CMA decisions on accounting should provide general guidance rather than impose detailed rules. Given this ambiguity, the way in which the accounting decision is drafted may provide clues as to whether the parties regard it as binding—for example, whether it is drafted in mandatory or discretionary terms.[182]

The strength of these provisions, as well as the transparency framework, discussed below, can be attributed to the concerted efforts of an informal group of key negotiators from developed and developing countries, including the EU, Australia, New Zealand, South Africa, Switzerland, the US, and others, as well as the Singaporean diplomat who facilitated the formal negotiations. This informal group, which came to be called 'friends of rules', formed after Lima when its members realized that the rules of the game, of profound importance to the integrity of the agreement, were getting short shrift in a process focused primarily on the headline political issues.

B. Registering NDCs

The NDCs referred to in Article 4.2 are to be recorded in a public registry maintained by the secretariat.[183] The US, Canada, and New Zealand, among others, favored this approach, arguing that housing contributions outside the treaty would enable their speedy and seamless updating. Others were concerned that if contributions were housed outside the agreement, parties would enjoy excessive discretion in revising their contributions, potentially even downwards. To address this concern, the Paris Agreement permits parties to adjust their contributions only with a view to enhancing the level of ambition and subject to CMA guidance.[184] The Paris decision also calls on the CMA to adopt modalities and procedures for the operation and use of the public registry,[185] which could potentially circumscribe the discretion parties have. In any case, notwithstanding the fact that contributions are housed outside the instrument, the entire structure of the agreement, and Article 4 in particular, underscores that NDCs are a crucial element of the Paris Agreement.

C. Progression in NDCs

In addition to the array of obligations relating to NDCs, the Paris Agreement sets a firm expectation that parties' NDCs will progress from each five-year cycle to the next. The relevant provision reads:

Each Party's successive nationally determined contribution will represent a progression beyond the Party's then current nationally determined contribution, and reflect its highest possible ambition, reflecting its common but differentiated responsibilities and respective capabilities, in the light of different national circumstances.[186]

---

[182] See Chapter 3, Section II.D.3 for a full discussion of the status of COP decisions.
[183] Paris Agreement, Art 4.12.   [184] Ibid, Art 4.11.
[185] Decision 1/CP.21 (n 19) para 29.   [186] Paris Agreement, Art 4.3.

Progression could potentially be reflected in several ways. For example, it could be demonstrated through more stringent numerical commitments of the same form, ie a decrease in emissions intensity from a base year over a previous intensity target, or an increase in absolute reductions over an earlier absolute reduction target. It could also be reflected in the form of commitments. For instance, parties that have undertaken sectoral measures might take on economy-wide emissions intensity or business-as-usual deviation targets, or those that currently have economy-wide emissions intensity or business-as-usual deviation targets might take on economy-wide absolute emissions reduction targets.

This provision applies to 'each Party' not to 'Parties' in general. The use of the auxiliary verb 'will' signals an expectation, but not an obligation, that each party will undertake more ambitious actions over time.[187] Many developing countries advocated 'progression' as a way of ensuring that developed countries did not take on commitments less rigorous than their Kyoto commitments. The notion of progression also formed the basis for Brazil's 'concentric differentiation' approach that envisioned gradual progression by all parties in the type and scale of their commitments, reflected in Article 4.4, which recommends that developed countries undertake economy-wide absolute emission reduction targets, and encourages developing countries to move over time toward economy-wide emission reduction or limitation targets.[188]

As noted above, the provision on progression is not prescriptive in relation to how progression (in form or rigor) is defined and it is silent on who determines progression. Each party will, in practice, decide for itself what its contributions will be and hence how its contribution will reflect its 'highest possible ambition' and the principle of CBDRRC. Nevertheless, the standards of progression and highest possible ambition are arguably objective rather than self-judging, so parties' national determinations will be open to comment and critique by other states as well as by civil society organizations.

In addition to the expectation that parties will undertake more ambitious mitigation contributions over time, the Paris Agreement provides that '[t]he efforts of all Parties will represent a progression over time'.[189] This crosscutting provision extends the progression principle beyond mitigation to areas such as adaptation and support. It differs from the mitigation progression provision in two respects. First, it applies to 'all Parties' not 'each Party', indicating that it could be interpreted as a collective rather than an individual expectation. Second, it uses the term 'efforts' rather than 'nationally determined contributions', which captures a wider range of actions, including not only mitigation contributions,[190] but also adaptation planning and implementation,[191] and provision of financial resources to developing

---

[187] The notion of progression first found reflection in the Lima decision. See Lima Call for Climate Action, para 10.

[188] See Views of Brazil on the Elements of a New Agreement under the Convention Applicable to All Parties (6 November 2014) <http://www4.unfccc.int/submissions/Lists/OSPSubmissionUpload/73_99_130602104651393682-BRAZIL%20ADP%20Elements.pdf> accessed 20 January 2017.

[189] Paris Agreement, Art 3.   [190] Ibid, Art 4.2.   [191] Ibid, Art 7.9.

countries.[192] Both provisions on progression, however, are similar in that they use the auxiliary verb 'will' and thus establish expectations rather than obligations of more ambitious actions over time. A final occurrence of 'progression' in the Paris Agreement is in relation to the mobilization of finance, which developed countries are urged, 'as part of the global effort', to take the lead on.[193] This provision is phrased in passive language and as a recommendation.

Even though some of these provisions place collective or individual expectations on parties, and progression is initially self-determined, together they bear tremendous significance, as they are designed to ensure that the regime as a whole moves toward ever more ambitious and rigorous actions—that there is a 'direction of travel' for the regime, as it were. Since developed and developing countries are starting from different points, reflected in their self-differentiated NDCs, the principle of progression also implies that differentiation will continue in successive cycles of NDCs, at least into the near future.

D. Ambition cycle

The expectation of progression, together with the global stocktakes to assess collective progress toward long-term goals, discussed below, and the binding obligation on each state to communicate an NDC every five years, informed by the outcomes of the global stocktake, form what has come to be characterized as the 'ambition cycle' of the Paris Agreement. This ambition cycle, intended to promote progressively stronger NDCs over time, was viewed as crucial by many states, since the NDCs submitted in the run-up to Paris were acknowledged by states themselves to be insufficient.[194] The Paris Agreement and the decision accompanying it establish the following time-line for the ambition cycle:

- In 2018, parties will convene a 'facilitative dialogue' focusing on mitigation, to take stock of their collective progress in achieving the emission goals set forth in Article 4.1.[195]

- By 2020, parties with NDCs running to 2025 are requested to communicate a new NDC, informed by the facilitative dialogue. Parties with NDCs running to 2030 may continue their existing NDC or update it.[196]

- By 2020, parties are invited to communicate their mid-century, long-term low GHG emission development strategies.[197]

- In 2023, the CMA will conduct its first global stocktake, addressing adaptation and finance as well as mitigation.[198]

- By 2025, all parties must communicate their successive NDC, informed by the global stocktake, nine to twelve months before the next CMA.[199]

---

[192] Ibid, Art 9.1.   [193] Ibid, Art 9.3.
[194] See Synthesis Report on the aggregate effect of the INDCs (n 37).
[195] Decision 1/CP.21 (n 19) para 20.   [196] Ibid, paras 23 and 24.
[197] Ibid, para 35.   [198] Paris Agreement, Art 14.2.
[199] Decision 1/CP.21 (n 19) para 25.

- In 2028, the CMA will conduct its second global stocktake, which will inform the successive NDC that each party is required to communicate by 2030.

The ambition cycle will continue on a five-year basis indefinitely. Although the Paris Agreement does not itself specify a common time frame for NDCs, and the initial NDCs submitted prior to the Paris conference have different end dates, the agreement provides that the CMA shall consider common time frames in the course of elaborating the Agreement's rules.[200]

VI. MARKET-BASED APPROACHES (ARTICLE 6)

Market-based approaches such as emissions trading and the Clean Development Mechanism (CDM) were central features of the Kyoto Protocol architecture, but for most of the ADP negotiations, it was unclear whether states would agree to include market-oriented language in the Paris Agreement. The fact that more than half the INDCs submitted by parties contemplated the use of international carbon markets[201] suggested broad support for inclusion of a market-based provision. But a small number of states, led by Bolivia, strongly opposed such a provision. In the end, supporters of market mechanisms succeeded in including a separate article on markets. As a concession to market opponents, Article 6 never refers directly to 'markets', and expressly recognizes the importance of non-market approaches,[202] but not market approaches. Nevertheless, in effect, it provides for two market-based mechanisms.

First, Article 6.2 recognizes that parties may engage in 'cooperative approaches' to achieve their NDCs, involving the use of 'internationally transferred mitigation outcomes'—the new jargon for emissions trading and other mechanisms to link national climate policies. To ensure environmental integrity, parties must apply 'robust accounting rules'—including to ensure that emission reductions are not double counted—consistent with guidance to be adopted by the CMA. Because parties' NDCs are highly heterogeneous, developing this common accounting system is likely to pose difficult but not insurmountable challenges.[203]

Second, Article 6.4 establishes a new mechanism to 'promote the mitigation of GHG emissions while fostering sustainable development' (christened by many

---

[200] Paris Agreement, Art 4.10.

[201] International Carbon Action Partnership (ICAP), *Emissions Trading Worldwide: International Carbon Action Partnership: Status Report 2016* (Berlin: ICAP, 2016) (64 INDCs said they planned to use markets, and 25 said they were considering using markets); Environmental Defense Fund and International Emissions Trading Association, 'Carbon Pricing: the Paris Agreement's Key Ingredient' (April 2016) <http://www.ieta.org/resources/Resources/Reports/Carbon_Pricing_The_Paris_Agreements_Key_Ingredient.pdf> accessed 20 January 2017.

[202] Paris Agreement, Art 6.8.

[203] See Daniel Bodansky *et al.*, 'Facilitating Linkage of Climate Policies through the Paris Outcome', *Climate Policy* (2015) <http://www.tandfonline.com/doi/abs/10.1080/14693062.2015.1069175?journalCode=tcpo20> accessed 20 January 2017.

as the 'sustainable development mechanism' or SDM and by others as the 'mitigation mechanism'). Like the CDM, the new mechanism will generate emission reduction offsets that another country can use to fulfill its NDC. But, in contrast to the CDM, the SDM will not be limited to project-based reductions, and might involve emission reduction policies or programs. In addition, it will be able to generate offsets for emission reductions in developed as well as developing countries, thus merging the roles of the CDM and joint implementation under the Kyoto Protocol. The Paris Agreement and decision task the CMA to designate a supervisory body for the new mechanism, as well as to develop rules, modalities, and procedures, drawing on the experience gained from the existing FCCC and Kyoto Protocol mechanisms.[204]

VII. ADAPTATION (ARTICLE 7)

As discussed above in relation to 'scope' of the Paris Agreement, most developing countries have long argued for parity between mitigation and adaptation in the climate regime, and thus sought to include strong provisions on adaptation in the Paris Agreement. They had limited success, however, perhaps in part because adaptation provides primarily local benefits, so that countries have an incentive to adapt regardless of what other countries are doing, making the case for collective action less compelling.

The Paris Agreement contains one hard law provision and several soft law provisions relating to adaptation. Parties are obliged to ('Each Party shall') engage in adaptation planning and implementation of adaptation actions. Parties are nudged ('Parties should') to submit and update adaptation communications (possibly as part of their NDCs) identifying priorities and needs, for listing on a public registry,[205] and to strengthen cooperation on adaptation.[206] Many of these provisions are qualified by phrases like, 'as appropriate', which permit discretion.[207] The Paris Agreement also tasks the CMA with developing modalities to recognize the adaptation efforts of developing countries.[208]

In addition, the adaptation article in the Paris Agreement includes several contextual provisions.[209] For instance, Article 7.2 recognizes that adaptation is a global challenge. Article 7.5 acknowledges that adaptation action should follow a country-driven approach. And Article 7.6 recognizes the importance of support for

---

[204] Paris Agreement, Art 6.7; Decision 1/CP.21 (n 19) para 37(f). For a detailed discussion of Article 6, see Andre Marcu, 'Carbon Market Provisions in the Paris Agreement (Article 6)' (Centre for European Policy Studies, January 2016) <https://www.ceps.eu/system/files/SR%20No%20128%20ACM%20Post%20COP21%20Analysis%20of%20Article%206.pdf> accessed 20 January 2017.

[205] Paris Agreement, Art 7.10 read with Art 13.8. The agenda for the post-Paris negotiations mandates further work on adaptation communications as a component of NDCs, which will likely lead to the creation of an adaptation registry. Revised Provisional Agenda, Proposal by the Co-Chairs (20 May 2016) FCCC/APA/2016/L.1.

[206] Paris Agreement, Art 7.7.   [207] See eg ibid, Arts 7.5, 7.7(a), 7.9, 7.10, and 13.8.

[208] Ibid, Art 7.3.   [209] See eg ibid, Arts 7.2, 7.4, 7.5, and 7.6.

adaptation efforts. These provisions do not prescribe—whether in mandatory, recommendatory or even cajoling terms—a particular course of action. Instead, they provide context, construct a narrative, capture shared understandings, and generate mutual reassurances about the nature of the adaptation problem and particular ways of addressing it. In so doing, these provisions perform a critical function and were essential to the Paris package.

An excellent example of a contextual provision is Article 7.4, in which parties recognize that the current need for adaptation is significant, that greater levels of mitigation can reduce the need for additional adaptation efforts, and that greater adaptation needs can involve greater adaptation costs. Although this provision does not require any particular conduct from parties, it was nevertheless extremely important for vulnerable countries. Many developing countries had stressed the links between mitigation ambition (or lack thereof) and the need for enhanced adaptation. Indeed, the African Group had proposed a quantifiable adaptation goal that would assess adaptation impacts and costs flowing from the agreed temperature goal.[210] Implicit in this proposal was an assumption that the worst impacts of climate change would be borne by vulnerable countries that had contributed little thus far to creating the problem, and that such adaptation costs should be raised and borne by developed countries. But, perhaps because of its potential financial implications, this proposal by the African Group proved unpalatable to developed and some developing countries. The Paris Agreement thus contains only a qualitative adaptation goal in Article 7.1, namely to enhance adaptive capacity, strengthen resilience, and reduce vulnerability to climate change. In deference, however, to the concerns of many vulnerable countries, Article 7.4 recognizes the critical inter-linkages between adaptation, mitigation, and support.[211] Although only a descriptive provision, it signals a shared understanding that was crucial to the acceptability of the larger political package.

Finally, it is worth noting that the Paris Agreement also endorses the aim that scaled up financial resources should achieve a balance between adaptation and mitigation, and specifically recognizes the need for 'public and grant-based resources' for adaptation.[212]

VIII. LOSS AND DAMAGE (ARTICLE 8)

As discussed in Chapter 5, the issue of loss and damage has been on the table since the beginning of the UN climate regime, with small island states and other

---

[210] See Submission by Swaziland on behalf of the African Group (n 155).

[211] The Paris Agreement also implicitly endorses, in the global stocktake provision, the inter-linkages between the achievement of long-term goals, including in relation to temperature, and efforts related to mitigation, adaptation, and means of implementation. Paris Agreement, Art 14.

[212] Ibid, Art 9.4.

vulnerable countries investing considerable negotiating capital on it. At the 2013 Warsaw conference, parties established the Warsaw International Mechanism for Loss and Damage Associated with Climate Change Impacts (WIM) to address loss and damage associated with impacts of climate change in particularly vulnerable developing countries.[213] Parties disagreed on whether loss and damage should be addressed as part of adaptation or as a distinct issue.[214] Many vulnerable countries believe that the topic of loss and damage is distinct from adaptation, and encompasses issues of liability and compensation, while developed countries prefer to address the issue within the framework of adaptation.[215] At the Warsaw conference, parties agreed to establish the new mechanism 'under the Cancun Adaptation Framework', but to provide for a review in 2016.[216] The following year, at the Lima conference, parties agreed to a two-year work plan for the executive committee of the WIM.[217] As the review of the mechanism for loss and damage was slated for 2016, many developed countries believed the issue would not be addressed in Paris. But given the salience of the topic to vulnerable countries, they successfully pushed to include a provision on loss and damage in the Paris Agreement.

Although Article 8 is arguably of greater symbolic than substantive significance, it is important for two reasons. First, it expressly brings the issue of loss and damage within the scope of the Paris Agreement. Second, it is a freestanding article, thus, arguably, separating loss and damage from adaptation, as developing countries have long sought. As the price for agreeing to include Article 8, however, the US insisted on adding a paragraph to the Paris COP decision stating that 'Article 8 does not involve or provide a basis for any liability or compensation,'[218] thereby stripping loss and damage of some of its most distinctive elements.[219] Some of the areas of cooperation and facilitation identified in Article 8 are, in fact, forms of adaptation, aimed at preventing damage, including early warning systems, emergency preparedness, and comprehensive risk assessment and management. Nevertheless, Article 8 gives loss and damage a toehold in the regime, which developing countries are likely to use to advance the issue going forward.

[213] Decision 2/CP.19, 'Warsaw international mechanism for loss and damage associated with climate change impacts' (31 January 2014) FCCC/CP/2013/10/Add.1, 6.
[214] Karen Elizabeth McNamara, 'Exploring Loss and Damage at the International Climate Change Talks', *International Journal of Disaster Risk Science*, 5/3 (2014): 242.
[215] See generally Meinhard Doelle, 'Loss and Damage in the UN Climate Regime', in Daniel A. Farber and Marjan Peeters (eds), *Elgar Encyclopedia of Environmental Law vol 1: Climate Change Law* (Cheltenham, UK: Edward Elgar, 2016) 617.
[216] Decision 2/CP.19 (n 213) para 1.
[217] Decision 2/ CP.20, 'Warsaw International Mechanism on Loss and Damage' (2 February 2015) FCCC/CP/2014/10/Add.1, 2.
[218] Warsaw decision, para 51.
[219] See contra M.J. Mace and Roda Verheyen, 'Loss, Damage and Responsibility after COP21: All Options Open for the Paris Agreement', *Review of European, Comparative and International Environmental Law*, 25/2 (2016): 197.

IX. SUPPORT (ARTICLES 9, 10, AND 11)

A. Finance

In the lead-up to Paris, finance was expected to be one of the most difficult 'crunch' issues to resolve, given the seemingly unbridgeable gap between developing countries, which sought new financial commitments in the Paris Agreement, and developed countries, which insisted that they could not accept any new commitments and sought to broaden the donor pool. In the end, however, developing countries were willing to settle for modest advancements in the Paris Agreement, making resolution of the finance issue possible.

The FCCC requires Annex II parties to provide financial assistance to developing countries for mitigation and adaptation.[220] In the Copenhagen Accord, developed countries committed to a goal of mobilizing $100 billion per year in climate finance by 2020, in order to assist developing countries in mitigating and adapting to climate change. The Copenhagen pledge encompassed money from both public and private sources, and was made 'in the context of meaningful mitigation actions' by developing countries, as well as transparency on implementation.[221] A recent report of the Organization for Economic Co-operation and Development (OECD) found that $62 billion in climate finance was mobilized in 2014, up from $52 billion in 2013.[222] These figures are disputed, however, because of methodological questions about what counts as climate finance.[223] Against this backdrop, the Paris Agreement's provisions on finance are rather modest.

1. Financial commitments

Article 9 obliges developed countries to provide financial resources to assist developing countries with adaptation and mitigation, 'in continuation of their existing obligations under the Convention'.[224] It is the latter clause that permitted the US to accept this mandatory construction of their financial obligations. Article 9 also creates a number of new reporting requirements (including biennial reports that include projected levels of public finance), and introduces a new substantive norm, albeit soft, recommending that the mobilization of climate finance 'should represent a progression beyond previous efforts'.[225]

---

[220] FCCC, Arts 4.3 and 4.4.   [221] Copenhagen Accord, para 8.

[222] OECD, 'Climate Finance in 2013–2014 and USD 100 Billion Goal' (report by the OECD in collaboration with the Climate Policy Initiative, 2015) <http://www.oecd.org/env/cc/Climate-Finance-in-2013-14-and-the-USD-billion-goal.pdf> accessed 20 January 2017.

[223] Climate Change Finance Unit, Ministry of Finance, Government of India, 'Climate Change Finance, Analysis of a Recent OECD Report: Some Credible Facts Needed' (2015) < http://pibphoto.nic.in/documents/rlink/2015/nov/p2015112901.pdf > accessed 20 January 2017.

[224] Paris Agreement, Art 9.1.   [225] Ibid, Art 9.3.

2. Donor pool

In a departure from the sharp differentiation in the FCCC, the Paris Agreement 'encourages' other parties to 'provide or continue to provide support voluntarily'.[226] This provision is considerably weaker than developed countries had sought. It encourages rather than requires or recommends the provision of support, and is silent as to who should do so (as compared to earlier formulations that specified countries 'with capacity' or 'in a position' or 'willing' to do so). Nevertheless, this provision could prove significant, by beginning to break down the wall between donor and recipient countries. Along similar lines, the Paris Agreement calls on developed countries to take the lead in mobilizing climate change, but as 'part of a global effort'.[227]

3. Mobilization goal

The US and other developed countries succeeded in excluding a reference to the Copenhagen $100 billion per year mobilization goal from the Paris Agreement. Instead, the only quantitative finance goal appears in the accompanying COP decision, which extends developed countries' existing $100 billion mobilization goal through 2025 and provides that the parties shall set a new collective quantified goal prior to 2025 (not explicitly limited to developed countries), using the $100 billion per year figure as a floor.[228]

Finance, as discussed below, will be part of the 2023 global stocktake. Like the Copenhagen Accord, the Paris Agreement recommends that the provision of scaled-up support should aim to achieve a balance between mitigation and adaptation.[229]

B. Technology

In relation to technology, the Paris Agreement creates a technology framework to provide overarching guidance to the work of the convention's technology mechanism in promoting and facilitating enhanced action on technology development and transfer.[230] It also makes support available to accelerate, encourage, and enable innovation through collaborative approaches to research and development and by facilitating access to technology.[231] Information relating to technology support will also feed into the global stocktake.[232]

C. Capacity-building

The Paris Agreement urges parties to cooperate to enhance the capacity of developing countries to implement the agreement,[233] and requires them to regularly

---

[226] Ibid, Art 9.2.   [227] Ibid, Art 9.3.   [228] Decision 1/CP.21 (n 19) para 53.
[229] Paris Agreement, Art 9.4.   [230] Ibid, Arts 10.3 and 10.4.
[231] Ibid, Arts 10.5 and 10.6.   [232] Ibid, Art 10.6.   [233] Ibid, Art 11.3.

communicate on these actions.[234] It also provides a hook to develop appropriate institutional arrangements for capacity-building.[235]

X. OVERSIGHT SYSTEM (ARTICLES 13, 14, AND 15)

The Paris Agreement establishes an oversight system to ensure effective implementation of its provisions, as well as to assess collective progress toward the agreement's long-term goals. This oversight system is vital to the conceptual apparatus of the agreement, and forms, along with the rules relating to NDCs, part of the 'top down' element of the agreement's hybrid architecture.

A. Transparency (Article 13)

Since the Paris Agreement does not contain binding obligations of result in relation to the content of parties' NDCs, the agreement's transparency framework is the main mechanism to hold states accountable for doing what they say they will do.[236] The premise is that peer and public pressure can be as effective as legal obligation in influencing behavior, an issue that has long been debated in the literature on soft law.[237]

Developing countries have traditionally resisted strong reporting and review requirements. Until now, the climate regime has addressed their concerns by differentiating between their commitments and those of developed countries. The 2010 Cancun Agreements, for example, established two systems: IAR for developed countries, and ICA for developing countries.[238] A crunch issue in Paris was whether to move away from the bifurcated approach of the Cancun Agreements to a common transparency system for both developed and developing countries.

Until the final days of the Paris conference, many developing parties, in particular the LMDCs, argued for a bifurcated system that placed differing transparency requirements on developed and developing countries. The Umbrella Group,[239] the EU and the Environmental Integrity Group eventually prevailed, however, and the Paris Agreement's transparency system, albeit not explicitly characterized as 'common' or 'unified', reflects an enhanced framework applicable to all. It addresses differentiation not through bifurcation between developed and developing countries, but through a pragmatic tailoring of commitments to capacities.[240] It provides for

---

[234] Ibid, Art 11.4.   [235] Ibid, Art 11.5.

[236] See generally Harro van Asselt, Håkon Sælen, and Pieter Pauw, 'Assessment and Review under a 2015 Climate Change Agreement' (Nordic Council of Ministers 2015) <http://norden.diva-portal.org/smash/get/diva2:797336/FULLTEXT01.pdf> accessed 20 January 2017.

[237] See Shelton, Commitment and Compliance (n 28); David Victor, Kal Raustiala, and Eugene B. Skolnikoff (eds), *The Implementation and Effectiveness of International Environmental Commitments: Theory and Practice* (Cambridge, MA: MIT Press, 1998).

[238] Cancun Agreements LCA, paras 44, 46(d), 63, and 66.

[239] The Umbrella Group usually includes Australia, Canada, Japan, New Zealand, Kazakhstan, Norway, the Russian Federation, Ukraine, and the US.

[240] See nn 107–114 above and accompanying text.

'built in flexibility, which takes into account Parties' different capacities',[241] offers flexibility to those developing countries that 'need it in the light of their capacities',[242] and creates a new capacity-building initiative for transparency to assist developing countries.[243]

The Paris Agreement's transparency framework for action and support is comparatively robust, particularly given that it applies to developing as well as developed countries. It places extensive informational demands on all parties[244] and creates several review mechanisms.[245] The purpose of the transparency framework is to ensure clarity and tracking of progress toward achieving parties' NDCs and adaptation actions,[246] as well as to provide clarity on support provided and received by parties.[247] Toward this end, all parties are required biennially[248] to provide a national inventory report of GHG emissions and removals and information necessary to track progress in implementing and achieving mitigation contributions.[249] Further, developed countries are required to provide information on financial, technology and capacity-building support they provide to developing countries.[250] Article 13 also recommends that each party provide information related to climate impacts and adaptation[251] and that developing countries provide information on the support they need and receive.[252] It is worth noting that there is a hierarchy in the legal character of the informational requirements placed on parties. Informational requirements in relation to mitigation are mandatory individual obligations applicable to all ('each Party shall'). Informational requirements in relation to finance are mandatory collective obligations for developed countries ('developed country Parties shall') and recommendations for developing countries ('developing country Parties should'). Informational requirements in relation to adaptation are recommendations ('each Party should'), and allow parties discretion ('as appropriate').

The information submitted by all parties in relation to mitigation and by developed country parties on the provision of support will be subject to a technical expert review.[253] This review will consider the support provided to parties, the implementation of their NDCs, and the consistency of the information they provide with the common modalities, procedures, and guidelines adopted by the CMA.[254] In addition each party is expected to participate in a 'facilitative, multilateral consideration of progress' with respect to the implementation and achievement of its NDC, as well as its efforts in relation to finance.[255]

It is unclear, at this point, how these review processes will be conducted, who will conduct them, what their outputs will be, how, if at all, these outputs will feed into the global stocktake, and how they will relate to implementation and compliance. The Paris Agreement provides that the enhanced transparency framework is to build

---

[241] Paris Agreement, Art 13.1.   [242] Ibid, Art 13.2.
[243] Decision 1/CP.21 (n 19) para 84.   [244] Paris Agreement, Art 13.
[245] Ibid, Art 13.11.   [246] Ibid, Art 13.5.   [247] Ibid, Art 13.6.
[248] Decision 1/CP.21 (n 19) para 90.   [249] Paris Agreement, Art 13.7.
[250] Ibid, Art 13.9.   [251] Ibid, Art 13.8.   [252] Ibid, Art 13.10.
[253] Ibid, Art 13.11.   [254] Paris Agreement, Art 13.12.   [255] Ibid, Art 13.11.

on the existing transparency arrangements under the FCCC, and that the CMA is to draw on these arrangements (including national communications, biennial reports, IAR and ICA) in developing modalities, procedures, and guidelines for the enhanced transparency framework. These modalities, procedures, and guidelines are to be developed by 2018 and will supersede the existing arrangements following the submission of parties' final biennial reports and biennial update reports.[256]

B. Global stocktake (Article 14)

The transparency framework is complemented by a 'global stocktake' every five years to assess collective progress toward long-term goals.[257] The global stocktake performs a crucial function in the context of 'nationally determined' contributions. It allows a collective assessment of whether national efforts add up to what is necessary to limit temperature increase to well below 2° C.

The Paris Agreement provides broad guidance on the nature, purpose, tasks and outcome of the stocktake, but leaves the mechanics to be determined by the CMA.[258] The Paris Agreement envisions the stocktake as a 'comprehensive and facilitative'[259] exercise—thus reinforcing the fact that the Paris Agreement addresses not only mitigation but also adaptation and support, and that it is primarily a facilitative rather than a prescriptive instrument.

The purpose of the stocktake is to 'assess the collective progress towards achieving the purpose of this Agreement and its long term goals'.[260] The 'purpose' of the agreement is stated in Article 2, and includes the long-term temperature goal and the context for implementation. It is unclear what the 'long term goals' are. While mitigation,[261] adaptation,[262] and finance[263] goals, with varying levels of precision, are identified in the agreement, there are no identifiable goals in relation to technology and capacity-building. This introduces an element of uncertainty into the assessment of progress.

Moreover, the stocktake is authorized to consider 'collective', not individual, progress. Although AILAC, AOSIS, and the EU had proposed individualized assessments of performance, the LMDCs, among others, successfully averted such assessments from becoming part of the global stocktake process.

The agreement sets various tasks for the stocktake, as, for instance, reviewing the overall progress made in achieving the global goal on adaptation.[264] It also identifies initial inputs to the stocktake, including information provided by parties on finance,[265] available information on technology development and transfer,[266] and information generated through the transparency framework.[267] Other inputs

---

[256] Decision 1/CP.21 (n 19) para 98.   [257] Paris Agreement, Art 14.
[258] Decision 1/CP.21 (n 19) paras 99–101.
[259] Paris Agreement, Art 14.1. In relation to the stocktaking process for adaptation, further details are offered in Article 7.14.
[260] Ibid.   [261] Ibid, Art 4.1.   [262] Ibid, Art 7.1.
[263] Ibid, Art 2.1(c), read with Decision 1/CP.21 (n 19) para 53.
[264] Paris Agreement, Art 7.14(d).   [265] Ibid, Art 9.6.   [266] Ibid, Art 10.6.
[267] Ibid, Arts 13.5 and 13.6.

will be identified in the years to come.[268] The inclusion of information generated through the transparency framework as an input to the stocktake is of particular significance, since it suggests that the stocktake could consider the past performance of parties in implementing their NDCs.

The global stocktake is required to assess collective progress 'in the light of equity and the best available science'.[269] The inclusion of 'equity' was a negotiating coup for several developing countries, in particular the African Group, that had long championed the need to consider parties' historical responsibilities, current capabilities and development needs in setting expectations for NDCs.[270] It is unclear at this point how equity, yet to be defined in the climate regime, will be understood and incorporated in the global stocktake. Nevertheless, the reference to equity leaves the door open for a dialogue on equitable burden sharing, as well an assessment of whether states are contributing as much as they should, given their responsibilities and capabilities, although admittedly this will be difficult to reach agreement on.

Finally, the outcome of the stocktake is to inform parties in updating and enhancing their actions and support 'in a nationally determined manner'.[271] This is a carefully balanced provision. On the one hand, it links the outcome of the stocktake with the process of updating parties' contributions,[272] thus generating strong expectations that parties will enhance the ambition of their actions and support, informed by the findings of the stocktake. On the other hand, it underscores the 'nationally determined' nature of actions and support, thus addressing concerns over loss of autonomy and external ratchets. In this respect LMDCs, in particular China and India, prevailed over AILAC, AOSIS, and the EU, which had sought more prescriptive language to link the outcome of the stocktake with future NDCs.

The first stocktake is set to take place in 2023,[273] once the mechanics of the stocktake have been worked out. There was a felt need for an earlier stocktake to guide parties, especially those with contributions set to five-year time frames, in updating and revising their contributions. Parties agreed therefore to convene a 'facilitative dialogue' in 2018 to take stock of the collective efforts of parties in relation to the agreement's long-term mitigation goal and to inform the preparation of the next round of NDCs.[274]

The global stocktake is cleverly designed to ensure both that it influences NDCs and that it is palatable to all, even the LMDCs, for whom any assessment process was anathema, as it would potentially impinge on sovereign autonomy. The global stocktake is a facilitative process. It assesses collective not individual progress. It assesses collective progress on support as well as on mitigation. It will consider not just science but also equity in determining the adequacy of collective progress. And, finally, ratcheting of contributions as a result of the stocktake, if any, will be left to

---

[268] Decision 1/CP.21 (n 19) para 99 (identifying sources of input 'including but not limited to').
[269] Paris Agreement, Art 14.1.
[270] See Submission by Swaziland on behalf of the African Group (n 155).
[271] Paris Agreement, Art 14.3.   [272] Ibid, Art 4.9.   [273] Ibid, Art 14.2.
[274] Decision 1/CP.21 (n 19) para 20.

national determination, albeit with built-in expectations based on the outcome of the stocktake.

C. Implementation and compliance mechanism (Article 15)

The Paris Agreement establishes a mechanism to facilitate implementation of and promote compliance with its provisions, but the skeletal provision establishing this new mechanism provides only minimal guidance on how it will work. Article 15 indicates that the mechanism is to be 'transparent, non-adversarial and non-punitive', but it does not describe the relationship, if any, between the transparency framework and the new mechanism, and leaves the mechanism's modalities and procedures to be negotiated in the years to follow.[275] Article 15 does provide that the mechanism will address both implementation of and compliance with the agreement, that it is to consist of an expert-based facilitative committee, and that the committee is to function in a transparent, non-adversarial, and non-punitive manner.[276] This guidance addresses concerns of those who feared—across the developed-developing country divide—that the Paris Agreement would recreate a Kyoto-like compliance committee with an enforcement branch and serious consequences for non-compliance. However, the fact that the Paris Agreement addresses 'compliance' and not just implementation is a significant achievement for the EU, AOSIS, and Norway, which had pushed for inclusion of a compliance mechanism in the negotiations.

XI. INSTITUTIONS (ARTICLES 16–19)

The Paris Agreement uses the existing institutional structure of the FCCC, including the FCCC COP (which is to serve as the Meeting of Parties to the Paris Agreement,[277] with states that are not party to the Paris Agreement participating as observers),[278] the FCCC's subsidiary bodies, and its secretariat.[279] In addition, numerous subsidiary bodies and institutional arrangements under the Convention have been mandated ('shall') to serve the Paris Agreement. These include the Green Climate Fund and the Global Environment Facility, the Least Developed Countries Fund, the Special Climate Change Fund,[280] the standing committee on finance,[281] the technology mechanism,[282] appropriate institutional arrangements for capacity-building,[283] and the forum on the impact of the implementation of response measures.[284] Further subsidiary bodies and institutional arrangements can be mandated to serve the agreement through a decision of the CMA.[285]

---

[275] Paris Agreement, Art 15.3, and Decision 1/CP.21 (n 19) paras 102 and 103.
[276] Paris Agreement, Art 15.2.   [277] Ibid, Art 16.1.   [278] Ibid, Art 16.2.
[279] Ibid, Arts 17 and 18.   [280] Ibid, Art 9.8 and Decision 1/CP.21 (n 19) para 58.
[281] Decision 1/CP.21 (n 19) para 63.   [282] Paris Agreement, Art 10.3.
[283] Ibid, Art 11.5.   [284] Decision 1/CP.21 (n 19) para 32.
[285] Paris Agreement, Art 18.

XII. FINAL CLAUSES (ARTICLES 20–28)

The Paris Agreement includes a standard set of final clauses. Parties must express their consent to be bound by means of ratification, accession, acceptance, or approval.[286] Entry into force involves a 'double trigger', requiring acceptance by at least fifty-five states that account for at least 55% of global GHG emissions.[287] The Paris Agreement was opened for signature at a high-level signature ceremony convened by the Secretary General in New York on 22 April 2016, 'Earth Day'.[288] A record 175 FCCC parties signed the agreement on this day,[289] and the Paris Agreement entered into force on 4 November 2016, less than a year after it was adopted.[290]

The Paris Agreement incorporates by reference the FCCC's provisions on amendments,[291] adoption and amendment of annexes,[292] and dispute settlement.[293] Reservations are expressly disallowed,[294] but parties may withdraw by giving one year's notice, beginning three years after the agreement's entry into force.[295]

XIII. NEXT STEPS

The Durban Platform had envisaged the Paris Agreement as taking effect from 2020.[296] The Paris Agreement, however, entered into force on 4 November 2016—much sooner than expected. Several factors contributed to the Paris Agreement's extraordinarily rapid entry into force. States wanted to harness the political momentum and goodwill generated in Paris before it dissipated. Many states were also concerned about the impact the US elections could have on the Paris Agreement, given the threat by Donald Trump, now the President, to 'cancel' the Paris Agreement.[297] The agreement's entry into force before the US election could potentially insulate it from the vicissitudes of American electoral politics for four years, when withdrawal

---

[286] Ibid, Art 20. See Chapter 3, Section II.C.

[287] Ibid, Art 21. The penultimate version of the negotiating text had also included bracketed language providing that the agreement would not enter into force prior to 2020, but this language was not included in the final text, allowing the agreement's early entry into force in November 2016. See FCCC Legal Affairs Programme, 'Entry into Force of the Paris Agreement: legal requirements and implications'(7 April 2016) <https://unfccc.int/files/paris_agreement/application/pdf/entry_into_force_of_pa.pdf> accessed 20 January 2017.

[288] Decision 1/CP.21 (n 19) paras 1–4.

[289] See for a list of signatories, FCCC, 'List of 175 signatories to Paris Agreement' <http://newsroom.unfccc.int/paris-agreement/175-states-sign-paris-agreement/> accessed 20 January 2017.

[290] See for the status of ratification and the most recent number of signatures, FCCC, 'Paris Agreement—Status of Ratification' <http://unfccc.int/paris_agreement/items/9444.php> accessed 20 January 2017.

[291] Paris Agreement, Art 22.   [292] Ibid, Art 23.   [293] Ibid, Art 24.

[294] Ibid, Art 27.   [295] Ibid, Art 28.   [296] Durban Platform, para 4.

[297] 'Donald Trump would "cancel" Paris climate deal', *BBC News* (27 May 2016) <http://www.bbc.com/news/election-us-2016-36401174> accessed 20 January 2017.

first becomes legally possible.[298] Indeed, the EU fast tracked its approval of the Paris Agreement in order to take the Paris Agreement over the emissions threshold necessary for entry into force.[299] But entry into force of the Paris Agreement, albeit very important, is merely the first step in its successful implementation. Much of the legal framework created by the Paris Agreement is yet to be fleshed out. The post-Paris negotiations have crucial gap-filling work to do.[300]

For states that have submitted INDCs, their INDCs must be converted into NDCs. Unless a state decides otherwise, this will happen automatically when a state submits its instrument of ratification, acceptance, approval or accession—in essence, removing the 'I' from INDC, leaving the substance of the contribution unchanged.[301] But the Paris COP decision does not prohibit a state from making substantive changes to its contribution before finalizing it.

The Paris COP decision establishes an Ad hoc Working Group on the Paris Agreement (APA), and tasks it with preparing for the agreement's entry into force and the first meeting of the CMA. The APA's main job will be to develop guidance on up-front information and accounting, and to elaborate rules, modalities, and guidelines relating to the transparency framework, the global stocktake, and the implementation and compliance mechanism, for adoption by the CMA.[302] The strength and rigor of these 'top down' elements of the Paris Agreement will play an important role in ensuring that parties' successive NDCs represent a progression from past ones, and that they reflect parties' highest possible ambition. Such ambition will be necessary to bridge the considerable gap between current emissions trajectories and least-cost 2° C and 1.5° C scenarios.

The negotiations in the APA will provide an early indicator of how much the Paris Agreement reflects a stable political equilibrium. In the UN climate regime, issues are rarely settled fully and parties often push to regain ground they had previously ceded. In Paris, many developing countries accepted the move away from binary differentiation only reluctantly, so it remains to be seen whether and how they seek to reintroduce it when elaborating the Paris Agreement's rules.

---

[298] Paris Agreement, Art 28. However, should the US decide to withdraw from the FCCC, its withdrawal from the FCCC and the Paris Agreement would take effect simultaneously a year after the official notice of such withdrawal is received. Ibid, read with FCCC , Art 25. See Daniel Bodansky, 'Legal Note: Could a Future President Reverse U.S. Approval of the Paris Agreement?' (Arlington, VA: Center for Climate and Energy Solutions, October 2016) <https://www.c2es.org/docUploads/legal-note-could-future-president-reverse-us-approval-paris-agreement.pdf> accessed 20 January 2017.

[299] Ibid, Art 21.

[300] See FCCC, 'Taking the Paris Agreement Forward: Tasks arising from Decision 1/CP.21' (March 2016) <http://unfccc.int/files/bodies/cop/application/pdf/overview_1cp21_tasks_.pdf > accessed 20 January 2017.

[301] Decision 1/CP.21 (n 19) para 22.

[302] See, for a list of tasks identified by the secretariat, FCCC, Taking the Paris Agreement Forward (n 300). See also Revised Provisional Agenda, Proposal by the Co-chairs (20 May 2016) FCCC/APA/2016/L.1. 2018 has since been set as the deadline for completing these tasks.

XIV. CONCLUSION

The Paris Agreement is a landmark in the UN climate negotiations. Notwithstanding long-standing and seemingly intractable differences, parties harnessed the political will necessary to arrive at an agreement that is long-term, rules-based, and applicable to all. The Paris Agreement contains ambitious goals, extensive obligations, and comparatively rigorous oversight. Admittedly, the goals are aspirational, the obligations are largely procedural, and the mechanics of the oversight mechanisms have yet to be fleshed out. Differentiation too has come to acquire a new more nuanced form. Despite its many tenuous compromises and infirmities, the Paris Agreement represents a hard fought deal among 196 nations. Countries across the developed and developing country divide made significant concessions from long-held positions in the closing hours of the conference, thus making the final agreement possible.

Many difficult issues remain, however, and much of the hard work lies ahead. The process of elaboration in the post-Paris negotiations will reveal the degree to which the Paris Agreement resolved issues or merely papered over them. For example, the Paris Agreement did not resolve the issue of burden sharing among parties. But, whether resolvable or not, this issue will continue to underpin both the negotiations and actions taken by parties in the years to come. Many developing countries, including Brazil, China, and India, were among those that helped bring the Paris Agreement into force. However, these countries, although rapidly growing, continue to face serious developmental challenges and have other compelling priorities. Many have limited resources to devote to the significant energy transformations required to bend their emissions curve in line with $2°$ C or $1.5°$ C scenarios. The declaration accompanying India's ratification of the Paris Agreement offers a useful illustration of these tensions.[303] India's declaration highlights its development agenda, in particular poverty eradication and basic needs provision; notes India's assumption of unencumbered access to cleaner sources of energy, technologies, and financial resources; and asserts that its ratification is based on a fair and ambitious global commitment to combating climate change.[304] Given limited resources, it remains to be seen to what extent many countries, even with the best intentions, will be able to make the transformational changes required domestically to meet the global temperature limit.

Further, the Paris Agreement takes a 'broad then deep' approach to emissions reductions, first expanding coverage of emissions limits, and then seeking depth of commitments.[305] That the Paris Agreement has broad appeal is evident both in its rapid entry into force as well the fact that parties' NDCs cover 99% of global emissions. However, the NDCs are, if not shallow, at least insufficient, given the scale of the challenge. The design of the Paris Agreement, with its focus on progression

---

[303] FCCC, Paris Agreement—Status of Ratification (n 290).   [304] Ibid.
[305] See Chapter 2, Section IV.B.

and highest possible ambition of successive NDCs, aspires to depth of mitigation commitments over time. But it is uncertain whether such an incremental and iterative approach will produce sufficiently rapid change to meet the global temperature limit agreed to in Paris, in particular the 1.5° C aspirational goal.

These concerns notwithstanding, the Paris Agreement justifies cautious optimism about the future of the international climate regime. Of course, it is only one of many contributors to climate policy. Success or failure in combating climate change will depend as much or more on other factors, such as domestic politics and technological change. But the willingness of states to come together and agree on a comprehensive, universal, long-term, and in many ways ambitious agreement bodes well for our chances of limiting dangerous global warming.

SELECT BIBLIOGRAPHY

Bodansky D., 'The Paris Climate Agreement: A New Hope?', *American Journal of International Law*, 110/2 (2016): 288.

Bodansky D. and Rajamani L., 'Key Legal Issues in the 2015 Climate Negotiations' (Arlington, Virginia: Center for Climate and Energy Solutions, June 2015).

Doelle M., 'The Paris Agreement: Historic Breakthrough or High Stakes Experiment?', *Climate Law Special Issue*, 6/1–2 (2016): 1.

Klein D. *et al.* (eds), *The Paris Climate Agreement: Analysis and Commentary* (Oxford University Press, forthcoming 2017).

Oberthür S. and Bodle R., 'Legal Form and Nature of the Paris Outcome', *Climate Law Special Issue*, 6/1–2 (2016): 40.

Rajamani L., 'The Devilish Details: Key Legal Issues in the 2015 Climate Negotiations', *Modern Law Review*, 78/5 (2015): 826.

Rajamani L., 'Ambition and Differentiation in the 2015 Paris Agreement: Interpretative Possibilities and Underlying Politics', *International and Comparative Law Quarterly*, 65/2 (2016): 493.

Rajamani L., 'The 2015 Paris Agreement: Interplay Between Hard, Soft and Non-Obligations', *Journal of Environmental Law*, 28/2 (2016): 337.

Saverisi A., 'The Paris Agreement: A New Beginning', *Journal of Energy and Natural Resources Law*, 34/1 (2016): 16.

'Special Issue: The Paris Agreement', *Review of European, Comparative and International Environmental Law*, 25/2 (2016): 139.

Voigt C. and Ferriera F., 'Differentiation in the Paris Agreement', *Climate Law Special Issue*, 6/1–2 (2016): 58.

Werksman J., 'The Legal Character of International Environmental Obligations in the Wake of the Paris Climate Change Agreement' (University of Edinburgh: Brodies Environmental Law Lecture Series, 9 February 2016).

Subjects/ Addressee	Provisions that create obligations	Provisions that generate expectations	Provisions that Recommend	Provisions that Encourage	Provisions that set aspirations	Provisions that capture understandings
Individual (Each Party or A Party)	**Mitigation:** 4.2: 'Each Party **shall** prepare, communicate and maintain successive nationally determined contributions that it intends to achieve. Parties **shall** pursue domestic mitigation measures, with the aim of achieving the objectives of such contributions.'[306] 4.9: 'Each Party **shall** communicate' a nationally determined contribution (NDC) every five years. 4.17: 'Each party' to an agreement to act jointly '**shall**' be responsible for its emission level as set out in the terms of its joint fulfilment agreement. **Adaptation:** 7.9: 'Each Party **shall, as appropriate,**' engage in adaptation planning processes and the implementation of actions.	**Mitigation:** 4.3: Each Party's successive NDC '**will** represent a progression' beyond the Party's then current NDC.	**Adaptation:** 7.10: 'Each Party **should, as appropriate,** submit and update periodically an adaptation communication.' **Transparency:** 13.8 'Each Party **should** also provide information' related to climate change impacts and adaptation... **as appropriate.**'			

(Continued)

306 It is unclear whether the reference to 'Parties' in the second sentence of Article 4.2 should be read as referring implicitly to 'Each Party', given the use of the term 'Each Party' in the first sentence, or whether it was a deliberate reference to the parties plural. Thus, it appears here as well as in the relevant row below.

Table 7.1 Continued

Subjects/ Addressee	Provisions that create obligations	Provisions that generate expectations	Provisions that Recommend	Provisions that Encourage	Provisions that set aspirations	Provisions that capture understandings
	Transparency: 13.7: 'Each Party **shall** regularly provide' information on national inventories and to track progress in implementing its NDC. 13.11: '[e]ach Party **shall** participate in a facilitative, multilateral consideration of progress' with respect to efforts on finance, and 'implementation and achievement' of its NDC.				**Mitigation:** 4.1: 'Parties **aim to** reach global peaking of greenhouse gas emissions as soon as possible.'	
Collective or Cooperative 'Parties' or 'All Parties'	**Education, Awareness, Public Participation:** 12: 'Parties **shall** cooperate in taking measures, **as appropriate**, to enhance climate change education, training, public awareness, public participation and public access to information.'		**Adaptation:** 7.7: 'Parties **should** strengthen their cooperation on enhancing action on adaptation.' **Loss & Damage:** 8.3: 'Parties **should** enhance understanding, action and support, including through the Warsaw International Mechanism, **as appropriate**, on a cooperative and facilitative basis with respect to loss and damage associated with the adverse effects of climate change.' **Capacity-building:** 11.3: All Parties **should** cooperate to enhance the capacity of developing country Parties to			

Blanket 'Parties' or 'All Parties'	Cross-cutting:	Cross-cutting:	Sinks:	Technology:	Market-based Approaches:
	3: '… all Parties **are to** undertake and communicate ambitious efforts as defined in Articles 4, 7, 9, 10 and 11…'[307]	3: '… all Parties **are to** undertake and communicate ambitious efforts as defined in Articles 4, 7, 9, 10 and 11…'[309]	5.2: 'Parties are **encouraged** to take action to implement and support' REDD+.	10.1: 'Parties **share a long-term vision** on the importance of fully realizing technology development and transfer in order to improve resilience to climate change and to reduce greenhouse gas emissions.'	6.1: 'Parties **recognize** that some Parties choose to pursue voluntary cooperation in the implementation of their nationally determined contributions.'
	Mitigation:	3: 'The efforts of all Parties **will** represent a progression over time, while recognizing the need to support developing country Parties for the effective implementation of this Agreement.'	**Finance:**		6.8: 'Parties **recognize** the importance of integrated, holistic and balanced non-market approaches being available to Parties.'
	4.2 … Parties **shall** pursue domestic mitigation measures, with the aim of achieving the objectives of such contributions.'[308]	**Mitigation:**	9.2: 'Other [than developed country] Parties are **encouraged** to provide or continue to provide such support voluntarily.'		**Adaptation:**
	4.8: In communicating their NDCs, 'all Parties **shall** provide the information necessary for clarity, transparency, and understanding.'	4.14: 'In the context of their nationally determined contributions, when recognizing and implementing mitigation actions with respect to anthropogenic emissions and removals, Parties **should** take into account, as appropriate, existing methods and guidance under the Convention.'			7.2: 'Parties **recognize** that adaptation is a global challenge faced by all.'
	4.13: 'Parties **shall** account' for their NDCs. In accounting for their NDCs, 'Parties **shall** promote environmental integrity, transparency, accuracy, completeness, comparability and consistency; and ensure the avoidance of double counting,'	4.19: 'All Parties **should** strive to formulate and communicate long-term low greenhouse gas emission development strategies.'			
		Sinks:			
		5.1: 'Parties **should** take action to conserve and enhance, as appropriate, sinks and reservoirs of greenhouse gases.'			

(Continued)

---

307 The phrase 'are to' in Article 3 is ambiguous, and is understood as an imperative by some and an expectation by others, so it appears in both columns.
308 See n 306 above.   309 See n 307 above.

Table 7.1 Continued

Subjects/Addressee	Provisions that create obligations	Provisions that generate expectations	Provisions that Recommend	Provisions that Encourage	Provisions that set aspirations	Provisions that capture understandings
	4.16: Parties that have reached an agreement to act jointly 'shall notify the secretariat of the terms of that agreement' including the emission level allocated to each Party. 4.15: 'Parties shall take into consideration' in implementing this Agreement the concerns of countries most affected by the impact of response measures **Market-based Approaches:** 6.2: 'Parties shall,' where engaging in cooperative market approaches 'promote sustainable development and ensure environmental integrity and transparency, including in governance, and shall apply robust accounting.' **Technology:** 10.2: 'Parties … shall strengthen cooperative action on technology development and transfer.' **Capacity-building:** 11.4: 'All Parties, enhancing the capacity of developing country Parties shall regularly communicate on these actions or measures on capacity-building.'					7.4: 'Parties **recognize** that the current need for adaptation is significant and that greater levels of mitigation can reduce the need for additional adaptation efforts, and that greater adaptation needs can involve greater adaptation costs.' 7.5: 'Parties **acknowledge** that adaptation action should follow a country-driven, gender-responsive, participatory and fully transparent approach.' 7.6: 'Parties **recognize** the importance of support for and international cooperation on adaptation efforts.' **Loss & Damage:** 8.1: 'Parties **recognize** the importance of averting, minimizing and addressing loss and damage associated with the adverse effects of climate change.'

| Developed country Parties | **Finance:**
9.1: 'Developed country Parties **shall** provide financial resources to assist developing country Parties with respect to both mitigation and adaptation in continuation of their existing obligations under the Convention.'
9.5: 'Developed country Parties **shall** biennially communicate indicative quantitative and qualitative information' relating to provision and mobilization of finance.
9.7: Developed country Parties **shall** provide transparent and consistent information on support for developing country Parties provided and mobilized through public interventions biennially.'
Transparency:
13.9: 'Developed country Parties **shall**, and other Parties that provide support should, provide information on financial, technology transfer and capacity-building support provided to developing country Parties.' | **Mitigation:**
4.4: 'Developed country Parties **should** continue taking the lead by undertaking economy-wide absolute emission reduction targets.'
Finance:
Article 9.3: 'As part of a global effort, developed country Parties **should** continue to take the lead in mobilizing climate finance from a wide variety of sources.'
11.3: 'Developed country Parties **should** enhance support for capacity-building actions in developing country Parties.' |

(Continued)

Table 7.1 Continued

Subjects/ Addressee	Provisions that create obligations	Provisions that generate expectations	Provisions that Recommend	Provisions that Encourage	Provisions that set aspirations	Provisions that capture understandings
Developing country Parties			**Mitigation:** 4.4: Developing country Parties **should** continue enhancing their mitigation efforts.' **Capacity-building:** 11.4: 'Developing country Parties **should** regularly communicate progress made on implementing capacity-building plans, policies, actions or measures to implement this Agreement.' **Transparency:** 13.9: … 'and other Parties that provide support **should**, provide information on financial, technology transfer and capacity-building support provided to developing country Parties.' **Capacity-building:** 13.10: 'Developing country Parties should provide information on financial, technology transfer and capacity-building support needed and received.'	**Mitigation:** 4.4: Developing country Parties 'are **encouraged** to move over time towards economy-wide emission reduction or limitation targets in the light of different national circumstances.' **Finance:** 9.5: Other (than developed country) Parties providing resources 'are **encouraged** to communicate biennially such information on a voluntary basis.' **Finance:** 9.7: Other (than developed country) Parties 'are **encouraged** to' provide information on support for developing countries mobilized through public interventions.		

No addressee (passive voice)	**Mitigation:** 4.5: 'Support **shall** be provided to developing country Parties for the implementation of this Article.' **Adaptation:** 7.13: 'Continuous and enhanced international support **shall** be provided to developing country Parties for the implementation' of relevant adaptation actions. **Technology:** 10.6: 'Support, including financial support, **shall** be provided to developing country Parties for the implementation of this Article.' **Transparency:** 13.14: 'Support **shall** be provided to developing countries for the implementation of this Article.' 13.15: 'Support **shall** also be provided for the building of transparency-related capacity of developing country Parties.'

8

Climate Governance beyond the United Nations Climate Regime

I. INTRODUCTION

The climate change problem implicates virtually every aspect of society and every economic sector. So it is perhaps not surprising that it engages institutions of every kind, both public and private, at every scale, from local to global.[1] One study identified seventy transnational institutions that perform governance functions related to climate change—by setting standards, providing and disseminating information, building capacity, and managing projects.[2] Some of these transnational institutions involve public actors, others are private, and still others involve public–private partnerships. And this list of seventy institutions does not include the many international organizations involved in the climate change problem, such as the International Maritime Organization (IMO), the International Civil Aviation Organization (ICAO), and the World Bank, or the countless institutions that operate within a single state, rather than transnationally. As of January 2017, the Lima to Paris Action Agenda (LPAA) and its associated 'NAZCA' portal, which records actions by sub- and non-state actors, lists approximately 12,500 commitments, more than 2,000 from cities, a roughly equal number from private companies, and more than 230 from civil society organizations.[3]

This groundswell of activity provides political support for the Paris Agreement, helps enhance the credibility of states' existing nationally determined contributions (NDCs), and could catalyze stronger NDCs in the future. But it could also supplement the UN climate regime or even substitute for it, if the inter-governmental process were to falter (for example, because countries withdraw from the Paris

[1] This paragraph is drawn from Daniel Bodansky, 'Multilateral Climate Efforts Beyond the UNFCCC' (Arlington, VA: Pew Center on Global Climate Change, November 2011) <http://www.c2es.org/publications/multilateral-climate-efforts-beyond-unfccc> accessed 20 January 2017.

[2] Kenneth W. Abbott, 'The Transnational Regime Complex for Climate Change', *Environment and Planning C: Government and Policy*, 30/4 (2011): 571; see also Matthew J. Hoffmann, *Climate Governance at the Crossroads: Experimenting with a Global Response after Kyoto* (Oxford University Press, 2011) (describing climate governance 'experiments' by cities, states, regions, citizen groups, and corporations).

[3] 'NAZCA' stands for the Non-State Actor Zone for Climate Action. It was launched in 2014 by the Peruvian presidency of COP20. For a current listing of NAZCA commitments, see <http://climateaction.unfccc.int> accessed 20 January 2017.

Agreement due to domestic political changes, a distinct possibility for the US under the administration of President Donald Trump). Even the most optimistic estimates of the contributions put forward by states both at the 2009 Copenhagen conference and the 2015 Paris conference show that there is a significant gap between countries' pledges and the reductions necessary to keep global warming below 2° C.[4] Many see the proliferation of initiatives outside the UN climate regime as a critical means of 'wedging' this gap.[5] As one commentator argues, '[r]elying on national governments alone to deliver results is not enough ... The real action on climate change around the world is coming from governors, mayors, corporate chief executives and community leaders. They are the ones best positioned to make change happen on the ground'.[6] Thus far, however, tracking the degree to which sub- and non-state actions have actually been responsible for reducing emissions has proven challenging, making assessment of these claims difficult.[7]

The complex, decentralized architecture of climate governance has been theorized in many ways—for example, in terms of a 'transnational regime complex',[8] 'polycentricity',[9] 'multi-level governance',[10] or 'fragmentation'.[11] Regardless of the label used, climate change governance outside the FCCC has four central features:

- First, it is multi-level: it operates through institutions at different geographic scales, ranging from global to regional to national to sub-national.

- Second, it is multi-actor, involving both public and private institutions, including states, sub-national governments, international organizations, environmental and other civil society organizations, and business.[12]

- Third, it involves different degrees of legalization, from 'hard law' rules set forth in treaties such as the International Convention for the Prevention of Pollution from Ships (MARPOL 73/78)[13] and the Montreal Protocol on

[4] United Nations Environment Programme (UNEP), 'The Emissions Gap Report 2015: A UNEP Synthesis Report' (Nairobi: UNEP, November 2015).
[5] Angel Hsu *et al.*, 'Towards a New Climate Diplomacy', *Nature Climate Change*, 5/6 (2015): 501; see also Jon Hovi *et al.*, 'Climate Change Mitigation: A Role for Climate Clubs?', *Palgrave Communications* (10 May 2016) <http://www.palgrave-journals.com/articles/palcomms201620> accessed 20 January 2017.
[6] Daniel C. Esty, 'Bottom-Up Climate Fix', *The New York Times* (21 September 2014).
[7] Angel Hsu *et al.*, 'Track Climate Pledges of Cities and Companies', *Nature*, 532/7599 (2016): 303.
[8] Abbott, Transnational Regime Complex (n 2); Robert O. Keohane and David G. Victor, 'The Regime Complex for Climate Change', *Perspectives on Politics*, 9/1 (2011): 7.
[9] Elinor Ostrom, 'Polycentric Systems for Coping with Collective Action and Environmental Change', *Global Environmental Change*, 20/4 (2010): 550; Hari M. Osofsky, 'Polycentrism and Climate Change', in Daniel A. Farber and Marjan Peeters (eds), *Encyclopedia of Environmental Law vol 1: Climate Change Law* (Cheltenham, UK: Edward Elgar, 2016) 325.
[10] Jacqueline Peel, Lee Godden, and Rodney J. Keenan, 'Climate Change Law in an Era of Multi-Level Governance', *Transnational Environmental Law*, 1/2 (2012): 245; see also Harriett Bulkeley *et al.*, *Transnational Climate Change Governance* (Cambridge University Press, 2014).
[11] Harro Van Asselt, Francesco Sindico, and Michael A. Mehling, 'Global Climate Change and the Fragmentation of International Law', *Law and Policy*, 30/4 (2008): 423.
[12] Peter Newell, Philipp Pattberg, and Heike Schroeder, 'Multiactor Governance and the Environment', *Annual Review of Environment and Resources*, 37 (2012): 365.
[13] International Convention for the Prevention of Pollution from Ships (adopted 2 November 1973) 1340 UNTS 184, amended by Protocol of 1978 Relating to the International Convention

Substances that Deplete the Ozone Layer, to 'soft law' norms such as the 'gold standard' for carbon credits[14] or the 'Carbon Neutral protocol'.[15]

- Fourth, it is polycentric, in that there is no central, organizing authority.

II. MULTI-LEVEL CLIMATE GOVERNANCE

Although the theory of multi-level governance is comparatively recent,[16] the fact of multi-level governance is not. Once political communities organize at more than the local level, governance operates at multiple scales. International law has always, to some degree, had a multi-level character, in that international institutions generally act through national governments rather than directly, and international law depends for its implementation primarily on states. Traditionally, however, international law's multi-level character has been circumscribed by its focus on the national rather than the sub-national level and on governmental rather than non-governmental actors.

Multi-level governance involves horizontal relationships between institutions at the same hierarchical or geographical level, vertical relationships between institutions at different levels,[17] and diagonal relationships between institutions at different levels in different countries.[18] Multilateral institutions such as the FCCC, IMO, and World Bank have horizontal relationships with one another, as well as vertical relationships with states and non-governmental actors. States relate horizontally to one another bilaterally and multilaterally; they have vertical relationships with international institutions above and sub-national actors below; and sometimes they have diagonal relations with sub-national actors in other states. And sub-national and private actors have horizontal relationships with one another (for example, through networks like the Compact of Mayors[19] and the C40 Cities

---

for the Prevention of Pollution from Ships (adopted 17 February 1978, entered into force 2 October 1983) 1340 UNTS 61 (MARPOL 73/78).

[14] The gold standard is a voluntary standard developed by the World Wildlife Fund and other international NGOs in 2003 to determine whether carbon mitigation projects actually reduce greenhouse gas emissions. For discussion of the gold standard, see Chapter 6, Section V.B.2.

[15] The CarbonNeutral Protocol was developed by a private company in 2002 to evaluate carbon neutral certification programs. See CarbonNeutral <http://www.carbonneutral.com> accessed 20 January 2017.

[16] See generally Ian Bache and Matthew Flinders (eds), *Multi-Level Governance* (Oxford University Press, 2004).

[17] Thijs Etty *et al.*, 'Transnational Dimensions of Climate Governance', *Transnational Environmental Law*, 1/2 (2012): 235.

[18] Hari M. Osofsky, 'Is Climate Change "International"? Litigation's Diagonal Regulatory Role', *Virginia Journal of International Law*, 49/3 (2009): 585.

[19] The Compact of Mayors was launched in 2014 by UN Secretary General Ban Ki-moon and former New York City mayor, Michael Bloomberg, who serves as the Secretary-General's Special Envoy for Cities and Climate Change. It involves the principal cities' networks, including C40 and Local Governments for Sustainability (which still uses the acronym, ICLEI, originally standing for International Council for Local Environmental Initiatives).

Climate Leadership Group[20]); vertical relationships with national and international institutions; and diagonal relationships with institutions at other levels in other governance hierarchies. Theories of multi-level governance seek to explore these relationships—horizontal, vertical, and diagonal—between the multitude of governance institutions.

Multi-level governance can be hierarchic or polycentric. In a hierarchic system, some institutions have primacy over others.[21] Hierarchy is most common among vertically related institutions—that is, those with different geographic scales. For example, international law asserts its priority over national law by stipulating that national law does not provide a justification for violating a state's international obligations.[22] Similarly, within states, national law is usually superior to local law, so national climate policies constrain the actions of sub-national units. But hierarchy can also exist among horizontally related institutions. For example, in the international system, the UN Charter provides for its own primacy over other treaties.[23]

Polycentric systems, in contrast, have multiple nodes of authority, with overlapping jurisdiction but no hierarchical ordering.[24] In a polycentric system, multiple institutions are potentially able to address the same issue, creating the risk of duplication of effort and conflict. The relationships of international organizations are generally polycentric: their jurisdiction can overlap and none is superior to any other. The same is true of the state system, which is premised on the principle of sovereign equality.

The concepts of hierarchy and polycentrism are both ideal types; many systems of multi-level governance have elements of both. A federal system such as the United States (US), for example, has polycentric features, since the jurisdiction of federal and state governments overlap.[25] States can develop their own climate policies, employing the same types of regulatory instruments (such as emissions trading) as the federal government. But American federalism also has a hierarchic character, in that federal law is supreme over state law, in case of conflict. Similarly, many environmental treaties—including the FCCC and the Kyoto Protocol—set minimum standards that bind states; but they do not displace national sovereignty, since they permit states to adopt national climate change policies that go beyond what is required internationally, as many states have done.

The overlapping jurisdiction entailed by polycentric governance has both advantages and disadvantages. On the positive side, allowing multiple institutions to

---

[20] On C40, see n 145 below and accompanying text.
[21] Kenneth W. Abbott, 'Strengthening the Transnational Regime Complex for Climate Change', *Transnational Environmental Law*, 3/1 (2014): 57, 64–5 (contrasting nested, overlapping and parallel systems of governance).
[22] International Law Commission (ILC), 'Responsibility of States for Internationally Wrongful Acts' in Report of the International Law Commission on its fifty-third session (23 April–1 June and 2 July–10 August 2001) UN Doc A/56/10, Art 32.
[23] United Nations, Charter of the United Nations (24 October 1945) 1 UNTS XVI (UN Charter), Art 103.
[24] Ostrom, Polycentric Systems (n 9).
[25] Daniel C. Esty, 'Revitalizing Environmental Federalism', *Michigan Law Review*, 95/3 (1996): 570.

address the same issue allows for experimentation and flexibility. Institutions operating at a local scale can serve as laboratories to try novel approaches, without risk to the larger governance units.[26] Even when governance institutions have no formal relationships, they can still learn from one another. To the extent that an approach is successful at one scale, it can serve as a model for other jurisdictions either at the same or higher scales. One state can imitate the success of another; or an approach can work its way up from the local to the national to the international level. For example, California's regulations have often served as a model for other states and for US federal regulation.[27] And the US experience with the sulphur dioxide allowance trading program in the early 1990s served as the inspiration for the Kyoto Protocol's emissions trading system.[28]

A decentralized, multi-level approach can also reduce the risks of gaps in a regime since, if one institution is not addressing a significant aspect of a problem, another institution can step in. The Kyoto Protocol does not address black carbon, for example—an aerosol that contributes to global warming but is not, strictly speaking, a greenhouse gas (GHG). So there is a role (discussed in Section IV.C below) for other institutions to fill this gap, including the Arctic Council[29] and the Convention on Long-Range Transboundary Air Pollution (LRTAP Convention).[30]

These positive effects of polycentric governance can be strengthened through the development of networks, which reduce transaction costs, facilitate the diffusion of ideas and technologies, and promote solidarity and cooperation.[31] For example, networks of cities such as the C40 Cities Climate Leadership Group play an important role in sharing information about zoning and transportation policies, developing standardized methodologies for municipal emissions inventories, building capacity, and giving voice to local communities at the national and international levels.[32]

Finally, different governance bodies can complement and reinforce one another, given their different constituencies, competencies, and capacities. Cities have

---

[26] *New State Ice Co v Liebmann*, 285 US 262, 311 (Brandeis, J., dissenting, 1932) ('a single courageous state may, if its citizens choose, serve as a laboratory, and try novel social and economic experiments without risk to the rest of the country').

[27] David Vogel, 'Trading Up and Governing Across: Transnational Governance and Environmental Protection', *Journal of European Public Policy*, 4/4 (1997): 556.

[28] On the influence of national policy on international policy, see generally Elizabeth R. DeSombre, *Domestic Sources of International Environmental Policy: Industry, Environmentalists and U.S. Power* (Cambridge, MA: MIT Press, 2000).

[29] See generally Timo Koivurova and David L. VanderZwaag, 'The Arctic Council at 10 Years: Retrospect and Prospect', *University of British Columbia Law Review*, 40/1 (2007): 121. For more on the Arctic Council, see n 113 below and accompanying text.

[30] Convention on Long-Range Transboundary Air Pollution (adopted 13 November 1979, entered into force 16 March 1983) 1302 UNTS 217 (LRTAP Convention).

[31] R.A.W. Rhodes, 'Policy Network Analysis', in Robert E. Goodin, Michael Moran, and Martin Rein (eds), *Oxford Handbook of Public Policy* (Oxford University Press, 2006) 1425.

[32] On C40, see n 145 below and accompanying text; on the role of cities, see J. Corfee-Morlot *et al.*, *Cities, Climate Change and Multilevel Governance* (Paris: OECD, 2009) 81–2; Michele M. Betsill and Harriett Bulkeley, 'Cities and the Multilevel Governance of Climate Change', *Global Governance*, 12/2 (2006): 141, 143.

greater local knowledge than national and international institutions—knowledge that can be useful to higher-level institutions in developing implementation strategies and in administering programs to transfer technologies or build capacity. The Montreal Protocol regime furthers the UN climate regime's goals by declining to fund projects that replace ozone-depleting substances (ODS) with GHGs. And the World Trade Organization (WTO) could reinforce the UN climate regime by working to phase out energy subsidies.[33] These complementary activities can arise organically, or they can be orchestrated by an institution that self-consciously encourages or employs other like-minded institutions to perform particular tasks, such as monitoring or capacity-building, for which an institution has particular strengths.[34]

Although polycentric governance has benefits, it also creates the potential for confusion, duplication of effort, forum shopping, and even conflict—the concerns emphasized in the literature on 'fragmentation'.[35] Locally-determined policies can conflict with national policies; national policies with international policies; and one international policy with another, as sometimes occurs in the trade and environment arena. And even when there are no policy conflicts, the sheer number of similar institutions and networks can produce inefficiencies and tensions.[36]

At least three approaches can be used to avoid such conflicts. One possibility is for institutions to divide up issues, *ex ante*, on a geographic or functional basis. For example, among vertically-related institutions (ie those at different levels), issues can be matched with institutions based on their geographic scale. This type of division of labour is the basis for the principle of subsidiarity within the EU, which provides that the EU will not intervene when an issue can be addressed effectively by the member states.[37] Similarly, among institutions operating over the same geographic scale, issues can be allocated to the institution with the greatest functional expertise.[38] The UN climate regime, for example, provides for a division of labor: it addresses most GHG emissions, but does not regulate emissions of GHGs governed by the Montreal Protocol, and provides that emissions from international transport should be addressed by the relevant UN specialized agency—IMO in the case of maritime emissions, and ICAO in the case of emissions from civil aviation.[39]

[33] World Bank, *Subsidies in the Energy Sector: An Overview* (Washington, D.C.: World Bank, July 2010). On the trade regime and energy subsidies, see Chapter 9, Section IV.B.5.
[34] See generally Kenneth W. Abbott, Philipp Genschel, Duncan Snidal, and Bernhard Zangl (eds), *International Organizations as Orchestrators* (Cambridge University Press, 2015).
[35] See Van Asselt, Sindico, and Mehling, Global Climate Change and the Fragmentation of International Law (n 11).
[36] For example, networks of cities include the C40 Cities Climate Leadership Group, the World Mayors Council on Climate Change, Cities for Climate Protection, the Large Cities Climate Group, and ICLEI's Local Governments for Sustainability.
[37] Antonio Estella, *The EU Principle of Subsidiarity and Its Critique* (Oxford University Press, 2003); George A. Berman, 'Taking Subsidiarity Seriously: Federalism in the European Community and the United States', *Columbia Law Review*, 94/2 (1994): 331.
[38] The international rules relating to jurisdiction attempt to avoid horizontal conflicts among states through the rule of territoriality and the correlative limits on extra-territorial jurisdiction.
[39] Kyoto Protocol, Art 2.2.

Second, umbrella institutions can be created to coordinate and harmonize the activities of similar, overlapping institutions—for example, through the creation of a registry or registries, to give some order to the various mechanisms for recording and assessing climate actions.[40]

Finally, to the extent conflicts arise, they can be addressed on a case-by-case basis through conflict rules—for example, the *lex specialis* rule, which provides that the more specialized rule prevails over the more general one; or the later-in-time rule, which provides that later agreements prevail over earlier ones.[41]

III. PUBLIC AND PRIVATE CLIMATE GOVERNANCE

Climate change governance is not only multi-level; it is also multi-actor. It is not the exclusive preserve of governmental and inter-governmental actors, but also involves a wide variety of non-state actors. The roles and relationships between public and private actors can be conceptualized in terms of what Kenneth Abbott and Duncan Snidal call a 'governance triangle',[42] whose three vertices are the state, civil society organizations (CSOs), and business ('the firm'). International law generally focuses on the top part of the triangle, which encompasses state-led activities such as the UN climate regime, regional and sub-national emissions trading systems, and the initiatives of sub-national governments such as provinces and cities. But climate change governance is also exercised by:

- Business, through mechanisms such as the Verified Carbon Standard (VCS), which was developed by the World Business Council for Sustainable Development, the International Emissions Trading Association, and other private groups.[43]

- Environmental groups and other CSOs—for example, through the Gold Standard.[44]

- Business in collaboration with governmental actors—for example, through the International Organization for Standardization (ISO) GHG accounting standard.[45]

---

[40] Thomas Hale, 'Design Considerations for a Registry of Sub- and Non-State Actions in the UN Framework Convention on Climate Change' (University of Oxford: Blavatnik School of Government, 24 February 2014) <http://www.bsg.ox.ac.uk/sites/www.bsg.ox.ac.uk/files/documents/2014-UNFCC-ClimateRegistry-PolicyMemo.pdf> accessed 20 January 2017.

[41] VCLT, Art 30 (later-in-time rule). On ways of resolving conflicts, see generally Harro van Asselt, *The Fragmentation of Global Climate Governance: Consequences and Management of Regime Interactions* (Cheltenham, UK: Edward Elgar, 2014).

[42] Kenneth Abbott and Duncan Snidal, 'The Governance Triangle: Regulatory Standards Institutions and the Shadow of the State', in Walter Mattli and Ngaire Woods (eds), *The Politics of Global Regulation* (Princeton University Press, 2009) 44.

[43] Verified Carbon Standard <http://www.v-c-s.org> accessed 20 January 2017.

[44] On the Gold Standard, see n 14 above.

[45] International Organization for Standardization News, 'New ISO 14064 standards provide tools for assessing and supporting greenhouse gas reduction and emissions trading' (3 March 2006)

- CSOs in collaboration with governmental actors.
- CSOs and business in collaboration with one another—eg through the Carbon Disclosure Project.[46]
- Governments, CSOs, and business acting together—eg to protect forests through REDD+.[47]

These joint activities have a variety of rationales, including reducing transaction costs and promoting shared interests. But some may be understood in terms of 'club' theory, in which comparatively small groups of actors form clubs in order to exclude others and produce private benefits, such as lower energy costs or new technologies.[48]

Public and private governance institutions can relate to one another in a variety of ways. Private actors can seek to influence public actors by providing information and technical analysis, raising public awareness, and producing demonstration effects.[49] Conversely, states can enlist private actors in an effort to implement their policies. Finally, private actors can operate independently and seek to influence sub- and non-state actors directly.[50] For example, the Carbon Disclosure Project works directly with companies to get them to disclose their emissions,[51] and Fossil Free pressures universities and other organizations to divest from fossil fuel companies.[52]

Because only states can establish legally binding rules, the various private initiatives by CSOs and business involve standards that are formally non-binding. Nevertheless, private governance can exert significant authority through network effects, public opinion, and peer pressure. If most of the firms in a particular sector agree on a common standard, for example, other firms may feel the need to conform. If a standard is accepted by the public and influences consumer behavior, producers may feel pressured to adopt it, in order not to be disadvantaged in the marketplace. If the fossil fuel divestment movement mounts a campaign

<http://www.iso.org/iso/home/news_index/news_archive/news.htm?refid=Ref994> accessed 20 January 2017.

[46] CDP: Driving Sustainable Economies <https://www.cdp.net/fr> accessed 20 January 2017. For an assessment, see Daniel C. Matisoff *et al.*, 'Convergence in Environmental Reporting: Assessing the Carbon Disclosure Project', *Business Strategy and the Environment*, 22/5 (2013): 285.

[47] REDD+ stands for Reductions in Emissions from Deforestation and Forest Degradation. It was originally proposed by the Coalition of Rainforest Nations in 2005 to incentivize the protection of forests. See generally Christina Voight (ed), *Research Handbook on REDD+ and International Law* (Cheltenham, UK: Edward Elgar, 2016).

[48] See Richard B. Stewart, Michael Oppenheimer, and Bryce Rudyk, 'Building Blocks for Global Climate Protection', *Stanford Environmental Law Journal*, 32/2 (2013): 12.

[49] Abbott, Strengthening the Transnational Regime Complex (n 21), 68.   [50] Ibid, 67.

[51] The Carbon Disclosure Project is an investor initiative started in 2000 for voluntary reporting of emissions by business. See generally Florence Depoers, Thomas Jeanjean, and Tiphaine Jérôme, 'Voluntary Disclosure of Greenhouse Gas Emissions: Contrasting the Carbon Disclosure Project and Corporate Reports', *Journal of Business Ethics*, 134/3 (2016): 445.

[52] Samuel Alexander, Kara Nicholson, and John Wiseman, *Fossil Free: The Development and Significance of the Fossil Fuel Divestment Movement* (University of Melbourne: Melbourne Sustainable Society Institute, 2014).

against a university, the university may decide to divest in order to avoid negative publicity.[53] In all of these ways, private climate governance can exercise significant authority over behavior. As with any exercise of authority by private, unelected, non-democratic actors, this raises legitimacy concerns.[54]

IV. CLIMATE GOVERNANCE BY OTHER MULTILATERAL INSTITUTIONS

At the global level, the FCCC has served as the hub of efforts to address the threat of climate change. But many other multilateral institutions have become engaged in climate-related work.[55] These include UN specialized agencies such as IMO and ICAO, which address emissions from maritime shipping and civil aviation respectively; political forums such as the Group of 8 (G-8), the Group of 20 (G-20), and the Security Council, which now routinely include climate change on their agendas; and the Major Economies Forum (MEF), a high-level meeting of seventeen major developed and developing states.

Efforts to address the climate change issue in multilateral forums other than the UN climate regime have several rationales:

- First, in institutions with a track record of success, such as the Montreal Protocol, participants have developed working relationships that help instil trust and promote cooperation.

- Second, institutions with a sectoral focus, such as IMO and ICAO, have a tradition of cooperation that can help facilitate agreement and allow a response tailored to the specific nature of the sector.[56]

- Third, some institutions have procedural rules that make agreement more likely. For example, in contrast to the consensus rule in the FCCC, IMO allows decisions to be made by a qualified majority vote—a voting rule that allowed the adoption of mandatory efficiency standards for new ships, despite opposition by China, Brazil, and Saudi Arabia (see Section IV.A.1 below).

---

[53] Julie Ayling and Neil Gunningham, 'Non-State Governance and Climate Policy: The Fossil Fuel Divestment Movement', *Climate Policy* (2015) <http://dx.doi.org/10.1080/14693062.2015.1094729> accessed 20 January 2017.

[54] Julia Black, 'Constructing and Contesting Legitimacy and Accountability in Polycentric Regulatory Regimes', *Regulation and Governance*, 2/2 (2008): 137; Benjamin Cashore, 'Legitimacy and the Privatization of Environmental Governance: How Non-State Market-Driven (NSMD) Governance Systems Gain Rule-Making Authority', *Governance*, 15/4 (2002): 503.

[55] This section draws on materials from Bodansky, Multilateral Climate Efforts Beyond the UNFCCC (n 1); see also Harro van Asselt, 'Alongside the UNFCCC: Complementary Venues for Climate Action' (Arlington, VA: Center for Climate and Energy Solutions, May 2014) <http://www.c2es.org/docUploads/alongside-the-unfccc.pdf> accessed 20 January 2017.

[56] On sectoral agreements, see generally Daniel Bodansky, 'International Sectoral Agreements in a Post-2012 Climate Framework' (Arlington, VA: Pew Center on Global Climate Change, May 2007) <http://www.c2es.org/docUploads/International%20Sectoral%20Aggreements%20in%20a%20Post-2012%20Climate%20Framework.pdf> accessed 20 January 2017.

- Finally, some institutions, such as the LRTAP Convention, provide a regional forum for action, where established relations may make it easier to achieve agreement around shared interests and objectives.

Addressing the climate change issue in other multilateral forums is unproblematic when the UN climate regime delegates action to the other institution, or when outside activities supplement or complement the FCCC. In the case of IMO and ICAO, for example, the Kyoto Protocol specifically directed Annex I parties to address emissions from international transport in the relevant UN specialized agencies,[57] so the UN climate regime has effectively assigned this part of the climate change problem to IMO and ICAO. Similarly, in the case of the Montreal Protocol, decisions to fund projects that replace hydrofchlofofluorocarbons (HCFCs) with chemicals other than hydrofluorocarbons (HFC) complement the UN climate regime, by furthering the Kyoto Protocol's limits on HFC emissions. Finally, efforts under the LRTAP Convention to reduce emissions of black carbon supplement the UN climate regime, by focusing on a part of the climate change problem that neither the FCCC nor the Kyoto Protocol addresses.

But addressing climate change through other multilateral forums raises concern when it competes with the FCCC process. For example, regulation of HFCs under the Montreal Protocol could be seen as competing with the Kyoto Protocol, which already regulates HFCs.[58] As noted earlier, although regulatory competition has potential benefits, it raises the risks of forum shopping, lack of policy coherence and, more generally, the fragmentation of international law.[59]

Pursuing the climate change issue outside the UN climate regime also raises the question of whether the principles set forth in Article 3 of the FCCC apply—in particular, the principle of common but differentiated responsibilities and respective capabilities (CBDRRC).[60] This question has arisen in the work of IMO and ICAO to limit maritime and aviation emissions. Neither IMO nor ICAO applies the principle of CBDRRC in its other work; instead, they seek to regulate ships and planes uniformly, regardless of nationality. In general, IMO has chosen to apply the same principle of non-discrimination in its climate change work, rather than differentiate between the obligations of developed and developing countries.[61] But this approach remains controversial.

---

[57] Kyoto Protocol, Art 2.2.

[58] Sebastian Oberthür, Claire Dupont(-roche Kelly), and Yasuko Matsumoto, 'Managing Policy Contradictions between the Montreal and Kyoto Protocols: The Case of Fluorinated Greenhouse Gases', in Sebastian Oberthür and Olav Schram Stokke (eds), *Managing Institutional Complexity: Regime Interplay and Global Environmental Change* (Cambridge, MA: MIT Press, 2011) 115.

[59] Harro Van Asselt, 'Legal and Political Approaches in Interplay Management: Dealing with the Fragmentation of Global Climate Governance', in Oberthür and Stokke, ibid, 59.

[60] For discussion of CBDRRC, see Chapter 1, Section V.C.

[61] Sophia Kopela, 'Climate Change, Regime Interaction, and the Principle of Common But Differentiated Responsibility: The Experience of the International Maritime Organization', *Yearbook of International Environmental Law*, 24/1 (2014): 70.

A. Bunker emissions

Aviation and maritime emissions each account for about 2% of annual carbon dioxide (CO_2) emissions, and these are rapidly growing.[62] Attributing these emissions (often referred to as 'bunker emissions') to a particular country is difficult. For this reason, the Kyoto Protocol does not include bunker emissions in its national emissions targets. Instead, it directs Annex I parties to address emissions from international transport through the relevant specialized agencies: IMO in the case of maritime transport, and ICAO in the case of civil aviation.[63]

1. International Maritime Organization

A 2014 IMO study[64] estimated that international maritime shipping accounts for CO_2 emissions of about 900 million tons.[65] Although this is a relatively small fraction (2.7%) of total global GHG emissions, maritime emissions are expected to double or even triple by mid-century in the absence of mitigation policies.[66]

In 2011, the parties to MARPOL 73/78—the IMO agreement regulating pollution from ships—adopted an amendment to Annex VI (addressing air pollution) on energy efficiency for ships.[67] The amendment:

- Requires new ships to meet an energy efficiency design index (EEDI), which specifies CO_2 emission limits per capacity mile for different types and sizes of vessels.

- Requires all ships to adopt and implement a ship-specific energy efficiency management plan.

---

[62] International Maritime Organization (IMO), 'Greenhouse Gas Emissions' <http://www.imo.org/en/OurWork/environment/pollutionprevention/airpollution/pages/ghg-emissions.aspx> accessed 20 January 2017; International Civil Aviation Organisation (ICAO), 'Aircraft Engine Emissions' <http://www.icao.int/environmental-protection/Pages/aircraft-engine-emissions.aspx> accessed 20 January 2017. See generally Alice Bows-Larkin, 'All Adrift: Aviation, Shipping, and Climate Change Policy', *Climate Policy*, 15/6 (2015): 681; FCCC, 'Emissions from fuel used for international aviation and maritime transport (international bunker fuels)' <http://unfccc.int/methods/emissions_from_intl_transport/items/1057.php> accessed 20 January 2017.

[63] Kyoto Protocol, Art 2.2.

[64] This section draws on Daniel Bodansky, 'The Regulation of Emissions from Ships: The Role of the International Maritime Organization', in H. Sheiber, N. Olifer, and M. Kwon (eds), *Ocean Law Debates: The 50-Year Legacy and Emerging Issues for the Years Ahead* (Leiden: Brill, forthcoming 2017).

[65] IMO, *Third Greenhouse Gas Study* (London: IMO, 2014), Table 1. The International Energy Agency estimate of GHG emissions from international shipping is lower—about 1.7% of global GHG emissions—and there is debate about whether the IMO or IEA methodology is more reliable. See David McCollum, Gregory Gould, and David Greene, 'Greenhouse Gas Emissions from Aviation and Marine Transportation: Mitigation Potential and Policies' (Arlington, VA: Pew Center on Global Climate Change, December 2009) <http://www.c2es.org/docUploads/aviation-and-marine-report-2009.pdf> accessed 20 January 2017, 6. The 2014 IMO report estimated that of overall GHG emissions from shipping, the vast majority (about 97%) were CO_2, mostly in exhaust gas.

[66] IMO, ibid, 34.

[67] Marine Environment Protection Committee (MEPC), 'Amendments to MARPOL Annex IV on Regulations for the Prevention of Air Pollution from Ships by Inclusion of New Regulations on Energy Efficiency from Ships' Resolution MEPC.203(62) (adopted 15 July 2011, entered into force 1 January 2013) IMO Doc. MEPC 62/24/Add.1, Annex 19.

A big question in the development of the Annex VI amendments was whether and how the principle of CBDRRC would apply. Essentially, states took three positions. Some developed states, including the US, argued that the principle of CBDRRC does not apply to IMO's work on GHG emissions, especially in light of IMO's non-discrimination and no-more-favourable-treatment principles. In contrast, China and India argued that CBDRRC applies, and that it requires that the obligations of developed and developing countries to limit maritime emissions be differentiated along the lines of the Kyoto Protocol, trumping IMO's non-discrimination principle.[68] In the middle, the IMO secretariat argued that even if CBDRRC is relevant to IMO's work on GHG emissions, it does not conflict with IMO's principle of non-discrimination, since non-discrimination applies to ships, whereas CBDRRC applies to countries.[69]

Ultimately, developed countries succeeded in reflecting the 'no more favourable treatment' principle in the MARPOL Annex VI amendment. The amendment does not differentiate between vessels flagged, owned, or operated in developed versus developing countries; instead, its regulations apply equally to all vessels.[70] As a result, the amendment was opposed by China, Brazil, and Saudi Arabia. Nevertheless, it was eventually approved by a vote of 49-5 (with 2 abstentions), pursuant to MARPOL Article 16, which allows annexes to be amended by a two-thirds majority of the parties.[71] The amendment entered into force on 1 January 2013.

The MARPOL Annex VI amendment is significant in several ways. First, it establishes the first mandatory emission standards for a sector. Second, its requirements apply uniformly, with no differentiation between ships flagged in developed and developing countries.[72] Instead, the amendment addresses the issue of differentiation through the inclusion of a provision to promote technical co-operation and assistance for developing countries. Third, the amendment's adoption by a majority vote represents the first time that a decision relating to climate change has been taken over the objection of a significant group of countries.

---

[68] Kopela, Climate Change, Regime Interaction, and the Principle of Common But Differentiated Responsibility (n 61).

[69] IMO, 'Legal Aspects of the Organization's Work on GHG Emissions from Ships in the Context of the UNFCCC and the Kyoto Protocol' (1 April 2011) <http://www.imo.org/OurWork/Environment/PollutionPrevention/AirPollution/Documents/Third%20Intersessional/11-Legal_final.pdf> accessed 20 January 2017.

[70] The only concession to developing countries was that parties may waive the new requirements for four years.

[71] IMO, Report of the Marine Environment Protection Committee on its sixty-second session (26 July 2011) IMO Doc. MEPC 62/24 (Report of MEPC 62) para 6.110. Brazil, Chile, China, Kuwait, and Saudi Arabia voted against the amendment, and Jamaica and St Vincent and the Grenadines abstained. After the adoption of the amendment, Brazil, China, India, Saudi Arabia, and Venezuela made statements objecting to the vote. 'Statements by the Delegations of Brazil, China, India, Saudi Arabia and the Bolivarian Republic of Venezuela and the Observers of the Pacific Environment and Clean Shipping Coalition after the Adoption of Amendments to MARPOL Annex VI', in Report of MEPC 62, IMO Doc. MEPC 62/24/Add.1, Annex 20.

[72] Although some countries argued that, by failing to differentiate between developed and developing countries, the Annex VI amendment violates the FCCC, the IMO Legal Office concluded that the principles of the UN climate regime do not limit the outcomes of IMO's decision-making process. See IMO, Legal Aspects (n 69).

MARPOL allows countries that voted against the Annex VI amendment to opt out of the new requirements. In the end, although five countries voted against the amendment, only Brazil lodged a formal reservation.[73] Nevertheless, its flag vessels will still need to meet the new standards if they wish to call on the ports of states that accepted the amendment. Moreover, shipbuilders are likely to comply with the new standards for all new vessels, regardless of where a ship is expected to be flagged, since failure to comply with the standards will lower the potential resale value of the ship. For these reasons, the new MARPOL standards are likely to be applied universally, despite Brazil's reservation.

The vote to adopt the Annex VI amendments in 2011 did not resolve the differences regarding CBDRRC. A solution was finally reached two years later, through the adoption of an IMO resolution with preambular language that took 'cognizance' of the IMO principles of non-discrimination and no-more-favorable treatment as well as the FCCC principle of CBDRRC, without specifying their applicability to MARPOL.[74] The resolution also established an ad hoc expert working group on facilitation of transfer of technology for ships, to identify developing country technology needs as well as barriers to technology transfer.

IMO's work on maritime emissions is ongoing and one option still under consideration is the development of a market-based mechanism for international shipping. However, the focus of IMO's recent work has been on data collection and analysis, including new requirements for the collection and reporting of data on fuel consumption.[75]

2. International Civil Aviation Organization

In many respects, civil aviation is similar to maritime shipping:

- Civil aviation is a highly international industry, making a global sectoral approach appropriate.

- Currently, emissions from international civil aviation are relatively low, accounting for only about 1.3% of global CO_2 emissions.[76] But aviation emissions are growing rapidly, and are projected to increase by four- to six-fold by 2050 in the absence of new policies, despite continued improvements in efficiency.[77]

[73] IMO, *Status of Multilateral Conventions and Instruments in Respect of which the International Maritime Organization or its Secretary-General Performs Depositary or Other Functions, as at 10 October 2016* (London: IMO, 2016) 166.

[74] IMO, 'Promotion of Technical Cooperation and Transfer of Technology Relating to the Improvement of Energy Efficiency of Ships' Res. MEPC.229 (65) (17 May 2013) IMO Doc. MEPC 65/22, Annex 4.

[75] IMO provisionally approved new data reporting requirements in 2016. 'Amendments to MARPOL Annex VI (Data Consumption System for Fuel Oil Consumption)' Res. MEPC.278(70) (27 October 2016). The requirements are expected to enter into force on 1 March 2018.

[76] ICAO, 'Top 3 Misconceptions about CORSIA' <http://www.icao.int/environmental-protection/Pages/A39_CORSIA_FAQ6.aspx> accessed 20 January 2017.

[77] Gregg Fleming and Urs Ziegler, 'Environmental Trends in Aviation to 2050', in *ICAO Environmental Report 2013: Aviation and Climate Change* (Montreal: ICAO, 2013) 22, 25.

- Emissions from civil aviation could be reduced significantly using existing technologies—for example, through the use of new lightweight materials and more efficient engines to increase the fuel efficiency of aircraft, by substituting lower-carbon fuels for existing sources, and, to a lesser extent, by operating aircraft in ways that use less fuel. According to one estimate, these measures could together reduce emissions from civil aviation by 50% by 2050 as compared to business-as-usual projections.[78] While this would represent a significant improvement compared to the no-policy case, aviation emissions would still double by 2050, given the expected quadrupling of air travel.

ICAO is the UN specialized agency responsible for governance of international civil aviation. Established in 1944 by the Convention on International Civil Aviation[79] (often referred to as the Chicago Convention), ICAO develops policies, standards and guidance in the field of international civil aviation. Within ICAO, the Committee on Aviation Environmental Protection (CAEP) has principal responsibility for environmental matters.

In October 2010, the ICAO Assembly adopted a consolidated resolution on climate change, setting global goals of (1) improving average fuel efficiency by 2% annually, and (2) achieving carbon-neutral growth starting in 2020 (in effect, stabilizing global CO_2 emissions at 2020 levels).[80] The resolution made international aviation the first sector to adopt global emissions goals, although the resolution characterized the goals as 'aspirational' and the contributions of states to achieving the goals as 'voluntary', and specifically noted that the 2% fuel efficiency goal and the 2020 stabilization goal do not 'attribute specific obligations to individual states'.[81] States also agreed to develop a global CO_2 efficiency standard for aircraft, analogous to the EEDI standard developed by IMO for new ships.

Like IMO, ICAO decisions can be made by a qualified majority vote. As a result, the ICAO Assembly was able to adopt its 2010 resolution despite opposition by China, India and Brazil. A number of countries entered reservations to particular aspects of the Assembly resolution, including China, which objected to the inclusion of developing country emissions in the 2020 stabilization goal; the EU, which criticized the 2020 goal as too weak;[82] and the US, which objected to language suggesting that developing countries might have lesser requirements.

A complicating factor in the ICAO discussions was the unilateral decision by the EU in 2012 to extend the scope of its emissions trading system (EU-ETS) to

---

[78] McCollum, Gould, and Greene, Greenhouse Gas Emissions from Aviation and Marine Transportation (n 65) 14.

[79] Convention on International Civil Aviation (adopted 7 December 1944, entered into force 4 April 1947) 15 UNTS 295.

[80] ICAO, 'Consolidated Statement of Continuing ICAO Policies and Practices Related to Environmental Protection – Climate Change' ICAO Assembly Res A37-19: Resolutions adopted at the thirty-seventh session by the Assembly (8 October 2010) 55, paras 4, 6.

[81] Ibid, para 5.

[82] The EU had sought a global goal of reducing emissions from civil aviation by 10% from 2005 levels by 2020.

emissions from all flights that land in or depart from EU member states.[83] The threat of unilateral action by the EU both politicized the climate change issue within ICAO and served as an important driver of ICAO action. US airlines filed suit in British courts to enjoin implementation of the EU directive, on the ground that the directive violated customary international law by regulating emissions outside the EU's airspace; violated Article 2.2 of the Kyoto Protocol, which directs Annex I states to address international aviation emissions through ICAO; and violated the Chicago Convention through its imposition of additional charges. The case was transferred to the European Court of Justice (ECJ), which upheld the EU directive in 2011.[84] Nevertheless, in response to strong and concerted pressure from China, India, and the US,[85] among others, the EU agreed to suspend the directive temporarily, in order to allow progress to be made in ICAO to develop a global market-based measure to limit emissions from civil aviation.[86]

Following suspension of the EU directive, work within ICAO to find a multilateral solution to aviation emissions proceeded with greater urgency. ICAO's work focused on two approaches: aircraft efficiency standards and a market-based measure (MBM).[87] In February 2016, the CAEP preliminarily approved a CO_2 performance standard for new aircraft, which will be phased in between 2020 and 2028, starting with new models and eventually applying to all models currently being produced. Then, in October 2016, as part of a basket of measures, ICAO adopted the first global market-based measure for an entire sector, the Carbon Offset and Reduction Scheme for International Aviation (CORSIA), which is intended to implement ICAO's goal of carbon neutral growth from 2020 and is projected to offset an estimated 2.5 billion tons of aviation emissions over the fifteen years of the program.[88]

CORSIA will require covered airlines to offset emissions above 2020 levels through purchases of emission reduction credits from outside the aviation sector (for example, REDD+ and the Paris Agreement's new market mechanism). It will

---

[83] Directive 2008/101/EC of the European Parliament and of the Council of 19 November 2008 amending Directive 2003/87/EC so as to include aviation activities in the scheme for greenhouse gas emission allowance trading within the Community (Text with EEA relevance) (13 January 2009) *Official Journal of the European Union* L8/3.

[84] Case C-366/10, *Air Transport Association of America v Secretary of State for Energy and Climate Change* [2011] ECR I-3755.

[85] India and China opposed the EU measure as contrary to the principle of CBDRRC, while the US opposed it on the ground it was an impermissible exercise of extraterritorial jurisdiction. See Joanne Scott and Lavanya Rajamani, 'EU Climate Unilateralism', *European Journal of International Law*, 23/2 (2012): 469.

[86] European Union, 'Stopping the clock of ETS and aviation emissions following last week's International Civil Aviation Organisation (ICAO) Council', Press Release (12 November 2012) <http://europa.eu/rapid/press-release_MEMO-12-854_en.htm> accessed 20 January 2017.

[87] ICAO Environment, 'Carbon Offsetting and Reduction Scheme for International Aviation (CORSIA)' <http://www.icao.int/environmental-protection/Pages/market-based-measures.aspx> accessed 20 January 2017.

[88] ICAO Assembly Resolution A39-3 (6 October 2016). For a number of perspectives on a market-based measure for international aviation, see 'Special Issue on Aviation and Climate Change', *Carbon and Climate Law Review*, 2016/2 (2016): 91.

start with a pilot and first phase, running from 2021–23 and 2023–26, respectively, in which participation will be voluntary. These will be followed by a second phase, beginning in 2027, in which all states are expected to participate, except those in exempt categories, including least developed countries, small island states, and those with aviation activity below a set threshold. Overall, the scheme is expected to cover about three-quarters of anticipated emissions growth. A key issue in the negotiation of CORSIA was whether airlines' offset requirements would be based on their individual emissions growth (which would put the heaviest burden on fast-growing airlines in developing countries), or the sector's total growth (which would make established, slower-growing airlines responsible for offsetting global growth based on their proportionate share of overall aviation activity). CORSIA adopts a 'dynamic approach', under which airlines' offset requirements will initially be tied to global emissions growth, but will over time shift to their individual growth.

As in IMO, there was considerable debate in ICAO about the degree to which CORSIA would differentiate among states. CORSIA does not establish different offsetting requirements for different categories of states, as a few developing countries had sought. But it does reflect differentiation in a number of other ways, including by making participation voluntary in the pilot and first phases, exempting LDCs and small island states, providing for capacity-building, and requiring established airlines to share some of the burden of offsetting emissions growth by fast-growing airlines in developing countries. In order to reflect ICAO's principle of non-discrimination, its offsetting requirements do not apply to routes serviced by airlines of exempt countries.

B. Ozone-depleting substances

The depletion of the ozone layer predated climate change as a matter of international concern, and the international ozone regime[89] influenced the design of the FCCC.[90] Although ODS are potent GHGs,[91] they are not addressed under the FCCC regime.[92] Instead, the climate regime has deferred to the Montreal Protocol, which provides for the reduction and phase-out of a wide range of ODS, including carbon tetrachloride, methyl chloroform, HCFCs, and methyl bromide.[93]

---

[89] The ozone regime consists of the Vienna Convention on the Protection of the Ozone Layer (adopted 22 March 1985, entered into force 22 September 1988) 1513 UNTS 324, the Montreal Protocol, and the associated amendments and decisions of the parties.

[90] Oberthur, Dupont(-roche Kelly) and Matsumoto, Managing Policy Contradictions between the Montreal and Kyoto Protocols (n 58).

[91] For example, CFC-11 has a global warming potential (GWP) of 4660, meaning that it is 4660 times more potent, molecule for molecule, than CO_2, over a 100-year time horizon, and CFC-12 has a GWP of 10,200. IPCC, Climate Change 2013: The Physical Science Basis (2013), Appendix 8.A.

[92] The FCCC's commitments apply only to 'greenhouse gases not controlled by the Montreal Protocol,' FCCC, Arts 4.1(a), 4.2(a), and the Kyoto Protocol emissions targets do not include any ODS. Kyoto Protocol, Annex A (listing gases covered).

[93] The Montreal Protocol has 197 parties, and has resulted in the phase-out of more than 98% of all of the chemicals it controls. UNEP, *Key Achievements of the Montreal Protocol to Date* <http://ozone.unep.org/Publications/MP_Key_Achievements-E.pdf> accessed 20 January 2017.

The Montreal Protocol's reductions in ODS have yielded a significant climate bene-fit.[94] Initially, these climate benefits were simply a by-product of the effort to protect the ozone layer, but, in 2007, the Montreal Protocol parties first explicitly included climate considerations in their decision-making, when they agreed to accelerate the phase-out schedule for HCFCs by ten years—from 2030 to 2020 for 'Article 2 par-ties' (in effect, developed countries) and from 2040 to 2030 for 'Article 5 parties' (ie developing countries with per capita consumption of ODS below a set threshold).[95] The HCFC decision is projected to result in a reduction of emissions of twenty-five $GtCO_{2e}$ between 2010 and 2050—a net contribution to climate change mitigation 'far larger', according to one study, than the reduction from the Kyoto Protocol's first commitment period targets.[96]

Following the adoption of the HCFC decision, attention turned to HFCs, which the Montreal Protocol has indirectly encouraged as non-ozone-depleting substitutes for HCFCs. Although HFCs do not deplete the ozone layer, they are extremely potent GHGs—depending on the gas, as much as 10,800 times more powerful per molecule than CO_2 over a 100-year time horizon[97]—and are included in the basket of six gases regulated by the Kyoto Protocol. So, in encouraging HFCs, the Montreal Protocol has worked at cross-purposes to the UN climate regime. HFCs today account for only about 2% of global GHG emissions,[98] but this figure is projected to grow rapidly, due to increased demand for air conditioning and refrigeration, par-ticularly in developing countries. According to one estimate, by mid-century, HFCs will contribute the equivalent of 5.5–8.8 Gt of CO_2 per year (roughly comparable to total US GHG emissions today) and will account for 9–19% of global GHG emissions,[99] although there is considerable uncertainty about these figures, and the IPCC's representative concentration pathways have 'substantially lower projected growth'.[100]

Initially, some countries questioned regulating HFCs under the Montreal Protocol, because they are not ozone-depleting substances. But, in November 2015, the Montreal Protocol parties agreed to the Dubai Pathway, which initiated

[94] Guus J.M. Velders *et al.*, 'The Importance of the Montreal Protocol in Protecting Climate', *Proceedings of the National Academy of Sciences*, 104 (2007): 4814.

[95] Decision XIX/6, 'Adjustments to the Montreal Protocol with Regard to Annex C, Group I Substances (Hydrochlorofluorocarbons)' (21 September 2007) UNEP/OzL.Pro19/7, 33. Under the Montreal Protocol, 'Article 5 parties' are developing countries whose consumption of certain controlled substances is below 0.3 kilograms per capita. 'Article 2 parties' are all other parties.

[96] Velders, Importance of Montreal Protocol (n 94); see also D.W. Fahey and M.I. Hegglin, *Twenty Questions and Answers about the Ozone Layer: 2010 Update* (Geneva: World Meteorological Organization, 2011), Q61 (estimating that the Montreal Protocol's contribution to climate change mitigation has been five to six times larger than the Kyoto Protocol's contribution during the first commitment period).

[97] IPCC, Climate Change 2013: Physical Science Basis (n 91) Appendix 8.A.

[98] IPCC, Climate Change 2014: Mitigation of Climate Change (2014) 123.

[99] Guus J.M. Velders *et al.*, 'The Large Contribution of Projected HFC Emissions to Future Climate Forcing', *Proceedings of the National Academy of Sciences*, 106/27 (2009): 10949.

[100] IPCC, Climate Change 2013: Physical Science Basis (n 91) 701.

negotiations to phase down the production and use of HFCs.[101] The negotiations concluded the following October at the Kigali conference.

The Montreal Protocol provides two procedures for revisions: first, an amendment procedure to add new chemicals to the protocol's regulatory regime, which requires ratification by two thirds of the protocol parties and binds only those states that ratify,[102] and, second, an 'adjustment' procedure to increase the stringency of controls on substances that the protocol already regulates, which applies to all parties and requires only a two-thirds vote, representing a majority of both Article 5 parties and non-Article 5 parties.[103] The 2007 decision to accelerate the phase-out schedule for HCFCs took the form of an adjustment. In contrast, the Kigali decision to phase down HFCs took the form of an amendment, since the Montreal Protocol does not currently regulate HFCs, and the amendment will apply only to states that give their affirmative consent.

The Kigali Amendment, adopted in October 2016, establishes a detailed schedule to phase down the production and use of HFCs.[104] It requires most 'Article 2 parties' to begin reducing production and use of HFCs in 2019 and to reduce by 85% relative to 2011–13 levels by 2036.[105] It also commits most 'Article 5 parties' to a freeze in 2024 and a phase-down schedule leading to 80% reductions by 2045 relative to 2020–22 levels. A small number of Article 5 countries, including India, Pakistan, and the Gulf states, will have an additional four years in which to get started, and have a different baseline. The amendment envisages trade measures against non-parties by 2030. The amendment also provides for periodic reviews of technology development every five years, in order to consider whether to strengthen the ambition of the reduction schedule. A group of donor countries agreed to provide $80 million to support developing countries in taking early action. The reductions, when fully implemented, will avoid an estimated eighty billion tons of CO_2 equivalent emissions by 2050, and could avoid up to $0.5°$ C of warming by the end of the century.[106]

C. Black carbon and other short-lived climate forcers

Black carbon is a carbonaceous aerosol that is a major component of soot. The biggest single source of black carbon globally is biomass burning in agriculture and forestry, which accounts for about 40% of total emissions. Although black carbon

---

[101] Decision XXVII/1, 'Dubai Pathway on Hyrdrofluorocarbons' (5 November 2015) UN Doc. UNEP/OzL.Pro.27/13.

[102] The amendment procedures for the Montreal Protocol are set forth in its parent agreement, the Vienna Convention (n 89) Art 9.

[103] Montreal Protocol, Art 2.9.

[104] Decision XXVIII/1, 'Further Amendment of the Montreal Protocol' (15 November 2016) UNEP/OzL.Pro.28/12, 31. The text of the Kigali Amendment is set out in Annex I. Ibid, 46.

[105] Belarus, Kazakhstan, Russia, Tajikistan, and Uzbekistan have a slightly slower phasedown schedule.

[106] Jeff Tollefson, 'Nations Agree to Ban Refrigerants that Worsen Climate Change', *Nature* (15 October 2016) <http://www.nature.com/news/nations-agree-to-ban-refrigerants-that-worsen-climate-change-1.20810> accessed 20 January 2017.

is not a GHG, it contributes to global warming by directly absorbing visible sunlight, darkening snow, and influencing cloud formation. According to some studies, black carbon is the second biggest contributor to global warming after CO_2.[107] But there is still no scientific consensus concerning its quantitative contribution to climate change.[108]

In contrast to CO_2 and other GHGs, which stay in the atmosphere for decades or centuries, black carbon has a short atmospheric lifetime, ranging from days to weeks, and is often referred to as a 'short-lived climate forcer' (SLCF). Other SLCFs include tropospheric ozone, methane, and some HFCs (the latter two of which are regulated under the Kyoto Protocol).

The short atmospheric lifetime of black carbon has several important consequences. First, reducing emissions has an immediate effect on concentration levels and hence on temperature. Controlling black carbon could thus play a crucial role in slowing global warming in the near term. Second, black carbon is not well-mixed in the atmosphere, so its effects are largely regional. The climate effects are particularly intense in snow-covered areas, where deposition of black carbon darkens snow and ice, increasing their absorption of sunlight and hence making them melt more rapidly. As a result, in addressing black carbon emissions, what matters is not just the total amount of the reductions, but also where the reductions occur. Reductions would be particularly beneficial in areas where the emissions are deposited in ice-covered areas such as the Arctic, and could potentially reduce warming of the Arctic by about two-thirds over the next thirty years.[109]

Because black carbon has largely regional impacts, proposals to regulate black carbon have focused on the LRTAP Convention, a regional agreement covering Europe, Russia and North America, which includes all of the Arctic circumpolar countries.[110] Adopted in 1979 under the auspices of the UN Economic Commission for Europe (UNECE), the LRTAP Convention now has seven protocols addressing different types of pollutants, including sulphur dioxide, nitrogen oxides, volatile organic compounds, ammonia, heavy metals, and persistent organic pollutants, as well as the 1999 Gothenburg Protocol, which adopts a multi-pollutant, multi-effect approach.

In 2009, the LRTAP Convention Executive Body created an ad hoc expert group on black carbon under the Gothenburg Protocol, which issued its report in 2010, recommending amendment of the protocol. In 2012, the twenty-five Gothenburg

---

[107] T.C. Bond *et al.*, 'Bounding the Role of Black Carbon in the Climate System: A Scientific Assessment', *Journal of Geophysical Research: Atmospheres* 118 (2013): 5380, 5381. One study estimated black carbon forcing as 25–88% of CO_2 forcing. V. Ramanathan and G. Carmichael, 'Global and Regional Climate Changes Due to Black Carbon', *Nature Geoscience*, 1 (2008): 221.

[108] IPCC, Climate Change 2013: The Physical Science Basis (n 91), 718 (noting 'wide' uncertainties); LRTAP Convention, Black Carbon: Report by the Co-Chairs of the Ad Hoc Expert Group on Black Carbon (2010) UN Doc. ECE/EB.AIR/2010/7 and Corr.1, 6.

[109] UNEP/WMO, *Integrated Assessment of Black Carbon and Tropospheric Ozone* (Nairobi: UNEP, 2011) 3.

[110] LRTAP Convention (n 30).

Protocol parties adopted (1) an amendment[111] that adds fine particulate matter as a regulated pollutant and specifically identifies black carbon as a component of fine particulate matter, and (2) a guidance document on reporting of black carbon emissions. When the amendment comes into force, it will require parties to reduce their emissions of fine particulate matter by 22% from 2005 levels by 2020. However, these requirements will apply only to the protocol parties, a group that does not include China, India, or any other developing country.

In parallel with the LRTAP Convention, the US and six partners established the Climate and Clean Air Coalition to Reduce Short-Lived Climate Pollutants (CCAC) in 2012. CCAC is administered by the United Nations Environment Programme (UNEP) and is open to membership by states, international organizations, and non-state actors (including sub-state initiatives like the C-40 cities coalition, civil society groups, scientific organizations, and business). As of August 2016, fifty states, sixteen international organizations, and forty-five non-state actors had become CCAC partners. In joining CCAC, states commit to controlling and reducing their emissions of SLCFs. In addition, CCAC has undertaken several sectoral initiatives.[112]

Finally, the Arctic Council has also begun to consider the problem of black carbon. The Arctic Council was established in 1996 as a high-level intergovernmental forum.[113] Its permanent participants include not only the eight Arctic states, but also representatives of Arctic indigenous peoples. In 2009, the Arctic Council established a Task Force on Short-Lived Climate Forcers, which issued a report in 2013 recommending measures to reduce emissions of black carbon and methane. The Arctic Contaminants Action Program also has a variety of projects relating to black carbon and is working to complete a black carbon emissions inventory in 2017.

D. UN Security Council

The impacts of climate change—including sea-level rise, droughts, floods, extreme weather events, and migration flows—could cause instability and conflict and thus have significant security implications.[114] The Security Council has responsibility under Chapter VII of the UN Charter for addressing threats to international peace and security. The issue of climate change was first brought before the Security Council in 2007 by the United Kingdom, and was raised again in 2011 (by Germany) and 2013 (by Pakistan). China, Russia, and most developing countries have questioned the link between climate change and international security, and argue that climate change should be considered by the FCCC and the General

---

[111] Decision 2012/2, 'Amendment of the Text and Annexes II to the 1999 Protocol and the Addition of New Annexes X and XI' (4 May 2012) UN Doc ECE/EB.AIR/111/Add.1, 6.

[112] Birgit Lode, 'The Climate and Clean Air Coalition to Reduce Short-Lived Climate Pollutants (CCAC)', *ASIL Insights*, 17/20 (2013).

[113] Koivurova and VanderZwaag, Arctic Council at 10 Years (n 29).

[114] See generally Jürgen Scheffran *et al.* (eds), *Climate Change, Human Security and Violent Conflict: Challenges for Societal Instability* (Heidelberg: Springer-Verlag, 2012).

Assembly, not the Security Council. The Security Council debate in 2007 led to a UN General Assembly Resolution[115] and a Report by the Secretary-General.[116] Following the 2011 Security Council debate, the Council president issued a statement expressing the Council's concern that climate change may, 'in the long run, aggravate certain existing threats to international peace and security' and that the loss of territory by small island states resulting from sea-level rise could have security implications.[117]

E. Informal political forums

Climate change is addressed not only in regulatory institutions such as IMO and ICAO, but also in various informal political forums—some focused specifically on climate change, such as the Major Economies Forum on Energy and Climate (MEF), and others with a more general remit, in which climate change is only one of many agenda items. These forums involve smaller groups of countries and are sometimes described as 'clubs',[118] although few are 'clubs' in the strict economic sense, that is, groups that exclude others in order to provide private benefits.[119] Although supporters of the 'starting small' strategy argue that it could produce stronger collective action and greater emission reductions, empirical studies suggest that, thus far, climate clubs have served primarily as 'forums for political dialogue' and 'have achieved very little in terms of actual emissions reductions'.[120]

1. Major Economies Forum on Energy and Climate

The MEF is a 'minilateral'[121] forum intended to complement the FCCC negotiations by allowing more informal discussions among the major developed and developing countries. The seventeen countries that comprise the MEF[122] account for more than 80% of global GHGs,[123] so an agreement among them could largely address the climate change problem.

---

[115] General Assembly Resolution 63/281, 'Climate change and its possible security implications' (11 June 2009) UN Doc. A/RES/63/281.

[116] UN Secretary-General, 'Climate change and its possible security implications' (11 September 2009) UN Doc A/64/350.

[117] 'Implications of Climate Change Important when Climate Impacts Drive Conflict' (20 July 2011) UN Doc SC/10332.

[118] Lutz Weischer, Jennifer Morgan, and Milap Patel, 'Climate Clubs: Can Small Groups of Countries Make a Big Difference in Addressing Climate Change?', *Review of European Community and International Environmental Law*, 21/3 (2012): 177.

[119] See Hovi, Climate Change Mitigation: A Role for Climate Clubs? (n 5).   [120] Ibid.

[121] The term, 'minilateral', is used in contrast to 'multilateral' to refer to cooperation among a smaller number of countries. See Moises Naim, 'Minilateralism', *Foreign Policy* (June 21, 2009) (defining minilateralism as bringing to the table 'the smallest number of countries needed to have the largest possible impact on solving a particular problem').

[122] Australia, Brazil, Canada, China, the EU, France, Germany, India, Indonesia, Italy, Japan, Korea, Mexico, Russia, South Africa, the United Kingdom, and the US. Major Economies Forum on Energy and Climate <http://www.majoreconomiesforum.org/> accessed 20 January 2017.

[123] World Resources Institute, CAIT Climate Data Explorer <http://cait.wri.org/> accessed 20 January 2017.

The MEF is the successor to the Major Economies Meeting on Energy Security and Climate Change (MEM), launched by US President George W. Bush in 2007, which emerged from a felt need among developed countries (and, in particular, the US) for the 'major emitters' to have an opportunity to address climate change and energy issues, shorn of the shackles of the seemingly cumbersome UN process and the constraints of the Kyoto negotiations (that included neither large developing countries like China and India, which did not have mitigation targets, nor the US, which had rejected it). At the time, the US opposed the negotiation of any new UN climate change instrument, and many feared that the MEM was an attempt by the US to bypass the UN climate regime. The Obama Administration re-launched the MEM as the MEF in order to dispel these fears. The MEF is explicitly intended to complement rather than displace the FCCC process, by providing political leadership and direction to the UN climate regime. Since its inception, the MEF has met several times a year and has provided an opportunity for senior officials from key countries to meet informally, without the distractions that often accompany the annual climate conferences, in order to better understand each other's views. Although it has helped incubate ideas, the MEF has been hampered in its efforts to broker deals among major emitters by the fact that most developing countries prefer to negotiate in the FCCC process, where they feel a greater sense of empowerment and ownership.

2. G-8/G-20

Several 'G' clubs also provide political direction to the climate regime. These 'G' clubs are informal meetings generally held at the leaders or ministerial level. They are distinguishable from negotiating coalitions and groups[124] in that have formal membership, rotating presidencies, and mandates covering a broader universe than climate change. These 'G' clubs forge policy statements, but they do not develop common negotiating positions.

The G-8 is the oldest G club, and comprises the eight largest developed country economies,[125] which account for roughly half of global GDP and a third of global GHG emissions. Beginning in 1990, G-8 leaders have regularly included language on climate change in their communiqués,[126] and have had a separate agenda item on climate change since 2003. At the 2005 Gleneagles Summit, G-8 leaders adopted a 'plan of action' on climate change, clean energy, and sustainable development and established a dialogue to monitor implementation.[127] But, generally, G-8 meetings have served as a forum for leaders to provide political guidance for the FCCC process. For example, in 2009, during the run-up to the Copenhagen

---

[124] The negotiating coalitions active in the climate change negotiations are discussed in Chapter 3, Section II.B.2.

[125] France, Germany, Italy, the United Kingdom, Japan, the US, Canada, and Russia (since 1998).

[126] David Sandalow and Hannah Volfson, 'G8 Summit Leaders' Statements, Climate Change Language 1990-2004' (Washington: Brookings Institution, 30 June 2005).

[127] Gleneagles Plan of Action: Climate Change, Clean Energy, and Sustainable Development (9 July 2005) <https://www.gov.uk/government/uploads/system/uploads/attachment_data/file/48584/gleneagles-planofaction.pdf> accessed 20 January 2017.

conference, the G-8 leaders adopted goals of limiting global warming to no more than 2° C and reducing global emissions by 50% (and their emissions by 80%) by 2050.[128] The 2° C goal was endorsed in the 2009 Copenhagen Accord and formally adopted into the FCCC process in the 2010 Cancun Agreements, but the 50% emissions reduction by 2050 goal proved too controversial to be adopted by the UN climate regime. The G-8 has since 2005 also invited the leaders of the five largest developing countries in a G-8+5 formation for separate sessions.[129]

The G-20 is a parallel club involving both developed and developing countries. It was established in 1999, in the aftermath of the 1997 financial crisis, to address economic issues. Originally a meeting of finance ministers, the G-20 became a leaders' summit in 2008. G-20 members represent 90% of global GDP and account for 84% of fossil fuel emissions. Although the mandate of the G-20 focuses on promoting economic growth, the G-20 has recently begun to include climate change on its agenda. But progress in the G-20 on climate change has been modest compared to that in the G-8.[130] The 2009 G-20 meeting called for the phase out over the medium term of 'inefficient' fossil fuel subsidies,[131] and the 2015 meeting characterized climate change as 'one of the greatest challenges of our time'.[132]

3. Bilateral initiatives

In addition to plurilateral forums, bilateral climate cooperation between countries has also played a critical role in reaching a climate deal and shaping its contours, and will likely play a role in implementing it. The US and the EU, in particular, and the French in the lead up to the Paris conference, proactively sought out bilateral relationships and understandings with China, India and Brazil, among others.[133] These served as parallel frameworks for dialogue in support of the formal FCCC process. For instance, the political breakthrough in the Paris Agreement on

---

[128] L'Aquila Declaration on Responsible Leadership for a Sustainable Future (8 July 2009) para 65 <http://www.g8italia2009.it/G8/Home/Summit/G8-G8_Layout_locale-1199882116809_Atti.htm> accessed 20 January 2017.

[129] G8+5 Academies' Joint Statement, 'Climate Change and the Transformation of Energy Technologies for a Low Carbon Future' (May 2009) <http://www.nationalacademies.org/includes/G8+5energy-climate09.pdf> accessed 20 January 2017.

[130] Doug Koplow and Steve Kretzmann, 'G20 Fossil Fuel Subsidy Phase Out: A Review of Current Gaps and Needed Changes to Achieve Success' (November 2010) <http://priceofoil.org/content/uploads/2010/11/OCI.ET_.G20FF.FINAL_.pdf > accessed 20 January 2017.

[131] G20 Leaders' Statement, The Pittsburgh Summit (24–25 September 2009) <https://www.treasury.gov/resource-center/international/g7-g20/Documents/pittsburgh_summit_leaders_statement_250909.pdf> accessed 20 January 2017.

[132] G20 Leaders' Communique, Antalya Summit (15–16 November 2015) <http://www.consilium.europa.eu/en/meetings/international-summit/2015/11/15-16/> accessed 20 January 2017.

[133] See eg EU-China Joint Statement on Climate Change, European Council, Brussels (29 June 2015) <http://www.consilium.europa.eu/en/press/press-releases/2015/06/29-eu-china-climate-statement/> accessed 20 January 2017; Joint Statement on the First US-India Strategic and Commercial Dialogue, US Department of State, Office of the Spokesperson, Washington DC (22 September 2015); Jennifer Helgeson, 'France & Brazil: A Common Call to Climate Change Action in the Amazon!' (30 November 2009) <http://www.climaticoanalysis.org/post/france-brazil-a-common-call-to-climate-change-action-in-the-amazon/#> accessed 20 January 2017.

the principle of CBDRRC, reflected in the addition of the phrase 'in light of different national circumstances', emerged out of a US-China statement in 2014.[134] In addition, such bilateral cooperation between key countries helped structure and channel initiatives and projects, as for instance on technology between India and the US.[135]

V. SUB-NATIONAL CLIMATE GOVERNANCE

Although climate change is a quintessentially global problem that requires a global solution, local and regional institutions also play important roles in climate governance. Climate change implicates many policies that have traditionally been addressed at the regional and local levels, such as land-use planning, transportation, and waste management. An Australian study found that local authorities 'have a degree of influence over half of all GHG emissions',[136] and the International Energy Agency estimates that cities account for more than 70% of global CO_2 emissions.[137] So local and regional governmental policies can have a tremendous effect on the climate change problem, for better or worse. A city can invest in mass transit and thereby reduce reliance on cars, for example, or it can adopt zoning rules that encourage urban sprawl. It can adopt building codes that encourage energy efficiency, waste management practices that minimize methane emissions from landfills, and coastal zone management laws that require developers to consider sea level rise, or it can continue business as usual.

Not only do local governments have authority over many aspects of the climate change problem, agreement is often easier to achieve at the local level, where people's values and interests are more homogeneous than at the national or international levels. In the US, for example, many cities and states have been able to adopt ambitious climate change policies, even while climate policy at the national level remains gridlocked. Under the Mayors' Climate Protection Agreement, for example, the mayors of more than one thousand US cities, with a total population of nearly ninety million people, pledged to meet or beat the Kyoto Protocol's emissions target in their communities.[138] Similarly, California has enacted an ambitious emissions trading program,[139] even though similar proposals in Congress failed to be adopted. As of 2016, more than twenty cities, states and regions around the world

---

[134] US-China Joint Announcement on Climate Change, Beijing, China (12 November 2014) <https://obamawhitehouse.archives.gov/the-press-office/2014/11/11/us-china-joint-announcement-climate-change> accessed 20 January 2017.

[135] Joint Statement on the First US-India Strategic and Commercial Dialogue (n 133).

[136] Betsill and Bulkeley, Cities and the Multilevel Governance of Climate Change (n 32) 143.

[137] International Energy Agency, *World Energy Outlook* (Paris: OECD/IEA, 2008) 180.

[138] US Conference of Mayors Climate Protection Agreement <http://www.usmayors.org/climate-protection/agreement.htm> accessed 20 January 2017. In contrast to the Compact of Mayors and the C40 initiative (see nn 19–20 above), the Mayors' Climate Protection Agreement involves only US mayors.

[139] Center for Climate and Energy Solutions (C2ES), *California Cap-and-Trade Program Summary* (Arlington, VA, January 2014).

had adopted carbon pricing instruments such as an emissions trading program or a carbon tax, with those in China covering the largest volume of emissions (approximately 1 $GtCO_2e$), through pilot emissions trading systems in seven cities.[140]

Provinces and localities not only contribute to climate change; they are also affected by it. Climate change will have significant impacts on cities, for example, through heatwaves, flooding, and reductions in water supply. As an OECD study observes, '[t]he fate of the Earth's climate and the vulnerability of human society to climate change are intrinsically linked to the way the cities develop over the coming decades and century'.[141]

The vertical relationships between local and national climate change policies can be top-down, bottom-up, or hybrid. In a highly centralized state such as France, the national climate change program includes a variety of local policies, which are imposed from the top-down. In implementing these policies, local governments act essentially as agents of the national government. Top-down policies can also circumscribe local and regional governments—for example, by imposing uniform national standards or pre-empting local action. In such cases, national policies represent a ceiling rather than a floor.[142]

In bottom-up systems, by contrast, local and regional authorities have significant autonomy to develop their own climate change policies, which may percolate up to the national level. In the US, for example, the federal government granted a waiver that allowed California to develop its own emissions standards for automobiles, which require a 34% reduction in GHG emissions by new cars by 2025.[143]

The vertical relationship between local and national authorities can also have a hybrid form. Rather than either imposing national standards or taking a totally hands-off approach, the national government may promote local action from the top-down through financial assistance, but still leave local governments with significant autonomy to develop their own climate policies from the bottom-up.

Ordinarily, local governance is not directly relevant to international law. International law regulates the behavior of states, not sub-national actors such as provinces or cities. As a result, even though much governance takes place at the local level, local institutions typically have little interaction with international institutions. To the extent international norms filter down to the local level, it is only through the mediation of national law.

Although climate change is no exception to this general rule, it is unusual in that local policies to address climate change are not purely local; they are linked

[140] World Bank and Ecofys, *State and Trends of Carbon Pricing: 2015* (Washington, D.C.: World Bank, 2015) 10.

[141] Corfee-Morlot *et al.*, Cities, Climate Change and Multilateral Governance (n 32) 13.

[142] For a general discussion of environmental federalism, see Michael D. Jones, Elizabeth A. Shanahan, and Lisa J. Hammer, 'Environmental Policy', in Donald P. Haider-Market (ed), *The Oxford Handbook of State and Local Government* (Oxford University Press, 2014) 778; see also Jonathan H. Adler, 'When Is Two a Crowd? The Impact of Federal Action on State Environmental Regulation', *Harvard Environmental Law Review*, 31/1 (2007): 67.

[143] California Air Resources Board, 'California's Advanced Clean Car Program' <https://www.arb.ca.gov/msprog/acc/acc.htm> accessed 20 January 2017.

transnationally with local policies in other countries in order to share information and promote common values.[144] The C40 Cities Climate Leadership Group, for example, is a network of more than eighty megacities, which represent 600 million people and more than 25% of the global economy.[145] It was preceded by the ICLEI Cities for Climate Protection Program, which included more than 1000 cities from around the world.[146] Similarly, sub-national jurisdictions that have adopted emissions trading programs have, in some cases, linked up with one another to create transnational carbon markets.[147] An example is the linkage of the California and Quebec emissions trading systems that began in 2014. These sub-national groupings represent an alternative method to international law to achieve policy integration.

VI. JUDICIAL GOVERNANCE

Traditionally, courts and tribunals have played a comparatively modest role in the development and implementation of international environmental law.[148] Although most multilateral environmental agreements (MEAs)—including the FCCC—provide for some system of dispute settlement, few cases have been brought either internationally[149] or domestically[150] to interpret or enforce these agreements, and the same is true for customary international law. Instead, political institutions have

---

[144] Betsill and Bulkeley, Cities and the Multilevel Governance of Climate Change (n 32) 143 (twenty-eight transnational networks of subnational governments in Europe).

[145] C40 was initiated in 2005 by the Mayor of London, Ken Livingstone, and was led by former New York City Mayor Michael Bloomberg from 2010 to 2013.

[146] ICLEI stands for International Council for Local Environmental Initiatives. It was founded in 1990 and now goes by the name, Local Governments for a Sustainable Future. See also n 19 above.

[147] See generally Matthew Ransom and Robert N. Stavins, 'Linkage of Greenhouse Gas Emissions Trading Systems: Learning from Experience' (Washington, D.C.: Resources for the Future, November 2013).

[148] There is an extensive literature on the role of adjudication in addressing climate change, including: Jacqueline Peel and Hari M. Osofsky, *Climate Change Litigation: Regulatory Pathways to Cleaner Energy* (Cambridge University Press, 2015); William C.G. Burns and Hari M. Osofsky (eds), *Adjudicating Climate Change: State, National, and International Approaches* (Cambridge University Press, 2009); Michael Faure and Marjan Peeters, *Climate Change Liability* (Cheltenham: Edward Elgar, 2011); Richard Lord *et al.* (eds), *Climate Change Liability: Transnational Law and Practice* (Cambridge University Press, 2012); Michael J. Faure and Andre Nollkaemper, 'International Liability as an Instrument to Prevent and Compensate for Climate Change', *Stanford Journal of International Law*, 43 (2007): 123. For a critique of climate change litigation, see Eric A. Posner, 'Climate Change and International Human Rights Litigation: A Critical Appraisal', *University of Pennsylvania Law Review*, 155/6 (2007): 1925.

[149] Roda Verheyen and Cathrin Zengerling, 'International Dispute Settlement', in Cinnamon P. Carlarne, Kevin R. Gray, and Richard G. Tarasofsky (eds), *The Oxford Handbook of International Climate Change Law* (Oxford University Press, 2016) 417; Cesare Romano, 'International Dispute Settlement', in Daniel Bodansky, Jutta Brunnée, and Ellen Hey (eds), *Oxford Handbook of International Environmental Law* (Oxford University Press, 2007) 1036.

[150] Burns and Osofsky (eds), Adjudicating Climate Change (n 148). For a general discussion of the role of national courts, see Daniel Bodansky and Jutta Brunnée, 'The Role of National Courts in the Field of International Environmental Law', *Review of European Community and International Environmental Law*, 7/1 (1998): 11.

been the dominant players in the international environmental law process: inter-governmental negotiations and legislatures in the development of norms, and the executive branch in their application.

Recently, this situation has begun to change, both in international environmental law generally and, more particularly, in the area of climate change law.[151] A growing number of climate change cases have been initiated both internationally and domestically, reflecting a greater role by courts and tribunals in climate change governance:[152]

- At the international level, an Inuit group filed a petition before the Inter-American Commission on Human Rights in 2005, alleging that the US had violated their human rights, including the rights to culture, life, health, and shelter, by failing to reduce its emissions.[153]

- Between 2004 and 2006, several environmental non-governmental organizations (NGOs) filed petitions to the World Heritage Committee, arguing that climate change was a threat to the Great Barrier Reef, Waterton-Glacier National Park, and other world heritage sites.[154]

- A number of island states, led by Palau, proposed in 2012 that the General Assembly request an advisory opinion from the International Court of Justice regarding the 'responsibilities of States, under international law, to ensure that activities carried out under their jurisdiction or control that emit greenhouse gases do not damage other States'.[155]

- At the national level, the US Supreme Court held in *Massachusetts v EPA* that CO_2 is a pollutant that can be regulated by the Environmental Protection

---

[151] Recent environmental cases include the *MOX Case* between Ireland and the United Kingdom (Permanent Court of Arbitration, 2 July 2003), the *Pulp Mills Case* between Argentina and Uruguay (see Chapter 2, Section III.A.1), and the *Aerial Herbicide Spraying Case* between Ecuador and Colombia, which was resolved through a settlement by the parties; see ICJ Press Release 2013/20 <http://www.icj-cij.org/docket/files/138/17526.pdf> accessed 20 January 2017.

[152] A compendium of cases related to climate change is maintained by the NGO, Climate Justice, and can be found at: <http://www.climatelaw.org> accessed 20 January 2017.

[153] Petition to the Inter-American Commission on Human Rights Seeking Relief from Violations Resulting from Global Warming Caused by Acts and Omissions of the United States (7 December 2005) <http://www.inuitcircumpolar.com/inuit-petition-inter-american-commission-on-human-rights-to-oppose-climate-change-caused-by-the-united-states-of-america.html> accessed 20 January 2017. See also Chapter 9, Sections II.D.1 and II.E.1.

[154] World Heritage Committee, Decision 29 COM 7B.a, 'General Issues: Threats to World Heritage Properties' (9 September 2005) Doc WHC-05/29.COM/22, 36; Decision 30 COM 7.1, 'Issues Relating to the State of Conservation of World Heritage Properties: The Impacts of Climate Change on World Heritage Properties' (23 August 2006) Doc WHC-06/30.COM/19, 7. See generally Erica J. Thorson, 'The World Heritage Convention and Climate Change: The Case for a Climate Change Mitigation Strategy beyond the Kyoto Protocol', in Burns and Osofsky (eds), Adjudicating Climate Change (n 148) 255. Articles 4 and 6 of the World Heritage Convention require parties not to take 'any deliberate measures which might damage directly or indirectly' world heritage sites located in another country.

[155] Yale Center for Environmental Law and Policy, 'Climate Change and the International Court of Justice' (2013) <https://papers.ssrn.com/sol3/papers.cfm?abstract_id=2309943##> accessed 20 January 2017. For further discussion of a possible ICJ case, see Chapter 2, Section III.B.2.

Agency (EPA) under the Clean Air Act.[156] Meanwhile, in Canada, the environmental NGO, Friends of the Earth, brought a case alleging that the Canadian government had violated the Kyoto Protocol Implementation Act, by failing to comply with the protocol.[157]

- The Land and Environment Court of New South Wales, Australia, found that environmental impact assessments of coal-mining projects must consider emissions from the subsequent burning of the coal.[158]

- In a negligence case brought by a Dutch Foundation and hundreds of individuals, *Urgenda Foundation v The State of the Netherlands,* a Dutch court found in June 2015 that the government's 20% emissions reduction target breached its duty of care to take mitigation measures, and ordered the government to adopt at least a 25% reduction target.[159]

- Most recently, the Lahore High Court in Pakistan, in a September 2015 decision in *Leghari v Federation of Pakistan,* found that the government had made 'no progress' in implementing its National Climate Policy and Framework, held that this failure violated citizens' human rights, and ordered the establishment of a commission to oversee implementation of the government's adaptation plan.[160]

Adjudication relating to climate change varies along several dimensions, including its function, the source of law involved, and the tribunal that hears the case. The following sections consider each of these issues.

A. Functions of litigation

Climate change litigation can serve several potentially overlapping functions. Some cases seek to limit GHG emissions, for example, by compelling legislative or regulatory action.[161] The World Heritage Committee petitions, for example, sought an opinion that the World Heritage Convention obligates states parties to reduce their emissions in order to protect world heritage sites threatened by climate change, such as the Great Barrier Reef. Until recently, both international and domestic tribunals were reluctant to find that international law requires governments to reduce national emissions, given the far-reaching political implications such a ruling would have. In the case involving the Great Barrier Reef, the World Heritage Committee found that the issue of emissions mitigation was being addressed in the

---

[156] *Massachusetts v EPA,* 549 U.S. 497 (2007).
[157] *Friends of the Earth v Canada,* 2008 FC 1183 [2009] 3 F.C.R. 201.
[158] *Gray v Minister of Planning* [2006] LGERA 258; Brian J. Preston, 'The Influence of Climate Change Litigation on Governments and the Private Sector', *Climate Law,* 2/4 (2011): 485.
[159] *Urgenda Foundation v. The State of the Netherlands,* C/09/456689/HA ZA 13-1396 (judgment of 24 June 2015); see Jolene Lin, 'The First Successful Climate Negligence Case: A Comment on *Urgenda Foundation v the State of the Netherlands*', *Climate Law,* 5/1 (2015): 65.
[160] *Leghari v Federation of Pakistan,* Lahore High Court Green Bench, Case No. W.P. No. 25501/2015.
[161] See Preston, Influence of Climate Change Litigation (n 158).

UN climate regime, and instead focused on the problem of adapting world heritage sites to the impacts of climate change.[162] Similarly, in the Canadian case brought by Friends of the Earth, the court found that the issue of whether Canada had violated the Kyoto Protocol was a political question, and concluded that it had 'no role to play reviewing the reasonableness of the government's response to Canada's Kyoto commitments'.[163] However, a number of national cases have held that the government can or must take into account climate change in its regulatory and administrative decision-making. For example, the plaintiffs were successful in *Massachusetts v EPA* in arguing that US federal law allows the Environmental Protection Agency to regulate GHG emissions, since this outcome left decisions about emissions mitigation in the hands of EPA rather than the courts. Cases involving permitting decisions by the government have also had some success, since they concern the legality of particular projects under existing national law, rather than requiring the courts to make broad, politically-charged rulings about international duties to reduce emissions. New Zealand courts, for example, have held that the government must consider, in deciding whether to permit the construction of wind farms and coal-fired power plants, the effect of a proposed project on GHG emissions.[164] Australian courts have also held that permitting decisions regarding power plants must take into account the effects on GHG emissions.[165]

More recently, several courts have gone even further and have directly ordered the government to take stronger climate action. In the *Urgenda Case*, described above, a Dutch court ordered the government to adopt a stronger emissions reduction target.[166] And in the *Leghari Case*, also described above, Pakistan's Lahore High Court ordered the establishment of a commission to oversee implementation of the government's adaptation plan.[167]

Another category of cases involves tort claims for climate change damages. Although such claims can have a deterrent effect on future emissions, their immediate goal is to provide compensation to the victims.[168] One of the main barriers to such cases is the problem of defining climate change damages and attributing them to particular actors.[169] At present, the most that science can say is that climate

---

[162] See n 154 above and accompanying text.

[163] *Friends of the Earth v Canada*, 2008 FC 1183 [2009] 3 F.C.R. 201. The Canadian court of appeals subsequently upheld the lower court ruling, and the Supreme Court declined to hear the appeal.

[164] *Genesis Power Ltd. v Franklin District Council*, Decision No. A 148/2005; *Greenpeace New Zealand v Northland Regional Council and Might River Power Limited*, High Court of New Zealand, Auckland Registry, CIV 206-404-004617 (2006).

[165] William C.G. Burns and Hari M. Osofsky, 'Overview: The Exigencies that Drive Potential Causes of Action for Climate Change', in Burns and Osofsky (eds), Adjudicating Climate Change (n 148) 1, 23.

[166] See n 159 above and accompanying text.

[167] See n 160 above and accompanying text.

[168] David A. Grossman, 'Tort-Based Climate Litigation', in Burns and Osofsky (eds), Adjudicating Climate Change (n 148) 193.

[169] Christina Voight, 'Climate Change and Damages', in Carlarne, Gray, and Tarasofsky (eds), Oxford Handbook of International Climate Change Law (n 149) 464.

change increases the likelihood or intensity of a particular kind of event, like a heat wave or storm, not that climate change is the 'but for' cause.[170]

Finally, even if unsuccessful, climate change litigation can help raise public awareness.[171] By focusing on particular victims and particular impacts, litigation helps give climate change damages a human face. As David Hunter notes, the Inuit petition 'tells a story about the impacts of climate change in human terms far removed from the antiseptic discussion[s] of GHG concentrations or global mean temperatures that have traditionally predominated international climate negotiations'.[172] Similarly, petitions to the World Bank Inspection Panel cannot compel a project to be stopped. But, by focusing attention on the harms caused by the project, a petition can help mobilize public opposition and thereby influence decisions about whether to allow or modify the project.

B. Source of law

Climate change litigation also varies depending on the source of law involved. A few cases have alleged violations of international law. For example, the *Friends of the Earth Case* in Canada alleged violations of the FCCC and the Kyoto Protocol. The proposal by Palau to request an advisory opinion from the ICJ would have explicitly focused on the responsibility of states under international law. Similarly, the Inuit petition alleged violations of international human rights law, the World Heritage petitions concerned putative duties to mitigate emissions under the World Heritage Convention, and a Nigerian decision on natural gas flaring by oil companies found that flaring violated the human rights of the local population, not only under the Nigerian constitution, but also under the African Charter on Human and Peoples' Rights.[173]

In some cases, national courts have employed international norms for interpretive purposes. In *Leghari*, for example, the Lahore High Court looked to the principles of sustainable development, precaution, and inter-generational equity in finding that the Pakistani government violated the fundamental rights of its citizens by failing to implement its climate change adaptation policy. Similarly, in *Urgenda*, the Dutch court looked to international norms such as the 2° C temperature limit in finding that the government had breached its duty of care by failing to take stronger mitigation measures.[174]

---

[170] See Myles Allen *et al.*, 'Scientific Challenges in the Attribution of Harm to Human Influence on Climate', *University of Pennsylvania Law Review*, 155/6 (2007): 1353.

[171] David B. Hunter, 'The Implications of Climate Change Litigation: Litigation for International Environmental Law-Making,' in Burns and Osofsky (eds), Adjudicating Climate Change (n 148) 357.

[172] Ibid, 360.

[173] *Jonah Gbemre v Shell Petroleum Development Co. Nigeria Ltd et al.* (2005) FHCNLR (Nigeria), (2005) AHRLR 151 (NgHC 2005). On the *Gbemre Case*, see Amy Sinden, 'An Emerging Human Right to Security from Climate Change: The Case against Gas Flaring in Nigeria', in Burns and Osofsky (eds), Adjudicating Climate Change (n 148) 173.

[174] See Lin, First Successful Climate Negligence Case (n 159).

Many of the cases to date, however, have involved national rather than international law. The cases brought in US courts, for example, have concerned the Clean Air Act,[175] the National Environmental Policy Act,[176] public nuisance law,[177] and the Endangered Species Act.[178] A German case requiring disclosure of the climate change impacts of projects supported by the German export credit agency was decided on the basis of the German Access to Environmental Information Act.[179] And New Zealand and Australian cases concerning power plant permits involved the Resource Management Act of 1991 in the New Zealand cases, and the Victorian Planning and Environment Act in the Australian case.[180] In most instances, national laws such as these establish more precise obligations than international agreements such as the FCCC or the World Heritage Convention, and thus provide a stronger basis for judicial governance.

C. Forum

A third variable in climate change litigation is the forum where a case is brought. In addition to national courts, possibilities at the international level include:[181]

- The International Court of Justice. Since few states currently accept the compulsory jurisdiction of the ICJ, an ICJ ruling would most likely take the form of an advisory opinion.[182]

- The International Tribunal for the Law of the Sea (ITLOS), which has jurisdiction over cases involving the UN Convention on the Law of the Sea,[183] the 1995 Fish Stocks Agreement,[184] and other related

---

[175] *Massachusetts v EPA*, 549 U.S. 497 (2007).

[176] *Friends of the Earth v Watson*, 2005 US Dist. LEXIS 42335 (2005). The government ultimately settled the case in 2009, agreeing to consider climate change impacts attributable to federally-supported projects.

[177] *American Electric Power v Connecticut*, 131 S.Ct. 2527 (2011) (Clean Air Act displaces federal common law right to injunctive relief based on public nuisance); *Native Village of Kivalina v ExxonMobil Corp*, 696 F.2d 849 (9th Cir. 2012) (Clean Air Act displaces federal public nuisance claim for damages).

[178] See Brendan R. Cummings and Kassie R. Siegel, 'Biodiversity, Global Warming, and the United States Endangered Species Act: The Role of Domestic Wildlife Law in Addressing Greenhouse Gas Emissions', in Burns and Osofsky (eds), Adjudicating Climate Change (n 148) 145.

[179] Hans-Joachim Koch, Michael Lührs and Roda Verheyen, 'Germany', in Lord *et al.* (eds), Climate Change Liability (n 148) 376, 414.

[180] Burns and Osofsky, Overview (n 165) 22–4.

[181] Verheyen and Zengerling, International Dispute Settlement (n 149) 417.

[182] For a discussion of climate change adjudication in the ICJ as well other international courts and tribunals, see Philippe Sands, 'Climate Change and the Rule of Law: Adjudicating the Future of International Law', *Journal of Environmental Law*, 28/1 (2016): 19.

[183] United Nations Convention on the Law of the Sea (adopted 10 December 1982; entered into force 16 November 1994) 1833 UNTS 3.

[184] Agreement for the Implementation of the Provisions of the UN Convention on the Law of the Sea Relating to the Conservation and Management of Straddling Fish Stocks and Highly Migratory Fish Stocks (adopted 4 August 1995; entered into force 11 December 2001) 2167 UNTS 3.

agreements, and could consider claims concerning damage to the marine environment.[185]

- The dispute settlement panels and the Appellate Body under the WTO's Dispute Settlement Understanding, which could provide a forum for disputes involving national climate policies that implicate trade law.[186] Some cases, involving feed-in tariffs for renewable energy, have already wound their way through this system.[187]

- The International Centre for the Settlement of Investment Disputes (ICSID). Several ICSID cases have arisen that tangentially relate to climate change, involving the issuance of permits for coal fired plants. Claims might also be possible challenging subsidies for renewable energy.

- The Permanent Court of Arbitration, which has considered a case brought by an investor in a joint implementation project concerning the transfer of emission reduction units.[188]

- Regional human rights tribunals, such as the Inter-American Commission or Court of Human Rights, as in the Inuit case described earlier.[189]

However, although international cases like the Inuit petition have attracted a great deal of attention, they have not been successful thus far, except as a means of raising public awareness. Given the weaknesses of international dispute settlement procedures—in particular, the lack in most cases of compulsory jurisdiction or enforcement authority—international adjudication is unlikely to provide effective relief, either in reducing emissions or compensating victims.[190] Even if small island states succeeded, for example, in obtaining an advisory opinion from the ICJ that states have a responsibility to reduce emissions, this would at best put pressure on states in the FCCC to reach a stronger agreement, rather than directly cause them to reduce their emissions.

Litigation in national courts, by contrast, has had somewhat greater success, particularly in challenging particular government decisions, such as approving permits to construct power plants or providing export credits for energy projects in other countries. As noted earlier, generally these cases have been based on domestic law, although a few domestic courts have based their decisions, in part, on international norms.

---

[185] See William C.G. Burns, 'Potential Causes of Action for Climate Change Impacts under the United Nations Fish Stocks Agreement,' in Burns and Osofsky (eds), Adjudicating Climate Change (n 148), 314.

[186] See Chapter 9, Section IV.B.3.   [187] See ibid, Section IV.B.5.b.

[188] *Naftrac Limited v State Environmental Investment Agency of Ukraine* (4 December 2012), described in Verheyen and Zengerling, International Dispute Settlement (n 149) 423.

[189] See n 153 above and accompanying text.

[190] See also Chapter 2, Sections III.B and III.C, for a discussion of the problems in finding state responsibility for climate change harms.

D. Assessment

It is still too early to tell how significant judicial governance will be. Cases such as *Urgenda* and *Leghari* suggest that national courts are more willing to play a significant role in overseeing national climate change policy. But the Inuit and World Heritage Cases internationally, and the *Friends of the Earth Case* in Canada, suggest that there may be limits to the role of litigation in addressing climate change. As even supporters of climate change litigation admit, litigation is a second-best option; 'an international regime that involves all states and that provides for the action that science tells us is needed to avert dangerous climate change would be the preferred approach'.[191]

VII. POLYCENTRIC GOVERNANCE OF THE CARBON MARKET

Over the past decade, the global carbon market has grown significantly.[192] Emissions trading systems have now been adopted at virtually every level of governance—at the global level by the Kyoto Protocol; at the regional level by the EU; at the national level by countries like Kazakhstan, New Zealand, South Korea, and Switzerland; and at the subnational level by individual states and provinces like British Columbia, California, Ontario, Quebec, Saitma, and Tokyo, as well as regional groupings such as the Regional Greenhouse Gas Initiative (RGGI).[193] As of 2015, thirty-nine countries and twenty-three subnational jurisdictions either had implemented or were scheduled to implement carbon pricing instruments. Although the international carbon markets created in connection with the UN climate regime are the largest (in particular, the Clean Development Mechanism (CDM)), the World Bank estimates that national, regional, and local carbon pricing initiatives cover about 13% of global GHG emissions.[194]

Linkage of existing or emerging regional, national and sub-national emissions trading systems can produce a number of benefits, including, in particular, greater cost-effectiveness. But given the considerable differences in the design of emissions trading systems—for example, in terms of the economic sectors and GHGs covered, the time frames, and the methods for allocating allowances—linkage generally requires, at a minimum, the development of common rules on issues such as

---

[191] Jutta Brunnée, *et al.*, 'Introduction', in R. Lord *et al.* (eds), Climate Change Liability (n 148) 3, 6.

[192] This section draws on Daniel Bodansky, 'Climate Change: Transnational Legal Order or Disorder', in Terence C. Halliday and Gregory Shaffer (eds), *Transnational Legal Orders* (Cambridge University Press, 2016) 287.

[193] World Bank and Ecofys, State and Trends of Carbon Pricing (n 140) 10–11; Torbjorg Jevnaker and Jorgen Wettestad, 'Linked Carbon Markets: Silver Bullet, or Castle in the Air?', *Climate Law*, 6/1-2 (2016): 142, 144.

[194] World Bank and Ecofys, Carbon Pricing Watch 2016 <https://openknowledge.worldbank.org/bitstream/handle/10986/24288/CarbonPricingWatch2016.pdf?sequence=4&isAllowed=y> accessed 20 January 2017.

accounting; measurement, reporting and verification (MRV); allowance tracking; and carbon offsets.[195] In the absence of a global regime, linkages are beginning to develop in a decentralized, bottom-up manner, through the negotiation of agreements between jurisdictions with emissions trading systems, under which each jurisdiction recognizes the emissions allowances of the others.[196] In 2014, California and Quebec officially linked their programs and held a shared auction, and a number of other linkages between national and sub-national programs are planned. Heterogeneity among carbon pricing instruments makes linkage more complex, but not impossible.[197]

Compared to the embryonic state of linkages among emissions trading systems, the rules regarding carbon credits reflect a higher degree of order. A multiplicity of transnational carbon standards have been developed to certify credits for GHG emissions reduction projects, including both public standards, like the rules developed by the Kyoto Protocol's CDM,[198] and thirty privately developed standards, including the Verified Carbon Standard, the GHG protocol, and the Gold Standard, which are used in voluntary markets. According to one survey, '[e]ach standard has a slightly different focus and none has so far managed to establish itself as the industry standard'.[199] Nevertheless, there is 'surprising evidence of policy convergence' among standards.[200] 'Although there is an explosion in the number of private standards post-Kyoto, clearly some have emerged as more important—and indeed more credible—than others.'[201] The EU-ETS is, at present, the major driver of the carbon credit market, so the standards it applies for credits entering the EU-ETS are extremely influential.[202] In addition, the Kyoto Protocol's standards for carbon credits have a high degree of prestige and have become embedded in private standards, reflecting a degree of concordance among global, regional, national, and privately developed norms, and suggesting that the protocol will have 'long-term

---

[195] Dallas Burtraw, *et al.*, 'Linking by Degrees: Incremental Alignment of Cap-and-Trade Markets' (Resources for the Future, April 2013); Andreas Tuerck *et al.*, 'Linking Carbon Markets: Concepts, Case Studies, and Pathways', *Climate Policy*, 9 (2009): 341.

[196] See generally Ranson and Stavins, Linkage of Greenhouse Gas Emissions Trading Systems (n 147).

[197] Gilbert E. Metcalf and David Weisbach, 'Linking Policies When Tastes Differ: Global Climate Policy in a Heterogeneous World' (Cambridge, MA: Harvard Project on International Climate Agreements, 28 May 2010).

[198] For a discussion of the CDM, see Chapter 6, Section V.B.

[199] Anja Kollmuss, Helge Zink, and Clifford Polycarp, 'Making Sense of the Voluntary Carbon Market: A Comparison of Carbon Offset Standards' (Stockholm: Stockholm Environment Institute, March 2008) vi.

[200] Jessica Green, 'Order Out of Chaos: Public and Private Rules for Managing Carbon', *Global Environmental Politics*, 13/2 (2013): 2.

[201] Ibid, 14.

[202] The EU-ETS has stimulated a voluminous literature, including A. Denny Ellerman, Frank J. Convery, and Christian de Perthuis, *Pricing Carbon: The European Emissions Trading Scheme* (Cambridge University Press, 2010), and Jon Birger Skjaerseth and Jorgen Wettestad, *EU Emissions Trading: Initiation, Decision-Making and Implementation* (Surrey, UK: Ashgate Publishing, 2008). For a recent assessment, see 'Symposium: The EU Emissions Trading System: Research Findings and Needs', *Review of Environmental Economics and Policy*, 10/1 (2016): 89.

residual effects', even if it does not continue post 2020.[203] More generally, the inter-connections in the carbon market between internationally negotiated rules (such as those for the CDM), national and sub-national rules, and private standards suggest a 'blurring' of 'the boundaries between "public" and "private" governance'.[204]

VIII. POLYCENTRIC GOVERNANCE AND THE UN CLIMATE CHANGE REGIME

Like most inter-governmental organizations, the UN climate regime has been state-centric. The original General Assembly mandate for the FCCC negotiations recognized the importance of engaging civil society, but saw this as occurring primarily at the national level, through 'a broad-based preparatory process ... involving, as appropriate, the scientific community, industry, trade unions, non-governmental organizations and other interested groups'.[205] Although the mandate also invited NGOs 'to make contributions to the negotiating process', this was on the 'understanding that these organizations shall not have any negotiating role'.[206]

Since then, the FCCC has accredited more than 2000 NGOs and 100 international organizations as observers,[207] some of which have played a significant informal role in the FCCC process—for example, by providing information and analysis, making proposals, and lobbying governments. But NGOs have not had a formal role in the negotiations, nor, until recently, has the FCCC regime tried to engage directly with the climate change activities of sub- and non-state actors.

This separation between the UN climate regime and the broader set of actions by non-state actors to address climate change began to change in the four-year process leading to the Paris Agreement. Non-state actors played a significant role in the technical examination process organized under the ADP's Workstream II, which explored ways of enhancing the ambition of pre-2020 climate actions. The Lima to Paris Action Agenda (LPAA) organized by the Peruvian and French COP presidencies focused on actions by non-state actors to reduce emissions, and established the NAZCA portal to record these actions.[208] And the UN Secretary-General's Climate Summit in 2014 brought together leaders from governments, the private sector, and civil society, and helped catalyze a number of public, private, and joint initiatives to reduce emissions.[209]

---

[203] According to Green, 79% of private carbon standards recognize the Kyoto Protocol's rules. Green, Order Out of Chaos (n 200) 2.

[204] Ibid, 3.

[205] UNGA Res 45/212, 'Protection of global climate for present and future generations of mankind' UNGA (21 December 1990) UN Doc. A/RES/45/212, para 3.

[206] Ibid, para 19.

[207] Numbers are as of 2016 <http://unfccc.int/parties_and_observers/observer_organizations/items/9524.php> accessed 20 January 2017.

[208] On NAZCA, see n 3 above.

[209] Climate Summit 2014: Catalyzing Action <http://www.un.org/climatechange/summit/> accessed 20 January 2017.

Early in the Paris process, some harbored the hope that the Paris Agreement would explicitly recognize the role of sub- and non-state actors in combating climate change, or might even allow non-state actors to sign.[210] But the FCCC process is conservative by nature, and making such a radical departure from the norms of multilateral environmental agreements gained little traction in the negotiations. Instead, the only mention in the Paris Agreement of non-state actors appears in the preamble, which recognizes 'the importance of the engagements of ... various actors ... in addressing climate change'.[211]

However, the COP decision that adopted the Paris Agreement includes a more fulsome section on 'non-party stakeholders'—a category that includes civil society organizations, the private sector, financial institutions, cities, and other subnational authorities. The decision welcomes their efforts, invites them to scale these efforts up, and invites them to demonstrate their efforts via the NAZCA portal.[212]

Going forward, actions by sub- and non-state actors could play several possible roles in relation to the Paris Agreement:

- First, they could play a supportive role, by bolstering the credibility of NDCs and providing political support. For example, the Paris Pledge for Action promises support for implementing the Paris Agreement, and has been signed by more than 600 companies, 180 investors, and 110 cities and regions.[213]

- Second, actions outside the FCCC could help close the gap between the Paris Agreement's NDCs and its long-term temperature goal. To do this, however, non-state actors would need to demonstrate that their initiatives are additional to the emission reductions promised in states' NDCs.

- Third, actions by civil society and the private sector could be catalytic in promoting stronger NDCs in the future through policy innovation, demonstration effects, and political mobilization.

- Finally, polycentric climate governance could help compensate for any future loss of momentum in the UN climate regime.

IX. CONCLUSION

Supporters of polycentric governance of the climate change issue argue that tackling discrete dimensions of the issue at multiple levels, by multiple actors, can facilitate targeted, incremental progress. Given the infirmities of inter-state negotiations and uncertainties about the success of any individual negotiating process (the UN climate regime included), diversifying one's portfolio of policy approaches helps

---

[210] Esty, Bottom-Up Climate Fix (n 6).   [211] Paris Agreement, preambular recital 15.
[212] Decision 1/CP.21, 'Adoption of the Paris Agreement' (29 January 2016) FCCC/CP/2015/10/ Add.1, 2, paras 133–4.
[213] Paris Pledge for Action <http://www.parispledgeforaction.org/about/> accessed 20 January 2017.

reduce the risk of failure. But better accounting will be needed to assess the efficacy of initiatives by sub- and non-state actors to reduce emissions.[214]

SELECT BIBLIOGRAPHY

Abbott K.W., 'The Transnational Regime Complex for Climate Change', *Environment and Planning C: Government and Policy*, 30/4 (2011): 571.

Bulkeley H. *et al., Transnational Climate Change Governance* (Cambridge University Press, 2014).

Etty T. *et al.*, 'Transnational Dimensions of Climate Governance', *Transnational Environmental Law*, 1/2 (2012): 235.

Newell P., Pattberg P., and Schroeder H., 'Multiactor Governance and the Environment', *Annual Review of Environment and Resources*, 37 (2012): 365.

Okereke C., Bulkeley H., and Schroeder H., 'Conceptualizing Climate Governance Beyond the International Regime', *Global Environmental Politics*, 9/1 (2009): 58.

Peel J., Godden L., and Keenan R.J., 'Climate Change Law in an Era of Multi-Level Governance', *Transnational Environmental Law*, 1/2 (2012): 245.

Rabe B., 'Beyond Kyoto: Climate Change Policy in Multilevel Governance Systems', *Governance: An International Journal of Policy, Administration and Institutions*, 20/3 (2007): 423.

---

[214] Hsu *et al.*, Track Climate Pledges of Cities and Companies (n 7).

9

Intersections between International Climate Change Law and Other Areas of International Law

I. INTRODUCTION

The climate change problem has tremendous scope, both in its causes and its effects. On the one hand, virtually every aspect of human development contributes to climate change, including energy production, transportation, agriculture, and industry. On the other hand, climate change will have a wide variety of impacts—on low-lying and coastal areas, agriculture, human health, and biodiversity, among others.

Given the breadth of its causes and effects, the issue of climate change intersects with many areas of international law. For example:

- Global warming could leave many people without adequate food or lodging, and threaten their economic and social rights. Conversely, the measures adopted to address climate change could also raise human rights concerns.

- Climate impacts—and, in particular, sea-level rise—could cause large-scale displacement of people, both internally and across borders.

- Measures to address climate change could affect products from different countries differently, raising trade concerns. Or countries with policies to address climate change could use trade measures against countries that lack comparable policies or that decline to accept commitments under the UN climate regime.

This chapter maps the intersections between international climate change law and the three areas of international law implicated by the examples listed above: human rights law, the law relating to displacement and migration, and trade law. While there are other areas of intersection,[1] the three topics considered in this chapter illustrate the crosscutting nature of climate change as an issue. Each of them has given rise to significant scholarly debate and international practice, making them

---

[1] For example, investment law, intellectual property law, and energy law.

especially well-suited to exploring the interactions between international climate change law and international law more generally.

II. CLIMATE CHANGE AND HUMAN RIGHTS

A. Introduction

It is now 'beyond debate' that the adverse effects of climate change will, in their severity, threaten a range of human rights,[2] including the rights to life, health, food, and housing.[3] Indeed, Mary Robinson, a former UN High Commissioner for Human Rights, has called climate change 'the greatest threat to human rights in the twenty-first century'.[4] In addition, measures taken to mitigate and adapt to climate change have the potential to impinge on human rights.[5]

In the last decade, interest in the subject of climate change and human rights has grown tremendously.[6] Litigators have begun to bring claims asserting that climate

---

[2] This section draws from Daniel Bodansky, 'Introduction: Climate Change and Human Rights: Unpacking the Issues', *Georgia Journal of International and Comparative Law*, 38/3 (2010): 511; Lavanya Rajamani, 'Human Rights in the Climate Change Regime: From Rio to Paris', in John H. Knox and Ramin Pejan (eds), *The Human Right to a Healthy Environment* (Cambridge University Press, 2017, forthcoming); and Lavanya Rajamani, 'The Increasing Currency and Relevance of Rights-Based Perspectives in the International Negotiations on Climate Change', *Journal of Environmental Law*, 22/3 (2010): 391.

[3] Office of the High Commissioner for Human Rights (OHCHR), 'Understanding Human Rights and Climate Change: Submission of the Office of the High Commissioner for Human Rights to the 21st Conference of the Parties to the United Nations Framework Convention on Climate Change' (26 November 2015) <http://www.ohchr.org/Documents/Issues/ClimateChange/COP21.pdf> accessed 20 January 2017. See eg Human Rights Council (HRC) Res 32/33, 'Human Rights and Climate Change' (18 July 2016) UN Doc A/HRC/RES/32/33. The human rights approach to climate change is also discussed in Intergovernmental Panel on Climate Change (IPCC), *Climate Change 2014: Mitigation of Climate Change* (Cambridge University Press, 2014) 1027. The phrase 'beyond debate' was used by John Knox on 3 December 2015. OHCHR, 'COP21: "States' human rights obligations encompass climate change"—UN expert' (Paris, 3 December 2015) <http://www.ohchr.org/EN/NewsEvents/Pages/DisplayNews.aspx?NewsID=16836&LangID=E> accessed 20 January 2017.

[4] Quoted in Report of the Special Rapporteur on the issue of human rights obligations relating to the enjoyment of a safe, clean, healthy and sustainable environment (1 February 2016) UN Doc A/HRC/31/52, 7.

[5] HRC Res 32/33 (n 3) preambular recital 5; HRC Res 29/15, 'Human Rights and Climate Change' (22 July 2015) UN Doc A/HRC/RES/29/15, preambular recital 3; HRC Res 26/27, 'Human Rights and Climate Change' (15 July 2014) UN Doc A/HRC/RES/26/27, preambular recital 3; HRC Res 18/22, 'Human Rights and Climate Change' (17 October 2011) UN Doc A/HRC/RES/18/22, preambular recital 4.

[6] This literature is part of a broader literature on human rights and the environment, which dates back to the 1972 Stockholm Declaration, and has proliferated over the last fifteen years. See generally Donald K. Anton and Dinah L. Shelton, *Environmental Protection and Human Rights* (Cambridge University Press, 2011); John Bonine and Svitlana Kravchenko, *Human Rights and the Environment: Cases, Law, and Policy* (Durham, NC: Carolina Academic Press, 2008); Alan Boyle and Michael Anderson (eds), *Human Rights Approaches to Environmental Protection* (Oxford University Press, 1996). The 2007 Male' Declaration on the Human Dimension of Global Climate Change was the first intergovernmental instrument addressing the human rights implications of climate change. Male' Declaration on the Human Dimension of Global Climate Change (14 November 2007) <http://www.ciel.org/Publications/Male_Declaration_Nov07.pdf> accessed 20 January 2017. For a general

change is implicated in human rights violations,[7] and the academic community has explored the theoretical and practical issues involved.[8] The Office of the High Commissioner of Human Rights (OHCHR) has initiated a stream of work on Human Rights and Climate Change,[9] producing an initial report on the subject in 2009.[10] The Human Rights Council has adopted a series of resolutions alerting states to the inter-connections between human rights and climate change, and reminding them of their obligations under human rights instruments.[11] In 2012, motivated largely by concerns about climate change, it appointed an independent expert (now titled special rapporteur) to focus on human rights and the environment, and it has instructed other special rapporteurs (including the special rapporteurs on housing, migrants, internally displaced persons, and food) to consider the implications of climate change for their mandates.[12]

Proposals to treat climate change as a human rights problem raise many fundamental questions. Theoretically, what does it mean to conceptualize climate change in human rights terms? In other words, how would a human rights approach differ from an approach that treated climate change as an environmental, economic, or scientific problem? Normatively, does it make sense to approach climate change as a human rights issue? What are the advantages and disadvantages of a human rights approach to climate change? Descriptively, what does human rights law say about climate change and, conversely, what does climate change law say about human rights?

description of the growing focus on the relationship of climate change and human rights, see Report of the Special Rapporteur (n 4) 3–7.

[7] See Chapter 8, Section VI.

[8] See eg, Stephen Humphreys (ed), *Human Rights and Climate Change* (Cambridge University Press, 2010); John H. Knox, 'Climate Change and Human Rights Law', *Virginia Journal of International Law*, 50/1 (2009): 163; Siobhan McInerney-Lankford, Mac Darrow, and Lavanya Rajamani, *Human Rights and Climate Change: A Review of the International Legal Dimension* (Washington, D.C.: The World Bank, 2011); Timo Koivurova, Sébastien Duych, and Leen Heinämäki, 'Climate Change and Human Rights', in Erkki J. Hollo, Kati Kulovesi, and Michael Mehling (eds), *Climate Change and the Law* (Dordrecht: Springer, 2013) 287; Sheila R. Foster and Paolo Galizzi, 'Human Rights and Climate Change: Building Synergies for a Common Future', in Daniel A. Farber and Marhan Peeters (eds), *Elgar Encyclopedia of Environmental Law vol. 1: Climate Change Law* (Cheltenham, UK: Edward Elgar, 2016) 43; John H. Knox, 'Human Rights Principles and Climate Change', in Cinnamon P. Carlarne, Kevin R. Gray, and Richard Tarasofsky (eds), *The Oxford Handbook of International Climate Change Law* (Oxford University Press, 2016) 213; Philippe Cullet, 'Human Rights and Climate Change: Broadening the Right to Environment', in Carlarne *et al.*, Oxford Handbook of International Climate Change Law, ibid, 495; Eric A. Posner, 'Climate Change and International Human Rights Litigation: A Critical Appraisal', *University of Pennsylvania Law Review*, 155/6 (2007): 1925; Amy Sinden, 'Climate Change and Human Rights', *Journal of Land Resources & Environmental Law*, 27/2 (2007): 255; Stephen M. Gardiner *et al.* (eds), *Climate Ethics: Essential Readings* (New York: Oxford University Press, 2010); Henry Shue, *Climate Justice: Vulnerability and Protection* (Oxford University Press, 2014).

[9] See generally OHCHR, 'Human Rights and Climate Change' <http://www.ohchr.org/EN/Issues/HRAndClimateChange/Pages/HRClimateChangeIndex.aspx> accessed 20 January 2017.

[10] Report of the Office of the United Nations High Commission for Human Rights on the Relationship between Climate Change and Human Rights (15 January 2009) UN Doc A/HRC/10/61.

[11] See HRC Res 32/33 (n 3); HRC Res 29/15 (n 5); HRC Res 26/27 (n 5); HRC Res 18/22 (n 5).

[12] Report of the Special Rapporteur (n 4) 5.

B. Distinguishing features of a human rights approach to climate change

In many respects, the environmental perspective on climate change is similar to the human rights perspective. The policy debate about climate change has always focused on its human impacts—the harms to coastal communities, drought-prone areas, agriculture, human health, and human welfare more generally. In addition, human rights are less absolutist than some believe, and, like environmental law, can involve balancing tests. The relatively few environmental cases that have been decided thus far by international human rights tribunals recognize that 'states have discretion within wide limits to determine how to strike the balance between environmental harm and the benefits of the activities causing it'.[13] Finally, a focus on minimum thresholds 'beneath which no one is to be allowed to sink'[14] does not fundamentally distinguish human rights law from climate change law. Environmental law also frequently defines minimum or maximum thresholds. For example, the FCCC defines its objective in terms of a maximum threshold level of greenhouse gas (GHG) concentrations, above which dangerous climate change would occur.[15] The Paris Agreement supplements this concentration threshold with a temperature change threshold of 'well below 2° C' (and an aspirational aim of 1.5° C).[16]

Nevertheless, there are important differences between the human rights and environmental approaches. Most obviously, human rights law defines obligations states owe to individuals, whereas international environmental law focuses primarily on obligations that states owe to one another. As a result, human rights law highlights the harms to individuals caused by environmental problems such as climate change.

Human rights regimes also tend to be more legalistic than international environmental regimes.[17] Significantly, the paradigmatic institution established by human rights treaties is the expert committee, composed largely of lawyers. In contrast, the central institution established by multilateral environmental agreements (MEAs) is the conference of the parties (COP), whose primary task is political, namely to direct the implementation and evolution of the regime. Even the more specialized implementation committees established by some MEAs are generally composed of governmental rather than independent experts, and take a political rather than a strictly legal approach to compliance questions.[18]

The more obviously 'political' character of international environmental regimes is reflected not only in their institutional and procedural arrangements, but also in

---

[13] Knox, Climate Change and Human Rights Law (n 8) 196.

[14] Henry Shue, *Basic Rights: Subsistence, Affluence, and U.S. Foreign Policy* (Princeton University Press, 2nd edn, 1996) 18.

[15] FCCC, Art 2.   [16] Paris Agreement, Art 2.

[17] This paragraph and the next two are drawn from Daniel Bodansky, 'The Role of Reporting in International Environmental Treaties: Lessons for Human Rights Supervision', in Philip Alston and James Crawford (eds), *The Future of the UN Human Rights Treaty System* (Cambridge University Press, 2000) 361.

[18] See Chapter 6, Section VI.

their substantive obligations, which often reflect political compromises struck in order to achieve agreement. Of course, human rights agreements also are the product of negotiation, but with an important difference. In human rights agreements, the end point of the negotiations is a common core of human rights to be respected. In contrast, multilateral environmental negotiations often involve a process of outright horse-trading that results in different requirements for different countries, but by virtue of that fact, also allows more stringent and specific requirements to be adopted than would otherwise be possible.

Another important difference between international environmental law and human rights law is that international environmental law depends on reciprocity while human rights law does not. International environmental law is grounded in the need for mutual action. Most international environmental problems—including climate change—cannot be addressed by individual states acting alone; they require collective effort. In contrast, human rights obligations do not depend on reciprocity. One state's respect for human rights does not depend on, and may not be conditioned on, compliance by other states.

C. Advantages and disadvantages of a human rights approach to climate change

Regardless of the degree to which a human rights approach to climate change is conceptually distinctive, it offers a number of practical advantages over the intergovernmental negotiating process, which make it attractive to environmentalists. First, if the activities that contribute to climate change threaten the enjoyment of human rights, then current practices may be illegal, irrespective of whether governments agree internationally to mandatory emissions cuts. Legal arguments can be made under existing law about what countries *must* do, not simply policy arguments about what they *should* do.

Human rights law provides not only legal arguments, but also forums in which to make those arguments. In contrast to international environmental law, where dispute resolution mechanisms are in short supply, human rights law has tribunals to hear complaints and rapporteurs to investigate more general situations.[19] These

---

[19] At the global level, tribunals include the Human Rights Committee established by the International Covenant on Civil and Political Rights and the Committee on Economic, Social and Cultural Rights established under the International Covenant on Economic, Social and Cultural Rights. See International Covenant on Civil and Political Rights (adopted 16 December 1966, entered in force 23 March 1976) 999 UNTS 171 (ICCPR) Art 28; Optional Protocol to the International Covenant on Economic, Social and Cultural Rights (adopted 10 December 2008, entered in force 5 May 2013) UN Doc A/63/435 (allowing individual petitions to the Committee on Economic, Social and Cultural Rights). Regional tribunals include the Inter-American Commission of Human Rights (IAComHR), Inter-American Court of Human Rights (IACtHR) and the European Court of Human Rights (ECtHR). In addition, human rights claims can potentially be pursued in national courts. See generally Richard Lord *et al.*, *Climate Change Liability: Transnational Law and Practice* (Cambridge University Press, 2012). See also William C.G. Burns and Hari M. Osofsky (eds), *Adjudicating Climate Change: State, National, and International Approaches* (Cambridge University Press, 2009). See also Chapter 8, Section VI.

procedures give victims of climate change a forum in which they possess greater power than in inter-governmental negotiations, where they have little influence.[20]

Moreover, by focusing on the harms suffered by particular individuals and groups, human rights procedures help put a human face on climate change and make the impacts more concrete. Politicians have long understood that people respond more to individual stories than to general statistics.[21] Human rights cases serve as vehicles for telling the stories of those affected by climate change, and they can thus help mobilize public opinion and build political support for policy change.[22]

More generally, characterizing a problem as a human rights question elevates its standing relative to other issues. It gives the problem greater moral urgency and appeals to additional constituencies beyond environmentalists. In this regard, it serves a similar function as efforts to characterize climate change as an energy security or military security problem.

These potential advantages notwithstanding, a human rights approach also has important limitations. Although many forums exist in which to raise human rights claims, enforcement is often challenging. There are serious hurdles in terms of establishing the existence or scope of binding obligations (given the contextual and soft language used in the relevant treaties), jurisdiction (since states frequently do not recognize the jurisdiction of international dispute settlement forums), causation (between the GHG emissions of a state and impacts suffered by particular individuals), and damage (since much of the impact of climate change may be felt only in the future). In these ways, the climate change problem exposes the fault lines and limits of international dispute resolution.[23] Further, some human rights may be derogated from during times of emergency.

In addition to these pragmatic difficulties in enforcing human rights, there is an ethical concern that a human rights focus is excessively anthropocentric, and does not give due consideration to the intrinsic value of the environment.[24] It does not consider, for instance, the many species that are likely to face extinction as a result of global warming. A human rights approach also risks paying excessive homage to present generations at the expense of future generations. In seeking to concretize, prevent, and address harms to individuals and communities, harms to future generations—which by their very nature are abstract, unknown, and perhaps even unknowable—may stand compromised. The focus on concrete harms to current generations could militate against mitigation efforts that impose short-term costs on individuals with the expectation of long-term gains for society as a whole.

---

[20] Sinden, Climate Change and Human Rights (n 8) 264–5.

[21] As Joseph Stalin is said to have remarked, 'The death of one man is a tragedy. The death of millions is a statistic'. See David B. Hunter, 'The Implications of Climate Change Litigation: Litigation for International Environmental Law Making', in Burns and Osofsky, Adjudicating Climate Change (n 19) 357 and references contained therein.

[22] International Council on Human Rights Policy, *Climate Change and Human Rights: A Rough Guide* (Geneva: International Council on Human Rights Policy, 2008) 41.

[23] See Chapter 2, Sections III.C and IV.C.1 and Chapter 8, Section VI.

[24] See Catherine Redgwell, 'Life, the Universe and Everything: A Critique of Anthropocentric Rights', in Boyle and Anderson, Human Rights Approaches to Environmental Protection (n 6) 71, 87.

D. Which human rights are affected by the impacts of climate change?

There are at least two ways in which to apply a human rights optic to the climate change issue. The first focuses on how climate change affects the realization and enjoyment of established human rights, including the rights to life, food, water, shelter, health, and self-determination. The second considers the implications for climate change of a putative, autonomous human right to a healthy or clean environment.

1. Extending the ambit of existing rights to address climate impacts

Many established human rights are likely to be impaired by climate impacts including:

- The right to life, which is protected by virtually all human rights instruments.
- The rights to adequate food, water, and shelter.
- The right to the highest attainable standard of health.
- The right to self-determination.[25]

Although few cases have considered the human rights implications of climate change, it is well established that environmental harms (more generally) have pervasive effects on human rights.[26] In his separate opinion in the *Gabčíkovo-Nagymaros Case,* Judge Weeramantry recognized the protection of the environment as a '*sine qua non* for numerous human rights such as the right to health and the right to life itself'.[27] The European Court of Human Rights (ECtHR) in its landmark judgment in *Lopez Ostra,* held that 'severe environmental pollution may affect individuals' well-being and prevent them from enjoying their homes in such a way as to affect their private and family life adversely'.[28] In a series of cases following *Lopez Ostra,* the European Court recognized that severe environmental pollution may affect an individual's well-being and rights.[29] The court was clear, however, that

---

[25] HRC Res 32/33 (n 3); HRC Res 29/15 (n 5); HRC Res 26/27 (n 5); HRC Res 18/22 (n 5); HRC, Report on Relationship between Climate Change and Human Rights (n 10).

[26] Report of the Independent Expert on the issue of human rights obligations relating to the enjoyment of a safe, clean, healthy and sustainable environment, John H. Knox: Mapping Report (30 December 2013) UN Doc A/HRC/25/53, 6 (describing 'overwhelming support' for the view that 'environmental degradation can and does adversely affect the enjoyment of a broad range of human rights').

[27] *Gabčíkovo-Nagymoros Project (Hungary/Slovakia)* (Judgment) [1997] ICJ Rep 7, Separate Opinion of Vice-President Weeramantry, 88, 91.

[28] *Lopez Ostra v Spain* (1994) 20 EHRR 277, para 51.

[29] See eg *Guerra and others v Italy* (1998) 26 EHRR 357; *Taskin v Turkey* (2006) 42 EHRR 50; *Moreno Gomez v Spain* (2005) 41 EHRR 40; *Fadeyeva v Russia* (2007) 45 EHRR 10; *Tatar v Romania* App no 67021/01 (ECtHR, 27 January 2009); *Dubetska and others v Ukraine* App no 30499/03 (ECtHR, 10 February 2011). For cases balancing the societal interest in economic development with the human rights of particular claimants, see eg *Rayner and Powell v UK* (1990) 12 EHRR 355; *Hatton v UK* (2002) 34 EHRR 1. For cases relating to natural events see eg *Budayeva and others v Russia* App

environmental harm can constitute a human rights violation only if it impacts a person's enjoyment of a protected right. As the European Court stressed in *Kryatatos v Greece*, 'the crucial element which must be present … is the existence of a harmful effect on a person's private or family sphere and not simply the general deterioration of the environment'.[30]

Cases based on environmental harms have also been considered by the Human Rights Committee under the International Covenant on Civil and Political Rights (ICCPR),[31] and by the Inter-American Commission of Human Rights (IAComHR) and the Inter-American Court of Human Rights (IACtHR) under the American Declaration of the Rights and Duties of Man and the American Convention on Human Rights, respectively.[32] Indeed, the only climate change case brought thus far before an international tribunal was the Inuit petition to the IAComHR.[33] The petitioners alleged in that case that thinning of sea ice, changes in snowfall, melting of permafrost, and changes in animal movements caused by climate change have resulted in violations of the Inuit's rights to property, health, life, the means of subsistence, residence, movement, the inviolability of the home, and the benefits of culture, all of which are protected by the American Declaration of the Rights and Duties of Man. The Inter-American Commission held the case to be inadmissible, without offering any reasons. Cases in national courts have fared better. For instance, in *Gbemre v Shell Petroleum Development Corporation*,[34] the Nigerian Federal High Court held that the practice of gas flaring in the Niger Delta, which at

---

nos 15339/02, 21166/02, 20058/02, 11673/02, and 15343/02 (ECtHR, 20 March 2008); *Özel and others v Turkey*, App nos 14350/05, 15245/05, and 16051/05 (ECtHR, 17 November 2015).

[30] *Kyrtatos v Greece* (2005) 40 EHRR 16, para 52.

[31] See eg *Sara et al. v Finland*, Communication no 431/1990 (24 March 1994) UN Doc CCPR/C/50/D/431/1990; *Chief Bernard Ominayak and Lubicon Lake Band v Canada*, Communication no 167/1984 (10 May 1990) UN Doc CCPR/C/38/D/167/1984; *Ilmari Lansman et al. v Finland*, Communication no 511/1992 (8 November 1994) UN Doc CCPR/C/52/D/511/1992; *Apirana Mahuika et al. v New Zealand*, Communication no 547/1993 (16 November 2000) UN Doc CCPR/C/70/D/547/1993; *Andre Brun v France*, Communication no 1453/2006 (23 November 2006) UN Doc CCPR/C/88/D/1453/2006; *Bordes and Temeharo v France*, Communication no 645/1995 (22 July 1996) UN Doc CCPR/C/57/D/645/1995; *E.H.P. v Canada*, Communication no 67/1980 (27 October 1982) CCPR/C/OP/1.

[32] See eg IAComHR: Organization of American States (OAS), 'Report on the Situation of Human Rights in Ecuador' (24 April 1997) OEA/Ser.L./V/II.96 Doc. 10 rev. 1; *Case of the Mayagna (Sumo) Awas Tingni Community v Nicaragua*, Inter-American Court of Human Rights Series C No 79 (31 August 2001); *Case of Yanomami Indians v Brazil*, Case no 7615 (Brazil), Res no. 12/85, Inter-American Commission of Human Rights (5 March 1985) OEA/Ser.L/V/II.66 Doc.10 rev. 1; *Case of Maya indigenous community of the Toledo District v Belize*, Case no 12.053, Report no 40/04, Inter-American Commission of Human Rights (12 October 2004) OEA/Ser.L/V/II.122 Doc. 5 rev. 1, 727; *Case of La Oroya Community v Perú*, Case no 1473.06, Report no 76/09, Inter-American Commission of Human Rights (5 August 2009); *Saramaka People v Suriname*, Inter-American Court of Human Rights Series C No 172 (28 November 2007).

[33] Petition to the Inter-American Commission on Human Rights Seeking Relief from Violations Resulting from Global Warming Caused by Acts and Omissions of the United States (7 December 2005) <http://www.inuitcircumpolar.com/uploads/3/0/5/4/30542564/finalpetitionicc.pdf> accessed 20 January 2017 (Inuit Petition).

[34] *Jonah Gbemre v Shell Petroleum Development Co. Nigeria Ltd et al.* (2005) FHCNLR (Nigeria), (2005) AHRLR 151 (NgHC 2005).

the time contributed more to climate change than all other sources in Sub-Saharan Africa, violated constitutional rights to life and dignity.[35]

2. Recognizing a right to a healthy or clean environment

In addition to the application of existing rights to environmental issues, several non-binding international instruments[36] recognize and protect a stand-alone right to a healthy or clean environment. A number of regional human rights instruments also recognize a stand-alone environmental right, although none at the global level.[37] Stand-alone environmental rights are recognized in more than ninety national constitutions as well.[38] The Ksentini Report, commissioned by the UN Sub-Commission on Prevention of Discrimination and Protection of Minorities, records as early as 1994 'universal acceptance' of a range of environmental rights at the national, regional, and international levels.[39]

In all these cases, national and international, a putative stand-alone environmental right could logically be extended to cover climate protection. However, since the scope and content of stand-alone environmental rights, where they exist, are highly indeterminate, it is unclear what recognition of such a right would add. To what qualitative level should the environment be protected—clean, safe, healthy, decent, or satisfactory?[40] In the climate context, what degree of temperature increase is acceptable? Even limiting global warming to 2° C or 1.5° C, as the Paris Agreement aspires to do, would result in some climatic changes and consequent human

---

[35] Ibid.

[36] See eg UNGA Res 2398 (XXII), 'Problems of the Human Environment' (3 December 1968) UN Doc A/RES/2398(XXII); Stockholm Declaration, preamble; 'Hague Declaration on the Environment' (11 March 1989) (1989) 28 ILM 1308; UNGA Res 45/94, 'Need to ensure a healthy environment for the well-being of individuals' (14 December 1990) UN Doc A/RES/45/94.

[37] Regional agreements recognizing a stand-alone environmental right include the African Charter on Human and Peoples' Rights (adopted 27 June 1981, entered into force 21 October 1986) 1520 UNTS 217, Art 24 (right to a 'general satisfactory environment'); Additional Protocol to the American Convention on Human Rights in the Area of Economic, Social and Cultural Rights (Protocol of San Salvador) (adopted 17 November 1988, entered into force 16 November 1999) OAS Treaty Series No 69, reprinted in (1989) 28 ILM 156 (1988 San Salvador Protocol), Art 11 ('right to a healthy environment'); the Arab Charter on Human Rights (adopted 22 May 2004, entered into force 15 March 2008) <http://hrlibrary.umn.edu/instree/loas2005.html> accessed 20 January 2017, Art 38 ('right to a healthy environment'). A general reference to the environment in the context of sustainable development is to be found in the Treaty for the Establishment of the East African Community (signed 30 November 1999, entered into force 7 July 2000) 2144 UNTS 235.

[38] Report of the Independent Expert on the issue of human rights obligations relating to the enjoyment of a safe, clean, healthy, and sustainable environment, John H. Knox: Compilation of Good Practices (3 February 2015) UN Doc A/HRC/28/61, 15. Portugal was the first country to adopt a constitutional 'right to a healthy and ecologically balanced human environment'. Report of the Independent Expert on the issue of human rights obligations relating to the enjoyment of a safe, clean, healthy, and sustainable environment, John H. Knox: Preliminary Report (24 December 2012) UN Doc A/HRC/22/43, 5.

[39] See Fatma Zohra Ksentini, 'Human Rights and the Environment, Final Report' E.CN.4/Sub.2/1994/9 (6 July 1994).

[40] See Dominick McGoldrick, 'Sustainable Development and Human Rights: An Integrated Conception', *International and Comparative Law Quarterly,* 45/4 (1996): 796, 811.

impacts. Against which of the numerous existing standards, benchmarks, or thresholds should the qualitative level of protection be assessed? How, for instance, do we distinguish the climate impacts that are acceptable from those that are not, given that impacts differ between people and communities? How should achievement of a clean environment be prioritized against other important social objectives, such as provision of energy and food? And, to what extent should these rights be justiciable? These questions are yet to be authoritatively considered and resolved.

E. Nature of duties

The fact that climate change impacts the enjoyment of human rights does not mean that climate change itself constitutes a human rights violation. Climate change entails a human rights violation only if there is an identifiable duty that an identifiable duty-holder has breached. Claims that climate change violates human rights thus raise three issues. First, what types of duties are involved? Second, who has these duties? Third, to whom are these duties owed?

1. Types of duties

Human rights scholars often distinguish between the duty to respect, the duty to protect, and the duty to fulfill.[41] The duty of states to respect human rights is the most familiar and the least controversial. States may not act in ways that deprive individuals of their rights. For example, states may not engage in torture, commit extrajudicial killings, or deliberately starve civilians. These negative duties are duties to refrain from particular types of actions. In the climate change context, the duty to respect has implications for government activities that directly contribute to climate change—for example, emissions of carbon dioxide (CO_2) from government facilities and from military activities. It might also apply to government decisions that regulate private conduct—for example, decisions about whether to grant oil leases or to permit the construction of a coal-fired power plant.

In contrast to the duty to respect—a primarily negative duty not to engage in actions that adversely affect the enjoyment of a human right—the duty to protect or ensure is a positive duty that requires states to take action to prevent non-governmental actors from infringing on human rights.[42] For example, the

---

[41] Knox, Climate Change and Human Rights Law (n 8) 179–80.

[42] See eg Decision of the African Commission on Human and Peoples' Rights in *Social and Economic Rights Action Centre (CERAC) and the Centre for Economic and Social Rights (CESR) v Nigeria*, Communication no 155/96 (27 October 2001) (Ogoniland Case) para 57 (states have a duty to 'protect [their] citizens ... from damaging acts that may be perpetrated by private parties'); IAComHR, Report on the Situation of Human Rights in Ecuador (n 32) 88 (states have 'an obligation ... to take reasonable measures to prevent such risk [to life or health] or the necessary measures to respond when persons have suffered injury'). See generally Knox Mapping Report (n 26) 16–17.

Convention on the Elimination of Racial Discrimination not only prohibits states from engaging in discrimination themselves; it also requires states to protect individuals against private discrimination—for example, through the enactment of anti-discrimination laws.[43] The duty to protect is violated through omissions rather than through acts.

In the context of climate change, the duty to protect against the impairment of human rights resulting from climate change might include a duty to regulate private emissions that contribute to climate change, as well as a duty to undertake adaptation measures to limit the harms caused by global warming. In a case with potential implications for climate change, the ECtHR held in *Budayeva v Russia* that Russia had a positive obligation to put in place legislative and administrative frameworks to provide an effective deterrent against threats to the right to life caused by natural events such as mudslides.[44] To the extent that many of the impacts of climate change will manifest themselves in such seemingly natural events, the court's recognition that states have an obligation to mitigate the impacts of such events, and prepare for them, is significant.

Important questions regarding the duty to protect include: Is the duty one of due diligence, negligence, or strict liability? To what extent may a state balance protection of human rights against other important societal objectives such as economic development? To which activities does the duty apply—only activities within a state's territory or also activities by its nationals elsewhere? To what extent does the duty to protect against climate change vary depending on a state's resources and circumstances—in other words, to what extent should the duty to protect be differentiated?[45] And to what extent do states have a heightened duty to protect in relation to specially vulnerable groups, such as indigenous peoples, women and children?[46]

In addition to the duties to respect and protect, some human rights institutions have interpreted human rights law as imposing a duty to take positive steps to fulfill or facilitate the satisfaction of human rights. For example, the Committee on Economic, Social and Cultural Rights (CESCR) has found that the International Covenant on Economic, Social and Cultural Rights (ICESCR) requires states 'to adopt appropriate legislative, administrative, budgetary, judicial, promotional, and other measures towards the full realization of the right to health', including 'national policies aimed at reducing and eliminating pollution of air, water, and

---

[43] International Convention on the Elimination of All Forms of Racial Discrimination (adopted 21 December 1965, entered into force 4 January 1969) 660 UNTS 195, Art 2.

[44] *Budayeva v Russia* (2014) 59 EHRR 2.

[45] In this regard, the ICESCR provides that each state should take actions 'to the maximum of its available resources'. See ICESCR, Art 2.1.

[46] The Special Rapporteur on human rights and the environment answered this question in the affirmative, concluding in his 'mapping report' that states have additional obligations with respect to particularly vulnerable groups. See Knox Mapping Report (n 26) 19–21.

soil'.[47] According to the CESCR, states have a duty, 'at the very least', to 'ensure the satisfaction of minimum essential levels' of economic, social, and cultural rights.[48] Similarly, the notion of a duty to fulfill might imply that rich states have a duty to provide assistance to poorer states to help them mitigate or adapt to climate change.[49]

A particular human right may thus involve a variety of correlative duties. Consider, for example, the different ways in which the right to life might be implicated by environmental harms. First, a state could violate the right to life by taking actions that cause environmental harm. In the *Yanomami Case*, for example, the IAComHR found that the Brazilian government had violated the Yanomami's right to life by constructing a highway that allowed non-Yanomami people to move into the region where the Yanomami had traditionally lived, causing fatal diseases.[50] Alternatively, a state could violate the right to life by failing to prevent environmental harms caused by private actors—for example, through lack of adequate regulation. For example, in *E.H.P. v Canada*, the Human Rights Committee concluded that the storage of nuclear wastes near the petitioner's home raised 'serious issues with regard to the obligation of States parties to protect human life'.[51] Finally, a state might violate the right to life by failing to take positive steps to protect the environment.

The type of duty implicated by allegations of human rights violations caused by climate change is not always clear. For example, the Inuit petition to the IAComHR argued that the United States (US) was violating the rights of Inuit people through its 'acts and omissions regarding climate change', including its 'regulatory actions and inactions'. Using the language of the duty to respect, the petition asserted that the US has 'an international obligation not to deprive the Inuit of their own means of subsistence'. Using the language of the duty to protect, it also asserted that the 'United States has an obligation to protect the Inuit's human rights to life and personal security'.

A statement by the environmental group bringing the petition argued:

> Protecting human rights is the most fundamental responsibility of civilized nations. Because climate change is threatening the lives, health, culture and livelihoods of the Inuit, it is the responsibility of the United States, as the largest source of greenhouse gases, to take immediate and effective action to protect the rights of the Inuit.[52]

---

[47] Economic and Social Council, 'General Comment No. 14: The Right to the Highest Attainable Standard of Health (Article 12 of the International Covenant on Economic, Social and Cultural Rights)' (11 August 2000) UN Doc E/C.12/2000/4, paras 33, 36.

[48] Economic and Social Council, 'General Comment 3: The Nature of States Parties' Obligations (Article 2, para 1 of the Covenant)' (14 December 1990) UN Doc E/1991/23, para 10.

[49] Article 2 of the ICESCR requires states 'to take steps, individually and through international assistance and cooperation ... , with a view to achieving progressively the full realization of the rights recognized in the present Covenant'. But, as Stephen Humphreys notes, 'the extent to which this exhortation comprises an obligation remains deeply contested'. Stephen Humphreys, 'Introduction: Human Rights and Climate Change', in Humphreys, Human Rights and Climate Change (n 8) 10.

[50] *Case of Yanomami Indians* (n 32).   [51] *E.H.P. v Canada* (n 31) para 8.

[52] Inuit Petition (n 33) 7.

This statement could be interpreted as asserting a failure by the US to respect the human rights of Inuit, to the extent that acts by the US are responsible for the harms suffered by the Inuit; a failure to protect the human rights of Inuit, by failing to regulate private conduct; or a failure to fulfill the human rights of Inuit, by failing to help the Inuit adapt to climate change.

Finally, in addition to substantive duties to respect, protect, and fulfill human rights, states have a number of procedural duties relating to the environment, including duties to assess environmental impacts, facilitate public participation, and provide access to remedies for environmental obligations.

2. Duty holders

Since climate change is attributable primarily to emissions by private actors, a crucial question is whether the duties to respect, protect, and fulfill apply to private actors as well as to states and, if so, to what degree. International criminal law demonstrates that international law can, in some cases, impose duties directly on individuals, and some have proposed that corporations have duties to respect human rights.[53] So human rights law could, in theory, impose a duty on private actors to respect human rights by limiting their emissions of GHGs.[54] In *Gbemre v Shell Petroleum Development Corporation*,[55] a Nigerian court found that Shell had violated the fundamental rights to life and dignity of person and to a 'clean, poison-free, pollution-free healthy environment' under both Nigerian law and the African Charter on Human and Peoples' Rights. In the Philippines, in an important climate-related human rights investigation, the Philippines Commission on Human Rights ordered forty-seven oil, coal, and mining companies to respond to allegations of gross human rights violations resulting from their carbon production and emission processes.[56]

Generally, however, human rights law—like international environmental law—imposes duties on states rather than on corporations. If this is true in relation to climate change, then human rights law limits the activities of non-state actors only to the extent that states have a duty to protect against climate change by regulating private activities that impair the enjoyment of human rights and providing a remedy against the responsible actors.

---

[53] See Stephen R. Ratner, 'Corporations and Human Rights: A Theory of Legal Responsibility', *Yale Law Journal*, 111/3 (2001): 443.

[54] See Peter Newell, 'Climate Change, Human Rights and Corporate Accountability', in Humphreys, Human Rights and Climate Change (n 8) 126.

[55] *Jonah Gbemre* (n 34). See Amy Sinden, 'An Emerging Human Right to Security from Climate Change: The Case against Gas Flaring in Nigeria', in Burns and Osofsky, Adjudicating Climate Change (n 19) 173.

[56] See John Vidal, 'World's Largest Carbon Producers Face Landmark Human Rights Case', *The Guardian* (27 July 2016) <https://www.theguardian.com/environment/2016/jul/27/worlds-largest-carbon-producers-face-landmark-human-rights-case> accessed 20 January 2017; Petition Requesting for Investigation of the Responsibility of the Carbon Majors for Human Rights Violations or Threats of Violations Resulting from the Impacts of Climate Change (Quezon City, Philippines, 9 May 2016) <http://www.greenpeace.org/seasia/ph/PageFiles/735232/Climate_Change_and_Human_Rights_Petition.pdf> accessed 20 January 2017.

3. Duty beneficiaries

A final issue concerns the geographic scope of human rights duties. Are the duties to respect, protect, and fulfill owed only to individuals or groups within a state's territory, or do they extend to people in other countries, giving them correlative rights? Generally, the answer to this question depends on whether human rights law applies extraterritorially and can hence restrict what a government or a company does in another country. But, in the climate change context, defining the geographic scope of the rights holders is necessary even when a government acts, or fails to act, within its own territory, since GHG emissions do not respect borders: emissions purely within a state's territory affect the enjoyment of human rights by people everywhere, although to differing degrees.[57] The question arises, therefore, of whether the extraterritorial effects of GHG emissions mean that states owe human rights duties to people throughout the world. The Inuit petition, for example, was brought on behalf not only of the Inuit living in Alaska, but elsewhere in the Arctic region, including in Russia, Canada, Norway, and Finland.

F. Human rights implications of response measures

In addition to the impacts of climate change itself on the enjoyment of human rights, the measures undertaken by states and private actors in response to climate change can raise human rights issues in two ways. First, response measures may affect the enjoyment of substantive human rights, such as the right to food and the rights of indigenous peoples.[58] This is true of both mitigation and adaptation policies. On the mitigation side, policies to slow deforestation or to increase reforestation, for example, could affect forest communities. The use of corn to produce ethanol could raise the price of agricultural products and thereby impact the right to food. And investments in expensive new emissions control technologies could divert resources from other uses and undermine a country's ability to provide an adequate standard of living. Similarly, with respect to adaptation, relocation of people living in coastal or flood-prone areas could raise human rights issues, if done forcibly.[59]

Analyzing these response measures from the perspective of human rights is in many ways more familiar and straightforward than analyzing the impacts of climate change itself, and indeed the only references to human rights in the UN climate regime relate to the human rights implications of response measures.[60] When

---

[57] See generally Mark Gibney and Sigrun Skogly (eds), *Universal Human Rights and Extraterritorial Obligations* (Philadelphia: University of Pennsylvania Press, 2010). For an excellent discussion of these issues in the context of climate change, see Knox, Climate Change and Human Rights Law (n 8) 200–11.

[58] Naomi Roht-Arriaza, '"First Do No Harm": Human Rights and Efforts to Combat Climate Change', *Georgia Journal of International and Comparative Law*, 38/3 (2010): 593; see also Knox, ibid, 198–200.

[59] International Council on Human Rights, Climate Change and Human Rights Policy (n 22).

[60] See n 82 below and accompanying text.

a government acts to combat climate change, it must do so in ways that respect human rights. In this regard, measures to combat climate change are no different from measures to combat terrorism or crime. Forest policies, for example, should respect indigenous rights, biofuel policies should respect the right to food, and so forth.[61] More controversially, some commentators have proposed that climate change policy should distinguish between 'luxury emissions' and 'subsistence' or 'survival' emissions, which should not be cut because they are necessary for the enjoyment of basic human rights to food, water, and shelter.[62]

Second, a variety of well-established procedural rights have obvious implications for climate policymaking, both nationally and internationally, including the rights to freedom of expression and association, the right to information, the right to participate in government decision-making processes, and the right to access to remedies for harms.[63] Although these procedural rights apply universally, human rights law recognizes their importance, in particular, for specially vulnerable groups, such as women, children, indigenous peoples, and those living in extreme poverty. As the Special Rapporteur on Human Rights and the Environment notes, procedural rights are:

… rights whose free exercise makes policies more transparent, better informed, and more responsive … When directed at environmental issues, the exercise of such rights results in policies that better reflect the concerns of those most concerned and, as a result, that better safeguard their rights to life and health, among others, from infringement through environmental harm.[64]

G. Human rights in the UN climate regime

Although the human impacts of climate change have underpinned the climate negotiations from the start, the FCCC and the Kyoto Protocol do not contain any explicit references to human rights. The only explicit reference to a 'right' in the FCCC is in relation to sustainable development. FCCC, Article 3.4, in relevant part, reads: [t]he Parties have a right to, and should, promote sustainable development'. The right recognized here is 'to promote sustainable development' and not a

---

[61] See nn 67–68 below and accompanying text.

[62] Henry Shue, 'Subsistence Emissions and Luxury Emissions', *Law and Policy*, 15/1 (1993): 39; see also Paul Baer, Tom Athanasiou, and Sivan Kartha, *The Right to Development in a Climate Constrained World: The Greenhouse Development Rights Framework* (Berlin: Heinrich Böll Foundation, 2007) (proposing a 'greenhouse development rights' framework).

[63] These rights are protected by a number of human rights instruments, including the ICCPR (Arts 2, 19, 21, 22, and 25), and are also recognized in human rights instruments such as the Rio Declaration, principle 10, and, at the regional level in the Aarhus Convention. See Convention on Access to Information, Public Participation in Decision-making and Access to Justice in Environmental Matters (adopted 25 June 1998, entered into force 30 October 2001) 2161 UNTS 447. Human rights instruments also recognize the particular role of vulnerable groups, such as indigenous peoples, women, and youth. Report of the Special Rapporteur (n 4) 13–16.

[64] Knox Preliminary Report (n 38) 10. See also Svitlana Kravchenko, 'Procedural Rights as a Crucial Tool to Combat Climate Change', *Georgia Journal of International and Comparative Law*, 38/3 (2010): 613.

'right to development', which was unpalatable to many developed countries,[65] not only because of long articulated concerns with collective (as opposed to individual) rights, but also because, in the context of climate change, a right to development could translate into a right to emit.

The Cancun Agreements in 2010 contain the first explicit reference to human rights in the UN climate regime, urging states to 'fully respect human rights' in all climate change-related actions.[66] The Cancun Agreements also included, as one of the 'safeguards' relating to REDD+ (reducing emissions from deforestation and forest degradation in developing countries),[67] a requirement that parties respect the 'knowledge and rights of indigenous peoples and members of local communities'.[68]

In keeping with the growing focus internationally on the human rights implication of climate impacts, a number of states,[69] non-governmental organizations,[70] and international bodies[71] urged the inclusion of human rights concerns in the Paris Agreement.[72] In an effort to headline human rights, eighteen countries, led by Costa Rica, voluntarily pledged in February 2015 to 'enable meaningful collaboration between national representatives in these two processes [FCCC and

---

[65] See Susan Biniaz, 'Comma but Differentiated Responsibilities: Punctuation and 30 other ways negotiators have resolved issues in the international climate regime' (Columbia Law School–Sabin Centre for Climate Change Law, June 2016) <https://web.law.columbia.edu/sites/default/files/microsites/climate-change/files/Publications/biniaz_2016_june_comma_diff_responsibilities.pdf> accessed 20 January 2017, for an interesting back story on the provision, and its interpretation. Also discussed in Chapter 3, Section II.D.5.

[66] Cancun Agreements LCA, para 8.   [67] Ibid, para 70 and Appendix I.

[68] Ibid, Appendix I, para 2(c).

[69] See eg Submission of Chile on behalf of AILAC to the ADP on Human Rights and Climate Change (31 May 2015) <http://www4.unfccc.int/Submissions/Lists/OSPSubmissionUpload/195_99_130775585079215037-Chile%20on%20behalf%20of%20AILAC%20HR%20and%20CC.docx> accessed 20 January 2017; Proposal of Ecuador, Durban Platform (3 March 2013) <http://unfccc.int/files/documentation/submissions_from_parties/adp/application/pdf/adp_ecuador_workstream_1_20130301.pdf> accessed 20 January 2017, 2; EIG Surgical edits (19 October 2015) <http://unfccc.int/files/bodies/awg/application/pdf/adp2-11_ws1_eig_19oct2015.pdf> accessed 20 January 2017; EU Text Suggestions on Key Issues (19 October 2015) <http://unfccc.int/files/bodies/awg/application/pdf/151019_eu_proposed_edits_agreement.pdf> accessed 20 January 2017, 2; Textual insertions of the Philippines for the Draft Agreement (19 October 2015) <http://unfccc.int/files/meetings/bonn_oct_2015/application/pdf/textual_insertions_of_the_philippines_for_the_draft_agreement.pdf> accessed 20 January 2017.

[70] See eg Submission to the Ad Hoc Working Group on the Durban Platform for Enhanced Action Calling for Human Rights Protections in the 2015 Climate Agreement (7 February 2015) <http://unfccc.int/files/documentation/submissions_from_non-party_stakeholders/application/pdf/489.pdf> accessed 20 January 2017; Human Rights and Climate Change Working Group, Submission to the Ad Hoc Working Group on the Durban Platform for Enhanced Action Regarding Information, Views and Proposals Related to the Durban Platform Workplan Under Workstream 1 (1 March 2013) <http://unfccc.int/resource/docs/2013/smsn/ngo/303.pdf> accessed 20 January 2017; Submission to the ADP by the Mary Robinson Foundation—Climate Justice (1 March 2013) <http://unfccc.int/resource/docs/2013/smsn/un/306.pdf> accessed 20 January 2017.

[71] See eg OHCHR, 'A New Climate Change Agreement Must Include Human Rights Protections for All' (17 October 2014) <http://www.ohchr.org/Documents/HRBodies/SP/SP_To_UNFCCC.pdf> accessed 2 August 2016; OHCHR, 'The Effects of Climate Change on the Full Enjoyment of Human Rights' (30 April 2015) <http://www.thecvf.org/wp-content/uploads/2015/05/humanrightsSRHRE.pdf> accessed 20 January 2017.

[72] For an overview of the advocacy movement on human rights in the lead up to Paris, see generally Benoit Mayer, 'Human Rights in the Paris Agreement', *Climate Law*, 6/1 (2016): 109.

the Human Rights Council] to increase our understanding of how human rights obligations inform better climate action'.[73] In Paris, many parties sought an explicit human rights reference in an operative part of the agreement, in particular in Article 2,[74] which identifies the purpose of the Paris Agreement, sets the long-term temperature goal, and frames the implementation of the agreement. Early versions of Article 2.2 contained bracketed references to human rights.[75] Proponents hoped that a reference to human rights in this provision would help promote the protection of human rights in the implementation of the Paris Agreement.[76]

However, inclusion of a human rights provision in the operative part of the Paris Agreement proved difficult to secure, for several reasons. First and foremost, some parties believed that introducing human rights concerns into the 'purpose' of the Paris Agreement would dilute the climate objectives it contained,[77] and argued that other forums are more appropriate for furtherance of human rights objectives.[78] In addition, it was not obvious which rights, if any, should be singled out for protection in the context of implementing the Paris Agreement. There appeared to be broad consensus on rights such as those of women, but others such as the rights of those under occupation provoked fierce debate. The solution mooted was to include a generic reference to human rights, but this proved unacceptable to most parties, as each party or group of parties was invested in one or more specific rights to the exclusion of others.[79] In any case, some argued that a generic reference to rights would lead to greater conceptual fuzziness, and thus less certainty and predictability in implementing the Paris Agreement, as well as protection of the relevant human

---

[73] The Geneva Pledge for Human Rights in Climate Action, 13 February 2015 < http://www.forest-peoples.org/sites/fpp/files/news/2015/02/Annex_Geneva%20Pledge.pdf > accessed 20 January 2017.

[74] See in particular, Chile on behalf of AILAC to the ADP on Human Rights and Climate Change (n 69). See also for media reportage, Human Rights Watch, 'UN: Human Rights crucial in addressing climate change—Paris Agreement Should Ensure Transparency, Accountability and Participation' (3 December 2015) <https://www.hrw.org/news/2015/12/03/un-human-rights-crucial-addressing-climate-change> accessed 20 January 2017.

[75] Ad Hoc Working Group on the Durban Platform for Enhanced Action (ADP), Draft Paris Outcome, Revised draft conclusions proposed by the Co-Chairs (5 December 2015) FCCC/ADP/2015/L.6/Rev.1, Annex I: Draft Agreement and Draft Decision. See also Draft agreement and draft decision on workstreams 1 and 2 of the Ad Hoc Working Group on the Durban Platform for Enhanced Action (edited version of 6 November 2015, re-issued 10 November 2015), ADP.2015.11. InformalNote.

[76] Human rights references are included in Art 2.2 in earlier versions of the Negotiating text. See eg Draft Paris Outcome, Proposal by the President, Version 1 of 9 December 2015 at 15:00 <http://unfccc.int/resource/docs/2015/cop21/eng/da01.pdf> accessed 20 January 2017; Draft Agreement and Draft Decision (5 December 2015), ibid.

[77] See eg Government of Norway, 'COP 21: Indigenous Peoples, Human Rights and Climate Change' (7 December 2015) <https://www.regjeringen.no/no/aktuelt/cop21-indigenous-peoples-human-rights-and-climat-changes/id2466047/> accessed 20 January 2016.

[78] See eg New Zealand Submission to the Ad Hoc Working Group on the Durban Platform for Enhanced Action: Views on options and ways for further increasing the level of global ambition (28 March 2012) <http://unfccc.int/resource/docs/2012/adp1/eng/misc01.pdf> accessed 20 January 2017.

[79] See Indigenous Rising: An Indigenous Environmental Network Project, 'Indigenous Rights on the Chopping Block of UN COP21 Paris Climate Accord' (4 December 2015) <http://indigenous-rising.org/indigenous-rights-on-chopping-block-of-un-cop21-paris-climate-accord/> accessed 20 January 2017.

rights. These reasons, among others, dictated the eventual compromise to reflect selected human rights in the preamble, which provides context,[80] rather than in an operational provision of the Paris Agreement, which has greater legal gravitas.[81]

Eventually, the only explicit reference to human rights agreed to in the Paris Agreement occurs in the preamble. The relevant preambular recital reads:

Parties should, when taking action to address climate change, respect, promote, and consider their respective obligations on human rights, the right to health, the rights of indigenous peoples, local communities, migrants children, persons with disabilities and people in vulnerable situations, and the right to development, as well as gender equality, empowerment of women, and intergenerational equity.[82]

As discussed in detail in Chapter 7, this recital carefully circumscribes its impact. Notably, it addresses only the human rights aspects of response measures, and refers to parties' 'respective obligations', thus ensuring that no new human rights obligations are implied for states.

Parties had differing views on the existence, characterization, relative importance, and boundaries of the listed human rights. Some parties argued they did not have obligations with respect to some of the rights. Further, some parties conceived of certain rights as 'individual right' while others saw them as 'collective rights'. For instance, the Least Developed Countries (LDCs) consider the 'right to development' as a right belonging to individuals,[83] and Ecuador, as a right belonging to developing countries.[84] Additionally, some proposed human rights, such as the 'rights of people under occupation', proved so controversial that they are engaged, if at all, only by implication. In this instance, 'people in vulnerable situations' could arguably include those under occupation. Given the indeterminacy and vagueness of phrases such as this, countries wanted to make clear in the preambular recital that they did not necessarily subscribe to all of the listed rights.

Despite all of these caveats, however, the very inclusion of an explicit reference to human rights in the Paris Agreement was viewed by many as crucial, and may signal enhanced receptivity to rights concerns and discourses in the UN climate regime. Moreover, in addition to the explicit reference to human rights in the preamble, the Paris Agreement implicitly bolsters certain procedural rights, by requiring parties to

---

[80] Vienna Convention on the Law of Treaties (adopted 23 May 1969, entered into force 27 January 1980) 1155 UNTS 331, Art 31.2. The preamble is part of the context for purposes of interpretation of the treaty, including its object and purpose. See Anthony Aust, *Modern Treaty Law and Practice* (Cambridge University Press, 2nd edn, 2007) 425 (also noting that 'the preamble can be the most convenient place to put the leftovers of hopeless causes').

[81] See for a discussion of defining elements of legal character, Lavanya Rajamani, 'The 2015 Paris Agreement: Interplay between Hard, Soft and Non-Obligations', *Journal of Environmental Law*, 28/2 (2016): 337, 342–52. See also Daniel Bodansky, 'The Legal Character of the Paris Agreement', *Review of European, Comparative and International Law*, 25/2 (2016): 142.

[82] Paris Agreement, preambular recital 11.

[83] Angola on behalf of the Least Developed Countries Group—'surgical insertions' to co-chairs non-paper (v. 5 October 2015): ARTICLE 2: PURPOSE (19 October 2015) <http://unfccc.int/files/bodies/awg/application/pdf/adp2-11_art2_purpose_ldcs_19oct2015.pdf> accessed 20 January 2017.

[84] Ecuador, Views on options and ways for further increasing the level of ambition (28 March 2012) <http://unfccc.int/resource/docs/2012/adp1/eng/misc01.pdf> accessed 20 January 2017.

cooperate to enhance public participation and public access to information, measures whose importance is also affirmed in the preamble.[85]

III. CLIMATE CHANGE, MIGRATION, AND DISPLACEMENT

A. Introduction

The disruptions caused by climate change—including drought and flooding, extreme weather events, and sea level rise—are likely to trigger large scale movements of people. The Intergovernmental Panel on Climate Change (IPCC) in 1990 predicted that the 'gravest effects of climate change may be those on human migration'.[86] Although its recent pronouncements have been more guarded, the IPCC nevertheless states that climate change is projected to increase displacement of people.[87] The scope and scale of displacement, and the extent to which such displacement can be traced (primarily) to climate change, are, however, in dispute. There are no authoritative estimates of those likely to be displaced by climate impacts. 'Guestimates' vary from 25 million people at the conservative end,[88] to 1 billion in the middle,[89] and 2 billion at the high end.[90] These estimates vary in part because of the 'complex multi-causal' nature of human mobility and the uncertainties about climate change impacts.[91] Although there

---

[85] Paris Agreement, preambular recital 14.

[86] IPCC, *Climate Change: The IPCC Scientific Assessment (1990)* (Cambridge University Press, 1990) 20.

[87] IPCC, *Climate Change 2014: Synthesis Report* (Cambridge University Press, 2014) Summary for Policymakers (SPM), 16 ('Climate change is projected to increase displacement of people (medium evidence, high agreement). Populations that lack the resources for planned migration experience higher exposure to extreme weather events, particularly in developing countries with low income.').

[88] See Internal Displacement Monitoring Centre (IDMC), 'IDMC's Global Internal Displacement Database' <http://www.internal-displacement.org/database/> accessed 20 January 2017 (noting that on average 25 million are displaced internally every year due to disasters).

[89] Informal group on migration/displacement and climate change of the Inter-Agency Standing Committee (IASC), 'Climate Change, Migration and Displacement: Who will be affected?' (Working Paper, 31 October 2008) <http://unfccc.int/resource/docs/2008/smsn/igo/022.pdf> accessed 20 January 2017.

[90] Norman Myers, 'Environmental Refugees: An Emergent Security Issue' (13th Economic Forum, Prague, 22 May 2005) <http://www.osce.org/eea/14851?download=true> accessed 20 January 2017.

[91] IPCC, *Climate Change 2014: Impacts, Adaptation and Vulnerability* (Cambridge University Press, 2014) SPM, 20; M.K. Solomon and Koko Warner, 'Protection of Persons Displaced as a Result of Climate Change: Existing Tools and Emerging Frameworks', in Michael B. Gerrard and Gregory E. Wannier (eds), *Threatened Island Nations: Legal Implications of Rising Seas and a Changing Climate* (Cambridge University Press, 2013) 243, 281–4; See generally UK Government Office for Science, 'Foresight: Migration and Global Environmental Change – Final Project Report' (London: UK Government Office for Science, 2011) <https://www.gov.uk/government/uploads/system/uploads/attachment_data/file/287717/11-1116-migration-and-global-environmental-change.pdf> accessed 20 January 2017.

is a clear link between climate impacts and displacement,[92] individual mobility decisions are multi-faceted and other factors and pressures, including social, economic, and political, play important roles.[93] Climate change may also act as a 'force multiplier',[94] or 'impact multiplier and accelerator',[95] as it both displaces people and intensifies other factors that trigger human mobility. Scholars have suggested, therefore, that it is more sensible to approach 'climate related movement as part of global migration dynamics, rather than as a discrete, independent category'.[96]

Climate impacts can manifest themselves in slow-onset environmental degradation, such as 'sea level rise, increasing temperatures, ocean acidification, glacial retreat and related impacts, salinization, land and forest degradation, loss of biodiversity and desertification'.[97] Climate impacts can also manifest themselves in extreme weather events or rapid onset events, such as typhoons and hurricanes.[98] Both types of climate events could lead to human mobility. Such mobility could be temporary in so far as people flee their homes and return when the environmental threat has receded, or permanent in so far as the environmental changes endure. It could be a 'voluntary' adaptation strategy to cope with an increasingly hostile environment, or it could be 'forced' in so far as homes have been rendered uninhabitable and livelihoods unsustainable.[99] There is a thin line, however, between voluntary and forced movement,[100] and climate-induced displacement is best 'understood as a continuum, ranging from clear cases of forced to clear cases of voluntary movement, with a grey zone in between'.[101]

Climate-induced movements could be internal, within the same state, or cross international borders. Although the phenomenon of 'climate refugees' crossing borders in search of succour has a powerful hold on the popular imagination,[102]

---

[92] Submission from the Office of the United Nations High Commissioner for Refugees (UNHCR), 'Forced displacement in the context of climate change: challenges for states under international law' (25 May 2009) FCCC/AWGLCA/2009/MISC.5, 15.

[93] Jane McAdam, *Climate Change, Forced Migration and International Law* (Oxford University Press, 2012) 15–16.

[94] Antonio Gueterres, 'Millions Uprooted: Saving Refugees and the Displaced', *Foreign Affairs*, 87/5 (2008) <https://www.foreignaffairs.com/articles/2008-09-01/millions-uprooted> accessed 20 January 2017.

[95] UNHCR, 'Summary of Deliberations on Climate Change and Displacement' (Expert Roundtable on Climate Change and Displacement, Bellagio, 25 February 2011) <http://www.unhcr.org/4da2b5e19.pdf> accessed 20 January 2017, 2.

[96] Jane McAdam, 'Climate Change-Related Displacement of Persons', in Carlarne *et al.*, Oxford Handbook of International Climate Change Law (n 8) 519, 520.

[97] Cancun Agreements LCA, para 25.

[98] See Walter Kälin, 'Conceptualizing Climate-Induced Displacement', in Jane McAdam (ed), *Climate Change and Displacement: Multidisciplinary Perspectives* (Oxford: Hart Publishing, 2010) 81, 85.

[99] Ibid.

[100] Diane C. Bates, 'Environmental Refugees? Classifying Human Migration Caused by Environmental Change', *Population and Environment*, 23/5 (2002): 465, 467–8.

[101] International Organisation for Migration (IOM), 'Migration, Climate Change and the Environment: A Complete Nexus' <https://www.iom.int/complex-nexus> accessed 20 January 2017.

[102] Benoit Mayer, *The Concept of Climate Migration: Advocacy and Its Prospects* (Cheltenham, UK: Edward Elgar Publishing, 2016) 4–5.

internal displacement is likely to far outstrip cross-border displacement.[103] Among the existing international legal frameworks that govern displacement, some apply to internal movement and others to cross-border movement. In both cases, albeit more so in relation to cross-border displacement, there are considerable gaps in protection. In any case, whether the displacement is temporary or permanent, voluntary or forced, internal or cross-border, the most serious effects of climate change, including in relation to displacement, are predicted to disproportionately affect poor regions and countries and already vulnerable populations.[104]

B. Existing international protection

1. *Internal displacement*

The legal framework for the protection of internally displaced persons is contained in the 1998 Guiding Principles on Internal Displacement (GPID).[105] Although these are non-binding principles, they are widely accepted as codifying guarantees in international human rights law and international humanitarian law in relation to the protection of internally displaced persons.[106] Indeed, the 2005 World Summit Outcome endorsed these principles as 'an important international legal framework for the protection of internally displaced persons'.[107]

---

[103] See The Nansen Initiative: Disaster-Induced Cross-Border Displacement, 'Agenda for the Protection of Cross-Border Displaced Persons in the Context of Disasters and Climate Change' (Vol 1, December 2015) <https://nanseninitiative.org/wp-content/uploads/2015/02/PROTECTION-AGENDA-VOLUME-1.pdf> accessed 20 January 2017, 14. See generally IDMC, 'Global Estimates 2015: People Displaced by Disasters' (July 2015) http://www.internal-displacement.org/assets/library/Media/201507-globalEstimates-2015/20150713-global-estimates-2015-en-v1.pdf> accessed 20 January 2017.

[104] See eg Nansen Initiative, ibid. See also Report on Relationship between Climate Change and Human Rights (n 10) paras 42–54.

[105] United Nations Commission on Human Rights, Report of the Representative of the Secretary-General, Mr. Francis M. Deng, submitted pursuant to Commission resolution 1997/39, Addendum: Guiding Principles on Internal Displacement (11 February 1998) UN Doc E/CN.4/1998/53/Add.2, Annex (Guiding Principles on Internal Displacement). The GPID is complemented by the Inter-Agency Standing Committee's 'IASC Operational Guidelines on the Protection of Persons in Situations of Natural Disasters' (The Brookings-Bern Project on Internal Displacement, January 2011) <http://www.ohchr.org/Documents/Issues/IDPersons/OperationalGuidelines.pdf> accessed 20 January 2017. See generally Alice Edwards, 'Climate Change and International Refugee Law', in Rosemary Rayfuse and Shirley V. Scott (eds), *International Law in the Era of Climate Change* (Cheltenham, UK: Edward Elgar Publishing, 2012) 58, 62–5; McAdam, Climate Change, Forced Migration (n 93) 250–6; Katrina M. Wyman, 'Human Mobility and Climate Change', in Farber and Peeters (eds), Climate Change Law (n 8) 637, 639.

[106] Walter Kälin, *Guiding Principles on Internal Displacement: Annotation* (Washington, D.C.: American Society of International Law, 2nd edn, 2008) viii. See also UNHCR, Summary of Deliberations (n 95) para 19 (noting that these guiding principles reflect and consolidate existing international law). But see Marco Simons, 'The Emergence of a Norm Against Arbitrary Forced Relocation', *Columbia Human Rights Law Review,* 34/1 (2002): 95, 128 (noting although the GPID may soon attain the status of custom, they are not yet customary international law).

[107] UNGA Res 60/1, '2005 World Summit Outcome' (24 October 2005) UN Doc A/RES/60/1, para 132.

The description of internally displaced persons in the GPID could encompass those displaced due to climate impacts. Internally displaced persons are 'persons or groups of persons who have been forced or obliged to flee or to leave their homes or places of habitual residence, in particular as a result of or in order to avoid the effects of armed conflict, situations of generalized violence, violations of human rights or natural or human-made disasters, and who have not crossed an internationally recognized State border'.[108] Climate change is a 'human-made disaster' but since the GPID definition encompasses both human-made and natural disasters, it makes the 'attribution' question (whether human-made or natural) irrelevant,[109] and is widely accepted as applying to climate-induced displacement.[110]

The Guiding Principles identify needs and rights of the displaced at different stages of displacement—pre-displacement, displacement, and resettlement.[111] Of particular relevance in the climate context are the highlighted rights of the displaced to: life; dignity and physical, mental and moral integrity; liberty and security; liberty of movement, and freedom to choose one's home; seek safety and asylum elsewhere; know the fate of missing relatives; respect for family life and unity; an adequate standard of living; medical care and attention; recognition before the law; not be arbitrarily deprived of property and possessions; not be discriminated against; and education.[112] The Guiding Principles also address the provision of humanitarian assistance to the displaced[113] and their return, resettlement, and integration.[114]

Although the Guiding Principles are comprehensive and systematic in their coverage of the needs and rights relating to displacement, there are some difficulties with their application and effectiveness in the climate context. First, they apply only to those displaced by climate events, and not the totality of the population affected by such events.[115] Second, they appear designed primarily to address rapid onset disasters rather than slow onset processes such as sea level rise,[116] which require greater emphasis on 'positive obligations' of states to anticipate, plan ahead, and take measures to prevent or mitigate conditions that are likely to cause displacement.[117]

---

[108] Guiding Principles on Internal Displacement (n 105) para 2.

[109] See Kälin, Climate-induced displacement (n 98).

[110] UNHCR, Summary of Deliberations (n 95) para 19; Edwards, Climate Change and International Refugee Law (n 105) 64; McAdam, Climate Change-Related Displacement (n 96) 529.

[111] See McAdam, Climate Change, Forced Migration (n 93) 250–2.

[112] Guiding Principles on Internal Displacement (n 105) principles 10–23.

[113] Ibid, principles 24–7.   [114] Ibid, principles 28–30.

[115] Edwards, Climate Change and International Refugee Law (n 105) 64. It is worth noting, however, that the totality of the population is covered by the human rights obligations a state owes to its citizens, so they are not without protection.

[116] Ibid. See also Sumundu Atapattu, 'Climate Change, Human Rights and Forced Migration: Implications for International Law', *Wisconsin International Law Journal*, 27/3 (2009): 607, 618.

[117] UNGA, 'Protection of and assistance to internally displaced persons', Note by Secretary-General (9 August 2011) UN Doc A/66/285, para 54. See Brookings Institution, Georgetown University, and UNHCR, 'Guidance on Protecting People from Disasters and Environmental Change Through Planned Relocation' (7 October 2015)<https://isim.georgetown.edu/sites/isim/files/files/upload/GUIDANCE_PLANNED%20RELOCATION_14%20OCT%202015.pdf> accessed 20 January 2017 (for an attempt to create detailed guidance on planned relocation).

Third, they contain no monitoring or reporting mechanism. Finally, there are considerable gaps in the implementation of these principles, due perhaps to the lack of a reporting or monitoring mechanism and to limited political will and resources, including financial.[118] Nevertheless, a legal framework for protection of internally displaced persons exists, and can be readily applied in the climate (and natural disaster) context. The Nansen Initiative, discussed below, seeks to do so by identifying a series of effective practices that states should consider adopting, including reviewing domestic legislation and policies to bring them in line with the Guiding Principles.[119]

The Guiding Principles, although non-binding, are widely applied,[120] and have been incorporated and further concretized in legally-binding regional instruments such as the African Union Convention for the Protection and Assistance of Internally Displaced Persons (the Kampala Convention)[121] and the Protocol on the Protection and Assistance to Internally Displaced Persons (the Great Lakes Protocol).[122] These regional instruments seek to fill some of the gaps in the Guiding Principles; for instance the Kampala Convention contains compliance and monitoring mechanisms.[123] And they require state parties to enact legislation to 'domesticate the Guiding Principles'[124] and to provide a legal framework for implementation of the Guiding Principles within national legal systems.[125] The Kampala Declaration to the Kampala Convention is of particular relevance to climate-induced displacement, as it explicitly recognizes 'the increasing incidence of displacement caused by environmental factors, including climate change' and requires states to address

---

[118] Wyman, Human Mobility and Climate Change (n105) 639. See also Khalid Koser, 'Climate Change and Internal Displacement: Challenges to the Normative Framework', in Etienne Piguet *et al.* (eds), *Migration and Climate Change* (Cambridge University Press and UNESCO Publishing 2011) 289, 296–7 (discussing the limitations of the Guiding Principles).

[119] See Nansen Initiative (n 103) paras 99–103. See generally Francois Gemenne and Pauline Brucker, 'From the Governance of Internal Displacement to the Governance of Environmental Migration: What Can the Latter Learn from the Former?' (American Political Science Association Annual Meeting, 2013) <http://papers.ssrn.com/sol3/papers.cfm?abstract_id=2299802> accessed 20 January 2017.

[120] Guiding Principles on Internal Displacement (n 105) para 4. See UNGA Res 58/177, 'Protection of and Assistance to Internally Displaced Persons' (12 March 2004) UN Doc A/RES/58/177 (noting the increasing dissemination, promotion and application of the Guiding Principles on Internal Displacement when dealing with situations of internal displacement).

[121] African Union Convention for the Protection and Assistance of Internally Displaced Persons (adopted 23 October 2009, entered into force 06 December 2012) <https://treaties.un.org/doc/Publication/UNTS/No%20Volume/52375/Part/I-52375-08000002803f0260.pdf> accessed 20 January 2017 (Kampala Convention).

[122] Protocol on the Protection and Assistance to Internally Displaced Persons (adopted 15 December 2006, entry into force 21 June 2008) (Great Lakes Protocol). See generally Werner Scholtz, 'The Day After No Tomorrow? Persons Displaced Environmentally through Climate Change: AU Law to the Rescue?', *South African Yearbook of International Law,* 35 (2010): 36, 46. See also ASEAN Agreement on Disaster Management and Emergency Response (adopted 26 July 2005, entry into force 24 December 2009) <http://asean.org/?static_post=asean-agreement-on-disaster-management-and-emergency-response-vientiane-26-july-2005-3> accessed 20 January 2017.

[123] Kampala Convention (n 121) Arts 14.1 and 14.4.

[124] Great Lakes Protocol (n 122) Art 6.

[125] Ibid; Kampala Convention (n 121) Art 3.2.

climate change in an effort to find durable solutions to the problem of refugees and internally displaced persons.[126]

2. Cross-border displacement

There is no single legal framework for the protection of those displaced across national borders for climate-related reasons. Among the frameworks that may be relevant are those pertaining to international refugee law, international human rights law, and the law relating to statelessness.

a) International refugee law

Although the term 'climate refugee' is a powerful emotive and advocacy tool, most of those affected by climate-induced displacement are unlikely to fall within the definition of a 'refugee' under the 1951 Refugee Convention, which is limited to those who migrate to escape racial, religious, political, or ethnic persecution.[127] Climate-induced displacement is neither covered by this definition nor contemplated by the drafters.[128]

A refugee is defined as someone who, 'owing to a well-founded fear of being persecuted for reasons of race, religion, nationality, membership of a particular social group or political opinion, is outside the country of his nationality and is unable or, owing to such fear, is unwilling to ... return to it.'[129] Climate change, albeit human-made, cannot, absent considerable legal jugglery, be characterized as persecution.[130] Even if it could be so characterized, such persecution would need to be for reasons of race, religion, nationality, or membership of a particular social group or political opinion. Since the impacts of climate change are largely

---

[126] African Union, Kampala Declaration on Refugees, Returnees and Internally Displaced Persons in Africa (23 October 2009) Ext/Assembly/AU/PA/Draft/Decl.(I) Rev.1, preambular recital 5 and para 22.

[127] Convention Relating to the Status of Refugees (adopted 28 July 1951, entry into force 22 April 1954) 189 UNTS 137 (Refugee Convention). See McAdam, Climate Change, Forced Migration (n 8) 42–8. See also Alisa Ceri Warnock, 'Small Island Developing States of the Pacific and Climate Change: Adaptation and Alternatives', *New Zealand Yearbook of International Law*, 4 (2007): 247, 271–8; David Keane, 'The Environmental Causes and Consequences of Migration: A Search for the Meaning of "Environmental Refugees"', *Georgetown International Environmental Law Review*, 16/2 (2004): 209, 215; Tracey King, 'Environmental Displacement: Coordinating Effects to Find Solutions', *Georgetown International Environmental Law Review*, 18/3 (2006): 543, 551–4; Aurelie Lopez, 'The Protection of Environmentally Displaced Persons in International Law', *Environmental Law*, 37/2 (2007): 365, 377; Susan F. Martin, 'Climate Change, Migration and Governance', *Global Governance: A Review of Multilateralism and International Organizations*, 16/3 (2010): 397, 404–5; Tiffany T.V. Duong, 'When Islands Drown: The Plight of "Climate Change Refugees" and Recourse to International Human Rights Law', *University of Pennsylvania Journal of International Law*, 31/4 (2010): 1239, 1249–50.

[128] Kälin, Conceptualizing Climate-Induced Displacement (n 98) 88.

[129] Refugee Convention, Art 1.

[130] See McAdam, Climate Change, Forced Migration (n 93) 42. See also Christopher M. Kozoll, 'Poisoning the Well: Persecution, the Environment, and Refugee Status', *Colorado Journal of International Environmental Law and Policy*, 15/2 (2004): 271. But see Jessica B. Cooper, 'Environmental Refugees: Meeting the Requirements of the Refugee Definition', *New York University Environmental Law Journal*, 6/2 (1998): 480.

non-discriminatory, this is difficult if not impossible to establish.[131] It is also difficult to identify a 'persecutor' in this context, given the distributed responsibilities of states for causing climate change. The string of (thus far) unsuccessful claims by Pacific Islanders for asylum in Australia and New Zealand based on climate impacts illustrate the hurdles of using the Refugee Convention to address climate-induced displacement.[132] However, the New Zealand courts have not ruled out the application of the Refugee Convention, advocating instead a case-by-case approach.[133] In a narrow band of situations, those affected by climate-induced displacement may arguably fall within the definition of a 'refugee'. For instance, if people flee because of competition over resources arising from climate change, and they are denied access to resources because of their race, religion, nationality, membership of a particular social group, or political opinion, then they could qualify as refugees.[134] Victims of natural disasters may also qualify, if their government consciously withheld or obstructed assistance in order to punish or marginalize them on account of these characteristics.[135] However, in these cases, it is not the impacts of climate change itself that render a person a refugee; rather climate impacts render persons vulnerable to persecution on account of these characteristics.[136]

Regional instruments, such as the Organization of African Unity Convention[137] and the Cartagena Declaration on Refugees,[138] contain broader definitions of refugees. However, these too do not readily apply to those affected by climate-induced displacement, absent creative interpretation, which states are unlikely to accept.[139]

---

[131] McAdam, ibid, 46–7.

[132] See eg *Teitiota v The Chief Executive of the Ministry of Business, Innovation and Employment* [2015] NZSC 107; *AF (Kiribati)* [2013] NZIPT 800413; 1004726 [2010] RRTA 845 (Sept 2010) (Tonga). For a full list see McAdam, Climate Change-Related Displacement (n 96) 522.

[133] *AF Kiribati*, ibid, para 64.

[134] See Martin, Climate Change, Migration (n 127) 405; King, Environmental Displacement (n 127) 554; and Lopez, Protection of Environmentally Displaced Persons (n 127) 377–89.

[135] UNHCR, Summary of Deliberations (n 95) para 8; UNHCR, Forced Displacement (n 92) 21.

[136] Jane McAdam, 'From the Nansen Initiative to the Platform on Disaster Displacement: Shaping International Approaches to Climate Change, Disasters and Displacement', *University of New South Wales Law Journal*, 39/4 (2016): 1518.

[137] Organization of African Unity Convention Governing the Specific Aspects of Refugee Problems in Africa (adopted 10 September 1969, entry into force 20 June 1974) 1001 UNTS 45 (including in the definition of refugees those who flee 'events seriously disturbing public order'). Tamara Wood, 'Protection and Disasters in the Horn of Africa: Norms and Practice for Addressing Cross-Border Displacement in Disaster Contexts' (January 2015) <http://www.nanseninitiative.org/wp-content/uploads/2015/03/190215_Technical_Paper_Tamara_Wood.pdf> accessed 20 January 2017.

[138] Cartagena Declaration on Refugees (Colloquium on the International Protection of Refugees in Central America, Mexico and Panama, 22 November 1984) OAS Doc. OEA/Ser.L/V/II.66/doc.10, rev. 1, at 190–3 (1984–85) (including in the definition of refugees those who flee, inter alia, due to 'internal conflicts, massive violation of human rights or other circumstances which have seriously disturbed public order').

[139] See McAdam, Climate Change, Forced Migration (n 93) 48–9; and Alice Edwards, 'Refugee Status Determination in Africa', *African Journal of International and Comparative Law*, 14/2 (2006): 204, 225–7.

b) International human rights law

As the first section of this chapter demonstrates, human rights law is of tremendous salience in relation to climate change. In the context of displacement, it provides a useful complement to the protections afforded by international refugee law. It requires states to protect, in addition to 'refugees', people at risk of arbitrary deprivation of life, torture, or cruel, inhuman, or degrading treatment or punishment.[140] In particular, it prohibits states from sending refugees or asylum seekers to territories where they are at risk of arbitrary deprivation of life, torture, or cruel, inhuman, or degrading treatment or punishment.[141] This obligation is referred to as 'non-refoulement' in international law. In relation to climate-induced displacement, the climate impacts people are fleeing from would need to be established as amounting to 'cruel, inhuman or degrading treatment'. Courts have held that breaches of social and economic rights (as for instance destitution and 'dire humanitarian conditions'[142]) can amount to inhuman or degrading treatment. However, they have also carefully limited the meaning of cruel and inhuman or degrading treatment so that it cannot be extended to cover claims relating to generalized poverty, unemployment, or lack of resources and services.[143] Thus, claims that generalized climate impacts trigger a state's non-refoulement obligation would be difficult to maintain. In addition, it is worth noting that many of the worst impacts of climate change have yet to manifest themselves. As a result, those fleeing future or imminent impacts may not be able to establish that returning to their home state would, at that moment, cross the threshold into cruel and inhuman or degrading treatment.[144] A further factor relevant to the application of the principle of non-refoulement is that climate impacts are likely to result in large-scale rather than a trickle of movement. Although the fundamental obligation of non-refoulement applies and must be 'scrupulously observed' even in situations of mass influx,[145] such situations give rise to considerable difficulties for the receiving state. In these cases, states may (only) be required to provide 'temporary protection' that extends to admission to safety, respect for basic human rights, protection against refoulement, and safe return when conditions permit.[146] Safe return implies that the cause

---

[140] McAdam, ibid, 53.

[141] Sir Elihu Lauterpacht and Daniel Bethlehem, 'The Scope and Content of the Principle of *Non-refoulement*: Opinion', in Erika Feller *et al.* (eds), *Refugee Protection in International Law: UNHCR's Global Consultations on International Protection* (Cambridge University Press, 2003) 87, 89–93 and references therein.

[142] See eg *R v Secretary of State* 2005 UKHL 66.

[143] McAdam, Climate Change-Related Displacement (n 96) 525.

[144] Ibid, 525–6. See *AF (Kiribati)* (n 132).

[145] See Lauterpacht and Bethlehem, Non-refoulement (n 141) 119–21. See also Jean-Francois Durieux and Jane McAdam, 'Non-Refoulement through Time: The Case for a Derogation Clause to the Refugee Convention in Mass Influx Emergencies', *International Journal of Refugee Law*, 16/1 (2004): 4.

[146] UNHCR, 'Protection of Asylum Seekers in Situations of Large-Scale Influx', Executive Committee Conclusion No. 22 (XXXII) (21 October 1981) UN Doc 12A (A/36/12/Add.1). See Edwards, Climate Change and International Refugee Law (n 105) 73–76; see also Alice Edwards, 'Temporary Protection, Derogation and the 1951 Refugee Convention', *Melbourne Journal of International Law*, 13/2 (2012): 595.

that gave rise to the exodus is at an end, and if the cause persists, protection must continue. Thus, climate change claims, while not prima facie excluded, would need to be carefully argued, developed, and tailored to come within the ambit of states' non-refoulement obligation.[147]

Other rights and obligations may have a bearing on climate-induced displacement.[148] For instance, the 'right to a healthy environment' that has, as discussed in the previous section, been incorporated in regional instruments and many national constitutions, may be relevant in that severe climate impacts arguably breach this right. However, scholars question whether such a right, where it exists, can give rise to a 'right of sanctuary' relevant to climate-induced displacement, 'rather than merely a remedy under international law'.[149]

Another avenue that scholars have explored in relation to addressing climate-induced displacement is the emerging doctrine of 'responsibility to protect'.[150] This doctrine holds that 'sovereign states have a responsibility to protect their own citizens from avoidable catastrophe—from mass murder and rape, from starvation—but that when they are unwilling or unable to do so, that responsibility must be borne by the broader community of states'.[151] Although not conceived of in the context of climate change or designed to address situations of climate-induced harms, some argue that this doctrine can be extended to the climate context.[152] The 'responsibility to protect' in relation to climate change would entail a responsibility 'to seriously address carbon emissions', to take measures to address climate impacts, including displacement, and to provide 'permanent and durable solutions' for those displaced by climate change.[153] The criticisms that have hounded the 'responsibility to protect' doctrine, however—that such 'responsibilities' will likely be exercised in discretionary and politically-motivated ways—also apply here.[154]

c) Law relating to statelessness

Another legal framework that has potential application to cases of climate-induced displacement, in particular to the paradigmatic case of small island states at imminent risk of submersion, is the law relating to statelessness.[155] The situation of 'sinking islands' raises complex legal and technical questions, and strains against the traditional boundaries of

---

[147] McAdam, Climate Change, Forced Migration (n 93) 54.
[148] See generally McAdam, ibid, ch 3; Duong, When Islands Drown (n 127) 1252–61.
[149] Edwards, Climate Change and International Refugee Law (n 105) 71.
[150] Susan F. Martin, 'Forced Migration, the Refugee Regime and the Responsibility to Protect', *Global Responsibility to Protect*, 2/1 (2010): 38; Ben Saul and Jane McAdam, 'An Insecure Climate for Human Security? Climate-Induced Displacement and International Law', in Alice Edwards and Carla Frestman (eds), *Human Security and Non-citizens: Law, Policy and International Affairs* (Cambridge University Press, 2010), 357, 400–2.
[151] Report of the International Commission on Intervention and State Sovereignty, *The Responsibility to Protect* (Ottawa: International Development Research Centre, December 2001) xi.
[152] Saul and McAdam, Insecure Climate for Human Security (n 150) 24–5.   [153] Ibid.
[154] Ibid.
[155] See 'Climate Change and Statelessness: An Overview', Submission by UNHCR, IOM and Norwegian Refugee Council (NRC) to the AWG-LCA-6 (15 May 2009) <http://unfccc.int/resource/docs/2009/smsn/igo/048.pdf> accessed 20 January 2017, 12.

international law.[156] The treaties relating to statelessness—the 1954 Convention Relating to the Status of Stateless Persons,[157] and the 1961 Convention on the Reduction of Statelessness[158]—however, are unlikely to be of use to the inhabitants of sinking islands. First, these treaties are not universally ratified, so their provisions bind only a subset of states.[159] Second, these treaties are designed to address the situation of persons rendered stateless due to a conflict of laws or as a consequence of state succession, not those whose territories have disappeared or been rendered uninhabitable.[160] Further there is a strong presumption of continuity of states, since states continue to exist as long as other states continue to treat them as such.[161] In any case, since most of these islands will be rendered uninhabitable due to climate impacts such as loss of drinking water supplies and arable land well before they are submerged, the challenge is to find protective frameworks that apply to the planned and staggered migration of affected populations.[162]

C. Addressing gaps in protection

The considerable gaps in protection in relation to climate-induced displacement—in particular, cross-border displacement—have prompted a host of proposals seeking to address these gaps. Many scholars have proposed new treaty instruments[163] and institutional arrangements,[164] including as part

---

[156] Jane McAdam, ' "Disappearing States", Statelessness and the Boundaries of International Law', in Jane McAdam (ed), *Climate Change and Displacement: Multidisciplinary Perspectives* (Oxford: Hart Publishing, 2010) 105. See generally Michael B. Gerrard and Gregory E. Wannier (eds), *Threatened Island Nations* (n 6).

[157] Convention relating to the Status of Stateless Persons (adopted 28 September 1954, entry into force 6 June 1960) 360 UNTS 117.

[158] Convention on the Reduction of Statelessness (adopted 30 August 1961, entry into force 13 December 1975) 989 UNTS 175.

[159] As of 20 September 2016, the Convention Relating to the Status of Stateless Persons had eighty-nine parties, and the Convention on the Reduction of Statelessness had sixty-eight parties. United Nations Treaty Collection, 'Chapter V: Refugees and Stateless Persons' <https://treaties.un.org/Pages/ViewDetailsII.aspx?src=TREATY&mtdsg_no=V-3&chapter=5&Temp=mtdsg2&clang=_en> and <https://treaties.un.org/Pages/ViewDetails.aspx?src=IND&mtdsg_no=V-4&chapter=5&clang=_en> accessed 20 January 2017.

[160] Edwards, Climate Change and International Refugee Law (n 105) 78.

[161] McAdam, Disappearing States (n 156).   [162] Ibid.

[163] See eg Dana Z. Falstrom, 'Stemming the Flow of Environmental Displacement: Creating a Convention to Protect Persons and Preserve the Environment', *Colorado Journal of International Environmental Law and Policy,* 13 (2002): 1 ('The Convention on the Protection of Environmentally Displaced Persons'); Benoit Mayer, 'The International Legal Challenges of Climate-Induced Migration: Proposal for an International Legal Framework', *Colorado Journal of International Environmental Law and Policy,* 22/3 (2011): 357; Julien Betaille *et al.*, 'Draft Convention on the International Status of Environmentally-Displaced Persons', *Revue Européenne de Droit de L'environnement,* 4 (2008): 395; Bonnie Docherty and Tyler Giannini, 'Confronting a Rising Tide: A Proposal for a Convention on Climate Change Refugees', *Harvard Environmental Law Review,* 33/2 (2009): 349; David Hodgkinson *et al.*, 'The Hour When the Ship Comes In: A Convention for Persons Displaced by Climate Change', *Monash University Law Review,* 36/1 (2010): 69 (proposing a convention for climate change displaced persons).

[164] See eg King, Environmental Displacement (n 127) 543 (proposing an 'International Coordination Mechanism for Environmental Displacement' to address displacement when environmental degradation is a 'significant cause').

of the FCCC regime.[165] In addition to the fact that academic appetite for new instruments and arrangements far exceeds political appetite, these proposals, to varying degrees, suffer from crippling limitations.[166] Some of them are conceptually problematic in that their starting point is the existence of a distinct category of 'climate refugees' or 'climate exiles'. As discussed before, such a category is hard to define and delineate, as displacement is a multi-causal phenomenon. Even assuming such a category can be defined and delineated, proposals to address the needs and rights of 'climate refugees' may arbitrarily privilege those suffering from climate harms over those suffering from other harms, and climate events over geophysical events.[167] From a human rights perspective, it is rightly argued, the focus should be on the harm suffered, not its cause.[168] Some scholars, however, argue that 'victims' of climate-induced sea level rise deserve unique moral consideration.[169] Even if this is so, it is unclear that such moral consideration should translate into a dedicated legal instrument.

In light of these concerns about proposals for new instruments and arrangements, and the lack of political interest in such new instruments, scholars suggest that the preferable approach is to 'reinvigorate existing concepts' and 'consolidate gains',[170] and to build policy consensus over time on protection for those affected by climate-induced displacement. An influential initiative that sought to build such policy consensus was the Nansen Initiative on Disaster-Induced

---

[165] See eg Frank Biermann and Ingrid Boas, 'Preparing for a Warmer World: Towards a Global Governance System to Protect Climate Refugees', *Global Environmental Politics,* 10/1 (2010): 60 (proposing an additional protocol to the FCCC for 'Recognition, Protection and Resettlement of Climate Refugees'); Brendan Gogarty, 'Climate Change-Displacement: Current Legal Solutions to Future Global Problems', *Journal of Law, Information and Science,* 21/1 (2011): 167, 185–6 (proposing a new protocol on migration and displacement under the FCC); Angela Williams, 'Turning the Tide: Recognising Climate Change Refugees in International Law', *Law and Policy,* 30/4 (2008): 502 (proposing a set of regionally-based protocols to the FCCC to ensure greater participation and greater specificity based on regional requirements); Sujatha Byravan and Sudhir C. Rajan, 'The Ethical Implications of Sea-Level Rise Due to Climate Change', *Ethics and International Affairs,* 24/3 (2010): 239, 242 (proposing a treaty on climate migration).

[166] See generally Jane McAdam, 'Swimming Against the Tide: Why a Climate Change Displacement Treaty Is Not the Answer', *International Journal of Refugee Law,* 23/1 (2011): 2; International Bar Association, 'The Peninsula Principles on Climate Displacement within States' (18 August 2013) <http://displacementsolutions.org/wp-content/uploads/2014/12/Peninsula-Principles.pdf> accessed 20 January 2017; Jane McAdam, 'Refusing Refuge in the Pacific: (De)constructing Climate-Induced Displacement in International Law', in Piguet *et al.* (eds), Migration and Climate Change (n 118) 102–37; Katrina M. Wyman, 'Responses to Climate Migration', *Harvard Environmental Law Review,* 37/1 (2013): 167.

[167] Alexander Betts, *Survival Migration: Failed Governance and the Crisis of Displacement* (Ithaca: Cornell University Press, 2013).

[168] McAdam, Refusing Refuge in the Pacific (n 166); McAdam, Climate Change-Related Displacement (n 96) 532.

[169] Byravan and Rajan, Ethical Implications (n 165).

[170] Edwards, Climate Change and International Refugee Law (n 105) 63. See also in a similar vein McAdam, Refusing Refuge in the Pacific (n 166); Wyman, Responses to Climate Migration (n 166).

Cross Border Displacement,[171] a state-led bottom-up consultative process that led to the 2016 'Agenda for the protection of cross-border displaced persons in the context of disasters and climate change'.[172] The non-binding 'Protection Agenda', which sets out priority areas and recommendations for future work, was endorsed by 109 states.[173] And its recommendations are set to be implemented by the Platform on Disaster Displacement, the successor to the Nansen Initiative.[174]

The Nansen Initiative reflects the increasing political attention states have devoted in recent times to the protection gaps and challenges relating to those persons displaced due to climate-induced and natural disasters.[175] The 2015 Sendai Framework for Disaster Risk Reduction calls for enhanced action to prevent and mitigate displacement and to address internal and cross-border displacement risk.[176] The 2016 World Humanitarian Summit identifies disaster and climate-induced displacement as a humanitarian challenge,[177] and a number of its participants called for an 'international mechanism and legal framework for the protection of people displaced by the adverse impacts of climate change'.[178] The UN Secretary-General's Agenda for Humanity calls on states to '[a]dopt an appropriate international framework, national legislation and regional cooperation frameworks by 2025 to ensure countries in disaster-prone regions are prepared to receive and protect those displaced across borders without refugee status'.[179] And the New York Declaration, an outcome of the 2016 UN Summit on Refugees and Migrants, both recognizes that people may move due to the adverse effects of climate change as well as commits governments to addressing the drivers of large-scale movements, including climate change.[180]

---

[171] Nansen Initiative (n 103). See for further details on the Nansen Initiative and its various outcome documents <http://disasterdisplacement.org/resources/> accessed 20 January 2017.

[172] Ibid.

[173] Ibid and see The Nansen Initiative, Global Consultation Conference Report, Geneva, 12–13 October 2015 (Geneva: The Nansen Initiative, December 2015) <https://www.nanseninitiative.org/wp-content/uploads/2015/02/GLOBAL-CONSULTATION-REPORT.pdf> accessed 20 January 2017.

[174] See generally Platform on Disaster Displacement, Follow-up to the Nansen Initiative <http://disasterdisplacement.org/> accessed 20 January 2017.

[175] See generally for a discussion of recent developments McAdam, From the Nansen Initiative (n 136).

[176] Third World Conference on Disaster Risk Reduction, 'Sendai Framework for Disaster Risk Reduction 2015–2030' (18 March 2015) UN Doc A/CONF.224/CRP.1.

[177] See UNGA, 'Outcome of the World Humanitarian Summit', Report of the Secretary-General (23 August 2016) UN Doc A/71/353, para 23.

[178] Chair's Summary by the United Nations Secretary General, 'Standing Up for Humanity: Committing to Action' (Istanbul: World Humanitarian Summit, 23–24 May 2016) <https://consultations.worldhumanitariansummit.org/bitcache/5171492e71696bcf9d4c571c93dfc6dcd7f361ee?vid=581078&disposition=inline&op=view> accessed 20 January 2017, 5.

[179] UNGA, 'One Humanity: Shared Responsibility', Report of the Secretary-General for the World Humanitarian Summit (2 February 2016) UN Doc A/70/709, Annex, 55.

[180] UNGA, 'New York Declaration for Refugees and Migrants'(13 September 2016) A/71/L.1, paras 1, 43.

D. Climate-induced displacement and migration in the UN climate regime

The FCCC does not address climate-induced displacement,[181] but it nevertheless provides various hooks for the protection of those displaced due to climate impacts. In the last decade, submissions by states and observers such as the UNHCR, the International Organization for Migration, and the Norwegian Refugee Council[182] have highlighted the need for protection frameworks, both within and outside the climate regime, leading to an increasing incorporation of migration and displacement concerns in COP decisions and the Paris Agreement.

Although the FCCC does not contain any explicit references to displacement or migration, concerns about these problems are arguably addressed in various provisions of the FCCC. The FCCC defines 'adverse effects' as including 'deleterious' effects on 'human health and welfare', which plausibly includes the protection concerns that arise in the context of displacement. Article 3 recognizes that the 'specific needs and special circumstances of developing country Parties, especially those that are particularly vulnerable to the adverse effects of climate change ... should be given full consideration.' And Article 4.8 further provides that parties should give 'full consideration to actions necessary ... to meet the specific needs and concerns of developing countries arising from the adverse effects of climate change'. Among these needs and concerns are those relating to displacement and migration.

These concerns were brought to the fore in the negotiations following the Bali Action Plan. AOSIS,[183] LDCs,[184] Argentina,[185] Bolivia,[186] Egypt,[187] Ghana,[188] Tuvalu,[189] and Swaziland (on behalf of a group of African countries)[190] were among those that raised concerns relating to climate-induced displacement. Many of these parties argued that developed countries have enhanced responsibility toward those affected by climate-induced displacement, and thus are required to provide funding[191] and, in some cases, accept climate migrants and 'refugees'.[192] Others

---

[181] See eg David Hodgkinson *et al.*, 'Copenhagen, Climate Change "Refugees" and the Need for a Global Agreement', *Public Policy,* 4/2 (2009): 159 (arguing that the FCCC is 'not designed for and cannot appropriately address the problem of climate change displacement'); and see generally Christine Gibb and James Ford, 'Should the United Nations Framework Convention on Climate Change Recognize Climate Migrants?', *Environmental Research Letters,* 7/4 (2012): 1.

[182] Submission by UNHCR, IOM and NRC, Climate Change and Statelessness (n 155); UNHCR, Forced Displacement (n 92).

[183] Submission from Alliance of Small Island States (18 December 2009) FCCC/AWGLCA/2009/MISC.8, 15, 20.

[184] Submission from Lesotho (13 March 2009) FCCC/AWGLCA/2009/MISC.1, 51, 52.

[185] Submission from Argentina (27 October 2008) FCCC/AWGLCA/2008/MISC.5, 10, 13.

[186] Submission from Bolivia (10 December 2010) FCCC/AWGLCA/2010/MISC.8/Add.2, 1, 3; See also Submission from Bolivia (30 April 2010) FCCC/AWGLCA/2010/MISC.2, 14, 14–39.

[187] Submission from Egypt (3 March 2008) FCCC/AWGLCA/2008/MISC.1, 23.

[188] Submission from Ghana (30 April 2010) FCCC/AWGLCA/2010/MISC.2, 42, 43–4.

[189] Submission from Tuvalu (22 May 2009) FCCC/AWGLCA/2009/MISC.4/Add.1, 9, 14.

[190] Submission from Swaziland (13 March 2009) FCCC/AWGLCA/2009/MISC.1, 78.

[191] Submission from Bolivia (30 April 2010) (n 186).

[192] Submission from Bangladesh (19 May 2009) FCCC/AWGLCA/2009/MISC.4, 26 (Part I). See also Submission from Bolivia, ibid; and Submission from Ghana (n 188).

focused on their submissions on building national capacity to enhance adaptation efforts and plan migration, where necessary,[193] and on enhancing coordination and cooperation across national, regional, and international levels.[194] Observers and non-state actors also played an active role in highlighting the issue of climate-induced displacement and migration.[195] Due to the concerted efforts of a range of state and non-state actors, the Cancun Agreements contain the first explicit reference in the UN climate regime to migration and displacement.

The Cancun Agreements recognize the need for '[m]easures to enhance understanding, coordination and cooperation with regard to climate-induced displacement, migration and planned relocation, where appropriate, at the national, regional and international levels'.[196] It is noteworthy, however, that this reference appears in a paragraph 'invit[ing] all Parties' to enhance actions on adaptation. The provision neither requires that parties take such actions (to the extent that COP decisions can do so), nor does it single out developed countries for enhanced responsibility, as many developing countries had proposed. Carefully circumscribed though this provision is, it nevertheless proved critical in catalyzing and spurring research, information exchange, and policy development on climate-induced displacement, in particular through the influential state-led multi-stakeholder Nansen Initiative.[197]

The Cancun Agreements also created an Adaptation Committee and launched a work program on loss and damage.[198] Since Cancun, the discussion on climate-induced displacement and migration has been considered in the context of adaptation and loss and damage.[199] In the context of adaptation, consideration is underway on ways to address displacement and migration concerns in national adaptation planning.[200] In the context of loss and damage, the Warsaw International Mechanism's executive committee has been tasked, as part of its initial two-year work plan, to enhance understanding and expertise on the impacts of climate change on migration, displacement, and human mobility, and the application of such understanding and expertise.[201]

In the negotiations of the Paris Agreement too, several Parties and observers urged the inclusion of references to human mobility.[202] Culminating a decade-long

---

[193] Submission from Lesotho (n 184).   [194] Submission from Ghana (n 188).

[195] Koko Warner, 'Climate Change Induced Displacement: Adaptation Policy in the Context of the UNFCCC Climate Negotiations' (Background Paper, UNHCR Expert Roundtable, Bellagio, May 2011) <http://www.unhcr.org/4df9cc309.pdf> accessed 20 January 2017.

[196] Cancun Agreements LCA, para 14(f).   [197] See Nansen Initiative (n 103).

[198] Cancun Agreements LCA, para 26.

[199] See eg Submission from Bolivia *et al.* (19 November 2012) FCCC/SBI/2012/MISC.14/Add.1, 3, 5, 7, 10; Submission from Gambia on behalf of the LDCs, (19 November 2012) FCCC/SBI/2012/MISC.14/Add.1, 16, 21, 24; Submission from Ghana (19 November 2012) FCCC/SBI/2012/MISC.14/Add.1, 29, 30; Submission of UNHCR *et al.*, 'Human mobility in the context of loss and damage from climate change: Needs, gaps, and roles of the Convention in addressing loss and damage' (19 November 2012) FCCC/SBI/2012/MISC.14/Add.1, 36.

[200] See Koko Warner *et al.*, 'National Adaptation Plans and human mobility', *Forced Migration Review,* 49 (May 2015) <http://www.fmreview.org/climatechange-disasters/warner-kaelin-martin-nassef.html> accessed 20 January 2017.

[201] FCCC, 'Initial two-year workplan of the Executive Committee of the Warsaw International Mechanism for Loss and Damage' <http://unfccc.int/adaptation/workstreams/loss_and_damage/items/8805.php> accessed 20 January 2017, action area 6.

[202] See eg Submission from Republic of Ecuador (28 March 2012) FCCC/ADP/2012/MISC.1, 17 (3 March 2013) <http://unfccc.int/files/documentation/submissions_from_parties/adp/application/

effort to mainstream climate-induced displacement and migration into the UN climate regime, the Paris Agreement contains an explicit reference to 'migrants' in a preambular recital. This recital recommends that 'Parties should, when taking action to address climate change, respect, promote, and consider their respective obligations on human rights ...' including the rights of 'migrants'. As discussed, earlier in this chapter, this recommendation is limited by the reference 'their respective obligations',[203] suggesting thereby that parties are required to do so only to the extent that they have existing obligations in relation to the rights of migrants. Notably, however, several NDCs contain references to migration and displacement, primarily in the internal context.[204]

In addition, the COP decision accompanying the Paris Agreement requests the executive committee of the Warsaw International Mechanism to establish a task force to develop recommendations for integrated approaches to avert, minimize, and address displacement related to the adverse impacts of climate change.[205] In the lead up to Paris, LDCs had championed the establishment of a climate change displacement coordination facility,[206] but this proved too controversial to be accepted. The task force, however, could help 'transform the information-oriented agenda of Cancun into an action-oriented agenda'.[207] How effectively it does this remains to be seen.

IV. CLIMATE CHANGE AND TRADE

Perhaps the most controversial and difficult interface issues arise in the relationship between climate change law and international trade law. Many domestic measures to address climate change affect international trade and therefore present issues

---

pdf/adp_ecuador_workstream2_20130301.pdf> accessed 20 January 2017 ('climate refugees'); Input by G-77 and China (19 October 2015) <http://unfccc.int/files/bodies/awg/application/pdf/g77_adaptation_rev2.pdf> accessed 20 January 2017 (proposing a 'displacement coordination facility'); Recommendations from the Advisory Group on Climate Change and Human Mobility, 'Human Mobility in the Context of Climate Change UNFCCC—Paris COP 21' (November 2015) <http://www.internal-displacement.org/assets/publications/2015/201511-human-mobility-in-the-context-of-climate-change-unfccc-Paris-COP21.pdf> accessed 20 January 2017.

[203] See Section II.G above.

[204] See INDCs from the Republic of Chad (1 October 2015), Egypt (16 November 2015), Republic of Kirbati (26 September 2015), Republic Of Malawi (8 October 2015), Republic Of Mauritius (28 September 2015), Nigeria (28 November 2015), Papua New Guinea (30 September 2015), etc, in FCCC, 'INDCs as communicated by Parties' <http://www4.unfccc.int/Submissions/INDC/Submission%20Pages/submissions.aspx> accessed 20 January 2017. See also Dina Ionesco, 'COP21 Paris Agreement: A Stepping Stone for Climate Migrants', *International Organisation for Migration Newsdesk* (23 December 2015) <https://weblog.iom.int/cop21-paris-agreement-stepping-stone-climate-migrants> accessed 20 January 2017.

[205] Decison 1/CP.21, 'Adoption of the Paris Agreement' (29 January 2016) FCCC/CP/2015/10/Add.1, para 49.

[206] See Submission by Nepal on behalf of the Least Developed Countries Group on the ADP Co-Chairs' Non Paper of 7 July 2014 on Parties Views and Proposal on the Elements for a Draft Negotiation Text <http://www4.unfccc.int/submissions/Lists/OSPSubmissionUpload/39_99_130584499817551043-Submission%20by%20Nepal%20ADP_21%20Oct%202014.pdf> accessed 20 January 2017.

[207] McAdam, From the Nansen Initiative (n 136).

under international trade law. These include not only direct trade measures, such as border tax adjustments and import restrictions that states take to ease potential competitive disadvantages for domestic industries subject to costly climate policy requirements, but also general environmental policies such as carbon taxes, emission trading schemes, energy efficiency standards, and subsidies for renewable energy. Depending on their purpose and design, all of these measures could conceivably run afoul of the obligations imposed by international trade law. Given the magnitude of climate policies' economic implications, the potential for conflict between climate action and the international trade regime is immense, so trade law considerations are often front and center as states develop national (and subnational) climate policy measures.

In order to promote states' shared interest in free trade, the World Trade Organization (WTO) regime imposes a range of limitations ('disciplines' in trade law parlance) on states' freedom to devise national policy measures, including climate-related measures. However, WTO law also leaves states considerable flexibility to choose among different policies. Thus, even when a climate measure violates one of WTO's trade disciplines, a state may be able to justify the measure under one of the exceptions that WTO law recognizes. In order to be justifiable, however, a measure must be genuinely intended to achieve climate policy goals and not constitute an arbitrary or disguised restriction on trade. The balance to be struck is reflected also in the FCCC, which emphasizes the importance of a 'supportive and open international economic system', and underscores that 'measures taken to combat climate change, including unilateral ones, should not constitute a means of arbitrary or unjustifiable discrimination or a disguised restriction on international trade'.[208]

This section provides an overview of the key features of the WTO regime, focusing on its basic rules and dispute settlement process. It then surveys the legal issues on which 'trade and environment' cases have turned to date, and highlights the potential implications for climate policy. It concludes by offering brief reflections on the approach that the UN climate regime has taken to trade issues, and the opportunities that may exist not only to minimize the potential for conflict between trade and climate policy, but also to harness the potential for mutually supportive policies.

A. The World Trade Organization

Global trade rules were first set out in the 1947 General Agreement on Tariffs and Trade (1947 GATT).[209] The 1947 GATT served as the principal global trading arrangement until 1994, when the 'Uruguay Round' of trade talks (1986–94)

---

[208] FCCC, Art 3.5. See also below, Section IV.E.
[209] General Agreement on Tariffs and Trade (adopted 30 October 1947, entered into force 1 January 1948) 55 UNTS 188 (1947 GATT).

culminated in the creation of the WTO,[210] the membership of which comprises 164 states.[211] The Uruguay Round produced a series of agreements that constitute the global rulebook for international trade.[212] For present purposes, the most significant of these are the Agreement Establishing the World Trade Organization (WTO Agreement),[213] the revision of the GATT 1947 into the GATT 1994 (GATT),[214] the General Agreement on Trade in Services (GATS),[215] the Agreement on Subsidies and Countervailing Measures (SCM Agreement),[216] the Anti-Dumping Agreement,[217] and the Agreement on Trade-Related Investment Measures (TRIMs Agreement).[218] The Uruguay Round agreements also include the Agreement on the Application of Sanitary and Phytosanitary Measures (SPS Agreement) and the Agreement on Technical Barriers to Trade (TBT Agreement), which supplement the relevant GATT provisions in their respective areas of coverage. The SPS Agreement deals with specific risks (notably food safety) to human health and animal and plant health regulations,[219] while the TBT Agreement aims to ensure that technical regulations, standards, and conformity assessment procedures outside of the SPS context are non-discriminatory and do not create unnecessary obstacles to trade.[220] In addition to these substantive agreements, the Uruguay Round established a new system for settling disputes, set forth in the WTO Dispute Settlement Understanding (DSU).[221] By joining the WTO, states agree to be bound by virtually all of the WTO agreements, including those mentioned above.[222]

---

[210] Final Act Embodying the Results of the Uruguay Round of Multilateral Trade Negotiations (adopted on 15 April 1994, entered into force 1 January1995) 1867 UNTS 14.

[211] See World Trade Organization (WTO), 'Members and Observers' <https://www.wto.org/english/thewto_e/whatis_e/tif_e/org6_e.htm> accessed 20 January 2017.

[212] See WTO, 'WTO Legal Texts' <https://www.wto.org/english/docs_e/legal_e/legal_e.htm> accessed 20 January 2017. For a general overview of trade law, see Michael J. Trebilcock, *Understanding Trade* Law (Cheltenham, UK: Edward Elgar, 2011). For a helpful overview on the most climate-relevant agreements, see Susanne Droege *et al.*, *The Trade System and Climate Action: Ways Forward under the Paris Agreement* (Climate Strategies, Working Paper, October 2016) 15–20 <http://climatestrategies.org/wp-content/uploads/2016/10/Trade-and-climate-ways-forward-1.pdf> accessed 20 January 2017.

[213] Agreement Establishing the World Trade Organization (adopted 15 April 1994, entered into force 1 January 1995) 1867 UNTS 154 (WTO Agreement).

[214] General Agreement on Tariffs and Trade 1994 (15 April 1994) LT/UR/A-1A/1/GATT/1 (the GATT).

[215] General Agreement on Trade in Services (15 April 1994) LT/UR/A-1B/S/1 (GATS).

[216] Agreement on Subsidies and Countervailing Measures (15 April 1994) LT/UR/A-1A/9 (SCM Agreement).

[217] Agreement on Implementation of Article VI of the General Agreement on Tariffs and Trade 1994 (15 April 1994) LT/UR/A-1A/3 (The Anti-Dumping Agreement).

[218] Agreement on Trade-Related Investment Measures (15 April 1994) LT/UR/A-1A/13 (TRIMs Agreement).

[219] Agreement on the Application of Sanitary and Phytosanitary Measures (15 April 1994) LT/UR/A-1A/2 (SPS Agreement). To date, the SPS Agreement has not played a major role in the climate context, although, in principle, it could apply. See n 271 below and accompanying text.

[220] Agreement on Technical Barriers to Trade (15 April 1994) LT/UR/A-1A/10 (TBT Agreement).

[221] Understanding on Rules and Procedures Governing the Settlement of Disputes (15 April 1994) LT/UR/A-2/DS/U1 (DSU).

[222] WTO Agreement, Art II.2.

For the purposes of introducing readers to the broad contours of the interplay between the trade and climate regimes, this section focuses on the global rule system of the WTO. It is important to note, however, that alongside this system, an array of bilateral and regional trade agreements have been negotiated.[223] Unlike the WTO agreements, many of these bilateral and regional agreements also contain investment chapters, including, most controversially, investor-state dispute settlement regimes.[224] These dispute settlement processes have begun to emerge as another site for foreign challenges to domestic climate policies, in this case by corporations proceeding directly against states.[225] More recently, states have sought to streamline the increasingly unwieldy multitude of trade arrangements through mega-regional agreements, such as the EU-Canada Comprehensive Economic and Trade Agreement (CETA), the EU-US Transatlantic Trade and Investment Partnership (TTIP), the Trans-Pacific Partnership (TPP), and the Regional Comprehensive Economic Partnership (RCEP) between Asia-Pacific states.[226] However, the negotiation of these mega-regional trade agreements has proven to be difficult and, in Europe and North America, has met with considerable political and civil society resistance.[227]

B. GATT principles

The GATT 1947 made no specific mention of the environment.[228] In contrast, the preamble to the WTO Agreement explicitly recognizes that trade relations should

---

[223] As of February 2016, 625 regional trade agreements had been notified to the WTO. See Droege *et al.*, Trade System and Climate Action (n 212) 11–12.

[224] See eg North American Free Trade Agreement (adopted 17 December 1992, entered into force 1 January 1994) (1993) 32 ILM 289 (NAFTA) ch XI. For an overview, see Gary Clyde Hufbauer and Cathleen Cimino-Isaacs, 'How Will TTP and TTIP Change the WTO System?', *Journal of International Economic Law*, 18/3 (2015): 679, 682. See also generally, Jorge E. Viñuales, *Foreign Investment and the Environment in International Law* (Cambridge University Press, 2012).

[225] See eg 'U.S. wind power firm awarded $28M after NAFTA challenge', *CBC News* (14 October 2016) <http://www.cbc.ca/news/business/windstream-ontario-nafta-dispute-1.3805486> accessed 20 January 2017. For more background, see International Centre for Trade and Sustainable Development, 'NAFTA wind energy dispute ramps up' (18 February 2016) <http://www.ictsd.org/bridges-news/bridges/news/nafta-wind-energy-dispute-ramps-up> accessed 20 January 2017.

[226] See Hufbauer and Cimino-Isaacs, TTP and TTIP (n 224); Slow Yue Chia, 'Emerging Mega-FTAs: Rationale, Challenges and Implications', *Asian Economic Papers*, 14/1 (2015): 1.

[227] See eg Paul Waldie, 'Growing European anti-trade movement threatens Canada-EU deal', *The Globe and Mail* (1 June 2016) <http://www.theglobeandmail.com/report-on-business/international-business/european-business/growing-european-anti-trade-movement-threatens-canada-eu-deal/article30229924/> accessed 20 January 2017.

[228] On the legal approach to 'trade and environment' issues, see generally Gary Hufbauer and Meera Fickling, 'Trade and the Environment', in Amrita Narlikar, Martin Daunton, and Robert M. Stern (eds), *The Oxford Handbook on The World Trade Organization* (Oxford University Press, 2012) 719; Daniel Bodansky and Jessica C. Lawrence, 'Trade and Environment', in Daniel Bethlehem *et al.* (eds), *The Oxford Handbook of International Trade Law* (Oxford University Press, 2009) 505, 521. For general treatments of the relationship between the trade and climate regimes, see Rafael Leal-Arcas, *Climate Change and International Trade* (Cheltenham: Edward Elgar, 2013); Tracey Epps and Andrew Green, *Reconciling Trade and Climate: How the WTO Can Help Address Climate Change* (Cheltenham, UK:

allow 'for the optimal use of the world's resources in accordance with the objective of sustainable development, seeking both to protect and preserve the environment and enhance the means for doing so in a manner consistent with the [parties'] respective needs and concerns at different levels of economic development'.[229] This provision marks the first time that a multilateral trade agreement recognized sustainable development as one of its guiding principles. It has come to play an important role in the interpretation of the core principles of the GATT and, in particular, the exceptions to its trade disciplines.[230]

1. Trade disciplines

The basic obligations of the GATT include the following trade disciplines:[231]

- Most-favored-nation (MFN) principle (Article I): States must treat 'like' products alike, regardless of a product's country of origin or destination; they cannot discriminate between products from different countries. For example, the US cannot adopt climate policies that treat products from China any less favorably than like products from the United Kingdom.

- Tariff 'bindings' (Article II): The GATT specifies the maximum permissible tariff on long lists of goods, set forth in 'tariff bindings' contained in a schedule to the GATT. Most of the trade negotiation rounds since 1947 have focused on adding further types of goods to the tariff bindings (for example, agricultural products), and progressively lowering the permissible tariffs. However, the GATT permits border tax adjustments (BTAs) (as opposed to border taxes), so long as the charge imposed on imported products is equivalent to internal taxes imposed on 'like' domestic products (Article II.2(a)). For example, when a state institutes a domestic carbon tax, it might adopt BTAs that impose equivalent taxes on imported products.

- National treatment principle (Article III): Once goods have been imported from another country, the importing country must treat them no less favorably than 'like products' produced domestically. For example, countries may not adopt climate policies that discriminate between local and foreign products through higher taxes or stricter regulations.

- Subsidies and countervailing duties (Article XVI): Subsidies allow producers to sell products at less than their normal price. For example, climate policy considerations may lead countries to subsidize renewable energy or energy

---

Edward Elgar, 2010); Gary Clyde Hufbauer, Steve Charnovitz, and Jisun Kim, *Global Warming and the World Trading System* (Washington, D.C.: Peterson Institute for International Economics, 2009).

[229] WTO Agreement (n 213), preamble.

[230] See WTO, *United States—Import Prohibition of Certain Shrimp and Shrimp Products—Report of the Appellate Body* (12 October 1998) WT/DS58/AB/R, para 153 (observing that the preamble gives 'color, texture and shading' to the interpretation of the WTO Agreements, including the GATT).

[231] For a basic overview, see WTO, 'Principles of the Trading System' <https://www.wto.org/english/thewto_e/whatis_e/tif_e/fact2_e.htm> accessed on 20 January 2017.

efficient products. The GATT prohibits export subsidies and allows the importing state to impose countervailing duties on subsidized goods.

- No quantitative restrictions (Article XI): The GATT prohibits, with certain exceptions, bans or restrictions on imports or exports other than tariffs.

These basic GATT disciplines are clarified and further developed through other agreements under the WTO umbrella. For example, the TBT Agreement elaborates upon GATT Articles I and III, in order to ensure that technical regulations, standards, or related procedures do not violate the MFN principle or discriminate between domestic and imported products. Similarly, the SCM Agreement elaborates GATT Article XVI and other subsidy-related provisions of the GATT, by disciplining both the use of subsidies and actions countries might take to counter their effects.

2. Exceptions

Under the WTO, trade restrictive measures that violate the GATT's trade disciplines can nevertheless be permissible in order to achieve certain policy objectives, enumerated in Article XX on 'General Exceptions'. For present purposes, the most relevant exceptions to the trade disciplines allow measures:

- 'necessary to protect human, animal or plant life or health' (Article XX(b)); or
- 'relating to the conservation of exhaustible natural resources if such measures are made effective in conjunction with restrictions on domestic production or consumption' (Article XX(g)).

The exceptions set out in Article XX, however, are prefaced by an introductory paragraph commonly referred to as the Article XX 'chapeau', which provides that trade measures may 'not be applied in a manner which would constitute a means of arbitrary or unjustifiable discrimination between countries where the same conditions prevail, or a disguised restriction on international trade'. In other words, assessing whether or not a measure can be justified under Article XX entails a two-step analysis: determining, first, whether the measure falls under one of the exceptions, and, second, whether it is applied consistently with the chapeau requirements.

Many environment-related disputes have turned on whether a trade-restrictive measure that fits within the parameters of Article XX(b) or (g) is *applied* in a manner that meets the requirements of the chapeau. For example, in the *Shrimp/Turtle Case*, the WTO Appellate Body confirmed that trade-restrictive sea turtle protection measures adopted by the US fit within the Article XX(g) exception because sea turtles are 'exhaustible natural resources' within the meaning of the article.[232] The Appellate Body also confirmed that Article XX(g) could be used to justify measures intended to protect natural resources beyond a state's jurisdiction, since the migratory nature of

---

[232] *Shrimp/Turtle* (n 230) para 129.

sea turtles established a sufficient nexus to the US.[233] Nevertheless, the US initially lost the *Shrimp/Turtle Case* because its measures were found to have been applied in an arbitrary fashion, in part because the US had not made sufficient efforts to arrive at a multilateral solution.[234] In response, the US revised its measures and attempted to negotiate a multilateral solution, and the Appellate Body subsequently concluded that the revised measures did meet the chapeau requirements.[235]

While the first challenges to national policies aimed at climate change mitigation have now made their way through the WTO dispute settlement system,[236] none of them entailed consideration of GATT Article XX(b) or (g). Still, it seems safe to say that climate policies may come within the ambit of Article XX(b) when they aim to protect humans, animals, or plants from the negative effects of climate change.[237] Policy measures aimed at conserving 'plant and animal species that may disappear as a result of global warming' may also be justifiable as 'relating to the conservation of exhaustible natural resources' under Article XX(g).[238] Indeed, in the *Shrimp/Turtle Case*, the Appellate Body observed that the 'words of Article XX(g), "exhaustible natural resources", ... must be read by a treaty interpreter in the light of contemporary concerns of the community of nations about the protection and conservation of the environment'.[239] Two years earlier, in the *US-Gasoline Case*, a WTO panel had found a policy to reduce the depletion of clean air to fall under Article XX(g).[240] It seems plausible to argue, therefore, that the global climate itself is an 'exhaustible natural resource', which would bring mitigation policies within the ambit of Article XX(g), since they relate to the conservation of that exhaustible natural resource. Hence, the main issues in justifying trade-related climate measures are likely to revolve around the design features and application of the measures in question, in order to satisfy the Article XX chapeau.

3. The dispute settlement process

The WTO's DSU establishes one of the strongest dispute settlement procedures in contemporary international law.[241] Prior to the WTO, under the GATT 1947,

---

[233] Ibid, paras 72 and 168. [234] Ibid, paras 160–86.

[235] WTO, *United States—Import Prohibition of Certain Shrimp and Shrimp Products, Recourse to Article 21.5 of the DSU by Malaysia—Report of the Appellate Body* (22 October 2001) WT/DS58/AB/RW, paras 153–4 (confirming the compatibility of the adjusted US measures with the Article XX chapeau).

[236] See below Section IV.B.3.

[237] See WTO, *United States—Standards for Reformulated and Conventional Gasoline—Panel Report* (29 January 1996) WT/DS2/AB/R, para 6.21.

[238] Ludivine Tamiotti *et al.*, *Trade and Climate Change* (United Nations Environment Programme and WTO, June 2009) xix.

[239] *Shrimp/Turtle* (n 230) para 129.

[240] *US-Gasoline* (n 237) para 6.37. See also WTO, *United States—Standards for Reformulated and Conventional Gasoline—Report of the Appellate Body* (29 April 1996) WT/DS2/AB/R, 9–10, 14–22 (noting that the US had not appealed on this issue and therefore only reviewing other aspects of the Panel's interpretation of Article XX(g)).

[241] On the WTO dispute settlement system, see generally David Palmeter and Petros C. Mavroidis, *Dispute Settlement in the World Trade Organization: Practice and Procedure* (Cambridge University Press,

three-member panels were appointed by the GATT Council to hear disputes between parties that could not be solved by consultation or mediation.[242] These panels could make only recommendations, which required adoption by the GATT Council to become binding upon parties. Moreover, the GATT operated under a rule of positive consensus, which meant that any contracting state, including the respondent, could block referral of a dispute to a panel or the adoption of a panel report by the Council.[243] The WTO's DSU considerably strengthened the GATT's dispute settlement procedure, by establishing a predictable and strict timetable for the dispute settlement process,[244] an appeals procedure,[245] and a Dispute Settlement Body (DSB) to administer the dispute settlement process.[246] The DSU also replaced the positive consensus rule with one of 'negative' (or reverse) consensus. Under this rule, panel reports are adopted 'unless a party to the dispute formally notifies the DSB of its decision to appeal or the DSB decides by consensus not to adopt the report'.[247] Likewise, reports of the Appellate Body are adopted unless the DSB decides otherwise by consensus.[248]

4. *The relationship between trade rules and climate protection measures*

a) Unilateral or multilateral measures?
Trade-related environmental measures (TREMs) can be adopted either unilaterally or multilaterally.[249] Given the difficulties of international standard-setting, most environmental standards are still developed at the national level. However, trade measures like those in the Montreal Protocol (banning imports and exports of ozone depleting substances from/to non-parties), the Basel Convention (limiting exports of hazardous wastes),[250] and CITES (banning trade in certain endangered species),[251] have become a relatively common feature of MEAs; they are included in some twenty of the more than 250 MEAs currently in force.[252] In addition, international standard-setting bodies, such as the Codex Alimentarius Commission

---

2nd edn, 2004); WTO, *A Handbook on the WTO Dispute Settlement System* (Cambridge University Press, 2004).

[242] WTO, 'Historical Development of the WTO Dispute Settlement System' <https://www.wto.org/english/tratop_e/dispu_e/disp_settlement_cbt_e/c2s1p1_e.htm> accessed 20 January 2017.
[243] Ibid.   [244] DSU (n 221) Art 20.
[245] Ibid, Art 17. For general overviews of the reformed system, see WTO, 'WTO Bodies involved in the dispute settlement process' <https://www.wto.org/english/tratop_e/dispu_e/disp_settlement_cbt_e/c3s1p1_e.htm> accessed 20 January 2017; WTO, WTO Dispute Settlement Mechanism (n 241).
[246] DSU, ibid, Art 2. For disputes concerning one of the WTO agreements, all WTO members are represented in the DSB.
[247] Ibid, Art 16.4.   [248] Ibid, Art 17.14.
[249] This section and the next are drawn from Bodansky and Lawrence, Trade and Environment (n 228) 519–24.
[250] Basel Convention on the Control of Transboundary Movements of Hazardous Wastes and their Disposal (adopted 22 March 1989, entered into force 5 May 1992) 1673 UNTS 57 (Basel Convention).
[251] Convention on International Trade in Endangered Species of Wild Fauna and Flora (adopted 3 March 1973, entered into force 1 July 1975) 993 UNTS 243 (CITES).
[252] WTO, 'The Doha mandate on multilateral environmental agreements (MEAs)', <https://www.wto.org/english/tratop_e/envir_e/envir_neg_mea_e.htm> accessed on 20 January 2017.

and the International Organization for Standardization, have developed a growing number of product standards relating to health and the environment.[253]

In general, multilateral environmental measures pose less of a danger to trade than unilateral national measures, and are hence favored by the trade regime.[254] National measures raise three types of concerns. First, to the extent that they privilege domestic producers, they prompt concerns about protectionism. Second, even when national measures are not adopted for protectionist reasons, they inhibit trade indirectly, by making it more difficult for producers to sell a single homogeneous product globally. Finally, unilateral national measures can raise sovereignty issues when they are used to pressure other countries to change their environmental policies. Developing countries, in particular, have expressed this concern, criticizing the imposition of developed country environmental standards on countries of the global South as 'eco-imperialism,' which values environmental protection over the lives of the world's poor and ignores problematic aspects of the developed country policies, such as agricultural subsidies.[255]

Multilateral measures are less susceptible to all three of these problems. The fact that a measure has been accepted by a large number of states reduces the potential for protectionism.[256] Moreover, uniform international standards do not present additional impediments to trade (beyond those set forth in the standards themselves), since producers need to learn about only a single standard and can produce a single, uniform product. Finally, although multilateral trade measures can be used coercively—as UN Security Council sanctions illustrate—they typically are seen as more legitimate and less susceptible to abuse than unilateral measures, because they result from a more broadly participatory process.[257]

For these reasons, trade law displays a marked preference for multilateral measures. Article 104.1 of the North American Free Trade Agreement (NAFTA), one of the aforementioned regional trade agreements,[258] goes so far as to create an explicit exemption for measures adopted pursuant to enumerated MEAs.[259] Although the WTO agreements do not specifically exempt MEAs from their strictures, the decision in the *Shrimp/Turtle Case*, with its emphasis on multilateral negotiations,[260]

---

[253] Steve Charnovitz, 'International Standards and the WTO', *GW Law Faculty Publications & Other Works*, Paper 394 (2005) <http://scholarship.law.gwu.edu/faculty_publications/394> accessed 20 January 2017.

[254] See Hufbauer *et al.*, Global Warming (n 228) 100.

[255] See eg, Paul K. Driessen, *Eco-Imperialism: Green Power, Black Death* (Bellevue, WA: Merril Press, 2003); Bradly J. Condon and Tapen Sinha, *The Role of Climate Change in Global Economic Governance* (Oxford University Press, 2013) 41–9; Rafael Leal-Arcas, 'Unilateral Trade-related Climate Change Measures', *The Journal of World Investment & Trade*, 13/6 (2012): 875.

[256] Even multilateral measures may raise questions of fairness, particularly in the context of multilateral trade measures adopted by parties to an MEA against non-parties.

[257] Multilateral agreement does not fully eliminate the problem of coercion, since it may simply reflect powerful states' success in forcing their will on other states. For a discussion of the legitimacy of Security Council sanctions, see David Caron, 'The Legitimacy of the Collective Authority of the Security Council', *American Journal of International Law*, 87/4 (1993): 552.

[258] See nn 223–224 above and accompanying text.

[259] See NAFTA (n 224) Art 104 (Relation to Environmental and Conservation Agreements).

[260] See n 234 above and accompanying text.

suggests a similar result. The preference for international standards is even clearer in the SPS and TBT Agreements, which create a safe harbor for health and technical standards that conform to international standards.[261]

Although the trade regime encourages WTO members to act multilaterally when possible, it does not exclude the use of unilateral measures.[262] In some cases, international standards do not exist, and agreement is not possible, so the choice is not between unilateral and multilateral action, but between action and inaction.[263] Moreover, as both the SPS and TBT Agreements recognize, WTO Members have different values, traditions, and regulatory cultures, so uniform standards may not be appropriate.[264]

The ultimate acceptance of a unilateral measure in the *Shrimp/Turtle Case*, after the US made a good faith effort to negotiate multilateral turtle conservation measures,[265] was taken as positive news by many environmental activists, particularly those who see unilateral action as a frequent prerequisite of multilateral cooperation and upward harmonization.[266] However, developing countries have questioned the fairness of the decision. To say, as the *Shrimp/Turtle Case* implied, that a developed country like the US can unilaterally adopt trade-restrictive environmental measures so long as it makes an attempt to negotiate, ignores the fact that the negotiating playing field may be far from level. Because of the enormous differentials between developed and developing countries in both market and 'discursive' power, some commentators argue that developed states can essentially decide on a rule, go through a formal negotiating process, and then adopt a trade-restrictive environmental regulation unilaterally, regardless of any objection by developing country trading partners.[267]

b) Direct and indirect trade restrictions

Traditionally, an important threshold question in considering the compatibility of an environmental measure with the trade regime was whether the measure

---

[261] SPS Agreement (n 219) Art 3.2; TBT Agreement (n 220) Art 2.4.

[262] The SPS and TBT Agreements allow WTO members to set a higher level of standards than international standards, guidelines, or recommendations in pursuing legitimate objectives such as environmental protection. See SPS Agreement (n 219) Art 3.3 and TBT Agreement (n 220) Art 2.4. Similarly, Principle 12 of the Rio Declaration provides only that environmental measures should be based on international consensus 'as far as possible'.

[263] Daniel Bodansky, 'What's So Bad about Unilateral Action to Protect the Environment?', *European Journal of International Law*, 11/2 (2000): 339.

[264] As the Appellate Body has noted, 'it is undisputed that WTO Members have the right to determine the level of protection of health that they consider appropriate in a given situation'. See WTO, *European Communities—Measures Affecting Asbestos and Asbestos-Containing Products—Report of the Appellate Body* (12 March 2001) WT/DS135/R, WT/DS135/AB/R, para 168.

[265] *US—Shrimp (Article 21.5—Malaysia)* (n 235), para 153.

[266] See Steve Charnovitz, 'Free Trade, Fair Trade, Green Trade: Defogging the Debate', *Cornell International Law Journal*, 27/3 (1994): 459, 493–8.

[267] Gregory Shaffer, 'Power, Governance, and the WTO: A Comparative Institutional Approach', in Michael Barnett and Robert Duval (eds), *Power in Global Governance* (Cambridge University Press, 2005) 130; Donald McRae, 'Trade and the Environment: Competition, Cooperation or Confusion?', *Alberta Law Review*, 41/3 (2003): 745, 757.

limits trade directly or indirectly. On their face, the trade disciplines imposed by the GATT—surveyed above—focus primarily on direct restrictions on trade. By contrast, the GATT does little to limit the authority of WTO members to adopt governmental measures of a more general character, not directed at trade, except to prohibit them from doing indirectly what they cannot do directly, namely to inhibit trade by preferring domestic over foreign goods.

Within this framework, whether or not an environmental measure is specifically directed at trade structures the rest of the analysis. TREMs, such as the restrictions on trade in endangered species and hazardous wastes envisaged in CITES and the Basel Convention, are *prima facie* prohibited and are inconsistent with the GATT (Article XI), unless they can be justified under one of the Article XX exceptions. In contrast, more general environmental measures are permissible, unless they afford 'less favourable treatment' to 'like' foreign products in violation of GATT Article III (national treatment), or to 'like' products from different countries in violation of GATT Article I (MFN).[268] Hence, analysis of TREMs traditionally tended to focus on the scope of the Article XX exceptions, whereas analysis of general environmental measures tended to focus on the concepts of 'likeness' and 'less favorable treatment'.

As the trade regime has evolved, however, this distinction between TREMs and other measures may have lost much of its significance. On the one hand, the WTO Appellate Body's interpretation of the Article XX exceptions in the *Shrimp/Turtle Case* suggests that TREMs are permissible as long as they are not applied in a manner that constitutes an 'arbitrary and unjustifiable restriction on trade'[269]— in essence, a non-discrimination norm that is similar to, although arguably more relaxed than, the one found in Article III. On the other hand, as the trade regime has made room for certain direct restrictions on trade, it has imposed increasingly stringent disciplines on more general governmental measures—in particular, as the TBT and SPS Agreements seek to ensure that technical and health standards do not serve as non-tariff barriers to trade. According to some observers, this evolution has led to the paradoxical result that the trade regime may subject general environmental measures to more, not less, stringent disciplines than directly trade-restrictive measures.[270] For example, SPS measures must meet the SPS Agreement's requirements regarding risk assessment and scientific evidence,[271] whereas trade-restrictive

---

[268] WTO, *Dominican Republic—Measures Affecting the Importation and Internal Sale of Cigarettes—Panel Report* (26 November 2004) WT/DS302/R, para 96; See also, WTO, *Turkey—Measures Affecting the Importation of Rice—Panel Report* (21 September 2007) WT/DS334/R; WTO, *European Communities—Measures Affecting Asbestos and Products Containing Asbestos—Panel Report* (18 September 2000) WT/DS135/R.

[269] See nn 232–235 above and accompanying text.

[270] Steve Charnovitz, 'The World Trade Organization and Environmental Supervision', *International Environment Reporter*, 17/2 (1994): 89, 92 (discussing the irony of WTO's rigid rules on health and environment in the context of its soft stance on protectionism).

[271] See WTO, *European Communities—Measures Concerning Meat and Meat Products (Hormones)—Panel Report* (18 August 1997) WT/DS26/R/USA. In principle, the SPS Agreement could apply in the climate context. See World Bank/Standards and Trade Development Facility, 'Climate Change and Trade: The Link to Sanitary and Phytosanitary Standards' (WTO Secretariat, 2011) <http://www.

environmental protection measures must satisfy only Article XX, which, as noted above, requires simply that conservation measures not constitute an 'arbitrary or unjustifiable' restriction on trade.

c) The role of the 'likeness' standard

States have a variety of domestic policy measures to address climate change at their disposal. For example, they might adopt energy efficiency standards for cars or appliances; impose a carbon tax on electricity, manufacturing sectors, or certain fuels; adopt an emissions trading program; require carbon footprint labeling of products; or subsidize renewable energy or energy efficient products. Which of these national climate measures raise trade concerns, and why?

Ordinarily, states are free to adopt environmental product standards so long as these standards do not violate a WTO discipline—for example, the national treatment rule by discriminating against 'like' foreign products (GATT Article III), or the MFN rule by discriminating among 'like' products from different countries (GATT Article I). If they do violate a WTO discipline, the question becomes whether the discrimination is justifiable under GATT Article XX(b) or (g). In determining whether a national environmental standard is discriminatory, the first step of the analysis tends to focus on the 'likeness' of the products involved.

d) Criteria for assessing 'likeness'

The WTO Appellate Body, in the *Asbestos Case*, indicated that 'likeness' must be assessed on a case-by-case basis.[272] It also set out several criteria to assist the assessment: the physical properties of products; the extent to which products are capable of serving the same or similar end uses; the extent to which consumers perceive and treat the products as alternative means to perform particular functions or satisfy particular demands; and the international classification of the products for tariff purposes.[273] The case concerned a ban by France on the use of construction materials containing asbestos. Canada challenged the relevant measures, inter alia, under GATT Article III. Initially, the dispute settlement panel held that the French measures violated Article III because asbestos products were 'like' certain cement-based construction products, but concluded that the measures could be justified under GATT Article XX(b) as necessary to protect human life or health. By contrast, the Appellate Body considered that the health risks associated with asbestos were relevant also in applying the aforementioned criteria for assessing 'likeness', and thus in assessing whether the measures were discriminatory in the first place. The Appellate Body concluded that, given these risks, asbestos products had different physical properties and were subject to different consumer tastes than cement-based construction products—hence they were not 'like' products.

oie.int/doc/ged/D13282.PDF> accessed 20 January 2017 (considering the role of SPS standards in relation to risks linked to rising temperatures and extreme weather events). However, given its focus on food safety measures and measures aimed at plant or animal health (eg pest protection), it seems unlikely that the SPS Agreement would find application to trade-related climate policy measures.

[272] See *EC—Asbestos* (n 264) paras 101 and 102.   [273] Ibid, para 101.

For the purposes of assessing the GATT (or TBT) compatibility of climate policy measures, the *EC-Asbestos Case* suggests that states have considerable room to impose general product-related standards. A state would not violate GATT Articles I or III, for example, by imposing fuel or energy efficiency requirements impacting the import of cars or appliances that do not meet those standards. The same arguably applies to the compatibility of carbon footprint labeling requirements,[274] although it is possible that requiring the inclusion of transport-related emissions in the footprint might be found to discriminate against, or among (depending on distance), otherwise 'like' foreign products.[275] Furthermore, under the TBT Agreement, states must show that environmental standards such as labeling requirements are an effective and appropriate means of fulfilling legitimate policy objectives (ie for present purposes, objectives under GATT Articles XX(b) and (g)).[276]

e) Processes and production methods (PPMs) and 'likeness'

A more difficult question is whether states could regulate or tax products based on, say, the GHG intensity of the products' manufacturing process. GATT dispute settlement panels have held that the 'likeness' of products must be assessed on the basis of the properties of the products themselves, thus excluding from the analysis non-product-related 'processes and production methods' (PPMs). For example, in the first *Tuna/Dolphin Case*, the panel held that canned tuna products could not be distinguished based on whether or not the tuna was caught in a 'dolphin-safe' manner.[277] The decision preceded the adoption of the WTO Agreement and did not become binding under the old GATT dispute settlement system. Nonetheless, it raised significant concerns among environmental advocates, who feared it would preclude states from taking into account environmental harms resulting from the production process (such as emissions of CO_2 or other pollutants) in designing domestic policies or MEAs.[278]

---

[274] See Meinhard Doelle, 'Climate Change and the WTO: Opportunities to Motivate State Action on Climate Change through the World Trade Organization', *Review of European, Comparative and International Environmental Law*, 13/1 (2004): 85, 99. But note that, to the extent that a carbon footprint label focuses on emissions from the production process, the questions raised in the next section will arise.

[275] See Vicki Waye, 'Carbon Footprints, Food Miles and the Australian Wine Industry', *Melbourne Journal of International Law*, 9/1 (2008): 271.

[276] See WTO, *European Communities—Trade Description of Sardines—Report of the Appellate Body* (26 September 2002) WT/DS231/R, WT/DS231/AB/R; Eric Vranes, 'Climate Labeling and the WTO: The 2010 EU Ecolabelling Programme as a Test Case under WTO Law', *European Yearbook of International Economic Law*, 2 (2011): 205 (discussing life-cycle labeling, including emissions from the production process).

[277] See *United States—Restrictions on Imports of Tuna*, GATT Panel Report (3 September 1991) DS21/R–39S/155, unadopted, para 5.42. A second *Tuna-Dolphin* case concerned a complaint by the EU about the impact of the US measures on 'intermediary' nations, ie nations that process tuna caught in a state covered by the US measures. See *United States—Restrictions on Imports of Tuna*, GATT Panel Report (16 June 1994) DS29/R444, unadopted.

[278] For a discussion see eg Daniel C. Esty, *Greening the GATT: Trade, Environment and the Future* (Washington, D.C.: Institute for International Economics, 1994) 29, 34–5.

Many trade experts continue to argue that environmental impact should not be a legitimate criterion for finding products unlike, and governments should not be able to discriminate between products based on their production methods.[279] Several developing country WTO members have also opposed including PPMs in the likeness analysis. Fearing loss of market-access and competitive advantage, they have accused developed-country NGOs and governments of using production methods as thinly veiled pretexts for protectionism.[280] Environmentalists, by contrast, have argued that it is essential for environmental regulations to target environmentally harmful production methods, for example, through taxes or regulations that favor 'clean' energy sources over 'dirty' ones. In their view, the trade regime's focus on whether environmentally-friendly and -unfriendly products are 'like,' in order to determine whether governments can permissibly distinguish between them, gets the analysis backward.[281]

While the question whether PPMs are appropriately considered in the assessment of product 'likeness' has not been resolved, it is beyond doubt that there is scope for justifying PPM measures under GATT Article XX.[282] The WTO Appellate Body, for example, while emphasizing the trade system's preference for internationally negotiated solutions to international problems, has also held that individual states are entitled to take extraterritorial, PPM-related environmental impacts into account, provided there is a sufficient link to the regulating state's efforts 'to protect human, animal or plant life or health' or to conserve 'exhaustible natural resources' (GATT Articles XX(b) or (g)), and so long as the environmental measures satisfy the chapeau of Article XX. Hence, in the *Shrimp/Turtle Case*, the Appellate Body ultimately found a measure not dissimilar to the one at issue in the *Tuna/Dolphin Case* (ie standards relating to fishing methods) to be justified under GATT Article XX(g).[283] In other words, WTO law would appear to leave room for states to take measures addressing the climate impacts of the production process—for example, CO_2 emissions from the generation of electricity or the manufacturing of goods.[284] Whether this flexibility can be provided through a more expansive interpretation of the 'likeness' standard of Articles

[279] This paragraph is drawn from Bodansky and Lawrence, Trade and Environment (n 228) 526.

[280] See Jagdish Bhagwati, 'The Question of Linkage', *American Journal of International Law*, 96/1 (2002): 126, 133.

[281] See eg William J. Snape and Naomi B. Lefkovitz, 'Searching for GATT's Environmental Miranda: Are "Process Standards" Getting "Due Process"?', *Cornell International Law Journal*, 27/3 (1994): 777.

[282] For detailed treatments, see eg Steve Charnovitz, 'The Law of Environmental "PPMs" in the WTO: Debunking the Myth of Illegality', *Yale Journal of International Law*, 27/1 (2002): 59; Christiane R. Conrad, *Processes and Production Methods (PPMs) in WTO Law: Interfacing Trade and Social Goals* (Cambridge University Press, 2011).

[283] See nn 232–235 above and accompanying text.

[284] See also Doelle, Climate Change and the WTO (n 274) 98; Bradly J. Condon, 'Climate Change and Unresolved Issues in WTO Law', *Journal of International Economic Law*, 12/4 (2009): 895; Johannes Norpoth, 'Mysteries of the TBT Agreement Resolved? Lessons to Learn for Climate Policies and Developing Country Exporters from Recent TBT Disputes', *Journal of World Trade*, 47/3 (2013): 575.

I and III,[285] or whether it will require application of the Article XX exceptions, remains to be seen.[286]

5. Trade-related climate measures

In principle, trade-related measures could serve a variety of purposes in promoting climate policies. First, they could be used to induce other countries to change their environmental policies, as the aforementioned Montreal Protocol and the US Pelly Amendment illustrate.[287] In the climate context, there has been discussion of the use of trade measures against states that do not put a price on carbon or that otherwise have weak domestic standards.[288] To date, however, states have shown restraint in resorting to such assertive measures.

Second, environmental measures limiting trade could be used to defend a country that adopts a carbon tax or emissions trading system against 'unfair' competition from countries with lower environmental standards. Arguably, countries that do not put a price on carbon are, in effect, providing their businesses with a subsidy. In response, some environmentalists argue that countries should be allowed to level the playing field by imposing an eco-duty or BTA, particularly in cases involving transboundary or global harms.[289] Such defensive measures would force foreign companies to internalize the environmental costs of their production processes (at least with respect to exports to countries with BTAs), pressure environmentally weak states to implement more stringent protection measures, and minimize 'leakage' of emissions to lower-cost jurisdictions that do not put a price on carbon.[290]

The following discussion considers two trade-related climate policy measures that have received recent attention.

---

[285] See Tamiotti *et al.*, Trade and Climate (n 238).

[286] See also Section IV.B.5.b below (discussing the potential relevance of the WTO Appellate Body report in the *Canada—Renewable Energy* case for the future evolution of the PPM debate).

[287] The Pelly Amendment allows the US President to restrict the import of fishery or wildlife products from countries that diminish the effectiveness of international fishery or endangered species programs. 22 USCA § 1978 (West 1990 &Supp 1994); see also Steve Charnovitz, 'Environmental Trade Sanctions and the GATT: An Analysis of the Pelly Amendment on Foreign Environmental Practices', *American University Journal of International Law & Policy*, 9/3 (1994): 751.

[288] See eg William Nordhaus, 'Climate Clubs: Overcoming Free-riding in International Climate Policy', *American Economic Review*, 105/4 (2015): 1339.

[289] But, as critics note, once the lack of environmental standards is recognized as a subsidy or grounds for dumping charges, it is a 'slippery slope' to recognize other government expenditures (or the lack thereof) as subsidies. GATT Secretariat, 'Trade and the Environment' (3 February 1991) GATT/ 1529 20.

[290] See Bodansky and Lawrence, Trade and Environment (n 228) 520–1; Jacob Werksman, James A. Bradbury, and Lutz Weischer, 'Trade Measures and Climate Change Policy: Searching for Common Ground on an Uneven Playing Field' (Washington, D.C.: World Resources Institute, 2009); Harro van Asselt and Thomas Brewer, 'Addressing Competitiveness and Leakage Concerns in Climate Policy: An Analysis of Border Adjustment Measures in the US and the EU', *Energy Policy*, 38 (2010): 42.

a) Border adjustments

So far, jurisdictions that have instituted emissions trading schemes have tended to address international competitiveness concerns through the initial allocation of a certain number of free allowances to industries exposed to international competition.[291] However, border adjustment measures have been a steady staple of the salient debates as well.[292] With respect to a domestic carbon tax, for example, countries might consider BTAs that impose an equivalent tax on imported products. BTAs have been common in many other contexts, including cigarette, alcohol, or fossil fuel taxation.[293] In the case of a domestic emissions trading system, however, border adjustments have not yet been implemented in practice, perhaps because the design of such measures would have to overcome a range of practical challenges, related to the methods for assessing product-specific carbon emissions and to the carbon price fluctuations that commonly arise in the context of emission trading systems.[294] Furthermore, it remains unclear, and disputed, whether a border adjustment involving, for example, a duty on importers to surrender emission reduction units corresponding to a certain carbon content of imported products can be considered to be a border tax adjustment within the meaning of the trade regime in the first place.[295]

From a WTO perspective, leaving aside highly technical matters, such as what constitutes a tax adjustment (as opposed to a tax, duty, or subsidy),[296] the key questions concerning border measures revolve around some of the same issues as those engaged by other trade restrictions. In the case of a BTA, for example, the first question to answer is whether the tax imposed on imported products is in conformity with GATT Article II:2(a), which permits only charges that are equivalent to those imposed on a 'like' domestic product.[297] In other words, the 'likeness' questions

---

[291] See Tamiotti *et al.*, Trade and Climate (n 238), 98–100. Depending on how such free allowance, or other 'phase-in', schemes are structured, they may themselves violate trade disciplines, such as those imposing restrictions on subsidies.

[292] See Werksman *et al.*, Trade Measures and Climate Change Policy (n 290) (discussing the border adjustments contemplated in the context of the US American Clean Energy and Security Act (ACESA)); van Asselt and Brewer Addressing competitiveness (n 290) (discussing the border adjustments considered under ACESA and the EU emissions trading system (EU ETS)).

[293] Tamiotti *et al.*, Trade and Climate (n 238) 100.

[294] For brief overviews, see ibid (101–2); van Asselt and Brewer, Addressing competitiveness (n 290) 43. See also Sofia Persson, 'Practical Aspects of Border Carbon Adjustment Measures—Using a Trade Facilitation Perspective to Assess Trade Costs', *ICTSD Global Platform on Climate Change, Trade Policies and Sustainable Energy, Issue Paper No. 13* (International Centre for Trade and Sustainable Development, Geneva, 2010), 19 <http://www.ictsd.org/downloads/2011/05/persson-ictsd-practical-aspects-of-border-carbon-adjustment-measures.pdf> accessed 20 January 2017; Charles E. McLure, Jr., 'A Primer on the Legality of Border Tax Adjustments for Carbon Prices: Through a GATT Darkly', *Climate Change Law Review*, 4 (2011): 456.

[295] We thank Harro van Asselt for this observation. See also Droege *et al.*, Trade System and Climate Action (n 212) 32.

[296] See Joost Pauwelyn, 'U.S. Federal Climate Policy and Competitiveness Concerns: The Limits and Options of International Trade Law', NI WP 07-02 (Nicholas Institute for Environmental Policy Solutions, Duke University, April 2007), 17–27. For a comprehensive treatment, see Kateryna Holzer, *Carbon-related Border Adjustment and WTO Law: The Case of Trade in Goods* (Cheltenham, UK: Edward Elgar, 2014).

[297] Note that border adjustments can also take the form of tax rebates upon export of a product, in which case the question becomes whether or not the export adjustment amounts to an inappropriate

considered above and the criteria set out in the *EC-Asbestos Case* will play a central role in relation to border adjustments.[298] Moreover, in the event of discrimination between 'like' products, a further question is whether the discrimination is justified by one of the GATT Article XX exceptions.[299] In this context, as highlighted by the Appellate Body report in the *Shrimp/Turtle Case*, both the design and application of the border measure will be key in making that determination.[300]

b) Subsidies

Subsidies for the renewable energy sector, especially so-called 'feed-in tariffs' (FITs), have ushered a new era of climate change-related trade disputes at the WTO, involving not only the GATT, but also the SCM Agreement, which focuses on subsidies and countervailing duties, and the TRIMs Agreements. FITs have emerged as a popular policy tool to incentivize the uptake of renewable energy through long-term contracts by government to purchase electricity at set prices from individual renewable energy producers.[301]

Thus far, the WTO decisions on FITs have focused not on their general permissibility, but rather on the 'domestic content' requirements included in some FIT schemes, which mandate that a certain percentage of goods used in the production process of renewable energy projects be sourced locally.[302] In two recent WTO cases, FITs involving domestic content requirements were found to violate the GATT's national treatment principle as well as the TRIMs Agreement, but neither case ruled on whether FITs were subsidies as defined in the SCM Agreement, much less prohibited subsidies. As many commentators have noted, greater clarity is needed on the features that bring national measures, including climate-related

---

subsidy under the SCM Agreement (n 216). See generally Tamiotti *et al.*, Trade and Climate (n 238) 104–5; Aaron Cosbey, 'Border Carbon Adjustment' (International Institute for Sustainable Development, August 2008) <https://www.iisd.org/pdf/2008/cph_trade_climate_border_carbon. pdf> accessed 20 January 2017, 3. See also Persson, Practical Aspects (n 294) 5 (on policy reasons that might militate against export adjustments).

[298] See Section IV.B.4 above.

[299] See Cosbey, Border Carbon Adjustment (n 297) 3–4.

[300] On design options generally, see Persson, Practical Aspects (n 294) 5–11; Jennifer Hillman, 'Changing Climate for Carbon Taxes: Who's Afraid of the WTO', Climate and Energy Paper Series 2013 (German Marshall Fund 2013); Pauwelyn, US Federal Climate Policy (n 296). On the trade law dimensions, see Werksman *et al.*, Trade Measures and Climate Change Policy (n 290) 5–7 (discussing how the border adjustments considered in the context of the US ACESA fare in relation to GATT Article XX); Gary Hufbauer and Meera Fickling, 'Climate Negotiations, EITE Industries, and the WTO: Facing the Conflicts', *International Trade Journal*, 25/3 (2011): 276; Christine Kaufmann and Rolf H. Weber, 'Carbon-related Border Tax Adjustment: Mitigating Climate Change or Restructuring International Trade?', *World Trade Review*, 10/4 (2011): 497.

[301] See Steve Charnovitz and Carolyn Fischer, '*Canada – Renewable Energy*: Implications for WTO Law on Green and Not-So-Green Subsidies', *World Trade Review*, 14/2 (2015): 177.

[302] Marie Wilke, 'Feed-in Tariffs for Renewable Energy and WTO Subsidy Rules: An Initial Legal Review' (International Centre for Trade and Sustainable Development, Geneva, 2011) <http://www. ictsd.org/downloads/2011/11/feed-in-tariffs-for-renewable-energy-and-wto-subsidy-rules.pdf> accessed 20 January 2017, 17–18.

policies, within the definition of subsidies, such that they could be challenged under the SCM Agreement.[303]

In *Canada—Certain Measures Affecting the Renewable Energy Generation Sector*,[304] the EU and Japan challenged a FIT program introduced by the province of Ontario to promote wind energy generation and to provide incentives for investment in the manufacturing of renewable energy technology. The complaint focused on the scheme's requirement to source a certain level of component parts and services from local producers.[305] The challenges were based on Article 2.1 of the TRIMS Agreement, Article III:4 of the GATT, and Articles 3.1(b) and 3.2 of the SCM Agreement. Both the WTO panel and Appellate Body found Ontario's domestic content requirements to be inconsistent with GATT Article III:4 and Article 2.1 of the TRIMs Agreement. However, there was no conclusive ruling on the question whether the domestic content requirements amounted to a prohibited subsidy under the SCM Agreement.[306] While the Appellate Body provided a roadmap for a future assessment of this issue, it concluded that it did not have sufficient factual findings on the record to reach a decision on whether the FIT provided a subsidy within the meaning of the SCM Agreement at all.[307]

---

[303] Article 1.1(a) and (b) of the SCM Agreement (n 216) stipulates that a subsidy is 'a financial contribution by a government or any public body within the territory of a member' that confers a 'benefit' on an enterprise. Both components of the definition have given rise to WTO dispute settlement, with the concept of 'benefit' being the most controversial and difficult to pin down. On the question whether FITs are subsidies within the four corners of the SCM Agreement, see eg Charnovitz and Fischer, Canada—Renewable Energy: Implications (n 301) 192–8. On climate-related subsidies in general, see eg Andrew Green, 'Trade Rules and Climate Change Subsidies', *World Trade Review*, 5/ 3 (2006): 377, 393–6; Robert Howse, 'Climate Mitigation Subsidies and the WTO Legal Framework: A Policy Analysis' (International Institute for Sustainable Development, May 2010) <https://www.iisd. org/pdf/2009/bali_2_copenhagen_subsidies_legal.pdf> accessed 20 January 2017, 6–7.

[304] WTO, *Canada—Certain Measures Affecting the Renewable Energy Sector—Panel Report* (19 December 2012) WT/DS412/R, WT/DS426/R; *Canada—Certain Measures Affecting the Renewable Energy Generation Sector—Report of the Appellate Body* (6 May 2013) WT/DS412/AB/R and WT/DS426/AB/R.

[305] For a summary, Charnovitz and Fischer, Canada—Renewable Energy: Implications (n 301) 179–81.

[306] Articles 3.1(b) and 3.2 of the SCM Agreement (n 216) prohibit subsidies 'contingent, whether solely or as one of several other conditions, upon the use of domestic over imported goods'. Note that subsidies that do not fall within the category of automatically 'prohibited' subsidies may nonetheless be 'actionable' subsidies within the meaning of Article 5 of the SCM Agreement (n 216), which give the affected state the right to impose countervailing duties. Article 8 of the SCM Agreement also envisaged a category of 'non-actionable', and hence permissible, subsidies, including 'assistance to promote adaptation of existing facilities to new environmental requirements imposed by law and/or regulations' (Article 8.2(c)). However, these exemptions were 'provisional' only (Article 31) and their application has not been extended. See Howse, Climate Mitigation Subsidies (n 303) 4.

[307] While the Appellate Body concluded that the FIT contracts entailed a 'financial contribution', it found itself unable to determine whether that contribution conferred a benefit on the FIT recipient. For a detailed discussion, see Charnovitz and Fischer, Canada—Renewable Energy: Implications (n 301) 192–8. Note that, in the meantime, Ontario had removed the domestic content requirement from its FIT scheme. See 'Changes relating to domestic content requirements for microFIT after July 25, 2014' <http://microfit.powerauthority.on.ca/faqs/microfit-domestic-content-after-25-july-2014> accessed 20 January 2017.

India—Certain Measures Relating to Solar Cells and Solar Modules also involved a mandatory domestic content requirement.[308] As in the *Canada—Renewable Energy* dispute, the panel and Appellate Body found the domestic content requirements to be inconsistent with both GATT Article III:4 and Article 2.1 of the TRIMs Agreement. In contrast to Canada in the *Renewable Energy Case*,[309] India attempted to justify its FIT measures under GATT Article XX, although it relied on Article XX(d) (allowing measures necessary to secure compliance with domestic laws or regulations) and Article XX(j) (allowing measures 'essential to the acquisition or distribution of products in ... short supply'), rather than on the environmental exceptions under Article XX(b) and (g). India invoked Article XX(j) to argue that the domestic content requirements were justified on the grounds that the lack of domestic manufacturing capacity in solar cells and modules, and/or the risk of a disruption in imports, made these 'products in general or local short supply' within the meaning of the provision.[310] Regarding Article XX(d), India argued that the domestic content requirements of its solar power scheme were necessary to 'secure compliance with laws and regulations', pointing to various international instruments, including the FCCC, as well as to domestic laws.[311] Both arguments were rejected by the panel and Appellate Body.[312]

Neither case considered whether, absent a domestic content requirement, WTO law allows states to use a FIT to subsidize renewable energy, on the basis of renewable energy's environmental and climate benefits. Can any conclusions be drawn from WTO jurisprudence about the permissibility of environmentally-oriented subsidies, based on the 'likeness' or 'unlikeness' of energy from clean or 'climate friendly' sources, as opposed to sources relying on, say, fossil fuels? Several scholars have criticized the WTO law on subsidies for its insufficient ability to distinguish between 'desirable' and 'undesirable' subsidies.[313] However, *Canada—Renewable Energy* contains subtle hints that electricity from clean energy sources may not be 'like' electricity from carbon-intensive sources.[314] For example, in its general observations about the parameters for assessment under the SCM Agreement, the

---

[308] WTO, *India—Certain Measures Relating to Solar Cells and Solar Modules—Panel Report* (24 February 2016) WT/DS456/R, and Report of the Appellate Body (16 September 2016) WT/DS456/AB/R.

[309] Charnovitz and Fischer, Canada—Renewable Energy: Implications (n 301) 189.

[310] *India—Solar Cells* (n 308) paras 7.237–7.264.

[311] Ibid, paras 7.285–7.301 (international instruments); paras 7.302–7.319 (domestic).

[312] Ibid, para 5.154.

[313] See generally Alan O. Sykes, 'The Questionable Case for Subsidies Regulation: A Comparative Perspective', *Journal of Legal Analysis*, 2/2 (2012): 473. On the specific question of distinctions between subsides in the climate context, see Howse, Climate Mitigation Subsidies (n 303); Luca Rubini, 'Ain't Wastin' Time No More: Subsidies for Renewable Energy, the SCM Agreement, Policy Space, and Law Reform', *Journal of International Economic Law*, 15/2 (2012): 525.

[314] See Charnovitz and Fischer, Canada—Renewable Energy: Implications (n 301) 200–2; Avidan Kent and Vyoma Jha, 'Keeping Up with the Changing Climate: The WTO's Evolutive Approach in Response to the Trade and Climate Conundrum', *The Journal of World Investment and Trade*, 15/1–2 (2014): 258, 261; Rob Howse, 'Securing Policy Space for Clean Energy under the SCM Agreement: Alternative Approaches', in *Clean Energy and the Trade System Group: Proposals and Analysis* (International Centre for Trade and Sustainable Development, December 2013).

Appellate Body held that the relevant markets were the 'competitive markets for wind and solar ... generated energy',[315] rather than the market for electricity from any source of power, as the panel had considered. The Appellate Body also remarked that the government's electricity preferences may reflect consumer attitudes toward different energy sources,[316] an observation that may be relevant not only in the context of the SCM Agreement, but also in assessing under GATT Articles I and III whether electricity from clean sources is a 'like' product to energy from other sources.[317] Perhaps most significantly, the Appellate Body observed that 'fossil fuel resources are exhaustible, and thus fossil energy needs to be replaced progressively if electricity supply is to be guaranteed in the long term',[318] notwithstanding the fact that Canada did not raise a GATT Article XX(g) defense. One might put this observation down to mere 'greenwashing' of its report,[319] but the similarities between the Appellate Body's phrasing and the wording of GATT Article XX(g) suggest there may be some scope for justifying clean energy subsidies on environmental grounds. However, it is important to note in this context that, unlike the GATT and the TRIMS Agreement, the SCM Agreement does not contain a general exceptions provision like Article XX. Thus, although it has been suggested that Article XX is,[320] or should be,[321] applicable to subsidies that fall under the SCM Agreement, this is not a foregone conclusion.

It is also worth noting that, to date, disputes concerning the WTO compatibility of subsidies have focused on measures taken to promote renewable energy, and have not challenged fossil fuel subsidies.[322] But some commentators have identified the question whether fossil fuel subsidies could be challenged under WTO law as likely to move up on the trade policy agenda.[323] From a climate policy perspective, the issue is of great importance,[324] given the pervasive nature of fossil fuel subsidies, which far exceed renewable energy subsidies.[325] In principle, fossil fuel subsidies are covered by relevant WTO agreements, such as the GATT, the SCM Agreement

---

[315] See *Canada—Renewable Energy*, Appellate Body Report (n 304), para 5.178.
[316] Ibid, para 5.177.
[317] See Charnovitz and Fischer, Canada—Renewable Energy: Implications (n 301) 201–2.
[318] See *Canada—Renewable Energy*, Appellate Body Report (n 305), para 5.186.
[319] See Charnovitz and Fischer, Canada—Renewable Energy: Implications (n 301) 207.
[320] See Howse, Climate Mitigation Subsidies (n 303) 17.
[321] See eg Green, Trade Rules (n 303) 407–10.
[322] See Henok Birhanu Asmelash, 'Energy Subsidies and WTO Dispute Settlement: Why Only Renewable Energy Subsidies Are Challenged', *Journal of International Economic Law*, 18 (2015): 261.
[323] Droege *et al.*, Trade System and Climate Action (n 212) 33. See also Karl Mathiesen, 'G7 nations pledge to end fossil fuel subsidies by 2025', *The Guardian*, 27 May 2016, <https://www.theguardian.com/environment/2016/may/27/g7-nations-pledge-to-end-fossil-fuel-subsidies-by-2025> accessed 20 January 2017.
[324] See eg International Energy Agency (IEA), *World Energy Outlook Special Report 2015: Energy and Climate Change* (Paris: IEA, 2015) (discussing the role of fossil-fuel subsidy phase-outs in meeting global climate policy goals).
[325] Note that different approaches to estimating the total value of global fossil fuel subsidies prevail; see IEA, 'World Energy Outlook: Energy Subsidies' <http://www.worldenergyoutlook.org/resources/energysubsidies/> accessed 20 January 2017; David Coady *et al.*, *How Large Are Global Energy Subsidies?* (International Monetary Fund (IMF) Working Paper, WP/15/105, 2015) 17–22 <http://www.imf.org/external/pubs/ft/survey/so/2015/NEW070215A.htm> accessed 20 January 2017.

and the TRIMs Agreement. However, the application of these agreements to fossil fuel subsidies has proven difficult in practice, due to lack of information about the scope and nature of such subsidies, and the lack of clarity as to whether they fit the definitional criteria of (prohibited) subsidies.[326]

C. Trade in the UN climate regime

Unlike other environmental agreements, such as CITES, the Basel Convention, and the Montreal Protocol,[327] the agreements that make up the UN climate regime neither rely on trade restrictions to advance mitigation goals nor take a position on recourse to such measures in the climate context. This arms-length stance should not be surprising, considering the divergent views on the appropriateness of trade measures to support climate policy goals.[328] Furthermore, given the scale of the potential trade issues raised by climate policies, the relationship between trade law and the climate regime implicates a host of politically sensitive issues.

As noted at the beginning of this section, the FCCC emphasizes the importance of a 'supportive and open international economic system'. However, in stating that 'measures taken to combat climate change, including unilateral ones, should not constitute a means of arbitrary or unjustifiable discrimination or a disguised restriction on international trade',[329] FCCC Article 3.5 limits itself to reiterating the rule contained in GATT Article XX.[330] In other words, the FCCC neither condones nor forbids the use of trade measures; it refers parties to existing trade law—the rule framework surveyed in this section. The Kyoto Protocol maintains the FCCC's neutral approach, but also reflects the concerns of developing countries,[331] stipulating that Annex I parties 'shall strive to implement' their climate policies and

---

[326] See Asmelash, Energy Subsidies (n 322) 267; Chris Wold, Grant Wilson, and Sara Foroshani, 'Leveraging Climate Change Benefits through the World Trade Organization: Are Fossil Fuel Subsidies Actionable?', *Georgetown Journal of International Law*, 43/3 (2012): 587. See also nn 303, 306–307 above and accompanying text.

[327] See nn 250–251 above and accompanying text.

[328] Developing countries, for example, have expressed grave concern about trade-restrictive climate policies, especially unilateral ones. See eg Proposals by India for inclusion of additional agenda items in the provisional agenda of the seventeenth session of the Conference of the Parties, FCCC/CP/2011/INF.2 (21 September 2011) (advocating a prohibition of unilateral trade measures in the climate context). By contrast, other FCCC parties, including the EU and the US, have taken concrete steps toward deploying trade measures. See van Asselt and Brewer, Addressing Competitiveness (n 290).

[329] FCCC, Art 3.5. See also Rio Declaration, principle 12: '... Unilateral actions to deal with environmental challenges outside the jurisdiction of the importing country should be avoided. Environmental measures addressing transboundary or global environmental problems should, as far as possible, be based on an international consensus.'

[330] See Chapter 5, Section III.C.5. See also Daniel Bodansky, 'The United Nations Framework Convention on Climate Change: A Commentary', *Yale Journal of International Law*, 18/2 (1993): 451, 502.

[331] Under a proposal by the G-77/China, Annex I parties were to be required 'to ensure' that climate policies and measures had 'no adverse impacts' on socio-economic conditions in developing countries. See Joanna Depledge, 'Tracing the Origins of the Kyoto Protocol: An Article-by-Article Textual History' (25 November 2000) FCCC/TP/2000/2, paras 116–25 (on the negotiating history of the provision).

measures 'in such a way as to minimize adverse effects, including ... effects on international trade, and social, environmental and economic impacts on other Parties, especially developing country Parties'.[332]

In the development of the climate regime since Kyoto, trade issues have consistently loomed in the background, but the regime has continued to take a hands-off approach. The Cancun Agreements, for example, reiterated the principles set out in FCCC Article 3.5.[333] During COP17 in Durban, India attempted, in vain, to place a discussion of unilateral trade measures on the agenda, asking that parties 'expressly prohibit' such measures.[334] The Paris outcome, for its part, does not address trade issues at all, so the approach of FCCC Article 3.5 remains authoritative. However, the silence of the Paris Agreement on trade issues in no way suggests that these issues have been resolved—far from it. The 'forum on the impact of the implementation of response measures', first convened pursuant to the Cancun Agreements,[335] provides one setting in which the relationship between trade and climate policies will continue to be discussed.[336] Once dominated by the specific concerns of oil-exporting countries, the response measures topic has come to be intertwined with broader concerns by developing countries about the 'adverse impacts of mitigation actions',[337] including the trade-related impacts of the kinds of domestic measures canvassed in this section.[338]

These issues will assume heightened importance to the extent that the accelerated pace and scope of domestic climate actions entailed by the Paris Agreement's provisions on progression and ambition prompt trade law challenges to domestic policies.[339] However, whether the necessarily case-by-case nature of WTO dispute settlement can produce the needed clarification of the relationship between the trade regime and implementation actions under the Paris Agreement is uncertain,[340] as

---

[332] Kyoto Protocol, Art 2.3. The provision refers, in particular, to the developing country parties identified in FCCC Arts 4.8 and 4.9.

[333] Cancun Agreements LCA, para 90.

[334] See Proposals by India for inclusion of additional agenda items in the provisional agenda of the seventeenth session of the Conference of the Parties, FCCC/CP/2011/INF.2 (21 September 2011).

[335] Cancun Agreements LCA, para 93. The COP decision adopting the Paris Agreement provides that the Forum will continue to serve the Agreement. Decision 1/CP.21 (n 205) paras 33–4.

[336] The Paris Agreement itself provides a toe-hold for this topic, by recognizing that parties 'may be affected not only by climate change, but also by the impacts of the measures taken in response to it' (Preamble), and by providing that, in implementing the agreement, parties 'shall take into consideration ... the concerns of Parties with economies most affected by the impacts of response measures, especially developing country Parties' (Art 4.15).

[337] The anchor for these debates in the climate regime is FCCC Article 4.8.

[338] For a detailed discussion, see Nicholas Chan, 'The "New" Impacts of the Implementation of Climate Change Response Measures', *Review of European, Comparative and International Environmental Law*, 25/2 (2016): 228.

[339] See also Ingrid Jegou, Sonja Hawkins, Kimberly Botwright, 'A landmark universal emissions-cutting deal offers both hope and challenges as stakeholders move to implementation', *Bridges Africa*, 5/2 (10 March 2016) <http://www.ictsd.org/bridges-news/bridges-africa/news/what-role-for-trade-and-investment-in-the-new-climate-regime> accessed 20 January 2017; Ilmi Granoff, 'Trade Implications of Climate Policy after the Paris Outcome', *Trade Hot Topics*, Issue 130 (Commonwealth Secretariat, 2016) <http://unctad14.org/Documents/U14ditc_d01d_FGE_Cont2_en.pdf> accessed 20 January 2017, 4–6.

[340] See Droege *et al.*, Trade System and Climate Action (n 212) 34.

is the scope for a more comprehensive approach to climate policy measures under the auspices of the WTO.[341] At least in the medium term, greater opportunities for proactive approaches may exist in plurilateral settings, such as the ongoing efforts by a sub-set of WTO members to arrive at an Environmental Goods Agreement that would eliminate tariffs on a broad range of 'green' goods.[342] Other opportunities to harmonize standards or to elaborate common rules for trade-related climate measures may exist under the regional and mega-regional trade agreements mentioned at the beginning of this section,[343] and might help allay some of the political and civil society concerns about these agreements.[344] It is too soon to know how these various efforts will play out. Yet one thing seems safe to predict: since the climate regime has left the resolution of the tensions between trade and climate policy considerations to trade law, standard setting and dispute settlement in the latter area will play significant roles in shaping bottom-up climate action.

SELECT BIBLIOGRAPHY

'Report of the Special Rapporteur on the issue of human rights obligations relating to the enjoyment of a safe, clean, healthy and sustainable environment' (1 February 2016) UN Doc A/HRC/31/52, 7.

Anton D.K. and Shelton D.L., *Environmental Protection and Human Rights* (Cambridge University Press, 2011).

Bonine J. and Kravchenko S., *Human Rights and the Environment: Cases, Law, and Policy* (Durham, NC: Carolina Academic Press, 2008).

Boyle A. and Anderson M. (eds), *Human Rights Approaches to Environmental Protection* (Oxford University Press, 1996).

Conrad C.R., *Processes and Production Methods (PPMs) in WTO Law: Interfacing Trade and Social Goals* (Cambridge University Press, 2011).

Doelle M., 'Climate Change and the WTO: Opportunities to Motivate State Action on Climate Change through the World Trade Organization', *Review of European Community and International Environmental Law*, 13/1 (2004): 85.

Droege S. *et al.*, 'The Trade System and Climate Action: Ways Forward under the Paris Agreement' (Climate Strategies, Working Paper, October 2016) <http://climatestrategies.

---

[341] See ibid, 11 (discussing the limited progress made, for example, in the WTO's Committee on Trade and Environment), and ibid, 34–8 (discussing various reform options, including amendments, waivers and authoritative interpretations of the WTO agreements).

[342] See International Centre for Trade and Sustainable Development, 'Environmental goods agreement negotiators agree roadmap for conclusion', BIORES: Analysis and News on Trade and Environment (4 August 2016) <http://www.ictsd.org/bridges-news/biores/news/environmental-goods-agreement-negotiators-agree-roadmap-for-conclusion> accessed 20 January 2017. The participants include major trading nations, such as Canada, China, Japan, the US, and the EU. But see also Arthur Neslen, 'Trade deal threatens Paris climate goals, leaked documents show', *The Guardian* (20 September 2016) <https://www.theguardian.com/environment/2016/sep/20/global-trade-deal-threatens-paris-climate-goals-leaked-documents-show> accessed 20 January 2017 (suggesting that a new Trade in Services Agreement between the EU and twenty-two other countries could make it harder for governments to favor clean energy over fossil fuels).

[343] See Leal-Arcas, Climate Change and International Trade (n 228) 405–16; Droege *et al.*, Trade System and Climate Action (n 212) 38–9.

[344] See n 227 above and accompanying text.

org/wp-content/uploads/2016/10/Trade-and-climate-ways-forward-1.pdf> accessed 20 January 2017.

Edwards A., 'Climate Change and International Refugee Law', in Rayfuse R. and Schott S.V. (eds), *International Law in the Era of Climate Change* (Cheltenham, UK: Edward Elgar Publishing, 2012) 58.

Holzer K., *Carbon-related Border Adjustment and WTO Law: The Case of Trade in Goods* (Cheltenham, UK: Edward Elgar, 2014).

Howse R., 'Climate Mitigation Subsidies and the WTO Legal Framework: A Policy Analysis' (International Institute for Sustainable Development, May 2010) <https://www.iisd.org/pdf/2009/bali_2_copenhagen_subsidies_legal.pdf> accessed 20 January 2017.

Hufbauer G.C., Charnovitz S., and Kim J., *Global Warming and the World Trading System* (Washington, D.C.: Peterson Institute for International Economics, 2009).

Knox J.H., 'Human Rights Principles and Climate Change', in Carlarne C.P., Gray K.R., and Tarasofsky R. (eds), *The Oxford Handbook of International Climate Change Law* (Oxford University Press, 2016) 213.

Leal-Arcas R., *Climate Change and International Trade* (Cheltenham, UK: Edward Elgar, 2013).

McAdam J. (ed), *Climate Change and Displacement: Multidisciplinary Perspectives* (Oxford: Hart Publishing, 2010).

McAdam J., *Climate Change, Forced Migration and International Law* (Oxford University Press, 2012).

McAdam J., 'From the Nansen Initiative to the Platform on Disaster Displacement: Shaping International Approaches to Climate Change, Disasters and Displacement', *University of New South Wales Law Journal*, 39/4 (2016, forthcoming).

Rajamani L., 'Human Rights in the Climate Change Regime: From Rio to Paris', in Knox J.H. and Pejan R. (eds), T*he Human Right to a Healthy Environment* (Cambridge University Press, 2017).

Wyman K.M., 'Human Mobility and Climate Change', in Farber D.A. and Peeters M. (eds), *Elgar Encyclopedia of Environmental Law Series vol 1: Climate Change Law* (Cheltenham, UK: Edward Elgar, 2016).

10

Conclusion

I. THE EVOLUTION OF INTERNATIONAL CLIMATE CHANGE LAW: A BRIEF RECAP

Unlike many areas of international environmental law, international climate change law has not followed a straight pathway from soft to hard law, from a bottom-up to a top-down architecture, from more general to more precise obligations, or from greater to less differentiation. Instead, it has taken a long and winding road, which better reflects a Hegelian[1] than a Whig[2] view of history, moving dialectically from thesis to antithesis to synthesis, rather than progressing unidirectionally toward greater stringency and effectiveness. In this story, the Kyoto Protocol represents the thesis, the Copenhagen Accord the antithesis, and the Paris Agreement the synthesis. The Kyoto Protocol was moulded by the dominant paradigm at the time: it prescribes a legally binding, top-down architecture, consisting of quantitative targets and timetables to limit greenhouse gas emissions, coupled with a complex system of international rules on accounting and compliance. The Copenhagen Accord was in many respects the polar opposite: a political agreement built around bottom-up pledges giving states tremendous flexibility. The Paris Agreement represents a hybrid of the two: it is a legally binding instrument with some non-binding elements, and combines bottom-up, nationally determined contributions (NDCs) with internationally negotiated rules to promote ambition and accountability.[3]

When the climate issue first emerged in the late 1980s, many did not appreciate how difficult it would be to address politically and had unrealistically high expectations. In many respects, the high-water mark of ambition came in 1988, in the Toronto Declaration, which called for a 20% reduction in *global* CO_2 emissions by 2005 and the establishment of a global fund financed by a tax on fossil fuels.[4]

---

[1] Julie E. Maybee, 'Hegel's Dialectics', in Edward N. Zalta (ed), *Stanford Encylopedia of Philosophy* (Fall 2016 edition) <http://plato.stanford.edu/entries/hegel-dialectics/> accessed 20 January 2017.

[2] Herman Butterfield, *The Whig Interpretation of History* (London: George Bell and Sons Ltd, 1931) (according to Whig interpretation, history is a story of progress).

[3] See Chapters 1, 5, 6, and 7.

[4] Proceedings of the World Conference on the Changing Atmosphere: Implications for Global Security, held in Toronto from 27 to 30 June 1988, (1988) WMO No. 710.

By contrast, almost three decades later, with emissions almost 50% higher than in 1990, the political difficulties of addressing climate change have become painfully apparent, and the 2015 Paris Agreement sets a more modest goal, calling for a peaking of global emissions as soon as possible and at unspecified levels.[5]

Initially, many countries saw the ozone regime as a model for tackling climate change. The ozone problem had been addressed through the framework convention/protocol approach, beginning with the 1985 Vienna Convention, which established the basic system of governance, followed by the 1987 Montreal Protocol on Substances that Deplete the Ozone Layer, which prescribed internationally negotiated, quantitative limits on national production and consumption of ozone-depleting substances (ODS). Reflecting this approach, the UN climate regime began with the 1992 FCCC, followed by the 1997 Kyoto Protocol and the 2001 Marrakesh Accords. The FCCC established the regime's basic objective, principles, and institutions, while the Kyoto Protocol imposed legally binding limits on Annex I party emissions, and the Marrakesh Accords elaborated the protocol's rules.[6]

But, here, the stories of the ozone and climate regimes diverge. From its inception, the Montreal Protocol steadily progressed both in breadth and depth. Originally, it required parties to freeze and then halve their consumption and production of five chlorofluorocarbons (CFCs), the principal ODS, and to freeze their consumption and production of three halons.[7] Subsequently, through a series of adjustments and amendments, the parties to the Montreal Protocol added dozens of ODS to its list of controlled substances, and progressively ratcheted up the stringency of its control measures, so that, today, the protocol regulates almost 100 chemicals and requires the complete phase-out of most ozone-depleting substances.[8] In addition, the parties created a Multilateral Fund to entice developing countries to join, and a non-compliance procedure to promote implementation and compliance.

In contrast, the Kyoto Protocol did not trigger a process leading to greater depth and breadth. Its second commitment period targets apply to a smaller fraction of global emissions than the first commitment period targets, and may never enter into force. And the Kyoto Protocol emission targets will almost certainly not be extended beyond 2020, when the second commitment period ends. Instead, the climate regime moved in a different direction, retreating in depth in order to promote greater breadth. The 2009 Copenhagen Accord and 2010 Cancun Agreements established a non-legally binding system of bottom-up pledges, which attracted much broader participation than the Kyoto Protocol's legally binding emission targets. Only then did the 2015 Paris Agreement begin to deepen the Copenhagen/Cancun architecture, by incorporating it in a legally binding instrument, with multilateral rules to promote ambition and oversight. The climate regime's approach to differentiation has followed a similarly winding path, starting with moderate differentiation in the FCCC, reflected in its distinction between the

---

[5] See Chapter 7, Section IV.   [6] See Chapters 4, 5, and 6.
[7] Montreal Protocol, Art 2.
[8] United Nations Environment Programme, *Handbook for the Montreal Protocol on Substances that Deplete the Ozone Layer* (7th edn, 2006) 6–12.

common commitments of all parties and the differentiated commitments of Annex I and Annex II parties, then moving to radical differentiation in the Kyoto Protocol, which completely excluded non-Annex I parties from any new commitments, and most recently adopting a more nuanced, non-annex based approach to differentiation in the Paris Agreement.[9]

Meanwhile, as the UN climate regime has struggled to make progress over the last decade, the broader landscape of international climate change law has diversified. The International Maritime Organization (IMO) and the International Civil Aviation Organization (ICAO) have addressed emissions from maritime transport and international civil aviation. States have agreed to regulate hydrochlorofluorocarbons (HCFCs) and hydrofluorocarbons (HFCs), two particularly potent groups of greenhouse gases, through the Montreal Protocol, and to address black carbon through the Convention on Long-range Transboundary Air Pollution. And cities, regional governments, and non-governmental actors have pursued a wide variety of initiatives to mitigate and adapt to climate change.[10]

The development of international climate change law reflects many factors. Science has been a key driver from the beginning. Scientific developments first put climate change on the policy agenda in the 1980s, and mounting scientific concern about the risks of climate change has underpinned political pressure to address the problem ever since. The IPCC's First Assessment Report in 1990 provided the impetus for the FCCC, the Second Assessment Report in 1995 for the Kyoto Protocol, the Fourth Assessment Report in 2007 for the Copenhagen Accord, and the Fifth Assessment Report in 2013 for the Paris Agreement. Although the mitigation measures adopted under the Kyoto Protocol, Copenhagen Accord, and Paris Agreement have tended to reflect politics more than science, science has influenced other elements of the regime. The FCCC and Kyoto Protocol's comprehensive, multi-gas approach, for example, reflected the scientific understanding at the time of the causes of climate change. And the Paris Agreement's temperature goals of 2° C or 1.5° C were based on a scientific assessment of the maximum warming to which the world can safely adapt.

From the beginning, however, scientific and environmental concerns about the impacts of climate change have been counterbalanced by economic concerns about the costs of limiting emissions. Many countries have been wary of accepting legally binding emission targets because of their potential impacts on economic development and competitiveness. The solution in the Paris Agreement was to allow parties to nationally determine their mitigation contributions, and to rely on transparency and oversight to encourage implementation, rather than on legal enforcement.[11]

Transformations in the world economy have also played an important role in the development of international climate change law. In 1990, when the negotiations of the FCCC began, developed countries accounted for about 70% of global emissions. Since then, developing country emissions have tripled and now account

---

[9] See Chapters 4, 5, 6, and 7.   [10] See Chapter 8, Sections II and III.
[11] See Chapter 7.

for almost 60% of global emissions.[12] The Chinese economy alone has grown more than ten-fold,[13] and its emissions have quadrupled. In 1990, US emissions were roughly double those of China, but by 2014, the situation had reversed, with Chinese emissions roughly doubling those of the US.[14] These trends have led to an increasing focus in international climate change law on developing as well as developed country emissions, reflected most importantly in the Paris Agreement's mitigation regime, which applies to all parties, as well as in the complementary actions in ICAO to address emissions from civil aviation and in the Montreal Protocol to address the use of HFCs.[15]

Concerns about equity and climate justice have been another important influence on the evolution of international climate change law. Developing countries such as China and India have consistently argued that developed countries should take the lead in responding to climate change, since they were responsible for causing the problem and have greater capacity to respond. Cumulative emissions between 1850 and 2012 for Annex I countries are about 2.4 times those of non-Annex I countries,[16] and per capita CO_2 emissions for most developing countries remain significantly below those of most developed countries. India's per capita emissions in 2013 were 1.7 tons, for example, as compared to 7.3 tons for the EU and 16.6 tons for the US.[17] Meanwhile, developed countries have stressed the global nature of the climate change problem and the need for all countries to take action. The fight over how obligations should be differentiated has played itself out across all of the different sites of international climate change law, including the UN climate regime, IMO, ICAO, and the Montreal Protocol.

Perhaps the most important factor in the development of international climate change law has been learning from experience. The hybrid approach in the Paris Agreement reflects the lessons learnt from the Kyoto Protocol and the Copenhagen Accord. The Kyoto Protocol arguably tried to do too much too soon, by imposing legally binding, absolute limits on national emissions, and attracted relatively little participation; the Copenhagen Accord tried to attract universal participation by giving states flexibility, but produced insufficient ambition. The Paris Agreement tries to strike a balance between the two.[18] In the meantime, the slow progress in

---

[12] International Energy Agency, *CO_2 Emissions from Fuel Combustion: Key CO_2 Emission Trends* (2016) Figure 4.

[13] 'GDP Statistics from the World Bank: China' <https://knoema.com/mhrzolg/gdp-statistics-from-the-world-bank?country=China> accessed 20 January 2017.

[14] European Commission, Emission Database for Global Atmospheric Research, 'CO_2 Time Series 1990-2014 Per Region/Country' <http://edgar.jrc.ec.europa.eu/overview.php?v=CO2ts1990-2014&sort=des9> accessed 20 January 2017.

[15] See Chapters 7 and 8.

[16] CO_2 emissions from Annex I countries from 1850 to 2012 were 937,952 $MtCO_2$ and from non-Annex I were 388,623 $MTCO_2$. Data for Cumulative Total CO_2 Emissions Excluding Land-Use Change and Forestry from 1850 to selected years—2012 from World Resources Institute (WRI), 'CAIT Climate Data Explorer' <http://cait.wri.org/> accessed 20 January 2017.

[17] Jos G.J. Olivier *et al.*, *Trends in Global CO_2 Emissions: 2014 Report* (The Hague: PBL Netherlands Environmental Assessment Agency, 2014) <http://edgar.jrc.ec.europa.eu/news_docs/jrc-2014-trends-in-global-co2-emissions-2014-report-93171.pdf> accessed 20 January 2017, 49, Table A1.2.

[18] See Chapters 5, 6, and 7.

the UN climate regime in the 2000s led to efforts to address the climate change problem elsewhere, in international institutions such as IMO, ICAO, and the Montreal Protocol; at the sub-national level by regions and cities; and by non-state actors through private and public–private initiatives.[19]

II. DISTINCTIVE FEATURES OF INTERNATIONAL CLIMATE CHANGE LAW

International climate change law is not a self-contained body of law.[20] It is anchored in the general rules, principles, and law-making practices of public international law and international environmental law,[21] and intersects with other fields of international law, including most notably human rights, migration, and trade law.[22] And yet international climate change law does have certain distinctive features, most evident in the evolution of the UN climate regime[23] and in its increasing enmeshment with diverse transnational, national, sub-national, and private standard-setting activities.[24]

First, it largely reflects a managerial rather than an enforcement-oriented approach.[25] Recourse to international or domestic litigation has been relatively limited to date, arguably due to both the complex and polycentric nature of the climate challenge and the conceptual and practical constraints of the relevant legal frameworks.[26] Within the UN climate regime, the Kyoto Protocol's compliance procedures and mechanisms encompass some quasi-judicial and enforcement-oriented elements, including, most notably, the compliance committee's enforcement branch and the range of consequences for non-compliance by Annex I parties with their target-related commitments.[27] However, these aspects of Kyoto's compliance system are closely tied to the protocol's particular features, especially its binding emission targets for Annex I parties, market mechanisms, and sharp differentiation between Annex I and non-Annex I parties' commitments. Such an enforcement-oriented approach is less apt in the context of the Paris Agreement, with its non-legally binding NDCs, required of all parties.[28] Instead, the Paris Agreement draws on the climate regime's extensive experience with measurement, reporting and verification (MRV) to ensure implementation. Sophisticated MRV requirements were first elaborated under the FCCC, and have continued to be crucial components of the Kyoto Protocol and Paris Agreement's oversight systems. Another managerial tool, the provision of financial and technological assistance for developing countries' implementation (and adaptation) efforts, also has been a prominent topic in the climate regime since its inception. More recently, the creation of the Green

---

[19] See Chapter 8.   [20] See Chapter 1.   [21] See Chapters 2 and 3.
[22] See Chapter 9.   [23] See Chapters 4 to 7.   [24] See Chapter 8.
[25] See generally Abram Chayes and Antonia Handler Chayes, *The New Sovereignty: Compliance with International Regulatory Agreements* (Cambridge, MA: Harvard University Press, 1995).
[26] See Chapters 2 and 8.   [27] See Chapter 6, Section VI.B.
[28] See Chapter 7, Section X.C.

Climate Fund was a key element of the parties' efforts to go beyond the Kyoto Protocol and develop a comprehensive and long-term legal framework for global climate action. In short, the climate regime's strong emphasis on transparency, peer pressure, and assistance, combined with its continued efforts to keep the spotlight on the urgency of the climate challenge, makes it a quintessentially managerial regime. This approach meshes with the underlying assumptions that states broadly agree on the need to combat climate change and that a successful climate regime must therefore manage factors that hinder climate action (such as lack of knowledge, lack of trust, and capacity problems), rather than seek to enforce such action.

A second distinctive feature of the climate regime is the centrality of differentiation as an issue. The climate regime is unique in its explicit articulation of common but differentiated responsibilities and respective capabilities as one of its guiding principles. But the meaning of this principle has been contested from the start, and has shifted over time, from a categorical approach in the FCCC and the Kyoto Protocol, based on lists of parties in annexes, to a more nuanced, tailored approach in the Paris Agreement.

A third, related, feature of international climate change law is its experimentation with legal form. Building on the experience gained under other multilateral environmental agreements, the climate regime has developed an innovative approach to the blending of formally binding and non-binding elements. The Paris Agreement represents a carefully calibrated mix of formal treaty law, decisions of the parties, and domestic standard setting, integrated into the regime through non-legally binding NDCs. This hybrid approach to legal form goes hand-in-hand with an equally careful meshing of substantive and procedural elements. Most notably, the legally binding procedural commitments in the Paris Agreement (ie to prepare, communicate, and maintain NDCs; to provide clear, transparent, and understandable information on NDCs; and to account for NDCs),[29] in conjunction with the non-legally binding normative expectations it enshrines (in relation to, for instance, highest possible ambition, progression over time, and leadership from developed countries), serve to discipline and guide domestic action.

The climate regime's experimentation with legal form connects to a fourth distinctive feature of international climate change law—its polycentricity. Today, the UN climate regime is only one of many sites of global climate governance. A diverse array of institutions—formal and informal, public and private, and situated at multiple levels of governance, ranging from local to global—are taking action to address climate change.[30] The UN climate regime operates alongside these other efforts and recognizes their importance.[31] Through this multiplicity of institutions and approaches, international climate change law reflects the fact that climate change is a multidimensional problem, which implicates virtually every aspect of society and every economic sector.

---

[29] Paris Agreement, Arts 4.2, 4.8, and 4.13.   [30] See Chapter 8.
[31] Paris Agreement, preambular recital 15 ('recognizing the importance of the engagements of all levels of government and various actors … in addressing climate change').

The central role of economic activity in both generating and reducing GHG emissions accounts for a further distinctive feature of international climate change law: its market orientation. The establishment of market mechanisms to reduce emissions was a hotly contested issue in the FCCC negotiations.[32] The debate was resolved in favor of market mechanisms in the Kyoto Protocol, and the Paris Agreement continues to recognize their use.[33] But the UN climate regime is hardly alone in its recourse to market-based mechanisms to address climate change. Other international institutions have considered the use of market mechanisms to help curb emissions from particular sectors, such as shipping and aviation,[34] and a growing number of regional, national, and sub-national carbon trading systems have helped build a global carbon market from the bottom up.[35] Finally, as national and sub-national standard setting, carbon pricing, and labelling schemes assume greater importance, international trade law is playing an increasingly prominent role in shaping both the global marketplace and polycentric climate governance.[36]

III. EFFECTIVENESS OF INTERNATIONAL CLIMATE CHANGE LAW

Since climate change emerged as an international issue three decades ago, states have expended enormous effort and spilt much ink negotiating a series of international instruments to address the problem. In addition to the instruments of the UN climate regime, including the 1992 FCCC, 1997 Kyoto Protocol, 2001 Marrakesh Accords, 2009 Copenhagen Accord, 2010 Cancun Agreements, and 2015 Paris Agreement, states also negotiated the 2011 MARPOL Annex VI amendments to address emissions from ships, the 2016 Kigali Amendment to the Montreal Protocol to address HFCs, and the 2016 ICAO global market-based measure to address aviation emissions.[37] But numerous though these agreements are, it is difficult to assess to what extent international climate change law, and the UN climate regime in particular, have been effective in responding to climate change.

Effectiveness has multiple meanings.[38] Effectiveness, at its simplest, refers to the extent to which the regime in question improves the state of the underlying problem,[39] or achieves the objectives or purposes for which it was intended.[40] The

---

[32] See Chapter 5, Section IV.B.2.
[33] See Chapter 6, Section V, and Chapter 7, Section VI.   [34] See Chapter 8, Section IV.
[35] Ibid, Section VII.   [36] See Chapter 9, Section IV.
[37] See Chapter 8, Section IV.
[38] See generally Daniel Bodansky, *The Art and Craft of International Environmental Law* (Cambridge, MA: Harvard University Press, 2010) ch 12.
[39] See Kal Raustiala, 'Compliance & Effectiveness in International Regulatory Cooperation', *Case Western Reserve Journal of International Law*, 32/3 (2000): 387, 393.
[40] Andreas Hasenclever, Peter Mayer, and Volker Rittberger, 'Interests, Power, Knowledge: The Study of International Regimes', *Mershon International Studies Review*, 40/2 (1996): 117 (noting that 'a regime is effective to the extent that it achieves the objectives or purposes for which it was intended and to the extent that its members abide by its norms and rules').

purpose of international climate change law is to prevent dangerous climate change and adapt to its adverse impacts. Have the international agreements brokered over the last twenty-five years put us on track to limiting temperature increase and managing the adverse impacts of climate change?

This is an inherently difficult question to answer, as the chain of actions linking the legal regime to the environmental outcome is 'complex, uncertain and discontinuous'.[41] As some scholars have noted, social and political structures are complex, ecological systems are in perpetual evolution, and establishing causal links between the regime and the observed results is a problem-ridden task.[42] However, it is worth noting that GHG emissions have steadily increased in the last several decades. Indeed, in the first decade of the twenty-first century, emissions grew at a faster pace (2.2% per year) than over the last three decades of the twentieth century (1.3% per year).[43] There are many reasons for this growth in GHG emissions, but whatever the precise causes, the inadequacies of international climate change law form part of the explanatory context. The FCCC contained only a stabilization target, and for Annex I countries alone.[44] The Kyoto Protocol's first commitment period targets covered just 24% of 2010 global GHG emissions.[45] Its second commitment period attracted even fewer countries and thus covers less than 12% of 2012 global GHG emissions.[46] The Cancun pledges for the pre-2020 period cover 83% of global emissions, but these pledges are modest, and even assuming full implementation (without conditions),[47] there will be a considerable gap between countries' pledges and the emissions pathways consistent with limiting temperature increase to 2° C or 1.5° C.[48] Efforts to persuade countries to enhance the ambition of their 2020 targets have thus far proven fruitless.[49] The NDCs submitted by parties in the context of the Paris Agreement cover an impressive 99% of global emissions, but these too are at considerable variance with emissions pathways consistent with the agreement's long-term temperature goal.[50] Nor has the UN climate regime, or activities elsewhere, led to significant adaptation efforts. It appears therefore that

[41] Konrad von Moltke, 'Research on the Effectiveness of International Environmental Agreements: Lessons for Policy Makers' (Paper prepared for the Final Conference of the EU Concerted Action on Regime Effectiveness, Institut d'Educació Contínua (IDEC), Barcelona, 9–12 November 2000) 4–5.

[42] Ibid.

[43] United Nations Environment Programme (UNEP), *The Emissions Gap Report 2015: A UNEP Synthesis Report* (Nairobi: UNEP, November 2015) 3.

[44] See Chapter 5, Section IV.B.1.

[45] Igor Shishlov, Romain Morel, and Valentin Bellassen, 'Compliance of the Parties to the Kyoto Protocol in the First Commitment Period', *Climate Policy*, 16/6 (2016): 768.

[46] This includes the emissions share of Australia, Belarus, EU-28, Iceland, Kazakhstan, Norway, Switzerland, Ukraine in 2010, excluding LULUCF. WRI, CAIT Climate Data Explorer (n 16).

[47] See US Climate Action Network, 'Who's On Board with the Copenhagen Accord?', <http://www.usclimatenetwork.org/policy/copenhagen-accord-commitments> accessed 20 January 2017.

[48] UNEP, 'Bridging the Emissions Gap: A UNEP Synthesis Report' (Nairobi: UNEP, November 2011) 9.

[49] See Chapter 6, Section X.

[50] FCCC, Aggregate effect of the intended nationally determined contributions: an update, Synthesis report by the secretariat (2 May 2016) FCCC/CP/2016/2, figure 2.

international climate change law has not put the world on track to achieving its stated goals.

A second, more modest, way of assessing effectiveness is to ask whether international climate change law has induced changes in state behavior in the 'right' direction—that is, toward greater mitigation and adaptation to climate change.[51] Has international climate change law improved upon 'business as usual' GHG emissions trajectories? Has it helped bend the emissions curve downward toward the desired temperature limit of 'well below 2°C', which was agreed in Paris? Have states and other actors done more to adapt to climate change than they would have done if international climate change law had not developed? Some scholars argue that assessing effectiveness through behavioral change rather than by environmental outcome is a more sensible way of measuring the effectiveness of a rule or regime, since many factors, in addition to the rule or regime, contribute to the environmental outcome.[52] However, assessing behavioral change is also a difficult and speculative exercise, as it requires a counterfactual assessment, dependent on questionable assumptions, of what would have happened in the absence of international climate change law, under 'business as usual'. Nevertheless, it is worth noting that aggregate global GHG emissions levels associated with the implementation of states' NDCs are expected to be 'sizeably lower' than in pre-Paris trajectories (although still considerably higher than least-cost 2° C and 1.5° C scenarios).[53] Global average per capita emissions are also expected to decline as a result of the effect of the NDCs.[54] Perhaps more importantly, in terms of assessing behavioral change, the FCCC secretariat's review of parties' NDCs indicates a 'clear and increasing trend' toward taking national actions to address climate change.[55] It also reveals the 'increasing prominence of climate change on national political agendas'.[56] These developments are reflected in the scope and scale of the NDCs as compared to the Cancun pledges. Under Cancun, a total of sixty-one parties presented quantified emission targets of one kind or another, while in their NDCs 155 parties have communicated such targets.[57]

A third way of assessing effectiveness is to ask whether the climate regime has done as well as possible politically. Was the Paris Agreement as successful as possible, given the numerous political constraints that parties face in addressing climate change both internationally and domestically? Or was a more ambitious deal within reach? Could the negotiators have done better? Answering this question is even more difficult than assessing behavioral effectiveness, since it depends on subtle and unprovable assumptions about what is politically achievable at a given time—what trade-offs between ambition and participation are possible. Some observers have argued that the UN climate regime has been dysfunctional for much of its history, and that a different governance structure, involving fewer states, might have

---

[51] Raustiala, Compliance & Effectiveness (n 39).   [52] Ibid, 394.
[53] FCCC, Aggregate effect of the intended nationally determined contributions (n 50) para 38 and figure 2.
[54] Ibid, para 37.   [55] Ibid, para 51.   [56] Ibid, para 52.   [57] Ibid, para 48.

been able to make more progress.[58] But many, if not most, observers would agree that the Paris Agreement was a considerable diplomatic achievement and that its rules go as far—or further—than seemed achievable, when the negotiations began, in promoting transparency and progression.[59]

A final metric for assessing the effectiveness of international climate change law is the degree to which it has increased the salience of the climate change problem and helped generate greater attention, concern, and political will. Has international climate change law created a dynamic that will enable and catalyze stronger action in the future? In this respect, the jury is still out with respect to the Paris Agreement. But the fact that both the Copenhagen and Paris conferences commanded unprecedented levels of participation, not just from heads of states and governments, but also from a wide range of stakeholders, is encouraging.

IV. LOOKING AHEAD

The adoption within the space of a year of the Paris Agreement, the 2016 Kigali Amendment to the Montreal Protocol to address HFCs, and the 2016 ICAO global market-based measure to address aviation emissions, and the Paris Agreement's extraordinarily rapid entry into force, represent a step change in the international effort to address climate change. The Paris Agreement was a breakthrough in establishing a legal architecture applicable to all, which was able to bridge the divide between developed and developing countries. The ICAO decision establishes the first sector-based market mechanism. And the Kigali Amendment provides for the phasedown of an important class of GHGs. Together, this triptych of agreements is a testament to the importance placed on climate change by the international community. What is more, these inter-governmental agreements are bolstered by a 'groundswell' of activity at multiple levels by multiple actors to address climate change.

But impressive though these agreements and activities are, they still fall short of putting the world on a pathway to limiting climate change to below 2° C, much less 1.5° C. And the agreements all require further elaboration, so international climate change law is still very much a work in progress. Under the Paris Agreement, the parties need to elaborate rules relating to transparency, accounting, the new market mechanism, the global stocktake, and the agreement's implementation and compliance mechanism. The strength and rigor of these 'top-down' elements of the Paris Agreement will play an important role in determining the agreement's success in encouraging progressively more ambitious action over time. In the case of the ICAO market-based measure, states need to elaborate the requirements for

---

[58] David G. Victor, *Global Warming Gridlock: Creating More Effective Strategies for Saving the Planet* (Cambridge University Press, 2011) 210–15.
[59] See Chapter 7.

emission offsets. And the Kigali Amendment still needs to be accepted by states and to enter into force.

Moreover, notwithstanding the spirit of optimism that pervaded international climate change law in 2015–2016, many difficult issues remain. Although all three instruments found ways around the conundrum of differentiation,[60] the issue of burden sharing will likely persist, given the disparities among countries in wealth, historical and per capita emissions, and circumstances. Developing states are likely to continue to push for increased financing and easier access to technologies. And as the costs of climate change mount, particularly for poor, vulnerable countries, the issue of compensation for climate-related damages is likely to move to the fore.

Finally, the rapid progress of recent years could be undermined by a host of exogenous factors. The 2016 US presidential election is a dramatic illustration. But other possibilities, such as turmoil in Europe or a downturn in the Chinese economy, would also have serious implications for the climate regime.

It is important to recognize that international climate change law, while important, is only one of many determinants of climate policy. It is as much a reflection as a driver of political will, probably more. It can facilitate but rarely force states to act. It depends, ultimately, on the desire of states to combat climate change. If there is a will, international climate change law can provide—and has provided—the way, by organizing international cooperation, setting standards, and encouraging action, primarily by states, but also, to some degree, by non-state actors. The Paris Agreement and the various instruments adopted by ICAO, IMO, the Montreal Protocol parties, cities, regions, business, and civil society groups reflect the growing public concern about climate change. But whether this concern will translate into sufficient action to prevent dangerous climate change remains to be seen.

---

[60] Susan Biniaz, 'I Beg to Differ: Taking Account of National Circumstances under the Paris Agreement, the ICAO Market-Based Measure, and the Montreal Protocol's HFC Amendment' (New York: Sabin Center for Climate Change Law) <http://columbiaclimatelaw.com/files/2017/01/Biniaz-2017-01-Taking-Account-of-National-Circumstances.pdf> accessed 20 January 2017.

Index

Printed and bound by CPI Group (UK) Ltd, Croydon, CR0 4YY